College Transfer Success

CUSTOM EDITION FOR NASH COMMUNITY COLLEGE

Staley

CENGAGE
Learning·

Australia • Brazil • Japan • Korea • Mexico • Singapore • Spain • United Kingdom • United States

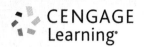

College Transfer Success: Custom Edition for Nash Community College

FOCUS on Community College Success, Third Edition
Constance Staley

© 2014, 2012, 2010 Cengage Learning. All rights reserved.

For product information and technology assistance, contact us at
Cengage Learning Customer & Sales Support, 1-800-354-9706

For permission to use material from this text or product,
submit all requests online at **cengage.com/permissions**
Further permissions questions can be emailed to
permissionrequest@cengage.com

This book contains select works from existing Cengage Learning resources and was produced by Cengage Learning Custom Solutions for collegiate use. As such, those adopting and/or contributing to this work are responsible for editorial content accuracy, continuity and completeness.

Compilation © 2015 Cengage Learning

ISBN: 978-1-305-74823-1

WCN: 01-100-101

Cengage Learning
20 Channel Center Street
Boston, MA 02210
USA

Cengage Learning is a leading provider of customized learning solutions with office locations around the globe, including Singapore, the United Kingdom, Australia, Mexico, Brazil, and Japan. Locate your local office at:
www.international.cengage.com/region.

Cengage Learning products are represented in Canada by Nelson Education, Ltd.

For your lifelong learning solutions, visit **www.cengage.com/custom.**

Visit our corporate website at **www.cengage.com.**

Brief Contents

Focus on Community College Success (Staley)

Contents vi

Acknowledgments xii

Meet the Cast xv

Introduction to Students xxi

FOCUS Entrance Interview xxiii

Chapter 1   Getting the Right Start.. 1

Chapter 2   Building Dreams, Setting Goals.................................... 27

Chapter 3   Learning Styles and Studying 47

Chapter 4   Managing Your Time, Energy, and Money 81

Chapter 5   Thinking Critically and Creatively................................ 113

Chapter 6   Learning Online 137

Chapter 7   Engaging, Listening, and Note-Taking in Class 169

Chapter 8   Reading, Writing, and Presenting 199

Chapter 9   Developing Memory, Taking Tests................................ 231

Chapter 10   Building Relationships, Valuing Diversity 267

Chapter 11   Choosing a College Major and Career.......................... 301

Chapter 12   Creating Your Future 321

FOCUS Exit Interview 345

Notes 349

Index 361

ACA 122 Student Resource Workbook 1

Acknowledgments

It's been said that "Achievement is a *we* thing, not a *me* thing, always the product of many heads and hands." There are so many people to thank that this acknowledgements section could be as long as a chapter of *FOCUS*! However, here I'll at least mention those who have contributed the most, including all the students over the last 35-plus years who have taught me more than I've ever taught them.

Family Let me start at the center of my life. My deepest thanks go to Steve, my Sean-Connery-look-alike husband (How do I put up with it?), who almost forgot what I looked like over the last few years. As I *FOCUS*ed away in my attic office day after day and night after night, he brought me too many cups of coffee to count. I cherish his devotion. My daughters, Shannon and Stephanie, helped bring some much-needed balance to my life, and aside from being the most adorable children on the planet, my grandtwins, Aidan and Ailie, have been a living learning laboratory for me. As young children mastering one new thing after another, they truly have taught me about of the pure joy of learning. And to my beautiful nearly-90 Mom, who lovingly alternated between urging me to "slow down and relax" and "hurry up and finish," thanks for all your motherly love.

Reviewers The list of reviewers who have contributed their insights and expertise to *FOCUS on Community College Success* is long. I'd like to especially thank Regina Lewis of Pikes Peak Community College for her willingness to serve as consulting editor of *FOCUS on Community College Success*. And my heartfelt thanks to the reviewers who helped inform the third edition revisions: Beverly Brucks, Illinois Central College; Mark Deitrick, Community College of Beaver County; Amy Harrell, Nash Community College; Amber Morgan, Greenville Technical College; Carlos Rivera, Essex County College; Rebecka Sare, Polk State College; René Sawyer, Greenville Technical College; Lynnae Selberg, Grand Rapids Community College; Claudia Swicegood, Rowan-Cabarrus Community College; Susan Todd, Jefferson College; Kirstin Wiley, Bluegrass Community and Technical College.

I'd be remiss to ignore the valuable input gained from reviewers of the previous edition of *FOCUS on Community College Success* that helped shape this book: Lynda Bennett, Blue Mountain Community College; Beverly Brucks, Illinois Central University; Susannah Chewning, Union County Community College; Colleen Courtney, Palm Beach State College; Myra Cox, City Colleges of Chicago, Harold Washington; Traci-Dale Crawford, Thomas Nelson Community College; Jean M. Davis, Florida Community College at Jacksonville; Melanie Deffendall, Delgado Community College; Anne Dickens, Lee College; Gregory Dieringer, University of Akron; Michael Discello, Pittsburgh Technical Institute; Sammie Dortch, City Colleges of Chicago, Harold Washington; Shirley Flor, San Diego Mesa College; Wendy Grace, Holmes Community College; Evelyn Green, City Colleges of Chicago, Harry Truman; Laurene M. Grimes, Lorain County Community College; Anne M. Gupton, Mott Community College; William Hysell, Mohawk Valley Community College; Cynthia S. Johnson, Palm Beach Community College; Benjamin G. Kramer, New River Community College;

Joseph Kornoski, Montgomery County Community College; Judy Kronen-berger, Sinclair Community College; Carol Kushner, Dutchess Community College; Christine Landrum, Mineral Area College; Lois Lawson-Bridell, Gloucester County College; Amelia Leighton, Jackson Community College; Jeanine Long, Southwest Georgia Technical College; Sandra Mahon, Community College of Allegheny County; Michael G. McCreary, Florida Community College at Jacksonville; Cherie Meador, Daley College; Mark A. Mills, Florida Community College at Jacksonville; Jennifer D. Morrison, J. Sargeant Reynolds Community College; Mita Noor, Los Angeles Pierce College; Bob Noyes, Tidewater Community College; Bonnie Porter Pajka, Luzerne County Community College; Kate Pandolpho, Ocean County College; Patricia Parma, Palo Alto College; Richard Patete, Keiser University; Gail Platt, South Plains College; Mary Poole, Madisonville Community College; Cristina Rodriguez, Los Angeles Pierce College; Janet Sims, Cleveland Community College; Camilla Swain-Ledoux, Ivy Technical College; Ivanhoe Tejeda, City Colleges of Chicago, Harold Washington; Karla Thompson, New Mexico State University Carlsbad; Carrie Tomko, University of Akron; Janice Woods, Mohave Community College.

The Wadsworth Team   No book, of course, gets very far without a publisher, and *FOCUS* has had the best publishing team imaginable: the dynamic, highly people-skilled Annie Todd, Director of Developmental Studies; the best-in-the industry, innovative, energetic Shani Fisher, Executive Editor; the meticulous, multitalented Julia Giannotti, Senior Development Editor; true professionals who combed pages and probably did more than I'll ever know, Cathy Brooks, Content Project Manager; and Associate Editor, Joanna Hassel, for her work on all the outstanding supplements to *FOCUS*; the obviously talented Art Director, Pam Galbreath; and Ed Dionne, Project Manager at MPS North America. I'd like to especially thank Larry Harwood, the master photographer who took photos of the *FOCUS* cast on the University of Colorado at Colorado Springs campus. And heartfelt thanks to Wadsworth's Annie Mitchell and Sean Wakely, who believed in this project from the very start; Sylvia Shepherd, whose creative vision shaped much of this book, and Lauren Larsen, whose wit and wisdom formed the basis for several of the early chapters.

Other Contributors   I'd also particularly like to thank the "*FOCUS* All-Stars," as I call them, who modeled for the photo shoots and starred in the "Inside the *FOCUS* Studio" videos. They followed artistic direction like pros, and they make this book unique. I'd also like to thank my colleagues at UCCS who have helped me develop many of the ideas in this book, whether they know it or not—all the Freshman Seminar faculty past and present. I also can't go without thanking the many authors who granted me permission to use their work and three essential scholars who allowed me to use, apply, and extend their instruments throughout the book: Neil Fleming, Brian French, and John Bransford. And thanks to my expert student research assistants; to Meg Foster from J. Sargeant Reynolds Community College for updating the Instructor's Resource Manual; and to Aren Moore, who worked with me to create the "props" for each chapter's opening case study, and the dynamic, groundbreaking, multimedia *FOCUS*points for each chapter. And finally, I'd like to thank Matt McClain, the comedy writer who brought his innovative humor to the learning process through podcast summaries of the chapters and television scripts for the website TV shows. He took the "big ideas" from *FOCUS* chapters and made them memorable to students by using their own best loved media.

Above all, *FOCUS* has taught me truly to focus. Writing a book takes the same kind of endurance and determination that it takes to get a college degree. My empathy level for my students has, if anything, increased—and I am thankful for all I've learned while writing. It has been a cathartic experience to see what has filled each computer screen as I've tapped, tapped, tapped away. Ultimately, what I have chosen to put into each chapter has told me a great deal about who I am, what I know (and don't), and what I value. There's no doubt: I am a better teacher for having written this book. May all my readers grow through their *FOCUS* experience, too.

Chapter 1: Darnell Williams / Calil

Hometown: Colorado Springs, Colorado

Major: History with a secondary education emphasis

Lessons Learned: Calil noticed many similarities between himself and the *FOCUS* Challenge Case character he portrayed, besides playing football and watching movies. Calil, too, had problems with the transition from high school to college. He admits he was a student who "coasted" through his senior year of high school, which made his first year of college more difficult.

Toughest First-Year Class: English, like Darnell, because he wasn't fully aware of the instructor's expectations.

Advice to New Students: "Determination is the key to success. If you are determined, there is nothing in the world that can stop you."

Chapter 2: Sylvia Sanchez / Alycia

Hometown: I've lived all over Colorado. I consider the whole state to be my hometown!

Major: Nursing with a minor in psychology

Lessons Learned: Alycia is still learning lessons about college. She keeps growing and discovering new things about herself and has made lifelong friends. She plans to remember college as the best years of her life!

Toughest First-Year Class: Anatomy ... It was hard to study *all* the time.

Advice to New Students: "Listen to your heart; it will lead you to the right place. Take every opportunity that comes to you because college is about finding out who you are and what you want from life."

©Larry Harwood Photography. Property of Cengage Learning.

Chapter 3: Tammy Ko / Jessica

Hometown: Manitou Springs, Colorado

Major: Marketing

Lessons Learned: Juggling a part-time job while in school, Jessica loved meeting new people, but she regretted not talking to other students about which instructors and courses to take toward her marketing major. In order to succeed, she says, you've "gotta give it all you've got!"

Toughest First-Year Class: Microeconomics because it wasn't like high school courses that just required memorizing a lot of facts.

Advice to New Students: "Talk to other students to learn about the best instructors, and make sure you are studying something that you are interested in."

©Larry Harwood Photography. Property of Cengage Learning.

Chapter 4: Derek Johnson / Derrick

Hometown: Colorado Springs, Colorado

Major: Communications/Recording Arts

Lessons Learned: Even though he's not married and has no children, Derrick and his case study character have much in common—too much to do and too little time! Derrick felt his biggest mistake in college was not asking enough questions in class. He knows now he should ask for clarity on content or assignments he doesn't understand.

Toughest First-Year Class: English because he and his instructor had differing opinions, but he communicated through the tough spots and earned an "A."

Advice to New Students: "Surround yourself with positive people. As the saying goes, 'You are the company you keep.' I've seen many of my friends drop out because the people they called friends were holding them back from their full potential."

Free Time: composing music and producing films

Chapter 5: Desiree Moore / Regina

Hometown: Colorado Springs, Colorado

Major: MA Communication

Lessons Learned: Organization, time management, study groups, and note cards

Toughest First-Year Course: Psychology because in this class I had to be very organized to keep my notes in order. There were only two exams in this class during the entire semester. I did not organize my notes or my time very well.

Advice to New Students: "Get to know your professors, ask questions, and have a study buddy."

Free Time: In my free time, I work out at the gym. I also spend quality time with my son.

Chapter 6: Dario Jones / Orlando

Hometown: Fountain, Colorado

Major: MA, Communication

Lessons Learned: Start strong, work hard, and finish strong

Toughest First-Year Course: Math 099

Advice to New Students: "Get to know your instructors and fellow classmates. Ask questions in class when you're not sure about something."

Free Time: What free time? To relax, I listen to jazz or classical music, or I'll channel surf until I find something interesting to watch.

Chapter 7: Rachel White / Shannon

Hometown: Denver, Colorado

Major: Philosophy

Lessons Learned: Go to class!

Toughest First-Year Course: Intro to Geography (it might have been easier if I'd gone to class).

Advice to New Students: "Balance fun and schoolwork, so you don't get burned out on either one!"

Free Time: Acting and improv

Chapter 8: Katie Alexander / Christina

©Larry Harwood Photography. Property of Cengage Learning.

Hometown: Colorado Springs, Colorado. Because she went to college in her hometown, Christina really enjoyed the opportunity college provided to meet new people.

Major: Nursing

Lessons Learned: Spending her free time with her friends watching movies, going bowling or dancing, and just hanging out, Christina found that like her *FOCUS* Challenge Case character, she, too, would make up excuses to get out of studying and doing her homework. She quickly learned the importance of reading and taking notes. "As weird as it may sound, reading cuts your end study time by more than half. Reading the material ahead of time helps you understand everything so much better."

Advice to New Students: "Stay motivated. College is going to *fly* by! If you stay motivated and get good grades, it really will be over before you know it."

Chapter 9: Kevin Baxter / Dave

©Larry Harwood Photography. Property of Cengage Learning.

Hometown: St. Paul, Minnesota

Background: Portraying a student returning to school after fifteen-plus years in the working world, Dave is currently a professor of chemistry at University of Colorado at Colorado Springs.

College Memories: Dave remembers how much he liked the different social environment college provided after graduating from high school.

Toughest First-Year Course: English Composition because writing wasn't exactly his forte.

Advice to New Students: "Study hard, and use your time wisely."

Free Time: Woodworking, hiking, and climbing

Chapter 10: Kia Washington / Charmaine

Hometown: Colorado Springs, Colorado

Major: Psychology and Sociology

Toughest First-Year Course: General psychology because there was so much to learn in such a short period of time.

Lessons Learned: Charmaine learned how to manage her time more effectively, as well as the necessity of keeping yourself healthy in mind, body, and spirit, something she felt her *FOCUS* Challenge Case character could have benefited from.

Advice to New Students: "Remember to have fun in everything that you do, both academically and otherwise. Take care of yourself first, and don't feel as though you have to do everything all the time; sometimes the best parts of life come during moments of down time. This is where you are able to truly reflect on what it is you're doing and remember why you're doing it in the first place!"

Chapter 11: Ethan Cole / Josh

Hometown: Fort Morgan, Colorado

Major: Sociology

Lessons Learned: Like his *FOCUS* Challenge Case character, Josh noticed that he, too, didn't always push himself to reach his potential. But he learned through his first-year seminar course that he is responsible for himself and that instructors aren't like high school teachers. They will let you fail a class if you don't do what you need to. It's up to you.

Advice to New Students: "Not only did getting involved on campus help me have more fun in school, but it has also helped me academically. It has taught me how to manage my time and has made it so much easier for me to participate with confidence in class. Just make sure you get what you need to do done, and you will enjoy your college experience so much more."

Free Time: "Free time? What's that?! I'm too busy to have free time!" (But he secretly admits he snowboards, plays guitar, draws, and spends time with friends.)

Chapter 12: Anthony Lopez / Luis

©Larry Harwood Photography. Property of Cengage Learning.

Hometown: Aguascalientes, Mexico

Major: Spanish with an emphasis on secondary education

Lessons Learned: Luis is extremely involved on campus and within his community—he is President of the Association of Future Teachers, sings with his church choir, plays intramural soccer, and works for the Air Force on weekends. Luis thinks one mistake he made in his first term was that he procrastinated with homework because his new freedom let him think he could have fun first and study later, but he quickly learned he was wrong.

Advice to New Students: "Be smart and be involved, but always do your homework first. If you are involved on campus, you will meet people that will help make your college experience easier and more fun."

MEET THE AUTHOR: Constance Staley

©Larry Harwood Photography. Property of Cengage Learning.

Hometown: Pittsburgh, Pennsylvania (although she never actually lived there. Instead, she lived all over the world and went to ten schools in twelve years.)

Background: Connie has taught at the University of Colorado at Colorado Springs for more than 35 years after getting a bachelor's degree in education, a master's degree in linguistics, and a Ph.D. in communication.

College Memories: Connie remembers loving her public speaking class as a first-year student and having tons of friends, but being extremely homesick for her family.

Advice to New Students: "Earning a college degree is hard work, takes a long time, and requires a substantial investment of your time, energy, and resources. But it's the best investment you can make in your own future—one you'll never regret."

Free Time: Spending time with her husband, her two daughters, and her boy/girl grandtwins; relaxing at her cabin in the mountains; and traveling around the country to speak to other professors who also care about first-year students and their success.

Dear Reader,

This book is different. It won't coerce, coddle, caution, or coax you. Instead, it will give *you* the tools you need to coach yourself. Ultimately, this book is about you, your college career, and your career beyond college. It's about the future you will create for yourself.

FOCUS on Community College Success stars a cast of my own students (several colleagues, and one of my daughters), like a stage play. One student "actor" is featured in each chapter's opening case study. All twelve cast members reappear throughout the book, so that you'll get to know them as you read. I've been teaching for more than 35 years now and worked with thousands of students. Each case study is about a real student (with a fictitious name) that I've worked with or a mixture of several students. You may find you have some things in common with them. But whether you do or not, I hope they will make this book come to life for you. You'll also be able to meet these "actors" electronically in *FOCUS TV* videos on the book's CourseMate website.

I love what I do, and I care deeply about students. I hope that comes through to you as a reader. You'll see that I've inserted some of my personality, had a bit of fun at times, and tried to create a new kind of textbook for you. In my view, learning should be engaging, personal, memorable, challenging, and fun.

Most importantly, I know that these next few years hold the key to unlock much of what you want from your life. And from all my years of experience and research, I can tell you straightforwardly that what you read in this book works. It gets results. It can turn you into a better, faster learner. *Really?* you ask. Really! The only thing you have to do is put all the words in this book into action. That's where the challenge comes in.

Becoming an educated person takes time, energy, resources, and focus. At times, it may mean shutting down the six windows you have open on your computer, and directing all your attention to one thing in laser-like fashion. It may mean disciplining yourself to dig in and stick with something until you've nailed it. Can you do it? I'm betting you can, or I wouldn't have written this book. Invest yourself fully in what you read here, and then decide to incorporate it into your life. If there's one secret to college success, that's it.

So, you're off! You're about to begin one of the most fascinating, liberating, challenging, and adventure-filled times of your life. I may not be able to meet each one of you personally, but I *can* wish you well, wherever you are. I hope this book helps you on your journey.

Constance Staley

INFORMATION ABOUT YOU

Name _____

Student Number _____   Course/Section _____

Instructor _____

Gender _____   Age _____

Although you may not have experienced life as a new college student for long, we're interested in how you expect to spend your time, what challenges you think you'll face, and your general views of what you think college will be like. Please answer thoughtfully.

Your Background

1. **Ethnic Identification (check all that apply):**

____ American Indian or Alaska Native   ____ Native Hawaiian or Other Pacific Islander   ____ Asian

____ Hispanic/Latino   ____ Black or African American   ____ White

____ Mixed Race (for example, one Caucasian parent and one Asian)   ____ Prefer not to answer

2. **Is English your first (native) language?**

____ yes   ____ no

3. **Did your parents graduate from college?**

____ yes, both   ____ yes, father only   ____ yes, mother only   ____ neither   ____ not sure

Your Previous School Experience

4. **If you are entering college soon after completing high school, on average, how many total hours per week did you spend studying outside of class in high school?**

____ 0–5   ____ 6–10   ____ 11–15   ____ 16–20   ____ 21–25
____ 26–30   ____ 31–35   ____ 36–40   ____ 40+   ____ I am a returning student and attended high school some time ago.

5. **What was your high school grade point average when you graduated?**

____ A+   ____ A   ____ A−   ____ B+   ____ B
____ B−   ____ C+   ____ C   ____ C−   ____ D or lower
____ I don't remember.   ____ I earned a GED.

6. **Did you go to college elsewhere before enrolling in this one?**

____ yes   ____ no   ____ I've attended more than one other college.

Information About This Semester/Quarter

7. How many credit hours are you taking this term?

____ 6 or fewer   ____ 7–11   ____ 12–14   ____ 15–16   ____ 17 or more

8. Where are you living this term?

____ with my immediate family   ____ with a relative other than my immediate family

____ on my own   ____ other (please explain)

Working While in College

9. In addition to going to college, do you expect to work for pay at a job (or jobs) this term?

____ yes   ____ no

10. If so, how many hours per week do you expect to work?

____ 1–10   ____ 11–20   ____ 21–30   ____ 31–40   ____ 40+

YOUR COLLEGE EXPECTATIONS

Your Reasons and Predictions

11. Why did you decide to go to college? (Check all that apply.)

____ because I want to build a better life for myself.   ____ because I want to build a better life for my family.

____ because I want to be well off financially in the future.   ____ because I need a college education to achieve my dreams.

____ because my friends were going to college.   ____ because my family encouraged me to go.

____ because it was expected of me.   ____ because I want to prepare for a *new* career.

____ because I want to continue learning.   ____ because the career I am pursuing requires a degree.

____ because I was unsure of what I might do instead.   ____ other (please explain) _____

12. How do you expect to learn best in college? (Check all that apply.)

____ by looking at charts, maps, graphs   ____ by looking at color-coded information   ____ by looking at symbols and graphics

____ by listening to instructors' lectures   ____ by listening to other students during in-class discussions   ____ by talking about course content with friends or family

____ by reading books   ____ by writing papers   ____ by taking notes

____ by going on field trips   ____ by engaging in activities   ____ by actually doing things

13. The following sets of opposite descriptive phrases are separated by five blank lines. Put an X on the line between the two that best represent your response, like this: For me, high school was easy ____:__X__:____:____:____ hard

I expect my first term of college to:

challenge me academically	____:____:____:____:____	be easy
be very different from high school	____:____:____:____:____	be a lot like high school
be exciting	____:____:____:____:____	be dull
be interesting	____:____:____:____:____	be uninteresting
motivate me to continue	____:____:____:____:____	discourage me
be fun	____:____:____:____:____	be boring
help me feel a part of this school	____:____:____:____:____	make me feel like an outsider

14. How many total hours per week do you expect to study outside of class for your college courses?

____ 0–5   ____ 6–10   ____ 11–15   ____ 16–20   ____ 21–25
____ 26–30   ____ 31–35   ____ 36–40   ____ 40+

15. What do you expect your grade point average to be at the end of your first term of college?

____ A+   ____ A   ____ A–   ____ B+   ____ B
____ B–   ____ C+   ____ C   ____ C–   ____ D or lower

Your Strengths, Personality, and Interests

16. Please identify your *strengths*—personal characteristics that will contribute to your college success. (Check all that apply.)

____ a. I am good at building relationships.

____ b. I can usually convince others to follow my plan.

____ c. I like to win.

____ d. I work toward future goals.

____ e. I like to be productive and get things done.

____ f. I have a positive outlook on life.

____ g. I'm usually the person who gets things going.

____ h. I enjoy the challenge of learning new things.

____ i. I am focused.

____ j. I can usually look at a problem and figure out a plan of action.

____ k. I work to keep everyone happy.

____ l. I'm a take-charge kind of person.

____ m. I help other people develop their talents and skills.

____ n. I'm a very responsible person.

____ o. I can analyze a situation and see various ways things might work out.

____ p. I usually give tasks my best effort.

17. How confident are you in yourself in each of the following areas? (1 = very confident, 5 = not at all confident)

____ overall academic ability   ____ technology skills

____ mathematical skills   ____ physical well being

____ leadership ability   ____ writing skills

____ reading skills   ____ social skills

____ public speaking skills   ____ emotional well being

____ study skills   ____ teamwork skills

18. For each of the following pairs of descriptors, which set sounds most like you? (Please choose between the two options on each line and place a checkmark by your choice.)

____ Extraverted and outgoing   or   ____ Introverted and quiet

____ Detail-oriented and practical   or   ____ Big-picture and future-oriented

____ Rational and truthful   or   ____ People-oriented and tactful

____ Organized and self-disciplined   or   ____ Spontaneous and flexible

19. *FOCUS* is about 12 different aspects of college life. Which are you most interested in applying to yourself in your academic work? (Check all that apply.)

____ Getting the right start   ____ Learning styles and studying

____ Building dreams, setting goals   ____ Thinking critically and creatively

____ Managing time, energy, and money   ____ Engaging, listening, and note-taking in class

____ Learning online   ____ Developing memory, taking tests

____ Reading, writing, and presenting   ____ Choosing a college major and career

____ Building relationships, valuing diversity   ____ Creating a future

Your Challenges

20. Of the 12 aspects of college life identified in the previous question, which do you expect to be most challenging to apply to yourself in your academic work? (Check all that apply.)

_____ Getting the right start

_____ Building dreams, setting goals

_____ Managing time, energy, and money

_____ Learning online

_____ Reading, writing, and presenting

_____ Building relationships, valuing diversity

_____ Learning styles and studying

_____ Thinking critically and creatively

_____ Engaging, listening, and note-taking in class

_____ Developing memory, taking tests

_____ Choosing a college major and career

_____ Creating a future

21. Which one of your current classes do you expect to find most challenging this term and why?

Which class? (course title _or_ department and course number) _____

Why? _____

Do you expect to succeed in this course? _____ yes _____ no _____ Perhaps (please explain): _____

22. Please mark your _top three areas of concern_ relating to your first term of college by placing 1, 2, and 3 next to the items you choose (with 1 representing your top concern).

_____ I might not fit in.

_____ I might have difficulty making friends.

_____ I might not be academically successful.

_____ My performance might disappoint my family.

_____ My personal life might interfere with my studies.

_____ My studies might interfere with my personal life.

_____ I might have financial difficulties.

_____ My job might interfere with my studies.

_____ My studies might interfere with my job.

_____ My social life might interfere with my studies.

_____ My studies might interfere with my social life.

_____ My instructors might not care about me as an individual.

_____ I might not finish my degree.

_____ I might not manage my time well.

_____ I might be bored in my classes.

_____ I might feel intimidated by my instructors.

_____ I might feel overwhelmed by all I have to do.

_____ other (please explain)_____

Your Future

23. How certain are you now of the following (1 = totally sure, 5 = totally unsure)?

_____ Finishing your degree or certificate

_____ Finishing your degree or certificate at this school

_____ Sticking with the major you've chosen

_____ Continuing on to work toward a bachelor's or advanced degree

24. What are you most looking forward to in college?

25. Describe the best outcomes you hope for at the end of this first semester/quarter. Do you expect to achieve them? Why or why not?

chapter 1 Getting the Right Start

READINESS CHECK

How this chapter relates to YOU

1. When it comes to getting the right start in college, what are you most unsure about, if anything?

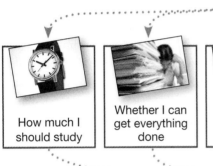

| How much I should study | Whether I can get everything done | What different instructors expect | Whether I can give it my best shot | Whether college is right for me |

2. What is most likely to be your response? Circle it.

| I'll check with my instructors. | I'll ask my classmates. | I'll see how things go and adjust. | I'll wait and eventually figure it out. |

3. What would you have to do to increase your likelihood of success? Will you do it this quarter or semester?

Example: *Find out now before it's too late. Yes!*

How YOU will relate to this chapter

What are you most interested in learning about? Put checkmarks by those topics.

☐ Who goes to community college and why

☐ What different types of degrees are available

☐ How to display academic professionalism

☐ Why developmental courses are important

☐ How to master a syllabus

☐ Why college success courses work

● How motivated are you to learn more about getting the right start in college? (5 = high, 1 = low) ____

● How ready are you to read now? ____ (If something is in your way, take care of it if you can. Zero in and focus.)

● How long do you think it will take you to complete this chapter? If you start and stop, keep track of your overall time. ____ hour(s) ____ minutes

1

Darnell Williams

© Larry Harwood Photography. Property of Cengage Learning.

Quite honestly, Darnell Williams hadn't found high school all that challenging. Playing football his last two years had made it bearable. But at his school, if you showed up and had a pulse, you could count on passing your courses. There wasn't anything in particular he really wanted to do after high school, so he didn't do much of anything except hang out with friends, watch movies, and play an occasional game of football. But the truth was that Darnell had a hard time focusing, especially on school. After a year had gone by and his friends all started scattering, Darnell decided to go to the community college in his hometown. Maybe something there would appeal to him.

But after two weeks, Darnell admitted that he didn't find his classes all that engaging. Although he was strong physically from working out for football, he knew he was out of shape academically. He didn't do any homework in high school, but how much would he have to do here? Because Darnell had no idea which classes to take, he figured he'd just get some required courses out of the way during his first term. He'd always heard people say, "College is about your communication skills, like writing and speaking. If your basic skills are good, and you're willing to work hard, you'll do fine." Based on that advice, he'd enrolled in two courses: Developmental English and Public Speaking. But between the two, he'd already cut class three times. And Developmental English? Seriously? Darnell knew that writing had never been his strong suit, but it had to be better than that!

CINEMA
Good Only Date Sold
ADMIT ONE
048107

belle23/Shutterstock.com

Earlier that morning, Darnell had received an e-mail from his best friend, Curtis, at the large state university two hours from home. It read like this:

Man, I hope I can make it here! I wish I'd taken more college prep courses. In high school, we could just memorize things like math formulas; even if we didn't understand them, we could do well on tests. Here, there aren't as many exams, and if I blow just one, I'm in big trouble. How long B4 midterms 4 you? AFAIK, I'm already off to a rough start. I gotta just T+. GTG LTR Curtis

Toward the end of the message, Darnell noticed that Curtis had slipped into the usual e-mail abbreviations like T+ for "think positively" and AFAIK for "as far as I know." *I wish I could write like that in my composition class*, Darnell thought.

Then it hit him. He went to his "sent mail" folder and looked up yesterday's e-mail to his public speaking instructor: "sorry i missed ur class on

Laurin Rinder/Shutterstock.com

Fall Football Schedule

	OPPONENT	TIME
er 6	Colorado State	7:00 PM ET
er 11	at Toledo	9:00 PM ET
ber 19	Wyoming	3:30 PM ET
er 1	at West Virginia	7:30 PM ET
er 1	at Texas	7:00 PM ET
er 10	Kansas	9:00 PM ET
er 17	at Kansas State	3:30 PM ET
ber 24	Missouri	9:00 PM ET
er 31	Texas A&M	3:30 PM ET
ember 7	at Iowa State	9:00 PM ET
		7:30 PM ET

© Cengage Learning

Course Schedule
Main Campus
FALL SEMESTER
Williams, Darnell

Title	Hrs	Days	Meeting Times	Bldg	

Wednesday my dog was sick D. ps was anything due?" He wondered whether that kind of informal writing would fly in messages to college professors. Darnell was used to texting; that's how he usually wrote. And after sending the message, he had wondered just how important attendance was. In high school, nobody seemed to care if you cut class. But here? Even though he and Curtis were at different schools, it seemed they both noticed a big difference between high school and college. Looking back, high school seemed like a piece of cake. In college, you actually had to get assignments done on time and pay attention to the instructor's high standards.

Darnell wondered if he'd be more motivated in college if he could have signed up for some courses he'd actually been interested in, like Sports in Society or Modern American Cinema. Sports and movies were two of his favorite things. At the moment, Darnell had absolutely no idea what to major in. Should he get a certificate or go on for a four-year degree? He was—as his college put it—an "undecided" student.

Professor Monroe had already begun when Darnell walked into class, and she shot a scowl in his direction. As he sat down at his computer station in the writing lab next to an older, grand-motherly-looking lady and a young businessman in a suit and pulled up the course website, his mind went totally blank. In high school, he hadn't been required to write anything longer than a few paragraphs. *I'm going to blame this stress on my senior-year English teacher, Mr. Forester. This is his fault. He should have done a better job of preparing us for college,* Darnell decided.

Just then, Professor Monroe was reminding the students that they'd get back their first graded essays today. "I have to be honest with you, class," she'd warned, "I expected more from you, and frankly, I'm disappointed in your work. We have a lot of work to do this term!" *Ouch!* Darnell thought to himself. *I hope she's not talking about me! Maybe I shouldn't have handed anything in. At least then I wouldn't get a paper back with red marks all over it!*

Darnell held his breath as he looked at the paper she handed him, and then he saw it. At the top there was no grade at all—no red marks— nothing but the teacher's note that said, "See me." What could that possibly mean? *This college thing is going to be more challenging than I thought,* he said to himself. One thing was clear to him: If he wanted to do well, he'd probably have to cut back on movies and sports and learn how to be a real college student. *There should be a class to help with all this stuff!* he thought to himself. *That would take out the guess-work and help me know exactly how to be successful.*

EAST HIGH SCHOOL
OFFICIAL TRANSCRIPT

STUDENT INFORMATION
FULL NAME: Darnell Williams
PARENTS/GUARDIAN: Michael and Joan Williams

ACADEMIC RECORD

SCHOOL YEAR: 2007–2008   GRADE LEVEL: 9th

Course Title	Credit Earned	Final Grade
English I	1.0	B
Mathematics I	1.0	C
Biology w/lab	1.0	C
Geography	1.0	B
World History	1.0	B
Spanish I	1.0	B
Phys Ed	1.0	B
Film Appreciation	0.5	A

SCHOOL YEAR: 2008–2009   GRA

Course Title
English II
Mathematics II
Chemistry w/lab
Computer Lab
Ancient Civilizations
Spanish II
Phys Ed

1. Do you have anything in common with Darnell? If so, what steps are you taking to help make sure you're successful?

2. Why do you think the instructor didn't give Darnell a grade? Would a teacher's note that says "See me" always indicate a problem?

3. In your experience, what are some of the main academic differences between high school and college? How did you read and study in high school, and how do you think that will change in college?

You're in College Now

academic having to do with education

Congratulations! You're in college. You've just started a new chapter of your life! As the saying goes, "The first step toward getting somewhere is to decide that you are not going to stay where you are." In choosing to go to community college, that's what you've decided. You're *not* going to stay where you are. Your journey has begun. This chapter will launch you on your journey by covering the basics. You may already know much of this information, but not everyone does. So, let's start at the beginning.

Why do people go to community college? Generally, people go to a community college to improve their skills or gain completely new ones. Many community college students differ from four-year college students in ways like these: they attend school part-time, support themselves, work full-time, are single parents, waited to go on to college, or got their high school degrees in nonstandard ways.[1] (In fact, if you don't yet have a high school diploma or GED, your community college may be able to help you with that.)

GED stands for **g**eneral **e**ducation **d**evelopment; passing these tests is an alternative to earning a traditional high school diploma

> **Reason 1: Transitioning from High School to College.** If you just finished high school, you may see college as the obvious next step. Like Darnell, you'll find college to be a very different game. Think of it this way: Darnell arrived at college, playing what he thought was a decent game of checkers. But he quickly discovered that his instructors expected him to play chess. He'd been successful in high school, and to the inexperienced eye, college

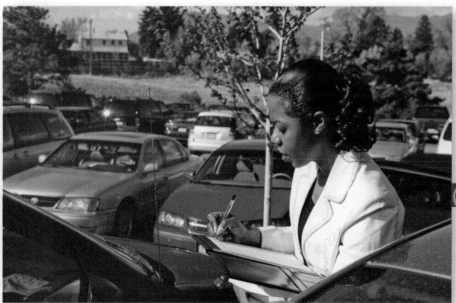

> **First say to yourself what you would be; and then do what you have to do.**
>
> *Epictetus, Greek philosopher,*
> *55–135* A.D.

looked like the same game board. After all, school is school, right? Wrong! Darnell quickly discovered that college is a new game with different rules!

marketplace of ideas a place where many ideas are exchanged freely

Other students you know may have gone off to college somewhere else. But you considered things like cost and convenience and chose a college in your own community. A community college is a *real* college—a **marketplace of ideas**, where you can try out all kinds of new things. According to one study, more community college students than students at four-year schools report more opportunities to speak in class and get to know their instructors. A community college that focuses on teaching—and on you—can be a good place to be.[2]

A community college can also be a great place to test the waters. Before plunging into a university setting (often with higher tuition rates), you want to see if college is right for you. After you get into the rhythm of your classes, you may decide you've made a good decision. Or you may decide to wait until your life is less complicated or your head is in the right place.

> **Reason 2: Going Back to School after a Break.** Perhaps you've tried college before and quit. But now you've decided to get back on the road to success. Maybe you're absolutely committed to making it this time, so you're more motivated. Something may have changed in your life, or you worked to save up for college for a while, or you've been a stay-at-home mom, or you have an employer now who will help foot your tuition bill.

One of the most interesting things about community colleges is the amazing mix of students from all walks of life. You're just as likely to be sitting beside a grandmother who's decided it's her turn now, a soldier who's just come back from overseas, or a businessman gaining credentials for a promotion. Adult community college students are practical, self-directed learners who want to build on their past experiences and apply what they learn to their everyday lives. Does that describe you?[3]

Or perhaps you're returning to school to gear up with a select course or two. For example, maybe you have a new job that requires giving presentations, and the thought of it terrifies you. So you take a course to help you overcome your fear of public speaking. You don't necessarily want a degree; you just want to take a course or two. There's probably no better place than a community college to meet those kinds of focused needs.

❝ ❞

The road to success is lined with many tempting parking spaces.

Traditional proverb

Who goes to community college? Take a look at these statistics:

> 44 percent of all college students nationwide attend community colleges.

> 46 percent of community college students are 25 or older. The average age is 28 years old.

> 61 percent are female.

> 33 percent are parents.

> 42 percent are the first in their families to go to college.

> 85 percent work full- or part-time.

> 33 percent are minority students, with the Latino population increasing most rapidly.[4]

Earning a Two-Year Degree

If you're in college to earn a degree, an associate's degree will prepare you to go one of two ways in a relatively short amount of time: (1) into a career or (2) on to further education. If you want a career-oriented associate's degree, in two years you can train for one of the fastest-growing jobs in the economy by taking approximately twenty classes. The best jobs for the future requiring a two-year degree include becoming a nurse, environmental technician, paralegal, fashion designer, dental hygienist, occupational therapist, or radiologic technologist.[5] If you prefer hands-on coursework and a career like one of these is your goal, a community college is exactly the right place for you. (It's also quite possible that you couldn't prepare for some of these specific degrees at a four-year institution.)

Instead of a career-oriented associate's degree, you may want to earn a fairly general two-year degree to apply toward a bachelor's degree at a university. Part of the coursework you'll complete to get an associate's degree will consist of core requirements or general education courses, like writing and speaking, that apply to any career field. If those are your plans, you'll leave your community college with transferable courses when the time comes.[6]

Perhaps instead of a two-year associate's degree, you want to specialize even further and finish your coursework sooner, so instead you opt for a certificate. Certificates generally require fifteen to as many as fifty credits, and you'll most likely only take courses that apply specifically to the career field you're preparing for. You set your sights on a target and finish your certificate program in as little as one year, sometimes less.[7]

One of the biggest differences between an associate's degree and a certificate is that the courses you take for an associate's degree usually transfer to a four-year school and include core requirements, general courses like speaking, writing, and math.[8] That may not be true of certificate programs. So if you think you may want to earn a bachelor's degree at some point, choose an associate's degree. It's up to you. How soon do you need a job? What interests you? How hands-on do you want your course of study to be?[9]

Academic Professionalism: What Instructors Will Expect from You

Imagine this: You've just landed a new job, and it's a good one, one you really wanted. How do you know what to do and how to act? What will your boss expect from you? Should you just show up whenever it's convenient, take on this job on top of others you already have, and start firing off casual e-mails and texts about business? ["what up with the Johnson report i thought jules was gonna write that"] Probably not—at least not if you want to be successful. You'll want to display workplace professionalism by noting how professionalism is defined in your new organization, and then start doing those things right away. The same thing is true in college: If you want to be successful, you have to display academic professionalism. It's a theme you start now and carry with you into your career. How is academic professionalism defined? If you surveyed community college instructors across the country, they'd give you advice like this:

1. **Don't just pile on.** College isn't just "one more thing" to add to the daily agenda of your life. You may have to give something up (like watching every single TV show you love every week) to give it all you've got. Some people hope they'll be able to just add college to an already-long list of obligations. But when they add one more thing, the entire stack crumbles. Something in your life will need adjusting to make room for coursework. You may have to reduce your hours at work for a while, or tell your aunt that you can't watch her kids on Thursday nights so she can go to class, because you have to go to class, too. Put college at the top of your list of obligations.

2. ***Choose* to go to class.** Let's face it: Life is complicated. It involves overlapping demands and making choices on a minute-by-minute basis. Your boss wants a piece of you, your kids (if you have any) want your attention while you try to study, your friend wants to go to the movies the night before your midterm exam, the bills keep mounting, and on and on. Some students choose to miss class to pick up a relative at the airport or shop with a friend who's in town, for example, and just skip class. Sometimes true emergencies in your personal life will interfere with your academic life. If you're ill, for example, call or e-mail your instructor beforehand, if for no other reason than to be courteous. But your instructors will expect you to plan nonemergencies around your already scheduled (and paid-for!) classes. Many things in your life are important—it's true—but while you're in school, coming to class and doing your coursework are the right choices to make. Unfortunately, many community college students sabotage themselves within the first few weeks of classes by skipping class (25 percent), turning in an assignment late (33 percent), or not turning an assignment in at all (24 percent). Don't allow yourself to become one of these statistics![10]

3. **Don't be an ostrich!** Some students fall prey to "the Ostrich Syndrome." If reading or homework assignments seem too hard or feel like busywork, they just don't do them. Instead, they bury their heads in the sand and pretend like nothing's at stake. Somehow they may even think that they can't get a bad grade if they don't turn in an assignment for the instructor to grade. It goes without saying (but here it is anyway) that "ostriching" is the opposite of academic professionalism. Always do your best work and submit it on time. If the assignment is due on October 1, it's due on October 1. Honest-to-goodness realism and continuous upkeep in your courses work wonders in college, just as they do in the workplace.

4. **Show respect.** One thing instructors dislike is getting a sense from students that school isn't a top priority. When you breeze in late or sneak out early, you're communicating that you don't value school, your instructor, and your classmates, whether you realize it or not. If you criticize a classmate or your instructor in public—even if you think it's constructive—that's disrespectful, too. And when you whip out your cell phone to see how many "likes" you have after your last Facebook post, or text your boyfriend about where to go for dinner, everyone knows where your head is. When you're in class, be in class.

5. **Know the rules.** Your college has policies you need to know about up front. What constitutes cheating? How can you avoid plagiarism? Who should you talk to if you have a concern about your grade? Do instructors accept texts and cell phone calls? What kind of writing will they expect in e-mails? Even when it comes to everyday things—like weather cancellations—your college has policies and procedures to guide you.

6. **Take charge.** When it comes right down to it, who is responsible for your success? None other than you! Even though you may be afraid to speak up or not want

An ostrich with its head in the sand is just as blind to opportunity as to disaster.

Anonymous

> **If everyone is moving forward together, then success takes care of itself.**
>
> *Henry Ford, American industrialist (1863–1947)*

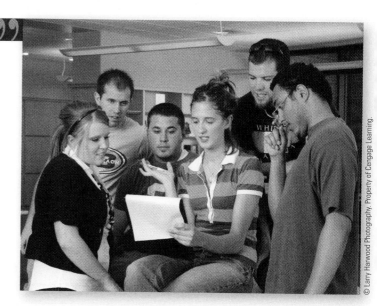

to admit that you're fuzzy about something, your instructors will rely on *you* to let them know that. They aren't mind readers. Do what you need to do: get help, take advantage of instructors' office hours, or hire a tutor. Don't sit idly by while success drifts away.

7. **Invest enough time.** In high school you may have done well without trying very hard. A teacher may have forgiven a late assignment, provided opportunities for extra credit, or graded on a curve so that everyone passed. But college is different. In college, it's important to get ready for class beforehand by reading and doing assignments, and then jump in once you're there. Bring your books, notebook, and pen, and sit up straight, too, just like mom always used to say. College isn't a place to just slide by or wing it. It's a place to put your best foot forward. That may mean rewriting a paper three times or rereading a textbook chapter more than once. Academic professionalism requires you to invest as much time as it takes.

8. **Learn to work in groups.** Your instructors know the value of teamwork later in your career, so they'll expect you to work with your classmates in class, outside of class, or online. They may even think it's important enough to assign points for group projects in the course syllabus. Even though you may prefer to work alone, teamwork skills are highly valued in today's workplace, and you'll learn things from other students that you might not learn from your instructor.[11]

9. **Check your email regularly.** Sure, you can talk to an instructor on the phone or text a classmate with a question about an assignment. But the primary means of communication in college is e-mail. Most colleges will send all "official correspondence" (like bills) this way, and many professors will use campus e-mail to communicate with you. If you never check your school e-mail account, but instead only use your personal account, you'll miss important information. ("What? The instructor's sick today? I just drove 20 miles to get here!") Your campus IT department or an online helpsheet can tell you how to forward one e-mail account to the other so that you're always up to speed. Believe it or not, this one simple thing trips up more students than you would ever imagine!

10. **Engage!** Students who soak up all they can enjoy college most. When they're in class, they're tuned in. Sure, Professor Whoever may not be quite as entertaining as your favorite TV star, and going to class isn't as much fun as the latest box office smash hit. But college is about becoming an *educated* person, not an *entertained* one.

Academic Responsibilities: How to Help Yourself Succeed

learning curve a measure of how long it takes you to learn something and how hard it is

Any time you start something new, there's a learning curve involved. The best thing to do is to admit it, decide what to do, and start climbing! Beyond conducting yourself as a professional student, what other things will help you succeed? Here are some additional responsibilities.

Develop a Degree Plan and Plan Your Coursework

In some ways, college is like a journey with parts of the itinerary planned for you. You can't just hitchhike wherever you like. It's more like a guided tour planned by experts in the areas you'd like to explore. You can choose to go left or right at particular moments, but much of the trip is planned in advance.[12] If you'd like to become a nurse, for example, your coursework will be prescribed for you. However, everyone appreciates the focused knowledge of nurses when they need one!

concentration focused effort; specialization

core basic

Some courses will count toward your major or area of concentration, and some will satisfy core requirements. Core requirements often make students wonder: "I'm never going to be another Stephen King. Why do I have to suffer through writing courses I'll never use?" The key words in that last sentence are *never use*. You'll speak and write and think and solve problems in any career. Even though you're in college to prepare for a career, becoming a more knowledgeable person in general should be a big part of your mission.

Most community colleges will ask you to fill out a degree plan up front. You'll plan your coursework for each semester or quarter from now until you've finished. Not only do you end up taking the right courses, but you can watch your progress as you go.

If you decide to transfer to a four-year institution later to get a bachelor's degree, it's likely you can bring many of your associate's degree credits (up to 60 credit hours or half the credits you'll need for a four-year degree) from your community college courses with you. That wouldn't be true unless community colleges were considered to be **real** colleges and coursework was seen as equivalent. However, it is your responsibility to know what courses will transfer to the particular transfer institution you may have in mind. Do some digging on your own by calling an advisor at that school for information that will help you with your planning now. Find out **exactly** which courses will transfer into the major you're considering. And remember that there's a difference between whether a course will **transfer** (for general credit) or **count** (toward a specific degree).

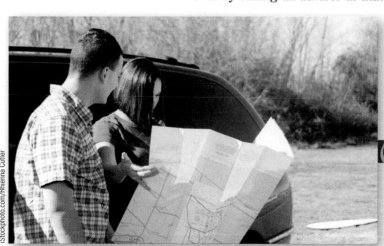

> **If you don't know where you are going, you might wind up someplace else.**
>
> *Yogi Berra, major league baseball player and manager*

Why Do I Have to Take This Class?

Here is a road map, or a sample degree plan, for Darnell, assuming he decides to get a general Associate of Arts Degree at his community college. (The requirements at your community college will be different from this example.)

GREAT BLUFFS COMMUNITY COLLEGE

DEGREE TRACKING WORKSHEET ◄———

NAME___Darnell Williams___ EMAIL ADDRESS___dwilliams@gbcc.edu___

STUDENT NUMBER___123-45-6789___ PHONE___555-9876___

GENERAL STUDIES

Associate of Arts Degree

Program Course #	Course Title	Term (to be) Taken	Term Hours	Grade A = 4 B = 3 C = 2 D = 1 F = 0	Notes
ENGL 090	English Composition I	Fall 2013	3	?	
HIST 103	United States History I		3		
	Foreign Language		5		
GBCC 100	College Success		3		
SPE 115	Public Speaking	Fall 2013	3	?	
ENGL 102	English Composition II		3		
HIST 104	United States History II		3		
	Foreign Language (must be the same language)		5		
	Humanities		3		
PSC 205	United States Government		3		
	Literature		3		
	Visual and Performing Arts		3		
SOC 103	Introduction to Sociology		3		
	Mathematics		3		
	Humanities		3		
PSC 206	State and Local Government		3		
	Natural Science I		3–4		
	Natural Science II		3–4		
	Unrestricted Elective		3		
	Unrestricted Elective		3		

(Adapted from Austin Community College website. Available at www3.austincc.edu/catalog/fy2008/deggens01.rtf)

To complete this activity, visit your academic advisor to get a degree plan for the associate degree or certificate program you're most interested in now. (You may change your mind later.) Fill it in with the help of your advisor, looking ahead to which courses you'll take, semester by semester (or quarter by quarter). Use this degree plan as a working document as you progress through your program.

> The simple act of paying attention can take you a long way.

—KEANU REEVES, AMERICAN ACTOR

Reason 1. They do the right things at the wrong times.

There are many reasons why college students lose their focus. This book will examine some of the most common reasons. See if any of them apply to you.

One reason many of us lose our FOCUS is because we aren't truly present. We don't pay attention. Perhaps we do the right things, but we do them at the wrong times. If you're a morning person, and math is your toughest course, study math in the mornings! The same goes for night owls. In order to be completely present for challenging tasks, ready to give all our attention, we must know ourselves and our own natural rhythms.

TRY It!

On the chart below, put a circle around your peak energy times. Now go back to the list of times, and put a checkmark by your regular study times. Do they match up? Are you studying when you're most effective? If not, can you rearrange things so that you are?

Time		Time	
8 A.M.	_____	4 P.M.	_____
9 A.M.	_____	5 P.M.	_____
10 A.M.	_____	6 P.M.	_____
11 A.M.	_____	7 P.M.	_____
12 A.M.	_____	8 P.M.	_____
1 P.M.	_____	9 P.M.	_____
2 P.M.	_____	10 P.M.	_____
3 P.M.	_____	11 P.M.	_____

Be Advised! Advising Mistakes Students Make

One of the most important relationships you'll have as a community college student is the one you build with your academic advisor. On your campus, this person may be an advisor, a counselor, or a faculty member who can steer you toward courses you can handle and instructors you can learn best from. An advisor can keep you from taking classes that bog you down academically or unnecessary ones that take you extra time to earn your degree. Here's a list of advising mistakes students make, from real advisors who work with college students every day.

1. **Not using the campus advising office or your faculty advisor.** If you don't get regular advice from an advisor, counselor, or a designated faculty member who's serving as your advisor, your degree may take longer and cost more money. It's that simple. It's your college career, after all, and it's important that you and your advisor work as partners.

2. **Not planning ahead.** Some students walk into the advising office or e-mail an advisor and expect help right away, and sometimes that works. However, planning ahead is a better option. Planning ahead includes making an appointment, looking through the course offerings, making a list of questions to ask, and thinking in advance about which days you can attend classes based on your work schedule, how many classes you can take, and on which days of the week. And, if you're leaving your advisor a voice-mail, remember to include all of this important information. What's wrong with this message? "Hi, this is Tony. I have a question about my schedule. Please call me back, OK?" Tony who? And what's his phone number? Or how about an e-mail like this from

hotchick13@email.com? "Do I need to take English 090? Please let me know." Exactly who is "hotchick13"?

3. **Procrastinating.** It's important not to put off advising appointments. To drop a class, you may need to meet a deadline. Or you may need help from an advisor to solve a problem with a faculty member, but by the time you get around to it, the instructor has already left campus for the summer. If you deal with problems right away, while they're small, they may be reversible. (And it's always a good idea to discuss dropping a class with the instructor first.)

4. **Skipping prerequisites.** Some students want to skip the required pre-requisites. They think they can handle the work. They think prereqs are a waste of time and money when, actually, they're in place because hundreds of students before you have shown that these classes help you succeed. And in some cases, students who haven't taken a prereq are actually disenrolled from the course that requires it.

prerequisites courses that you need to take before advancing on to other ones

5. **Choosing the wrong major.** Sometimes students lock on to a major because someone else thinks it's a good idea or because a particular career field pays well, not because they enjoy the subject and are suited for it. Staying motivated is hard when you're not interested in something. Advisors can help you figure out which major is right for you.

6. **Taking too many credits or too few.** Some students are overly optimistic and think they can handle a heavier course load than the other factors in their lives will permit. Other students may underestimate the number of courses they should take, which increases the time it takes them to finish school. An advisor can help you stay on target.

7. **Ignoring problems.** If you run into difficulty and end up on academic probation, for example, an advisor or college official will work with you to get you back on track. But you must agree to that bargain and accept the help, possibly by signing a contract of steps you must take to reverse the situation.

8. **Being afraid to drop a course.** Sometimes, when you've tried everything (for example, tutoring, extra help sessions, and the campus learning center), but you're still not succeeding in a course, the best thing to do may be to drop the course by filling out a drop form (online or on paper) and submitting it. Then retake the course later. That option is better than just not going to class and assuming that by not coming, you've dropped the course. Colleges require deliberate action from you. It's always best to know your school's rules and talk with your instructor first. *And beware that dropping a course may affect your financial aid.*[13]

Make the Grade: Computing Your GPA

One of the most important things to learn as a new college student—and fast—is what grade point averages (GPAs) are and how they work. Your GPA is an indication of how well you're doing, and you keep track of it over time, term by term. Your academic record will follow you for the rest of your life! Some students don't realize how grade points add up. They end up on academic probation, even

GPA an average of all your grades for a single semester or a running average across all your coursework

if they only have one failing grade. Let's say you're taking four courses this term, and you earn the following grades:

Course	Credits	Final Grade	Grade Point Value
English Composition	3 credits	C (2 points)	6
College Algebra	3 credits	F (0 points)	0
College Success	3 credits	B (3 points)	9
Public Speaking	3 credits	D (1 point)	3
TOTAL	**12 credits**		**18 grade points**

You may look at this record and think, *Not bad. I passed three of my four courses.* But divide that Grade Point Value column total (18) by the total number of credits (12), and you get 1.5.

GPA = Grade Point Value ÷ Total Number of Credits

At most schools, a 1.5 GPA puts you on academic probation, and eventually, you may be facing suspension. That can be a discouraging way to start, and digging yourself out of a GPA hole once you're there takes a very long time, like paying off credit card debt.

Not only is it important to keep track of your grades over the whole term, but it's also important to keep track of your grade in each course. If you stop going to your math class because it's too hard or because you don't like the teacher, your grade will suffer. If an assignment is worth 25 percent of your grade, and you don't turn it in, the highest grade you can possibly earn, even if you do everything else perfectly, is a 75 percent or "C." You may think, *but it's only one assignment.* It is only one assignment, but it counts as one-quarter of your grade. In college, everything counts. The typical grading scale in college is:

A = 90–100%   B = 80–89%   C = 70–79%
D = 60–69%   F = 59% and below

Realize the Value of Developmental Courses

As a rule, community colleges have what's called an open-door admissions policy. That means that anyone who wants to get an education is invited in. You don't have to get a certain score on the SAT or ACT standardized national tests, and you don't have to have a

Problems are only opportunities in work clothes.

Henry J. Kaiser, American industrialist (1882–1967)

particular GPA in high school to be admitted. That's a good thing. As a nation, we are opening the doors of education to everyone, and our society as a whole benefits in many ways. Education improves the quality of life.[14]

But when restrictions are removed, more variety is a natural result, right? Think of it this way: If every student at your community college had to be over six feet tall to be admitted, then you and all your classmates would tower over the general public. But if anyone of any height could attend, you'd see a range from very short to very tall. Some people would need steps to reach high places, and others would have to duck under low ceilings. But variety presents challenges. Community colleges are characterized by variety, and they've devised ways to make it work. Here's how.

New community college students bring standardized test scores or take placement tests that help schools know where to *place* them. If you're "short" on some necessary skills for success, like reading, writing, or math, they'll place you in a developmental (sometimes called *remedial*) class to help you catch up fast. Some students see these courses negatively, thinking they're a waste of time or money. Not so! Don't get discouraged if you're in one or more of these classes. They're insurance that you will grow into the skills you'll need.

developmental designed to develop or improve a skill

If you're enrolled in a developmental class, you're in good company. In one study of 35 community colleges that are all part of a proposal to increase student success, 37 percent of incoming students required one remedial course, 26 percent required two courses, and 22 percent required three courses—for a total of 85 percent. And note this piece of good news: In a related study, students who earned a C or better in a developmental course during their first semester were, from that point forward, more likely to stay in school and succeed than students who weren't required to take a developmental course in the first place![15] In another study, students who took a developmental writing course earned higher English grades in later courses and higher GPAs overall than students who did not.[16] If you're enrolled in a developmental class, perhaps you're beginning to see its value *now*. If you don't see the value yet, chances are you'll greatly appreciate what it did for you *later*.

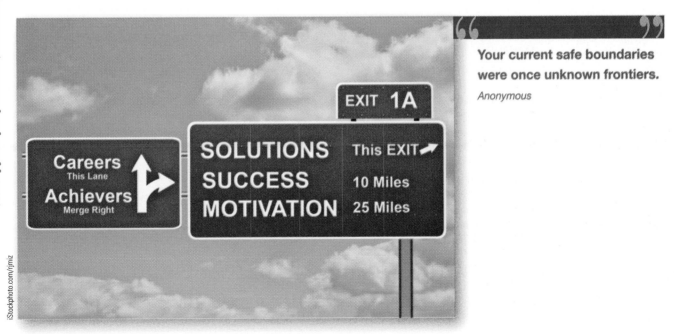

iStockphoto.com/rjmiz

Your current safe boundaries were once unknown frontiers.

Anonymous

BOX 1.1

Analyzing a Syllabus

Take a look at this example syllabus to see what you think. What is this professor like? Do you get a sense of her standards and values from her syllabus? Will this be a challenging course? Take a close look at a syllabus from one of your current classes. Analyze it, just as this one has been analyzed, and make a list of things you learn about specific aspects of the syllabus that can help you be successful.

> Some community colleges have a syllabus template or standard format so that your syllabus for each class will look basically the same and contain similar kinds of information.

> Pay attention to the course description. It's a summary of what you can expect.

> You can buy the textbook from your college bookstore or order it online. But often textbooks are "customized" with portions inserted from different books or material that pertains to your own campus. You must buy those books from your campus bookstore. Even though textbooks cost money, they are a critical investment. Trying to get by without one puts you at a disadvantage right from the start.

> The instructor has devoted a substantial portion of the syllabus to this topic, and she has spelled out her expectations in detail. Professional conduct must be important to her.

> This syllabus actually continues on for several more pages and includes three other things: (1) a campus statement about academic honesty and plagiarism, (2) due dates for each assignment, and (3) specific information on how speeches will be graded.

> Send the instructor an e-mail the first week of class, introducing yourself and discussing your thoughts about how this class will help you. Remember, however, that in college, you must use good grammar and correct spelling in ALL your writing, including e-mails.

> It's appropriate to ask the instructor what she prefers to be called: Regina, Ms. Lewis, Professor Lewis, and so on.

GREAT BLUFFS COMMUNITY COLLEGE
COURSE SYLLABUS

Course ID: SPE 115
Term: Fall 2013
Instructor: Regina Lewis
Office: Vail Hall 501
Office Hours: MW 10:00–11:00 a.m., TR 2:00–3:00 p.m., by appointment only

Course Title: Public Speaking
Credit Hours: 3
E-mail Address: regina.lewis@gbcc.edu
Office Phone: 555–1234

Course Description: This course combines the theory of speech communication with oral performance skills. Emphasis is on researching, organizing, and preparing speeches and analyzing the needs and interests of your particular audience. Although this is primarily a performance class, you will also build your writing and researching skills.

Prerequisites/Co-Requisites: ENG 090, REA 090

Course Textbook: *Public Speaking: Concepts and Skills for a Diverse Society,* 2013. Cengage Learning.

Professional Conduct in Class: Students are responsible for knowing and abiding by the "Standards of Conduct" listed in the 2013–2014 GBCC Catalog (beginning on page 10). Your cell phone or pager should be turned off, set to vibrate only, or left at home. Eating, sleeping, social discussions, or doing reading or homework for other classes are distracting behaviors and communicate indifference and disrespect for this learning environment and subject matter. Children should not be brought to class. Getting up and coming in and out during class (unless you are sick, of course) is distracting to your classmates. These activities are unacceptable in academic environments and qualify as examples of inappropriate conduct in class, which may result in your academic withdrawal from the class.

Online Course Management System (CMS): e-CC (pronounced EASY). All students have access to the materials posted on the CMS website through the Internet from a campus computer lab or from home.

Attendance: If you must miss a class for an emergency, you must still submit assigned work by the due date. Please provide documentation to indicate that the absence was due to a situation beyond your control. There are no excused absences without documentation. In order to receive credit for attendance, you must attend the ENTIRE class period. IF YOU MISS A CLASS, IT IS YOUR RESPONSIBILITY TO CONTACT A CLASSMATE FOR NOTES AND ASSIGNMENTS. NO MAKEUP WORK IS ALLOWED.

Grading: Assignments must be turned in on time and speeches must be presented on schedule. Grades for makeup speeches are automatically reduced by 20 percent. Only one makeup day will be scheduled for speeches missed due to emergencies! THERE ARE NO MAKEUP EXAMS OR WRITTEN ASSIGNMENTS.

Americans with Disabilities Act (ADA): Any student eligible for academic accommodations because of a learning or physical disability should speak with the instructor during the first week of class and contact the Office of Support Services.

Speeches: You will be required to give a minimum of five speeches.
- SP 1: Informative 5 mins. (+ or −1 min.) (1 visual aid) Prep and speaking outline required.
- SP 2: Career (Impromptu) Speaking on the spot!
- SP 3: Ceremonial 3 mins. (+ or −1 min.) (1 quote) Prep and speaking outline required.
- SP 4: Persuasive 7 mins. (+ or −1 min.) (2 visual aids and 2 sources) Prep and speaking outline required. You must have a partner for the opposition.
- SP 5: Public Speaking Outside the Box 10 mins. (+ or −2 mins.) (Poster, flyer, 2 visual aids) Presented in TV studio.

Source: Regina Lewis, Pikes Peak Community College. Used by permission.

Master the Syllabus

You'll get a syllabus (or course schedule) for most all of the college classes you'll take. If the syllabi (plural of syllabus) for your courses are available online, check them often to keep up with any changes in the schedule or new assignments. If you have a hard copy, keep it handy and refer to it often. Think of a syllabus as:

> a preview of what to expect during every class

> a road map for where the course will take you

> a contract between you and your instructor

> a summary of all the assignments and how much they count toward your grade

> a tool that lists reading and homework to help you prepare for class

> evidence of an instructor's standards, grading system, and values

Avoid the PCP Syndrome: Use Campus Resources

The convenience of community college can also be a drawback. Because you're going to college in your own community, it's easy to develop a drive-through mentality. You show up for classes and then hightail it for work or home right away. Some experts describe this phenomenon as the "PCP Syndrome: Parking Lot, Class, Parking Lot." What's wrong with that? you ask. When you've finished grocery shopping, you get back in your car and go home, right? You don't cruise the aisles and hang around.

But going to college is very different from shopping for groceries. Your campus has many things available for you to take advantage of: student clubs, special presentations, musical events, and learning resource centers, for example. You may never find out about these "free samples" if you're not there. You won't make new friends or get to know your instructors, two practices that are essential to your success.[17] The danger is that when the going gets rough, which can happen during exam time, you may be tempted to retreat to what you're most familiar with—your life before college—and abandon your efforts. Whatever the problem, there's a place to go for help on campus. Even if your campus doesn't have every possible kind of support center right there, your advisors or instructors can always direct you to services off campus.

Remember that "HELP" is not a four-letter word. Getting help when you need it isn't a stigma; it's smart. Take this example: In 1979, Diana Nyad achieved the record for open-water swimming a distance of 102.5 miles. But it took 51 other people to help her reach her goal (guides to check winds and currents, divers to look for sharks, and NASA nutrition experts to keep her from losing more than the 29 pounds she lost during that one swim).[18] Your campus has all kinds of resources available for the taking, but you must take them. They won't come to you. Here are some of the FAQs new college students often ask:

> **How can I meet other students?** Take advantage of favorite gathering spots on campus. If you're finding it hard to meet people, could it be because you're not around? To meet people, it helps to be where they are.

> **What if I need help with a challenging course?** Many campuses have support centers: a science learning center or a math learning center, for example. Or particular courses may offer what's called supplemental instruction, extra help beyond class sessions with basic course materials or homework assignments. You may be able to work with a tutor, too—a student who's extra-good at math, for example. Check out whatever options are available to you, and use them, rather than struggle on your own if you're not getting results.

> **I'm thinking of dropping a class. How do I do it?** The Office of the Registrar or Office of Admissions and Records is where to go. They also help with things like transferring credits and getting transcripts if you've attended college somewhere before or plan to transfer. Think through the results of dropping a class, however. Will doing so change your financial aid status, for example?

> **What if I need a counselor?** College is a time of change. Your relationships may be affected or you may suffer from symptoms of stress. If your campus has a counseling center and you need to use its services, do so. And if you find yourself in the middle of a real crisis, call the campus hotline for immediate help.

> **How can I find out if I have a learning disability?** Check to see whether your campus has a learning center or a special office that helps with learning disabilities. You can work with a specialist there who can help. If you've been diagnosed with a learning disability before, bring your documentation to that office for their records and let your instructors know. They can help, too.

> **What if I have a technology crisis?** Your campus probably has a computer help desk, where techies can often solve what sounds like a complicated problem, with simple advice. Also, use the campus computer labs. They may have better computers than yours at home, and you can make good use of blocks of time between classes.

> **Are health services available to students?** Many campuses have a student health center where you can find a range of free or inexpensive services—everything from flu shots to strep throat tests to birth control advice if you're sexually active.

iStockphoto.com/walik

> ❝ **One hundred percent of the shots you don't take don't go in.** ❞
>
> *Wayne Gretzky, called the greatest ice hockey player of all time*

> **What do I want to be when I grow up?** Thinking ahead to a career when you finish college is sometimes hard when so much is going on at the moment. What do you like to do? What people skills do you have? Visit your campus's career center. Experts there can help you discover a major and career that will work for you.

> **Is child care available?** Many campuses have inexpensive child care available. Being able to drop off a child in the morning right on campus and pick him up after your classes are over can be a real help.

> **Where can I buy my books?** Textbooks are a big investment these days, and it's important to buy the right editions for your classes. Should you buy them from your campus bookstore or order online? Buying books

EXERCISE 1.3

Top Ten Resources Your Campus Offers

Make a list of ten resources your campus offers that can help you succeed in your coursework. For example, does your campus have a health center, a day care center, or a learning center? Visit each location, and identify specific ways you will use each office or service.

Name of office/service	Contact information	How will I use this resource?
1.		
2.		
3.		
4.		
5.		
6.		
7.		
8.		
9.		
10.		

online may save you money, although you'll have to wait for shipment. The bookstore is a much quicker option, and it's a good idea to find out where it is, no matter where you buy your books. You'll most likely need it for other school supplies. Renting your books or buying an e-book that you can read online may be an option, too.

> **Where can I get other pieces of information I may need?** Try your campus website, the school bulletin or catalog, the student handbook, or the school newspaper.

> **What if I need the help of Campus Security?** If you feel unsafe walking to your car late at night or you need information about parking permits on campus, check with the Campus Security or Public Safety Office. They're there for your protection.

What's the bottom line? Get to know your campus and its full range of offerings—and take advantage of everything that's in place to help you be as academically successful as possible.

Toughing It Out: What College Takes

What does it mean to succeed? Actually, success is difficult to define, and different people define success differently. Right now in college, you may think of success in terms of the money you'll make after you finish. But is success just about money? Is it about fame? Status? According to motivational author Robert Collier, "Success is the sum of small efforts, repeated day in and day out." Perhaps to you, success is somewhere off in the distant future, and it happens more or less suddenly, like winning the lottery.

Actually, success begins right now. You should be the one to define what success will look like in your life, but generally, success is *setting out to do something that means something to you, and then being fully engaged while doing it.* It's that simple. And it applies to your college experience as well. It starts now.

In order to understand your own definition of success in college, first you need to ask yourself why you're here. Why *did* you come—or return—to college, anyway? Do you want to develop into a more interesting, well-rounded, educated human being? Are you working toward a degree that leads to a specific career? Do you have children and want an education in order to give them a better life? This book will provide you with an honest look at what that takes, including plenty of opportunities to ask yourself questions about these things. It will also offer you tools you can use throughout your college courses and in your life beyond college.

Some students think going to college is like any other financial transaction: buying a gallon of milk, for example. You pay the cashier the money, and the milk now belongs to you. They think if they pay tuition, the college credits should be theirs. Not so. There's much more to it than that. A college education requires more than a financial commitment. It requires you to invest your ability, your intellect, your drive, your effort—and yourself. College has to do with more than the brain matter found between your ears.

The Good News and the Bad News (Benefits and Obstacles)

What's the good news about going to college? The benefits are wide-reaching and long-lasting. Think about how this list applies to you.

1. **Higher earning potential.** College increases your potential to earn money. It's that simple. On average, people with associate's degrees earn 20 to 30 percent more than those with a high school diploma only. Experts say that one-third of new job growth from 2008 until 2018 will require some education after high school.[19] And there's some evidence that jobs requiring certificates or associate's degrees will grow at an even faster rate than jobs requiring a four-year degree.[20] Sixty percent of jobs right now are held by people with post–high school education or training.[21]

2. **Lower unemployment rates.** College decreases your risk of unemployment. This is especially helpful when the economy takes a downturn. According to one recent major study, getting an associate's or bachelor's degree is a better investment today than the stock market, gold, or housing.[22]

3. **Wisdom.** College gives you opportunities to gain understanding about many things—politics, people, and current affairs to name a few. Beyond theories, facts, and dates, well-educated people know how to think critically, contribute to society, and manage their lives.

4. **Insight.** College students have the opportunity to understand themselves better as they learn different ways of doing things.

5. **Lifelong learning.** According to research, getting a college degree—even for a career that doesn't require one—leads to a happier, healthier life.[23] College students are prepared to become lifelong learners. It's not just about grades. It's about becoming the best student-learner you can be—inside or outside of the classroom. This one benefit will stay with you through the rest of your life.

What's the bad news? What obstacles may stand in your path? Darnell Williams isn't quite sure why he's in college. Will he be successful? It depends, doesn't it? Here's some evidence on what "it" consists of.

Some experts say that fewer than half of community college students reach their educational goals.[24] But who goes, who finishes later, and who

Always bear in mind that your own resolution to succeed is more important than any one thing.

Abraham Lincoln, 16th President of the United States (1809–1875)

iStockphoto.com/Pedrosa

transfers to another school are hard things to track. The risk factors for dropping out of college include working more than thirty hours per week, going to school part-time, being a single parent or having children at home, and being a first-generation college student.[25] However, more than 70 percent of community college students have at least one of these characteristics, and half have two or more.[26] It's true that going to college is "A Whole 'Nother World," as one major report's title says. Juggling a job, family, friends, transportation, tuition, and all the things that are impacted by the energy and effort it takes to go to college can be overwhelming. If you're a first-generation college student, you may not have a role model at home who can help you, because your parents didn't go to college. (That's why it's important to make connections with your classmates, instructors, and advisors who can guide you.)[27] Even though college may be more challenging for first-generation students, you can still be highly successful. Perhaps the most famous current example is Michelle Obama, who went from first-generation college student to First Lady.[28]

The important thing to keep in mind as you think about risk factors is that they alone cannot determine your ultimate level of success. Don't throw in the towel now if you had a child at age sixteen or are working thirty-five hours per week. These factors are presented merely as information to assist you on your journey. They are simply predictors—not *determiners*. Only you can determine your outcomes in life, and that includes college.

predictors something that indicates something in the future may happen

Plenty of people who have achieved great things in their lives got their start at a community college. Look at this impressive list:[29]

> Queen Latifah, rapper, actress, talk show host
> Gwendolyn Brooks, Pulitzer prize–winning poet
> Billy Crystal, actor and comedian
> Tom Hanks, actor
> Calvin Klein, designer
> Clint Eastwood, actor
> Joyce Luther Kennard, California Supreme Court justice
> Jim Lehrer, news anchor
> James Sinegal, CEO of Costco

Your effort, attitude, and willingness to get any help you need to succeed are all vital.

> I am only one,
> But still I am one.
> I cannot do everything,
> But still I can do something;
> And because I cannot do everything
> I will not refuse to do the something that I can do.

Edward Everett Hale, American author (1822–1909)

This Course Has a Proven Track Record

If you're reading this book, there's a good chance you're enrolled in a first-year seminar course, called something like First-Year Seminar, First-Year Experience, College Success, Learning Community, or any of a host of other names. These courses are designed to introduce you to college life, familiarize you with your own campus, and help you improve your academic skills. Do they work? According to experts, the answer is yes! Of course, you have to keep your part of the bargain, but in general, community college students who complete first-year seminars are much more successful. According to one study, community college students who took an orientation or college success course were seventy-two times more likely to graduate than students who didn't.[30] Take a look at the results of another major study in Figure 1.1.

Students who completed a college success course were more likely to stay in school, succeed academically, and transfer to universities. And students who completed a college success course and also needed to take developmental courses in one to three subject areas were even more likely to achieve these results! That's what this course is about: your success. Your instructor and your classmates are rooting for you. Now it's up to you!

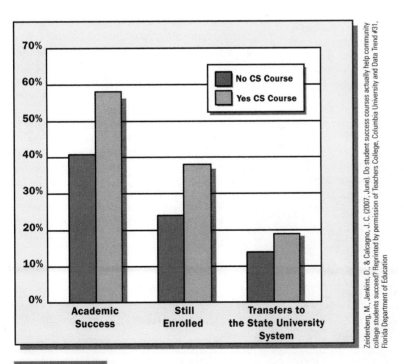

Zeidenberg, M., Jenkins, D., & Calcagno, J. C. (2007, June). Do student success courses actually help community college students succeed? Reprinted by permission of Teachers College, Columbia University and Data Trend #31. Florida Department of Education

FIGURE 1.1

Outcomes of Community College Students Completing a College Success Course and Those Who Did Not (1999–2000 through 2003–2004)

BOX **1.2**

Generation 1: First in the Family?

Did both your parents graduate from college? If not, you are a "first-generation college student." Quite an impressive title, isn't it? Being first at something has some definite pros. You're a trailblazer, a pioneer, someone to be looked up to. "Imagine, our son Dion with a college degree! Isn't that something?" But along with pros come potential challenges. Who will you go to for advice? Will your family understand what it takes? Will they support your efforts? At moments when your confidence is shaken, you may wonder: *Can a first-generation student be successful?* The answer? Of course! (Your author is a first-generation college graduate!) In the end, your success is up to you. As you begin your college career, take these suggestions to heart:

1. **Communicate with your family.** Research shows that the *quality* and *quantity* of communication about college that you engage in with your family is key to your success. Although they can't empathize because they haven't "been there and done that," they can listen and encourage you. Talk to them openly about your college experience.[31]

2. **Keep your stress level in check.** If your family puts extra pressure on you to perform, your stress level may increase dramatically. But stress isn't the best motivator. This is something you want to do, so hone in and hunker down. Pay particular attention to your instructors, keep track of due dates, and focus. All you can

do is your best. Think of it this way: you're "demystifying" college. You may just inspire Mom or Dad or your little brother to go to college one day too.[32]

3. **Get going.** Remember this: when the going gets tough, the tough get going. Sometimes first-generation students are tempted to drop out, scale back (from four classes to three, for example), avoid assessment (thinking, oddly, "If I don't turn my paper in, I can't get a bad grade on it"), or lower their own expectations ("I was hoping for a 4.0 GPA, but maybe a 2.0 will do"). Although sometimes these options may be the right ones, sabotaging your own efforts is never a good idea. Keep your eye on the prize—that degree you'll be the first one to earn in your family.[33]

4. **Find a true mentor.** Look for a particular professor or advisor to serve as a mentor—someone you can go to for advice and support. Just knowing that someone cares can be a powerful motivator. Ask this person to help you through rough patches or go to her to get recharged when your "academic batteries" are low.

5. **Get involved.** College may feel like a "foreign" culture to you. You may have conflicting emotions: excitement, confusion, and anxiety. You may not understand what instructors expect, how to fit in, or how to get it all done. But you won't learn these things if you aren't around. If you breeze in for your classes and bolt afterward, it will be harder to adjust to your new role. Ease into the campus culture and take full advantage of what it means to be in college. Make friends and feel the beat of campus life.[34]

If you follow this advice, you *can* be successful! If you're a first-generation college student, dog-ear or bookmark this page, and refer back to it whenever you need to.

Ryan McVay/Getty Images

> Though no one can go back and make a brand new start, anyone can start from now and make a brand-new ending.
>
> *Carl Bard*

How Do I Want to Be Different When I'm Done?

One thing is sure: College will change you. Most every high-intensity experience full of opportunities does. Take advantage, meet new people, and stretch yourself. You may notice that as a result of your college experience, your old relationships may "fit" differently. Your romantic partner may brag about you or secretly envy you. Your family may praise your efforts or hardly notice. But you will. If you finish what you've begun, you will watch yourself become a more sophisticated, more knowledgeable, more confident person. You can't help but be. Ask yourself now, at the beginning of your college experience, just how you'd like to change, and make it happen.

BOX 1.3 How to Read a Case Study

Each chapter of *FOCUS* will begin with a case study about a real student, marked as **STEP 1** and portrayed by a member of the *FOCUS* cast. (You'll see the cast members in photos throughout the book—and will perhaps almost feel you know them all by the end.) As you read the case, you may think: *Hmmm . . . this is an interesting story, but what does it have to do with me?* Make the most out of these case studies by following these suggestions:

- **Make a connection.** Although you may be a different age, gender, or ethnicity, look at the issues beneath the surface. Actually, you may have some things in common with the case study character, or you may know someone else who does. Are you tempted to make some of the mistakes Darnell is making? Is your best buddy worried about similar issues? Did your sister, who was in college before you, struggle with her writing class, as Darnell does?

- **Get engaged.** The case studies are designed to be a fully interactive and visual experience for you. You can gain a complete picture of the case study students by reading their

story *and* looking closely at the photos and visual examples. Learn even more about the students by looking at sample emails, notes, text messages, Facebook profiles, and other key visual examples of their lives.

- **Think critically.** Imagine yourself in a conversation with the case study students. What advice would you give them? How would you help them solve their problems? Becoming an active reader and critical thinker will help you build skills that will contribute to your success as a college student.

- **Prepare to learn.** The case study will preview all the topics you'll read about in the chapter. The chapters will provide you with strategies to deal with these challenges. Make sure you read each case thoroughly, watch for things you will learn in the chapter, and then answer the Reaction questions listed in **STEP 2**.

If you follow them through the book, these featured students will lead you into a rich, "FOCUSed" learning experience!

EXERCISE 1.4

Write Your Own Case Study

Everyone has a story. This is your opportunity to tell yours! Start by flipping through FOCUS and skimming the other Challenge cases. Perhaps your biggest challenge will be something like those facing Katie Alexander or Derek Johnson, or maybe your particular challenge doesn't appear in this book. (If you expect everything to be "smooth sailing" for you, you may prefer to write about a friend or relative beginning college, and that's acceptable too.) This exercise will allow you to personalize what you will learn in this class and identify possible issues that may interfere with your success in college early on. Here are the steps you will follow:

1. First, write your *CHALLENGE* story. Your instructor will give you specific guidelines, but in general, write a two-page case study that highlights your previous learning experiences, your   *(Continued)*

expectations for college, key pieces of your life outside of college that may interfere with your success, and the top challenges you are facing right now in college. You should write your story in the third person, and you may give yourself a fictional (but real-sounding) name. You may write, for example, "It was her first day of college, and the temperature outside had reached a record high. She rushed into the building from the parking lot so that the air conditioning would start cooling her down right away. But she had more than the temperature on her car thermometer on her mind. She was nervous. No one from her family had ever gone to college, and suddenly she felt pressure to impress them"—or whatever was true for you.

2. Choose personalized images to surround your story—a photo of you, other photos of people in the story, images that relate to the case, whatever you wish—and place them around the story. (Go to an online site that has free images you can choose from or download photos from your Facebook page, if you have one.) Your case should look something like one of the ones in *FOCUS*. You may use whatever e-tool you wish to create your case (PowerPoint or Word, for example), but your instructor may want you to turn in a paper copy. This part of the assignment should be two (facing) pages.

3. Write three to five *REACTION* questions to go along with your case. Start by thinking about issues where you need the most advice, and build your questions around those. You may want to ask your reader, "What's the primary challenge facing this new student? Describe it in your own words." or "Why is this issue (whatever it is) something that could interfere with college success?" Your instructor may ask you to answer these questions yourself or swap your case with a classmate and answer his or her questions. At the end of this course, you will look back at your beginning case study (CHALLENGE→REACTION) and write about the INSIGHT→ACTION learning that has taken place for you along the way.

step 3 INSIGHT *Now* What Do You Think?

At the beginning of this chapter, Darnell Williams faced a series of challenges as a new college student. Now after learning from this chapter, would you respond differently to any of the questions you answered about the "FOCUS Challenge Case"? Using what you learned in the chapter, write a paragraph ending Darnell's case study. What are some of the possible outcomes for Darnell?

step 4 ACTION Your Plans for Change

1. Identify one new thing you learned in reading this chapter. Why did you select the one you've selected? How will it affect what you do in your college classes?

2. Why are you going to community college? How do you see your college experience impacting your future?

3. How do you want college to change you? Why?

chapter 2 · Building Dreams, Setting Goals

How this chapter relates to **YOU**

1. When it comes to dreams, goals, and your own future, what are you most unsure about, if anything?

What I really want to do with my life

What I'm really good at

Whether my dreams are achievable

How to set realistic goals

If college will really help me

2. What is most likely to be your response? Circle it.

I'll keep thinking about it.

I'll ask for guidance from an expert on campus.

I'll see which courses really interest me.

I'll figure it out on my own.

3. What would you have to do to increase your likelihood of success? Will you do it this quarter or semester?

Example: Start working with an advisor or career counselor now! Yes!

How **YOU** will relate to this chapter

What are you most interested in learning about? Put checkmarks by those topics.

☐ How this book will help you learn

☐ What motivates you

☐ How your attitude can sabotage you

☐ Why you should distinguish between dreams and goals

☐ How to develop goals that work

How motivated are you to learn more about getting the right start in college?
(5 = high, 1 = low) ____

● How ready are you to read now? ____
(If something is in your way, take care of it if you can, zero in and focus.)

● How long do you think it will take you to complete this chapter? If you start and stop, keep track of your overall time.
____ hour(s) ____ minutes

Sylvia Sanchez

Artmin/Shutterstock.com

Her own apartment—finally! As Sylvia opened the new package of turquoise sheets for her bed she felt excited but at the same time, amazingly calm. Frankly, she couldn't believe her parents had agreed to it. But their response to the idea had been, "Sure, if you're willing to pay your own rent, we'll find plenty of uses for your room." So Sylvia had been counting off the days all summer, and frankly, it felt good to be on her own. No younger brothers and sisters squawking, no parents breathing down her neck, no grandparents living right next door, and no lame boyfriend thinking he could just hang around all the time. A fresh start—that's what she wanted. She stopped to check her cell phone—four new texts, probably all from him. And all those pictures of her he had posted on Facebook this morning! She wanted to write back and tell him to get over it, but she thought she'd better wait awhile for that. *Let's just see what college has to offer. That's smarter*, she admitted. Her three high school friends, and now roommates, hadn't arrived yet, so naturally Sylvia claimed the best bedroom. *They'd probably have done the same thing*, she reassured herself. *They should have gotten here earlier.*

Sylvia had always been smart—not brilliant, but smart enough to know how to play the game. She was always rushing around, doing a hundred things at once. Focusing wasn't her strong point, and multitasking didn't always get her the best grades, but truthfully, she'd never even cracked a book during her senior year and still passed all her classes. She always did her homework (that is, when she did any) in front of the TV while she played with the

dog, texted her friends, and checked her Facebook page. College, she imagined, would be a slightly harder version of high school. It couldn't be as hard as her parents had warned. She remembered their threats when she brought home a bad grade in high school: *You just wait until you start college!* How would they know? They'd never even been to college themselves. If all that propaganda from

Andesr/Shutterstock.com

Google, Inc.

https://mail.google.com/mail/?shva=1#inbc

File Edit View Favorites Tools Help

M Gmail - Inbox

Gmail Calendar Documents Photos Reader Web more ▾

Gmail

Search Mail   Search the Web   Show search options / Create a filter

Mail
Contacts
Tasks

Compose mail

Inbox
Buzz
Starred ☆
Important
Sent Mail
Drafts

Personal
Work
6 more▾

Archive   Report spam   Delete   ⊕ ⊖   Move to ▾   Labels ▾   More actions ▾   Refresh

	Carmen Kirby	Movie times for tonight...
	Maria Sanchez	Hi from mom!
	SingerTryOuts.com:	Try outs this Sunday!
	Al Sanchez	Hello from Dad.
	Maria Sanchez	Don't forget Grandma's BD!
	Maria Sanchez	Your sister got a new job!
	Constance Staley	Welcome to College Success!
	Al Sanchez	FW: Business opportunities on the rise!
	Maria Sanchez	Whiskers misses you!
	Alex Ortez	Which classes are you taking?
	Carmen Kirby	Movie times for tonight...

Sylvia Sanchez +

Search, add, or invite

Mom & Dad – last summer

Thursday 8:42 pm

parents and high school teachers were really true, no one would go to college! *How hard can it possibly be?* she asked herself. Her parents said they'd help financially when they could, but she wasn't expecting much. "And we're not paying for anything below a B!" her father had insisted. She just had to keep her grades up enough to hold onto her financial aid, and if she could manage to impress her parents, that wouldn't hurt, either. Her track record in school had never been all that great, but just maybe she could change that in college.

Of her four new college courses, Sylvia was least worried about her college success class. *Automatic A*, she predicted. *Everyone knows how to study. It's just common sense*, she thought to herself. But whether studying enough to "live up to her potential" was on her agenda was another thing. The thought of writing an essay every week for her English Composition class brought on major dread; in fact, she wasn't all that excited about any of her classes. There might be other, more compelling pursuits that took up her time in college, like meeting interesting people and finishing her demo CD.

The one thing Sylvia knew for sure was that she desperately wanted to make it in the music industry, and her parents desperately wanted her to major in business. "How many people actually become famous musicians?" they would ask. Her Dad grilled her regularly on the subject. "There are all kinds of possible careers if you earn a business degree, but how many people actually make it as musicians—even if they're good? What are the odds? College is the way to go, and a certificate in business makes sense." Your mother and I never had the chance; don't blow

this opportunity!" "Yeah, whatever . . ." was her usual retort.

But all Sylvia really wanted in life was to be behind a microphone in front of an audience. And the bigger the audience, the better. Someday—she just knew it—she'd sign a recording contract with a major record label. All her friends told her how good she was. They'd even encouraged her to try out for a TV singing competition. Imagine—fame and fortune. *Sylvia Sanchez, recording artist . . .* even her name had the right ring to it and eventually, everyone would recognize it. They'd download her top hits, and she'd have the clothes, hair, make-up, and money she'd always wanted.

As she stood at the foot of the bed, admiring her new sheets, Sylvia caught a glimpse of herself in the mirror on the wall. "Looking good!" she whispered. Was she referring to how her new bedroom was shaping up or how she'd made the right decision on what to wear?

Suddenly, Sylvia heard laughter in the hallway and realized it was her new roommates. They had hung out together in high school, but how would she like actually living with them? Would they start getting on one another's nerves? Deep down, Sylvia realized, she really did want to be successful in college. But she also wanted to live her own life and do her own thing. Still, she rationalized, *If this whole college thing doesn't work out, I'll move back home, pick up where I left off, get back my old job at the restaurant close to home, and wait for the future I* really *want.*

Elif Eren/Shutterstock.com

RAGMA IMAGES/Shutterstock.com

AP photo/PRNewsFoto/Epic Records, Pindyurin Vasily

© Cengage Learning

SDV 101: Academi
Focus on College

CHECK IT OUT!

"Excellence is achieved by the mastery of fundamentals"
Vince Lombardi

In this

• Empower yourself
→ to School

JOBS in BUSINESS!

ACME Business Professionals, Inc. is a rising company in North America that employs a wide range of business professionals. Currently seeking professionals ready to launch a career in business (marketing, finance, and sales).

JOB TITLE: Sales Associate, Midwestern Region

RESPONSIBILITIES:
• Assess current status of all existing business
• Provide current level of service or improve service to all clients
• Formulate plan to develop all new business opportunities
• Work with local interns to develop future staffing
• Select and train new associates
• Develop regional hiring/training opportunities
• Expand regional potential

SALARY: commensurate with experience and qualifications Acme Business Professionals, Inc. is known for its commitment to quality, diversity, and exceptional service.

TO APPLY: Send a current resume, along with a cover letter, to our Human Resources Department at Dana.Horner@acmepro.com.

Classified Ads

Course Schedule
Main Campus
FALL SEMESTER

© Cengage Learning

Student: Sanchez,

Course ID	Course T
PSYCH 100	INTRO TO
ENGL 130	ENGLISH
UNIV 101	COLLEGE
102	PHIL

Instructor

Work Schedule Week # 46

Fernando's Hideaway, South L

	Sunday	Monday	Tuesday	Wedensday	Thursday	Friday	
Abel, Nora	8-5	2-CL			8-5	9-6	
Collins, Becky	2-CL		9-6	2-CL		2-CL	
Sanchez, Sylvia		8-5	2-CL		9-6	8-5	
Harper, Alex			9-6	8-5	10-7	2-CL	

1. Is Sylvia sufficiently motivated to succeed in college? Why or why not?
2. Describe Sylvia's beliefs about her intelligence. Does she think college is mostly about effort or about ability? Is Sylvia a *learner* or a *performer*?
3. Is Sylvia's vision of becoming a famous singer a goal or a dream? Why?
4. Identify three things that show focus and might help Sylvia make good life management choices.
5. Are any elements of Sylvia's situation similar to your own college experience thus far?

Who Are You? And What Do You Want?

Imagine this voicemail greeting: "Hi. At the tone, please answer two of life's most important questions. Who are you? And what do you want?" Beep. Can you answer these questions right now? How much do you really know about yourself and what you want from this life of yours?

Don't worry. These aren't trick questions and there are no wrong answers. But there are some answers that are more right for you than others. College is a great time to think about who you are and what you want. In addition to learning about biology or history or business, college will be a time to learn about yourself: your motivation, values, dreams, and goals. You may make some of the most important choices of your life. Which major will you choose? Which career will you aim for? From this point on, it's up to you. Have you ever heard this phrase with 10 two-letter words: "If it is to be, it is up to me"? It's true.

Think about it: a college education is one of the best investments you can make. Once you've earned a college degree, it's yours forever. Someone can steal your car or walk away with your cell phone, but once you've earned a college degree, no one can ever take it from you. Your choice to go to college will pay off in many ways. So even if you aren't sure exactly how you want to spend the rest of your life right now, you can't go wrong by investing in your future.

This book starts with the big picture: managing your life. Notice the phrase is "managing your life"—not *controlling* your life. Let's face it: Many things in life are beyond our control. But you can manage your life by making smart choices, setting goals you can work toward, paying attention to your time and energy, and motivating yourself. As the title of this book states boldly, it's about focus.

For many of us, focusing is a challenge. We work too many hours, crowd our lives with obligations, and rush

> **What is important is to keep learning, to enjoy challenge, and to tolerate ambiguity. In the end there are no certain answers.**
>
> *Martina Horner, former President of Radcliffe College*

from one thing to the next. We think we're good at multitasking. We can surf the Internet, listen to our favorite music, watch a DVD, and read this chapter—all at the same time, right? But think about Gandhi's wise words applied to today's lifestyle: "There is more to life than increasing its speed." The truth is that over the long haul, the more time we spend multitasking, the less we're able to focus when we need to. Of course, it's not hard to multitask when you're doing simple things, like petting your dog and watching TV. But when you add in something that's academically challenging, you won't get much done, and chances are that it won't get done well. Recent research indicates that multitasking hurts your brain's ability to learn, and that what you learn while you're distracted by other things is harder to use and recall.[1] In fact, even though technology gives you quick access and new abilities, according to one study, when you're distracted by e-mail or phone calls, your IQ drops by 10 points.[2] Technology's stimulation gives your brain a squirt of dopamine, which can actually be addictive. And being constantly connected, research shows, can cause brain fatigue.[3] Or, here's another way to think about it. Remember those summer days when the temperature outside is above 100 degrees, and everyone's air conditioners are maxed out? The city may experience a brownout from the energy overload. Many experts say that multitasking causes a brownout in your brain; there's just not enough power to go around. The truth is your stress level can skyrocket when you "fragment" your attention in dozens of directions at the same time, and "rebooting" after you've interrupted yourself to bounce out to something else can take from seconds to hours.[4] Let's be honest: multitasking and learning don't mix very well. Succeeding in college requires you to know when to focus on just one urgent, important thing—and then to do it.

multitasking doing many different things at once

Of course, some people achieve success without a college degree, but by and large, they're the exception. Even Steven Spielberg, self-made billionaire in the film industry and winner of Academy Awards for *Schindler's List* and *Saving Private Ryan*, felt the need to finish the college degree he had started more than thirty years before. "I wanted to accomplish this for many years as a 'thank you' to my parents for giving me the opportunity for an education and a career, and as a personal note for my own family—and young people everywhere—about the importance of achieving their college education goals," he said. "But I hope they get there quicker than I did. Completing the requirements for my degree 33 years after finishing my principal education marks my longest post-production schedule."[5]

If you read this book carefully and follow its advice, it will help you become the best student you can possibly be. It will give you practical tools to help you manage your life. It will take you into your next level of education or into your career. And most of all, it will encourage you to become a true learner. That is this book's challenge to you as you begin your college experience.

Spending Time "in the System"

Spending time "in the system"? No, being in college isn't like being in jail—far from it. "The system" is the approach used in this book to help you learn: the Challenge → Reaction → Insight → Action system. It is based on the work of Dr. John Bransford and his colleagues, who together wrote an influential book called *How People Learn*.

Bransford believes learning is a chain reaction that might look something like this:

FIGURE 2.1

CRIA System: How People Learn

Source: Based on J. Bransford, et al. (2000). *How People Learn: Brain, Mind, Experience, and School.* Washington, DC: National Academy Press.

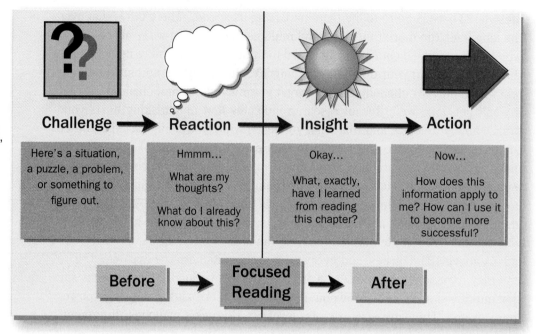

This Challenge → Reaction → Insight → Action learning chain reaction is integrated into *FOCUS* to help you learn. Each chapter takes you through "the system" by walking you through four steps:

STEP 1: Challenge. Whenever you're learning something new, the best place to start is by identifying what you think you already know. For example, each chapter's "Readiness Check" will ask you how this chapter will relate to you and how you'll relate to it. Then you'll continue by reading a case study about a new college student who's facing problems related to the topics in the chapter. Research shows that people generally learn more from examples of things going wrong than they can from examples of things going right. The challenges are real ones many students face. Perhaps you (or a classmate you know) are facing similar issues yourself. Read the case studies carefully and think about solutions that would help these students—before you read the chapter's content. Every chapter begins with a challenge as the first step of the learning chain reaction.

STEP 2: Reaction. After you read the case study, you are asked for your reaction by answering a few questions about it. What is the student in the case study doing wrong or right? What should the student do differently? Your instructor may ask you to discuss your reaction in class or answer the questions in writing. This step of the learning process shows you how much you already know—before you begin reading. It also shows you what you don't know and what you can learn by reading. The goal of this book is help you become a **deep learner**, as opposed to someone who skims the surface and simply rushes on to the next assignment and the next course. It will ask you to pause, **take stock**, focus, and think.

deep learner someone who learns everything they can about a topic

take stock evaluate your progress

STEP 3: Insight. At the end of each chapter, you'll be asked to revisit some of the questions you were asked in the chapter's opening Step 2: Reaction.

Surround yourself with people who take their work seriously, but not themselves, those who work hard and play hard.

Colin Powell, former U.S. Secretary of State

Rethinking your responses to the Challenge case will help you gauge how much you've learned. For example, Sylvia Sanchez dreamed of becoming a famous singer, a dream that could have become reality if things fell into place for her. But after reading about it in the chapter, you might decide that you really hadn't thought about it very deeply and there's more to it than you originally thought. The difference between Step 2 (your immediate reaction) and Step 3 (the new insights you've gained from reading) demonstrate that you've learned! After reading the chapter and discussing it in class, you'll know some research on the subject, the chapter's suggestions, examples you can apply, and your instructor's thoughts about how the case study student handled the challenges. You'll also gain some insights about yourself, if you face any of these issues, too.

STEP 4: Action. The final step in this learning chain reaction is about action. What have you learned that will change how you face similar challenges? Learning takes place when it relates to you personally, and insights have no impact unless they lead to change. The bottom line is: You must use your insights to take action. Think of this comparison. One day you feel tired, you notice that your clothes are tight, and you are suddenly aware that you're out of shape. You realize that you must eat healthier food and exercise more. But if you don't take action, it won't happen. To become real, new knowledge must lead to personal insights that result in action. What you learned by reading relates to you, and you must use it!

If you follow the system built into this book and use it as you read all your textbooks, the learning chain reaction will become automatic for you.

How Do You "Spend" Your Time?[6]

Add up the cost of going to college for an entire term: tuition for one semester/trimester/quarter, the total estimated cost of all the gas you will use to get to and from class for the term, books and supplies, a computer you may have bought, and child care or any other expenses related to your going to school. Put down everything you can think of. Divide that grand total by the number of hours you are in school (number of weeks class is in session multiplied by the number of hours you are scheduled to be in class). For example, if you are taking two 3-hour classes for a 16-week semester, the number you will divide your grand total by 96 (= 6 hours × 16 weeks). Completing this exercise will show you how much money each class session costs you—and the cost of missing class! Compare your "hourly rate" with that of your classmates and discuss the results as a group.

How Motivated *Are* You and *How* Are You Motivated?

Academic Intrinsic Motivation Self-Assessment

How intrinsically motivated are you? Read each of the following statements and circle the number beside each statement that most accurately represents your views about yourself.

	Completely Not True	Somewhat Not True	Neutral	Somewhat True	Completely True
1. I have academic goals.	1	2	3	4	5
2. I am confident I can complete my degree.	1	2	3	4	5
3. I determine my career goals.	1	2	3	4	5
4. I enjoy solving challenging, difficult problems.	1	2	3	4	5
5. I work on an assignment until I understand it.	1	2	3	4	5
6. I am confident I will finish a degree or certificate.	1	2	3	4	5
7. I determine the quality of my academic work.	1	2	3	4	5
8. I am pursuing college because I value education.	1	2	3	4	5
9. I feel good knowing that I determine how my academic career develops.	1	2	3	4	5
10. I have high standards for academic work.	1	2	3	4	5
11. Staying in college is my decision.	1	2	3	4	5
12. I study because I like to learn new things.	1	2	3	4	5
13. I enjoy doing outside readings in connection to my future coursework.	1	2	3	4	5
14. I am intrigued by the different topics introduced in my courses.	1	2	3	4	5
15. I study because I am curious.	1	2	3	4	5
16. I look forward to going to class.	1	2	3	4	5

	Completely Not True	Somewhat Not True	Neutral	Somewhat True	Completely True
17. I am excited to take more courses within my major.	1	2	3	4	5
18. I enjoy learning more within my field of study.	1	2	3	4	5
19. I like to find answers to questions about material I am learning.	1	2	3	4	5
20. I enjoy studying.	1	2	3	4	5
21. I have pictured myself in a career after college.	1	2	3	4	5
22. I am excited about the job opportunities I will have later.	1	2	3	4	5
23. I have pictured myself being successful in my chosen career.	1	2	3	4	5
24. I believe I will make a substantial contribution to my chosen profession.	1	2	3	4	5
25. I feel good knowing I will be a member of the professional community in my area of study.	1	2	3	4	5

Total each column, then add your scores across. ＿＿ + ＿＿ + ＿＿ + ＿＿ + ＿＿ =

＿＿＿＿ OVERALL SCORE

Continue reading to find out what your overall score means.

French, B. F., & Oakes, W. (2003). Measuring academic intrinsic motivation in the first year of college: Reliability and validity evidence for a new instrument. *Journal of the First Year Experience, 15(1)*, 83–102.

When it comes to getting a college education, where does motivation come into the picture? In general, motivation is your desire to put forth effort, even when the going gets rough. The word *motivation* comes from Medieval Latin, *motivus*, meaning "moving." What moves you to learn? There are many ways to define motivation, and different people are motivated by different things.

How motivated would you be to learn something difficult, like a new language, one you'd never studied before? Let's say that you were offered a chance to learn Finnish, a challenging language that is not related to English. For example, in Finnish *Kiitoksia oikein paljon* means "thank you very much." Finnish would be a challenge to learn. To determine your level of motivation, it would help to know your attitude toward Finland and Finnish people, whether you needed to learn Finnish for some reason, how you felt about learning it, whether you thought you could learn it successfully, whether you were rewarded in some way for learning it, and just how stimulating you found the learning process to be.[7] In other words, your motivation depends on many factors, right?

You'd probably be more motivated to learn Finnish if these sorts of things were part of the picture: (1) You were going to visit relatives in Finland and were excited about it; (2) you'd always been good at learning foreign languages and you expected to learn this one easily; (3) your boss was planning to transfer you to Helsinki as part of a big promotion; or (4) you enjoyed your Finnish language class, thought the instructor was a gifted teacher, and found the other students to be as motivated as you were. So, whose job is it to motivate you? Your instructor's? This book's? Yours? Can anyone else besides you motivate you? This book will ask you: How motivated *are* you to succeed in college? And *how* are you motivated?

To assess your own motivation, it's important to understand the difference between *extrinsic* and *intrinsic* motivation. People who are extrinsically, or externally, motivated learn in order to get a grade, earn credits, or complete a requirement, for example. They are motivated by things outside themselves. You could be motivated to learn Finnish to earn three credits or to get an A. People who are intrinsically, or internally, motivated learn because they're curious, fascinated, or challenged, or because they truly want to master a subject. They are motivated from within. You could be motivated to learn Finnish for the challenge, because you're curious about it, or because you find it fascinating. Let's be realistic, however. Extrinsic motivation is real and important. You need to earn college credits, and you'd rather get A's than F's. But how intrinsically motivated you are in college will have a great deal to do with just how successful you are. The motivation to become truly educated must come from within you.

extrinsically outside yourself

intrinsically inside yourself

FIGURE 2.2

Extrinsic versus Intrinsic Motivation

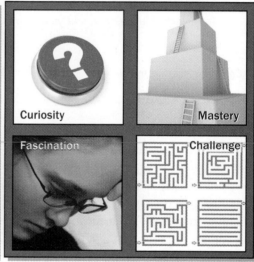

(clockwise from top left): Christopher Hall/Shutterstock.com; Yari/Shutterstock.com; Palto/Shutterstock.com; Pling/Shutterstock.com; Scott Maxwell/LuMaxArt/Shutterstock.com; Andy Dean Photography/Shutterstock.com; Yuri Arcurs/Shutterstock.com; Vasilius/Shutterstock.com.

You completed the Academic Intrinsic Motivation Scale (AIMS) in Exercise 2.2, which is designed to measure your intrinsic, or internal, motivation to succeed in college in terms of these four C-Factors:

1. **Curiosity.** Do you want to learn new things? Are you truly interested in what you're learning? Are you curious? Do you ask questions?

2. **Control.** Do you think working hard in your academic courses will pay off? Do you believe you can control how successful you'll be?

3. **Career outlook.** Are you goal oriented? Are you future oriented? Can you imagine yourself using what you learn in college to help you get a job you want?

4. **Challenge.** Does your college coursework challenge you? It is important that the level of challenge is right for you. Too much challenge can cause you to become frustrated and give up. Not enough challenge can cause you to lose interest.[8]

Think about it this way: If your overall score on the AIMS was 100–125, you're intrinsically motivated at a high level. If you scored between 75 and 99, you're intrinsically motivated at a moderate level, but increasing your intrinsic motivation may help you achieve more. If you scored below 75, a lack of intrinsic motivation could interfere with your college success. If you're intrinsically motivated, you'll use all the learning tools offered to you in *FOCUS*.

FOCUS has the factors involved in intrinsic motivation built in. These C-Factors appear at the end of each chapter. Choose to read one or two or perhaps all of them to boost your own motivation to learn and succeed:

 Curiosity: Each chapter includes a very short article on something that's related to college success. You'll read cutting-edge information that may make you curious to read more about it somewhere else.

 Control: You are encouraged throughout this book to apply what you are learning to a challenging task this term. You can apply the information to your toughest class, a challenging part of your job outside school or some other difficult situation.

 Career Outlook: Each chapter includes highly useful career advice you can start putting into practice now and carry with you into your new career after college. As you read these short articles, think about how they may apply to your future, and ask yourself whether you have the interest and motivation required to start using some of these techniques now.

 Challenge: In general, if a course is too challenging, you may be tempted to give up. If it's too easy, you may lose interest. Adjusting the level of challenge to what's right for you is key to keeping yourself motivated to learn. Test yourself. See if you can answer the "Challenge: Reality Check" questions that appear at the end of each chapter. For more practice online, access the CourseMate to take the Challenge Yourself Online Quiz.

EXERCISE 2.3

The Ideal Student

Create your own personal top-ten list of the characteristics (attitudes and actions) of an ideal student. Bring your completed list to your next class session so that all students can read their lists and create a master list that everyone can agree on. Put your initials next to each of the ten items on the master list that you promise to do throughout the term. Your personal top-ten list, which your instructor may discuss with you individually at a later time, will become your own list of goals for the course.

Give Yourself an Attitude Adjustment

There's a difference of opinion on the subject of attitude. Some people say attitude is not all that important. Attitude-schmattitude, they say. Others say that *attitude* is more important than aptitude. What do you think?

attitude state of mind or mental position

aptitude natural ability

© Larry Harwood Photography. Property of Cengage Learning.

You must motivate yourself EVERY DAY!

Matthew Stasior, motivational speaker

In research studies conducted by Rick Snyder at the University of Kansas, students who scored high on a measure of hope got higher grades. Snyder explained that students with high hopes set themselves higher goals and know how to work hard to attain them.

Quick quiz. How many times a day do you catch yourself saying "Whatever . . . ," and rolling your eyes? Whatever-ness—an attitude of boredom and impatience—takes a lot less effort than staying positive. Whether you realize it or not, whatevers chip away at your motivation, and they can cause you to give up on your dreams and goals. When it comes to your college education, one good thing you can do for yourself is to delete the word *whatever* from your vocabulary. Your education is much too important for whatevers—and so are you.

Five Ways to Adjust Your Attitude

The good thing about attitude is that you can change it yourself. As you think about benefits of fine-tuning your attitude, keep these five recommendations in mind:

1. **Know that you always have choices.** Regardless of circumstances—your income, your background, or your academic experiences—you always have a choice, even if it's limited to how you choose to view your current situation.

2. **Take responsibility for your own outcomes.** Coach Vince Lombardi used to have his players look in a mirror before every game and ask themselves, "Am I looking at the person who is helping me win or the one who is holding me back?" Blaming others simply diminishes your own power to work toward constructive responses to challenges.

3. **Turn down your negativity meter.** "Can't" and "won't" are two of the biggest obstacles to a healthy attitude. Also pay attention to how you describe things. Is the cup half empty or half full? State things in the positive rather than the negative (for example, "stay healthy" rather than "don't get sick"). Paying attention to positive role models whose traits you admire is also a great way to boost your outlook.

4. **Turn learning points into turning points.** Have you ever watched someone do something so badly that you've said to yourself, "I'm never going to do that! I'm going to do it differently!"? You can also choose to learn from your own mistakes and setbacks. They all offer some sort of lesson, even if it takes a bit of distance from the event to see what you can learn.

5. **Acknowledge your blessings.** Taking time at the end of each day to recognize and feel gratitude for the blessings in your life—no matter how large or small—is a great way to develop a positive attitude.

constructive responses
statements or actions that promote improvement

Statements That Ought to Be Outlawed in College . . . and Why

Because words reflect attitudes (and help shape them), listen for statements like these escaping from your mouth. They can negatively affect your attitude and therefore your learning:

- **"I thought college classes would be more interesting than they are."** Interesting is in the mind of the beholder.

- **"I didn't learn a thing in that class."** Actively search for what you can take away from a class, even if it didn't quite meet your expectations.

- **"The textbook is really dull. Why bother reading it?"** Reading may not be your favorite pastime, but you may learn more from a textbook than you can predict.

- **"The professor is soooo-o-o boring."** In life, we all interact with all types of personalities, so begin to appreciate differences in communication styles.

- **"Why do I have to take this required course? What's the point?"** The point is to broaden your horizons, expand your skills as a critical thinker, and become a lifelong scholar.

Care enough to give yourself every opportunity to do your best. And, yes, every class, every situation in life, is an opportunity. You're worth it.[9]

Ability versus Effort: What's More Important?

Successful people have several things in common: They love learning, seek challenges, value effort, and persevere even when things become difficult.[10] They demonstrate both ability and effort. These two things are the basic requirements for success. College is about both.

Think about some of the possible combinations of ability and effort. If you have high ability and exert great effort, you'll most likely succeed. If you have high ability and exert little effort, and still succeed, you've just proved how smart you must be! But if you have high ability and exert little effort and fail, you can

> **Ability is what you're capable of doing. Motivation determines what you do. Attitude determines how well you do it.**
>
> *Lou Holtz, former college football coach and ESPN sports analyst*

Theories of Intelligence Scale

What is intelligence? Are people born with a certain amount? Or can it be cultivated through learning? Using the following scale, write in the number that corresponds to your opinion in the space next to each statement. There are no right or wrong answers.

1	2	3	4	5	6
Strongly Agree	**Mostly Agree**	**Agree**	**Disagree**	**Mostly Disagree**	**Strongly Disagree**

_____ 1. You have a certain amount of intelligence, and you can't really do much to change it.

_____ 2. You can learn new things, but you can't really change your basic intelligence.

_____ 3. You can always substantially change how intelligent you are.

_____ 4. No matter how much intelligence you have, you can always change it quite a bit.

"Don't think of it as failure. Think of it as
time-released success."

Robert Orben

always claim you didn't have the time to invest or you didn't care, right? You can always say that you could have done well if you'd tried harder: "I could have written those Harry Potter books; I'm a great writer." If you had really tried for that kind of success, you wouldn't have been able to say that. That's a dangerous strategy, one that's

self-handicapping hurting your own chances to succeed

called "self-handicapping."[11] Some college students consciously or unconsciously apply this strategy. They exert little effort, perhaps because they have no confidence in themselves or because they fear failure, and then they rationalize when they don't do well.

Research shows that what you believe about your own intelligence—your *mindset*—can make a difference in how successful you'll be in college. At first glance this statement seems absurd. After all, you're either smart or you're not, right? Wrong.

The scaled questions demonstrate that there are two basic ways to define intelligence. Some of us are **performers**, who agree with statements 1 and 2, while others of us are **learners**, who agree more with statements 3 and 4. *Per-*

performers someone who is driven to appear smart

learners someone who is driven to learn, even by making mistakes

formers believe that intelligence is a fixed trait that cannot be changed. From the moment you're born, you have a certain amount of intelligence that belongs to you, and that's that. *Learners*, on the other hand, believe you can grow your intelligence if you capitalize on opportunities to learn. Whenever you tackle a tough challenge, you learn from it. The more you learn, the more intelligent you can become. Understanding which view of intelligence you believe in will make a difference in how you approach your college classes, and how successful you'll be.

Students who are taught the value of a learning mindset over a performance mindset can actually achieve more than students who don't.[12] In one study, college students' views of intelligence predicted the goals students valued in college. *Performers* were more likely to want to give up in challenging situations; learners wanted to try harder.[13] In one study that measured the electrical activity in college students' brains as they performed a difficult task, brain activity showed that *performers* cared most about whether their answers were right or wrong, whereas *learners* were interested in follow-up information they could learn from.[14] Yet another study showed that *learners* are more likely to buckle down academically, even when they feel depressed.[15] It's clear: Believing you're a *learner* provides advantages in motivation, achievement, enjoyment, and commitment.

Regardless of what you believe about your precise intelligence level, the fact is this: *Intelligence can be cultivated through learning.* And people's theories about their intelligence levels can be shifted.

What Drives You? Values, Dreams, and Goals

EXERCISE 2.5

Core Values Self-Assessment

What are your core values? What's most important to you—deep down inside? Review the following list and check off the items that you value. Don't spend too much time thinking about each one; just go with your initial gut reaction. For each item, ask yourself, "Is this something that's important to me?"

_____ Health	_____ Physical Appearance	_____ Financial wealth
_____ Fitness/Physical strength	_____ Independence	_____ Commitment
_____ Loyalty	_____ Honesty	_____ Compassion
_____ Academic achievement	_____ Children	_____ Leisure time
_____ Success	_____ Leadership	_____ Balance
_____ Happiness	_____ Family	_____ Friendship
_____ Social life	_____ Marriage/Partnership	_____ Recognition
_____ Athletics	_____ Spirituality	_____ Status
_____ Creativity	_____ Variety	_____ Wisdom
_____ Meaningful work	_____ Challenge	_____ Time spent alone
_____ Adventure	_____ Personal growth	_____ Other (list here)

Now review all of the items you checked off, and circle the five that are most important to you at this point in your life. Then rank them by putting a number next to each of the five circled values, with number one as your top priority. Finally, take stock. Is this the person you want to be? Is there anything about your values that you would like to change? If so, what's keeping you from making this change?

Before tackling the big questions about what you want to create with your life, it's important to first take a close look in the mirror. Who are you? What makes you tick? What do you **value**? What are your **goals**? Where will your **dreams** take you?

Values at the Core

What do you value in life? By taking time to examine your personal values, managing your life will become easier and make more sense. Values can be things you can't exactly see or touch, like love or respect, or things that are visible and real, like family or money. Understanding how they motivate you isn't as simple as it might seem. Values can change as you go through life. For example, if you're single now, you may value the freedom to meet a variety of potential romantic partners. Later, however, you may want a committed relationship because you want stability in your life. For this reason, it's important to look at your values from time to time and rethink them.

Another complicating factor is that values can conflict with one another. Suppose that you value honesty and kindness, and you are at a party and a friend asks you what you think of her new hair color. You honestly think it's hideous, but telling her so would hurt her feelings, thus violating your value of being kind. How do you respond? That would depend on which value is a higher priority for you. You have to make an on-the-spot decision about which value to

value something you think is important

goals something you make specific plans to achieve

dreams something you wish for

You are never given a wish without the power to make it come true. You may have to work for it, however.

Richard Bach, from Illusions

© Patrick Giardino/CORBIS

use. Once you define your values, however, they can help you make everyday choices as well as big decisions, like which major to pursue in college. For example, if academic achievement is one of your top values, the next time you have the urge to cut class, consider what that choice says about your value system. There is a great inner satisfaction that comes from living a life tied to core values.

Dreams versus Goals

Do you agree or disagree with this statement: "I can be anything I want to be"? You've probably heard this statement frequently. Your family and teachers all want you to have positive self-esteem, and certainly there are many career options available today. But is it true? Can you be *anything* you want to be? What's the difference between a dream and a goal?

As a student, you may dream of being a famous doctor or a famous athlete or just plain famous. That's the beauty of dreams—you can imagine yourself doing anything. When you're dreaming, you don't even have to play by the rules of reality. Dreams are fantasy-based—*you* in a perfect world. But when it's time to come back to reality, you discover that there are rules, after all. You may have dreamed of becoming a top-earning NBA player or a top fashion model when you were a child, but you have grown up to be the same height as Uncle Al or Aunt Sue—and that's not tall enough.

Dreams alone are not enough when it comes to creating your future. As professional life coach Diana Robinson says, "A dream is a goal without legs." And without legs, that goal is going nowhere. Dreaming is the first step to creating the future you want, but making dreams come true requires planning and hard work. Sylvia Sanchez wanted to become a famous singer because she likes music people always told her she was good. As she continues through college, however, she will come to understand herself better. The music industry might be challenging to break into, but that doesn't mean she should abandon her dream. She must find a realistic way to help her turn her dreams into goals. Just dreaming isn't enough. Dreams are exciting; you can let your imagination run wild. Goals are real; you must work out how to actually achieve your dreams.

Goal setting is an important part of the life management skills this book will help you develop. Your goals may not seem at all clear to you right now, but the important thing is to learn that there's a right way and a wrong way to set your

> **What you get by achieving your goals is not as important as what you become by achieving your goals.**
>
> *Zig Ziglar, Motivational speaker, writer, and trainer*

goals. The best way to ensure that the goals you set will serve you well is to make sure you *FOCUS*. Here's a brief overview of what that means.

F **Fit.** Your goal must fit your values, your character, and who you are as a person. Goals that conflict with any of these things will not only be difficult to accomplish, but they just won't work. If your goal is to become a writer for a travel magazine because you love adventure, but flying in planes terrifies you, you're in trouble.

O **Ownership.** Own your goal: See it, taste it, want it! It must be your goal, not someone else's goal for you. Ask yourself: Does the thought of achieving this goal get me fired up? Do I genuinely own this goal or do I feel I ought to have this goal because it sounds good or makes someone else happy?

C **Concreteness.** For any goal to be effective, it must be real. In other words, you must be able to describe your goal in detail: "To run a mile in less than six minutes by March 4th" is much more concrete than "to eventually run faster." The more concrete, the better.

U **Usefulness.** Goals must be useful. They must serve a purpose, and that purpose should be tied to your long-term vision of the person you want to become. For example, if you want to work for an international hotel some day, it would be useful to begin studying a foreign language now.

S **Stretch.** In the business world, people talk about stretch goals. These are goals that require employees to stretch beyond their usual limits to achieve something more challenging. Goals must be based in reality, but also offer you a chance to grow beyond the person you currently are.

Your goals should include both short- and long-term goals. Once your long-term goals are set (though they may shift over time as *you* shift over time), you will then want to set some short-term goals, which act as in-between steps to achieving your long-term goals.

Long-Term Goals What do I want to accomplish . . .	Short-Term Goals What do I want to accomplish . . .
In my lifetime?	This year?
In the next twenty years?	This month?
In the next ten years?	This week?
In the next three to five years?	Today?

Sharpen Your FOCUS

> **This constant, unproductive preoccupation with all the things we have to do is the single largest consumer of time and energy.**
>
> —KERRY GLEESON, TIME MANAGEMENT EXPERT

Reason 2: They're immobolized by worry.

It's easy to feel overwhelmed when you think about the big picture—school assignments, work demands, financial struggles, relationship ups and downs. The "big picture" is a gigantic puzzle that looms so large that it's hard to focus on any one individual piece. How much time do you spend worrying about how much is on your plate—as opposed to removing things one at a time in a systematic way? Sometimes the biggest enemy of focus is worry. Our ability to concentrate is hijacked by anxiety, pure and simple.

TRY It!

List the three items you worry about getting done most, and for each one, list three suggestions you should follow to improve your focus and your life.

1. _____
   a.
   b.
   c.
2. _____
   a.
   b.
   c.
3. _____
   a.
   b.
   c.

The Four C Factors: Just how motivated are YOU?

 CONTROL: *YOUR TOUGHEST CLASS*

Think about the courses you're enrolled in this term. Which one will be the toughest? Use the following chart to analyze your C-Factors for this course. Describe this course in terms of its challenge level, your curiosity about the subject, how much control you believe you have to succeed, and the way each class impacts your career outlook. Once you've determined the levels of challenge, curiosity, control, and career outlook, remember that it's your responsibility to adjust them. Look at Sylvia's entry above as a model. She has analyzed her responses to the Four C-Factors in one of her classes, Developmental English. Now do the same for your classes.

Course Title	Challenge	Curiosity	Control	Career Outlook	Adjustments Required
Developmental English	Very High: never been good at writing	Very Low: had a discouraging teacher in H.S.	Moderate: probably higher than it feels to me	Will need to know how to write in any job	Need to spend more time prewriting and going to the campus Writing Center for help

In your college classes this term, what is the relationship between the four C-Factors and your intrinsic motivation to learn? What can you change? For example, if you don't feel you have much control over how well you do, how can you change that?

_____

_____

_____

CURIOSITY: *KNOW THYSELF! HOW HARD CAN THAT BE?*

Socrates advised many centuries ago, "Know thyself." But David Dunning, professor of psychology at Cornell University and author of *Self-Insight: Roadblocks and Detours on the Path to Knowing Thyself*, says that most of us really don't know ourselves as well as we think we do. In fact, when we're asked to predict how well we'll do at something, and that prediction is compared to how well we actually did, most of us are off base. In one study, college students were given a pop quiz after they finished a task like memorizing a list of words or figuring out a problem. Then they were asked how well they thought they did.

In general, students who thought they did well sometimes performed in the bottom quarter, and students with the highest scores sometimes underestimated their performance.

Why is this so? Why aren't we all right on the mark? Specifically, why can't people tell when they're not doing a good job?

One reason Dunning offers is that people can't be expected to always know when they're not doing well. Because they don't necessarily know how to do what they're doing, they're simply not in a position to know how they actually did. That's why it's important to seek input from instructors about the quality of your work!

How closely does your own assessment of your how well you've completed your assignments and the feedback you get from your instructors match? How well do you know yourself in terms of the quality of your academic work? What have you learned about yourself as a learner so far?

_____

_____

_____

CAREER OUTLOOK: *TO THINE OWN SELF BE TRUE*

Expectations. They play a big role in our lives. Perhaps your family has talked about it for years: "Our Gabe is going to be a doctor. We've known it since we watched him play with his toy doctor's kit as a little kid." The story has been repeated so many times that it's now turned into a real expectation your family has for you.

But here's an important question: What do *you* want to do with your life? Although your family will most likely have an important perspective, figuring this out for yourself is one of the most important questions you begin to answer in college. Many college students change their majors at least once, and many adults change their careers, too.

Use college as an opportunity to truly get to know yourself. Pay attention to which disciplines fascinate you as a learner. Make decisions for the right reasons. A career that pays well but holds no real appeal for you may result in major dissatisfaction later on. Project some alternative futures for yourself based on various career possibilities. Imagine yourself wearing different career "hats." As a French Pulitzer Prize–winning author once said, "Be faithful to that which exists nowhere but in yourself." And set your own course.

Are there particular expectations related to getting an education that others have for you? How well do they align with your own dreams and goals? If there's disagreement, how do you plan to handle it?

_____

_____

_____

CHALLENGE: REALITY CHECK

How much did you learn? At the beginning of this chapter, you filled out a "Readiness Check" that asked how you thought this chapter would relate to you, and how you would relate to it. Now, fill out this "Reality Check" to find out.

1. How do people learn?

2. What is the difference between intrinsic and extrinsic motivation?

3. What's the difference between being a learner and being a performer?

4. How are dreams and goals different?

5. How long did it take? _____ hours _____ minutes. Before you began this chapter, you were asked to predict how long it would take you to complete it (total time, even if you read it in more than one sitting). Was your estimate on target, or will you revise it for the next chapter you'll read? _____

step 3 INSIGHT *Now* What Do You Think?

At the beginning of this chapter, Sylvia Sanchez faced a series of challenges as a new college student. Now after learning from this chapter, would you respond differently to any of the questions you answered about the "FOCUS Challenge Case"? Using what you learned in the chapter, write a paragraph ending to Sylvia's case study. What are some of the possible outcomes for her?

step 4 ACTION Your Plans for Change

1. Identify one new thing you learned in reading this chapter. Why did you select the one you've selected? How will it affect what you do in your college classes?

2. Do you have some of the same questions Sylvia does about your own level of motivation to achieve in college? How could you increase your motivation? How important might that be?

3. How do your own goals and dreams differ? How do you plan to turn your dreams into goals?

chapter 3 Learning Styles and Studying

READINESS CHECK

How this chapter relates to YOU

1. When it comes to learning and studying in college, what are you most unsure about, if anything?

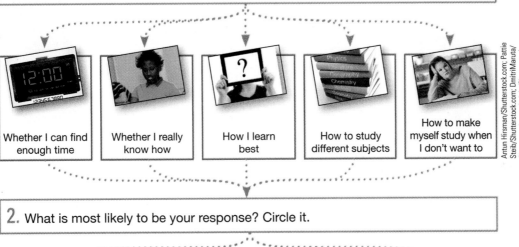

Whether I can find enough time | Whether I really know how | How I learn best | How to study different subjects | How to make myself study when I don't want to

2. What is most likely to be your response? Circle it.

I'll ask my instructors for suggestions. | I'll ask my classmates what they do. | I'll see how things go and adjust. | I'll probably just figure it out somehow.

3. What would you have to do to increase your likelihood of success? Will you do it this quarter or semester?

Example: *Read this book. Yes!*

How YOU will relate to this chapter

What are you most interested in learning about? Put checkmarks next to those topics.

☐ How learning changes your brain
☐ How people are intelligent in different ways
☐ How you learn through your senses
☐ How your personality type can affect your learning style
☐ What metacognition is and how it can help you
☐ How to apply your learning style to your study style
☐ How to become an intentional learner and make a master study plan

- How motivated are you to learn more about getting the right start in college? (5 = high, 1 = low) ____

- How ready are you to read now? ____ (If something is in your way, take care of it if you can, zero in and focus.)

- How long do you think it will take you to complete this chapter? If you start and stop, keep track of your overall time. ____ hour(s) ____ minutes

Tammy Ko

NORTH RIVER COMMUNITY CO

ENRO NOW

WWW.NORTHRIVERVIEWCC.E

As she walked out of her "Introduction to Criminology" class with her classmate Sam on a dark rainy afternoon, Tammy Ko noticed that her mood was in sync with the weather. "I had no idea what I was getting into," she confessed to Sam. It was obvious to Sam that Tammy and their professor lived in different worlds. Hers was filled with people and excitement. His was filled with dull lecture notes and complex theories in books.

Tammy was a first-semester student at the large community college in town. Even though she found college life hectic because of all the hours she had to work to pay her own tuition, Tammy was excited about working on her associate's degree in criminal justice. She wanted to get into her state's police academy and specialize in forensics, and she knew a degree would help her chances. The crime shows on TV were her favorites. She watched them all each week. She rationalized how much time it took by thinking of it as career development. The fun was picturing herself as an investigator solving headline cases: "Man Slain, Found in City Park" or "Modern Day 'Jack the Ripper' Terrorizes Las Vegas." She could envision herself hunched over laboratory equipment, testing intently for fibers or DNA, and actually breaking the case.

When she registered for classes, her academic advisor had told her that taking an "Introduction to Criminology" course from the sociology department would be a good idea. "It'll teach you how to think," he'd said, "and it'll give you the background you need to understand the criminal mind. At the end of this class," he said, "you'll know if you really want to pursue a career in forensics." *Maybe it would teach me how to think,* Tammy thought to herself now that the term was underway, *if only I could understand the professor. Forget understanding the criminal mind—I'd just like a glimpse into his!* Most of the time, Sam agreed with her just to keep the peace, although he always aced everything.

Professor Caldwell was quiet and reserved, and he seemed a bit out of touch. He dressed as if he hadn't bought a new piece of clothing in as many years

---

Program Description

Criminology

Although we think of criminology as a relatively new discipline, the foundations of criminology can be traced back over two centuries. Criminology is the "scientific study of the causes of crime and delinquency, crime control policies, institutions designed to control crime, and media depictions of crime, criminals, and victims." Criminology draws from many other disciplines, including: psychology, sociology, political science, economics, and others.

Criminology is a rapidly growing field of study, and has many possible career options, including: Federal Agent, Counselor, Drug Enforcement Agent, Probation Officer, Forensic Specialist, Victim Services Specialist, Litigation Manager, etc.

Course Work

First Year	Second Year
CRIM 103 – Introduction to Criminology	CRIM 315 – Advanced Criminology
CRIM 105 – Research Methods for Social Science	CRIM 318 – Juvenile Delinquency
ENGL 130 – Scientific Writing	CRIM 320 – Capital Punishment
CHEM 106 – General Chemistry I	PHIL 300 – Ethical Dilemmas in Criminal Justice
CHEM 108 – General Chemistry II	CRIM 350 – The Correctional System
MATH 135 – Calculus I	CRIM 360 – The Judicial System
MATH 136 – Calculus II	PSYC 310 – Abnormal Psychology
Elective – 3 credits	Electives – 6 credits

ELECTIVES
- CSI: Fact or Fantasy?
- Interview and Interrogation Techniques

as he'd been teaching. In class, he was very articulate, knowledgeable, and organized, with his handouts neatly piled on the desk, and he covered each day's material methodically, point by point. Tammy wished he'd leave his notes occasionally to explore other interesting things. Tammy had always preferred teachers who created exciting things to do in class over teachers who went completely by the book. Tammy's biggest complaint about Professor Caldwell was that he only talked about *theories* of criminology. When was he ever going to get to the hands-on part of the course? She couldn't help thinking, *When will we stop talking about theories and start working on real cases—like the ones on all those TV shows?*

To make matters worse, learning from lectures was not Tammy's strong suit. In fact, she really didn't know how to study, and furthermore she just flat out didn't enjoy it. Honestly, she avoided studying as much as she could. Her social life was her top priority. She hadn't done well on the first exam because she'd had to resort to memorizing things that didn't make much sense to her, and her D grade showed it.

The entire exam consisted of one question: "Compare and contrast two theories of criminology discussed in class thus far." Tammy hated essay tests. She was at her best on tests with right or wrong answers, like true–false or multiple-choice questions. Making sense out of spoken words that go by very quickly during a lecture and trying to psych out professors' preferred answers on essay tests were challenges to her.

But her "Introduction to Criminology" class was far from hands-on. In fact, Tammy had noticed that many of her teachers preferred *talking* about things to *doing* things. They seemed to take more interest in theories than in the real world. Too bad, she thought. *The real world is where exciting things happen.* Although she hated to admit it, sometimes Tammy couldn't wait for college to be over so that she could begin her career in the real world.

A few of Tammy's friends had taken Mr. Caldwell's classes, too. Her friends' advice was "Just try and memorize the stuff; that's all you can do." Regardless of what they happened to be talking about, somehow the conversation always came around to Mr. Caldwell and how impossible it was to learn in his classes.

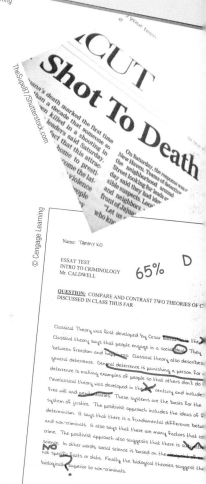

Michael J. Thompson/Shutterstock.com

© Cengage Learning

Name: TAMMY K.O

ESSAY TEST
INTRO TO CRIMINOLOGY
Mr. CALDWELL   65%   D

QUESTION: COMPARE AND CONTRAST TWO THEORIES OF C
DISCUSSED IN CLASS THUS FAR

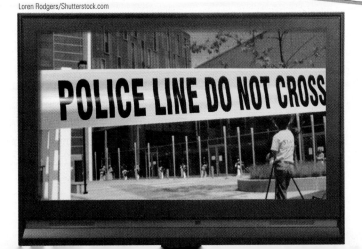

© Cengage Learning

NORTH RIVERVIEW POLICE
Requirements for Applicants

Prospective North Riverview Police Officers must meet all of the following minimum requirements. Requirements are determined by the City of North Riverview and the State Government.

QUICK CHECKLIST:

Be 19 years of age or older as outlined above.

Possess a high school diploma or GED.

Be a citizen of the United States.

Be free from convictions of disqualifying offenses.

Be personally examined by a State licensed physician.

Be personally examined by a State licensed psychologist.

Be subject to a thorough background investigation.

Successfully complete a basic police training course given at a commissioned, certified school.

Loren Rodgers/Shutterstock.com

POLICE LINE DO NOT CROSS

1. Do you have anything in common with Tammy? If so, how are you managing the situation so that you can be successful?

2. Is Tammy smart? If so, in what ways? What is she particularly good at?

3. What sensory modality does Tammy prefer for taking in information? Does she learn best by viewing information through charts and graphs, for example, or by talking and listening, by reading and writing, or by actually doing things?

4. Tammy says straightforwardly that she doesn't know how to study and dislikes doing it. In your view, what, specifically, should she do to succeed, not only in this class but in college?

Go to the Head of the Class: Learning and the Brain

EXERCISE 3.1

What Is Learning?

The following statements represent common student views on learning. Think about each statement, and mark it true or false based on your honest opinion.

_____ 1. Learning is often hard work and really not all that enjoyable.

_____ 2. Memorization and learning are basically the same thing.

_____ 3. The learning done in school is often gone in a few weeks or months.

_____ 4. In college, most learning takes place in class.

_____ 5. Learning is usually the result of listening to an instructor lecture or reading a textbook.

_____ 6. The best way to learn is by working alone.

_____ 7. Most students know intuitively how they learn best.

_____ 8. Teachers control what students learn.

_____ 9. Learning only deals with subjects taught in school.

_____10. The learning pace is controlled by the slowest learner in the class.

You probably noticed that many of these statements attempt to put learning in a negative light. How many did you mark true? This chapter will help you understand more about learning as a process and about yourself as a learner. As you read, your goal should be to use the insights you gain to become a better learner.

In one of his most famous plays, Shakespeare wrote, "O this learning. What a thing it is!" He was right. The fact that human beings can learn throughout their lives is an amazing characteristic. We learn language, numbers, and concepts right from the very start, and we keep learning until we draw our last breaths. But how do we do it, and more specific to this chapter, how do we learn at our best? In this chapter, you'll learn a great deal about yourself and your learning preferences, and you'll discover new ways to study so that you can learn more productively and efficiently. That kind of knowledge can definitely give you an advantage!

Let's start our exploration of the learning process close to home—in our own heads. What's going on up there, anyway? While your hands are busy manipulating test tubes in chemistry lab or your eyes are watching your psychology instructor's PowerPoint presentation, what's your brain up to? The answer? Plenty.

Use It or Lose It

The human brain consists of a complex web of connections between neurons or nerve cells. This web grows in complexity as it incorporates new knowledge. But if the connections are not reinforced frequently, you lose them. As you learn new things, you work to hardwire these connections, making them less likely to deteriorate. When your instructors repeat portions of the previous week's lecture or assign homework so you can practice material covered in class, they're helping you to form connections in your brain by using and reusing them—or, in other words, helping you to learn. Repetition is vital to learning. You must use and reuse information in order to hardwire it.

American humorist Will Rogers once said, "You know, you've got to exercise your *brain* just like your muscles." He was right. Giving your brain the exercise it needs—now and in your years after college—will help you form connections between neurons that, if you keep using them, will last a lifetime. From a biological point of view, that's what being a lifelong learner means. The age-old advice "use it or lose it" is true when it comes to learning.

Ask Questions and Hardwire Your Connections

Your instructors have been studying their disciplines for years, perhaps decades. They have developed extensive hardwired connections between their brain neurons. They are *experts*.

By contrast, you are a *novice*, or newcomer, to whatever discipline you're studying. You've not yet developed the brain wiring that your instructors have developed. That can lead to a potential problem. Sometimes instructors are so familiar with what they already know from years of traveling the same pathways in their brains that what you're learning for the first time seems obvious to them. Without even realizing it, they can expect what is familiar to them to be obvious to you. Think of how challenging it is when you try to teach something that you understand thoroughly to another person who doesn't, like teaching someone who has never used a computer before how to upload an assignment.

Because you're a novice, you may not understand everything your instructors say. Ask questions, check, clarify, probe, and persist until you do understand. Sometimes your confusion is not due to a lack of knowledge, but a lack of the *correct* knowledge. For example, you may study for a test by doing only one thing—reading and rereading the textbook. Actually, it's important to be familiar with many different ways to study and then choose the ones that work best for you.

Think of it this way. Some of the brain wiring you brought with you to college is positive and useful, and some actually hurts more than it helps. When you learn, you not only add new connections, but you rewire some old connections. While you're in college, you're under construction![1]

> **Movement is a medicine for creating change in a person's physical, emotional, and mental states.**
>
> —CAROL WELCH

Reason 3: They prefer to veg out.

Some people lose their focus because they've turned into couch potatoes. Their brains become as soft as their bodies. Research shows that just twenty minutes of exercise can help you become calm and focused for as long as twenty-four hours. Vigorous exercise helps you get rid of excess adrenaline and pumps in endorphins that block pain and anxiety.[2] Not only does exercise help you burn off cheeseburgers, recent brain-imaging and neurochemical studies indicate that "sweating makes you smart." Physical exercise helps reinforce existing connections and create new ones between brain wiring via a protein called BDNF (brain-derived neurotrophic factor). Brain wiring helps you process and store information, thus sharpening your ability to focus.

TRY It!

Keep an exercise log for a week. On a daily basis, record the type of physical activity, the length of time you do it, and the level of workout (mild, medium, or high exertion). Using an online exercise calculator, record the number of calories you burned. Finally, monitor your stress level to see if exercise helps lower it (1 = low, 10 = high).

Stockbyte/Photos.com

Photos.com/Jupiterimages; Photos.com/Jupiterimages; photos.com/Phil Date; Photos.com/Matthew Valentine; Photos.com/Stockbyte

	Sunday	Monday	Tuesday	Wednesday	Thursday	Friday	Saturday	TOTAL
Activity								
Time								
Exertion Level								
Calories Burned								
Overall stress level for the day (1 = low; 10 = high)								

Take Charge and Create the Best Conditions for Learning

Throughout this discussion, we've been talking about processes inside your brain. *Your* brain, not anyone else's. The bottom line is this: Learning must be *internally initiated*—by you. It can only be *externally encouraged*—by someone else. You're in charge of your own learning. Learning actually changes your brain.

Let's look at food as an analogy: If learning is a process that is as biological as digestion, then no one can learn for you, in the same way that no one can eat for you. The food in the refrigerator doesn't do you a bit of good unless you walk over, open the door, remove it, and start eating. It's there for the taking, but you must make that happen. To carry the analogy further, you eat on a daily basis, right? "No thanks, I ate last week" is a silly statement. Learning does for your brain what food does for your body. Nourish yourself!

Brain researchers tell us the best state for learning has many dimensions. Let's look at some of the most important ones.

1. **You're intrinsically motivated (from within yourself) to learn material that is appropriately challenging.**

> **Examine where your motivation to learn comes from.** Are you *internally* motivated because you're curious about the subject and want to learn about it or *externally* motivated to get an A or avoid an F? Can you generate your own internal motivation? This book has built-in reminders to boost your intrinsic motivation. Use them to your advantage as a learner.

> **Adjust the level of challenge yourself.** If you're too challenged in a class, you become nervous. Make sure you're keeping up with the workload and that you've completed the **prerequisites**. In many classes, you must know the fundamentals before tackling more advanced concepts. If you're not challenged enough, you can become bored and tune out. Your instructor will provide one level of challenge for everyone in the class. But it's up to you to fine-tune that challenge for yourself. Get extra help if you aren't quite up to the task, or bump up the challenge a notch or two if you're ahead of the game so that you're continually motivated to learn.

"When we come to know something, we have performed an act that is as biological as when we digest something."

Henry Plotkin, Darwin Machines and the Nature of Knowledge *(1994)*

prerequisite something that must be completed before something else

2. **You're appropriately stressed, but generally relaxed.**

> **Assess your stress.** According to researchers, you learn best in a state of *relaxed alertness,* a state of high challenge and low threat.[3] Although relaxed alertness may sound impossible, it can be achieved. No stress at all is what you'd find in a no-brainer course. Some stress is useful; it helps you learn. Stress can heighten your alertness and help you focus. How stressed are you—and why—when you get to class? Are you overstressed because you've rushed from your last class, you're late because you missed your bus, or because you haven't done the reading and hope you won't be called on? Prepare for class so that you're ready to jump in. Or instead of too much stress, are you understressed because you don't value the course material? Consider how the information can be useful to you—perhaps in ways you've never even thought of. Here's the vital question to ask yourself: How much stress do I need in order to trigger my best effort?

> **Pay attention to your overall physical state.** Are you taking care of your physical needs so that you can stay alert, keep up with the lecture, and participate in the discussion?

3. You're curious about what you're learning, and you look forward to learning it.

> **Get ready to learn by looking back and by looking ahead.** When you're about to cross the street, you must look both ways, right? Keep that image in mind because that's what you should do before each class. What did class consist of last time? Can you predict what it will consist of next time?

> **Focus on substance, not style.** Part of Tammy's bias against Mr. Caldwell focused on his appearance. Despite society's obsession with attractiveness, grooming, and fashion, a student's job is to ask, "What can I learn from this person?" Deciding an instructor isn't worth paying attention to because he doesn't dress well or because his hair style is outdated is just an excuse not to learn.

4. You search for personal meaning and patterns.

> **Ask yourself: What's in it for me?** Why is knowing this important? How can I use this information in the future? Instead of dismissing material that appears unrelated to your life, try figuring out how it *could* relate. You may be surprised!

> **Think about how courses relate to one another.** How does this new knowledge relate to things you're learning in other courses? Does sociology have anything to do with history? Psychology with economics?

5. Your emotions are involved, not just your mind.

> **Evaluate your attitudes and feelings.** Do you like the subject matter? Do you admire the teacher? Remember your high school teacher, Mr. Brown, whose class you just couldn't stand? Not every class will be your favorite. That's natural. But if a class turns you off as a learner, instead of allowing your emotions to take over, ask why and whether your feelings are in your best interest.

> **Make a deliberate decision to change negative feelings.** Fortunately, feelings can be changed. Hating a course or disliking a professor can only build resentment and threaten your success. It's possible to do a 180–degree turn and transform your negative emotions into positive energy.

6. You realize that as a learner you use what you already know in constructing new knowledge.[4]

> **Remember that passive learning is impossible.** When it comes to learning, you are the construction foreman, building on what you already know to construct new knowledge. You're not just memorizing facts someone else wants you to learn. You're a full partner in the learning process!

> **Remind yourself that constructing knowledge takes work.** No one ever built a house by simply sitting back or just hanging out.

It is not the answer that enlightens, but the question.

Eugene Ionesco, Romanian and French playwright (1909–1994)

> It is what we think we know already that often prevents us from learning.
>
> *Claude Bernard, French physiologist (1813–1878)*

Builders work hard, but in the end they have something to show for their efforts. In your college courses, identify what you already know, and blend new knowledge into the framework you've built in your mind. By constructing new knowledge, you are building yourself into a more sophisticated, more polished, and most certainly more educated person.

7. **You're given a degree of choice in terms of what you learn, how you do it, and feedback on how you're doing.**

> **Make the most of the choices you're given.** College isn't a free-for-all in which you can take any classes you like toward earning a degree. However, which electives you choose will be up to you. Or in a particular course, if your instructor allows you to write a paper or shoot a video, choose the option that will be more motivating for you. When you receive an assignment, select a topic that fires you up. It's easier to generate energy to put toward choices you've made yourself.

> **Use feedback to improve, and if feedback is not given, ask for it.** It's possible to get really good at doing something the wrong way. Take a golf swing or a swimming stroke, for example. Without someone intervening to give you feedback, it may be difficult to know how to improve. Your instructors will most likely write comments on your assignments to explain their grades. Evaluating your work is their job; it's what they must do to help you improve. Take their suggestions to heart and try them out.

All of us are already good learners in some situations. Let's say you're drawn to technology, for example. You're totally engrossed in computers and eagerly learn everything you can from books, classes, and online sources—and you sometimes totally lose yourself in a flow state as you're learning. No one has to force you to practice your technology skills or pick up an issue of *Wired* or *PC World*. You do it because you want to. In this case, you're self-motivated and therefore learning is easy. This chapter provides several different tools to help you understand your own personal profile as a learner so that you can try to learn at your best in *all* situations.

> The purpose of learning is growth, and our minds, unlike our bodies, can continue growing as long as we live.
>
> *Mortimer Adler, American philosopher, educator, and editor (1902–2001)*

Multiple Intelligences: *How Are You Smart?*

Multiple Intelligences Self-Assessment

Are people smart in different ways? How so? On each line, put check marks next to all the statements that best describe you.

Linguistic Intelligence: The capacity to use language to express what's on your mind and understand others ("word smart")

_____ I'm a good storyteller.

_____ I enjoy word games, puns, and tongue twisters.

_____ I'd rather listen to the radio than watch TV.

_____ I've recently written something I'm proud of.

_____ I can hear words in my head before I say or write them.

_____ When riding in the car, I sometimes pay more attention to words on billboards than I do to the scenery.

_____ In high school, I did better in English, history, or social studies than I did in math and science.

_____ I enjoy reading.

_____ TOTAL check marks

Logical-Mathematical Intelligence: The capacity to understand cause/effect relationships and to manipulate numbers ("number/reasoning smart")

_____ I can easily do math in my head.

_____ I enjoy brainteasers or puzzles.

_____ I like it when things can be counted or analyzed.

_____ I can easily find logical flaws in what others do or say.

_____ I think most things have rational explanations.

_____ Math and science were my favorite subjects in high school.

_____ I like to put things into categories.

_____ I'm interested in new scientific advances.

_____ TOTAL check marks

Spatial Intelligence: The capacity to represent the world visually or graphically ("picture smart")

_____ I like to take pictures of what I see around me.

_____ I'm sensitive to colors.

_____ My dreams at night are vivid.

_____ I like to doodle or draw.

_____ I'm good at navigating with a map.

_____ I can picture what something will look like before it's finished.

_____ In school, I preferred geometry to algebra.

_____ I often make my point by drawing a picture or diagram.

_____ TOTAL check marks

Bodily-Kinesthetic Intelligence: The capacity to use your whole body or parts of it to solve a problem, make something, or put on a production ("body smart")

_____ I regularly engage in sports or physical activities.

_____ I get fidgety (tap my foot, etc.) when asked to sit for long periods of time.

_____ I get some of my best ideas while I'm engaged in a physical activity.

_____ I need to practice a skill in order to learn it, rather than just reading or watching a video about it.

_____ I enjoy being a daredevil.

_____ I'm a well-coordinated person.

_____ I like to think through things while I'm doing something else like running or walking.

_____ I like to spend my free time outdoors.

_____ TOTAL check marks

Musical Intelligence: The capacity to think in music; hear patterns; and recognize, remember, and perhaps manipulate them ("music smart")

_____ I can tell when a musical note is flat or sharp.

_____ I play a musical instrument.

_____ I often hear music playing in my head.

_____ I can listen to a piece of music once or twice, and then sing it back accurately.

_____ I often sing or hum while working.

_____ I like music playing while I'm doing things.

_____ I'm good at keeping time to a piece of music.

_____ I consider music an important part of my life.

_____ TOTAL check marks

Interpersonal Intelligence: The capacity to understand other people ("people smart")

_____ I prefer group activities to solo activities.

_____ Others think of me as a leader.

_____ I enjoy the challenge of teaching others something I like to do.

_____ I like to get involved in social activities at school, church, or work.

_____ If I have a problem, I'm more likely to get help than tough it out alone.

_____ I feel comfortable in a crowd of people.

_____ I have several close friends.

_____ I'm the sort of person others come to for advice about their problems.

_____ TOTAL check marks

Intrapersonal Intelligence: The capacity to understand yourself, who you are, and what you can do ("self-smart")

_____ I like to spend time alone thinking about important questions in life.

_____ I have invested time in learning more about myself.

_____ I consider myself to be independent minded.

_____ I keep a journal of my inner thoughts.

_____ I'd rather spend a weekend alone than at a place with a lot of other people around.

_____ I've thought seriously about starting a business of my own.

_____ I'm realistic about my own strengths and weaknesses.

_____ I have goals for my life that I'm working on.

_____ TOTAL check marks

(Continued)

Naturalistic Intelligence: **The capacity to discriminate between living things and show sensitivity toward the natural world ("nature smart")**

_____ Environmental problems bother me.

_____ In school, I always enjoyed field trips to places in nature or away from class.

_____ I enjoy studying nature, plants, or animals.

_____ I've always done well on projects involving living systems.

_____ I enjoy pets.

_____ I notice signs of wildlife when I'm on a walk or hike.

_____ I can recognize types of plants, trees, rocks, birds, and so on.

_____ I enjoy learning about environmental issues.

_____ TOTAL check marks

Which intelligences have the most check marks? Write in the three intelligences in which you had the most number of check marks.

_____   _____   _____

Although this is an informal instrument, it can help you think about the concept of multiple intelligences, or MI. How are you smart?

Based on Armstrong, T. (1994). *Multiple intelligences in the classroom.* Alexandria, VA: Association for Supervision and Curriculum Development, pp. 18–20.

Have you ever noticed that people are smart in different ways? Consider the musical genius of Mozart, who published his first piano pieces at the age of five. Olympic Gold Medalist Lindsey Vonn started skiing when she was two years old. Not many of us are as musically gifted as Mozart or as physically gifted as Lindsey Vonn, but we all have strengths. You may earn top grades in math, and not-so-top grades in English, and your best friend's grades may be just the opposite.

According to Harvard psychologist Howard Gardner, people can be smart in the eight different categories you saw in Exercise 3.2. Most schools focus on particular types of intelligence, linguistic and logical-mathematical intelligence, reflecting the three R's: reading, writing, and 'rithmetic. But Gardner claims there are many different types of intelligence that can't be measured by traditional one-dimensional standardized IQ tests and represented by a three-digit number: 100 (average), 130 (gifted), or 150 (genius). Gardner defines intelligence as "the ability to find and solve problems and create products of value in one or more cultural settings."[5] One recent study showed that the three primary intelligences of community college students are intrapersonal, interpersonal, and bodily-kinesthetic.[6] What are yours?

So instead of asking the traditional question "How smart are you?" a better question is "How are you smart?" The idea is to find out how, and then apply this understanding of yourself to your academic work in order to achieve your best results.

Use Intelligence-Oriented Study Techniques

Do you sometimes wonder why you can't remember things for exams? Some learning experts believe that memory is intelligence-specific. You may have a good memory for people's faces but a bad memory for their names. You may be able to remember the words of a country-western hit, but not the dance steps that go with it. The Theory of Multiple Intelligences may explain why.[7]

Examine your own behaviors in class. If your instructors use their linguistic intelligence to teach, as many do, and your intelligences lie elsewhere, do you get frustrated? Instead of zeroing in on the lecture, do you fidget (bodily-kinesthetic), doodle (spatial), or socialize (interpersonal)? You may need to translate the information into your own personal intelligences, just as you would if your instructor speaks French and you speak English. This strategy might have worked for Tammy Ko from the "FOCUS Challenge Case." Mr. Caldwell's most developed intelligence is linguistic, whereas Tammy's are bodily-kinesthetic (manipulating test tubes) and interpersonal (interacting with people). Tammy's learning problems are partially due to her inability to translate from one set of intelligences (his) to another (hers). Creating flash cards, for example, or talking over the lectures with Sam might have really helped her. Take a look at this chart of possible intelligence-oriented study options:

Linguistic ---->	1. Rewrite your class notes. 2. Record yourself reading through your class notes, and play the recording as you study. 3. Read the textbook chapter aloud.
Logical Mathematical ---->	1. Create hypothetical conceptual problems to solve. 2. Organize chapter or lecture notes into a logical flow. 3. Analyze how the textbook chapter is organized and why.
Spatial ---->	1. Draw a map that demonstrates your thinking on course material. 2. Illustrate your notes by drawing diagrams and charts. 3. Mark up your textbook to show relationships among concepts.
Bodily–Kinesthetic ---->	1. Study course material while engaged in physical activity. 2. Practice skills introduced in class or in the text. 3. Act out a scene based on chapter content.
Musical ---->	1. Create musical memory devices by putting words into well-known melodies. 2. Listen to music while you're studying. 3. Sing or hum as you work.
Interpersonal ---->	1. Discuss course material with your classmates. 2. Organize a study group that meets regularly. 3. Meet a classmate before or after class for coffee and class conversation.
Intrapersonal ---->	1. Keep a journal to track your personal reactions to course material. 2. Study alone and engage in internal dialogue about course content. 3. Coach yourself on how to best study for a challenging class.
Naturalistic ---->	1. Search for applications of course content in the natural world. 2. Study outside (if weather permits and you can resist distractions). 3. Go to a physical location that exemplifies course material (for example, a park for your geology course).

Develop Your Weaker Intelligences

It's important to cultivate your weaker intelligences. Why? Because life isn't geared to one kind of intelligence. It's complex. A photo journalist for *National Geographic,* for example, might need linguistic intelligence, spatial intelligence, interpersonal intelligence, and naturalistic intelligence. Being well-rounded, as the expression goes, is truly a good thing. Artist Pablo Picasso once said, "I am always doing that which I cannot do, in order that I may learn how to do it."

Use your multiple intelligences to multiply your success. Remember that no one is naturally intelligent in all eight areas. Each individual is a unique blend of intelligences. But the Theory of Multiple Intelligences claims that we all have the capacity to develop all of our eight intelligences further. That's good news!

How Do You Perceive and Process Information?

Style—we all have it, right? What's yours? Baggy jeans and a T-shirt? Sandals, even in the middle of winter? A signature hairdo that defies gravity? When it comes to appearance, you have your own style. You know it, and so does everyone who knows you.

Think about how your mind works. For example, how do you decide what to wear in the morning? Do you turn on the radio or TV for the weather forecast? Stick your head out the front door? Ask someone else's opinion? Throw on whatever happens to be clean? We all have different styles, don't we?

perceive become aware of

So what's a learning style? A learning style is defined as your "characteristic and preferred ways of gathering, interpreting, organizing, recalling, and thinking about information."[8]

Here's one way of looking at things. The way you **perceive** information and the way you process it—your perceiving and processing preferences—are based in part on your senses. Which senses do you prefer to use to take in information—your eyes (visual-graphic or visual-words); your ears (aural); or all your senses, using your whole body (kinesthetic)? Which type of information sinks in best? Which type of information do you most trust to be accurate?

To further understand your preferred sensory channel, let's take this hypothetical example. Assume a rich relative you didn't even know leaves you some money, and you decide to use it to buy a new car. You must first answer many questions: What kind of car do you want to buy—an SUV, a sedan, a sports car, a van, or a truck? What are the differences between various makes and models? How do prices, comfort, and safety compare? Who provides the best warranty? Which car do consumers rate highest? How would you go about learning the answers to all these questions?

Learning how to learn is life's most important skill.

Tony Buzan, memory expert

© Holger Winkler/zefa/CORBIS

iStockphoto.com/Marcela Barsse

Visual. Some of us would **look**. We'd study charts and graphs comparing cars, mileage, fuel tank capacity, maintenance costs, and customer satisfaction. We learn through graphic representations that explain what could have been said in normal text format.

Johanna Goodyear/ Dreamstime.com

Aural. Some of us would **listen**. We'd ask all our friends what kind of cars they drive and what they've heard about cars from other people. We'd pay attention as showroom salespeople describe the features of various cars. We learn through sounds by listening.

Nadezda Firsova/ iStockphoto. com

Read/Write. Some of us would **read** or **write**. We'd buy a copy of *Consumer Reports* annual edition on automobiles, or copies of magazines such as *Car and Driver* or *Road and Track,* and write lists of each car's pros and cons. We learn through words by reading and writing.

Pascal Genest/iStockphoto.com

Kinesthetic. Some of us would want to **do it**. We'd go to the showroom and test-drive a few cars to physically try them out. We learn through experience when all our senses are activated.

What would you do? Eventually, as you're deciding which vehicle to buy, you might do all these things, and do them more than once. But learning style theory says we all have preferences for how we perceive and process information.

EXERCISE 3.3

VARK Learning Styles Assessment

Choose the answer that best explains your preference, and circle the letter. Please select more than one response if a single answer does not match your perception. ***Leave blank any question that does not apply.***

1. You are helping someone who wants to go downtown, find your airport, or locate the bus station. You would:
   (a) draw or give her a map.
   (b) tell her the directions.
   (c) write down the directions (without a map).
   (d) go with her.

2. You are not sure whether a word should be spelled "dependent" or "dependant." You would:
   (a) see the word in your mind and choose by the way different versions look.
   (b) think about how each word sounds and choose one.
   (c) find it in a dictionary.
   (d) write both words on paper and choose one.

3. You are planning a group vacation. You want some feedback from your friends about your plans. You would:
   (a) use a map or website to show them the places.
   (b) phone, text, or email them.
   (c) give them a copy of the printed itinerary.
   (d) describe some of the highlights.

4. You are going to cook something as a special treat for your family. You would:
   (a) look through the cookbook for ideas from the pictures.
   (b) ask friends for suggestions.
   (c) use a cookbook where you know there is a good recipe.
   (d) cook something you know without the need for instructions.

(Continued)

5. A group of tourists want to learn about the parks or wildlife reserves in your area. You would:
   (a) show them Internet pictures, photographs, or picture books.
   (b) talk about, or arrange a talk for them about, parks or wildlife reserves.
   (c) give them a book or pamphlets about the parks or wildlife reserves.
   (d) take them to a park or wildlife reserve and walk with them.

6. You are about to purchase a digital camera or cell phone. Other than price, what would most influence your decision?
   (a) Its attractive design that looks good
   (b) The salesperson telling me about its features
   (c) Reading the details about its features
   (d) Trying or testing it

7. Remember a time when you learned how to do something new. Try to avoid choosing a physical skill, like riding a bike. You learned best by:
   (a) diagrams and charts—visual clues.
   (b) listening to somebody explaining it and asking questions.
   (c) written instructions—for example, a manual or textbook.
   (d) watching a demonstration.

8. You have a problem with your heart. You would prefer that the doctor:
   (a) show you a diagram of what was wrong.
   (b) describe what was wrong.
   (c) give you a pamphlet to read about it.
   (d) use a plastic model of a heart to show what was wrong.

9. You want to learn a new software program, skill, or game on a computer. You would:
   (a) follow the diagrams in the book that came with it.
   (b) talk with people who know about the program.
   (c) read the written instructions that came with the program.
   (d) use the controls or keyboard and try things out.

10. You like websites that have:
    (a) interesting design and visual features.
    (b) audio channels where you can hear music, radio programs or interviews.
    (c) interesting written descriptions, lists and explanations.
    (d) things you can click on or try out.

11. Other than price, you would most be influenced in your decision to buy a new nonfiction book by:
    (a) a cover that looks appealing.
    (b) a friend talking about it and recommending it.
    (c) quickly reading parts of it.
    (d) its containing real-life stories, experiences, and examples.

12. You are using a book, CD, or website to learn how to take photos with your new digital camera. You would like to have:
    (a) diagrams showing the camera and what each part does.
    (b) a chance to ask questions and talk about the camera and its features.
    (c) clear written instructions with lists and bullet points about what to do.
    (d) many examples of good and poor photos and how to improve them.

13. You prefer a teacher or a presenter who uses:
    (a) diagrams, charts, or graphs.
    (b) question and answer, talk, group discussion, or guest speakers.
    (c) handouts, books, or readings.
    (d) demonstrations, models, field trips, role plays, or practical exercises.

14. You have finished a competition or test and would like some feedback. You would like to have feedback:
    (a) using graphs showing what you achieved.
    (b) from somebody who talks it through with you.
    (c) in a written format, describing your results.
    (d) using examples from what you have done.

15. You are going to choose food at a restaurant or cafe. You would:
    (a) look at what others are eating or look at pictures of each dish.
    (b) ask the server or friends to recommend choices.
    (c) choose from the written descriptions in the menu.
    (d) choose something that you have had there before.

16. You have to give an important speech at a conference or special occasion. You would:
    (a) make diagrams or create graphs to help explain things.
    (b) write a few key words and practice your speech over and over.
    (c) write out your speech and learn from reading it over several times.
    (d) gather many examples and stories to make the talk real and practical.

Source: N. Fleming. (2001–2011). VARK, a Guide to Learning Styles. Version 7.1. Available at http://www.vark-learn.com/english/page .asp?p=questionnaire. Adapted and used with permission from Neil Fleming.

Scoring the VARK

Let's tabulate your results.

Count your choices in each of the four VARK categories.	(a)	(b)	(c)	(d)
	Visual	Aural	Read/Write	Kinesthetic

Now that you've calculated your scores, do they match your perceptions of yourself as a learner? Could you have predicted them? The VARK's creators believe that you are best qualified to verify and interpret your own results.[9] Try the "just-in-time" VARK IT! suggestions that appear alongside as you read this book. They will help you apply your preferred VARK strategies and learn at your best.

Using Your Sensory Preferences

Knowing your preferences can help you in your academic coursework. If your highest score (by 4 or 5 points) is in one of the four VARK modalities, that particular learning modality is your preferred one.[10] If your scores are more or less even between several or all four modalities, these scores mean that you don't have a strong preference for any single modality. A lower score in a preference simply means that you are more comfortable using other styles. If your VARK results contain a zero in a particular learning modality, you may realize that you do indeed dislike this mode or find it unhelpful. You might want to reflect on why you don't like to use this learning modality. To learn more about your results and suggestions for applying them, see Figure 3.1 for your preferred modality.

Most college classes emphasize reading and writing; however, if your lowest score is in the read/write modality, don't assume you're academically doomed. VARK can help you discover alternative, more productive ways to learn the same course material. You may learn to adapt naturally to a particular instructor or discipline's preferences, using a visual modality in your economics class to interpret graphs and a kinesthetic modality in your chemistry lab to conduct experiments.

However, you may also find that you need to deliberately and strategically reroute your learning methods in some of your classes, and knowing your VARK preferences can help you do that. Learning to capitalize on your preferences and translate challenging course material into your preferred modality may serve you well. Remember these suggestions about the VARK, and try them out to see whether they improve your academic results.

1. **VARK preferences are not necessarily strengths.** However, VARK is an excellent vehicle to help you reflect on how you learn and begin to reinforce the productive strategies you're already using or select ones that might work better.

2. **If you have a strong preference for a particular modality, practice using it in many different ways.** (See Figure 3.1 later in this chapter.) Reinforce your learning by doing many things in that column.

3. **An estimated 60 percent of people are** multimodal**.** In a typical classroom of 30 students (based on VARK data):

    > 17 students would be multimodal,

    > 1 student would be visual,

    > 1 student would be aural,

    > 5 students would be read/write,

    > 6 students would be kinesthetic,

    and the teacher would most likely have a strong read/write preference![11]

4. **If you are multimodal, as most of us are, it may be necessary to use several of your modalities to boost your confidence in your learning.** Practice the suggestions for all of your preferred modalities.

5. **While in an ideal world, it would be good to try to strengthen lesser preferences, you may wish to save that goal for later in life.** Some experts suggest that college isn't the place to experiment. Grades count, and your continuing success will depend on how well you do. You may decide it's better to try to strengthen your current preferences now and work on expanding your lesser preferences later. This book will give you an opportunity to practice your VARK learning preferences—whatever they are—in each chapter. Ultimately, learning at your best is up to you.

Gaining the insights provided in this chapter and acting on them have the potential to greatly affect your college success. Understand yourself, capitalize on your preferences, build on them, focus, and learn!

multimodal preferring to use more than one sense

VARK It!

Aural: After you finish reading these five points about the VARK, try summarizing them aloud in your own words—until you can talk through all five.

What Role Does Your Personality Play?

One of the best things about college is having a chance to meet so many different types of people. At times you may find these differences intriguing. At other times, they may baffle you. Look around and listen to other students, and you'll start to notice. Have you heard students saying totally opposite things such as those listed here?

"There's no way I can study at home. It's way too noisy."

"There's no way I can study in the library. It's way too quiet."

"I'm so glad I've already decided on a major. Now I can go full steam ahead."

"I have no idea what to major in. I can think of six different majors I'd like to choose."

"My sociology instructor is great. She talks about all kinds of things in class, and her essay tests are actually fun!"

"My sociology instructor is so confusing. She talks about so many different things in class. How am I supposed to know what to study for her tests?"[12]

You're likely to run into all kinds of viewpoints and all types of people, but differences make life much more interesting! We're each unique. Perhaps your friends comment on your personality by saying, "She's really quiet," or "He's a 'party animal'," or "He's incredibly logical," or "She trusts her gut feelings." What you may not know is how big a role your personality plays in how you prefer to learn.

The Myers-Briggs Type Indicator® (MBTI) is the most well-known personality assessment instrument in the world. Each year, approximately two million people worldwide get a look into their personalities, their career choices, their interaction with others, and their learning styles by completing it. If you are able to complete the full Myers-Briggs Type Indicator in the class for which you're using this textbook, or through your college counseling center or learning center, do so. You'll learn a great deal about yourself.

The Myers-Briggs Type Indicator shows you your preferences in four areas:

E or I **What energizes you and where do you direct energy?** Do you get energy from other people (**E**xtravert) or do you go within yourself to find strength (**I**ntrovert)?

S or N **How do you gather information and what kind of information do you trust?** Do you trust your senses and factually based information (**S**ensor) or do you trust your gut feelings (i**N**tuition)?

T or F **How do you make decisions, arrive at conclusions, and make judgments?** Do you think things through logically (**T**hinker) or do you care about how others react and feel (**F**eeler)?

J or P **How do you relate to the outer world?** Do you prefer organization and structure (**J**udging) or do you like spontaneity and going with the flow (**P**erceiver)?

Each person is an exception to the rule.

Carl Jung, psychiatrist (1875–1961)

© Larry Harwood Photography. Property of Cengage Learning.

If you take the Myers-Briggs Type Indicator you should realize that it isn't about what you can do. It's about what you prefer to do. Here's an illustration. Write your name on the first line.

_____

_____

Now put the pen in your other hand, and try writing your name on the second line. What was different the second time around? For most people, the second try takes longer, is messier, probably feels strange, and requires more concentration. But could you do it? Yes. It's just that you prefer doing it the first way. The first way is easier and more natural; the second way makes a simple task seem like hard work! It's possible that you might have to try "writing with your other hand" in college—doing things that don't come naturally.

In the "FOCUS Challenge Case," Tammy was described as outgoing (**Ex**traverted) and hands-on (**S**ensing), whereas Mr. Caldwell was described as reserved (**I**ntroverted) and theoretical (i**N**tuitive). It's unlikely that Mr. Caldwell will change his teaching style, and even if he did, students in his class have a variety of learning styles. Whose style would he try to match? Both Tammy's personality and Mr. Caldwell's are similar to the most common types found in college classrooms. Although you couldn't be sure without looking at actual MBTI scores, you'd expect Tammy to be an ESFP. ESFP's are outgoing, like facts as opposed to theories, pay attention to the feelings of others, and prefer exploring options to following a structure. Based on the clues in the "Focus Challenge Case," you'd also expect Mr. Caldwell to be an INTJ—the opposite.

This chapter has covered learning from several different perspectives, and you now know more about yourself as a learner than you did before you read it. But you may be wondering: So how do Multiple Intelligences, VARK preferences, and personality traits (MBTI) work together to produce a unique learner? Although the three perspectives aren't intended to connect, let's look at this example to help you understand how each one would explain how people learn.

Let's say the person you sit by in your math class always asks you whether you want to join his study group. Based on what you've learned in this chapter, you'd be more likely to say yes if you:

1. **MI:** have *interpersonal* (or social) intelligence

2. **VARK:** are an *aural* learner who likes to discuss things

3. **MBTI:** are *extraverted* (you get energy from other people).

The three perspectives don't overlap; they're different. That's why this chapter presents all three. Each perspective explains how people learn in a different way.

Although simply knowing about these three perspectives is good, it's important to go further and act on that knowledge. As a single learner in a larger class, you will need to adjust to the teaching style of your instructor in ways such as the following:

> **Translate for maximum comfort.** The way to maximize your comfort as a learner is to find ways to translate from your instructor's preferences to yours. If you know that you prefer feeling over thinking, and your instructor's style is based on thinking, make the course material come alive by

VARK It!

Read/Write: In the margin, write a one paragraph self-description (that includes advice on how to study) based on your MI, VARK preferences, and personality type. Here's an example: "I'm an extravert with interpersonal and bodily-kinesthetic intelligences, and I prefer to use all my senses to learn (kinesthetic). I should study with friends and make flash cards or create practice quizzes."

personalizing it. How does the topic relate to you, your lifestyle, your family, and your future choices?

> **Make strategic choices.** Although learning preferences can help explain your academic successes, it's also important not to use them to rationalize your nonsuccesses. An introvert could say, "I could have aced that assignment if the instructor had let me work alone! I hate group projects." Become the best learner you can be at what you're naturally good at. But also realize that you'll need to become more versatile over time. In the workforce, you will not always be able to choose what you do and how you do it. Actively choose your learning strategies rather than simply hoping for the best. Remember: No one can learn for you, just as no one can eat for you.

> **Take full advantage.** College will present you with an extensive menu of learning opportunities. You will also build on your learning as you move beyond your general, introductory classes into courses in your chosen major—and across and between classes. Don't fall victim to the temptation to make excuses as some students do ("I could have been more successful in college if . . . I hadn't had to work so many hours . . . I hadn't had a family to support . . . my instructors had been more supportive. . . ." If, if, if. College may well be the most concentrated and potentially powerful learning opportunity you'll ever have. Ultimately, learning at your best is up to you.

There's a crack in everything. That's how the light gets in.

Leonard Cohen

BOX 3.1   Learning Disability? Five Ways to Help Yourself

Perhaps you were diagnosed with Attention-Deficit/Hyperactivity Disorder (ADHD) or dyslexia as a young child. If you're beginning your college career with a learning disability (LD), you're not alone. In a college or university with an enrollment of 25,000 students, for example, approximately 550 of those students have learning disabilities.[13] By some estimates, two-thirds of students with diagnosed LDs continue on to college after high school.[14] Does a learning disability mean all the odds are against you? No, but there are some important steps you must take to help yourself. Successful college students with LDs recognize, understand, and accept these steps, and develop compensating strategies to offset their LDs.

1. If you've been previously diagnosed with a learning disability, bring a copy of your evaluation or Individualized Education Plan (IEP) with you to campus. Some schools require documentation in order to use the institution's support services.

2. Locate the support services office on your campus and use it. These services are free

and can make all the difference in your success.

3. Learn more about your specific LD. Read about it. Visit credible websites. Understanding the ins and outs of what you're up against is important.

4. If you need special accommodations such as taking exams somewhere other than the classroom, schedule an appointment with your instructors early in the term to let them know. Having a learning disability doesn't mean you're required to do less work, but you'll get the support you need in order to do your best.

5. Remember that the advice in this book, which is helpful to all college students, can be even more useful to anyone with a learning disability. Time management strategies and study skills tailored to your specific LD are key.

Don't let fear of failure immobilize you. Instead, keep your eye on the goal and take charge of your own learning.[15]

Metacognition: Take Charge of How You Study

Do You Know How to Study?

To what extent do these ten statements apply to you? Write the number for each statement on the line preceeding it.

Never		Sometimes		Always
1	2	3	4	5

_____ 1. I keep going with things I have to learn rather than skipping over what I don't understand.

_____ 2. When I'm studying something difficult, I realize when I'm stuck and ask for help.

_____ 3. I make a study plan and stick to it in order to master class material.

_____ 4. I quiz myself as I'm studying to see what I understand and what I don't.

_____ 5. I talk through my problems, understanding things while I study.

_____ 6. After I study something, I think about how well it went.

_____ 7. I know when I learn best: morning, afternoon, or evening, for example.

_____ 8. I know how I study best: alone, with one other person, in a group, etc.

_____ 9. I know where I study best: at home, at the library, at my computer, etc.

_____ 10. I believe I'm in control of my own learning.

Now tally your scores on this informal instrument. If you scored between 40 and 50 total points, you have excellent metacognitive skills. If you scored between 30 and 40 points, your skills are probably average. However, note any items you rated down in the 1 to 2 range, and then continue reading this section of the chapter carefully.

Talk about needing to use a dictionary! What does the word *metacognition* mean? *Meta* is an ancient Greek prefix that is often used to mean *about*. For example, metacommunication is communicating *about* the way you communicate. ("I feel humiliated when you tease me in front of other people. Can you *not* do that?")

Because cognition means thinking and learning, metacognition is thinking about your thinking and learning about your learning. It's about identifying your learning goals, monitoring your progress, backing up or getting help when you're stuck, forging ahead when you're in the groove, and evaluating your results. Metacognition is about knowing yourself as a learner and about your ability (and motivation) to control your own learning. Some things are easy for you to learn; others are hard. What do you know about yourself as a learner, and do you use that awareness *intentionally* to learn at your best?[16]

These questions may seem simple, but how do you know:

1. When you've finished a reading assignment?

2. When your paper is ready to turn in?

3. When you've finished studying for an exam?

When you're eating a meal, you know when you're full, right? But when it comes to academic work, how do you know when you're done? Some students resort to answers like this to the question "How do you know when you're done?" Look at the range of students' answers:

> I just do.
> I trust in God.
> My eyelids get too heavy.
> I've been at it for a long time.
> My mom tells me to go to bed.
> I understand everything.
> I can write everything down without looking at the textbook or my notes.
> I've created a practice quiz for myself and get all the answers right.
> When my wife or girlfriend drills me and I know all the answers.
> When I can teach my husband everything I've learned.
> When I've highlighted, recopied my notes, made flash cards, written sample questions, tested myself, and so on.

Striving for success without hard work is like trying to harvest where you haven't planted.

David Bly, Minnesota politician

You can see that their answers become increasingly reliable as you progress down the list.[17]

Metacognition is about having an "awareness of [your] own cognitive machinery and how the machinery works."[18] It's about knowing the limits of your own learning and memory capabilities, knowing how much you can accomplish within a certain amount of time, and knowing what learning strategies work for you.[19] Know your limits, but at the same time, stretch.

Apply Your Learning Style to Your Study Style

Now that you've gained some insight into how you prefer to learn, it's time to apply those preferences to how you study. Are you the kind of student who re-reads a textbook page five times without having the information sink in? Do you procrastinate when it comes to reading assignments for your classes? If so, through this chapter, you may have discovered why. Perhaps your linguistic intelligence is relatively low. Perhaps Read/Write is your least preferred VARK modality. Perhaps your off-the-charts extraverted personality enjoys the company of others, not a book.

Metacognition means thinking about your thinking and learning about your learning—taking charge of your own learning—and maybe that's exactly what you need to do. Early on, this chapter advised you about "Creating the Best Conditions for Learning." Monitoring how you study and how well it's working is at the top of the list. Use this chart as your guide, and note the results. You may just see an improvement!

	Everyday Study Strategies	Exam Preparation Study Strategies
VISUAL iStockphoto.com/Marcela Barsse	• Convert your lecture notes to a visual format. • Study the placement of items, colors, and shapes in your textbook. • Put complex concepts into flowcharts or graphs. • Redraw ideas you create from memory.	• Practice turning your visuals back into words. • Recall the pictures you made of the pages you studied. • Use diagrams to answer exam questions, if your instructor will allow it.
AURAL Johanna Goodyear/ Dreamstime.com	• Read your notes aloud. • Explain your notes to another auditory learner. • Ask others to "hear" your understanding of the material. • Record your notes or listen to your instructors' podcasts. • Realize that your lecture notes may be incomplete. You may have become so involved in listening that you stopped writing. Fill your notes in later by talking with other students or getting material from the textbook.	• Practice by speaking your answers aloud. • Listen to your own voice as you answer questions. • Opt for an oral exam if allowed. • Imagine you are talking with the teacher as you answer questions.
READ/WRITE Nadezda Firsova/iStockphoto.com	• Write out your lecture notes again and again. • Read your notes (silently) again and again. • Put ideas and principles into different words. • Translate diagrams, graphs, etc., into text. • Rearrange words and "play"with wording. • Turn diagrams and charts into words.	• Write out potential exam answers. • Practice creating and taking exams. • Type out your answers to potential test questions. • Organize your notes into lists or bullets. • Write practice paragraphs, particularly beginnings and endings.
KINESTHETIC Pascal Genest/iStockphoto.com	• Recall experiments, field trips, etc. Remember the real things that happened. • Talk over your notes with another "K" person. • Use photos and pictures that make ideas come to life. • Go back to the lab, your manual, or your notes that include real examples. • Remember that your lecture notes will have gaps if topics weren't concrete or relevant for you. • Use case studies to help you learn abstract principles.	• Role-play the exam situation in your room (or the actual classroom). • Put plenty of examples into your answers. • Write practice answers and sample paragraphs. • Give yourself practice tests.

FIGURE 3.1

Visual, Aural, Read/Write, and Kinesthetic Learning Strategies

Becoming an Intentional Learner: Make a Master Study Plan

What's your favorite class this term? Or let's turn the question around: What's your least favorite class? Becoming an educated person may well require you to study things you wouldn't *choose* to study. Considering all you have to do, including your most and least favorite classes, what would making a master study plan look like? You've "been there, done that" all through your schooling, but do you *really* know how to study?

To begin, think about what you have to think about. What's your goal? Is it to finish your English essay by 10:00 P.M. so that you can start your algebra homework? Or is it to write the best essay you can possibly write? If you've allowed yourself one hour to read this chapter, but after an hour you're still not finished, you have three choices: keep reading, finish later, or give up entirely. What's in your best interest, honestly? See whether you find the following planning strategies helpful.

1. **Make sure you understand your assignments.** Understanding is critical to making a master plan. You can actually waste a great deal of time trying to read your instructor's mind after the fact: "Did she want us to *analyze* the play or *summarize* it?" When you leave class, make sure you're clear on what's been assigned.

2. **Schedule yourself to be three places at once.** Making a master plan requires you to think simultaneously about three different time zones:

   The past: Ask yourself what you already know. Is this a subject you've studied before? Have your study habits worked well for you in the past? How have you done your best work—in papers, on exams, on projects?

   The present: Ask yourself what you need to learn now. How interested are you in this material? How motivated are you to learn it? How much time will you devote to it?

   The future: Ask yourself how you'll go about learning it. Will you learn it using the strategies that work best for you? Which learning factors will you control? Will you do what you can to change what's not working?[20]

3. **Talk through your learning challenges.** There's good evidence that talking to yourself while you're studying is a good thing. Researchers find it helps you figure things out: *Okay, I understand the difference between a neurosis and a psychosis, but I'm not sure I can provide examples on my psychology test.* Once you've heard yourself admit that, you know where to focus your efforts next.[21] Or consider the possibility on "talking online" to other students worldwide at openstudy.com.

4. **Be a stickler.** Sticklers pay attention to details. They want to make sure everything is absolutely right. Have you ever thought about how important accuracy is? For example, if you were 99 instead of 100 percent accurate, that would mean that:

   > 500 airplanes in U.S. skies each day wouldn't be directed by air traffic controllers.[22] Disastrous!

   As you read and study, remember this example. Be thorough. Read the entire assignment. Pay attention to details. If you make a mistake, for example in solving a math problem, figure out exactly what went wrong so that you don't hold on to a bad academic habit. Rework the problem at least twice, write a few sentences describing the right way to solve it, and try another problem similar to it to see whether you really understand.[23] Accuracy counts!

5. **Take study breaks.** The human attention span is limited, and according to some researchers, it's shrinking, rather than expanding.[24] Plan to take brief scheduled breaks to

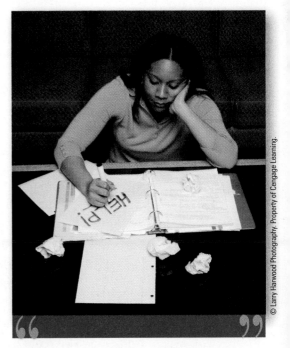

No one can become really educated without having pursued some study in which he took no interest.

T. S. Eliot, American-born poet (1888–1965)

© Larry Harwood Photography. Property of Cengage Learning.

stretch, walk around, or grab a light snack every half hour during study sessions. Of course, it's important to sit down and get back to work again. Don't let a quick study break to get a snack multiply into several hours of television viewing that wasn't in the plan.

6. **Mix it up.** Put a little variety into your study sessions by switching from one subject to another or from one mode of studying—for example, reading, self-quizzing, writing—to another. Variety helps you fight boredom and stay fresh (unless, of course, you're on the verge of a breakthrough). Even changing locations from time to time, rather than always studying in one place, stimulates your brain to reboot.[25]

7. **Estimate how long it will take.** Before starting an assignment, estimate the amount of time you will need to complete that assignment (just as you do at the start of each chapter of this book), and then compare that estimate with the actual amount of time the assignment took to complete. Getting into this habit helps you develop realistic schedules for future projects.

8. **Vary your study techniques by course content.** Studying productively is more than just learning a few general rules that apply to any type of subject matter. You need to zoom in on whatever subject or discipline it is that you're studying. Look over the pages of your textbook. Does the material synch with your learning style? Is it text-heavy (read/write)? Do graphs or charts explain the text and seem important? Are color-coding or bulleting used to call your attention to particular items (visual)? If the material isn't presented as you'd prefer, what can you do to "translate"? For example, if you're a kinesthetic learner, can you make flash cards? Can you create and complete practice tests? If you learn by listening, can you read the material aloud (aural)? And finally, what kind of exam (multiple-choice, essay, problem sets, etc.) does the material lend itself to? What are you likely to need to know, and what will you be asked to do on an exam? When you study math, it's important to do more than read. Working problem sets helps you actually develop the skills you need. When you study history, you study differently. You might draw a timeline of the events leading up to World War I, for example.[26]

9. **Study earlier, rather than later.** Whenever possible, study during the daytime, rather than waiting until evening. Research shows that each hour used for study during the day is equal to one and a half hours at night. Another major study showed that students who study between 6:00 p.m. and midnight are twice as likely to earn A's as students who put off their studying until after midnight.[27] And simply getting enough sleep can help you rachet up your GPA more than you'd expect.

10. **Create artificial deadlines for yourself.** Even though your instructors will have set deadlines for various assignments, create your own deadlines that precede the ones they set. Finish early, and you'll save yourself from any last minute emergencies that may come up, like crashed hard drives or empty printer cartridges.

11. **Treat school as a job.** If you consider the amount of study time you need to budget for each hour of class time, and you're taking 12–15 credits, then essentially you're working a 36–45 hour/week job on campus. Arrive at "work" early and get your tasks done during "business hours" so you have more leisure time in the evenings.

"Disciplined" Studying

Assume you are taking three classes this term: calculus, psychology, and music. For the three textbook pages here, describe how you would go about studying the material, based on what the content in these three subjects requires. Among other things, which particular VARK learning style preferences should be used: V, A, R, and/or K? Fill in specifics about how you would study each subject's textbook page. It's also important to annotate as you read, as shown here. Make notes to yourself in the margins or on sticky notes, reacting, explaining, or summarizing what you've learned or what is still fuzzy. In doing so, you'll be interacting with the material and personalizing it. Make connections; don't just let information float by and hope that something sticks. After you're done, compare notes with your classmates.

---

2   **Chapter P**   Preparation for Calculus

P.1   Graphs and Models

- Sketch the graph of an equation.
- Find the intercepts of a graph.
- Test a graph for symmetry with respect to an axis and the origin.
- Find the points of intersection of two graphs.
- Interpret mathematical models for real-life data.

Weird looking dude! But SMART!

RENÉ DESCARTES (1596–1650)

Descartes made many contributions to philosophy, science, and mathematics. The idea of representing points in the plane by pairs of real numbers and representing curves in the plane by equations was described by Descartes in his book *La Géométrie*, published in 1637.

The Graph of an Equation

In 1637 the French mathematician René Descartes revolutionized the study of mathematics by joining its two major fields—algebra and geometry. With Descartes's coordinate plane, geometric concepts could be formulated analytically and algebraic concepts could be viewed graphically. The power of this approach was such that within a century of its introduction, much of calculus had been developed.

The same approach can be followed in your study of calculus. That is, by viewing calculus from multiple perspectives—*graphically, analytically,* and *numerically*—you will increase your understanding of core concepts.

Consider the equation $3x + y = 7$. The point $(2, 1)$ is a **solution point** of the equation because the equation is satisfied (is true) when 2 is substituted for x and 1 is substituted for y. This equation has many other solutions, such as $(1, 4)$ and $(0, 7)$. To find other solutions systematically, solve the original equation for y.

$$y = 7 - 3x \qquad \text{Analytic approach}$$

Then construct a **table of values** by substituting several values of x.

x	0	1	2	3	4
y	7	4	1	-2	-5

Numerical approach

From the table, you can see that $(0, 7)$, $(1, 4)$, $(2, 1)$, $(3, -2)$, and $(4, -5)$ are solutions of the original equation $3x + y = 7$. Like many equations, this equation has an infinite number of solutions. The set of all solution points is the **graph** of the equation, as shown in Figure P.1.

NOTE en though we refer to the sketch shown in Figure P.1 as the graph of $3x + y = 7$, it really represents only a *portion* of the graph. The entire graph would extend beyond the page. ∎

In this course, you will study many sketching techniques. The simplest is point plotting—that is, you plot points until the basic shape of the graph seems apparent.

Graphical approach: $3x + y = 7$
Figure P.1

Point plotting—this graph really helps me understand the definition of parabola maybe that's because I'm a visual learner.

EXAMPLE 1   Sketching a Graph by Point Plotting

Sketch the graph of $y = x^2 - 2$.

Solution   First construct a table of values. Then plot the points shown in the table.

x	-2	-1	0	1	2	3
y	2	-1	-2	-1	2	7

The parabola $y = x^2 - 2$
Figure P.2

Finally, connect the points with a *smooth curve*, as shown in Figure P.2. This graph is a **parabola**. It is one of the conics you will study in Chapter 10. ∎

How would you study this? *Calculus, 9th Edition, by Ron Larson and Bruce H. Edwards.*

(Continued)

studies of the brain. Case studies lack formal control groups. This, of course, limits the conclusions that can be drawn from clinical observations.

Survey Method

Sometimes psychologists would like to ask everyone in the world a few well-chosen questions: "Do you drink coffee? How often per week?" "What form of discipline did your parents use when you were a child?" "What is the most dishonest thing you've done?" Honest answers to such questions can reveal much about people's behavior. But, because it is impossible to question everyone, doing a survey is often more practical.

In the **survey method,** public polling techniques are used to answer psychological questions (Tourangeau, 2004). Typically, people in a representative sample are asked a series of carefully worded questions. A **representative sample** is a small group that accurately reflects a larger population. A good sample must include the same proportion of men, women, young, old, professionals, blue-collar workers, Republicans, Democrats, whites, African Americans, Native Americans, Latinos, Asians, and so on as found in the population as a whole.

A *population* is an entire group of animals or people belonging to a particular category (for example, all college students or all single women). Ultimately, we are interested in entire populations. But by selecting a smaller sample, we can draw conclusions about the larger group without polling each and every person. Representative samples are often obtained by *randomly* selecting who will be included (▶▶ Figure 1.11). (Notice that this is similar to randomly assigning participants to groups in an experiment.)

How accurate is the survey method? Modern surveys like the Gallup and Harris polls are quite accurate. The Gallup poll has erred in its election predictions by only 1.5 percent since 1954. However, if a survey is based on a biased sample, it may paint a false picture. A *biased sample* does not accurately reflect the population from which it was drawn. Surveys done by magazines, websites, and online information services can be quite biased. Surveys on the use of guns done by *O: The Oprah Magazine* and *Guns and Ammo* magazine would probably produce very different results—neither of which would represent the general population. That's why psychologists using the survey method go to great lengths to ensure that their samples are representative. Fortunately, people can often be polled by telephone, which makes it easier to obtain large samples. Even if one person out of three refuses to answer survey questions, the results are still likely to be valid (Hutchinson, 2004).

Like me!

Internet Surveys

Recently, psychologists have started doing surveys and experiments on the Internet. Web-based research can be a cost-effective way to reach very large groups of people. Internet studies have provided interesting information about topics such as anger, decision making,

Survey method The use of public polling techniques to answer psychological questions.

Representative sample A small, randomly selected part of a larger population that accurately reflects characteristics of the whole population.

There's lots of phone polling during a presidential election year to get some idea of who will win.... It's important that the sample is representative and nonbiased. I like to learn kinesthetically so maybe I should look up some websites on polling...

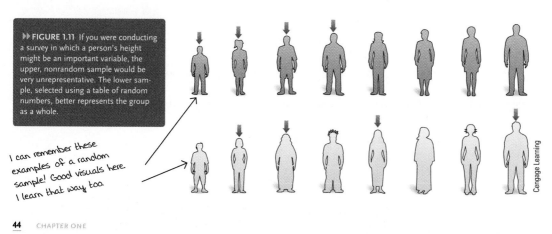

▶▶ **FIGURE 1.11** If you were conducting a survey in which a person's height might be an important variable, the upper, nonrandom sample would be very unrepresentative. The lower sample, selected using a table of random numbers, better represents the group as a whole.

I can remember these examples of a random sample! Good visuals here. I learn that way too.

Cengage Learning

44 CHAPTER ONE

How would you study this? *Psychology: A Journey, 4th Edition by Dennis Coon and John O. Mitterer.*

4

CHAPTER 1

The Basics of Music

Measures

As you performed the different meters, you may have lost your place momentarily. Even if you didn't, you can see that it would be difficult to play a long piece of music without losing one's place. For this reason, music is divided into **measures** with vertical lines called **bar lines**.

A bar line occurs immediately before an accented pulse. Thus, duple meter has two pulses per measure, triple meter has three pulses per measure, and quadruple meter has four pulses per measure. The following example shows the common meters again, this time with bar lines included. Notice how much easier it is to read and perform the meter when it is written this way.

Double bar lines have a special meaning: Their two most common uses are to signal the beginning of a new section in a large work and to mark the end of a work. Put double bar lines at the end of any exercises or pieces you write.

MUSIC IN *Action*

Hearing Pulse and Meter

As members of the class listen, clap a steady pulse without any noticeable accents. Slowly change the pulse to duple, triple, or quadruple meter. You may want to have a contest to see how quickly members of the class can detect the shift to a measured pulse.

Note Values

Learning to read music involves mastering two different musical subsystems: pitch notation and rhythmic notation. Pitch is indicated by the placement of a note on a five-line staff (the higher the note on the staff, the higher the pitch). You will learn about that later in this chapter. Rhythm, on the other hand, is written with

I remember learning about pitch and rhythm as a kid in my piano lessons with Mrs. Sauerbraten—or whatever her name was! Maybe being an aural learner helped me fake my way through all those lessons my parents paid for!

How would you study this? A Creative Approach to Music Fundamentals, 10th Edition, by William Duckworth.

Finally, what have you learned about studying and about yourself as a learner by completing this exercise?

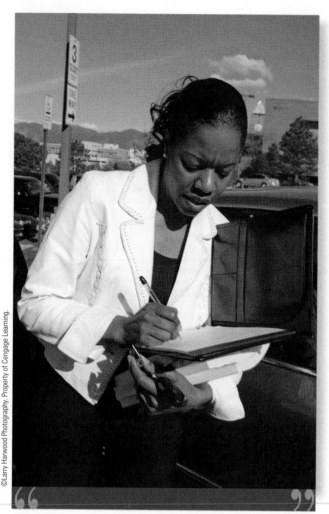

Education is learning what you didn't even know you didn't know.

—*Daniel J. Boorstin, American historian, 1914–2004*

12. Show up. Once you've decided to sit down to study, really commit yourself to showing up—being present emotionally and intellectually, not just physically. If you're committed to getting a college education, then give it all you've got! Get help if you need it. If you have a diagnosed learning disability, or believe you might, find out where help is available on your campus. One of the best ways to compensate for a learning disability is by relying on metacognition. In other words, consciously controlling what isn't happening automatically is vital to your success.[28]

Sprinting to the Finish Line: How to Study When the Heat Is On

Let's be realistic. Planning is important, but there will be the occasional time when you'll have to find some creative ways to survive the onslaught of all you have to study. You'll need to prioritize your time and make decisions about what to study. When you do need to find a way to accomplish more than is humanly possible, keep these "emergency preparedness" suggestions in mind:

1. **Triage.** With little time to spare, you must be efficient. Consider this analogy: If you're the physician on duty in the ER, and three patients come in at once, who will you take care of first: the fellow with strep throat, the woman with a sprained wrist, or the heart attack victim who needs CPR? Making decisions about priorities is called triage. Of all the material you need to study, ask what is most important, moderately important, and least important. For example, if you are earning an A− in art history, a B+ in geography, and a C− in math, you know which course most needs your attention. Evaluate the material and ask yourself which topics have received the most attention in class and in the textbook. Then focus your study time on those topics, rather than trying to study everything.

2. **Use every spare moment to study.** If flashcards work for you, take your flashcards with you everywhere, like on your daily bus ride or to the laundromat, for example. Organize your essay answer in your head while you're filling up at the pump. It's surprising: Small amounts of focused time do add up.

3. **Give it the old one-two-three-four punch.** Immerse all your senses in the precious little amount of time you have to study: *read, write, listen,* and *speak* the material.

4. **Get a grip on your gaps.** Honesty is the best policy. Rather than glossing over what you don't know, assess your knowledge as accurately as possible, and fill in the gaps.

5. **Cram, but only as the very last resort.** If you're ultrashort on time due to a real emergency, and you have studying to do for several classes, focus on one class at a time. Be aware: If you learn new information that is similar to something you already know, the old information can interfere. So if you're studying for a psychology test that contains some overlap with your sociology test, separate the study sessions by a day. Studies also show that cramming up to one hour before sleeping can help to minimize interference.[29] Nevertheless, continually remind yourself: What's my goal here? Is it to just get through twenty-five pages or is it to truly understand?

A Final Word about Studying and Learning

Albert Einstein said this: "Never regard study as a duty, but as the enviable opportunity to learn . . ." Studying and learning are what college is all about. Take his advice: Consider the opportunities before you to become an educated person, and take advantage of them all.

iStockphoto.com/Jacob Wackerhausen

> It's not that I'm so smart, it's just that I stay with problems longer.
>
> *Albert Einstein, American theoretical physicist (1879–1955)*

The Four C Factors: Just how motivated are YOU?

CONTROL: *YOUR TOUGHEST CLASS*

Reflect on yourself as a learner in your toughest class this term. How optimal are the conditions for learning? Put a check mark in the box if any of the following conditions are present.

Seven Conditions for Optimal Learning

1. ☐ You're intrinsically motivated to learn material that is appropriately challenging.

2. ☐ You're appropriately stressed, but generally relaxed.

3. ☐ You're curious about what you're learning, and you look forward to learning it.

4. ☐ You search for personal meaning and patterns.

5. ☐ Your emotions are involved, not just your mind.

6. ☐ You realize that as a learner you use what you already know in constructing new knowledge.

7. ☐ You're given a degree of choice in terms of what you learn, how you do it, and feedback on how you're doing.

If no boxes are checked, identify specific strategies discussed in this chapter that you could you use to create the best conditions for learning.

 CURIOSITY: *CAN YOU BUILD A BETTER BRAIN?*

Don't look now, but you're a very busy person! If you were watching a movie of your life at this moment, what would the scene look like? A cell phone in your hand, a website open on your computer screen, your iPod plugged in, and this book propped in your lap? So much to do, so little time! All we can hope for is that some scientist somewhere will invent a way to get a bigger, better brain! But let's face it: Brain enhancement surgery won't be available any time soon.

It is possible to build a better brain because the brain is more "plastic" than previously thought—not plastic like a Barbie doll, but plastic in that it can "reshape" itself, based on what science has discovered. In a fascinating book, *The Brain That Changes Itself*, Dr. Norman Doidge recounts miraculous stories of people with brain injuries whose brains have been rewired to work better. If you want some interesting reading, take a look.[30]

What's the secret to a healthy brain? New evidence shows that physical exercise helps our brains shrug off damage, reinforce old neural networks, forge new ones, and ultimately result in a better brain![31] A protein called BDNF (for brain-derived neurotrophic factor), sometimes referred to as "Miracle-Gro" for the brain, helps nerve cells in our brains grow and connect; it is important for development in the womb, but it's also important in adult brains. Simply put: It helps us learn. According to researchers, rats that eat a high-calorie, fast-food diet and have a couch-potato lifestyle have less BDNF in their brains. Omega-3 fatty acids found in fish normalize BDNF levels and counteract learning disabilities in rats with brain injuries.[32]

New research indicates that education is a great way to nourish our brains. People who are less educated have twice the risk of getting Alzheimer's disease in later life, and less educated people who have ho-hum, nonchallenging jobs have three to four times the risk. According to researchers, "College seems to pay off well into retirement." It can help you build a better brain![33]

Besides keeping your brain challenged in college, what are you doing to build a better brain?

_____

_____

_____

 CAREER OUTLOOK: *GET TRULY GRITTY*

True grit. Besides being the title of a famous novel and award-winning movie, what does it have to do with you? If you look up the word *grit*, you'll find this definition: "firmness of character; indomitable spirit; pluck."[34] People with grit have what it takes to hang in there. They tough things out despite huge obstacles that get thrown in their way. If an instructor in college or a colleague in the workplace says you have true grit, that's a compliment.

"Grit is a willingness to commit to long-term goals and to persist in the face of difficulty. Studies show that gritty people obtain more education in their lifetime and earn higher college GPAs.[35] Think of it this way: In college, grit explains the difference between two students who fail the same calculus test but respond very differently. One throws the exam in the trash can on the way out of the lecture hall and refuses to ever crack open the textbook again. The other vows to study differently and spend more time doing it. "I'm not going to let calculus get the better of me. I'm going to take control of my learning so that it gets the best from me!" See the difference? After college, in the workplace, grit has to do with how you react to being treated unfairly or badly—like being laid off just when you think your job is going particularly well.

The good news is that if you're short on grit, you can get more. Increasing your self-awareness, especially with help from experts, is the way to start. So when unexpected challenges surface—and they surely will—remember the quote earlier in this chapter: "There's a crack in everything. That's how the light gets in." Cracks are just cracks. They don't have to become breaks. And they can shed light on an otherwise dark situation. It's not the challenge itself that counts; it's how you respond to it.

How much grit do you have? Give one piece of evidence from your own experience this term. Identify a time when you showed grit or a time when having more could have helped you.

_____

_____

_____

CHALLENGE: REALITY CHECK

How much did you learn? At the beginning of this chapter, you filled out a "Readiness Check" that asked how you thought this chapter would relate to you, and how you would relate to it. Now, fill out this "Reality Check" to find out.

1. What does the term *multiple intelligences* mean? Can you name three different types of intelligences?

2. What does VARK stand for? Can you identify the letters as they relate to students' preferences for taking in information?

3. What's the definition of the word *metacognition*?

4. What can you do to become a more intentional learner? Identify three study habits you use now that you could change in order to study at your best.

5. How long did it take? _____ hours _____ minutes. Before you began this chapter, you were asked to predict how long it would take you to complete it (total time, even if you read it in more than one sitting). Was your estimate on target, or will you revise it for the next chapter you'll read?_____

INSIGHT *Now* What Do You Think?

At the beginning of this chapter, Tammy Ko faced a series of challenges as a new college student. Now, after learning from this chapter, would you respond differently to any of the questions you answered about the "FOCUS Challenge Case"? Using what you learned in the chapter, write a paragraph ending to Tammy's case study. What are some of the possible outcomes for her?

ACTION Your Plans for Change

1. How will you put the information from this chapter to good use, not only in this class but in any others you're enrolled in this term?

2. List your learning and personality preferences as you discovered them in this chapter here:

   Multiple Intelligences _____

   VARK _____

   MBTI _____

   What do you think these preferences reveal about you and how you learn?

3. If you apply your learning style to your study style, what will you actually change? Over the course of this term, note whether it helps you become more successful.

© Larry Harwood Photography. Property of Cengage Learning.

chapter 4 Managing Your Time, Energy, and Money

READINESS CHECK

How this chapter relates to YOU

1. When your time is limited, and you should be using it to study, what is most likely to derail you, if anything? Please circle one or more responses if any are generally true for you.

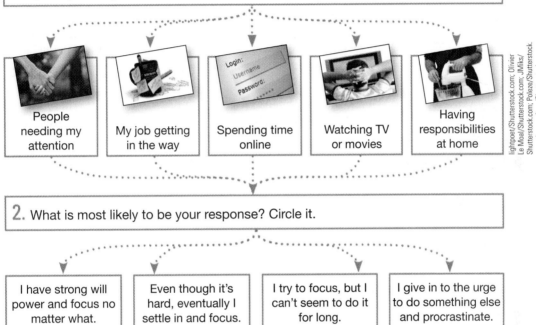

People needing my attention

My job getting in the way

Spending time online

Watching TV or movies

Having responsibilities at home

lightpoet/Shutterstock.com; Olivier Le Moal/Shutterstock.com; JMiks/Shutterstock.com; Poleze/Shutterstock.com; dragon_fang/Shutterstock.com

2. What is most likely to be your response? Circle it.

I have strong will power and focus no matter what.

Even though it's hard, eventually I settle in and focus.

I try to focus, but I can't seem to do it for long.

I give in to the urge to do something else and procrastinate.

3. What would you have to do to increase your likelihood of success? Will you do it now?

Example: Actually turn off my phone? Yes!

_____

_____

How YOU will relate to this chapter

What are you most interested in learning about? Put checkmarks by those topics.

☐ Why time management alone doesn't work
☐ How time management differs from energy management
☐ How to schedule your way to success
☐ How the P word can derail you
☐ How to realistically balance work, school, and your personal life
☐ How to manage your money

• How motivated are you to learn more about getting the right start in college? (5 = high, 1 = low) ___

• How ready are you to read now? ___ (If something is in your way, take care of it if you can, zero in and focus.)

• How long do you think it will take you to complete this chapter? If you start and stop, keep track of your overall time. ____ hour(s) ____ minutes

DEREK JOHNSON

twitter

What are you doing?

Heading to world history class. I have a 12 page paper due in a few weeks! This isn't fair!!

update

Home Profile Find People Settings

As Derek Johnson walked out of his World History class on Wednesday evening, he felt panicked. The instructor had just assigned a twelve-page paper, due one month from today. How could she? Derek thought. *Doesn't she realize how busy most returning students are?* The syllabus had mentioned a paper, but twelve pages seemed downright excessive. He sent a tweet complaining about it from his phone on his way to his next class. Twitter was quickly becoming Derek's favorite way to communicate.

When Derek had decided to go back to college five years after he graduated from high school, he hadn't quite realized what a juggling act it would require. First, there was his family—his wife, Justine, his four-year-old daughter, Taura, and another baby due before winter break. Then there was his job, which was really quite demanding for what he earned. He hoped that an associate's degree in accounting would help him get a job as an accounting assistant and possibly even move into the management ranks, where salaries were higher. Money was tight, and they always seemed to run out before payday. Add to that singing in his church choir, coaching the youth soccer league, competing in cycling races, and working out every morning at the gym. Derek had been a high school athlete, and physical fitness was a priority for him.

His head began to swim as he thought about all his upcoming obligations: his mother's birthday next week, his dog's vet appointment, his brother's visit, the training class he was required to attend for work. Something had to go, but he couldn't think of anything he was willing

MAKE TO-DO LIST!?

REMEMBER TO BUY MOM A BIRTHDAY GIFT!!!

REMEMBER:

COMPUTER TRAINING CLASS FOR WORK ON WEDNESDAY!

Community Center Gym Schedule

Monday	Tuesday	Wednesday	Thursday	Friday
Open Gym 6:30-8:30	Open Gym 6:30-8:30	Open Gym 6:30-8:30	Open Gym 6:30-8:30	Open Gym 6:30-8:30
Cycling Class 9:00-10:00	Taekwondo Class 9:00-10:00	Taekwondo Class 9:00-10:00	Kick Boxing 9:00-10:00	Cycling Class 9:00-10:00
Taekwondo Class 12:00-1:00	Yoga Class 12:00-1:00	Yoga Class 12:00-1:00	Yoga Class 12:00-1:00	Taekwondo Class 12:00-1:00
Yoga Class 3:00-4:00	Kick Boxing 3:00-4:00	Cycling Class 3:00-4:00	Taekwondo Class 3:00-4:00	Kick Boxing 3:00-4:00

MEMBERSHIP FEES - January 1 - December 31

Children	$10.00
Full-time Student	$30.00
Adult (18 and older)	$50.00
Senior	$40.00

to sacrifice to make time for a twelve-page paper. Maybe he'd have to break down and actually do some planning like the *compulsive* students he knew.

Still, the paper was to count as 25 percent of his final grade in the course. He decided he'd try to think of a topic for the paper on his way home. But then he remembered that his wife had asked him to stop at the store to pick up groceries. Somewhere on aisle 12, between the frozen pizza and the frozen yogurt, Derek's thoughts about his research paper vanished.

The following week, the instructor asked the students in the class how their papers were coming along. Some students gave long descriptions of their research progress, the amazing number of sources they'd found, and the detailed outlines they'd put together. Derek didn't raise his hand. Somehow, he never seemed to have enough time to plan—and therefore nothing ever seemed to get done.

A whole week has gone by, Derek thought on his way back to his car after class. *I have to get going!* Writing had never exactly been Derek's strong suit. In fact, it was something he generally disliked doing. Through a great deal of hard work, he had managed to earn a 3.8 GPA in high school—a record he planned to continue. A course in World History—a general education class that was not even a part of his major—was *not* going to ruin things! The week had absolutely flown by, and there were plenty of good reasons why his paper was getting off to such a slow start. Derek didn't waste time, except for occasionally watching his favorite TV shows while he studied and caught up on e-mail. Regardless, he rarely missed his nightly study time from 11:00 P.M.

to 1:00 A.M. Those two hours were reserved for homework, no matter what. The problem, of course, was keeping other things from crowding in.

At the end of class two weeks later, Derek noticed that several students lined up to show the instructor the first drafts of their papers. *That's it!* Derek thought to himself. *The paper is due next Wednesday. I'll spend Monday night, my only free night of the week, in the library. I can get there right after work and stay until 11:00 or so. That'll be five hours of concentrated time. I should be able to write it then.* Despite his good intentions, Derek didn't arrive at the library until nearly 8:00 P.M., and his work session wasn't all that productive. As he sat in his library stall, he found himself obsessing about things that were happening at work. His boss was offering him more hours. Considering that he really did want a degree, should he take on more, even though he didn't really like the job? Finally, when he glanced at his watch, he was shocked to see that it was already midnight! The library was closing, and he'd only written three pages. Where had the time gone?

On his way out to the car, his cell phone rang. It was Justine, wondering where he was. Taura was running a fever, and his boss had called about an emergency meeting at 7:00 A.M. *If one more thing goes wrong . . . ,* Derek thought to himself. His twelve-page paper was due in two days.

HISTORY PAPER OUTLINE

INTRO...

Borodaev/Shutterstock.com

6:30

CROM/Shutterstock.com

Studio 1One/Shutterstock.com

© Cengage Learning

© Cengage Learning

© Cengage Learning

WORLD HISTORY

Fall Semester Syllabus

Instructor: Julia Alexander
Office: Main Hall 320
Email: Julia.Alexander@campusmail.edu
Phone: 555-3424
Office Hours: 12:30-3pm daily

red Textbook:
History, 6th Edition. By William J. Duiker and Jackson J. Spielvogel ISBN

Exam:	10 @ 10 points each	100pts
nalysis:		100pts
ay:		50pts
		150pts
		100pts
		500pts

vilization and the Fertile Crescent
ne: *Agriculture and Mesopotamia*
vo: *The Nile Valley and the Near East*

Civilizations
ee: *The World of Homer*
: *Classical Greece and the Golden Age*
Rome: *The Rise of the Republic*
mperial Rome
Rome: *The Fall of the Empire*
China and the Far East
the Indian Subcontinent

Accounting Associate

Job Description

We are currently looking for a qualified Accounting As
educational, and industry experience. This is an entry l
graduates are encouraged to apply.

Job Responsibilities

Ensure timely collection of vendor A/R

Review, correct, and update sub ledger transactions a

Transaction review

Vendor follow-up and research

Vendor disputes

Inv

Campus Library

FALL SEMESTER HOURS

Monday – Thursday: 8 am – Midnight

Friday – Saturday: 8 am – 8 pm

1. What do you have in common with Derek? What time, energy, or money management issues are you experiencing in your life right now?
2. Describe the time-wasters that are a part of Derek's schedule. Do you think procrastination is an issue for Derek? What's behind his failure to make progress on his paper?
3. Suggest three realistic ways for Derek to balance work, school, and personal life.

Time Management Requires *FOCUS*

Before diving into the details of time management skills, let's clarify one important point. There's a sense in which the phrase *time management* is misleading. Let's say you decide to spend an hour reading an assigned short story for your literature class. You may sit in the library with your book propped open in front of you from 3:00 to 4:00 P.M. on the dot. But you may not digest a single word you're reading. You may be going through the motions, reading on autopilot. Have you managed your time? Technically, yes. Your planner says, "Library, short story for Lit 101, 3:00–4:00 P.M." But did you get results? Time management expert Jeffrey Mayer asks provocatively in the title of his book: *If You Haven't Got the Time to Do It Right, When Will You Find the Time to Do It Over?*. Now that's a good question!

Time management is not just about managing your time, it's about managing your attention. Attention management is the ability to focus your attention, not just your time, on a designated activity so that you produce a desired result. And that's a big challenge, because research shows that the human mind wanders about half the time[1]. Time management may get you through reading a chapter of your textbook, but attention management will make sure that you understand what you're reading. It's about *focus*. If you manage your attention during that hour, then you've managed your time productively. Without attention management, time management is pointless. And the good thing is that we can train our brains to focus.

Succeeding in school, at work, and in life is not just about what you do. It's about what gets done. You can argue about the effort you put into an academic assignment all you want, but it's doubtful your professor will say, "You know what? You're right. You deserve an A just for staying up late last night working on this paper." Activity and accomplishment aren't the same thing. Neither are quantity and quality. Just because the assignment asked for five pages and you turned in five, doesn't mean that you automatically deserve an A. Results count. So don't confuse being busy with being successful. Staying busy isn't much of a challenge; being successful is.

Here's a list of preliminary academic time-saving tips. However, remember that these suggestions won't give you a surefire recipe for academic success. To manage your time, you must also manage yourself: your energy, your behavior, your attention, your attitudes, *you*. Once you know how to manage all that, managing your time begins to work.

> In truth, people can generally make time for what they choose to do; it is not really the time but the will that is lacking.
>
> *Sir John Lubbock, British banker, politician, and archaeologist (1834–1913)*

> Have a plan for your study session; include suggested time limits for each topic or task.

> Don't confuse activity with accomplishment.
> 'Time = Success' is a myth.

Dr. Constance Staley, University of Colorado at Colorado Springs

Digital Vision/Getty Images

> Pay attention to what gets you off track. If you come to understand your patterns, you may be better able to control them.

> Turn off your phone or tell other people you live with that you don't want to be disturbed if a call comes in for you. Let them know what time they can tell callers to call you back.

> If you're working on your computer, work offline whenever possible. If you must be online to check sources, don't give in to the temptation to check your social networking account or e-mail every five minutes. According to a recent survey of over one million people, willpower is the one virtue human beings are least likely to recognize in themselves.[2] Whether it's resisting the third cupcake or staying on task to write a paper, willpower is sometimes hard to muster. But it can be cultivated by continually monitoring ourselves so that we're making decisions that are in our own best interest.

> Take two minutes to organize your workspace before beginning. Having the resources you need at your fingertips makes the session go much more smoothly, and you won't waste time searching for things you need.

> Focus. You can't do anything if you try to do everything. **Multitasking** may work for simple matters, such as scheduling a doctor's appointment while heating up a snack in the microwave. But when it comes to tasks that require brainpower, such as studying or writing, you need a single-minded focus. Remember that the more you multitask, the less able you are to focus. Believe it or not, multitasking actually slows you down. It may sound like the solution to time management, but it's not![3]

> Actually use a timer. Forty minutes is thought by some experts to be the optimum amount of time to focus on something before taking a break. It takes 30 minutes to really get in gear, and then you arrive at another 10 minutes of optimal productivity. If you aim for more than that, tedium can set in. And use a real, physical countdown timer. When you hear the "ding," you get a real feeling of accomplishment and a bit of relief from stress. Online timing tools can get buried under layers of other software applications. An actual timer can force you to face the challenge.[4]

> Monitor how your life works. There are different ways to manage time, and different ways work best for different people. Think of this analogy: Is time like ice or like water? A hard copy planner is a day-by-day record of solid blocks of time. But in today's world, solid blocks can melt away in seconds

multitasking doing two or more tasks at one time

as events around us change. Managing time may be less like moving around ice cubes and more like "going with the flow." Many dynamic e-tools are available to help you on a minute-by-minute basis, if you stay on top of how time flows in your life.[5] Whether it's an automatic, audible reminder from something you've entered into your Google calendar or an electronic "personal assistant" like Siri via your iPhone, these reminder systems can help you manage your obligations.[6]

Energy, Our Most Precious Resource

"We live in a digital time. Our rhythms are rushed, rapid-fire and relentless, our days carved up into bits and bytes. . . . We're wired up but we're melting down." So begins the bestselling book *The Power of Full Engagement: Managing Energy, Not Time, Is the Key to High Performance and Personal Renewal*. The authors, Jim Loehr and Tony Schwartz, have replaced the term *time management* with the term *energy management*. Their shift makes sense. Because most of us are running in overdrive most of the time, energy is our most precious resource.

Energy management experts say you can't control time—everyone has a fixed amount—but you can manage your energy. And in fact, it's your responsibility to do so. Once a day is gone, it's gone. But your energy can be renewed.

It's clear that some things are energy *drains:* bad news, illness, interpersonal conflict, time-consuming hassles, a heavy meal, rainy days. Likewise, some things are energy *gains* giving you a surge of freshness: a new job, good friends, music, laughter, fruit, coffee. It's a good idea to recognize your own personal energy drains and gains so that you know how and when to renew your supply.[7] Energy management experts say it's not just about *spending time*, it's about *expending energy:*

> physical energy
> emotional energy
> mental energy
> spiritual energy

Of the four dimensions of energy, let's take a closer look at the first two. To do your very best academically, it helps to be *physically* energized and *emotionally* connected. Physical energy is measured in terms of *quantity*. How much energy do you have—a lot or a little? Emotional energy, on the other hand, is measured by *quality*. What kind of energy do you have—positive or negative? If you put them together into a two-dimensional chart with *quantity* as the vertical axis and *quality* as the horizontal axis, you get something like Figure 4.1.

To do two things at once is to do neither.

Publius Syrus, Maxim 7, 42 B.C.

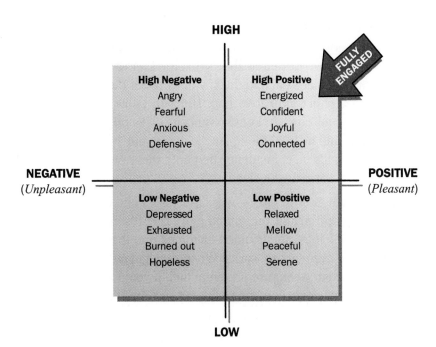

FIGURE 4.1

The Dynamics of Energy[8]

When you're operating in the upper right quarter of the chart, with high, positive energy, you're most productive, which makes sense. The question is, How do you get there? How do you make certain you're physically energized and emotionally connected so that you can do your best academically?

Get Physically Energized

To make sure you're physically energized, try these suggestions.

1. **Snap to your body's rhythm.** Have you noticed times of the day when it's easier to concentrate than others? Perhaps you regularly crash in the middle of the afternoon, for example, so you go for a chocolate fix or a coffee pick-me-up. Everyone has a biological clock. Paying attention to your body's natural rhythms is important. Plan to do activities that require you to be alert during your natural productivity peaks. That's better than plodding through a tough assignment when the energy just isn't there. Use low energy times to take care of mindless chores that require little to no brainpower.[9]

2. **Up and at 'em.** What about 8:00 A.M. classes? Don't use your body's natural rhythms as an excuse to sleep through class! ("I'm just not a morning person. . . .") If you're truly not a morning person, don't sign up for early morning classes. If you are coming off working a night shift, you may need some rest first. Sleeping through your obligations won't do much for your success—and you'll be playing a continual game of catch-up, which takes even more time. Some experts advise that you start your day as early as possible. Marking six items off your to-do list before lunch can give you a real high.[10]

3. **Sleep at night, study during the day.** Burning the midnight oil and pulling all-nighters isn't the best idea either. It only takes one all-nighter to

help you realize that a lack of sleep translates into a drop in performance. Without proper sleep, your ability to understand and remember course material is impaired. Research shows that the average adult requires seven to eight hours of sleep each night. If you can't get that much for whatever reason, take a short afternoon nap. Did you know that the Three Mile Island nuclear meltdown in Pennsylvania in 1979 and the Chernobyl disaster in the Ukraine in 1986 took place at 4 A.M. and 1:23 A.M., respectively? Experts believe it's no coincidence that both these events took place when workers would normally be sleeping.[11]

4. **"Burn premium fuel."** You've heard it before: Food is the fuel that makes us run. The better the fuel, the smoother we run. It's that simple. A solid diet of carbs—pizza, chips, and cookies—jammed into the fuel tank of your car would certainly gum up the works! When the demands on your energy are high, such as exam week, use premium fuel. If you don't believe this, think about how many people you know who get sick during times of high stress. Watch how many of your classmates are hacking and coughing their way through exams—or in bed, missing them altogether.

Get Emotionally Connected

Physical needs count, to be sure, but emotional connections are part of the picture, too. See whether you agree with these suggestions.

1. **Communicate like it matters.** Sometimes we save our best communicating for people we think we have to impress: teachers, bosses, or clients, for example. But what about the people we care about most in our lives? Sometimes these people get the leftovers after all the "important" communicating has been done for the day. Sometimes we're so comfortable with these people that we think we can let it all hang out, even when doing so is *not* a pretty sight. Communicate as if everything you said would actually come true— "Just drop dead," for instance—and watch the difference! Communicating productively with people we care about is one of the best ways to replenish our energy.

2. **Choose how you renew.** Finish this comparison: Junk food is to physical energy as _____ is to emotional energy. If you answered "TV," you're absolutely right. Most people use television as their primary form of emotional renewal, but, like junk food, it's not that nutritious and it's easy to consume too much. Try more engaging activities that affirm you: singing or reading or playing a sport.[12]

3. **Let others renew you.** Remember that people don't just make demands on your time; they also provide emotional renewal. There's pure joy in a child's laugh, a friend's smile, a father's pat on the back. These small pleasures in life are priceless—prize them!

We've focused on physical and emotional energy here, but remember that all four dimensions of energy—physical, emotional, mental, and spiritual—are interconnected. If you subtract one from the equation, you'll be firing on less than four cylinders. If you are fully engaged and living life to the fullest, all four dimensions of your energy equation will be in balance.

Sharpen Your FOCUS

> **There is more to life than increasing its speed.**
>
> —MOHANDAS K. GANDHI,
> INDIAN SPIRITUAL LEADER (1869–1948)

Reason 4. They burn out.

Why do people lose their focus? One reason is because they move so quickly that they never stop to look inside, let alone catch the scenery whizzing by around them. Their goal—whether they know it or not—is to just get through each busy day, cramming in more and more activities and obligations. Eventually, they burn out. Some people think that some form of spirituality can help people rebuild and regain their focus. For you, spirituality may mean a church, a type of organized religion, or simply looking inward to examine your life. According to a national study of 112,232 college students, four out of five first-year students are interested in spirituality, and nearly three-fourths report feeling a sense of connection with a higher power. Nearly half believe that college should help encourage their expression of spirituality.[13] Can college help you examine your values, find inner direction, ponder the meaning of life, and possibly help you slow down long enough to look at the big picture?

TRY It!

Do you think paying attention to your spiritual health has the potential to help you revitalize and sharpen your focus? To help you think about your answer to this question, respond to the items below:

1. It's easy to get caught up in day-to-day details, like kids, jobs, and bills. But many experts believe that you can sharpen your focus by taking time out to consider "life's bigger picture"—through yoga, meditation, prayer, or exercise, for example. Do you practice any of these? Do you think they might help? Why or why not?

2. Think about your college classes. Does "big picture" thinking come up (directly or indirectly) in any of them? If so, which class—and where has your thinking led you?

3. Make a promise to yourself to find time this week to free up your mind and slow down long enough to think more deeply than usual, and then pay attention to the results. What were they? Did your focus improve?

"I'll Study in My Free Time" ... and When Is That?

EXERCISE 4.1

Where Did the Time Go?

How do you spend your time? Complete this self-assessment to find out how you spend your time. Fill in the number of hours you spend doing each of the following, then multiply your answer by the number given (7 or 5 to figure weekly amounts) where appropriate.

	Number of hours per day
Sleeping:	_____ × 7 = _____
Personal grooming (for example, showering, shaving, putting on makeup):	_____ × 7 = _____
Eating (meals and snacks; include preparation or driving time):	_____ × 7 = _____
Commuting Monday through Friday (to school and work):	_____ × 5 = _____
Doing errands and chores:	_____ × 7 = _____
Spending time with family (parents, children, or spouse):	_____ × 7 = _____
Spending time with boyfriend or girlfriend:	_____ × 7 = _____

(Continued)

	Number of hours per week
At work:	____
In classes:	____
At regularly scheduled functions (church, clubs, etc.):	____
Socializing, hanging out, watching TV, talking on the phone, etc.:	____

Now add up all the numbers in the far right column, and subtract your total from 168, the number of hours in a week.

168 – _____ = _____. This is the total number of hours you have remaining in your week for that ever-important task of studying. You may wish to revise how much time you spend on other activities of your life, based on whether you're already short on hours without studying factored in.

Ask ten students when they study, and chances are at least eight will reply, "In my free time." The strange thing about this statement is that if you actually waited until you had free time to study, you probably never would. Truthfully, some students are amazed at how easily a day can race by without their ever thinking about cracking a book. This is why you should actually *schedule* your study time, but to do that, you should first be aware of how you're currently spending those twenty-four hours of each day.

Notice that Exercise 4.1 places studying at the bottom of the list, even though it's vital to your success in college. The exercise reflects a common attitude among college students, namely, that studying is what takes place after everything else gets done. Where does schoolwork rank on *your* list of priorities?

If succeeding in college is a top priority for you, then make sure that you're devoting adequate time to schoolwork outside the classroom. Most instructors expect you to study two to three hours outside of class for every hour spent in class. If it's a particularly challenging class, you may need even more study time. You can use the following chart to calculate the total number of hours you ought to expect to study—effectively—each week:

Credit hours for less demanding classes: ____ × 2 hours = ____ hours

Credit hours for typical/average classes: ____ × 3 hours = ____ hours

Credit hours for more challenging classes: ____ × 4 hours = ____ hours

Expected total study time per week = ____ hours

Remember, just putting in the time won't guarantee that you'll truly *understand* what you're studying. You need to ensure that your study time is productive by focusing your attention and strategically selecting study techniques that work best for you.

VARK It!

Kinesthetic: Try writing each item from your schedule today on sticky notes and arrange them in chronological order. Then try moving the sticky notes around to make the best use of your time and energy.

VARK It!

Visual: Think back over your day yesterday and draw it as a pie chart. If you showed time in class as RED, study time as BLUE, work as GREEN, and free time as WHITE, what would the overall results be? Are you using your time well?

Schedule Your Way to Success

Time Monitor

Can you remember how you spent all your time yesterday? Using the following Time Monitor, fill in as much as you can remember about how you spent your time yesterday, for the complete 24-hour period. Be as detailed as possible, right down to thirty-minute segments. If you were multitasking, put down your primary activity, and put an asterisk beside that time block. When you're finished, note how many asterisks are on your chart, and assess your overall productivity.

7:00 A.M. _____	3:00 _____	11:00 _____
7:30 _____	3:30 _____	11:30 _____
8:00 _____	4:00 _____	12:00 A.M. _____
8:30 _____	4:30 _____	12:30 _____
9:00 _____	5:00 _____	1:00 _____
9:30 _____	5:30 _____	1:30 _____
10:00 _____	6:00 _____	2:00 _____
10:30 _____	6:30 _____	2:30 _____
11:00 _____	7:00 _____	3:00 _____
11:30 _____	7:30 _____	3:30 _____
12:00 P.M. _____	8:00 _____	4:00 _____
12:30 _____	8:30 _____	4:30 _____
1:00 _____	9:00 _____	5:00 _____
1:30 _____	9:30 _____	5:30 _____
2:00 _____	10:00 _____	6:00 _____
2:30 _____	10:30 _____	6:30 _____

Now monitor how you use your time today (or tomorrow if you're reading this at night), or your instructor may have you complete this Time Monitor for a several days. Again, be very specific. At the conclusion of your record-keeping for this exercise, go back to Exercise 4.1, and check to see how accurate your estimates were.

There is no one right way to schedule your time, but if you experiment with the system presented in this book, you'll be on the right path. Eventually, you can tweak the system to make it uniquely your own. Try these eight steps to schedule your way to success!

Lame Excuses for Blowing Off Class

Do you find yourself skipping class at times in order to do something else: getting an oil change for your car, soaking up the sun's rays, or socializing with a friend on the phone? If so, ask yourself this: Would you walk into a gas station, put a big bill down on the counter to prepay for a tank of gas, and then put in a dollar's worth and drive off? Absolutely not, you say?

Would you buy a $10 movie ticket and then just toss it in the trash because you decided there was something else you'd rather do on the spur of the moment? No way!

Why, then, would you purchase much more expensive "tickets" to class—the average cost of an hour in class may be as high as $100, $150, or $200 or more—and then toss them in the trash by not attending? Don't you value your money more than that? More importantly, don't you value yourself more than that?

The next time you're tempted to opt out of your scheduled classes, ask yourself whether you really want to throw away money, in addition to the opportunity. Check your priorities, then put one foot in front of the other and walk into that classroom. In the long run, it's the best investment in your own future.

STEP 1: Fill out a "Term on a Page" Calendar. Right up front, create a "Term on a Page" calendar that shows the entire school term on one page. (See Exercise 4.3. This particular activity works best on paper. A month-by-month cell phone calendar won't let you see an entire term at once!) This calendar allows you to see the big picture. You will need to have the syllabus from each of your classes and your school's course schedule to do this step properly. The following items should be transferred onto your "Term on a Page" calendar:

> Holidays when your school is closed

> Exam and quiz dates from your syllabi

> Project or paper deadlines from your syllabi

> Relevant administrative deadlines (e.g., registration for the next term, drop dates)

> Birthdays and anniversaries to remember

> Important out-of-town travel

> Dates that pertain to other family members, such as days that your children's school is closed or that your spouse is out of town for a conference— anything that will impact your ability to attend classes or study

STEP 2: Invest in a Planner. Although it's good to have the big picture, you must also develop an ongoing scheduling system that works for you. Using the "It's all right up here in my head" method is a surefire way to miss an important appointment, fly past the deadline for your term paper without a clue, or lose track of the time you have left to complete multiple projects.

Take care of your minutes, and the hours will take care of themselves.

Lord Chesterfield, British statesman and diplomat (1694–1773)

EXERCISE 4.3

Term on a Page

Take a few minutes right now to create your own Term on a Page, using the charts in Figure 4.2.

Term _____ Year _____

FIGURE 4.2

Term on a Page

Month:	Sunday	Monday	Tuesday	Wednesday	Thursday	Friday	Saturday

Month:	Sunday	Monday	Tuesday	Wednesday	Thursday	Friday	Saturday

Month:	Sunday	Monday	Tuesday	Wednesday	Thursday	Friday	Saturday

Month:	Sunday	Monday	Tuesday	Wednesday	Thursday	Friday	Saturday

Month:	Sunday	Monday	Tuesday	Wednesday	Thursday	Friday	Saturday

Although your instructor will typically provide you with a class syllabus that lists test dates and assignment deadlines, trying to juggle multiple syllabi—not to mention your personal and work commitments—is enough to drive you crazy. You need *one* central place for all of your important deadlines, appointments, and commitments. This central place is a planner—a calendar book with space to write in each day. Most every successful person on the planet uses some kind of planner, whether paper or electronic.

When you go planner shopping, remember that you don't have to break the bank unless you want to. Many new college students find that an ordinary paper-and-pencil daily calendar from an office supply store works best. Having a full page for each day means you can write your daily to-do list right in your planner (more on to-do lists later), and that can be a huge help. Using an online calendar, like Google calendar, can work, too. But remember that unless you have a smart cell phone with Internet access, an online calendar won't be portable, and you'll have to remember to enter events later.

STEP 3: Transfer Important Dates. The next step is to transfer important dates for the whole term from your "Term on a Page" overview to the appropriate days in your planner. It's important to be able to see all of your due dates together to create a big picture, but it's equally important to have these dates recorded in your actual planner because you will use it more regularly—as the final authority on your schedule.

STEP 4: Set Intermediate Deadlines. After recording the important dates for the entire academic term, look at the individual due dates for major projects or papers that are assigned. Then set intermediate stepping-stone goals that will ultimately help you accomplish your final goals. Working backward from the due date, choose and record deadlines for completing certain chunks of the work. For example, if you have a research paper due, you could set an intermediate deadline for completing all of your initial research and other deadlines for the prewriting, writing, and rewriting steps for the paper.

STEP 5: Schedule Fixed Activities for the Entire Term. Next, you'll want to schedule in all fixed activities throughout the entire term: class meeting times and reading assignments, religious services you regularly attend, club meetings, and family activities. It's also a great idea to schedule brief review sessions for your classes. Of course, sometimes you'll be going directly into another class, but ten-minute segments of time before and after each class to review your notes help prepare you for surprise quizzes and improve your comprehension.

STEP 6: Check for Schedule Conflicts. Now, take a final look at your planner. Do you notice any major scheduling conflicts, such as a planned business trip smack dab in the middle of midterm

> **Nothing is so fatiguing as the eternal hanging on of an uncompleted task.**
>
> *William James, American psychologist and philosopher (1842–1910)*

exam week? Look for these conflicts now, when there's plenty of time to adjust your plans and talk with your instructor to see what you can work out.

STEP 7: Schedule Flextime. In all the scheduling of important dates, checking and double-checking, don't forget one thing. You do need personal time for eating, sleeping, exercising, and other regular activities that don't have a set time frame. Despite your planner, life will happen. If you get a toothache, you'll need to see a dentist right away. Several times each week, you can count on something coming up that will offer you a chance (or force you) to revise your schedule. The decision of how high the item ranks on your priority list rests with you, but the point is to leave some wiggle room in your schedule. One other good idea is to follow the "two-minute" rule. Do any work items that can be completed in two minutes right then, on the spot. Doing so will free you from nagging details as you plan for bigger items.[14]

STEP 8: Monitor Your Schedule Every Day. At this point, you've developed a working time management system. Now it's important to monitor your use of that system on a daily basis. Each night, take three minutes to review the day's activities. How well did you stick to your schedule? Did you accomplish the tasks you set out to do? Do you need to revise your schedule for the rest of the week based on something that happened—or didn't happen—today? This simple process will help you better schedule your time in the future and give you a sense of accomplishment—or of the need for more discipline—for tasks completed, hours worked, and classes attended.

To Do or Not to Do? There *Is* No Question

Part of your personal time management system should be keeping an ongoing to-do list. Although the concept of a to-do list sounds relatively simple, here are a few tricks of the trade.

Before the beginning of each school week, brainstorm all the things that you want or need to get done in the upcoming week. Using this random list of to-do items, assign a priority level next to each one. The A-B-C method is simple and easy to use:

A = must get this done; highest priority

B = very important, but not absolutely necessary to get done immediately

C = not terribly important, but should be done right away (time-sensitive)

The two factors to consider when assigning a priority level to a to-do item are *importance* and urgency, creating four time zones. Use Figure 4.3 as a guide.[15]

urgency in need of immediate attention

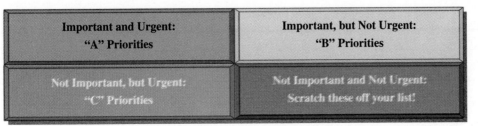

FIGURE 4.3

Time Zones

Important and Urgent: "A" Priorities	Important, but Not Urgent: "B" Priorities
Not Important, but Urgent: "C" Priorities	Not Important and Not Urgent: Scratch these off your list!

After you've assigned a time zone to each item, review your list of A and B priorities and ask yourself:

1. **Do any of the items fit best with a particular day of the week?** For example, donating blood may be a high priority task for you, yet you don't want to do it on a day when you have a sports event planned. That might leave you with two available days in the upcoming week that you can donate blood.

2. **Can any items be grouped together to make things easier?** For example, you may have three errands to run downtown on your to-do list, so grouping them together will save you from making three separate trips.

3. **Do any A and B priorities qualify as floating tasks that can be completed anytime, anywhere?** For example, perhaps you were assigned an extra-long reading assignment for one of your classes. It's both important and urgent, an A priority item. Bring your book to read while waiting at the dentist's office for your appointment, a B priority. Planning ahead can really help save time.

4. **Do any priorities need to be shifted?** As the days pass, some of your B priorities will become A priorities due to the urgency factor increasing. Or maybe an A priority will become a C priority because something changed about the task. This is normal.

Items you've marked with a C must be decided on a case-by-case basis. But don't let their urgency convince you that you should do them before you accomplish items on your A and B lists. As for those not important and not urgent to-do items, scratch them off the list right now. Life is too short to waste time on unimportant tasks. Give yourself permission to focus on what's important. Because time is a limited resource, one of the best ways to guarantee a successful college experience is to use it wisely. If you don't already use these tools on a regular basis, give them a shot. What do you have to lose except time?

EXERCISE 4.4

So Much to Do—So Little Time

Assume this is your to-do list for today (Monday). Assign each item one of the four time zones described earlier: A, B, and C (and strike through any items that are not urgent and not important). Finally, renumber the items to indicate which you would do first, second, and so forth.

Start time: 9:00 A.M., Monday morning, during the second week of the fall term.

1. _____ Return Professor Jordan's call before class tomorrow. He left a message saying he wants to talk to you about some problems with the assignment you turned in.

2. _____ Pick up your paycheck and get to the bank before it closes at 5:00 P.M. this afternoon.

3. _____ Call your mother to find out how grandma is doing in the hospital.

4. _____ Start figuring out how to go about your new assignment at work. Your boss seems nervous about it.

5. _____ Call your favorite aunt. She lives overseas in a time zone seven hours ahead of yours. Today is her fiftieth birthday.

6. _____ Stop by the Health Center to take advantage of free meningitis vaccinations today only.

7. _____ Listen to the new music you downloaded yesterday.

8. _____ Leave a note asking your boy- or girlfriend/sibling/child to please stop leaving messes everywhere. It's really aggravating.

9. _____ Read the two chapters in your history textbook for the in-class quiz on Wednesday.

10. _____ Watch the first episode of the new reality TV show you've been waiting for, at 9 P.M. tonight.

11. _____ Write a rough draft of the essay due in your composition class on Thursday.

12. _____ Invite an out-of-town friend to spend the weekend.

13. _____ Return the three library books that are a week overdue.

14. _____ Call your math Teaching Assistant and leave a message asking for an appointment during her office hours to get help with the homework due on Wednesday. Nearly everyone is confused about the assignment.

15. _____ Meet your best friend for dinner for his or her birthday at 6 P.M.

Outline the criteria you used for making your decisions. For example, did you base your answers on personal priorities, locations (combining tasks based on where you need to be to do them), urgency/importance, or some other principle? (Note that this exercise asks you to put these tasks in order, according to whatever principles from this chapter you choose—not to figure out how to multitask and accomplish several at once!) If you choose to call your aunt (5) while writing your essay (11), chances are she'll hear the tapping of the keys and the breaks in the conversation and know exactly what you're doing. It's important to base your choices not only on what's quick or convenient, but also on how much people and priorities mean to you.

How Time Flies!

According to efficiency expert Michael Fortino, in a lifetime, the average American will spend:

> Seven years in the bathroom

> Six years eating

> Five years waiting in line

> Three years in meetings

> Two years playing telephone tag

> Eight months opening junk mail

> And six months waiting at red lights[16]

What a waste of time! We can't do much about some of these items, but what *can* we do about other time-wasters? Plan—schedule—organize! Think about the issue of control in time management, and write in examples for the following:

1. Things you think you can't control, and you can't: _____

2. Things you think you can't control, but you can: _____

3. Things you think you can control, but you can't: _____

4. Things you think you can control, but you don't: _____

5. Things you think you can control, and you can: _____

Perhaps you wrote in something like *medical emergencies* for (1). You could have written in *family or friends bothering you while you study* for (2). For (4), maybe you could control how much *time you waste online*, but you don't. And for (5), perhaps you wrote in *your attention*. You're absolutely right. But what about (3)? Did anything fit there? Are there things you think you can control, but you can't? Try to think of something that would

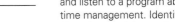

VARK It!

Aural: Go to the National Public Radio web site at www.npr.org, and listen to a program about time management. Identify three ideas that stuck in your head.

The bad news is time flies. The good news is you're the pilot.

Michael Altshuler, motivational speaker

fit into (3), and then think of creative ways you really could control this situation if you tried.[17] Have you ever thought about how much the issues of control and time management are related?

According to experts, there are four kinds of common problematic time management "P's" in the world. When it comes to time management, control is generally a good thing. You take control and become more productive. But take a look at these four "P's." They exert control in way that can bring counterproductive results!

> **The Preemptive.** Preemptives believe they are doing their best; in fact, they are continuously ahead of the game. They constantly, compulsively play "beat the clock." They're always way ahead of schedule. So what's wrong with that? Sometimes, nothing. But preemptives can gain a reputation of being non–team players, only out for themselves. They look like they're trying to impress everyone—or someone in particular, like the boss or teacher.

> **The People Pleaser.** People pleasers have the best of intentions, but they take on too much and sabotage their own effectiveness by trying to make others happy. Always saying yes to everyone may mean that there's no time left for their own work. Over time, they can even come to resent the very people they're trying to please and vice versa.

> **The Perfectionist.** Nothing is ever good enough for perfectionists. In effect, what they do is make other people play a waiting game while they continue to tinker with their projects to make them into some ideal they may never reach. They're control freaks, and they lead anxiety-ridden lives.

> **The Procrastinator.** Procrastinators are adrenaline junkies. They put things off until the 11th hour and then make a mad dash for the finish line, trailing a long list of excuses. Often, the root cause of procrastination is fear. Although the perfectionist will only accept an A+, the procrastinator is secretly afraid of not ever being able to achieve an A+. If she doesn't turn in an assignment, she can't find out just how good (or not) she is.[18]

EXERCISE 4.5

Are you a Preemptive, People-pleasing, Perfectionistic Procrastinator?

Do you know people who fit into each of these four problematic time management "P" categories? Do you fit into one of these categories? Work in groups or as a class to brainstorm ways of helping these people improve their time management skills. What advice would you give each type?

Preemptive	People Pleaser	Perfectionist	Procrastinator

Jupiterimages/Photos.com

Jupiterimages/Photos.com

Jupiterimages/Photos.com

Darko Novakovic/Photos.com

Photos.com

The "P" Word. Read This Section Now!... or Maybe Tomorrow...or...

Picture this: You sit down to work on a challenging homework assignment. After a few minutes, you think, *Man, I'm thirsty*, so you get up and get a soda. Then you sit back down to continue your work. A few minutes later, you decide that some chips would go nicely with your soda and you head to the kitchen. Again, you sit down to face the task before you, as you concentrate more on eating than on working. Ten minutes go by and a nagging thought starts taking over: *Must do laundry*. Up you go again to throw a load of clothes in the washer. Before long you're wondering where all the time went. Because you only have an hour left before class, you think, *Why bother getting started now? Doing this project will take much more time than that, so I'll just start it tomorrow*. Despite good intentions at the beginning of your work session, you've just succeeded in accomplishing zip, nada, nothing.

EXERCISE 4.6

Who, Me? Procrastinate?

Procrastination is a habit. It may show up as not getting around to doing your homework (if you don't turn it in, you can't get a bad grade on it—which almost guarantees that you'll get a bad grade on it), not vacuuming the carpet because it takes too much energy to lug the machine around, or not getting to work on time because your job is boring. What about you? Think about the following ten situations, and put a check mark next to each one to indicate the degree to which you normally procrastinate:

	Always	Sometimes	Never
1. Doing homework	____	____	____
2. Writing a paper	____	____	____
3. Studying for tests	____	____	____
4. Reading class material	____	____	____
5. Meeting with your academic advisor	____	____	____
6. Texting/e-mailing a friend	____	____	____
7. Playing a game/hanging out	____	____	____
8. Going to see a movie you've heard about	____	____	____
9. Meeting someone for dinner at a restaurant	____	____	____
10. Watching TV	____	____	____

If you are like many students, you checked "always" or "sometimes" more often for the first five items than you did for the last five. But procrastination isn't as simple as not procrastinating when you want to do something and procrastinating when you don't. You may actually hate vacuuming but decide to vacuum the entire house so that you don't have to face studying for a test. There are "layers" of procrastination and many reasons why people procrastinate. Which of these apply to you?

_____ Avoiding something you see as unpleasant   _____ Not realizing how important the task is

_____ Feeling overwhelmed by all you have to do   _____ Reacting to your own internal conflict

_____ Being intimidated by the task itself   _____ Protecting your self-esteem

_____ Fearing failure   _____ Waiting for a last-minute adrenaline rush

_____ Fearing success   _____ Just plain not wanting to

Congratulations! You—like thousands of other college students—have just successfully procrastinated! Researchers define procrastination as "need-lessly delaying tasks to the point of experiencing subjective discomfort."[19] And according to researchers, 70 percent of college students admit to procrastinating on their assignments.[20]

You may be in the majority, but alas, in this case, there's no safety in numbers! Academic procrastination is a major threat to your ability to succeed in college. And procrastination in the working world can actually bring your job, and ultimately your career, to a screeching halt. Plenty of people try to rationalize their procrastination by claiming that they work better under pressure. However, the challenge in college is that during some weeks of the term, every class you're taking will have an assignment or test due, all at once, and if you procrastinate, you'll not only generate tremendous anxiety for yourself, but you'll lower your chances of succeeding at any of them.

Before you can control the procrastination monster in your life, it's important to understand *why* you procrastinate. Think about all the instances in which you don't procrastinate: meeting your friends for dinner, returning a phone call from a friend, going to the store. Why are those things easy to do, but getting started on an assignment is difficult until you feel the jaws of a deadline closing down on you?[21] The reasons for procrastinating vary from person to person, but once you know your own reasons for putting things off, you'll be in a better position to address the problem from its root cause.

The next time you find yourself procrastinating, ask yourself why. Procrastination hurts your chances for success and gives you ready-made excuses if you don't succeed: "It's like running a full race with a knapsack full of bricks on your back. When you don't win, you can say it's not that you're not a good runner, it's just that you had this sack of bricks on your back."[22] In addition to understanding why you procrastinate, try these ten procrastination busters to help you kick the habit.

1. **Keep track (of your excuses).** Write them down consistently, and soon you'll be able to recognize them for what they are. Own your responsibilities—in school and in the rest of your life.

2. **Break down.** Break your project into its smaller components. A term paper, for example, can be broken down into the following smaller parts: prospectus, thesis, research, outline, small chunks of writing, and bibliography. Completing smaller tasks along the way is much easier than facing a threatening monster of a project.

3. **Trick yourself.** When you feel like procrastinating, pick some aspect of the project that's easy and that you would have to do anyway. If the thought of an entire paper is overwhelming you, for example, work on the bibliography to start. Starting with something—*anything*—that will get you into the rhythm of the work.

4. **Resolve issues.** If something's eating away at you, making it difficult to concentrate, take care of it. Sometimes you must deal with a bossy friend, your kids vying for your attention, or something equally intrusive. Then get down to work.

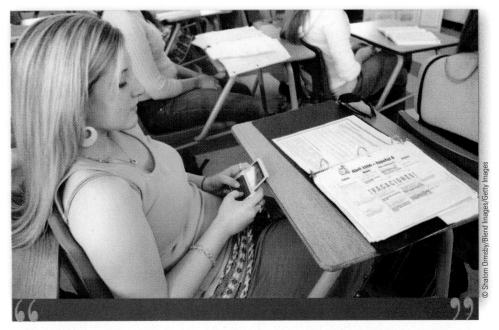

Things which matter most should never be at the mercy of things which matter least.

Johann Wolfgang von Goethe, German writer and scholar (1749–1832)

5. **Get real.** Set realistic goals for yourself. If you declare that you're going to finish a twelve-page paper in five hours, you're already doomed. Procrastinators are sometimes overly optimistic. They underestimate how much time something will take. Make it a habit to keep track of how long assignments take you in all your courses so that you can be increasingly realistic over time. And be specific. Instead of writing, "Finish Chapter 10" in your planner, write exactly what you need to do: "Finish reading Chapter 10, answer the discussion questions at the end, and e-mail my responses to my instructor."

6. **Capture killer B's.** You're working on Task A when Task B presents itself—perhaps it's a text or an e-mail, something that seems important at the time. Immediately capture the threatening "Killer B" by writing it in a paper notebook that's always by your side. Why paper? If you use an online journal, you'll be tempted to wander further online. You may end up in Timbuktu.com and make countless stops along the way.[23]

7. **Make a deal with yourself.** Even if it's only spending fifteen minutes on a task that day, do it so that you can see progress.

8. **Overcome fear.** Many of the reasons for procrastinating have to do with our personal fears. We may fear not doing something perfectly, or failing completely—or even the responsibility that comes with success to keep succeeding. But as Susan Jeffers, author and lecturer, states, "Feel the fear, and do it anyway!"

9. **Get tough.** Sometimes projects simply require discipline. The best way to complete a tough task is to simply dig in. Become your own taskmaster; "crack the whip" and force yourself to focus on those things that are high priorities, but perhaps not your idea of fun.

10. **Acknowledge accomplishment.** We're not talking major shopping sprees at Neiman Marcus here. We're talking reasonable, meaningful rewards that match up with how much effort you invested. Go buy yourself a small treat, call your best friend in another state, take a relaxing soak in the bathtub, or do something to celebrate your accomplishments—big and small—along the way. Acknowledgment, from yourself or others, is a great motivator for tackling future projects.

Beyond Juggling: *Realistically* Manage Work, School, and Personal Life*

Your personal time management needs depend on who you are and how many obligations you have. Today's college students are more diverse than ever. Increasing numbers of college students are also parents, part-time employees or full-time professionals, husbands or wives, community volunteers, soccer coaches, or Sunday school teachers. How on earth can you possibly juggle it all?

The answer? You can't. According to work-life balance expert Dawn Carlson, juggling is a knee-jerk coping mechanism—the default setting when time gets tight and it seems that nothing can be put on the back burner. If you, like millions of others, feel overworked, overcommitted, and exhausted at every turn, you may have already learned that you can't juggle your way to a balanced life. It's impossible.[24]

Now for the good news. Balance among work, school, and personal life is possible. All of us have three primary areas of our lives that should be in balance, ideally—meaningful work (including school), satisfying relationships, and a healthy lifestyle. In addition to work and relationships, we all need to take care of ourselves. See what you think of these five rebalancing strategies. The idea is you can't have it all, but you can have it better than you do now.

Alternating

If you use this strategy, your work-life balance comes in separate, concentrated doses. You may throw yourself into your career with abandon, and then cut back or quit work altogether and focus intensely on your family. You may give your job 110 percent during the week but devote Saturdays to physical fitness or to your kids or to running all the errands you've saved up during the week. Or you save Tuesdays and Thursdays for homework and go to classes Mondays, Wednesdays, and Fridays. People who use this strategy alternate between important things, and it works for them. An alternator's motto is "I want to have it all, but just not all at once."

Outsourcing

Outsourcing, or paying someone else to do something for you, is another solution. An outsourcer's motto might be "I want to have it all, not do it all." This strategy helps you achieve work–life balance by giving someone else some of

*Adapted from Sandholtz, K., Derr, B., Buckner, K., & Carlson, D. (2002). *Beyond juggling: Rebalancing your busy life.* San Francisco: Berrett-Koehler Publishing.

your responsibilities—usually in your personal life—to free up time for the tasks you care about most. If you have enough money, hire someone to clean the house or mow the lawn. If you don't, trade these jobs among family, friends, or neighbors who band together to help each other. Of course, there are ways this strategy could be misused by college students. Don't even think about outsourcing your research papers by having someone else write them or downloading them from the Internet with a charge card! Warning: This practice will definitely be hazardous to your academic health! In fact, your college career may be over!

Bundling

Bundling is efficient because it allows you to "kill two birds with one stone." Examine your busy life and look for areas in which you can double dip, such as combining exercising with socializing. If your social life is suffering because you have too much to do, take walks with a friend so that you can talk along the way. A bundler's motto is "I want to get more mileage out of the things I do by combining activities."

Techflexing

Technology allows us to work from almost anywhere, anytime, using technology. If you telecommute from home several days a week for your job, you might get up early, spend some time on e-mail, go out for a run, have breakfast with your family, and then get back on your computer. In the office, you use instant messaging to stay connected to family members or a cell phone to call home while commuting to a business meeting. Chances are you can telecommute to your campus library and do research online, register for classes online, and pay all your bills online, including tuition. Use technology, and the flexibility it gives you, to your advantage to merge important aspects of your life.

Simplifying

People who use this strategy have decided they don't want it all. They've reached a point where they make a permanent commitment to stop the craziness in their lives. The benefit of simplifying is greater freedom from details, stress, and the rat race. But there are trade-offs, of course. People may have to take a significant cut in pay in order to work fewer hours or at a less demanding job. But for them, it's worth it.[25]

These five strategies, used separately or in combination, have helped many people who are dealing with work, school, and family commitments at the same time. They all require certain trade-offs. None of these strategies is a magic solution.

But the alternative to rebalancing is more stress, more physical and emotional exhaustion, more frustration, and much less personal satisfaction. If you focus on rebalancing your life—making conscious choices and course corrections as you go—small changes can have a big impact. Work–life balance isn't an all-or-nothing proposition. It's an ever-changing journey. So take it one step at a time.

> Our attraction to a world of infinite possibility, information and complexity is here to stay. The challenge is how to participate productively in this new and turbulent world, and not be paralyzed by it.
>
> *David Allen, time management expert*

Time Is Money!

How Fiscally Fit Are You?

Have you ever heard the phrase "Time is money"? Before leaving the subject of time and energy management, let's look at how you manage your money as well. How good are you at managing your finances? Check one of the three boxes for each statement, to get a sense of how financially savvy you are.

	Always true of me	Sometimes true of me	Never true of me
1. At any given moment in time, I know the balance of my checking account.			
2. I use my credit card for particular types of purchases only, such as gas or food.			
3. I pay off my bills in full every month.			
4. I know the interest rate on my credit cards.			
5. I resist impulse buying and only spend when I need things.			
6. I have a budget and I follow it.			
7. I put money aside to save each month.			
8. When I get a pay raise, I increase the proportion of money I save.			
9. I keep track of my spending on a daily or weekly basis.			
10. I don't allow myself to get pressured by others into buying things I don't really need.			

Look over your responses. If you have more checks in the "Never true of me" column than you do in either of the two others, you may be able to put the information you're about to read to good use!

People say that "time is money." It's true. If you're so efficient with your time that you can call more customers or sell more products, then time does equal money. If your company is the first to introduce a hot new kind of cell phone or a zippy fuel-efficient car, you win. Even if better models come out next year, they may fall flat because people have already invested.

> **Don't tell me where your priorities are. Show me where you spend your money and I'll tell you what they are.**
>
> *James W. Frick (1924–), Former Vice President, University of Notre Dame*

Both time management and money management are key to your college success.

Studies show that working too many hours at a paid job increases your chances of dropping out of college.[26] Many students find themselves working more so that they can spend more, which in turn takes time away from their studies. They may take a semester off from college to make a pile of money and then never come back. Although there's evidence that working a moderate amount can help you polish your time and energy management skills, the real secret to financial responsibility in college is to track your habits and gain the knowledge you need to make sound financial decisions.

EXERCISE 4.8

Create a Spending Log

Take a look at this student's spending log, then complete one for yourself. Money has a way of slipping through our fingers. Choose one entire day that is representative of your spending, and use the chart on the next page to keep track of how you spend money. Write down everything from seemingly small, insignificant items to major purchases, and explain why you made each purchase. Your log may look something like this student's:

TIME	ITEM	LOCATION	AMOUNT	REASON
8–9 A.M.	coffee and bagel	convenience store	$3.50	overslept!
9–10 A.M.	computer paper	office supply store	$2.50	English paper due
10–11 A.M.	gas fill-up	gas station	$65.00	running on fumes!
11 A.M.– 12 P.M.	burger and fries	fast-food restaurant	$6.00	lunch on the run
12–1 P.M.	toiletries, etc.	drugstore	$18.00	out of stock
1–2 P.M.	bottled water	convenience store	$2.50	forgot to bring
2–3 P.M.	supplies	bookstore	$12.00	forgot to get earlier
3–7 P.M.	WORK			
7–8 P.M.	pizza	pizza place	$12.00	meet friends
8–9 P.M.	week's groceries	grocery store	$61.50	cupboard is bare!
9–10 P.M.	laundry	laundromat	$5.00	washer broken
10–11 P.M.	STUDY TIME			
11 P.M.– 12 A.M.	weekend movie, online tickets, DVDs, cell phone upgrade	Internet retail websites, phone service	$129.00 $20.00	friend's recommendations, need more minutes

This student has spent $337 today without doing anything special! When you analyze his expenditures, you can find patterns. He seems to (1) forget to plan, so he spends money continuously throughout the day, (2) spend relatively large amounts of money online, (3) be particularly vulnerable late at night, and (4) spend money grabbing food on the run. These are patterns he should be aware of if he wants to control his spending. He could pack food from home to save a significant amount of money, for example. Now create your own chart.

(Continued)

TIME	ITEM	LOCATION	AMOUNT	REASON
8–9 A.M.				
9–10 A.M.				
10–11 A.M.				
11 A.M. – 12 P.M.				
12–1 P.M.				
1–2 P.M.				
2–3 P.M.				
3–4 P.M.				
4–5 P.M.				
5–6 P.M.				
6–7 P.M.				
7–8 P.M.				
8–9 P.M.				
9–10 P.M.				
10–11 P.M.				
11 P.M.–12 A.M.				

What patterns do you notice about your spending? What kinds of changes will you try to make to curb any unnecessary spending?

VARK It!

Visual: Draw a bar graph of how much money you spend each month (housing, food, gas, clothes, etc.). Which column of the graph is tallest or longest. Should it be?

The Perils of Plastic

The "newly minted" Credit Card Act of 2009 has changed some things about how credit cards work. In 2008, before the law went into effect, college students carried a balance of $3,173 (a ten-year high), and a full 82 percent kept paying on a balance every month.[27] Under the new law, credit cards cannot be issued to people under the age of 21 unless they have an adult co-signer or can show proof that they have enough income. College students will need permission from parents or guardians to increase their credit limits. And those under 21 will be protected from "sneaky" credit card offers unless they opt to get them. Read up on credible Internet sites about the new law and the protections and restrictions it provides. If you already have a credit card or plan to get one, however, keep this general advice in mind.

1. **Think about the difference between needs and wants.** You may think you need particular things so that your friends will like you ("Hey,

let's stop for a burger"), so that you have a new item (like a new car you can't afford), or so that you look fabulous (like pricey manicures). Here's a rule of thumb: If buying something simply helps you move from acceptable to amazing, it's not an emergency. Do you really need a mocha latté every day? A regular old cup of coffee a day sets you back $500 per year!

2. **Leave home without it.** Don't routinely take your credit card with you. Use cash and save your credit card for true emergencies or essentials, like gas and groceries. Do you really want to risk paying interest on today's ice cream cone years from now?

3. **Don't spend money you don't have.** Only charge what you can pay for each month. Just because your credit card limit is $2,000 doesn't mean you need to spend that much each month. A vacation that costs $1,000 will take 12 years of minimal payments to pay off at an 18 percent interest rate. And that $1,000 trip will eventually cost you $2,115! One piece of good advice is to "live like a student while you are in school so you don't have to live like a student after you graduate."[28]

4. **Understand how credit works.** It's important to know the basics. According to one source, "Only 15% [of college students] have any idea how much their interest rate is, and fewer than one in 10 students know their interest rate, late fee and over-limit fee amounts."[29]

   Here are some terms you need to know:

   > **Credit reports.** Your credit history is based on (1) how many credit cards you owe money on, (2) how much money you owe, and (3) how many late payments you make. Bad grades on your credit report can make your life difficult later.

   > **Fees.** Credit card companies charge you in three ways: (1) annual fees (a fee you must pay every year to use the card); (2) finance charges (a charge for loaning you the money you can't pay back when your bill is due); and (3) late fees (for missing a monthly payment deadline). Think about what's most important to you—no annual fee, frequent flyer miles, or a lower interest rate—and shop around!

   > **The fine print.** How can you learn more? Read your credit card contract carefully. Credit card companies must give you certain important information, which is often on their website. Go to the Federal Reserve website for vital, bottom-line information, and search online to find out more about ways the new law could affect you.[30]

5. **Track your expenses.** All kinds of tools—technology-based and otherwise—can help you discover where your money actually goes. To control your spending, use a credit card with caution or use a debit card.

6. **If you're already in financial trouble, ask for help.** Talk to an expert who can help you figure out what to do.[31]

VARK It!

Aural: Working with another aural learner, take turns reading paragraphs of "The Perils of Plastic" section aloud. Talk over your own credit card spending and whether it's under control.

BOX 4.2

Top Ten Financial Aid FAQs

Financial aid. Like all good things, you have to know how it works. You can think of financial aid as complicated and time-consuming, or it can be the one thing that keeps you in school. Take a look at these questions students often ask about the mysteries of financial aid. Most students need financial help of some kind to earn a college degree. Here is some information to help you navigate your way financially.[32]

1. **Who qualifies for financial aid? Almost everyone!** You may not think you qualify for financial aid, but it's a good idea to apply anyway. You won't know until you apply, and some types of aid are based on criteria other than your income and assets.

2. **What does FAFSA stand for?** FAFSA stands for Free Application for Federal Student Aid. You apply online at fafsa.gov, or you can get a copy of the application by calling 1-800-4-FED-AID.

3. **What types of financial aid exist?** You can receive financial aid in the form of scholarships, fellowships, loans, grants, or work-study awards. Generally, scholarships and fellowships are for students with special academic, artistic, or athletic abilities; students with interests in specialized fields; students from particular parts of the country; or students from minority groups. Typically, you don't repay them. Loans and grants come in a variety of forms and from several possible sources, either federal or state government or private organizations. Loans must be repaid, but there are many loan programs to pay down your student loans if you pursue fields such as teaching, nursing, or public service. In addition, if you qualify for a need-based work-study job on or off campus, you can earn an hourly wage to assist in your educational expenses.

4. **When should I apply?** You can apply for financial aid any time after January 1 of the year you intend to go to college, but be mindful of your school's priority filing date to ensure you meet that deadline, as grant funds are limited. The FAFSA will require tax information from the previous year. Remember, you must be enrolled by the start of classes to receive funds.

5. **Do I have to reapply every year?** Yes. Your financial situation can change over time. Your brothers or sisters may start college while you're in school, for example, which can change your family's status.

6. **How can I keep my financial aid over my college years?** Assuming your financial situation remains fairly similar from year to year, you must demonstrate that you're making progress toward a degree in terms of credits and a minimum GPA. Remember that if you drop courses, your financial aid may be affected based on whether you're considered to be a full-time or part-time student.

7. **Who's responsible for paying back my loans?** You are. Others can help you, but ultimately the responsibility is yours and yours alone. If your parents forget to make a payment or don't pay a bill on time, you will be held responsible.

8. **If I leave school for a time, do I have to start repaying my loans right away?** Most loans have a grace period of six or nine months before you must begin repayment. You can request a forbearance or deferment if you need to postpone payments beyond your grace period.

9. **If I get an outside scholarship, should I report it to the Financial Aid office on campus?** Yes. They'll adjust your financial aid package if necessary, but the rules require that scholarships must be processed through the financial aid office.

10. **Where can I find out more?** Your best source of information is in the Office of Financial Aid right on your own campus. Or you can get information online at studentaid.ed.gov. Or call the Federal Student Aid Information Center at 1–800–433–3243, and ask for a free copy of *The Student Guide: Financial Aid* from the U.S. Department of Education.

The Four C Factors: Just how motivated are YOU?

 CONTROL: *APPLY NOW!*

In the chapter, Derek Johnson is taking a World History class. Read the following excerpt from one of Derek's course books, Voyages in World History *by Valerie Hansen, and consider the questions below. Before you start reading the excerpt (and setting your timer), take a minute to preview the questions you'll be asked.*

> Before the plague the Roman Empire had been an urban society where powerful people met at the marketplace each day to discuss their affairs, enjoying theater and circus performances alongside their poorer neighbors. By 600 such an urban type of life had become a memory. Starting in 541 and continuing to sometime in the ninth century, the population declined, cities shrank, the economy contracted, and tax revenues plummeted. In these centuries of declining tax revenues, the government minted far fewer coins than earlier, and a barter economy replaced the partially monetized economy. Craftsmen and merchants gave up their occupations to become farmers.
>
> Another consequence of these catastrophes was that the government could no longer afford to pay its soldiers. Instead, militias were formed by part-time soldiers who farmed the land during peacetime. When Islamic forces began to expand around 640, the Byzantine Empire ceded to the victorious Islamic armies large chunks of territory in Armenia and Africa.
>
> In contrast to the multiple officials of Roman times, the basic administrative unit of the Byzantine Empire during the seventh and eighth centuries was the *theme* (Greek plural form: *themata*) headed by a single governor. This governor heard legal disputes, collected taxes, and commanded the local militia. Society had also changed from Roman times. Few people knew Latin, and the high and low in rank led almost identical lives. Although some people possessed more land than others, they now worked the land alongside their poorer dependents. Slavery declined as well because no one could afford to feed slaves. Most of the people in the countryside were legally independent peasants who farmed the land intensively, often with two oxen and a plow, and grew only enough food to feed their own families.
>
> *Source:* Hansen, *Voyages in World History,* Brief. © 2013. Cengage Learning, page 205.

How long did it take you to read the excerpt from Voyages in World History? *How many times did your attention wander when you were reading this material? What "Killer B's" interrupted you? How can you deal with this issue when you're trying to read your assignments?*

_____

_____

_____

What are the dangers of multitasking when you're reading an excerpt from Voyages in World History *(or any of your assigned readings)?*

_____

_____

_____

Imagine you have the following tasks on your to-do list: Read a chapter in Voyages in World History, *write a two-page paper for your philosophy course, work out at the gym, take your aunt to a doctor's appointment, and work four hours at your part-time job. How would you prioritize these tasks? Be prepared to justify your decisions to your instructor or classmates.*

_____

_____

_____

CURIOSITY: *CHOOSE TO CHOOSE!*

Have you ever thought about how many dozens, if not hundreds, of choices you make each day? Psychologist and Professor Barry Schwartz, in his book *The Paradox of Choice: Why More Is Less,* believes that making nonstop choices can actually cause us to "invest time, energy, and no small amount of self-doubt, and dread." Choosing a new cell phone plan can take some people weeks while they research models of cell phones, minutes available, quotas of text messages, and Internet access, not to mention the fine print. Although being flooded with choices may feel luxurious, it can be stressful and even unrewarding. Paralysis, anxiety, and stress, rather than happiness, satisfaction, and perfection, can be the result of too much "more." Some of us, Schwartz says, are "maximizers"; we don't rest until we find the best. Others of us are "satisficers"; we're satisfied with what's good enough, based on our most important criteria. Of course, we all do some "maximizing" and some "satisficing," but generally, which are you? Here are Schwartz's recommendations to lower our stress levels in a society where more can actually give us less, especially in terms of quality of life:

1. **Choose to choose.** Some decisions are worth lengthy deliberation; others aren't. Be conscious of the choices you make and whether they're worth the return on your investment. "Maximize" when it counts, and "satisfice" when it doesn't.

2. **Remember that there's always greener grass somewhere.** Someone will always have a better job than you do, a nicer apartment, or a more attractive romantic partner. Regret or envy can eat away at you, and second-guessing can bring unsettling dissatisfaction.

3. **Regret less and appreciate more.** Although green grass does abound, so do sandpits and bumpy roads. That's an important realization, too! Value the good things you already have going for you.

4. **Build bridges, not walls.** Think about the ways in which the dozens of choices you've already made as a new college student give you your own unique profile or "choice-print": where you live, which classes you take, clubs you join, campus events you attend, your small circle of friends, and on and on. Remember that, and make conscious choices that will best help you succeed.[33]

Think about the last decision you made. How much time and energy did you spend making the decision? Did you maximize or sacrifice? What was the outcome?

_____

_____

_____

CAREER OUTLOOK: *WORK SMARTER, NOT HARDER*

Imagine yourself off to a great start, impressing everyone, especially your boss, in your long-awaited career after college. But something is gnawing at you. You can't help but notice your stress level inching up. One day, when you power up your office computer, you immediately see 250 new e-mails that weren't there yesterday. Aaaak!!! When you have multiple projects with deadlines, the bottom line question becomes "Which task do you do first when you're totally overwhelmed?"

Some people choose to become "workaholics". They come in early, leave late, and take work home with them. However, working more doesn't mean you care more or get more done. It just means you work more.[34] Instead of working harder, how about working smarter?

Try putting a whiteboard on your wall and spending the first hour prioritizing your day. Shut the door, turn everything off, and list your goals for the day by creating small boxes to represent your three main projects. Then explore how they can be chunked into smaller subprojects, and look for relationships among them and patterns across them. You'll be able to save yourself time and accomplish much more. Your whiteboard will help you prioritize prioritizing (and no, that's not a typo). You're moving the process of prioritizing right up to the top of your to-do list.

By prioritizing first, you're guaranteeing that you'll make greater headway than you would otherwise. You're working smarter, not harder. At the end of the day, you can look back at your "wake" in the imaginary river of your work life, satisfied with how far you've come from the shoreline. As someone once said, "Efficiency is intelligent laziness." Figure it out now. It's all about working smarter and getting things done.[35]

How can you practice prioritizing now to develop the skills you'll need in your eventual career?

_____

_____

_____

CHALLENGE: REALITY CHECK

How much did you learn? At the beginning of this chapter, you filled out a "Readiness Check" that asked how you thought this chapter would relate to you, and how you would relate to it. Now, fill out this "Reality Check" to find out.

1. What's the difference between time management, attention management, and energy management? How are they different, and what do they have in common?

2. What is the A-B-C method for prioritizing tasks? What does each letter represent, and how is the system used?

3. What percentage of college students admit to procrastinating on assignments? Why do they procrastinate? Does the fact that procrastination is so widespread (Everybody's doing it . . .) excuse it?

4. What percentage of college students with credit cards know how much interest they pay on their credit card bills?

5. How long did it take? _____ hours _____ minutes. Before you began this chapter, you were asked to predict how long it would take you to complete it (total time, even if you read it in more than one sitting). Was your estimate on target, or will you revise it for the next chapter you read?_____

step 3 INSIGHT _Now_ What Do You Think?

At the beginning of this chapter, Derek Johnson, a frustrated and disgruntled student, faced a challenge. Now after reading this chapter, would you respond differently to any of the questions you answered about the "FOCUS Challenge Case"? Using what you learned in the chapter, write a paragraph ending to Derek's case study. What are some of the possible outcomes for Derek?

step 4 ACTION Your Plans for Change

1. What's the most important thing you learned in reading this chapter?

2. How will you apply the information you've learned to yourself to improve your time, energy, and money management?

chapter 5 Thinking Critically and Creatively

READINESS CHECK

How this chapter relates to YOU

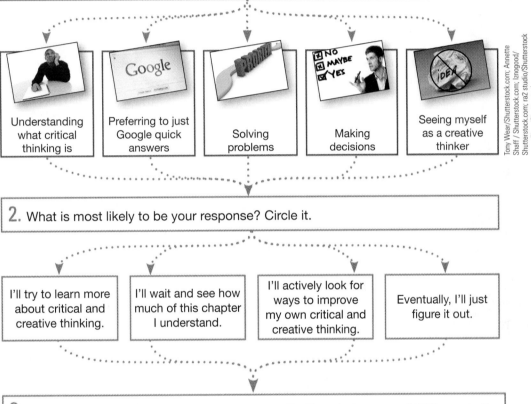

1. When it comes to thinking critically and creatively in your college classes, what do you find the most challenging, if anything?

Understanding what critical thinking is

Preferring to just Google quick answers

Solving problems

Making decisions

Seeing myself as a creative thinker

Tony Wear/Shutterstock.com; Annette Shaff / Shutterstock.com; Iznogood/ Shutterstock.com; ra2 studio/Shutterstock .com; Elnur/Shutterstock.com

2. What is most likely to be your response? Circle it.

I'll try to learn more about critical and creative thinking.

I'll wait and see how much of this chapter I understand.

I'll actively look for ways to improve my own critical and creative thinking.

Eventually, I'll just figure it out.

3. What would you have to do to increase your likelihood of success? Will you do it this quarter or semester?

Example: Really focus on this topic as the foundation for success in college. Yes!

How YOU will relate to this chapter

What are you most interested in learning about? Put checkmarks by those topics.

☐ How critical thinking and creative thinking are defined

☐ How a four-part model of critical thinking works

☐ How to analyze arguments, assess assumptions, and consider claims

☐ How to avoid mistakes in reasoning

☐ What metacognition is and why it's important

☐ How to become a more creative thinker

• How motivated are you to learn more about getting the right start in college? (5 = high, 1 = low) ___

• How ready are you to read now? ___

(If something is in your way, take care of it if you can; zero in and focus.)

• How long do you think it will take you to complete this chapter? If you start and stop, keep track of your overall time.

___ hour(s) ___ minutes

113

Desiree Moore

Anke van Wyk/Shutterstock.com

©Larry Harwood Photography. Property of Cengage Learning.

Simply put: Desiree Moore was a perfectionist. Her friends said she was "detail oriented." Her family said she was compulsive. Truthfully, though, she hadn't been all that successful in high school; her assignments were always turned in late, if at all, because they were never "finished." She'd always ask her teachers how long a paper should be and what topic she should write about. She wanted to get things right. Her teachers always advised her to stop "tweaking": "You spend so much time revising your assignments that nothing ever gets done." But she found it hard to take their advice.

High school had been so stressful that when she graduated, she took the first job that came along, as a receptionist for a small law firm. When the two lawyers announced they were going to retire, she started to job hunt immediately. She found another job as a telemarketer. But being hung up on all day wasn't all that much fun, so eventually she quit. She tried waiting tables and cleaning houses, but those jobs didn't hold much appeal either. Before she knew it, more than a few years had gone by, and Desiree realized she didn't have much to show for it. She needed more specialized skills in order to get a better job. When she thought back over all the jobs she'd had since high school, she realized that working with the two lawyers had been her favorite. So, Desiree decided to become a paralegal by earning a two-year degree at the big community college in

town. She would be the first person in her family to go to college! It was a good career field, and she could investigate legal cases, draft documents, and do research working alongside an attorney.

Her first semester consisted of two night classes: "Introduction to Paralegal Careers" and "Paralegal Ethics." But "Paralegal Ethics" was a very challenging course. The instructor, Mr. Courtney, a retired lawyer himself, had announced on the first day of class that he believed in the Socratic method of teaching, by asking questions of students instead of lecturing. "Socrates, perhaps the greatest philosopher of all time," he announced the first day, "is the 'father' of critical thinking. In this class, you'll learn to think critically. *Learning to think* is what college is all about." Mr. Courtney began every class session with a hypothetical story, and he always randomly chose a student to respond. His openings went something like this:

An attorney has just finished law school and opens a law office. He hires a legal

© Cengage Learning

Paralegal Associate's Degree Program

Courses offered:

- Introduction to the Law

- Torts & Personal Injury
- Contracts
- Legal Research, Writing & Civil Litigation
- Paralegal Ethics

- Criminal Law
- Business Law & Bankruptcy
- Constitutional Law and Criminal Procedure

© Cengage Learning

Paralegal Ethics Syllabus

Instructor: Samuel Courtney
Email Address: S.Courtney@campusmail.edu
Office Hours: MWF 8am–10am
Office Location: Main Hall 1020
Text: *Legal Ethics for Paralegals and the Law Office* (1st Edition) by Laura Morrison

Class Content:
- Understand ethical issues that paralegals may face
- Review the universal concepts of professional responsibility and ethical practices
- Define the roles of paralegals versus attorneys
- Recognize what activities constitute the
- Discuss possible solutions to ethical dilemmas

Class Method: Since philosophy is an important part of law, for our class method we will turn to one of the founding fathers of critical and philosophical thinking: Socrates. Consequently, we will be using the "Socratic method" when approaching course material. This means that instead of giving a lecture, I will ask you, the students, questions in order to create a lively discussion.

assistant, just out of college. He is eager to begin his new career, but he is also nervous because he's starting from scratch.

The lawyer's specialty is civil law, and several weeks go by before the phone even rings. His first potential client has a big problem. He wants to sue his next-door neighbor for keeping old cars, junk, and trash in his front yard. When he's asked the neighbor nicely to clean up his property, the neighbor has refused in threatening tones. The teenage sons who live in the home have ties to local gangs, and other neighbors are afraid. They all suspect the teenage boys of a series of unsolved robberies in the neighborhood. The neighborhood is getting a bad reputation, and home values in the area have fallen dramatically.

The lawyer, who desperately needs the work, decides to take the case. However, when the client fills out the contract, his legal assistant notices that the client's zip code is the same as her boss's. In fact, she recognizes the street name as one that's in the subdivision where the lawyer himself lives. Is this a problem? Would you say the lawyer has a "conflict of interest"? What should our legal assistant do?

One student responded with, "Yes, the lawyer lives in the same neighborhood as his client. He doesn't want his own property value to fall. According to our textbook, that's a conflict of interest." Another student said, "But the legal assistant should keep quiet and just do her job. She needs a paycheck. She shouldn't tell her boss what to do. It's none of her business." Mr. Courtney continued, "But what if the new client discovers that he and his lawyer live in the same neighborhood? Would the client see that as a possible conflict of interest? Could this damage the lawyer's legal career? What would *you* do if the legal assistant were you?" Mr. Courtney's questions seemed endless. Her best friend suggested that she look up his ratings online, but when she did, she found that students wrote about how much they had learned from him.

"What's important in college is thinking through problems," he said. "There aren't always clear right and wrong answers. The process of learning to think can be just as important as the answer itself."

Frankly, that explanation didn't sit well with Desiree. *If there aren't right answers, why go to college? The instructor knows the right answers. Why doesn't he just tell us?* Perfectionists like Desiree were always most comfortable when things were straightforward. Without fail, she always left Mr. Courtney's class with a headache from thinking so hard.

New attorney opens offi
  -civil law

Potential client:
  -wants to sue neighbor
  -won't clean trash in
  -possible gang connecti

Attorney takes case
  -but, attorney lives in sar
     neighborhood!

  PROBLEM!?

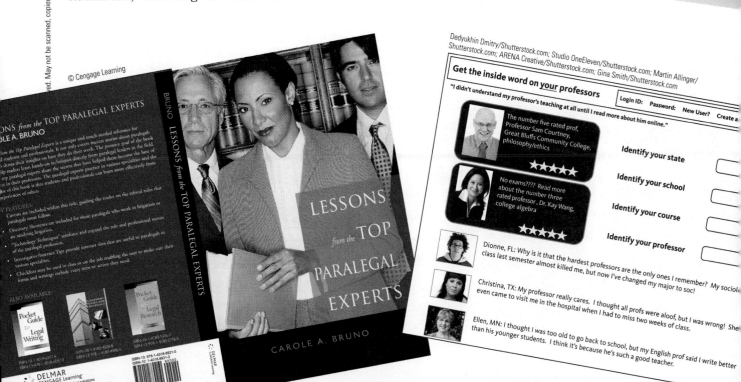

Get the inside word on your professors

"I didn't understand my professor's teaching at all until I read more about him online."

Login ID: Password: New User?   Create a

The number five rated prof. Professor Sam Courtney, Great Bluffs Community College, philosophy/ethics

★★★★★

No exams???? Read more about the number three rated professor , Dr. Kay Wang, college algebra

★★★★★

Identify your state

Identify your school

Identify your course

Identify your professor

Dionne, FL: Why is it that the hardest professors are the only ones I remember? My sociol class last semester almost killed me, but now I've changed my major to soc!

Christina, TX: My professor really cares. I thought all profs were aloof, but I was wrong! She even came to visit me in the hospital when I had to miss two weeks of class.

Ellen, MN: I thought I was too old to go back to school, but my English prof said I write better than his younger students. I think it's because he's such a good teacher.

BRUNO LESSONS *from the* TOP PARALEGAL EXPERTS

DELMAR

LESSONS *from the* TOP PARALEGAL EXPERTS

CAROLE A. BRUNO

Pocket Guide to Legal Writing

DELMAR CENGAGE Learning
For your lifelong learning solutions

1. Do you have anything in common with Desiree, like an instructor who teaches in a way you find difficult to understand? What specific steps are you taking to help yourself succeed?

2. Why does Desiree's instructor say that "learning to think is what college is all about"? What does he mean, and do you agree?

3. Do you agree with Mr. Courtney's statement that "there aren't always right answers"? If that's true, why is getting a college education so important?

4. Identify three things Desiree should do to get the most from Mr. Courtney's class.

Rethinking Thinking

Thinking is a natural, ongoing, everyday process we all engage in. In fact, we can't really turn it off, even if we try. We're always on. Everyone thinks all the time. We talk to ourselves in our heads. However, some experts say school teaches us how to just regurgitate what we've memorized, not how to think. Learning to think is what counts, and *focused thinking*—thinking critically and creatively—is what this chapter is about.

Picture this: You're in the library. It's late, and you're tired. You're supposed to be studying for your political science test, but instead of thinking about foreign policy, your mind begins drifting toward the vacation you took last summer, the great food you ate, and how much fun it was to be with your friends or family.

Would the mental process you're engaging in while sitting in the library be called *thinking?* For our purposes in this chapter, the answer is no. Here thinking is defined as a focused mental activity you engage in on purpose. You direct your thoughts toward a particular topic. You're the *active* thinker, not the *passive* daydreamer who is the victim of a wandering mind. Focused thinking involves zeroing in and managing your attention. It's deliberate, not accidental. You choose to do it for a reason.

Focused thinking is like a two-sided coin. Sometimes when you think, you *produce* ideas. That's what this chapter calls *creative thinking,* and that's something we'll deal with later. The other side of thinking requires you to *evaluate* ideas—your own or someone else's. That's *critical thinking*. The word *critical* comes from the Greek word for *critic* (*kritikos*), meaning "to question or analyze." You focus on something, sort through the information, and decide which ideas are most sensible, logical, or useful. When you're thinking critically, you're asking questions, analyzing arguments, assessing assumptions, considering claims, avoiding mistakes in reasoning, problem solving, decision making, and all the while, thinking about your thinking.

©Larry Harwood Photography. Property of Cengage Learning.

'Knowledge is power.' Rather, knowledge is happiness. To have knowledge, deep broad knowledge, is to know truth from false and lofty things from low.

Helen Keller, American author, activist, and lecturer (1880–1968)

Sharpen Your FOCUS

> **Blessed are the flexible, for they shall not be bent out of shape.**
>
> —MICHAEL MCGRIFFY, M.D.

Reason 5. They lack flexibility.

Have you ever stared at one thing so long that your vision blurred? You look hard, lock in, and eventually what you're staring at is out of focus. That's what can happen when you fixate on one way of doing things—the "right" way. Often, there's more than one right way, and one of the things you learn in college is how to decide what's what. You may not be able to do everything perfectly, as Desiree in the Focus Challenge Case wanted to. For her, procrastination was a way of giving herself permission to do a less than perfect job on a task that didn't require a perfect job in the first place.[1] For people like Desiree, developing flexibility can be a key to college success.

TRY It!

Choose one item on your "to-do" list this week that can be shifted down the list, and one item that should be shifted up. What's really important? In class, discuss whether perfectionism is a problem for you, and if so, what you can do about it.

What Is Critical Thinking?

Critical thinking is a particular kind of focused thinking. It is purposeful, reasoned, and goal-directed. It's thinking that aims to solve problems, calculate likelihood, weigh evidence, and make decisions.[2] In that sense, movie critics are critical thinkers because they look at a variety of standards (screenplay, acting, production quality, costumes, and so forth) and then decide how a movie measures up. When you're thinking critically, you're not just being critical. You're on the lookout for both faults and strengths. You're looking at how things measure up.[3]

Critical thinkers develop standards they can use to judge advertisements, political speeches, sales pitches, movies—you name it.[4] Critical thinking is not jumping to conclusions; buying arguments lock, stock, and barrel; accepting controversial ideas no matter what; or ignoring the facts.

Unfortunately, some people are noncritical thinkers. They may be biased or closed-minded. Other people are *selective* critical thinkers. When it comes to one particular subject, they shut down their minds. They can't explain their views, they're emotional about them, and they refuse to acknowledge any other position. Why do they believe these things? Only if they understand the *why,* can they explain their views to someone else or defend them under fire. The importance of *why* can't be overstated. Some people, of course, have already thought through their beliefs, and they understand their positions and the reasons for them very well. Arriving at that point is the goal of anyone who wants to become a better critical thinker.

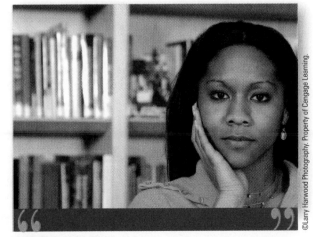

> **What we need is not the will to believe, but the will to find out.**
>
> Bertrand Russell, British philosopher, logician, and mathematician (1872–1970)

And Just Why Is Critical Thinking Important?

Some experts worry that colleges—and students—don't put enough emphasis on developing critical thinking skills, when they're actually the very foundation for college and life success.[5] Here is a list of reasons why it's important to improve your critical thinking skills. Beside each entry, mark the degree to which you'd like to refine your critical thinking skills in each area. How important is each of these items to you? On a scale from 1 to 5, with 5 representing the highest degree, would you like to:

1. _____ **Become a more successful college student?** Most college courses require you to think critically (in answering essay questions, for example). In one study of over 1,100 college students, higher scores on critical thinking skills tests correlated highly with better grades.[6] Critical thinkers, for example, can ask better questions in class. They recognize strategies their instructors use to encourage critical thinking ("How does that relate to our topic today?" "Can you give us an example?" "Let's look at this issue from another perspective.")[7] They learn to think like people who practice the disciplines they're studying—like a sociologist, biologist, or mathematician, for example.[8] There's even evidence that interaction with other students in activities outside of class can help you develop as a critical thinker.[9]

2. _____ **Become a better citizen?** Critical thinking is the foundation of a strong democracy. Voters must think critically about candidates' messages and whether they're likely to keep their campaign promises. It's easy to talk about balancing the budget or lowering taxes, but the truth is these highly complex tasks are very challenging to carry out. The American public must sift through information and examine politicians' arguments in order to keep our democracy strong.

3. _____ **Become a better employee?** A workforce of critical—and creative—thinkers helps the American economy thrive and individuals become more successful. The U.S. Department of Labor reports that today's jobs require employees who can deal with complex issues, learn and perform multiple tasks, analyze and deal with a wide variety of options, identify problems, perceive alternative approaches, and select the best approach.[10] Employers are "practically begging" for employees who can "think, collaborate, communicate, coordinate, and create."[11]

4. _____ **Become a smarter consumer?** In today's world, everyone wants your money. If you bought everything advertised in magazines or on television, you'd run out of money very quickly. Critical thinking will help you evaluate offers, avoid slick come-ons, and buy responsibly.

5. _____ **Build stronger relationships?** Critical thinking helps us understand our own and others' actions and become more responsible communicators. Whether with friends or romantic partners, relationships take work. Sometimes you have to listen between the lines for important clues to figure out what your partner really means. Actually, critical thinking is at the heart of every relationship you care about.

6. _____ **Become a lifelong learner?** Your education doesn't end when you get your diploma. In many ways the real exams begin afterward when you put your classroom learning to the test on the job. And in today's world you must continue to learn as you transition through jobs—personally and professionally. You'll need to keep expanding your skills, no matter what your career is.

Look over your responses to these six items. Now rank them 1 through 6, with 1 as your highest priority at this particular point in your life. Be prepared to explain your rankings in class.

A Four-Part Model of Critical Thinking

Now that we've defined critical thinking, let's ask an important related question: How do you do it? We'll look at the four primary components of critical thinking, and later in this chapter, we'll use a realistic news story, one that could take place near any community college campus, to allow you to apply what you've learned through a memorable example.

Take a look at Figure 5.1 to preview the four-part model of critical thinking. You'll see right away that your reasoning skills underlie everything. They are

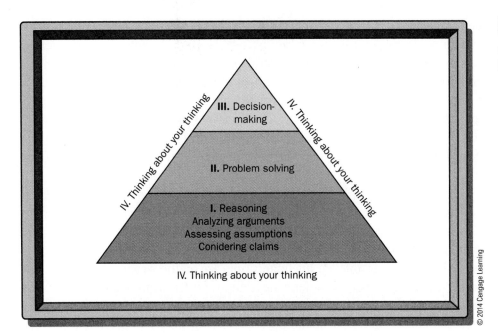

FIGURE 5.1

Critical Thinking Is Focused

© 2014 Cengage Learning

the foundation upon which your problem-solving and decision-making skills rest, and your metacognitive skills, or thinking about your thinking, surround all the focused thinking you do.

I. Reasoning: The Foundation of Critical Thinking

Reasoning, the foundation of critical thinking, is the ability to reach a conclusion from one or more arguments. A strong argument is convincing because it offers **evidence** to back up its claim. If no one would disagree with what you're saying, it's not an argument. It's obvious. "Grass is green" is not an argument. But "Cows that are grass-fed make the best meat" is (if supporting evidence is provided). Do you see the difference?

© 2014 Cengage Learning

evidence reasons why something is true, based on statistics, expert testimony, or examples

Think about your reasoning skills. How good are you at creating a sound argument? Let's say that you're trying to convince your friend that her cell phone conversation is making it difficult for you to study for a major exam. What evidence would you use to convince her? What's the likelihood of your success? Or how about this: How good are you at evaluating someone else's argument? For example, you're trying to decide whether an online discount is really a good deal. Would you take the advertiser's word for it, or would you compare prices on your own?

Throughout the rest of this chapter, ask yourself: Are there ways I can improve my reasoning skills? As you think about your own skills, consider these reasoning nuts and bolts that are essential parts of creating and evaluating arguments.

Analyzing Arguments Have you ever seen the *Monty Python Flying Circus* "Argument Clinic" sketch? In this bizarre skit a man comes to an "argument clinic" to buy an argument. The two arguers—"professional" and customer—engage in a long, "yes, it is"/"no, it isn't" squabble.

Critical thinking is about arguments. But most of us think of an argument as a back-and-forth disagreement. In the middle of the "Argument Clinic"

contradictory two people
saying opposite things

proposition a point

sketch, however, the customer actually makes an important point. He says that they're not really arguing; they're just **contradicting** each other. He continues, "An argument is a connected series of statements intended to establish a **proposition**." That's the kind of argument that's related to critical thinking.

Critical thinking is about an argument that *one* person puts forth, not a squabble between two people. An op-ed piece in the newspaper contains an argument. (Op-ed stands for the page "opposite the editorial page" that features signed articles expressing personal viewpoints.) Both attorneys—prosecution and defense—put forth their closing arguments at the end of a trial.

Arguments are said to be inductive or deductive. *Inductive* arguments go from specific observations to general conclusions. In criminal trials, the prosecution puts together individual pieces of evidence to prove that the defendant is guilty: eyewitnesses put him at the scene, the gun store salesman remembers selling him a pistol, and his fingerprints are on the weapon. Therefore, the prosecutor argues that the defendant is guilty. Other arguments are said to be *deductive*, meaning they go from broad generalizations to specific conclusions. All serial killers have a particular psychological profile. The defendant has this psychological profile. Therefore the defendant is the killer.

What do arguments do? They propose a line of reasoning. They try to persuade. Arguments contain clear reasons to believe someone or something. Arguments say A plus B equals C. Once you understand what an argument is, you must also understand that arguments can be sound or unsound. If I tell you that two plus two equals four, chances are good that you'll believe me. If, on the other hand, I tell you two plus two equals five, you'll flatly deny it. If I say "Cats have fur. Dogs have fur. Therefore dogs are cats," you'll tell me I'm crazy—because it's an unsound argument.

The standard we use to test the soundness of arguments is logic, which is a fairly extensive topic. Let's just say for our purposes here that arguments are sound when the evidence for them is reasonable, more reasonable than the evidence against them. The important point is that a sound argument provides at least one good reason to believe. Let's look at an example:

Few people think more than two or three times a year. I have made an international reputation for myself by thinking once or twice a week.

George Bernard Shaw, Irish literary critic, playwright, and essayist, 1925 Nobel Prize for Literature (1856–1950)

> *I don't see why all students have to take an introductory writing course. It's a free country. Students shouldn't have to take courses they don't want to take.*

Based on our definition, is this example an argument? Why or why not? Is the statement "It's a free country" relevant? What does living in a free country have to do with courses that community college students are required to take? Nothing. *Relevancy* is a condition needed for a sound argument.

Now look at this example:

> *I don't see why all first-year students have to take an introductory writing course. Many students have developed good writing skills in high school, and their entrance test scores are high.*

Is this second example an argument? Why or why not? The first example doesn't give you a good reason to believe the argument; the second example does. A true argument must contain at least one reason for you to believe it.

Here's another warning. Not everything that sounds like an argument is one. Look at this example:

Everyone taking Math 100 failed the test last Friday. I took the test last Friday. Therefore, I will probably get an F in the course.

Is that a sound argument—or is something missing? Even though all three statements may be true, when you put them together they don't make a sound argument. What grade has this student earned on earlier math tests? How many tests are left in the course? What other assignments figure into students' grades? The information present may not be adequate to predict an F in the course. *Adequacy* is another condition needed for a sound argument. This alternative, on the other hand, is a sound argument:

Everyone taking Math 100 failed the test last Friday. I took the test last Friday. Therefore, I earned an F on the test.

When you're assessing the soundness of an argument, you must look for two things: *relevance* and *adequacy*.[12]

Not all arguments are sound. Have you ever heard this story? A scientist came up with a new study to find out what makes people drunk, using himself in the experiment. The study went like this. On Monday night, he drank three tall glasses of scotch and water, mixed in equal amounts. The next morning, he recorded his results: intoxication. On Tuesday night, he drank three tall glasses of whiskey and water. On Wednesday night, he drank three tall glasses of rum and water. On Thursday night, he drank three tall glasses of vodka and water. Each morning, his recorded results were the same. He had become drunk. His totally wrong conclusion? Water makes people drunk.

Not only is it important to be able to construct sound arguments, but it's also important to be able to recognize them. As a consumer in today's information society, you must know when to buy into an argument, and when not to.

Assessing Assumptions When you're thinking critically, one of the most important kinds of questions you can ask is about the *assumptions* you or someone else is making, perhaps without even realizing it. Assumptions are things you take for granted, and they can limit your thinking. Consider this well-known puzzle, and afterward examine how the assumptions you brought with you interfered with solving it.

One day Kerry celebrated her birthday. Two days later her older twin brother, Harry, celebrated his birthday. How could that be?

You may have solved this puzzle if you were willing to question the underlying assumptions that were holding you back. (The answer is upside down at the bottom of this page.)

People reveal their basic assumptions in what they say. If you listen carefully, you can uncover them. "Go on for a bachelor's degree after I finish here? No way! As soon as I get my associate's degree, I'm done!" This student's underlying assumption is that college itself isn't as important as what comes afterward (like making money). This student may sit through her classes without getting

Kerry and Harry are not twins. Harry and his brother are twins, and they are older than Kerry.

Ablestock.com/Photos.com

engaged in the subject matter, and she checks off requirements as quickly as she can. Too bad.

Considering Claims Evaluating claims is one of the most basic aspects of reasoning. A claim is a statement that can be true or false, but not both. This is different from a fact, which cannot be disputed. What's the difference between a *fact* and a *claim*? Facts can't be disputed; claims can be true or false, but they must be one or the other, not both.

> *FACT: Ronald Reagan, George H. Bush, and Bill Clinton have been presidents of the United States during the last thirty years.*
>
> *CLAIM: Bill Clinton was the most popular American president in the last thirty years.*

The fact is obvious. The claim needs evidence to support it. As a critical thinker, it's important to use your reasoning skills to evaluate the evidence. Generally speaking, be wary of claims that

> are supported by unidentified sources ("Experts claim . . . ").

> are made by a person or company who stands to gain ("Brought to you by the makers of . . .").

> come from a single person claiming his experience as the norm ("I tried it and it worked for me!").

> use a bandwagon appeal ("Everybody's doing it.").

> mislead with statistics ("over half" when it's really only 50.5 percent).

On the other hand, we must also keep an open mind and be flexible in our thinking. If you get good evidence to support a view that contradicts yours, be willing to change your ideas. One way to evaluate the validity of claims is to use the Critical Thinking Pyramid (Figure 5.2). Consider claims by asking these four key questions: "Who?" "What?" "Why?" and "How?" Figure 5.2 shows how the questions progress from level 1 to 3.

Avoiding Faulty Reasoning Although we can certainly improve our critical-thinking skills, it's impossible to be perfect critical thinkers 100 percent of the time. As thinkers, we make mistakes, and sometimes others try to trick us with bad arguments. It's important to cultivate both types of critical thinking skills: your *productive* skills, which you use as a speaker and writer when you "produce" ideas, and your *receptive* skills, which you use as a reader and listener when you "receive" others' ideas. As responsible communicators, we must understand what a sound argument is and know how to construct one ourselves. We must also understand what a defective argument is so that we avoid getting sucked in when we shouldn't.

FIGURE **5.2**

The Focused Thinking Pyramid

Source: Adapted from Hellyer, R., Robinson, C., & Sherwood, P. (1998). Study skills for learning power. New York: Houghton Mifflin, 18.

Here is a top-ten list of logical fallacies, or false logic strategies, we can slip into—or others can use against us—if we're not careful. For each of the ten types, read through the example and then see whether you can come up with one of your own.

1. **False cause and effect** (assuming one cause for something when other causes are possible, too)

   I moved back home from my own apartment last month. I've failed every exam I've taken since. Living at home is blowing my GPA!

2. **Personal attack** (reacting to a challenge by attacking the challenger)

   How could anyone believe Mr. Courtney's views on ethics? We all know he's a very poor teacher.

3. **Unwarranted assumption** (taking too much for granted without evidence)

   You say community colleges give women equal opportunities. I say they don't. Reply: It's true. I read it on a website.

4. **Emotional appeal** (appealing to someone's feelings in order to gain acceptance of an argument)

   If you care about all the people hurt in this tragic accident, you'll dig deep into your pockets and send in a donation now.

5. **False authority** (attributing your argument to someone else in a supposed position of power to get you off the hook)

   I'd really like to be able to change your grade, but my Department Chair doesn't like me to do that.

Too often . . . we enjoy the comfort of opinion without the discomfort of thought.

John F. Kennedy, 35th president of the United States (1917–1963)

6. **Hasty conclusion** (jumping to a conclusion when other conclusions are possible)

   I'm sure that guy next to me in class stole my textbook when I wasn't looking. He's too cheap to buy his own.

7. **Straw man** (attempting to "prove" an argument by overstating, exaggerating, or oversimplifying the arguments of the opposing side)

   We should let students have more say in which courses they take. Reply: You actually want students to take any courses they want to? Oh, right, why don't we all just have a free-for-all instead?

8. **Shifting the burden of proof** (shifting the responsibility of proving an assertion to someone else because you have no evidence for what you assert)

   The policy forbidding any alcohol at campus events is working. Reply: No, it's not. Reply back: Oh yeah? Prove it.

9. **Oversimplification/overgeneralization** (reducing a complex issue to something very simple or stereotyping)

   College teachers have it made. They teach a couple classes a week for a few hours, and then they have free time the rest of the week. That's the kind of job I want!

10. **Either/or thinking** (taking only an extreme position on an issue when other positions are possible)

    Either we ban dating between students or we will be facing sexual harassment lawsuits.

II. Problem Solving: The Basic How-To's

When you have to solve a problem, your critical thinking skills should move front and center. Perhaps you need to find a way to earn more money. You run short each month, and the last few days before payday are nerve-racking. What should you do? Use a shotgun approach and try many different strategies at once, or come up with a more precise way to get the best results? See whether the following steps make sense to you and seem like something you might actually do.

© 2014 Cengage Learning

STEP 1: Define the problem. What is the exact nature of the problem you face? Defining the exact nature of the problem is something you must do if you hope to solve it. For example:

> Is it that you don't meter your spending and run out of money long before the next paycheck?

> Is it that you don't have a budget and you spend money randomly?

STEP 2: Brainstorm possible options. List all of the possible solutions you can come up with. For example:

> Pack food from home instead of hitting the fast-food joints so often.

> Stop ordering in pizza four nights a week when you get the munchies at midnight.

- Ask your boss for a raise. You've been doing a good job.
- Look for a job that pays more. Tips at the Pancake House where you work don't really amount to much.
- Capitalize on your particular skills to earn extra money. If you're a whiz at math, you could sign on as a math tutor on campus.

STEP 3: Set criteria to evaluate each option. For example:

- *Distance* is important. Your car isn't very reliable, so it would be good to find a job you can walk or ride your bike to.
- *Good pay* is important. In the past, you've always had low-paying jobs. You need whatever solution you arrive at to be worth your while.
- *Time* is important. You're taking a challenging load of classes, and you need to keep up your grades to keep your scholarship.

STEP 4: Evaluate each option you've proposed. For example:

- Pack food from home. (This is a good idea because you've already paid for that food, regardless of which solution you choose.)
- Stop ordering pizza when the munchies hit at midnight. (This is also a good option because unplanned expenses like this can mount up fast.)
- Ask your family to borrow money. (You'd really like to avoid this option. You don't want to seem like you're trying to take advantage of them.)
- Get a job that pays more. (Unfortunately, your campus is half an hour from the center of town where all the posh restaurants are.)
- Capitalize on your particular skills to earn extra money. (Tutors are paid more than minimum wage, and getting a job on campus would be convenient.)

STEP 5: Choose the best solution. In this case, it looks like getting a job on campus could fit the bill!

66 99

Everyone is entitled to their own opinion, but not their own facts.

Senator Daniel Patrick Moynihan (1927–2003)

66 99

Education is nothing more, nor less, than learning to think!

Peter Facione, professor, administrator, author, consultant, and critical thinking expert

Aspen Commons Apartment Complex Case Study

Great Bluffs Herald

Saturday, September 21, 2013

Start of School + Parties = Recipe for Death

Great Bluffs, Colorado It's that time of year again. The fall semester began last month at Great Bluffs Community College, and again this year, a student died of alcohol poisoning within the first three weeks of classes. Dante Lewis, a resident of an apartment complex near the school, Aspen Commons, was found dead yesterday morning. The body of the collapsed GBCC student was found in a third-floor apartment. An anonymous call to 9-1-1 came in at 6:15 a.m.: "We've got a guy here. We can't wake him, and we know he drank way too much last night." Lewis was pronounced dead on arrival at Great Bluffs General Hospital. The incident represented the second death from alcohol poisoning at Aspen Commons in as many years. Roland Bishop, GBCC's new president, is said to deeply mourn the loss of another new student. "No student should die during his first few weeks of college—what should be one of the most exciting times of his life. It's insane and very, very sad."

The Aspen Commons Apartment Complex has been warned that student parties among underage residents, where alcohol is served, should be discouraged.

President Bishop will convene a cross-college panel of faculty, staff, and students to investigate the incident and decide if any action should be taken by GBCC. Professor Juan Cordova, Sociology Department Chairperson, will head the new committee. A report with specific recommendations to President Bishop is expected by the end of the term. Alcohol is to blame for the deaths of 1,825 college students per year, according to figures from the National Institute on Alcohol Abuse and Alcoholism. About 599,000 students between the ages of 18 and 24 are injured annually while under the influence of alcohol, more than 696,000 are assaulted by another student who has been drinking, and more than 97,000 students are victims of alcohol-related sexual assault or date rape.

The average age of students at Great Bluffs Community College has dropped from 28 to 20 in recent years. Although many community college students live at home, many others live on their own in the community. Because it is within walking distance to GBCC, Aspen Commons is a popular choice. President Bishop's office indicates that it may enter into negotiations with the Colorado Housing Authority and with Clifford Industries, owners of Aspen Commons, about banning alcohol in the complex and requiring tenants to sign a no-alcohol agreement.

After this article appeared in the Great Bluffs Herald, many readers sent letters to the editor on September 22 and 23. Examine the following excerpts.

Trevor Ryan, GBCC Student: "My first few weeks at GBCC have been awesome, and living at Aspen Commons has been totally cool—one of the highlights of my life so far. I'd do it all over again tomorrow. But I didn't want to live at Aspen Commons just for the parties everyone talks about. It's a great place to live. All the students who live there say so."

Carlos Garcia, GBCC Student: "This whole incident has been very hard on me. Dante was my roommate. We've known each other since we were kids, and we moved into an apartment right after we graduated from high school last spring. I still can't believe this happened to him. Yeah, I was drinking at the party where he got totally wasted, too. But I lost track of him when I went to bed around midnight. If I had just stayed around, I'll bet I could have prevented what happened."

Ross Riley, Building Manager, Aspen Commons: "As building manager, I've seen my fair share of parties over the years. Sometimes things get out of control. I get a call in the middle of the night and end up calling the cops. Other residents complain about the noise. But it's not the apartment complex's problem. We just put a roof over people's heads. They make their own decisions about how to live."

Dr. Ruby Pinnell, ER Physician, Great Bluffs General Hospital: "As a doctor, I see all the damage today's young people are doing to themselves. The national study I spearheaded last year found that 31 percent of college students meet the clinical criteria for alcohol abuse, and 6 percent could be diagnosed as being alcohol-dependent. They don't realize that binge drinking could be risking serious damage to their brains now and actually cause increased memory loss later in adulthood. Many college males consume as many as 24 drinks in a row. These are very sad statistics."

Rufus Unser, Aspen Commons resident: "I've lived at Aspen Commons for 12 years now, and I'm just about to move into an assisted living facility because I'm 78 and my health is failing. I'm sick of rowdy parties, loud music late at night, and residents who run up and down the halls. I don't mind all the younger people who live in this complex, but I'd really like to get some sleep once in a while."

Sergeant Rick Fuller, Great Bluffs Police Department: "I've worked in the Great Bluffs Police Department for 15 years now, and I've seen a dramatic rise in the number of alcohol-related violence, crimes, and accidents. GBCC needs to do something. Their students are part of the problem, and they need to assume some responsibility."

Now that you've read the story from the **Great Bluffs Herald** *and the excerpts from letters to the editor, answer the following questions:*

1. What are the facts relating to the death of GBCC student Dante Lewis? How do you know they are facts and not claims?

2. Do you see logical fallacies in any of the letters to the editor of the *Great Bluffs Herald*? If so, which can you identify? What assumptions do the letter writers hold—right or wrong?

STEP 6: Plan how to achieve the best solution. When you talk with your advisor about applying for a job as a math tutor, you discover that you need a letter of recommendation from a math instructor. You e-mail your math instructor and set up a meeting for later in the week. When the letter is ready, you make an appointment to schedule an interview, and so forth.

STEP 7: Implement the solution and evaluate the results. A month or two after you take on the tutoring job, you evaluate whether this solution is really the best one. You may need to request more hours or different days. Or you may find that this job leads to a better one on campus. At any rate, you've used your critical thinking skills to solve a problem, systematically, logically, and effectively.

III. Decision Making: What's Your Style?

The kinds of arguments we're discussing in this chapter lead to decisions, and it's important to make good ones! After you've evaluated an argument, you must often do something about it. Before you know it, you'll be deciding on a major if you haven't already, a career field, a place to live, a romantic partner—you name it.

When you have an important decision to make, your critical thinking skills should kick into action. The more important the decision, the more thoughtful the process of deciding should be. But people make decisions in different ways.

VARK It!

Visual: Using the steps listed in this section, draw a diagram of the problem-solving process.

Problem Solving for Yourself

Try out the seven-step problem-solving model for yourself. Think of a problem you're facing right now, and fill in your ideas for steps 1 through 7. When you're done, ask yourself whether filling in these steps helped you understand the problem and this problem-solving process better.

STEP 1: Define the problem.

STEP 2: Brainstorm possible options.

STEP 3: Set criteria to evaluate each option.

STEP 4: Evaluate each option you've proposed.

STEP 5: Choose the best solution.

STEP 6: Plan how to achieve the best solution.

STEP 7: Implement the solution and evaluate the results.

Alan J. Rowe and Richard O. Mason wrote a book called *Managing with Style* about four basic decision-making styles used by managers. Although you may not be a manager now, think about what your style may be when you do have a position of responsibility. Here are the four styles they describe. See which one sounds as if it might describe you.

©Hemera Technologies/
PhotoObjects.net/Jupiter Images

> **Directive.** This decision-making style emphasizes the here and now. Directives prefer structure and using practical data to make decisions. They look for speed, efficiency, and results, and focus on short-term fixes. Directive decision makers base their decisions on experience, facts, procedures, and rules, and they have energy and drive to get things done. On the downside, because they work quickly, they are sometimes satisfied with simple solutions when something else might work better.

> **Analytical.** This decision-making style emphasizes a logical approach. Analyticals search carefully for the best decision, and they sometimes get hung up with overanalyzing things and take too long to finally make a decision. They are sometimes considered to be impersonal because they may be more interested in the problem than in the people who have it. But they are good at working with data and doing careful analysis.

> **Conceptual.** This decision-making style emphasizes the big picture. Conceptuals are adaptable, insightful, and flexible, and they look for interesting, new solutions. They are sometimes too idealistic, but they take risks and are very creative.

VARK It!

Visual: Draw a graph (pie chart, bar graph, etc.) to represent your preference in using each of these decision-making styles. Which are your strongest and weakest?

VARK It!

Kinesthetic: Form groups, with each person taking one of the decision-making styles, and role-play scenarios to show what they're actually like.

Ian Scott/Shutterstock.com

©Hemera Technologies/
PhotoObjects.net/Jupiter Images

> **Behavioral.** This decision-making style emphasizes people. Behaviorals enjoy people and the social aspects of work. They use their feelings to assess situations, communicate well, and are supportive of others. On the other hand, they are sometimes seen as wishy-washy or are criticized because they can't make hard decisions or can't say no.

Whether you're in college to prepare for a career field or retool for a new one, eventually, you will have to make important decisions on a daily basis. It's useful to begin thinking about your decision-making style now.

IV. Thinking about Your Thinking

One of the most important aspects of critical thinking is that it evaluates itself. As you're solving problems, for example, you're thinking about how you're thinking. You're assessing your progress as you go, analyzing the strengths and weaknesses in your thinking, and perhaps even coming up with better ways to do it. We call that **metacognition**.

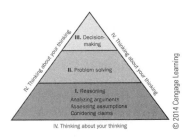

metacognition thinking about your thinking and learning about your learning

Novice or new learners don't stop to evaluate their thinking and make revisions. Expert or experienced learners do. Actually, whenever you're faced with learning something new, metacognition involves three elements. Ultimately, these elements should become the foundation of all your learning experiences so that you improve your metacognitive skills as you go.

> **Before: Develop a plan of action.** Ask yourself what you already know that can help you learn something new. What direction do you want to go in with your thinking? What should be your first task? How much time should you give yourself? Talk through your plan with someone else.

> **During: Monitor your plan.** While you're working, ask yourself how you're doing. Are you staying on track? Are you moving in the right direction? Should you slow down or speed up? What should you do if you don't understand what you're doing? Keep track of what works for you and what doesn't. Assume responsibility for your own thinking and learning.

> **After: Evaluate the plan.** How well did you do? Did you do better than expected or not as well as you expected? What could you have done differently? Can you apply what you just did here to future tasks? Give yourself some feedback.[13]

> And how is education supposed to make me feel smarter?

Homer Simpson, television cartoon character, The Simpsons

Becoming a Better Critical Thinker

Sharpening your critical thinking skills is vital because these skills underlie all the others in your academic toolkit. If you think well, you will be a better writer, a better presenter, a better listener, and a better reader. You will be more likely to engage more fully in your academic tasks because you will question, dig, analyze, and monitor yourself as you learn. Here are some suggestions for improving your skills. As you read them, think about yourself and how you learn.

If you have an apple and I have an apple and we exchange these apples, then you and I will still each have one apple. But if you have an idea and I have an idea and we exchange these ideas, then each of us will have two ideas.

George Bernard Shaw, Irish literary critic, playwright, and essayist, 1925 Nobel Prize for Literature (1856–1950)

1. **Admit when you don't know.** If you don't know enough to think critically about something, admit it, and then find out more. With the volume of information available in today's world, we can't possibly know everything about anything. But the good news is that information is everywhere. All you need to do is read, listen, point, and click to be well informed on many issues.

2. **Realize you have buttons that can be pushed.** We all have issues we're emotional about. That's normal. It's natural to feel strongly about some things, but it's also important to understand the reasons why so that you can tell your views to someone else. And of course, realize that you're not the only one with buttons. Your teacher, best friend, significant other, boss, and everyone else has them, too.

3. **Learn more about the opposition.** Many times, it's more comfortable to avoid what we don't agree with and reinforce what we already believe. But part of being a well-educated person means learning about the history, backgrounds, values, and techniques of people you disagree with so that you can anticipate and deal with their arguments more effectively.

4. **Trust and verify.** During the cold war, President Ronald Reagan liked to quote an old Russian saying to his Soviet counterpart, Mikhail Gorbachev: "Doveryay, no proveryay," or "Trust, but verify." Being a good critical thinker means achieving a balance between blind faith and healthy questioning.

5. **Remember that critical thinking is the foundation of all academic achievement.** There's nothing more important than learning to think critically. In college and in life, the skills discussed in this chapter will make you a better college student, a better citizen, a better employee, a smarter consumer, a better relational partner, and a better lifelong learner.

Creativity: "Thinking outside the ... Book"

Do you believe this statement? *Everyone has creative potential.* It's true. Most of us deny it, however. "Me, creative? Nah!" We're often unaware of the untapped ability we have to think creatively. Try this experiment. Look at the following list of words, and divide the list into two (and only two) different categories, using any rules you create. Take a few moments and see what you come up with.

dog, salad, book, grasshopper, kettle, paper, garbage, candle

Whenever this experiment is tried, people always come up with very creative categories. They may divide the words into things that you buy at a store

> A mind that is stretched to a new idea never returns to its original dimensions.
>
> *Oliver Wendell Holmes, American poet (1809–1894)*

(dog, salad, kettle, paper, candle), things that move on their own (dog, grasshopper), things that have a distinct smell (dog, candle, garbage), words that have two consonants, and so forth. People never say it can't be done; they always *invent* categories. Interesting, isn't it? Our minds are hungry for the stimulation of a creative challenge.

The fact is that intelligence has more to do with coming up with the right answer, and creative thinking has more to do with coming up with more than one right answer. Often we get so focused on the *right* answer that we rush to find it instead of exploring all the possibilities. Creative thinking is thinking outside the box, or in terms of getting an education, perhaps we should call it thinking outside the book. Going beyond the obvious and exploring possibilities are important parts of becoming an educated person. Employers report that many college graduates today have specific skills, but that what they rarely see "is the ability to use the right-hand side of the brain—creativity, working in a team."[14]

In Figure 5.2, we looked at the Focused Thinking Pyramid. Creative thinking is at the top of the pyramid: What if? It goes beyond critical thinking. It is predictive and multidimensional. It asks "What if . . . ?" questions. Here are some interesting ones: "What if everyone were allowed to tell one lie per day?" "What if no one could perceive colors?" "What if colleges didn't exist?" "If you looked up a word like *squallizmotex* in the dictionary, what might it mean?"[15]

According to creativity expert Alan Rowe, our creative intelligence demonstrates itself in four major styles. Each of us has aspects of all four styles of creativity.

> **Intuitive.** This creative style is best described as *resourceful*. If you are an Intuitive, you achieve goals, use common sense, and work to solve problems. You focus on results and rely on past experience to guide your actions. Managers, actors, and politicians are commonly Intuitives.

> **Innovative.** This creative style is best described as *curious*. Innovatives concentrate on problem solving, are organized, and rely on data. They use original approaches, are willing to experiment, and focus on step-by-step inquiry. Scientists, engineers, and inventors typically demonstrate the Innovative creative style.

> **Imaginative.** This creative style is best described as *insightful*. Imaginatives are willing to take risks, have leaps of imagination, and are independent thinkers. They are able to visualize opportunities, are artistic, enjoy writing, and think outside the box. Artists, musicians, writers, and charismatic leaders are often Imaginatives.

VARK It!

Read/Write: Write a one-sentence summary of each creativity style. Then, add a few sentences to the style that sounds most like you, and tell why.

> **Inspirational.** This creative style is best described as *visionary*. Inspirationals respond to societal needs, willingly give of themselves, and have the courage of their convictions. They focus on social change and the giving of themselves toward achieving it. They are often educators, motivational leaders, and writers.[16]

Which do you think is your predominant style? Think about how you can make the best use of your natural style. How will your creativity affect the major or *career* you choose? Most people have more than one creative style. Remember that motivation, not just intelligence, is the key to creativity. You must be willing to tap your creative potential and challenge yourself to show it.[17] According to *New York Times* best-seller, *A Whole New Mind*, "The future belongs to a very different kind of person with a very different kind of mind—creators and empathizers, pattern recognizers, and meaning makers. These people—artists, inventors, designers, storytellers, caregivers, consolers, big picture thinkers—will now reap society's richest rewards and share its greatest joys." (p. 1)

Ten Ways to Become a More Creative Thinker

Becoming a more creative thinker may mean you need to accept your creativity and cultivate it. Consider these suggestions on how to think more creatively.

FIGURE 5.3

The Pillow Method

Position 1—I'm right and you're wrong.

Position 2—You're right and I'm wrong.

Position 3—We're both right.

Position 4—We're both wrong.

1. **Find new eyes.** Find a new perspective on old issues. Here's an interesting example. Years ago, a group of Japanese schoolchildren came up with a new way to solve conflicts and build empathy for others' positions, called the Pillow Method. Figure 5.3 is an adaptation of it, based on the fact that a pillow has four sides and a middle, just like most problems. The middle, or *mu,* is the Zen expression for "it doesn't really matter." There is truth in all four positions. Try it: take a conflict you're having difficulty with at the moment, and write down all four sides and a middle.[18]

2. **Accept your creativity.** Many mindsets block creative thinking: "It can't be done!" "I'm just not the creative type." "I might look stupid!" Many people don't see themselves as creative. This perception can become a major stumbling block. If creativity isn't part of your self-image, you may need to change your image. Everyone has creative potential. You may just have to learn how to tap into yours.

3. **Make your thoughts visible.** For many of us, things become clear when we can see them, either in our mind's eye or displayed for us. Even Einstein, a scientist and mathematician, had a very visual mind. Sometimes if we write something down or sketch something out, we generate a new approach without really trying.

4. **Generate lots of ideas.** Thomas Edison held 1,093 patents, still the record. He gave himself idea goals. The rule he set for himself was that he had to come up with a major invention every six months and a minor invention every ten days.

5. **Don't overcomplexify.** In hindsight, many of the most creative discoveries are embarrassingly simple. Biologist Thomas Huxley said, after reading

> **A hunch is creativity trying to tell you something.**
>
> *Frank Capra, Italian American film director (1897–1991)*

Darwin's explanation of evolution: "How extremely stupid not to have thought of that!" But sometimes the most simple solution is the best one.[19]

6. **Capitalize on your mistakes.** Remember that Thomas Edison tried anything he could think of for a filament for the incandescent lamp, including a whisker from his best friend's beard. All in all, he tried about 1,800 things before finding the right one. Afterward he said, "I've gained a lot of knowledge—I now know a thousand things that won't work."[20]

7. **Let it flow.** Mihaly Csikszentmihalyi, the author of *Flow: The Psychology of Optimal Experience* and many other books on creativity, discovered something interesting. For his doctoral thesis, he studied artists by taking pictures of them painting every three minutes. He was struck by how engaged they were in their work, so engaged that they seemed to forget everything around them. He began studying other "experts": rock climbers, chess players, dancers, musicians, surgeons. Regardless of the activity, these people forgot the time, themselves, and their problems. What did the activities have in common? Clear, high goals and immediate feedback. Athletes call it being in the zone. The zone is described as the ultimate human experience, where mind and body are united in purpose. Csikszentmihalyi's suggestions for achieving flow are these: Pick an enjoyable activity that is at or slightly above your ability level, screen out distractions, focus all your senses and emotions, and look for regular feedback on how you're doing.[21]

> **I can't understand why people are frightened by new ideas. I'm frightened by the old ones.**
>
> *John Cage, American composer (1912–1992)*

8. **Bounce ideas off others.** One good way to become more creative is to use your family or friends as sounding boards. Sometimes just saying something out loud helps you understand more about it. Each person who provides a critique will give you a new perspective, possibly worth considering.

9. **Stop searching for the "right" answer.** This advice doesn't pertain to your upcoming math exam. But it does to apply to situations in which there are many ways to solve a problem. There may be more than one acceptable solution. A fear of making mistakes can hold you back.

10. **Detach your self-concept.** For most of us, creativity is often linked to self-concept. An idea is your brainchild, and you want it to win people over. You've invested part of yourself in giving birth to it. But there's nothing like self-criticism to shut down your creative juices. Your idea may not succeed on its own, but it may feed into someone else's idea and improve it. Or an idea you have about this problem may inform the next problem that challenges you. In the end, in addition to finding a workable solution, what's important is engaging in the creative process with others.

CONTROL: *YOUR TOUGHEST CLASS*

Look over the "Ten Ways to Become a More Creative Thinker" in this chapter and choose one of these items to write about. Which piece of advice will be most useful to you? Is there a way you can use your natural creativity to improve your chances in your toughest class? For example, item 6 might be a good idea to use in your math class. When you get an exam back, look it over, analyze your mistakes, and then come up with creative new ideas to improve your score next time—now that you know what didn't work last time. Item 10 might be something to work on if you always fear the essays you write for your composition class won't measure up.

1. Find new eyes.

2. Accept your creativity.

3. Make your thoughts visible.

4. Generate lots of ideas.

5. Don't overcomplexify.

6. Capitalize on your mistakes.

7. Let it flow.

8. Bounce ideas off others.

9. Stop searching for the right answer.

10. Detach your self-concept.

Which of the ten items listed above will you try, and in which of your current classes? (If you're only enrolled in one class, provide an example for that one.)

_____

_____

_____

CURIOSITY: *ARE YOU TALENTED?*

Who me? Creative? Talented? Gifted? Nah! Some people say: "I'm not creative. I have no talent. I'm just an ordinary guy." Other people settle for good instead of reaching for great: "I'm pretty good. I'm good enough. I have enough to get by." What does it take to become a truly great thinker, a great creator, a great athlete, a great musician, a great anything? According to Daniel Coyle, best-selling author of the acclaimed book, *The Talent Code*, talent is something you grow into, not something you're born with. In his research, Coyle discovered that talent is grown by a combination of three principles:

1. **Deep Practice:** Deep practice isn't just practicing regularly or even practicing a great deal, it's practicing a certain way: very slowly and deliberately. That's how your brain gains mastery. Deep practice is also based on stops and starts, mistakes, analyzing what went wrong, and trying over and over again until you can do it perfectly. The trick, Coyle says, is to reach just beyond your grasp.

2. **Ignition:** Any kind of practice, let alone deep practice, would be torture unless you really cared. Something or somebody must light a spark in you and ignite the fire that fuels your learning. You must be motivated from within to be great. Only then, with this burst of magnetic attraction to a skill, are you willing to work toward greatness.

3. **Master Coaching:** To become truly great, it takes an older, wiser, and more experienced teacher, someone who can show you things you don't see in yourself and help you reach your potential. To become truly excellent, someone must show you precisely how.

So the next time someone asks you whether you're creative, talented, or gifted, you may want to explore what it would take before immediately answering. Talent, according to Daniel Coyle, is something that can be grown depending on how much you want it and how hard you're willing to work to get it.

Think about your talents, or talents you'd like to have. What can you do to hone your current talents, or develop new talents? How do the three principles listed above apply to you and your talent?

CAREER OUTLOOK: *EXAMINE YOUR THINKING*

Consider a job that you've held in the past. If someone asked you to come up with five adjectives that describe the most memorable boss you've ever had, what words would come to you? Words like *encouraging, smart, visionary, responsive, or supportive*—or words like *hasty, unfair, mean, hypocritical, or irrational*? What do all the words you think of have in common? Were they mainly *positive* or *negative*?

When asked this question, most people go in one direction: either entirely positive or negative. No one ever says, "What I really love about my boss is his critical nature. He doesn't miss a single mistake I make."[22] It's natural to lean one way or the other; that's one reason why critical thinking skills are a useful tool in the workplace. They can help you adjust your thinking appropriately and keep you from getting locked into particular patterns, especially negative ones.

In the workplace, the most desirable kind of thinking is "realistic optimism." It's not blind faith or false hope; it's looking for the best in things and then working to make them happen. It's accepting what's going on around you, but at the same time admitting what needs to be changed. It's about resilience, "getting back on the horse," and trotting on. It's a productive pattern of thinking.[23]

If "realistic optimism" sounds like an oxymoron to you, have faith! Remember the words of the environmentalist and founder of Patagonia, the well-known outdoor gear company: "There's no difference between a pessimist who says, 'Oh, it's hopeless, so don't bother doing anything,' and an optimist who says, 'Don't bother doing anything, it's going to turn out fine anyway.' Either way, nothing happens." It's your thinking and your career, and you're in the driver's seat. You want to do things, go places, and make things happen. That's what it's all about.

How does this section apply to your current or a recent job? Can you think of an example of how "realistic optimism" could help you in a real-life scenario from your work experience?

How much did you learn? At the beginning of this chapter, you filled out a "Readiness Check" that asked how you thought this chapter would relate to you and how you would relate to it. Now, fill out this "Reality Check" to find out.

1. What's the difference between thinking and critical thinking?

2. Define *metacognition* in your own words.

3. Identify three specific types of faulty reasoning.

4. What's the difference between critical thinking and creative thinking?

5. How long did it take? _____ hours _____ minutes. Before you began this chapter, you were asked to predict how long it would take you to complete it (total time, even if you read it in more than one sitting). Was your estimate on target, or will you revise it for the next chapter you'll read?_____

step 3 INSIGHT *Now* What Do You Think?

At the beginning of this chapter, Desiree Moore, a frustrated student, faced a challenge. Now, after reading this chapter, would you respond differently to any of the questions you answered about the "FOCUS Challenge Case"? Using what you learned in the chapter, write a paragraph ending to Desiree's case study. What are some of the possible outcomes for Desiree?

step 4 ACTION Your Plans for Change

1. What's the most important thing you learned in reading this chapter? Why did it have an impact on you?

2. What will you change about the way you try to learn in your classes or perform on the job as a result of reading it?

© Larry Harwood Photography. Property of Cengage Learning.

chapter 6 Learning Online

How this chapter relates to YOU

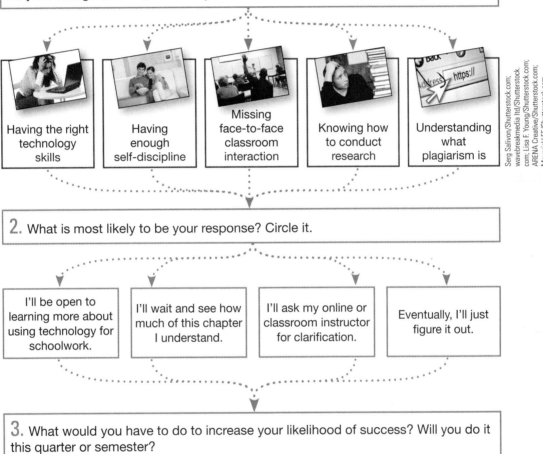

1. When it comes to online learning, using technology, and doing research for your college classes, what are you most concerned about, if anything?

| Having the right technology skills | Having enough self-discipline | Missing face-to-face classroom interaction | Knowing how to conduct research | Understanding what plagiarism is |

Serg Salivon/Shutterstock.com; wavebreakmedia ltd/Shutterstock.com; Lisa F. Young/Shutterstock.com; ARENA Creative/Shutterstock.com; MaverickLEE/Shutterstock.com

2. What is most likely to be your response? Circle it.

| I'll be open to learning more about using technology for schoolwork. | I'll wait and see how much of this chapter I understand. | I'll ask my online or classroom instructor for clarification. | Eventually, I'll just figure it out. |

3. What would you have to do to increase your likelihood of success? Will you do it this quarter or semester?

Example: Increase my self-discipline to be successful at online tasks. Yes!

How YOU will relate to this chapter

What are you most interested in learning about? Put checkmarks by those topics.

☐ How to develop useful strategies for online classes

☐ How to use technology to become more academically successful

☐ How to cultivate your research skills

☐ What information literacy skills are and why they're important

☐ What plagiarism is and how to avoid it

• How motivated are you to learn more about getting the right start in college? (5 = high, 1 = low) ____

• How ready are you to read now? ____ (If something is in your way, take care of it if you can, zero in and focus.)

• How long do you think it will take you to complete this chapter? If you start and stop, keep track of your overall time.

____ hour(s) ____ minutes

DARIO JONES

CLM/Shutterstock.com

Robert Kyllo/Shutterstock.com

Ben Mitchell/Shutterstock.com

Jack Haefner/Shutterstock.com

Ever since grade school, Dario Jones had been called a geek. It was a label he hated, but, honestly, most people probably thought of him that way. As a kid, Dario lived for computer games. He played them nearly every waking hour. In high school, he'd shower in record time, throw on whatever clean clothes he could find, and use any spare minutes for computer games. When he got home, he'd log right back on again. His Dad tried threatening him: "You'll lose your eyesight and flunk out of school." Once when he was younger, he faked a sore throat and played World of Warcraft at home for a week while his parents were at work. As he got older, his Dad warned: "You'll never get a date." But Dario wasn't worried. Online relationships were enough. Real-life relationships were too much trouble. After high school, he joined the Army, and now that he was finally back from 18 months in Afghanistan, his cyber life was much more exciting than ever. Dario spent more time—even sacrificing precious hours of sleep—surfing the Internet, envisioning how he could improve websites, and grooming his Facebook page than he spent talking to any living being.

Evgeny Karandaev/
Shutterstock.com

Then one day the obvious truth dawned on him. Now that he was a civilian, he was going to have to get a job—plain and simple. He had joined the Army because he really didn't know what he wanted to do next, and he figured he'd gain some skills there. But now that he was home, he wondered how those skills would translate into a different career—and whether he had the right skills.

Eventually, Dario made a decision. He would use his G.I. benefits and go to college. Because he was such a technology fan, maybe being a web designer would be a good field for him. And as he Googled opportunities, he found that he could get an entire degree online! What could be more perfect than that? Sitting in real classrooms with all those college kids didn't appeal to him at all. Besides, now that he was back from some pretty intense experiences while deployed, fighting for parking spots and being in crowded classrooms would just add to his stress, and that was something he didn't need. The images of the past 18 months were still very much alive in his memory. Besides, online courses had to be easier than real classes, and that one thing sealed the deal.

© Larry Harwood Photography. Property of Cengage

Copyright © Mike Margol / Photo Edit

But Dario quickly discovered that his considerable tech skills might not be enough. Besides that, all three classes had major assignments that would require a serious time commitment. The first week, he stayed up late, listening to online lectures, downloading handouts, and posting responses on the discussion board. Then before he knew it, he got an e-mail from the instructor in his toughest class, "Fundamentals of Internet Business," reminding him that he needed to post two of his own responses to her questions and respond to two classmates' comments each week. "Your comments need to be substantive, Dario, not just quick entries like, 'I really liked the online lecture for Chapter 6' or 'Good point, Keisha.' And you need to keep up," she wrote. "I didn't hear from you for two weeks." *That kind of criticism is a definite turn-off,* Dario thought to himself. If he hadn't already paid tuition, he would have been tempted to drop out of the course entirely.

The worst part was that his toughest class required a research paper. The assigned topic was Globalization and Internet Commerce. Even though he had always considered himself to be a technology expert, frankly, he didn't know where to start. *Step one,* Dario thought to himself, *is to Google.* He always Googled everything: the directions to a new Mexican restaurant—his favorite food—or some little-known fact that he wondered about, like how many Chihuahuas were sold in the United States last year. (He had just bought one.) But when he Googled "Internet Commerce," he got 22 million hits. *Better regroup,* he advised himself.

But how? Should he go to a real library or try to do his research online in the comfort of his own apartment? Physically going to a library seemed unnecessary when so much information was available online. Then he had a flash of inspiration: Wikipedia. He found a page on "Electronic Commerce." At least that was a start—that is, until he looked at his instructor's handout on the assignment. Students were discouraged from using Wikipedia as a primary research source. The handout said, "Information literacy is required." He got another idea: He'd close Wikipedia and go back to Googling. This time he'd try "Electronic Commerce." *Ah, only 7 million hits this time.* He was on a roll. He plugged in "E-Commerce," "E-Business," and "Globalization." He tried "Global Issues," but before he knew it, he found himself knee-deep in articles about "Global Warming." He was so far afield now that he couldn't find his way back to his topic. Should he shut everything down and start over or just give up?

At the last minute, Dario panicked. He found a few useful things online, and cut and pasted from the Internet until he'd filled five pages. At least he had something to turn in. He wondered if this was the way to do research and whether he'd broken any rules. *Well, I can always go back into the military,* he thought to himself. But to be honest, he really wanted to make an entirely new life for himself as a civilian.

Yuri Samsonov/Shutterstock.com

Luciana Bueno/Shutterstock.com

Christopher John Coudriet/Shutterstock.com

© Cengage Learning

Fundamentals of Internet Busir
CS 112

Research Paper Guideline

TOPIC: Globalization and Internet Commerce

For this assignment you will write a 10 page research paper ir relationship between globalization and Internet commerce. Y focus on how globalization has affected Internet commerce, b relationship may be a two-way street. In other words, look a commerce has changed the pace of globalization in the 21st ce

POTENTIAL AREAS OF RESEARCH FOCUS:

- What is Globalization?
- Free Trade
- tional Corporations

© Cengage Learning

Wikipedia Foundation, Inc

W http://en.wikipedia.org/wiki/Electronic_commerce

File Edit View Favorites Tools Help

W Electronic commerce - Wikipedia, the free encyclopedia

Help us provide free content to the world by donating today!

article | discussion | edit this page | history

Electronic commerce

From Wikipedia, the free encyclopedia

WIKIPEDIA
The Free Encyclopedia

Electronic Commerce, commonly known as (electronic marketing) e-commerce or eCo consists of the buying and selling of products or services over electronic systems such as other computer networks. The amount of trade conducted electronically has grown extrao

Fundamentals of Internet Business
CS 112

Instructor: Dr. Greg Otis
Office: Hansford Hall 230
Office Hours: T, W 2:00-4:00 PM

Description:

e of research tools
ay use any one of

Web Design
Certific

Learn How to E
Website Wi⁴

1. In your view, is Dario addicted to technology? Can being too dependent on technology be a problem? Why?

2. Do you have anything in common with Dario? For example, do you think (or have you found) that online classes are easier or harder than face-to-face courses? Why?

3. The instructor's assignment required "information literacy." What is information literacy? Dario was tech-savvy, but did he have the right skills? Why or why not?

4. Did Dario plagiarize his paper—or did he simply find the sources he needed and use them? Give the reasons behind your answer.

Taking Online Classes: E-Learning versus C-Learning

What do an American soldier just back from Afghanistan, a single mother of twin toddlers in California, and a victim of cerebral palsy in New York have in common? All three are taking the same online course in psychology. Instead of c-learning (traditionally, in the **c**lassroom), they're engaging in ***distance education*** or e-learning (**e**lectronically, online). E-learning is one kind of technology you may well run into during your time in college.

Hybrid, or blended, courses are part online and part on-ground in varying proportions.

Of course, most of your college courses are hybrids, or blended, courses: they each have an online component and a classroom component. You e-mail your professor, use software to track your progress, upload assignments and download handouts, but you still go to a physical classroom with classmates once or twice a term, or perhaps even every week. That's why they're called hybrid (like cars: part electricity and part gasoline) or blended (when mediated and face-to-face learning are meshed) classes. If you haven't already, chances are you'll be engaged in distance learning in a totally online environment for at least one of your college classes. In fact, 65 percent of college students whose institutions offer online courses have already taken at least one.[1] Distance education, as totally online classes are sometimes called, is gaining momentum fast at community colleges, and the demand for these courses hasn't peaked yet.[2]

What are the differences between e-learning and c-learning? E-learning is sometimes defined as structured learning that takes place without a teacher at the front of the room. If you're an independent, self-motivated learner, e-learning can be a great way to learn, because *you* are in control.

> *You control when you learn.* Instead of that dreaded 8:00 A.M. class—the only section that's open when you register—you can schedule your e-learning when it's

> It was not so very long ago that people thought that semiconductors were part-time orchestra leaders and microchips were very small snack foods.
>
> *Geraldine Ferraro, Democratic politician, 1935–2011*

© Stockbyte/Getty Images

convenient for you. If you want to do your coursework at midnight in your pajamas, who's to know?

> *You control how you learn.* If you are an introvert, e-learning may work well for you. You can work thoughtfully online and take all the time you need to reflect. If you are an extravert, however, you may become frustrated by the lack of warm bodies around. Jumping into threaded discussions and chatting online may satisfy some of those needs, but you may miss real people sitting next to you. If you're a kinesthetic learner, the keyboard action may suit you well. Because you're working independently, you can do whatever you need to do to accommodate your own learning style.

> *You control how fast you learn.* You know for a fact that students learn at different rates. With e-learning, you don't have to feel you're slowing down the class if you continue a line of questioning or worry about getting left in the dust if everyone else is way ahead of you.

E-learning can be a very effective way to learn, but it does require some adjustments. Here are some suggestions for making the best of your online learning opportunities:

1. **Work hard.** Many students think that fully online courses will be easier than going to class. After all, you won't have to shower, get dressed, drive through traffic, and cruise the campus for 15 minutes to find a parking spot. These factors, in and of themselves, should be big time savers. Unless your class requires a webcam (to record yourself for an online public speaking class, for example), you're virtually invisible. But think about it this way: in an online course, you will have to do many of the things that your instructor normally does for you. In a classroom, she may simply walk around and pass out handouts. Online, you'll have to locate them on the course website, download them, and print them out yourself. You'll need to read everything carefully, both the items posted on the course management shell itself (like the course calendar, syllabus, reminder messages, instructions for each assignment) and every document you download. Instead of taking a seat in the classroom to listen to your professor lecture at the front of the room, you will have to get the information yourself by downloading lecture notes, PowerPoint slides, or videos of your instructors' lectures. Some studies show that students work harder and longer online. The belief that online courses are easier is a myth.

2. **Keep up.** Even though you may be "invisible" in online courses, you can't "hide." You'll likely have to keep up by posting regularly to the class blog or online discussion board and comment on your classmates' posts every week. Dario from this chapter's Challenge case received an e-mail from his instructor, asking where he was. If you decide to "take a vacation" in the middle of your online course, your instructor may inquire about your whereabouts, too. Just as you'd do for a face-to-face class, consider setting aside a specific time each week for your online course, like Tuesday and Thursday afternoons, and commit to reserving that time for online coursework.

3. **Get advice from other online students.** The first time you take an online course, ask a friend or classmate who has experience with this type of course for advice. That person may save your hours of online wandering

with a few simple tips. Besides finding out how to navigate the course online, ask what student services are available online, like advising, tutoring, financial aid, enrollment, and tuition payments.

4. **Communicate your needs to your instructor.** If this is your first online course, ask your instructor for a general assessment of how much time he expects you to set aside each week. Think about the three hours or so you usually spend per week in a face-to-face class or lab, and use that as a rule of thumb. (Of course, specifics depend on what else you have going on and your individual learning style preferences. And when you begin to see the grades you earn on the assignments you turn in, you may decide to invest more time on your own.) Remember, too, that your instructor won't be able to see your "huh?" looks when you don't understand something. Take direct action by e-mailing her, for example, instead of hiding behind your computer screen and hoping for the best. "The best" usually doesn't come to you; you'll have to work for it. On the other hand, before you fire off a quick question, re-read the assignment. It may be that you just missed something simple, and your question is actually unnecessary.

5. **Stay in touch with other students in the course.** Rather than isolating yourself, which is a mistake, use e-mail to communicate with your cyber classmates to build an online learning community. They may be able to clarify an assignment or coach you through a tough spot.

learning community group of students who help one another learn.

6. **Take notes.** When you're sitting through an in-class lecture, you handwrite notes to review later. Likewise, if you're reading lecture notes online, open a Word document and switch back and forth for your own note-taking purposes. Or open an e-tool, like evernote.com, which can work well for note taking.

7. **Keep your antivirus program up to date.** When you upload assignment files, you run the risk of infecting your instructor's computer with whatever viruses your computer may have. Make sure your antivirus software is up to date!

8. **Create a productive learning environment.** Because you'll most likely do your e-learning at home, make sure the environment is right for learning. If your computer is next to the TV or your kids are acting up to get attention, move to another location that's calm, properly lit, and quiet.

9. **Use each login session as an opportunity to review.** Begin each online session by reviewing what you did or how much progress you made last time. Physically logging on can become a signal to take stock before moving forward with new course material.

10. **Organize, organize, organize!** In your face-to-face classes, you can keep courses separate in your mind by remembering where the different classrooms are located, for example, and who your classmates and teachers are. By contrast, in online courses you usually sit down in front of your same computer, and you might never even meet your classmates or teacher. You'll have to find ways to separate and organize materials for each class either physically by using hard copy files or electronically by using folders on your computer or thumb drive.

Any occurrence requiring undivided attention will be accompanied by a compelling distraction.

Robert Bloch, American fiction writer, (1917–1994)

11. **Call on your time management skills.** Create a "Term-on-a-Page" master calendar, mark the due dates for each class, and review it at the beginning of every week. If your e-course is self-paced, you'll need to plan ahead, schedule due dates, and above all discipline yourself to make continual progress. For many students, this very thing is the biggest challenge of online courses. The instructor isn't there with you, insisting that you turn in assignments. If you're sharing a computer with other family members, you'll need to create a master schedule of who can use the computer when. Remember that you may need to be online at particular times to engage in class chats or discussions.

12. **Have a back-up plan.** Technology crashes from time to time, and system **platforms** go down, sometimes just when you need them. Get to know your campus tech support staff, and don't hesitate to contact them in an emergency. Work ahead, so that you don't fall behind if the dreaded "blue screen" suddenly appears, signaling a tech failure. Watch for campus emails about system down time for scheduled upgrades, and work around it. In other words, take responsibility. If your paper is late because you left your thumb drive in the car, and your car is at your sister's house, expect to have points deducted. Most online instructors abide by syllabus rules, and they expect you to do the same.[3]

> **platform** the course management system (CMS) your campus uses, like Blackboard or Moodle, sometimes with a title for your school, like GBCConline.

EXERCISE 6.1

A Day in the Life of an Online Student

You wake up and look out the window. It's a beautiful day, and—lucky you—it's your day off from work! While having your morning coffee, you log on to Facebook. You see a few new posts on your wall and some new pictures from last weekend. You check your e-mail and find a tempting new Groupon, a few e-mails from friends, and an e-mail from the instructor of your online class. Oh no, you think. I haven't done anything for my online class in a while, and there's a big assignment due tomorrow! With a sigh you glance out the window one more time. It looks like you won't be able to spend the day relaxing outside like you thought.

Assume this is what your day looks like. For each entry in your hypothetical "day timer," look at the obstacles that may get in your way, and describe how you'll address them.

8:00 A.M.

You pour yourself another cup of coffee and sit down to work on your online course, but you start to wander, electronically. Maybe you should see how many of your friends "like" the new photos you uploaded to your Facebook page. Before you know it, an hour and a half has gone by and you get up to get a snack.

SOLUTION:

_____

_____

10:00 A.M.

You successfully get yourself back on task, but you've hit another snag. You have the syllabus somewhere, and you have lots of questions about the assignment. Your instructor gave you her contact info, but you can't afford to wait very long for a response.

SOLUTION:

_____

_____

(Continued)

10:30 A.M.

Now that you have clarification on the assignment, you dig into your work. You need to find four different sources for your research, but you're not having much luck. You try one Google search after another, but the websites don't seem to have what you're looking for.

SOLUTION:

_____

_____

11:00 A.M.

You've finally located some reliable and useful resources for your assignment. As you continue to work, you find yourself copying and pasting a useful word here and there into your paper. Pretty soon, you're clicking and dragging phrases, then sentences into your assignment. Am I plagiarizing? you wonder.

SOLUTION:

_____

_____

12:00 P.M.

You're working hard, finding good resources, and using them ethically. Your phone rings. It's one of your friends, inviting you to lunch and a movie this afternoon. You glance at your watch. You've been working on this project for a couple of hours now; haven't you earned a little break?

SOLUTION:

_____

_____

7:00 P.M.

Looking back on the day, you've accomplished a lot. You've coped with understanding the assignment clearly, finding good resources and using them well, and managing your time. You're pretty happy with your work, but you wish there was a way to get some feedback on the assignment before you email it to your instructor.

SOLUTION:

_____

_____

11:00 P.M.

Turn in for the night. Tomorrow is a new "Day in the Life of an Online Student."

Technology Skills: Wireless, Windowed, Webbed, and Wikied

Ah, technology . . . Does it make our lives simpler or more complicated? Like Dario, are you pulled into games like World of Warcraft? Do you live to text? Do you run, not walk, to any nearby computer to check your Facebook account? Or, on the other hand, do you hate the thought of facing your e-mail after you haven't had access for awhile? Did you find yourself answering "yes" to any of these questions—or maybe answering "yes" to all of them?

Many of us have a love–hate relationship with technology: We love the convenience but hate the dependence. But in college, your techno-skills will be another key to your success. You'll need to know things like how to produce an essay in Microsoft Word, how to give a PowerPoint presentation, and how to use course management systems like Blackboard. "Whoa! Wait a minute," you say. "I'm no expert at all of that!" You don't have to be an expert, but you do need to know the basics and be willing to learn more. Dario considered himself to be a technology expert, but his expertise was more about *entertainment* than *education*. In college, you'll be using technology to enhance your education.

Your community college may have invited you to enroll with a Twitter or Facebook invitation. Your school will provide you with an e-mail account and send you official college documents, like your tuition bill and weather alerts, over e-mail. You will take entire courses or parts of courses online so that you can learn on your own time at your own pace. Many of your instructors will use course management systems, YouTube clips, streaming video, and websites in the classroom to increase your learning. (And the good news is that many college students say it helps.[4]) So the time to start building your skills is now! Just how useful is the Internet to college students? The answer is that just like anything else, the Internet has pros and cons.

The Internet: The Good, the Bad, and the Ugly

The Good Students who enter college right after high school are the leading consumers of digital technology in the United States.[5] In one study, 79 per cent of college students reported that the Internet has had a positive impact on their college academic experience.[6] For many of us, the Internet is how we get our news, our research, our entertainment, and our communication. When it comes to all the potential benefits of the Internet, think about advantages like these:

> **Currency.** While some of the information posted on the Internet isn't up to date, much of it is current. This is especially important during a crisis or a national emergency, for example, when it's important to get news fast. Reports, articles, and studies that might take months to publish in books or articles are available on the web as soon as they're written.

currency timely

> **Availability.** The Internet never sleeps. If you can't sleep at 2:00 A.M., the Internet can keep you company. It can be a good friend to have. Unlike your real instructor, who teaches other classes besides yours and attends marathon meetings, Professor Google is always in. For the most part, you can check your e-mail or log onto the Internet from anywhere, any time.

> **Scope.** You can find out virtually anything you want to know on the Internet, from the recipe for the world's best chocolate chip cookie to medical advice on everything from Athlete's Foot to Zits. (Of course, real human beings are usually a better option for serious questions.)

scope range, capacity

> **Interactivity.** Unlike other media, the Internet lets you talk back. You can write a letter to the editor of a newspaper and wait for a reply, or you can push buttons on your phone in response to an endless list of menu questions ("If you want directions in English, press 1 . . .") and finally get to a real-live human being. But the Internet lets you communicate instantly and constantly. You can instant message to your heart's content, if you want to; add to your Facebook page daily; or edit a Wikipedia entry whenever you like.

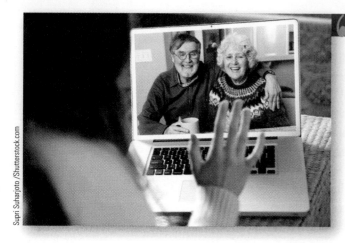

Supri Suharjoto /Shutterstock.com

> Technology is nothing. What's important is that you have a faith in people, that they're basically good and smart, and if you give them tools, they'll do wonderful things with them.

> *Steve Jobs, founder of Apple Computer*
> *(1955–2011)*

> **Affordability.** The number of Internet users worldwide now tops 2 billion; 273 million Americans are on the Net today.[7] For most of us, when it comes to the Internet, the price is right. After you buy a computer and pay a monthly access fee, you get a great deal for your money.

The Bad Too much of a good thing—anything—can be bad. When something becomes that central to our lives, it carries risks. Here are some Internet dangers worth thinking about:

> **Inaccuracy.** Often we take information presented to us at face value, without questioning it. But on many Internet sites, the responsibility for checking the accuracy of the information presented there is yours. Bob's Statistics Home Page and the U.S. Census Bureau's website are not equally valid. Not everything published online is true or right.

> **Laziness.** It's easy to allow the convenience of the Internet to make us lazy. Why go through the hassle of cooking dinner when you can just stop for a burger on the way home? The same thing applies to the Internet. Why not just do what Dario did and find information somebody else has already posted on the Internet, and use it? What's wrong with that? For one thing, if you don't give the rightful author credit, that's plagiarism, which can give you a zero on an assignment or even cause you to fail a course. But another thing worth considering is that the *how* of learning is as important as the *what*. If all you ever did was cut, paste, and download, you wouldn't learn how to do research yourself. College helps you learn skills you will need later—critical thinking, research, and writing skills, for example—in your career. You may never have to give your boss a five-page paper on the humor of Mark Twain—as you might your literature instructor—but you may need to write a five-page report on your customers' buying trends over the last six months.

> **Overdependence.** A related problem with anything that's easy and convenient is that we can start depending on it too much. National studies report that many of us lack basic knowledge. We can't name the Chief Justice of the Supreme Court or the President of Pakistan. Without even realizing it, we may think: Why bother learning a bunch of facts when you can just check quickly online? Are we so dependent on the Internet that we're relying on it for information we should learn or know?[8]

VARK It!

Visual: Monitor the time you spend online for one day. Draw a pie chart showing the time you spent online and doing other things (school, work, TV, etc). Do the results surprise you?

VARK It!

Kinesthetic: Find the browsing history on your web browser. How many of the websites are time-wasters and how many were used for work or school?

> **For a list of all the ways technology has failed to improve the quality of life, please press three.**
>
> *Alice Kahn, technology author*

The Ugly The Internet can be used in foul ways. Spam, viruses, spyware, and phishing cost American consumers billions of dollars in damage last year, affecting 40 percent of U.S. households.[9] Take a look at one student's social networking page in Figure 6.1 to see whether you can guess where things are headed.

Like the hypothetical Victoria Tymmyns (or her online name, VicTym) featured in Figure 6.1, some students publish inappropriate, confidential, and potentially dangerous information on their social media pages. Victoria has posted her address, phone numbers, and moment-by-moment location. Look at the final entries on her page to find out what potential threat she may be facing. Aside from the risk of serious harm, other types of "danger" can result from bad judgment, too. What some students post just for fun can later cost them a job opportunity. If your webpage has provocative photos of you or descriptions of rowdy weekend activities that you wouldn't want your grandmother to see, remove them! (Employers regularly check these sources for insider information on applicants.) "Living out loud," as social networking is sometimes called, requires constant vigilance so that the details of your life aren't on display. Some recent research indicates that younger users are more sensitive to keeping things offline than older users.[10] To avoid "social insecurity," keep these five useful suggestions in mind:

1. Use a password with at least eight letters and numbers, like FO34$&CuS.

2. Don't include your full birth date. Identity thieves can use this information.

3. Take advantage of privacy controls. Use the options provided to you, like choosing the "Friends Only" option. Be sure not to check the box for "Public Search Results." Search engines can find your Facebook profile on and off Facebook if you do.

4. You wouldn't put a "No One's Home" sign on your door, so don't post it as your status.

5. Don't post your child's name in a caption. If someone else does, remove it.[11]

What does all of this have to do with you? Everything! It's important to remember that the Internet itself is neutral. It can be used constructively or destructively, based on the choices you make. It can be an exciting, invigorating, essential part of your college experience. Use it wisely!

ISpy.com   GBCC

View More Photos of Me

Status   edit

Doin' shots at Annie Oakley's!

RMSU Friends

425 friends at GBCC See All

Seymore Bonz   N.O. Body

Friends in Other Networks

Cal (12)
UF (40)
CMU (6)
KSCC (7)
GBCC (425)

Basic Info [edit]
Name:	Victoria Tymmyns
Looking For:	A Good Time
Residence:	456 Pine Valley
Birthday:	June 12, 1990

Contact Info [edit]
Email:	VicTym@gbcc.edu
AIM Screenname	VicTym
Mobile:	719.111.1112
Current Address:	123 Fake St.
	Great Bluffs, CO 80900

Personal Info [edit]
Activities:	Drinkin' at "Annie Oakley's" every Fri. night.
	Karaoke at "All That Jazz" every Sat. night.
Favorite Music:	Black Flag, NIN, DK, the Clash
Favorite Movies	Shrek, Dracula

Work Info [edit]
Company:	Common Grounds Coffee Shop
Schedule:	Work M – F 7AM –2PM

The Wall [edit]

 N.O. Body wrote: at 11:00am August 1, 2013
Saw u dancing at Annie Oakley's!! Whatta hottie! We should meet.

 N.O. Body wrote: at 1:00pm August 1, 2013
Aw come on! U know u want to meet me!

 N.O. Body wrote: at 3:02pm August 1, 2013
Still no response? What's up? Do u wanna play or not?

 Seymore Bonz wrote: at 4:27pm August 1, 2013
R we still hookin up w/the gang at Annie Oakley's tonight?
Meet you guys at the front door at 10.

 N.O. Body wrote: at 5:20pm August 1, 2013
Sounds fun. Maybe i'll see u there.

 Bay-Bee Face wrote: at 10:17pm August 2, 2013
Can you believe how we much we rocked last night? What was the deal with that guy
who kept staring at us? He gave me the creeps!! You switched shifts w/Mary right?
Working at 4?

 N.O. Body wrote: at 12:39pm August 2, 2013
Gee, BTW u were dressed, I just assumed u liked being stared at… U looked really
cute at work.

 N.O. Body wrote: at 2:21pm August 3, 2013
What's the matter sweetheart? U looked unhappy to see me at work today. Why
didn't u talk to me? BTW, nice house u got. Who knew you lived in such a nice neighborhood.

 N.O. Body wrote: at 12:57pm August 5, 2013
Nice dog u have. Ur parents must be outta town—no one's been home all night.

 N.O. Body wrote: at 7:26pm August 5, 2013
U never showed up for ur shift today. I waited all day for u. Saw your friends.
They said somebody poisoned your dog. That's a shame—such a yappy
little thing. I hate stuck-up women. Guess I'll just have to find u in person…

FIGURE 6.1

Fictional Ispy.com page

Companion, M. (2006). Victoria Tymmyns Ispy.com. Used with permission.

Sharpen Your FOCUS

TRY It!

> *Oh sleep! It is a gentle thing, Beloved from pole to pole.*
>
> —SAMUEL TAYLOR COLERIDGE,
> ENGLISH CRITIC AND POET (1772–1834)

Reason 6: They're exhausted.

Let's face it: It's hard to focus when you're dead tired. You're so weary that you can't get your eyes to focus, much less your brain. What's keeping you up at night? Worry? Financial stress? Internet games? According to sleep experts, you should be getting seven or more hours per night, or a minimum of forty-nine hours per week. Some students, like Dario from the FOCUS Challenge Case, choose to stay up until the wee, small hours of the morning. Or perhaps you have a baby at home who keeps you up at night or a job working the night shift. Life happens. But the choices you make—whatever the situation—will determine the degree to which you can focus when you need to.

Keep a sleep log for a week. When you wake up, write down the number of hours of sleep you've gotten.

Sun.	Mon.	Tues.	Wed.	Thur.	Fri.	Sat.

Are you surprised to see the actual numbers? Is there much variation from night to night? From weekdays to weekends? Formulate a new strategy to become better rested. Scientists now know that the amount of sleep you get can affect your ability to focus, your health, your weight, and your grades![12]

Use Technology to Your Academic Advantage

Despite the pros and cons, technology plays a big role in all of our lives, especially the lives of college students. The truth of the matter is that technology skills are increasingly important in all academic disciplines—as well as any profession.[13] A recent study of 3,000 students at 1,179 two-year colleges and universities reports that technology use is widespread in higher education. See how many of these items apply to you. For example:

Technology Ownership
87% of students own a laptop
70% of students own a USB thumb drive
67% own a Wi-Fi device or have access to Wi-Fi
66% own a stationary gaming device
62% own an iPod
55% own a smartphone

Technology Use
99% of students use e-mail
93% of students use text messaging
90% use Facebook
85% download videos
85% read Wikis
73% use a course management system like Blackboard
72% read blogs
70% use the Internet
70% engage in online forums or bulletin boards
55% use e-books or e-textbooks[14]

What academic benefits does technology provide? In one major study, students noted that it helps them:

> Access resources and information.
> Simplify administrative tasks (enrolling for classes, paying tuition bills, etc.).
> Track progress in classes.
> Commuicate with instructors and classmates.
> Make learning more engaging and relevant.[15]

How Tech-Savvy Are You?

Let's look at some specific technology applications you'll need to know in college, including types of software, search engines, course management systems, and other class-related possibilities. Match the examples on the right to the descriptions on the left.

a.

b.

c. SPEECH 115
Darnell Williams

Persuasive Speech

Why Movies Are the Best Way to Relax

d.

e.

f.

g.

h.

Exercise 6.2 Continued

1. _____ **Internet Domain Extensions**

Internet hostnames after the period in the URL (Uniform Resource Locator) describe where websites come from:

.gov = U.S. government (such as www.irs.gov, the Internal Revenue Service [or IRS])

.edu = education (such as www.gbcc.edu, Great Bluffs Community College)

.org = organizations or businesses (such as www.democratic.org, the Democratic Party, or nonprofit organizations, like www.americanheart.org, American Heart Association)

.mil = military (such as www.defenselink.mil, U.S. Department of Defense)

.com = commercial, buying and selling (such as www.realtor.com, National Association of Realtors)

.net = network or Internet provider (such as www.earthlink.net)

.int = international organizations (such as Interpol, Council of Europe, or NATO)[16]

2. _____ **Software**

College will require you to use several standard software applications to do your academic work:

Microsoft Word allows you to type, edit, alphabetize, index, footnote, and do many other things to prepare papers for your classes.

Microsoft PowerPoint, used as an electronic visual aid for oral presentations, allows you to create an on-screen guide for your listeners (and you, if you glance at it periodically and subtly for clues).

Microsoft Excel spreadsheets are good for tabulating, record keeping, and organizing. The industry standard for these applications is generally the Microsoft products listed here, although other possibilities exist. If you need help learning any of these applications, your campus techies, your instructors, or online tutorials (which can easily be found by Googling) can help. If you're a techie yourself, you can venture into other software applications like Flash, Camtasia, or iMovie to make your academic work look even more professional.

3. _____ **Search Engines**

Different search engines work best for different purposes, but these three are the most popular recommendations:[17]

Google (www.google.com) has a well-deserved reputation as the best search engine you can use. Its size is not disclosed anywhere, but it's generally thought to have the largest assets to search and 900,000,000 unique visitors per month.

Bing (www.bing.com) a Microsoft alternative to Google, organizes your responses to help you make better informed decisions. It is used by 165,000,000 unique visitors a month.

Yahoo (www.yahoo.com) can also help you get excellent search results, or allow you to use any of the other specialized search features.

4. _____ **Wikis**

Wikis are today's online, editable encyclopedias. (The word wiki means "fast" in the Hawaiian language.) Wikipedia is the largest of these sites, and anyone can add information or change content (currently at 21 million articles in more than 280 languages on the Wikipedia site). On the other hand, be aware that inaccurate information can be added just as easily as accurate information. Never consider Wikipedia to be the final word on anything.

5. _____ **Course Management Systems**

Many of your college classes will be conducted partially or wholly online, using a course management system, like Blackboard, eCollege, or Moodle. These shells help organize the online component of classes, and most students report having positive experiences with them. How do students use course management systems?

- To track grades, assignments, and tests
- To take sample tests and quizzes (or real ones)
- To get the course syllabus
- To turn in assignments online
- To access readings and other course materials
- To post to an online discussion[18]

6. _____ **Blogs**

Web logs, or blogs, can be thought of as online journals that are typically one person's reactions to current events or cultural issues, for example. Or you can think of them as websites that someone changes every day.[19] Your instructors may post a question or comment and ask you to blog your responses online and to respond to your classmates' blogs. Everyone can get to know you by your online personality, and some students say they become better writers by reading other students' responses to their writing. And professional blogs can be a great way to stay current on the career you go into.

7. _____ **YouTube**

YouTube is a video-sharing website where you can upload and watch video clips. You may want to insert one into a presentation you create as a class assignment or post one yourself related to your life as a student.

8. _____ **Textbook Websites**

Textbook websites, like the one you're using for *FOCUS on Community College Success,* can contain information and activities to enrich your learning experience, like videos, quizzes, and iAudio chapter summaries. Use these resources to help you master course material.

BOX 6.1

Other Need-to-Know Technology Definitions

VPN (Virtual Private Network): You may need to go through particular steps to connect to your campus databases from home. Tech experts on your campus can show you how to do this, or there may be an online tutorial on your campus's website.

Podcasts: Many professors now record their lectures for you to review later. Or you can listen to *FOCUS on Community College Success* and other textbooks' iAudio summaries for each chapter online.

PDF files: Using Adobe technology, you can create and edit documents that are formatted on your computer screen just as they would appear if they were published. PDFs look very professional, and there may be a time when you are asked to create one for a particular class.

Web 2.0: Web 2.0 is not a new version of the Internet. It refers to creative uses of it, like Facebook, Wikis, and blogs, where instead of just reading passively, users help create the content.

Viruses, Worms, and Trojan Horses: Pranksters (or vicious cyber attackers, for that matter) can infiltrate campus technology systems and infect individual computers or shut down a campus system entirely. The solution? Don't open attachments with suspicious names or ones from people you don't know. And keep your antivirus software up to date!

Mobile Apps: Apps, short for "applications," are Internet-based programs that allow you to work, read, or communicate online from your smartphone or other portable electronic device. In today's world, people are busy and don't stay in one spot. They want to work, learn, and study from anywhere at anytime.

QR Codes: QR (short for "quick response") codes are two-dimensional bar codes that you can scan, for example, from your cell phone (if you download an app). The code will take you to a website immediately for more information.

Tablet Computing: Mobile devices such as the iPad are seen as having rich potential for use as learning tools. There's no cell phone ringing or text message binging, and the image is larger, so you can do more with it. Both Mobile Apps and Tablet Computing are seen as the hottest trends in educational technology.[20]

Dropbox: Dropbox is a free (or paid) service that lets you store your files on the Internet, access them from anywhere, and share them with anyone.

Writing Effective Online Messages

Being a professional student doesn't just apply to how you act in class, like asking questions if you're unclear or turning in your assignments on time. Online communication has particular rules you must follow. For example, when you're writing discussion board posts in a hybrid or online course, it's important to be civil. "How could anyone ever possibly think that?" as a post to a classmate's entry may be honest, but it's hardly collegial. Instead, why not say, "That's something I hadn't thought of. Can you explain more about it?"? Think about the Golden Rule of online posts: How would you feel if a classmate shot down a good idea of yours? Be respectful. When classmates post an idea, they're putting their egos on the line—or so it feels. Remember that you can disagree with a classmate online, but never disrespect him or her personally. "I thought we were always supposed to use good grammar on this discussion board. Jerome's posts are full of mistakes." There's no need to put Jerome on the spot. On the other hand, using good grammar and correct spelling will be important to your instructor, so be conscientious in that regard.

Another thing your instructor will insist on is that your posts are sufficiently informative. When you are in a hurry, it's tempting to write as little as possible, like "Alicia is right on target!" as your entire entry. Tell why. Mention parts of her argument you agree with, and explain your endorsement. A discussion board is a place for online, back-and-forth dialogue, not Tweet-like comments for other people to decipher.

Of course IMs and text messages are used more often in social contexts than academic ones, but some of the same rules apply. "Breaking up" with your romantic partner by sending a text message would probably be perceived as a cowardly "low blow." Simply put: Certain situations call for certain types of messages.

E-mail that you send your instructor has netiquette (online etiquette) standards you should follow, too. Take a look at these widely accepted rules for academic settings:

1. **Don't send a message you don't want to risk being forwarded to someone else.** Doing so has caused many a fretful night. ("Aaaaakkk! What have I done?")

2. **Don't hit the "send" key until you've given yourself time to cool off, if you're upset.** You may want to edit what you've written.

3. **Don't forward chain e-mails.** At the very least, they're a nuisance, and sometimes they're illegal.

4. **Don't do business over your school e-mail account.** Sending all 500 new students an invitation to your family's restaurant grand opening is off-limits. Besides, sending messages to lots of people at once is called "spam," and it can really gum up the works.

5. **Don't spread hoaxes about viruses or false threats.** You can get into big trouble for that.

6. **Don't type in all CAPS.** That's called SHOUTING, and it makes you look angry.

7. **Don't be too casual.** Use good grammar and correct spelling. Your instructors consider e-mails to be academic writing, and they'll expect professionalism from you. "Hey Prof, this is a heckuva of a cool class!" may sound enthusiastic, but it's not professional. Language that you use for texts and IMs is not appropriate for academic correspondence.

8. **Don't forget important details.** Include everything the reader needs to know. For example, if you're writing to an instructor, give your full name and the name of the course you're writing about. Professors teach more than one class and have many students.

9. **Don't hit the "Reply to All" key, when you mean to hit the "Reply" key.** Many e-mail message writers have been horrified upon learning that hundreds or thousands of people have read something personal or cranky that was meant for just one reader.

10. **Don't forget to fill in the subject line.** That gives readers a chance to preview your message and decide how soon they need to get to it.

VARK It!

Read/Write: Read through some of your last texts, IM's, posts, or tweets. Have you made any of the mistakes listed on this page?

How *Not* to Win Friends and Influence People Online

All four of these e-mail messages from students violate the rules of netiquette. See whether you can identify the rule number above that's been violated in each case.

From Matt   Rule:_____

    Professor X,

    I just looked at the online syllabus for Academic Success 101. Why didn't you tell us that our first paper is due on Monday? I will be very busy moving into a new apartment this weekend. Writing an essay for your class is the last thing I want to have to think about.

From Tiffany   Rule:_____

    Prof X,

    i didn't know u were makin us write a paper over the weekend. i won't be able to do it. i hop you don't mind.

From Xavier   Rule:_____

    PROFESSOR X,

    I CAN'T GET MY PAPER DONE BY MONDAY. LET ME KNOW WHAT I SHOULD DO.

From Dameon   Rule:_____

    Hey, Section 3

    Can you believe our instructor? She assigns a big writing assignment after only one day of class! Who in their right mind would be remotely interested in sitting in their crummy little room writing a bunch of meaningless junk, when we haven't even learned anything yet? What kind of teacher are we stuck with here? Somebody out there respond to me, OK? I'm totally hacked off!

As a class, discuss your responses. Do you all agree on which rules were broken in the four examples provided? See whether you can create some new ones that violate other rules.

Research Skills and Your College Success

VARK It!

Visual: Download or ask for a map of your library. Identify the locations of various resources, such as computers, reference books, librarian's area, study rooms, and so on.

Many of your class assignments in college will require you to conduct research. Why? Aren't you in college to learn from your instructors? Why do they ask *you* to do research on your own?

There are unanswered questions all around us in everyday life. Some questions are simple; others are complex. How much time will it take to get across town to a doctor's appointment during rush hour? What can you expect college tuition to cost by the time your kids are old enough to go? What are the chances that someone you know who has cancer will survive for five years? Research isn't necessarily a mysterious thing that scientists in white coats do in laboratories. Research is simply finding answers to questions, either real questions you encounter every day or questions that are assigned to you in your classes. Doing research on your own can be a powerful way to learn, sometimes even more so than hearing answers from someone else, even if those people are your instructors. Going off to a research expedition in the library may sound like exhausting busywork, but the skills you stand to gain are well worth the effort.

Conducting research teaches you some important things about how to formulate a question and then find answers. And it's not just finding answers so that you can scratch a particular assignment off your to-do list. It's about learning an important process. When you get into the world of work, your instructors won't be there to supply answers, so knowing how to figure things out on your own will be key to your success. So, exactly what is college-level research?

What Research Is *Not*	What Research Is
Research isn't just going on a "search and employ" mission. It's not just seeing what all you can find and then using it to check off an assignment on your to-do list.	**Research starts with a question.** If an assignment is broad, as Dario's was, you must come up with a specific question to research yourself. (More about that later.)
Research isn't just moving things from Point A (the library) to Point B (your paper).	**Research is a process with a plan.** A plan was something Dario lacked. He jumped in without a question—or a plan.
Research isn't random rummaging through real or virtual files to find out something.	**Research is goal-oriented.** You've formulated a question, developed a plan, and now you begin to find answers by using both online sources and ones that sit on your library's shelves.
Research isn't doing a quick Internet search. The cutting and pasting Dario did to fill up his five pages is actually plagiarism!	**Research often involves breaking a big question into several smaller ones.**[21]

Navigating the Library

You've probably heard this since you were a child: "The library is your friend." As a young child, it was exciting to go to the library, choose a book, check it out with your own library card, and bring it home to read. Now, being "exiled" to the library to do research for a paper may seem like torture that can ruin a perfectly good weekend. But if you look at things differently, it can be a mind-expanding trip into places unknown. The truth is that in college the library should be more than just a friend. It should become your best friend! Beyond navigating the web to find research for your assignments, as many students do, it's important to learn your way around the actual, physical space of the library on your campus. The library has many useful resources, including real, very knowledgeable librarians who are there to help you. Asking a reference librarian for help can save you hours of unproductive digging on your own. Here are some of the resources your library offers and how you should use these resources when you're assigned a research project:

> **Card Catalog.** Explore your library's catalog that lists all of the books available to you. Card catalogs used to be actual cards in file cabinet drawers, but now most libraries put all the information about their holdings online. Go to your college's website, and from there you can find your way to your college library's home page. Click the library's catalog button. Let's say Dario follows these instructions and finds this book in his campus library's catalog: *The Global Internet Economy*, edited by Bruce Kogut. Cambridge, MA: MIT Press, 2003. The call number for the book is HC79.I55 G579, based on the Library of Congress classification system, which most college libraries use. (Some libraries, like your community's public library, may use the Dewey Decimal system. One advantage of the Library of Congress system is that books usually have the same number, no matter which library you find them in. That's not always true for the Dewey

VARK It!

Aural: Visit your library and interview a reference librarian. Ask about the services provided and other resources in the library.

I find that a great part of the information I have was acquired by looking up something and finding something else on the way.

Franklin P. Adams, American journalist and radio personality (1881–1960)

Decimal system.) The Library of Congress number identifies this item as a book about economics and information technology. Now, after identifying other possible useful books, Dario needs to make his way to campus and find the actual book on the shelf.

> **Databases.** If you go to your library's home page, you can link to the list of online databases it subscribes to. Databases identify articles from academic journals and sometimes contain entire articles online. Generally, different databases exist for different disciplines, for example:

Education	**ERIC** (Educational Resources Information Center)
Psychology	**PsycINFO**™
Business	**Business Source Premier**

But more general databases also exist. Dario might want to search through these:

Academic Search Premier

WilsonWeb OmniFile Full Text Mega

The key to making the most of databases is to find the right search words to plug into the database's search engine. That's where a short coaching session with a real reference librarian can be enormously helpful. You can have productive results or no results at all, just by slightly altering the search words you enter. Also, check Google Scholar online. It will search academic literature, including journal abstracts and articles, dissertations and theses, and books, across many different disciplines.

> **Stacks.** Physically walk through the stacks or collections of books and periodicals (journals, magazines, newspapers, and audiovisual resources, for example). Get to know the stacks in your library, and figure out how to find what you need. Look for the Library of Congress numbers posted on signs at the end of each row of books. When Dario finds the book he's looking for, he's likely to find other books in the library's "HC" section that would also be useful to him. That's why even though doing online research is convenient, there's no substitute for "being there."

Information Literacy and Your College Success

Much of the research you do for your college assignments will take place online. Information literacy is defined as knowing *when* you need information, *where* to find it, *what* it means, *whether* it's accurate, and *how* to use it. Simply put, it's "the ability to use technology to solve information problems." Information literacy includes five components, as seen in Figure 6.2. Think about them as a step-by-step process as we work through Dario's assignment.[22]

BOX 6.2

The Top Five Research Mistakes First-Year Students Make: Advice from a Reference Librarian

Are you guilty of any of these common mistakes first-year students make?

1. **Selecting a topic that is too broad.** Students often start out with a very general topic, and sometimes have a hard time narrowing the focus. Trying to write a paper on "recycling" sets you up for an impossible task. Entire books have been written on that subject. Figuring out which words to use can be tricky, too. If you search Google or databases by entering the word "green," you'll get everything from "lime, mint, olive, and avocado" (meaning shades of green, not foods) to "Kermit, the frog." Brainstorming different search words and noting the usable results is half the battle.

2. **Taking short cuts.** Major search engines are a great place to start, but don't stop there. Just using Google or Foxfire is the equivalent of academic "wimping out," like just grabbing something quick from a vending machine when there's so much more nutritious and satisfying food out there. Libraries buy many different electronic databases that have a wealth of information: articles, books, and book chapters, for example. Learn how to use these library databases and really mine them for information. Finding useful information takes time and patience!

3. **Devoting too little time.** Students frequently underestimate how long the research process will take. There are multiple steps required to doing thorough research. It's not a last-minute process, and procrastination isn't the answer. Even if you write like a pro, you can't complete a research paper in an hour or two. Just getting in materials you've ordered from another library can take several weeks.

4. **Not evaluating sources.** Many students don't look closely enough at the sources they find, and then they end up making poor choices or using the first items that come up in search results. Instead, as you scan your results, look for hints about authenticity and accuracy. Compare your findings with other authoritative sites. Note the domain extension (like .gov, for example). One hit may lead you to another, which leads you to yet another. Evaluate your search results and be selective about what you use. Not all sources are created equal; make sure yours are credible ones that support your argument.

5. **Copying and pasting.** Students sometimes use someone else's work without correct and thorough documentation of the source, especially when time is running out. You can end up plagiarizing unintentionally just because you don't understand how to cite your sources. Or you may intentionally cut and paste to save yourself time and effort. But either way, you're putting your academic success at high risk.

The biggest mistake students make is not asking the reference librarian for help at the beginning of the research process! That's why librarians are there—to provide guidance and help with all of the above. Continue reading this chapter for more strategies on making the most of your research time.[23]

Step 1. Define

Define what the assignment requires of you. Dario was assigned a *research* paper. He wasn't being asked to **summarize** or *evaluate* a topic. He was asked to *find out about it.* But "Globalization and Internet Commerce" is a huge topic. He must narrow it down and decide which specific research question (or questions) he wants to focus on.

summarize condense a longer work into a few essential statements

If you were assigned the paper Dario was assigned, and you knew very little about "Globalization and Internet Commerce," you might start as he did, by Googling your topic to help you define it. But the Internet is huge and unstructured. There's really no way to organize that much information into simple, neat categories.[24] And how do you whittle down 22 million hits? According to a recent study, less than 1 percent of Google users look further than the first page of their Google results, regardless of how many hits they get![25]

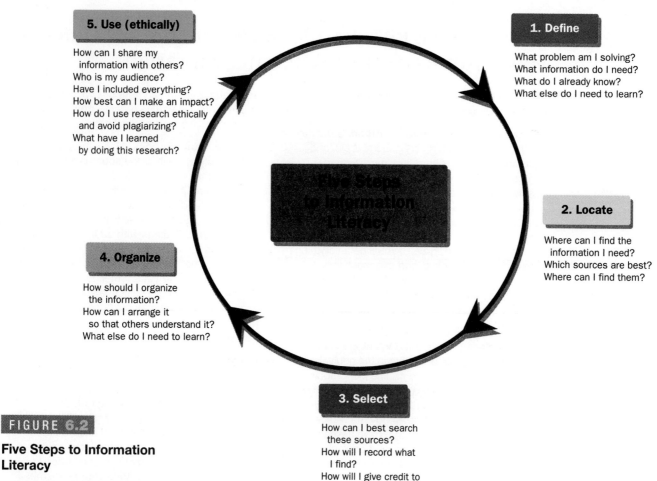

5. Use (ethically)

How can I share my
   information with others?
Who is my audience?
Have I included everything?
How best can I make an impact?
How do I use research ethically
   and avoid plagiarizing?
What have I learned
   by doing this research?

1. Define

What problem am I solving?
What information do I need?
What do I already know?
What else do I need to learn?

2. Locate

Where can I find the
   information I need?
Which sources are best?
Where can I find them?

4. Organize

How should I organize
   the information?
How can I arrange it
   so that others understand it?
What else do I need to learn?

3. Select

How can I best search
   these sources?
How will I record what
   I find?
How will I give credit to
   the sources?

Five Steps to Information Literacy

FIGURE 6.2

Five Steps to Information Literacy

Adapted from Wood, G. (2004, April 9). Academic original sin: Plagiarism, the Internet, and librarians. *The Journal of Academic Librarianship, 30*(3), 237–242. Reprinted by permission of Elsevier; Samson, S. (2010, May). Information literacy learning outcomes and student success. *Journal of Academic Librarianship, 36*(3), 202–10.

VARK It!

Multimodal (Visual/Aural):
Think about a current assignment for a class, and use this figure to talk through the questions for each step. Picture how you will actually move from one step to the other.

If you don't know anything about the topic you need to research—absolutely nothing at all—the Internet is a great place to start. You can type in "globalization" and "Internet commerce," and within the blink of an eye, information appears. The problem is that you now have too much information, and the challenge is knowing what to do next. Your college instructors will insist you go beyond the Internet and avoid relying too much on encyclopedias and Wikipedia. College requires you to do more research than you've probably done before, and to do it differently.

Dario could have used the websites that Google brought up to help him *define* a specific research focus, instead of being overwhelmed by the number of hits. Consider these more focused research topics or questions, which Google or Wikipedia could have led him to:

1. **Five Reasons to Go Global with Your Website** (Why is it a good idea?)

2. **Online Retail Businesses Will Explode over the Next Ten Years** (Where will it go in the future?)

3. **Three Problems with Doing E-Business Internationally: Language, Shipping, and Money** (What are the challenges of trying to make it happen?)

Let's take that last focused topic and run with it. Suppose you have an on-line business and you want to attract customers from around the world to expand it. That's a good idea, but how will you deal with translating what's on your website to other languages? How will you ship your product overseas for a reasonable cost? How will you deal with the exchange rate between the U.S. dollar and the currency used in other countries? Now we've taken a big, broad topic ("Globalization and Internet Commerce") and broken it down into three specific questions or subtopics to research. Your preliminary Google and Wikipedia searches can help you identify what the smaller chunks of your topic could be.

But they can't do *all* the work for you, and you can't stop there, as Dario did. You have to know what to do next. (If you think this process is challenging, you're not alone. In one study, only 35 percent of college students knew how to narrow a Google search!)[26]

Step 2. Locate

If you've identified electronic sources, bookmark them in a file labeled with the name of your project. If they're print resources, physically find them in the library. If they're not available in your own campus library, see whether it participates in an interlibrary loan agreement among libraries. Your own library may be able to borrow the resource from another library. (But be aware that this process may take up to two weeks or so. That's why it's important to start your research projects early!)

bookmark a way to save and organize websites in your web browser

Step 3. Select

The Information Age surrounds us with huge amounts of data of all kinds. With so much information available, how do we know what to believe? Whether or not it's true, we tend to think that if something is on television or in a book or online, it must be important. But in any of these cases, we need to exercise our critical thinking skills and turn them into critical searching skills. Just because information is published doesn't automatically make it right or true. In particular, some of the so-called research you encounter online may be bogus, containing inaccuracies or bias. You must read, interpret, and evaluate research to decide whether to use it. Use these five criteria to evaluate any website you come across:

1. **Currency.** How up to date is the information? Some websites don't list a date at the bottom of the screen (where copyright information is often found). If you don't see one, try using other hints on the site to get at how old the information is ("According to a study published in 1995 . . ."). You may find that you need to search for something more up to date.

2. **Accuracy.** How accurate is the information presented? If a website makes an unbelievable claim ("Grow a new head of hair in just six weeks!") or presents shaky statistics to make a case, it's important to be skeptical. Take responsibility to validate the information elsewhere.

3. **Authority.** Does the sponsor of the website have the credentials to post the information you see? Chances are "Steve's Picks" or "myfavoritemovies .com" is a collection of one person's opinions. Compare that to a film reviewer's site

> **Plans are only good intentions unless they immediately degenerate into hard work.**
>
> *Peter Drucker, management expert (1909–2005)*

Information Literacy and Your College Success   **159**

with information compiled by a professional film critic for a major newspaper. Which one would you trust more? You may not agree with Steve or the professional film critic, but one has credentials, and the other doesn't.

objectivity ability to not take sides, being neutral

4. **Objectivity.** Does the website sponsor have a reason to convince you of something, or is it presenting unbiased information? If the site wants you to order something online because it claims to have better products than those you can buy at a store, for example, you should be suspicious.

5. **Coverage.** If a website just presents one side of an issue or a very small piece of a larger picture, check to make sure you're getting all the information you need. If you're left wondering, *But what about . . . ?* you're probably having the right reaction.

EXERCISE 6.4

Critical Searching on the Internet

With these five criteria in mind, choose one of the following two assignments to complete. Each one will ask you to use your critical searching skills.

Assignment 1: Create a list of three websites that pertain to your intended major. (If you're not sure of your major right now, choose one to explore anyway.) Evaluate the websites, using the five criteria, to see which ones seem most useful to you as a student.

Assignment 2: Compare websites with contradictory information. Choose a controversial subject such as abortion, the death penalty, religion, politics, or some other subject of interest. Find three websites on your topic and compare them on the five criteria. Which of the three websites gets the highest marks? Why?

Step 4. Organize

Now that you have located the information you need, using a variety of sources, and selected those that will be most useful to you in your research project, it's time to organize. Dario's paper will be easier to write now that he has created three subtopics: language, shipping, and money. He should begin taking notes on index cards or highlighting pieces of information he wants to quote word-for-word (giving credit to the author) or paraphrase (putting information into his own words). He can literally put the index cards, printed articles, and photocopied pages from books he found while doing his research into three piles and work from those. Organization is the key to an excellent research paper. To help you keep track of the sources you find, you should follow these suggestions.

Don't agonize. Organize.

Florynce Kennedy, American lawyer and African American activist

Make sure you pay attention to details. Write the name of the book or article, author, place of publication, publisher, date, or URL at the top of an index card with your notes or on a photocopied page of information you plan to use. Here's an example of what two index cards (of the same paragraph) would look like:

[Ableson, H. Ledeen, K., & Lewis, H. (2008). *Blown to bits: Your life, liberty, and happiness after the digital explosion.* Boston, MA: Pearson Education, Inc.]

Direct Quote

"The Internet has caused drastic shifts in business practice. Customer service calls are outsourced to India today not just because labor costs are low there. Labor costs have always been low in India, but international telephone calls used to be expensive. Calls about airline reservations and lingerie returns are answered in India today because it now takes almost no time and costs almost no money to send to India the bits representing your voice." Blown to Bits, p. 12.

[Ableson, H. Ledeen, K., & Lewis, H. (2008). *Blown to bits: Your life, liberty, and happiness after the digital explosion.* Boston, MA: Pearson Education, Inc.]

Paraphrase

The Internet has changed the way we do business. Now people in places like India handle things like our airline reservations and lingerie returns, because the technology of cell phones has made long distance cheap.

If you have ideas of your own that don't come from any book, write them on cards or pages, too, and label them, "My Own Ideas."

> **Learn how to use Google Docs,** if you don't know how. Google Docs can serve as an alternative to index cards in some ways. For example, if you're called away on a trip and you plan to work on a paper for a class while you're away but forget to bring the stack of cards, you're out of luck. Google Docs, on the other hand, can be accessed via the Internet from anywhere. Simply create a gmail account for yourself, if you don't already have one, and choose the "Documents" tab. There you'll find all the documents you saved while doing research using your school library's online databases. You can open the articles, categorize them by subtopics, open them, or print them out. It's a great organizational tool for busy students.

Work is either fun or drudgery. It depends on your attitude. I like fun.

Colleen C. Barrett, President Emeritus and Corporate Secretary, Southwest Airlines

EXERCISE 6.5

Technology Project: Group Ad

Working with two or three classmates and using PowerPoint, Flash, or iMovie, create a television ad (as professional-looking as possible) for the course for which you're using this book. Use text, images, and music. The advertisement shouldn't be long—two or three minutes, or the length of the song you use—but it should describe what the course is about and why other students should take it. Be as creative as you like! Once you've created your presentation, play your ad for the class.

Step 5. Use (ethically)

You've done your research, and now it's time to share it with the world (or at least your instructor) either through the written word, the spoken word, or both. One of the most important things you can learn as a new student is not only how to *use* your research, but how to use *your* research. Some students think that because the Internet is out there, why not just use it? Other people have already made volumes upon volumes of prior research available. They've "been there; done that." Why reinvent the wheel? The reason is because the Internet is simply a tool, just like your library's online databases are tools. You must learn how to use the tool—the Internet—ethically. If your boss asks you for a report on the job, cutting and pasting from the Internet is unlikely to be an option. You must conduct your own research, analyze it, and compile it for a written report or oral presentation. We'll focus on developing speaking and writing skills elsewhere, but learning how to use the Internet ethically is a good place to start now.

Downloading Your Workload: The Easy Way Out?

EXERCISE 6.6

Plagiarism Survey[27]

When you're doing research for a class assignment, have you ever asked yourself questions like these? Jot down your own responses, and then see whether you can find the answers as you continue reading this section. Then discuss them as a class.

1. How do I put things into my own words?
2. How do I give credit to sources I use?
3. How do I do research methodically in steps so that I don't run out of time, leaving plagiarism as an attractive alternative?
4. If an assignment feels as though it's busy work that has nothing to do with my life, is plagiarism really such a bad thing?
5. Isn't anything published on the Internet free, valid, and available to use?

Source: Wood, G. (2004, April 9). Academic original sin: Plagiarism, the Internet and Librarians. *The Journal of Academic Librarianship, 30*(3), 237-242. Reprinted by permission of Elsevier.

One of the trickiest aspects of writing papers for your college courses can be expressed in these three words: *What is plagiarism?* First, you should understand the difference between *intentional* and *unintentional* plagiarism. Intentional plagiarism is deliberately downloading a paper from an online source or cutting and pasting text from a website or book, as Dario did, for example. However, you run the risk of committing unintentional plagiarism if you don't understand what plagiarism is or you forget which book you used, so you don't cite the words you've borrowed from someone else. Intentional plagiarism is cheating, pure and simple. Technology today makes plagiarism all too convenient and easy, but by the same token, finding plagiarism in students' papers has become easy for instructors, too. The bottom line? Follow the guidelines you get from your instructors. And if you don't understand them or your instructor assumes you already

> **The first principle is that you must not fool yourself, but you are the easiest person to fool.**
>
> *Richard P. Feynman (1918–1988), Nobel Prize Winner, Physics, 1965*

know them, ask questions. Both intentional and unintentional plagiarism can hurt you academically. These FAQs will help.

Q1: If I just list all the sources I used in writing a paper in the bibliography, won't that cover everything? List all your sources in the bibliography at the end of your paper, but also mention that they are others' ideas as you present them. Generally, it's a good idea to cite the original author soon after you present that idea in your paper. In a research paper, it's also useful to name the authors ("According to Staley, college success skills are critical in the first year of college.") Each discipline uses a particular format to cite references. These are called *style sheets*, such as:

> *MLA* (Modern Language Association) is often used in the humanities (English, art, and philosophy, for example).

> *APA* (American Psychological Association) is often used in the social sciences (psychology, communication, and sociology).

> *Chicago Manual of Style* is used in history.

Check with your instructor if you're not certain which one to use, and Google these terms to find the specifics of formatting.

Q2: Must I cite all my sources if I just put ideas into my own words? Yes, you must cite all your sources, even though you may think that your paper looks cluttered. In academic writing, you must cite all the information you use, whether you paraphrase it, quote it, or summarize it. Some students are even taught bad habits in high school, for example, "It's not plagiarism if you change every fifth word," so they write papers with a thesaurus close by. Unfortunately, that's not the way it works. Try reading what you'd like to paraphrase, and then cover the text with your hand and write what you remember. In this case, you'd still need to cite the reference, but because you're paraphrasing, you wouldn't use quotation marks.

Q3: But I didn't know anything at all about this subject before I started this assignment. Does that mean I should cite everything? Some ideas are common knowledge that need not be cited. For example, it's a well-known fact that the Civil War lasted from 1861 to 1865. If you cited this piece of common knowledge, who would you cite? Generally, however, your motto should be, "Better safe than sorry." As a rule, you must cite quotations, paraphrases, or summaries. If you use the exact words of someone else, put quotation marks around them, or if they're longer than four lines, indent them in a block. (And generally, only use long quotes if something has been said in a remarkable way.) Also cite specific facts you're

VARK It!

Read/Write: Reread a recent paper or assignment you've completed. Did you use your resources ethically, or might you have intentionally or unintentionally plagiarized?

VARK It!

Aural: With another aural learner, discuss the perils of plagiarism, and how you can work to avoid plagiarizing.

> Borrowed thoughts, like borrowed money, only show the poverty of the borrower.

Lady Marguerite Blessington, English socialite and writer (1789–1849) using as support and distinctive ideas belonging to others, even if you don't agree with them.

Q4: I've been doing a lot of reading for this paper. Now I'm not really sure which ideas came from others and which are my own. How do I avoid plagiarism? The best solution here is to take careful notes as you do your research and document where you found each piece of information. Avoid cutting and pasting text. That practice can backfire later when you can't remember what you've extracted and what represents your own thoughts and wording.

Now look back at your answers to the Plagiarism Survey in Exercise 6.6 at the beginning of this section and see whether you would change any of them.

EXERCISE 6.7

Plagiarism or Not?

In your opinion, is the following passage plagiarized? Compare these two examples:

Original passage: A new Northwestern University study provides the first biological evidence that bilinguals' rich experience with language "fine-tunes" their auditory nervous system and helps them juggle linguistic input in ways that enhance attention and working memory.

Source: Leopold, W. (2012, April 30). Bilingualism fine-tunes hearing, enhances attention. *Science Daily.* Available at http://www.sciencedaily.com/releases/2012/04/120430152033.htm.

Student paper: Bilinguals' use of more than one language fine-tunes their auditory nervous system and helps their attention and working memory.

Has this student committed plagiarism? Why or why not?

The Four C Factors: Just how motivated are YOU?

CONTROL: *YOUR TOUGHEST ASSIGNMENT*

Identify your most challenging assignment this term, one that will require you to use your research and information literacy skills. What is the specific assignment? For example, it could be "write a five-page paper in which you take a position on a controversial theme relating to our course topic." On a scale of 1 to 10 (with 10 being extremely difficult), how challenging do you expect this assignment to be? What would make the challenge more manageable? Describe your research assignment here.

_____

_____

_____

Now take a look at the website to the right and answer the following questions (without Googling):

1. Does this website appear to be authentic? Why or why not?

2. Would this service be useful to a student like you with a challenging research assignment?

3. In your opinion, is this website acceptable for college students to use? Why or why not?

4. Are there differences between the three available options and their degree of acceptability?

5. What's the difference between using these professional services and using the professional services of a campus reference librarian?

6. Do you know students who use "professional" research services? What are their views on the acceptability of these services?

7. If you were a college instructor, what would you tell your students about these services?

Can you identify online resources that might be helpful for your most difficult assignment? What online resources might be more harmful than helpful to your academic success?

_____

_____

_____

CURIOSITY: *ARE YOU CAUGHT IN THE NET?*

It's noon. You decide to check your online life while you chow down a giant burrito. Three wall entries and five new Facebook friend requests. *Who are these people?* you wonder. After a bit of browsing, you decide to update your photo albums by uploading several shots from your weekend adventures. Then you notice an amazing item on e-Bay that you've been looking for, and a bidding war is underway. You decide to join in, and you cast the winning bid. *Man, how am I going to pay for that?* you wonder. The clock ticks away. You order a new pair of shoes from your favorite website, and then check your watch. It's already 4:30. Four and a half hours have just gone by, and you have to catch the bus to get to campus in 10 minutes!

Does this scenario sound uncomfortably familiar? A few minutes start a chain reaction that stretches out for several hours. Just why is the Internet so addicting? Is it the novelty of things like Facebook or e-Bay? Is it because it allows us to do so much without moving from one spot?

Are you addicted? Ask yourself these questions: Do you obsess about your online life and get nervous if you haven't checked your e-mail or Facebook account for a while? Do you spend more time with your online friends than your real friends? Do you interrupt yourself constantly to check your e-mail or chat electronically with someone

Website advertisement (image)

Researchadvisors.com

All the help you need with time-consuming writing assignments!
Need a rush job? Call our hurry hotline @ 1-888-555-5555

Top topics | Top grades | Top staff

You have a paper to write for your history class, a midterm to prepare for in your calculus class, and a presentation due in your psychology class. Where do you put your time and effort? There's only so much of you to go around! Consider our affordable options and earn the grade you need!

There's no way I can get all this done—and still have a life! Help!

Option 1: Let our staff of qualified researchers put together an impressive bibliography on your topic. You'll be emailed a list of premium sources—each with a usable summary—and immediately, you're ready to write! No needless trips to the library, no hours of online searching. Let us do it for you! Prices start at just $39.95. Learn more…

Option 2: Upload your assignment and allow one of our talented writers to send you a first draft; then put on the finishing touches yourself to make the paper your own. A professional writer can give you the head start you need. Prices start at just $69.95. Learn more…

Option 3: Eliminate all the worry and stress, and let us handle everything for you. Give us specifics and a timeline, and we'll do the rest. Prices start at just $99.95. Learn more…

researchadvisors.com
Copyright © 2007-2009
researchadvisors.com is affiliated with the Alliance of Southwestern Colleges and Universities

iStockphoto.com/Antonio Nunes

while doing online research for your class projects? If the answers to the questions in this paragraph are yes, are you ready to consider that you may be overly dependent on the Internet?[28]

Don't get caught in the Net. Think about the impact it could have on your college success. Try these suggestions:

1. **Monitor your time online.** Estimate right now how much time you spend online per week. Then actually time yourself. Is your estimate accurate? Or are you way off base?

2. **Set limits.** Give yourself a hard-and-fast time limit, and stick to it.

3. **Shorten your online sessions.** Being online tends to distort time. You may think you've only been on for an hour, when three hours have actually gone by. Set an old-fashioned timer, and when it goes off, get up and do something else.

4. **Separate work and play online.** It's easy to find yourself on a fun-seeking detour when you're supposed to be working on a research paper. When work and play are combined, it's easy to lose track of what's what. You end up wasting time because it feels as if you're doing something productive when you really aren't.

5. **Take a tech vacation.** Without getting freaked out, think about this option: Turn off your computer for a day, and then extend the time to a week or more. Use a computer lab on campus to do your assignments, rather than tempting yourself to spend hours online at home. Train yourself to withdraw, little by little.

6. **Get a life.** Take up yoga, chess, or swimming. Make some new friends, start a relationship, or join a club on campus. Your real life might actually become more interesting.

7. **Talk to people who care about you—a family member or a counselor on campus.** Recognizing the problem and admitting it are the first steps. Being one-sided isn't healthy. There are experts and support groups available to help you deal with your problem and make your real life more fulfilling.[29]

Which website is your biggest distraction? Facebook, Craigslist, eBay, YouTube, or some other site? Which of the above suggestions might help you control your distractions best, and why?

_____

_____

_____

CAREER OUTLOOK: *"WRITE" YOUR REPUTATION*

You've just graduated from college and landed a great job. All that hard work paid off. But now what? How will people in—for example—a large company begin to form an impression of you? The simple answer is that they will *listen* to you—in meetings, during presentations, and while hanging around the proverbial water cooler. But how else will they judge you and your work? One way you may not have thought about yet provides great opportunity, but also significant risk. It can do you in quickly. At times it's ever so subtle; at other times it's totally in your face.

Imagine this example. Your new boss asks, "Can you get an e-mail out about that new policy?" As the eager company newbie, you reply, "Sure." You quickly compose an e-mail message to send out to everyone in the organization: **The new company policy will go into effect soon.** *Short and sweet,* you think and hit the "send" key.

But immediately, you get back a barrage of e-mails from other employees, "What company policy?" "There's a new company policy?" "What new shenanigans is the corporate office up to now?" The request from your boss sounded simple enough. But in your short, sweet message, you've just communicated something relatively meaningless: some new policy from somewhere is about to start sometime. Will your new colleagues assume you're uninformed, unthinking, or unconscious? Think about how composing that one message could start to shape your company reputation right out of the gate.

Instead, you could have sent out an e-mail message like this: **The new software system to report travel expenditures, which has been mandated by the corporate office in response to violations of company travel policy, will go into effect on November 1, 2013, upon the recommendation of the general manager's task force appointed to examine ways to streamline operations and cut company waste.** This message certainly isn't guilty of leaving out all the good stuff like the first one. In fact, you've overloaded your sentence with "TMI"—so much extraneous verbiage that most people will have to read it twice, if they read it at all. Your colleagues may assume you're as boring and stuffy as your message. Even people who haven't met you yet are forming an impression of you through your writing. Are you getting the idea? Pressure? Yes. Overstatement? No. Your writing broadcasts all kinds of information about you.[30] To make sure that people form the right impression of you, your writing must be clear, powerful, and bold. And actually, if you put some thought into it, the texting and tweeting you do now can help you develop the clear and concise business writing skills you'll need later.[31] (Our second bolded example above wouldn't fly as a tweet, would it? Too many characters.) Writing short, eye-catching, lively messages that people actually *will* read speaks volumes about your potential on the job. If you rock, make sure your writing rocks, too. That kind of writing tells people how effective you will be and "writes" your reputation for ongoing career success.

Looking at the two unsatisfactory messages above, rewrite the e-mail message one more time. Try to create a clear, concise, and effective message.

_____

_____

_____

CHALLENGE: REALITY CHECK

How much did you learn? At the beginning of this chapter, you filled out a "Readiness Check" that asked how you thought this chapter would relate to you, and how you would relate to it. Now, fill out this "Reality Check" to find out.

1. Identify one advantage and one disadvantage of online courses.
2. How would you define research? What steps are involved?
3. What is information literacy?
4. What are the five steps to information literacy?
5. In your own words, define *plagiarism*.
6. How long did it take? _____ hours _____ minutes. Before you began this chapter, you were asked to predict how long it would take you to complete it (total time, even if you read it in more than one sitting). Was your estimate on target, or will you revise it for the next chapter you'll read?_____

step 3 INSIGHT *Now* What Do You Think?

At the beginning of this chapter, Dario Jones faced a series of challenges as a new college student taking three online classes. Now after learning from this chapter, would you respond differently to any of the questions you answered about the FOCUS Challenge Case? Using what you learned in the chapter, write a paragraph ending to Dario's case study. What are some of the possible outcomes for Dario?

step 4 ACTION Your Plans for Change

1. Identify one new thing you learned in reading this chapter. Why did you select the one you've selected? How will it affect what you do in your college classes?

2. How much experience have you had conducting research? What sounds most challenging about the process?

3. How would you describe your technology skills? If you haven't had much experience with technology, how do you plan to increase your skills? If you have technology experience, how will you use your knowledge to your advantage in your college classes?

chapter 7 : Engaging, Listening, and Note-Taking in Class

READINESS CHECK

How this chapter relates to YOU

1. When it comes to engaging, listening, and note-taking in your college classes, what do you find most challenging, if anything?

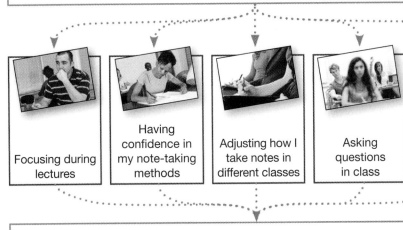

Focusing during lectures

Having confidence in my note-taking methods

Adjusting how I take notes in different classes

Asking questions in class

Using my class notes to study

2. What is most likely to be your response? Circle it.

I'll be open to learning more about this subject.

I'll wait and see how much of this chapter I understand.

I'll ask my instructor for clarification.

Eventually, I'll just figure it out.

3. What would you have to do to increase your likelihood of success? Will you do it this quarter or semester?

Example: Discipline myself to focus in class. Yes!

How YOU will relate to this chapter

What are you most interested in learning about? Put checkmarks by those topics.

☐ How to get engaged in class

☐ How to listen with focus to different kinds of lecture styles

☐ How to take good notes

☐ How to adjust your note-taking system and why

☐ How to ask questions in class

☐ How to use your notes to achieve the best results

● How motivated are you to learn more about getting the right start in college? (5 = high, 1 = low) ____

● How ready are you to read now? ____ (If something is in your way, take care of it if you can, so you can zero in and focus.)

● How long do you think it will take you to complete this chapter? If you start and stop, keep track of your overall time. ____ hour(s) ____ minutes

Rachel White

Every child goes through 'child development' and this process includes: walking, talking... children go through milestones at predictable time period.

2 month old babies explore environment, this is cognitive development, and emotional development is smiling and taking turns

Language development is when a baby learns first words, or learning parts of the body knowing when.

fine and gross motor skills: fine skills are when a child uses small muscles like drawing

fine

gross

Understanding CHILD Development 8th Edition

Rachel White's Caring Hands Childcare

**State Certified
-Home Childcare Service
Open 7:30am-5:30pm
ritious Meals, Preschool
Curriculum**

**Call Rachel White
719-555-5103
 an appointment**

TAKE ONE!!!

Caring Hands Childcare
719-555-5103

Caring Hands Childcare
719-555-5103

Caring Hands Childcare
719-555-5103

Caring Hands Childcare
719-555-5103

Caring Hands Childcare
719-555-5103

Caring Hands Childcare
719-555-5103

Caring Hands Childcare
719-555-5103

Caring Hands Childcare
719-555-5

Caring
71

Caring
71

Caring
71

All she ever wanted to be was a Mom. Rachel White loved kids. When she was one herself, she helped raise her six younger brothers and sisters. Her parents worked hard to support the family, so Rachel took over her mom's duties. With each new baby, Rachel got better at distinguishing between whiney cries, hurt cries, and hungry cries. It was Rachel who cooked their dinner most nights and took them to the park on Saturdays. It was almost as if they were Rachel's children. In fact, sometimes she pretended they were.

So as a senior, Rachel dropped out of high school and married her boyfriend, Mike. He loved kids, too, and when they found out they were expecting, he was as happy as she was that the "baby" was actually "babies." Twins ran in Mike's family, and it wasn't long until they had a real family with a little boy and a girl. But now with another baby on the way, Rachel realized that Mike's income wouldn't be enough. She wanted a big family like the one she'd grown up in, and she knew that getting an education was the best answer. The ideal career for a stay-at-home mom, she thought, would be to open a day care center in her own home. An associate's degree in Early Childhood Development would provide credentials. So she studied at night, earned her GED, and enrolled in two evening classes at her local community college. Mike would be so proud of her.

Despite a 40-minute commute in heavy traffic, Rachel was excited about her first class, Child Development I, as a new college student. But right away, several things caught her off guard. The young instructor was new to teaching, spoke with a foreign accent, and raced through the lecture. Because she'd been out of school for a while, Rachel felt as though she had forgotten how to be a student. As the instructor talked, she tried to take notes as quickly as she could, but how was she supposed to know what was important enough to write down? She looked around: What were other students writing? Was she the only one who couldn't keep up? The lecture began:

Child development is a process every child goes through. This process involves learning and mastering skills like sitting, walking, talking, skipping, and tying shoes. Children learn these skills, called developmental milestones, during predictable time periods. Children develop skills in five main areas of development: First, let's look at cognitive development. This is the child's ability to learn and solve problems. For example, this includes a two-month-old baby learning to explore the environment with hands or eyes or a five-year-old learning how to do simple math problems. Second, social/emotional development is the child's ability to interact with others, including helping themselves and self-control. Examples of this type of development would include a six-week-old baby smiling, a ten-month-old baby waving bye-bye, or a five-year-old boy knowing how to take turns in games at school. Third, speech and language development is the child's ability to both understand and use language. For example, this includes a 12-month-old baby saying his first words, a two-year-old naming parts of her body, or a five-year-old learning to say "feet" instead of "foots." Children also learn both fine and gross motor skills. Fine motor skills are the child's ability to use small muscles, specifically their hands and fingers, to pick up small objects, hold a spoon, turn pages in a book, or use a crayon to draw. Gross motor skills, on the other hand, are the child's ability to use large muscles. For example, a six-month-old baby learns how to sit up with some support, a 12-month-old baby learns to pull up to a stand holding onto furniture, and a five-year-old learns to skip.*

Rachel tried to pay attention to the instructor's words and copy down the writing scribbled all over the board,

*Source: Based on http://www.howkidsdevelop.com/developSkills.html#dev

but her mind seemed to drift to the flyers she'd create for her new day-care business, or whether she should call Mike at the break to tell him the twins seemed to be coming down with a cold. Why was it so hard to focus? Rachel wondered whether she should bring her laptop to take notes that way, but somehow she knew she wouldn't be able to resist the temptation to check her Facebook page every 15 minutes or so. Information seemed to fly out of her instructor's mouth at mach speed, and frankly, she used the foreign accent as an excuse for her troubles. Taking notes that quickly was just plain impossible. She tried giving her instructor quizzical looks to communicate "Slow down, please," but the instructor probably couldn't see Rachel's face in the back of the room.

Because she didn't catch all of what the instructor was talking about, asking questions in class would only prove that she wasn't paying attention. Trying to read and take notes from the textbook chapters *before* class was hard with her active and noisy kids. Instead, she tried to look like she was paying attention in class so that no one knew that her brain wasn't really there.

Rachel had thought about trying to stop in during her instructor's office hours sometime, but she hated the thought of rush-hour traffic. She could try making an appointment at another time, but did she really want to discuss how hard it was to concentrate in the class? It was too late in the term to drop the class, and she needed the credits for her degree. Still, she had to figure something out or this course was going to spoil her dream.

1. Do you have anything in common with Rachel? If so, how are you managing the situation so that you can be successful?

2. In terms of the title of this chapter—Engaging, Listening, and Note-taking in Class—how is Rachel doing? In your view, is she likely to pass the course? Why or why not?

3. List five mistakes Rachel is making.

4. Now list five things that Rachel should do immediately to improve her childhood development classroom experience.

Get Engaged in Class

engagement emotional and psychological commitment to a task

No, this chapter isn't about buying a ring and getting down on one knee. It's about your willingness to focus, listen, discuss, ask questions, take notes, and generally dive into your classes. It's about being a full participant in your learning, not just a spectator sitting on the sidelines. It's about not just memorizing information for exams and then forgetting it. You see, the secret to college success hinges on this one word: engagement.

Think about this analogy. How did you learn to swim? Did you watch swimming on TV? Did you get advice from your friends about swimming? Did you just Google it? No, you probably jumped in and got wet, right? The same thing is true with your college classes. The more willing you are to jump in and get wet, the more engaged you'll be in the learning process.

Follow the Rules of Engagement

Just as is the case with most places you can think of, college classrooms have rules about how to behave. You don't find people yelling in church or staring at other people in elevators or telling jokes at funerals. There are rules about how to behave in a variety of contexts, and college classrooms are no exception. In fact, the rules of engagement described here are a part of what this book calls academic professionalism, and preparing for class beforehand is at the top of the list. Despite their best intentions, some community college students "shoot themselves in the foot" without meaning to. They believe they're ready for college and motivated to achieve, but within the first few weeks of the term, they miss class (25%), turn in an assignment late (33%), or don't turn in an assignment at all (24%).[1] Although not all students see the value of academic professionalism and preparation, do more than your classmates—dare to prepare! If you follow these rules of engagement, your classes will be much more enjoyable, enriching learning experiences.

1. **Look ahead.** By checking your course syllabus before class, you'll be prepared for the upcoming topic. You'll also avoid the "oops" factor of sitting down, looking around, and noticing that everyone else knows something you don't about what's supposed to happen today.

2. **Do the assigned reading.** If you have a reading assignment due for class, do it, and take notes as you read. Write in the margins of your textbook or on sticky notes. Or take notes using one of many convenient online note-taking tools while you read. Question what you're reading, and enter into a mental conversation with the author. Having some background on the topic will allow

> When you can do the common things of life in an uncommon way, you will command the attention of the world.
>
> —*George Washington Carver, 1864–1943, horticulturist, chemist, and educator*

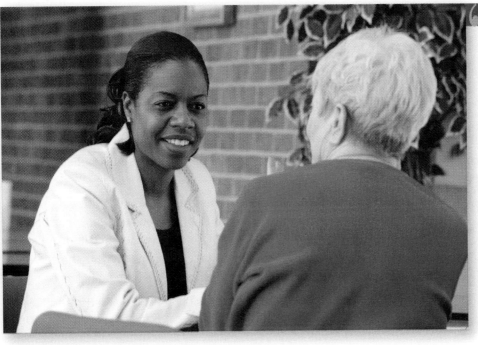

> **You cannot truly listen to anyone and do anything else at the same time.**
>
> M. Scott Peck, American author, (1936–2005)

you to listen more actively and participate more intelligently during any discussion: *Yes, I remember the chapter covering that topic,* you'll think when the instructor begins talking about something you recognize. Instead of hearing it for the first time, you'll *strengthen* what you've already read. According to one study, as few as one-third of your classmates will have done the assigned reading prior to class.[2] That little-known fact isn't a reason to excuse yourself from reading; instead it gives you insider information on how you can shine in class by comparison.

3. **Show up physically.** Not only is attending class important for your overall understanding of the material, but it may move your grade up a few notches. Even if attendance isn't required by your instructor, require it of yourself. Research says that missing classes is definitely related to your academic performance. And once you give yourself permission to skip one single class, it becomes easier to do it the next time, and the time after that. Studies indicate that on any given day, approximately one-third of your classmates will miss class, and that most students think that several absences during a term is "the standard."[3] Exercise good judgment, even if your classmates don't! Besides the importance of being there, it's essential to be on time and stay for the full class session. Students who arrive late and leave early are annoying not only to the instructor but also to their classmates. To everyone else, it looks like they don't value the other students or the class content. How would you like dinner guests to arrive an hour late, after you'd slaved over a hot stove all day? Your instructors have prepared for class, and they feel the same way. Build in time to find a parking place, hike to the building where class is held, or stop for a coffee. Do everything you can to avoid coming late and leaving early.

4. **Show up mentally.** Showing up means more than just occupying a seat in the classroom. It means thinking about what you bring to the class as a learner on any particular day. Do a mental readiness check when you arrive in class. If you're not ready, what can you do to rally for the cause?

5. **Choose your seat strategically.** Imagine paying $150 for a concert ticket, just like everyone else, and then electing to sit in the nosebleed section as high up and far away from the action as you could get. Sitting in the back means you're more likely to let your mind wander and less likely to hear clearly. Sitting in the front means you'll keep yourself accountable by being in full view of the instructor and the rest of the class. What's the best spot for great concentration? Front and center, literally—the "T zone"! In one study, students who sat at the back of a large auditorium were six times more likely to fail the course, even though the instructor had assigned seats randomly![4]

6. **Bring your tools.** Bring a writing utensil and notebook with you to every class. Your instructor may also ask you to bring your textbook, calculator, a blue book or scantron form for an exam, or other necessary items. If so, do it. Question: How seriously would you take a carpenter who showed up to work without a hammer, nails, and screwdriver? Get the point?

7. **Be aware that gab is not a gift.** In class, talking while others are speaking is inappropriate. And it's certainly not a gift—especially to your instructor. In fact, side conversations while your instructor is lecturing or your classmates are contributing to the discussion are downright rude. If you're seated next to a gabber, don't get sucked in. Use body language to communicate that you're there to learn, not to gab. If that's not enough, politely say something like "I really need to pay attention right now. Let's talk more later, okay?" Don't let other students cheat you out of learning.

8. **Choose to engage.** Engagement isn't something that just happens to you while you're not looking. It's a choice you make, and sometimes it's a difficult choice because the material isn't naturally appealing to you, or the course is a required one you didn't choose, or you're just in a bad mood. Choose to engage anyway. Instead of actively choosing to disengage in class by sleeping through lectures, surfing the Internet, or texting friends, choose to engage by leaning forward, listening, finding your own ways to connect to the material, and thinking of questions to ask. For many students, texting on their cell phones during class is particularly tempting. There's a reason why people are asked to turn off their cell phones before concerts, athletic events, or movies. Imagine being in a jam-packed theater trying to follow the film's plot, with cell phones going off every few seconds. You've paid good money to see a film. The same thing goes for your college classes.

9. **Focus.** After sitting down in class each day, take a moment to clear your head of all daydreams, to-do's, and worries. Take a deep breath and remind yourself of the opportunity to learn that lies ahead. Think of yourself as a reporter at a press conference, listening carefully because you'll be writing a story about what's going on. You *will* be writing a "story"—often in response to an essay question on an exam!

10. **Maintain your health.** Being sick can take its toll on your ability to concentrate, listen well, and participate. Prevent that from happening by getting enough sleep, eating well, and exercising. Remember, *energy management* is key to your ability to focus.

Listening with Focus

Listening with focus is more than just physically hearing words as they stream by. It's actually a complicated process that's hard work. You can't listen well when your energy is zapped, when you've stayed up all night, or when your stomach is growling fiercely. Focused listening means that you are concentrating fully on what's going on in class.

"Easy Listening" Is for Elevators—Focused Listening Is for Classrooms

Stores, restaurants, and elevators are known for their programmed, background easy listening music. Chances are you hardly notice it's there. Listening in class, however, requires actual skill, and you'll be doing a great deal of it as a college student. Experts estimate that the average student spends 80 percent of class time listening to lectures.[5]

Many of us think that listening is easy. If you happen to be around when there's something to listen to, you can't help but listen. Not so! Did you know that when you're listening at your best, your breathing rate, heartbeat, and body temperature all increase? Just as with physical exercise, your body works harder when you're engaged in focused listening. When all is said and done, listening is really about energy management.

Here are some techniques for improving your listening skills in the classroom. Read through the list, then go back and check off the ones you're willing to try harder to do in class this week.

Politeness is the art of choosing among one's real thoughts.

Adlai Stevenson II, U.S. Presidential candidate (1900–1965)

> **Calm yourself.** Take a few deep breaths with your eyes closed to help you put all those nagging distractions out of your mind during class time.

> **Be open.** Keep an open mind and view your class as yet another opportunity to strengthen your intellect and learn something new. Wisdom comes from a broad understanding of many things, rather than from a consistently limited focus what's going on in your own world.

> **Don't make snap judgments.** Remember, you don't have to like your instructor's wardrobe to respect his knowledge. Focus on the content he's offering you, even if you don't agree with it. You may change your mind later when you learn more. Don't jump to conclusions about content *or* style.

> **Assume responsibility.** Speak up! Ask questions! Even if you have an instructor with an accent who's difficult to understand, the burden of understanding course content rests with you. You will interact with people with all sorts of accents, voices, and speech patterns throughout your life. It's up to you to improve the situation.

> **Watch for gestures that communicate "Here comes something important!"** Some typical examples include raising an index finger, turning to face the class, leaning forward from behind the lectern, walking up the aisle, or using specific facial expressions or gestures.

> **Listen for speech patterns that subtly communicate "Make sure you include this in your notes!"** For example, listen for changes in the rate, volume, or tone of speech, longer than usual pauses, or repeated information.

VARK It!

Read/Write: Read this list of suggestions for improving your listening skills aloud. Choose one item to focus on, and coach yourself about how you'll do it.

> **Uncover general themes or roadmaps for each lecture.** See whether you can figure out where your instructor is taking you *while* he's taking you there. Always ask yourself, "Where's he going with this? What's he getting at? How does this relate to what was already said?"

> **Appreciate your instructor's prep time.** For every hour of lecture time, your teacher has worked for hours to prepare. Although she may make it look easy, her lecture has involved researching, organizing, creating a PowerPoint presentation, overheads, or a podcast, and preparing notes and handouts.

Listen Hard!

It's estimated that college students spend ten hours per week listening to lectures.[6] Instructors can speak 2,500–5,000 words during a fifty-minute lecture. That's a lot of words flying by at breakneck speed, so it's important to listen correctly. But what does *that* mean?

Think about the various situations in which you find yourself listening. You often listen to empty chit-chat on your way to class. "Hey, how's it going?" when you spot your best friend in the hallway is an example, right? Listening in this type of situation doesn't require a lot of brainpower. Although you wouldn't want to spend too much time on chit-chat, if you refused to engage in any at all, you'd probably be seen by others as odd, withdrawn, shy, or stuck up.

You also listen in challenging situations, some that are emotionally charged; for example, a friend needs to vent, relieve stress, or verbalize her anxieties. Most people who are blowing off steam aren't looking for you to fix their problems. They just want to be heard and hear you say something like "I understand" or "That's too bad."

Listening to chit-chat and listening in emotionally charged situations require what are called **soft listening skills**. You must be accepting, sensitive, and non-judgmental. You don't have to assess, analyze, or conclude. You just have to be there for someone else.

But these two types of listening situations don't describe all the kinds of listening you do. When you're listening to new information, as you do in your college classes, or when you're listening to someone trying to persuade you of something, you have to pay close attention, think critically, and ultimately make decisions about what you're hearing. Is something true or false? Right or wrong? How do you know? When you're listening to a person trying to inform you or to persuade you, you need **hard listening skills**. In situations like these, you must evaluate, analyze, and decide.

One mistake many students make in class is listening the wrong way. They should be using their hard listening skills, rather than sitting back and letting information float over them. Soft listening skills don't help you in class. You must listen intently, think critically, and analyze carefully what you're hearing. It's important to note that neither listening mode is better than the other. They are each simply better suited to different situations. But soft listening won't get you the results you want in your classes. You don't need to be there for your instructor; you need to be there for yourself.[7]

You may find many of your classes to be naturally fascinating learning experiences. But for others, you will need to be convinced. Even if you don't find Intro to Whatever to be the most engaging subject in the world, you may find yourself fascinated by your instructor. Most people are interested in other people. What makes him tick? Why was she drawn to this field? If you find it hard to get interested in the material, trick yourself by paying attention to the person delivering

Sharpen *Your* FOCUS

> **Speed is the blessing (and the curse) of the modern age. It is our drug of choice.**
>
> —EDWARD M. HALLOWELL, M.D., *CRAZY BUSY*

Reason 7. They are always rushing.

Are you hooked on speed? Do your days whiz by as you rush from thing to thing? Time management expert Edward Hallowell writes, "We go fast not just because we're busy, but because speed is fun. Speed grips attention. Speed excites. Speed speeds you out of boredom. Nothing is boring if it's fast enough." But what do we sacrifice when we choose to speed through life? The ability to focus! Focus is what is required when we need to zero in on important things. Ask yourself whether slowing down occasionally could help you truly sharpen your focus.

TRY It!

As you go through this week, make a point of slowing down—and accomplishing more. Keep a record of something you do each day—slower, longer, and better—by consciously remembering that "slow and steady wins the race."

Sunday _____

Monday _____

Tuesday _____

Wednesday _____

Thursday _____

Friday _____

Saturday _____

---

the message. Sometimes focusing on something about the speaker can help you focus on the subject matter, too. And you may just find out that you actually do find this class to be valuable. Although tricking yourself isn't always a good idea, it *can* work if you know what you're doing and why.

Get Wired for Sound

Increasingly instructors are providing podcasts and videocasts of their lectures so that you can *preview* the lecture in advance or *review* it after class. Some textbooks (like this one) offer chapter summaries you can listen to on the subway, in the gym, at home during a blizzard, or in bed while recovering from the flu, via your computer or digital-audio player.

Regardless of your learning style, recorded lectures allow you to re-listen to difficult concepts as many times as needed. You can take part in the live action in class and take notes later while re-listening to the podcast. In one study, students who re-listened to a lecture one, two, or three times increased their lecture notes substantially each time.[8] Of course, recorded lectures aren't meant to excuse you from attending class, and in order to take advantage of them, you actually have to find time to listen to them. They're supplemental tools to *reinforce* learning for busy students on the go, which is virtually *everyone* these days.[9]

> **The most basic and powerful way to connect to another person is to listen. Just listen. Perhaps the most important thing we ever give each other is our attention.**
>
> *Rachel Naomi Remen, physician and author*

Identify Lecture Styles So You Can Modify Listening Styles

Regardless of how challenging it is to listen with focus, being successful in college will require you to do just that—focus—no matter what class or which instructor. Sometimes your instructors are facilitators, who help you discover information on your own in new ways. Other times they are orators, who lecture as their primary means of delivering information. If you're not an aural learner, listening with focus to lectures will be a challenge for you.

Chances are you won't be able to change your instructors' lecturing styles. And even if you could, different students react differently to different lecture styles. But what you can do is expand your own skills as a listener—no matter what class or which instructor. Take a look at the lecture styles coming up and see whether you recognize them.

facilitators guides

orators public speakers

supplementary extra

Sophie Louise Phelps/
Shutterstock.com

iStockphoto.com/narvikk

VARK It!

Aural: With a partner, discuss the pros and cons of each lecture style. Do either of you have instructors that use any of these styles?

Kuzma/Shutterstock.com

Mladen Mitrinovic/
Shutterstock.com

Arkady/Shutterstock.com

> **The Rapid-Fire Lecturer:** You may have found yourself in a situation like Rachel's with an instructor who lectures so fast it makes your head spin. Listening and taking notes in a class like this are not easy. By the end of class, your hand aches from gripping your pen and writing furiously. Because there'll be no time to relax, you'll need to make certain you're ready for this class by taking all the suggestions in this chapter to heart. Read ahead so that you recognize points the instructor makes. Also take advantage of whatever supplementary materials this teacher provides in the way of audio support, online lecture notes, or PowerPoint handouts.

> **The All-Over-the-Map Lecturer:** Organization is not this lecturer's strong suit. Although the lecture may be organized in the lecturer's mind, what comes out is difficult to follow. In this case, it will be up to you to organize the lecture content yourself.

> **The Content-Intensive Lecturer:** This lecturer, determined to cover a certain amount of material in a particular amount of time, is hardly aware that anyone else is in the room. This teacher may use specific language related to the subject, which you will need to learn rapidly to keep up. Prepare yourself for a potentially rich learning environment, but be sure to ask questions right away if you find yourself confused.

> **The Review-the-Text Lecturer:** This lecturer will follow the textbook closely, summarizing and highlighting important points. You may assume it's not important to attend class, but watch out for this trap! Receiving the same information in more than one format (reading *and* listening) can be a great way to learn.

> **The Active-Learning Lecturer:** This lecturer may choose not to lecture at all or to alternate between short lectures and activities, exercises, and role plays. Although you may find it easier to get engaged in this type of class, and you'll most likely appreciate the teacher's creativity, remember that you are still responsible for connecting what happens in class to the course material itself. You will need to read, digest, and process the information on your own outside of class.

BOX 7.1

Listening Tips If English Is Your Second Language

It's normal to feel overwhelmed in the classroom as a new student, but especially if your first language isn't English. The academic environment in higher education can be stressful and competitive. It's even more stressful if you're also dealing with a new and different culture. You will need to give yourself time to adapt to all of these changes. In the meantime, here are some suggestions for improving your ability to listen well in class:

- Talk to your instructor before the course begins. Let her know that English is not your native language, but that you're very interested in learning. Ask for any suggestions on how you can increase your chances of success in the class. Your instructor will most likely be willing to provide you with extra help, knowing you're willing to do your part to overcome the language barrier.

- Try to get the main points of your instructor's lecture. You don't have to understand every word.

- Write down words to look up in the dictionary later. Keep a running list and check them all after class. Missing out on one important term can hurt your chances of understanding something else down the line.

- Don't be afraid to ask questions. If you're too uncomfortable to ask during class, make use of your instructor's office hours or e-mail address to get your questions answered. Also, teaching assistants and peer tutors may be available to help you.

- Use all support materials available for the class. Find out whether your instructor posts his notes on the course website or if they are available as handouts. Some instructors offer guided notes or skeleton outlines for students to fill in throughout the lecture. Some large lectures are videotaped for viewing by students at a later time. Make full use of podcasts of lectures, if they're available, so that you can listen more than once to portions you found confusing in class. Use any tools available to help reinforce lecture content.

- Team up with a classmate whose native language is English. Clarify your notes and fill in gaps.

- Form a study group with other classmates. Meet on a regular basis so that you can help one another. Remember: just because your native language isn't English doesn't mean you don't have something to offer the other members of your study group.

- Be patient. It will take some time to adjust to the accents of your various instructors. After a few weeks of class, you'll find it easier to understand what is being said.

- Practice your English comprehension by listening to talk radio or watching television or movies. You'll hear a variety of regional accents, for example, and broaden your understanding of American culture.

- Take an English as a Second Language course if you think it would help. It's important to keep up with the academic demands of college, and further development of your English skills may improve your comprehension and boost your confidence.

- If you continue to feel overwhelmed and unable to cope after several weeks in school, find out whether your campus has an International Students Office, and enlist support from people who are trained to help.[10]

Turn Listening Skills into Note-Taking Skills

How Well Do You Listen?

Now that you've read about focused listening, see how the following statements apply to you. Check the box that most applies to what you usually do in the classroom. Use this self-assessment to develop a plan for improvement, particularly so that you're listening at your best to take careful, useful notes.

Listening Statements:	Always True of Me	Sometimes True of Me	Never True of Me
I stay awake during class so that I can take good notes to use later while studying.	✓		
I maintain eye contact with the speaker.	✓		
I don't pretend to be interested in the subject.	✓		
I understand my instructor's questions.		✓	
I try to summarize the information in my notes.	✓		
I look for organizational patterns in the lecture and identify them in my notes (e.g., causes and effects, lists of items).		✓	
I set a purpose for listening, like trying to capture all the key ideas and examples that explain them.	✓		
I don't daydream during class, leaving gaps in my notes.		✓	
I try to predict the lecturer's next main point.		✓	
I take notes regularly.	✓		
I don't let external distractions such as loud noises, late-arriving students, and so on, interfere with my note-taking.		✓	
I try to determine the speaker's purpose.	✓		
I recognize that the speaker may be biased about the subject, but I don't let that affect my note-taking.	✓		
I write down questions the instructor poses during class.		✓	
I copy down main points and examples from the board or screen.	✓		
Total check marks for each column:	9	6	

Add up the check marks in each column to learn the results of your analysis. Pay particular attention to the total in the "Always True of Me" column.

13–15 "Always True of Me": You're probably an excellent listener, both in the classroom and in other situations. Keep up the good work.

10–12 "Always True of Me": You are a good listener, but you need to fine-tune a few of your listening skills.

7–9 "Always True of Me": You need to change some behaviors so that you get more out of your classes.

6 or less "Always True of Me" or 7 or more "Never True of Me": You need to learn better listening skills if you want to achieve academic success in college.[11]

Listening in class is one thing. Taking notes is quite another. You must be a good listener to take good notes, but being a good listener alone doesn't automatically make you a good note-taker. Note-taking is a crucial and complex skill, and doing well on tests isn't based on luck. It's based on combining preparation and opportunity—in other words, knowing how to take useful notes in class that work for you.

Actually, one reason that note-taking is so important in the learning process is that it uses all four VARK categories: *visual* (you see your instructor and the screen, if overheads or PowerPoint slides are being used), *aural* (you listen to the lecture), *read/write* (you write what you see and hear so that you can read it later to review), and *kinesthetic* (the physical act of writing opens up a pathway to the brain). Have you ever thought about it that way before?

According to one study, 99 percent of college students take notes during lectures, and 94 percent of students believe that note-taking is important.[12] These are good signs, but are these students taking notes correctly, as a result of focused listening? If 99 percent of college students are taking notes, why isn't nearly everyone getting straight A's? Here are some reasons:

> Students typically only record less than 40 percent of the lecture's main content ideas in their notes.[13]

> Only 47 percent of students actually review their notes later to see what they've written.

> Only 29 percent edit their notes later by adding, deleting, or reorganizing material.

> A full 12 percent do nothing other than recopy them verbatim.

> Some students never do anything with their notes once they leave class![14]

Does note-taking make a difference? Absolutely. During lectures, it serves two fundamental purposes: It helps you understand what you're learning at the time and it helps you preserve information to study later. In other words, both the *process* of note-taking (as you record information) and the *product* (your notes themselves) are important to learning. There is strong evidence that taking notes during a lecture leads to higher achievement than not taking notes, and working with your notes later increases your chances for academic achievement even more. Studies show that if you take notes, you have a 50 percent chance of recalling that information at test time versus a 15 percent chance of remembering the same information if you didn't take notes.[15]

Different Strokes for Different Folks: Note-Taking by the System and Subject

Now that we know just how important listening and note-taking are, let's ask a crucial question. Exactly how do you take *good* notes? Interestingly, when it comes to note-taking, "Different strokes for different folks" is literally true. Different note-taking systems work best for different lecture styles, different learning styles, and different subjects—math versus history, for example. If your instructor uses a "Rapid-Fire" lecture style, you'll need to write quickly, perhaps using abbreviations, no matter which note-taking system you use. If your instructor is an "All-Over-the-Map" lecturer, you may have to create the connections on paper as she talks about all kinds of ideas.

No matter which note-taking strategy you choose to use in a particular situation, an important question to ask is: What constitutes good notes? The answer is: writing an accurate, complete, organized account of what you hear in class (or read in your textbook, which is discussed later in this chapter). How do you know if your notes are good? Show them to your instructor and get input, or assess your strategy after you see your results on the first exam. Your note-taking skills should steadily improve as you evolve as a student.[16]

However you decide to take notes in a particular class, it's good to have some general goals:

1. **Capture main ideas.** Listen for an organizing pattern. Has the instructor been covering the subject by major time periods? Has she been listing contributors to the field by specific discoveries? What's her system? Listen for verbal clues your instructor emphasizes or repeats several times, notice what he writes on the board, or watch for major bullets or itemized steps on the screen. In the lecture Rachel was trying to focus on in class, her instructor made it easy to recognize main points by numbering them, "first," "second," and so forth. If portions of the lecture are highlighted verbally, these portions are probably important. Listen for signal words and phrases such as "There are three reasons . . . ," "On the other hand . . . ," "For example . . . ," and "In summary . . . ."

2. **Note whether a handout accompanies lecture materials.** If so, chances are that the information is considered to be important. If the instructor interrupts the lecture to give more detailed examples from a handout, he must consider doing so important enough to take up class time. Keep all handouts, and assume they'll be worth reviewing at exam time.

3. **Write down examples or key words from stories that will help anchor the main points.** If you were a classmate of Rachel's, you might not remember exactly when the social/emotional milestone begins to develop in children, but writing down the instructor's story about something funny her own little girl did may help trigger your memory.

4. **When in doubt, write it down.** If you're not sure whether to write something down, use the motto "Better safe than sorry." If you don't know a word the instructor uses, leave a blank to show you omitted something, or sound it out as you're writing and come back to it later. Put the lecture in your own words for the most part, but write down formulas, definitions, charts, diagrams, and specific facts verbatim. Also, write down good points made by classmates. Not all the words of wisdom in class will come from your instructor. If you've prepared for class by reading the assignment and listened to the lecture, and a classmate makes a point during a discussion that adds new information, write it down!

5. **Consider your learning style preferences.** If you're a visual learner, a note-taking system that works well for you may not work particularly well for a classmate who has a different learning style. Drawing all over your paper may help you see connections, whereas a classmate next to you is writing the same information down in a structured outline format. If a note-taking system seems awkward to you even after you've tried it for awhile, you may be better off trying a different one.

6. **Create a shorthand system that works.** When you're taking notes quickly, as you often do in class, you won't have time to write out every word your instructor utters. Use abbreviations or a shorthand system that you create for yourself. The last thing you want is to look at your notes as you begin to study for an exam and wonder what you meant by a string of letters that makes no sense now. So make an abbreviation "dictionary" for yourself that you use regularly, like this:

Symbol	Meaning	Example
→	leads to, produces, causes, makes	Practice → perfect.
←	comes from, is the result of	Tsunamis ← earthquakes
↑	increased, increasing, goes up, rises	Taxes ↑ 100% last year.
↓	decreased, decreasing, lowering	Salaries ↓ 10% this year.
#	number	Retry problem #3.
@	at	Due @ 4:00 p.m.
/	per	25 miles/gallon
p	page	Read p. 99.
pp	pages	Study pp 99–105.
¶	paragraph	Revise ¶ #4.
w/o	without	They revised w/o reading carefully.
?	question	Answer ? 1.
w/i	within	There are problems w/i the tax laws.
i.e.	that is	The SAT, i.e., a college entrance exam, is challenging.
e.g.	for example	Professionals, e.g., doctors and lawyers, have advanced degrees.
etc.	et cetera, so forth	Clinton, Reagan, etc., were popular presidents.
b/c	because	We pay taxes b/c it's the law.
b/4	before	Incidents b/4 the attack.
esp.	especially	Tobacco, esp. cigarettes, causes cancer.
min.	minimum	The min. wage may go up.
max.	maximum	The max. number of people in an elevator is 8.
gov't.	government	The gov't. helped the people.
ASAP	as soon as possible	Complete your certificate program ASAP.
wrt	write	wrt #3 (write number 3)
yr/yrs	year, years	She's 18 yrs old.

Based on http://www.english-zone.com/study/symbols.html

VARK It!

Read/Write: Add to this list by creating a few more abbreviations for one of your toughest classes, for example, hypothesis = hyp.

> **When you write down your ideas you automatically focus your full attention on them. Few if any of us can write one thought and think another at the same time. Thus a pencil and paper make excellent concentration tools.**
>
> —*Michael Leboeuf, American business author*

So what are the various note-taking methods? What are the steps involved in using each one? Knowing your options, developing your skills, and learning flexibility as a note-taker are keys to your success.

Outlining

Outlining is probably the oldest, and perhaps the most trusted form of taking notes. The problem, of course, is that not all instructors speak from an outline. Rachel's instructor probably did, and if Rachel had been able to focus, outlining may have worked well. Here's what Rachel's notes would have looked like. She'd listen for key points, like the five developmental milestones, and list examples beneath each one, like this:

Child Development 1, Week 4

1. Child development involves learning and mastering skills like sitting, walking, talking, skipping, and tying shoes.
   A. Developmental milestones are learned during predictable time periods.
   B. Children develop skills in five main areas of development:
      1. Cognitive development: ability to learn and solve problems.
         a. two-month-old baby learning to explore the environment with hands or eyes
         b. five-year-old learning how to do simple math problems
      2. Social/emotional development: ability to interact with others, including helping themselves and self-control.
         a. six-week-old baby smiling
         b. ten-month-old baby waving bye-bye
         c. five-year-old boy knowing how to take turns in games at school
      3. Speech/language development: ability to both understand and use language.
         a. 12-month-old baby saying his first words
         b. a two-year-old naming parts of her body
         c. a five-year-old learning to say "feet" instead of "foots"

She's listed the instructor's main points and several examples below each point to help her remember what it's about. At the end of the lecture, she could have included a **summary** of her notes. Summarizing is an excellent way to make sure you've understood the gist of all the information you've written down.

summary a condensed version of the main points

Summary:

Children reach developmental milestones in five areas at fairly predictable ages. These five areas are cognitive, social/emotional, speech/language, fine motor skills, and gross motor skills.

Of course, if your instructor's lecture is less organized, you can elect to use an informal variation of outlining, like listing bullets, and perhaps even color-coding them so they're easier to remember, as shown here:

> *Child Development 1, week 4*
>
> *Child development = learning & mastering skills*
> - *sitting*
> - *walking*
> - *talking*
> - *skipping*
> - *tying shoes*
>
> *Children develop skills in five main areas of development:*
> 1. *Cognitive development: ability to learn and solve problems.*
> 2. *Social/emotional development: ability to interact with others, including helping themselves and self-control.*
> 3. *Speech/language development: ability to both understand and use language.*

Even if your instructor is flashing PowerPoint slides on the screen, don't count on your memory to do all the work. You have to take notes yourself to help the information stick.

The Cornell System

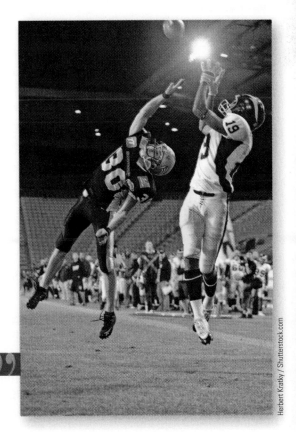

The Cornell system of note-taking, devised by educator Walter Pauk, suggests this. On each page of your notebook, draw a line from top to bottom about one and a half inches from the left edge of your paper. (Some notebook paper already has a red line there.) Take notes on the right side of the line. Your notes should include main ideas, examples, short phrases, and definitions, for example—almost like an outline.

Leave the left side blank to fill in later with key words or questions you'd like answered, as Rachel has done in Figure 7.1. After class, as you review your notes, put your hand or a sheet of paper over the right side and use the words or questions you've written on the left side as prompts to see whether you can remember what's on the right side.[17] By doing this to recall the lecture, you can get a good idea of how much of the information you've really understood.

> **Luck is what happens when preparation meets opportunity.**
>
> *Darrell Royal, football coach*

Herbert Kratky / Shutterstock.com

KEY WORDS AND QUESTIONS	SHORT PHRASES, EXAMPLES, DEFINITIONS
Child development	—Every child goes through.
Developmental milestones	—learning and mastering skills (sitting, walking, talking, skipping, tying shoes, etc.) — predictable time periods
Five main areas of development	1. Cognitive development Ability to learn and solve problems —two-month-old baby learning to explore the environment with hands or eyes —five-year-old learning to do simple math
Was it five main areas or six?	2. Social/emotional development Ability to interact with others, including helping themselves and self-control —six-week-old baby smiling —ten-month-old baby waving goodbye —five-year-old knowing how to take turns in games at school

© 2014 Cengage Learning

FIGURE 7.1

Child Development Milestones: Cornell System Example

Mind Maps

An alternative to the Cornell system, or a way to expand on it, is to create mind maps. Mind maps use both sides of your brain: the logical, orderly left side and the visual, creative right side. What they're particularly good for is showing the relationships among ideas. Mind maps are also generally a good note-taking method for visual learners, and even the physical act of drawing one may help you remember the information, particularly if you're a kinesthetic learner. To give mind mapping a try, here are some useful suggestions:

1. **Use extra-wide paper (11 × 17 inches or legal size).** You won't want to write vertically (which is hard to read) if you can help it.

2. **Write the main concept of the lecture in the center of the page.** Draw related concepts coming from the center.

3. **Limit your labels to key words so that your mind map is visually clear.**

4. **Use colors, symbols, and images to make your mind map livelier and more memorable.**

5. **Consider using software such as MindManager, MindManuals, Mind-Plugs, MindMapper, or MindGenius, which are all powerful brainstorming and organizing tools.** As you type, these programs will anticipate relationships and help you draw a mind map on screen.

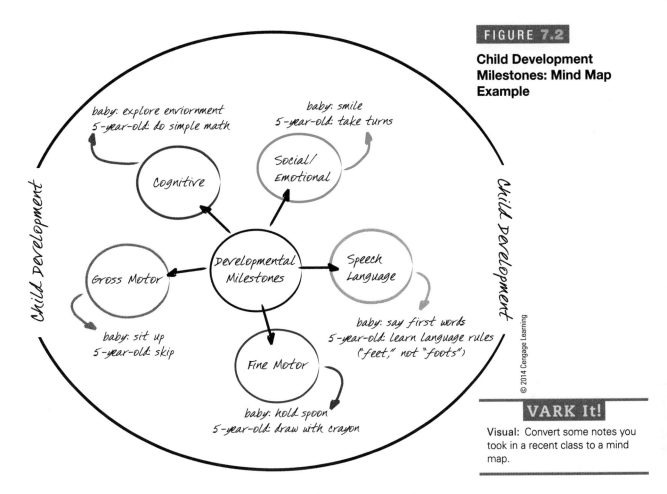

FIGURE **7.2**

Child Development Milestones: Mind Map Example

© 2014 Cengage Learning

VARK It!

Visual: Convert some notes you took in a recent class to a mind map.

Note-Taking on Instructor-Provided Handouts

PowerPoint Miniatures. Some instructors provide full-text lecture notes online or copies of their PowerPoint slides (three or six miniatures on a page). Instructors may hand out PowerPoint miniatures in class before the lecture, so you can follow along; hand them out after the lecture so that you still have to take your own notes but have the print outs of the miniatures as back-up; or e-mail them as attachments (see Figure 7.3). If you have copies of the PowerPoint slides to use during class, write in specifics on the lines provided next to each slide miniature, more or less as you would if you were using the Cornell System. Put down examples that are discussed in class but don't appear on the slide, or a story that will help you remember a main point on a slide. If they're handed out after

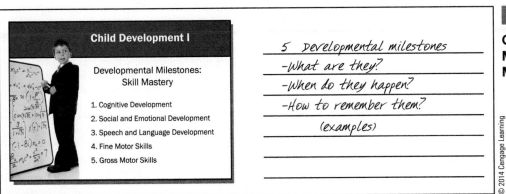

Photos.com

FIGURE **7.3**

Child Development Milestones: PowerPoint Miniatures Example

© 2014 Cengage Learning

class, transfer your own notes to the PowerPoint fill-in lines. If they're e-mailed to you before or after class, make sure you use them. They're "insurance" that you have access to what appeared in class on the screen. Tools such as these can be a valuable resource if you remember to use them. Don't rely on PowerPoints your instructors provide to the extent that you skip taking notes yourself in class altogether. Although it's helpful to have them available as a tool, you still need to take notes on your own to help you process the information you're listening to in class.

Guided Notes. Your instructor may actually help you to pay attention in class by providing what are called "Guided Notes," or copies of lecture outlines or Power-Point miniatures with key words missing, so that you must listen closely to "fill in the blanks." In one study, students in a college algebra class who used guided notes with problem sets they worked out together in groups liked their math class and did much better than comparable students who weren't using guided notes.[18]

Parallel Note-Taking. Because many instructors today provide e-support for lectures, either through web notes, hard copies of onscreen slides, lecture outlines, or a full transcript, parallel note-taking may be particularly useful, if you go about it in the right way.[19] Here's how it works, ideally.

If they're available, print out lecture notes before class and bring them with you, preferably in a ring binder. As your instructor lectures, use the back (blank) side of each page to record your own notes as the notes from the ongoing, real-time lecture face you. You can parallel what you're hearing from your instructor with your own on-the-spot, self-recorded notes, using a Cornell format on each blank page. It's the best of both worlds! You're reading, writing, and listening at the same time, fully immersing yourself in immediate and longer-lasting learning. Figure 7.4 illustrates how parallel note-taking might look for Rachel in her childhood development class.

FIGURE 7.4

Child Development Milestones: Parallel Note-Taking Example

[Fill in the blank page during actual lecture.]

My In-Class Lecture Notes

Every child develops skills like learning to sit up, walk, talk, skip, and tie shoes.

These are called developmental milestones, and they happen to most children around the same age.

Children learn skills in five main areas of development: cognitive, social/emotional, speech/language, fine, and gross motor skills:

[Print out instructor's notes and place in binder.]

Instructor's Lecture Notes

Child development is a process every child goes through. This process involves learning and mastering skills like sitting, walking, talking, skipping, and tying shoes. Children learn these skills, called developmental milestones, during predictable time periods. Children develop skills in five main areas of development: First, let's look at cognitive development. This is the child's ability to learn and solve problems. For example, this includes a two-month-old baby learning to explore the environment with hands or eyes, or a five-year-old learning how to do simple math problems. Second, social/emotional development is the child's ability to interact with others, including helping him or herself and self-control. Examples of this type of development would include a six-week-old baby smiling, a ten-month-old baby waving bye-bye, or a five-year-old boy knowing how to take turns in games at school.

Note-Taking by the Book

So far this chapter has discussed taking notes in class. What about taking notes as you read from a textbook? Is that important, too? The answer: absolutely! It's easy to go on auto-pilot as you read and have no idea what you read afterward! Instead, take notes in the margins, on sticky notes, or better yet, keep a spiral-bound notebook next to you, and fill it with your own words as you read. Jot down questions, summarize main points, or use the Cornell System. Actually, the best thing to do is to read a section, close the book, and write down what you remember. You'll prove to yourself what you absorbed and what you didn't. Then you can dive back into the textbook again and clarify concepts that are still fuzzy.[20]

Note-Taking by the Subject

Beyond figuring out which note-taking style seems to "fit" you best, think about times when the subject dictates that you vary your note-taking style. In your American History class, it may make sense to take your notes along a timeline of the beginning of World War II, for example (see Figure 7.5). Because your instructor and your textbook report key events that took place during World War II chronologically, along a time line, you might want your notes to reflect that.

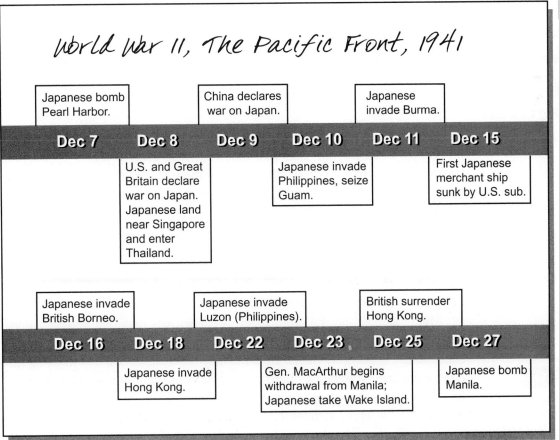

FIGURE 7.5

Timeline Example

Based on http://www.historyplace.com/unitedstates/pacificwar/timeline.htm

© 2014 Cengage Learning. All Rights Reserved. May not be scanned, copied, or duplicated, or posted to a publicly accessible website, in whole or in part.

Different Strokes for Different Folks: Note-Taking by the System and Subject   189

Notes, College Algebra 100, Wednesday, Oct. 5

Determine which of the x values are solutions to the equation

$$x^4 + x^3 - 5x^2 + x - 6 = 0$$

a) $x = -3$,   b) $x = -2$,   c) $x = 1$,   d) $x = 2$

STEPS TO SOLUTION	CALCULATIONS	RESULTS
1) Try answer a Substitute –3 into the equation for x and see if the equation is satisfied.	$(-3)^4 + (-3)^3 - 5(-3)^2 + (-3) - 6 \overset{?}{=} 0$ $81 \quad -27 \quad -45 \quad -3-6=0$ $0 = 0$	YES, because both sides are 0.
2) Try answer b Substitute –2 into the equation for x and see if the equation is satisfied.	$(-2)^4 + (-2)^3 - 5(-2)^2 + (-2) - 6 \overset{?}{=} 0$ $16 \quad -8 \quad -20 \quad -2-6=0$ $-20 \neq 0$	NO, because the two sides are unequal.
3) Try answer c Substitute 1 into the equation for x and see if the equation is satisfied.	$(1)^4 + (1)^3 - 5(1)^2 + 1 - 6 \overset{?}{=} 0$ $1 \quad +1 \quad -5 \quad +1-6=0$ $-8 \neq 0$	NO, because the two sides are unequal.
4) Try answer d Substitute 2 into the equation for x and see if the equation is satisfied.	$(2)^4 + (2)^3 - 5(2)^2 + 2 - 6 \overset{?}{=} 0$ $16 \quad +8 \quad -20 \quad +2-6=0$ $0 = 0$	YES, because both sides are 0.

FIGURE 7.6

Math Note-Taking Example

From http://www.math.armstrong
.edu/MathTutorial/exerciseSoln/
LinearEqSoln/LinearEq1Soln/
13LinearEq1.html

However, in your college algebra class, you may want to take notes very differently. Let's say, for example, that your instructor lectures by working problems on a white board or by projecting them on the screen. Then you are asked to work a problem and then talk it over with a classmate next to you. You may want to divide up your notes into columns by proposing a solution and then showing how you arrived at your answer. Having a record of how you worked a problem can be a valuable aid later when you're studying for a test that will probably contain algebra problems very much like the ones you solve regularly in class. Write everything down, and skip a few lines if there's something you want to fill in later (see Figure 7.6).

Mind mapping, on the other hand, is particularly useful in geology, physiology, biology, psychology, and education courses, where relationships among concepts are important.[21] Some students may make the mistake of thinking that mind maps are "scribbling," but the process of making connections on paper helps you make those same connections in your brain. Successful note-taking does mean "different strokes for different folks"—and different subjects. Be sure to make the right choices about which note-taking system makes the most sense for the course material being presented.

"Focused" Multitasking

One reason it's hard to focus in class is because of distractions. Like Rachel, you may be tempted to check your Facebook account or text someone about something that pops into your mind. Being pulled in different directions at once is what happens when you multitask. It breaks your concentration and disrupts your learning. Try this experiment instead. Let's call it "Focused Multitasking," meaning that all your attention is directed at one thing. Before you listen to an in-class lecture, divide into groups, with each group trying out a different note-taking strategy presented in this chapter. For example, Group 1 members should use outlines. Group 2 should use the Cornell System, Group 3 should create mind maps, and so on. Then begin the lecture. The lecture could be your instructor lecturing about this chapter of FOCUS. Or it could be something different, like listening to an NPR podcast that the instructor or the whole class chooses. You are intentionally using all of your VARK preferences at once to focus on a single topic. After the lecture, take a quiz provided by your instructor and see which note-taking group's method earns the highest score!

Ask and You Shall Receive

Even if you listen carefully to every word your instructor utters, it's likely you won't understand them all. After all, your instructor is an expert in the subject you're studying, and you're new to it. At some point or other, you'll need to ask questions. Even though that makes sense, not all students feel comfortable asking questions in class. Why? See whether you've excused yourself from asking questions for any of these reasons:

> I don't want to look stupid.

> I must be slow. Everyone else seems to be understanding.

> I'm too shy.

> I'll get the answer later from the textbook.

> I don't think my question is important enough.

> I don't want to interrupt the lecture. The instructor's on a roll.

> I'm sure the instructor knows what he's talking about. He must be right.

© Tomas Rodriguez/Corbis

> **He who is ashamed of asking is ashamed of learning.**
>
> *Danish Proverb*

If any of these reasons for not asking questions in class applies to you, the good news is . . . you're in good company. Many students think this way. The bad news, of course, is that your question remains unasked, and therefore unanswered.

The next time you find yourself in a situation where you don't understand something, consider these points.

1. **Remember that you're not in this alone.** Chances are you're probably not the only person in class who doesn't understand. Not only will you be doing yourself a favor by asking, but you'll also be helping someone else who's too shy to speak up.

2. **Ask academically relevant questions when the time is right.** As opposed to "Why do we need to know this?" or "Why did you make the test so hard?" ask questions to clarify information. Don't ask questions designed to take your instructor off on a tangent (to delay the impending quiz, for example). If you're really interested in something that's not directly related to the material being covered, the best time to raise the question would be during your instructor's office hours.

3. **Save *personally* relevant questions for later.** If your questions relate only to you (for example, you were ill and missed the last two classes), then don't ask in class. Set up an appointment with your instructor. You

tangent a sudden change of subject

impending upcoming

EXERCISE 7.3

How Much Does Asking Questions Help?

To demonstrate the value of asking questions, try this in-class exercise. A student volunteer, or class "lecturer," will briefly replace the instructor to describe to the rest of the class two different, simple figures she draws herself. Each figure should take up a full piece of paper. The rest of the class must then reproduce the drawings as accurately as possible on their own paper as the class "lecturer" describes each figure during two rounds. The point of the exercise is to replicate the two figures the class "lecturer" has drawn as accurately as possible from her description alone. The lecturer can't show the class her drawings; she must simply describe them.

Round 1: The volunteer should turn her back to the group (so she can't see them and they can't see her), hiding her paper from view, and give the class instructions for drawing Figure 1. No questions from the group are allowed. Keep track of the exact amount of time it takes for the rest of the class to listen to the instructions and complete the drawing. If this were an exam, the class would have to redraw the figure as closely as possible to the original to get an "A."

Round 2: Next, the volunteer should now turn around and face the class, giving instructions for drawing Figure 2. Students may ask questions of the "lecturer" to make sure they're getting the drawing right. Again, note the exact amount of time taken.

After both rounds of the exercise are done, the "lecturer" should ask class members whether they think their drawings look like the two originals, and count the number of students who think they drew Figure 1 correctly and the number of students who think they drew Figure 2 correctly. Then the "lecturer" should show the two original figures as drawn, and count the number of students who actually drew Figure 1 and Figure 2 correctly. Finally, as a group discuss the two rounds and the value of asking questions in lecture classes. Even though questions take more time, the results are usually much better.

Elapsed Time	# Think Correct	# Actually Correct
Round 1		
Round 2		

can also get answers by researching on your own, visiting or e-mailing your instructor, seeking out a teaching assistant or tutor, or working with a study group.

4. **Build on others' questions.** Your instructor isn't the only person who speaks in class. You must apply what you're reading in this chapter to listening to your classmates, too. Listen to the questions other students ask. Use their questions to spark your own. Perhaps another student has a unique way of looking at the issue being discussed that will spark an idea for a follow-up question from you. To your instructor good questions indicate *interest*, not *ignorance*.

Remember, your college education is an investment in your own future. You're here to learn, and asking questions is a natural part of that learning experience. Don't be shy—put that hand in the air!

Using Lecture Notes

Taking good notes is only part of the equation. To get the most value from your notes, you must actually *use* them. As soon as possible after class, take a few minutes to review your notes. If you find sections that are unclear, take time to fill in the gaps while things are still fresh in your mind. One instructor found that students who filled in any missing points right after class were able to increase the amount of lecture points they recorded by as much as 50 percent. And students who worked with another student to reconstruct the lecture immediately after class were able to increase their number of noted lecture points even more![22]

This part of the note-taking process is often overlooked, yet it is one of the most helpful steps for learning and recall. If you don't review your notes within twenty-four hours, there's good evidence that you'll end up *relearning* rather than *reviewing*. Reviewing helps you go beyond just writing to actually making sure you understand what you wrote. These three techniques help you get the best use of your notes: manipulating, paraphrasing, and summarizing.

> **Manipulating** involves working with your notes by typing them out later, for example. Some research indicates that it's not writing down information that's most important. Manipulating information is what counts. Work with your notes. Fill in charts, draw diagrams, create a mind map, underline, highlight, organize. Cut a copy of the instructor's lecture notes up into paragraphs, mix them up, and then put the lecture back together. Copy your notes onto flash cards. Manipulating information helps develop your reasoning skills, reduces your stress level, and can produce a more complete set of notes to study later.[23]

> **Paraphrasing** is the process of putting your notes into your own words. Recopy your notes or your instructor's prepared lecture notes, translating them into words you understand and examples that are meaningful to you. Paraphrasing is also a good way to self-test or to study with a classmate. If you can't find words of your own, perhaps you don't really understand the original notes. Sometimes students think they understand course material

VARK It!

Visual: As a visual learner, was this exercise easy for you because you could "picture" the images?

VARK It!

Multimodal: As a multimodal learner, you have an advantage because you are flexible. But you may have to use your two or three preferred modalities in order to be confident that you have learned something. Is this true for you?

Note-Taking 4-M

Practice your note-taking skills by doing this. Immediately after class, or during the lecture if your instructor allows, compare notes with a classmate by following these four steps:[24]

1. <u>M</u>atching—Look for content areas where your notes match those of your classmates.

2. <u>M</u>issing—Look for content areas where one of you has missed something important, and fill in the gaps.

3. <u>M</u>eaning—Talk about what this lecture means. Why was it included in the course? Do you both understand the lecture's main points?

4. <u>M</u>easuring—Quiz each other. Measure how much you learned from the lecture. Give each other some sample test questions to see whether you understand important concepts.

until the test proves otherwise, and then it's too late! Practice paraphrasing key concepts with a friend to see how well you both understand the material. Or ask yourself, *If I had to explain this to someone who missed class, what words would I use?*

> **Summarizing** is a process of writing a brief overview of all of your notes from one lecture. Imagine trying to take all your lecture notes from one class session and putting them on an index card. If you can do that, you've just written a summary. Research shows that students who use the summarizing technique have far greater recall of the material than those who don't.

Some students think that simply going over their notes is the best way to practice. Research shows that simply reading over your notes is a weak form of practice that does not transfer information into long-term memory.[25] You must actually *work with* the material, rearrange or reword it, or condense it to get the most academic bang for your buck. Active strategies always work better than more passive ones.

The Four C Factors: Just how motivated are YOU?

CONTROL: *YOUR TOUGHEST CLASS*

Think about your most challenging course this term. Use the following form to analyze the instructor's lecture style. Be careful not to be too obvious as you listen and analyze his or her style, of course, but after your chart is completed, decide what you can do as a listener to make adjustments in your toughest class. To get an idea of how to fill out the chart, look at what Rachel's entries for her child development class might have been. Filling out this chart may give you some insights about why one particular class is your toughest and help you modify your note-taking skills to what works best for that particular lecture style.[26]

COURSE	EXAMPLE: Child Development I	MY TOUGHEST CLASS
EMPHASIS *Content, students, or both?*	Teacher emphasizes content, primarily. She lectures for the full class period with little student interaction.	
ORGANIZATION *Structured or unstructured*	Lectures seem disorganized with notes written all over the board.	
PACE *Fast, slow, or medium?*	Very fast.	
VISUAL AIDS *Used? Useful?*	Board hard to see from the back of the room.	
EXAMPLES *Used? Useful?*	She needs to provide more real examples that students can relate to.	
LANGUAGE *Terms defined? Vocabulary understandable?*	The language isn't too hard, but I can't focus on what she's saying.	
DELIVERY *Animated via body language?*	Delivery style isn't lively and interesting. Instructor doesn't notice when students aren't paying attention.	
QUESTIONS *Encouraged?*	She rarely pauses to take questions.	

Now that you've analyzed your instructor's lecture style, what steps can you take to get more out of lectures in your toughest class?

_____

_____

_____

CURIOSITY: *QUIET YOUR MIND*

Have you ever noticed there's a play-by-play commentary going on inside your head, just like an NFL announcer during a big game: "On third down with no timeouts left. And here's the snap . . ." Compare that to your own play-by-play observations: "And here he comes . . . Dion's walking straight toward me. He's getting closer. Maybe this is my big chance. Should I start up a conversation with him, even though that might make me late for work?"

It's normal to have a silent conversation with yourself about what's going on around you, and it's perfectly human to think that what you hear in your own head is the most important thing on the planet. The question isn't whether or not it happens; it's whether that conversation is productive and useful, and if not, how to make it so.

Sometimes this ongoing, internal chatter makes it's hard to be fully present in your college classes because of three P's: pressure, preoccupation, and priorities. At that moment in the example above, Dion is a priority, so he gets inside someone else's head. But this person also needs to get to work on time. As you read earlier in *FOCUS*, productivity expert Kerry Gleeson believes, "This constant, unproductive preoccupation with all the things we have to do is the single largest consumer of time and energy." Do the three P's highjack your attention? If so, that's natural, but it's also important to find ways to quiet your mind when you need to.

Here are some tips on how to coach yourself to quiet your mind:[27]

- **Choose where to focus your attention.** Instead of allowing your mind to run you, make a conscious decision to run it. "Rule your mind, or it will rule you." – Horace (Roman poet, 65-8 BC)

- **Spend your free time; don't squander it.** Consider whether your free time is spent revitalizing or simply doing nothing in order to avoid unpleasant but necessary tasks. Short bouts of nothing can be liberating, but long bouts of nothing can be lead to stalling out or allowing negative thoughts to creep in.

- **Worry less; do more.** Worry is counterproductive; it drains us of the energy we need to get things done and keeps us from enjoying the present.

- **Forgive and forget.** Life is full of ups and downs, but it's important to keep moving. Focus on the present tense.

- **Be present.** Remember grade school? Your teachers would call the roll every morning, and you'd answer "present" or "I'm here." As American author James Thurber once wrote, "Let us not look back in anger, nor forward in fear, but around in awareness."

What steps can you take to put these suggestions into practice? Think about small and easy ways of changing your behaviors to quiet your mind and focus.

_____

_____

_____

CAREER OUTLOOK: *INCREASE YOUR SPQ*

Do you know people like this? When you start a story, they one-up you: "Oh, you think that's something? You should hear what I did. . . ." They spend their time (and yours) bragging about what they've done and how good they are at things. They "dot" every sentence with an "I." Let's face it: They're just plain annoying. Everything is about them.

Other people are humble. When it comes up in conversation that they won a full scholarship to your school, and you say, "Wow! That's incredible!" they say, "Oh, it was just good luck." When they get the top grade on the economics test that everyone else failed, they say, "I don't know. I just remembered stuff and wrote it down." You stand amazed.

But once you're settled into that new job after college, you have to show your stuff. No one will know exactly what you're capable of, nor can they read your mind (or your growing résumé) on a day-to-day basis. In order for your career to survive—and to thrive—you need high SPQ. What is SPQ? It's a fairly new fun, pop concept: Self-Promotion Intelligence (Quotient). It's vital to your career, and getting good at it can be a challenge.[28] It's not bragging; it's realizing what you have to offer and letting others know about it without turning them off. SPQ requires not only communication skills, but finesse. And it's not necessarily about being a superstar at one particular thing. It's recognizing your own particular blend of abilities—the combination of characteristics that makes you unique.

Start noticing exactly what makes you unique, and be prepared to talk about it, as if you were creating your own personal "brand." If you have a particular skill, become known as the go-to person for it. ("Ask Maria; she's great with PowerPoint!") Like an athlete, "play back" incidents in your head and remember what you did well (or not). Don't be afraid to speak up, even if you're an introvert. On the other hand, don't forget to ask questions of others and listen carefully to what they have to say about themselves. Volunteer for visibility by offering to write, speak, or run a meeting. Connect other people so that you become known as a networker. Use the pronoun "we" more than you use its complement, "I." (Rarely is anything accomplished by a single individual in isolation.) And finally, be generous in your praise of others; it will come back to you.[29]

What makes you unique? What makes up your personal "brand," and how you can let others know about it?

_____

_____

_____

CHALLENGE: REALITY CHECK

How much did you learn? At the beginning of this chapter, you filled out a "Readiness Check" that asked how you thought this chapter would relate to you, and how you would relate to it. Now, fill out this "Reality Check" to find out.

1. What does it mean to sit in the "T zone" in class and why is it important?

2. This chapter discusses "hard" and "soft" listening skills. What's the difference between the two and which one is the right one to use in class?

3. Identify three possible formats for taking notes in class.

4. Describe two effective ways of using your lecture notes to study.

5. How long did it take? _____ hours _____ minutes. Before you began this chapter, you were asked to predict how long it would take you to complete it (total time, even if you read it in more than one sitting). Was your estimate on target, or will you revise it for the next chapter you'll read?_____

step 3 INSIGHT *Now* What Do You Think?

At the beginning of this chapter, Rachel White, a frustrated student, faced a challenge. Now after reading this chapter, would you respond differently to any of the questions you answered about the "FOCUS Challenge Case"? Using what you learned in the chapter, write a paragraph ending to Rachel's case study. What are some of the possible outcomes for Rachel?

step 4 ACTION Your Plans for Change

1. What is the single most important point you will take from this chapter?
2. Do you have a class like Rachel's? What are you doing to cope?

chapter 8 Reading, Writing, and Presenting

READINESS CHECK

How this chapter relates to **YOU**

1. When it comes to reading, writing, and presenting in college, what do you find most challenging, if anything?

Understanding what I read

Struggling with writing assignments

Getting nervous speaking in front of others

Procrastinating on these types of assignments

Always completing and turning in assignments

2. What is most likely to be your response? Circle it.

I'll be open to learning how to improve my skills.	I'll wait and see how much of this chapter I understand.	I'll get help from a support center on campus.	Eventually, I'll just figure it out on my own.

3. What would you have to do to increase your likelihood of success? Will you do it this quarter or semester?

Example: Get help from an on-campus coach or tutor. Yes!

How **YOU** will relate to this chapter

What are you most interested in learning about? Put checkmarks by those topics.

☐ Why reading is important

☐ How to build reading skills

☐ How to read right

☐ How the writing process works

☐ What the seven C's (writing) and seven P's (presenting) are

☐ How to make your PowerPoint pop

• How motivated are you to learn more about getting the right start in college? (5 = high, 1 = low) ____

• How ready are you to read now? ____

   (If something is in your way, take care of it if you can, zero in and focus.)

• How long do you think it will take you to complete this chapter? If you start and stop, keep track of your overall time. ____ hour(s) ____ minutes

Katie Alexander

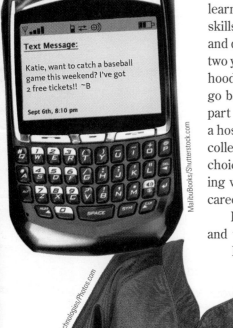

© Larry Harwood Photography.
Property of Cengage Learning.

College would be a lot more fun if it weren't for all the reading and writing required. That was Katie Alexander's take on things. She wasn't much of a student, actually. She much preferred playing softball or volleyball with her friends to sitting in one spot with a book propped open in front of her. Reading for fun wasn't something she'd ever even consider doing—at least not reading books. To Katie, reading 75 text messages a day was necessary; reading books was boring. *Anyway, why read the book when you can just watch the movie?* she always asked. Katie was an energetic, active, outgoing person, and "doing" and "socializing" were her things. Academic pursuits, like reading textbooks, writing papers, and giving presentations, definitely weren't.

Actually, this was Katie's second attempt at college. She'd gone to a small liberal arts school right after high school, but the self-discipline required just wasn't there. A specialist at the college officially diagnosed dyslexia, a learning disability that affects reading skills, and Katie became discouraged and dropped out. Working as a server for two years at a restaurant in her neighborhood helped her earn enough money to go back to school. She loved the people part of her waitressing job, and thought a hospitality degree from the community college close to home would be the right choice for her. Besides, how much reading would she possibly have to do for a career like that?

Because of her dyslexia, reading and writing papers were hard work for Katie. She was smart enough to make it in college—she was sure of that—and this time around, she was more motivated. But reading a long assignment, page by page, made her fidgety, and after she read something, she found it hard to summarize what it had been about. Reading took her a long time, so long that her mind wandered wherever it seemed to want to go. She found it hard to focus, and things just didn't seem to stick. Before she knew it, she was off in some other world, thinking about her friends, or her schedule at work, or everything else she had to do. Writing papers was just as hard, if not harder.

Back in grade school, Katie had been labeled as a slow reader. She was never in the top reading group, and although she resented the label, she didn't quite know what do to about it. The last time reading had actually been a subject in school was sixth grade. Now, eight years later, she was enrolled in a developmental reading class. Would it really help her?

Text Message:

Katie, want to catch a baseball game this weekend? I've got 2 free tickets!! ~B

Sept 6th, 8:10 pm

MalibuBooks/Shutterstock.com

Hemera Technologies/Photos.com

Katie

Oddphoto/Shutterstock.com

1027

PAY TO THE
ORDER OF *Great Bluffs Community College* $ 2159 00
    9-13-13   DATE

Two thousand one hundred and fifty nine & 00/100 DOLLARS

FOR

⑆ 22222222 ⑆ 000 ⑈   *Katie Alexander*

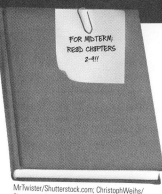

Katie's sister, Amanda, had always been an excellent student who loved to read, especially now that she'd gotten an e-reader for her birthday. Katie always wondered if Amanda's love of reading was due to the fact that she had been in a wheelchair since a car accident in the third grade. She couldn't be active or play sports. Katie's best friend, Brittney, however, had a different strategy. "There's so much required reading in all my classes that I don't even know where to start," Brittney admitted, "so I just don't do it. I go to class, listen to the lectures, and write down what the instructor has said on the essay tests. Katie, just learn to 'play the game'!"

Besides her developmental reading class, Katie was enrolled in two other classes: history and introduction to psychology. She knew she'd have plenty of reading to do there, and her friend Brittney's strategy definitely wasn't going to work. Professor Harris-Black had assigned a shocking number of chapters to read in their thick psychology textbook for the first exam. She didn't even go over the reading in class, and her lectures were about all sorts of things, much of which wasn't even related to the reading. Whenever Katie sat down to read a chapter, she found what to her were unfamiliar words and long, complicated phrases. The instructor had suggested that students read with a dictionary at their sides, but who'd ever want to keep stopping to look up words? You'd never finish!

With a midterm exam coming up in her psychology class next week, not to mention a paper and presentation due in her history class, Katie was beginning to panic. She'd only read one of the nine chapters assigned. In fact, she hadn't made it through the first chapter when she got discouraged and gave up. She knew the essay questions would be challenging. Winging it wouldn't work, and choosing to "watch the movie" instead of reading the book wasn't an option. Exactly what did psychology have to do with hospitality, she puzzled, and why did she have to take this course in the first place?

The night before the test, Katie decided to get serious. She sat down at her desk, armed with her yellow highlighter. As she began reading, however, she realized she didn't know exactly what to highlight because she didn't really understand what she was reading. Looking back at the page she had just finished, she saw that she had basically highlighted everything.

Exasperated, Katie told herself that she couldn't go to bed until she'd finished reading everything, no matter when that was. She started with the second chapter, because she'd read the first one, and by morning she'd be as ready as possible. Anyway, whether or not she did well wasn't up to her—it was up to Professor Harris-Black. She was the one making up the test.

Getting a good grade on her Introduction to Psychology midterm exam was probably out of the question, but if she could just manage to pass, Katie knew she would have to settle for that. On the other hand, she secretly hoped that maybe she'd just luck out.

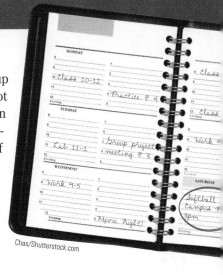

Psychology
Recommended Reading List

Treating the Troubled Family
    ackerman, N.W.
The Care and Feeding of Ideas
    adams, J. L.
Kinds of Minds
    Dennett, D.C.
The Dreaming Brain
    Clifford, James
Guilty by Reason of Insanity
    Lewis, D.O.
The Evolution of Consciousness
    Ornstein, R.
Beginner's Guide to Jungian Psychology
    Robertson, R.
anger: The Misunderstood Emotion
    Tavris, C.

```
ST# 34    OP#      TE#       TR#
          005749801035       3.38
          007065200750       2.97
          007065200750       2.97
          006025835503      14.96
          068113176369       4.97
          002340035457       0.93
          005963148202       3.87
          002340035458       0.93
          005920000731       SUBTOTAL   35.91
                    HST 15%    4.88
                    TOTAL     40.79
             DEBIT TEND       40.79
             CHANGE DUE        0.00
                 RT
GST/HST

Metro Sports Equipment

PURCHASE TRANSACTION RECORD
            40.79
CHEQUING     ************
RRN # :
AUTH # :
00 APPROVED-THANK YOU
TERMINAL ID:
```

Study Strategies for Students with Dyslex[...]

- Take advantage of multi-sensory learning metho[...]
  Study diagrams, look at charts
  Listen to the instructor's words
  Combine sensory input to create a more complete picture [...]

- Read through superficially first
  Look at the title page and intro
  Note the major headings and bullets
  Skim through the text to get the main ideas

- Read out loud
  Read out loud while highlighting, then read what you'[...]
  Listen to your voice as you emphasize important point[...]

- Organize your workspace
  Categorize papers and books for each subject
  Color-code assignments and papers to make organ[...]

- Improve your work methods
  Brainstorm at the beginning of a project
  Set priorities and outline your work strategy

- Prepare for tests
  Be sure to attend all classes leading up to the [...]
  Listen for clues and try to determine the form[...]
  Get a good night's sleep
  Take your time

1. Do you have anything in common with Katie? If so, in what ways, specifically?
2. Katie is probably an intelligent student, but she has decided that she dislikes reading, so she avoids it. How important will reading be as she continues to pursue a college degree? Is she likely to succeed her second time around?
3. How would you characterize Katie as a student? Identify five specific problems described in this case study that could interfere with her college success.
4. Identify three specific things Katie should do to get her college career on track.

Who Needs to Read?

What's so important about reading? Teachers seem to think it's important, but times have changed, haven't they? Now you can just skim predigested information on websites, get a summary of the day's news from television, and watch movies for entertainment. Who needs to read? Look around the next time you're in a doctor or dentist's waiting room. You'll see some people staring at the TV screen mounted on the wall, others plugged into iPods, and still others working with their smart phones. A few may be skimming through magazines, but does anyone ever pick up a book to actually read it cover to cover anymore? Does it matter?

The answer, according to many experts, is a definite yes, it does matter![1] Reading helped create civilization as we know it and taught us particular ways of thinking.

One fairly predictable result of doing anything less often is that eventually you may not do it as well. Practice helps you improve. Even an Olympic athlete who doesn't stick with training gets rusty after a while. As students read less,

No matter how busy you may think you are, you must find time for reading, or surrender yourself to self-chosen ignorance.

Confucius, Chinese philospher, 551–479 B.C.E.

Sharpen Your FOCUS

TRY It!

> **Make use of time, let not advantage slip.**
>
> —WILLIAM SHAKESPEARE

Reason 8. They miss opportunities.

When it comes to succeeding in college, you may feel like you're in the middle of a whirlwind, with obligations swirling around you. Everything's a blur, and you begin to lose your focus. You try hard: You buy a planner, fill in due dates, color code the level of priority of various items, and devote a good amount of time to getting yourself organized. Then you lose the planner or leave it in your car. You can't find the time to actually use the planner you've planned to use. Follow through and remember Shakespeare's wisdom: "let not advantage slip"! Turn opportunities into advantages, and keep your focus sharp.

Of course you're busy, but if you took five minutes— or even three—to review your planner before going to bed each night, time management might actually become a habit, rather than something you just can't find the time to do. Try reviewing your planner at the end of each day for one week, note your success by checking off each day you do it, and report your results in class.

Sunday	☐	Thursday	☐
Monday	☐	Friday	☐
Tuesday	☐	Saturday	☐
Wednesday	☐		

their reading skills deteriorate, and they don't enjoy doing it. On the other hand, the better you get at reading, the more you may enjoy it. Falling down every ten minutes the first time you get on skis isn't all that much fun, but once you can zip down the mountain like a pro, you begin to appreciate the sport.

Like Katie from the "FOCUS Challenge Case," reading may not be your favorite pastime. You may feel about reading like many people do about eating cauliflower. You know it's good for you, but you'd prefer to avoid it. However, this chapter wouldn't be worth its weight in trees if it didn't try to convince you otherwise. One aspect of reading Katie particularly dislikes is that reading is not a social or physical activity. You can read with someone else in the room, of course, or talk about what you read afterward with other people, but basically, reading is something you do alone. It's a solitary activity that involves you, words on a page, an invisible author, and your brain. You need to do it with a minimum of physical movement. Reading while playing a game of volleyball would be tough to pull off.

If you enjoy reading, congratulations! When you settle in with an exciting novel, you can travel to the far corners of the Earth, turn back the clock to previous centuries, or fast-forward to a future that extends beyond your lifetime. Whether or not you enjoy reading, it will be one of the primary skills you need to cultivate in college. According to one study, 85 percent of the learning you'll do in college requires careful reading.[2] First-year students often need to read and comprehend 150–200 pages per week in order to complete their academic assignments.[3]

What's more, reading skills go hand in hand with writing and presenting skills, which makes them even more important. The better you get at reading, the more likely you are to achieve academic success. Many of your classes will require intensive reading of complex material, including **primary sources** by

VARK It!

Aural: Why do (or don't) you enjoy reading? Talk through three reasons aloud with a classmate. Does listening to his or her arguments change your thinking at all?

primary sources works written by authors themselves, like the autobiography of Benjamin Franklin (that he wrote himself) original authors and scholarly research. If you complete reading assignments, and your classmates don't, think about how much ahead of the nonreaders *you* will be! But how do you learn to become a better, college-ready reader?

Build Your Reading Skills

Some people think reading should be second nature since we've all been doing it for many years now. Someone may understand an article they've just read immediately, whereas others ask, "How did you know that?" about something in the same passage. Learning to understand the process helps. In this chapter, we will look at some clues to help you become a better reader. It's not always as easy as it looks, especially in college. Books and articles you need to read for your classes are often challenging, and they can require a lot of self-discipline to read. Sometimes you may need to read a section or an entire chapter more than once! Perhaps you're in a developmental reading class to boost your skills. Or perhaps a language other than English is your native tongue. If so, this chapter can be especially useful to you.

Recognize the Building Blocks of English

One way to become a better reader is by gaining a deeper understanding of how English works. If you've been speaking it all your life, it seems natural. You open your mouth and speak, without pausing to think over every word choice. But even for many people who learned to speak English as children, *reading* English is a bigger challenge. Just what are some of the specific challenges?

© Zedcor Wholly Owned/
PhotoObjects.net/Jupiter Images

Sounds. English is spoken as a first or second language by 1.8 billion people. It's the designated "official" language in 54 countries.[4] English varies somewhat from one region of the country to another. If you live in the South, "pa" (as in "I'll have a slice of apple 'pa'") may be something you eat for dessert; in another part of the country, it's what you call your dad. The sound "tsk" you make when you mean "What a shame . . ." (tsk, tsk . . .) is an actual sound that might be the first sound in a word in other languages. In fact, when you were a six-month old baby, you could pronounce most any sound that exists in any language. But as you learn to speak as a young child, you discard sounds that aren't a part of your native language.

You already know a good deal about English that you're not even aware you know. If you entered a contest to name a new laundry detergent, you'd automatically use the "rules" for how English operates. For example, you know that you can't clump too many consonants together at the beginning of an English word, and you know that some sounds just don't go together, like "f" and "z." You'd never come up with "Buy new Fzuthoox!" People in the supermarket couldn't even pronounce it to ask a stocker, let alone find it on Aisle 9. If you're a new speaker of English, go to a website on English sounds and play the MP3 files. You can hear "pure" English online.[5]

© Zedcor Wholly Owned/
PhotoObjects.net/Jupiter Images

Syllables. Things get more complicated when sounds combine into syllables, like prefixes or suffixes. Some syllables are easy to understand, like the difference between the prefixes *pre-* and *post-* in preseason game versus postseason game. Or you know when you see the word *co-presenters*, that more than one person will be speaking. Other times, syllables are just plain puzzling. For example, typically, the prefix "in-" means "not." But why do *flammable* and *inflammable* mean exactly the same thing? Or when someone says your help is *valuable* or *invaluable*, why are both remarks equally complimentary? Go figure. Learning basic prefixes, suffixes, and word roots can help you decipher unfamiliar words you encounter in your reading.

Spelling. Here's where many of us get tripped up—and spellcheck isn't always the solution. (Did you notice the missing letter in the word spelled by the blocks?) To make things especially messy, English has many exceptions to its rules. Take a look at the Curiosity box at the end of this chapter to see some humorous examples of just how varied spelling is in English. When you try reading the poem out loud, you'll get the point quickly.

Vocabulary. Reading is about words. That's why it's important to put some muscle into your vocabulary. When you study a foreign language, your first task is to learn new vocabulary words so that you have something to say: "What time is it?" or "Where is the train station?" or "How much does this cost?" It's just as important, especially in college, to fill your mind with new words, too.

One of the best things you can do to become a better reader is to make friends with your dictionary. Even though it's annoying to stop every few minutes to look up a word, it's absolutely necessary. Sometimes it's important to break your stride, stop, and look up a word or phrase because what follows in the reading is based on that particular definition. Other times, these strategies might be appropriate:

Force yourself to reflect on what you read, paragraph by paragraph.

Samuel Taylor Coleridge, British poet (1772–1834)

> Keep a stack of blank index cards next to you, and write down the unknown word or phrase, the sentence it appears in, and the page number. Then when you have a sizable stack, or when you've scheduled a chunk of time, look up the whole stack.

> Try to guess the word's meaning from its **context** that helps to reveal its meaning. Remember Lewis Carroll's "Jabberwocky" poem from *Through the Looking-Glass*? Even though the poem contains fabricated words, when you read it, you infer that something was moving around sometime, somewhere, right?

> **'Twas brillig** ['*twas* usually indicates a time, as in 'twas daybreak],
>
> **and the slithy toves** [we don't know what *toves* are, but *slithy* sounds
> like a combination of slimy and slithering]

context words, sentences, and/or paragraphs around an unknown word that help you unlock its meaning

Often you can infer a word's meaning from how it's used or from other words around it, but not always. Many of your courses will require you to learn precise meanings for new terms. If you can't detect the meaning from the context, use your dictionary—and see it as a friend rather than an enemy.

EXERCISE 8.1

Word Hunt

You'll notice that this book defines some words that relate to your college education in the margins. That's not only a convenience; they're included to help remind you to stop and look up words as you read assignments for your other courses. Which other words are you looking up on your own as you read FOCUS? Highlight all the additional words you needed to look up in this chapter, and bring your list to class to compare with your classmates' lists.

Learn to "Read between the Lines"

We can move beyond the realm of sounds and words into the realm of sentences, inferences and main ideas. Being a good reader is like being a good detective. You have to watch for subtle clues and draw conclusions.

Inferences. Combining words into "complete thoughts" gives us sentences, and they can be complicated, too. The mere arrangement of words in a sentence can make a difference. From sentences and paragraphs, we create meaning and make **inferences**. For example, language experts talk about the difference between active and passive voice, often detectable by how words are arranged. For example:

inference a conclusion reached from hints or clues about something

---

EXERCISE 8.2

Two-Way Inferences

Part I. *Find a photo for this quote and bring it to class with you.*

"The secret of joy in work is contained in one word—excellence. To know how to do something well is to enjoy it."

—*Pearl Buck, Pulitzer Prize-winning American author, 1892–1973*

Part II. *Find a quote for the photo on the right and write it in the caption box below.*

iStockphoto.com/Daniel Bobrowsky

Mom (noticing the dent in the front fender): "Did you drive the car?"
You: "Yes, I drove the car." (Active voice, as in "I admit it.")

Compare that answer with "Um, the car was driven [by me]." (Passive voice, as in "the car was practically driving itself . . . ")

There's an inference (or conclusion) behind Mom's question, right? The dent is most likely your fault. Even a slight change in intonation or emphasis can make a difference in what two nearly identical sentences mean. Take this sign, for example, hanging in the men's room of a restaurant: "We aim to please. You aim, too, please."

Main Ideas. Reading longer sections of text requires that we look beyond sentences, down into the "guts" of a passage. This is where reading becomes interesting. How do you move beyond sounds, syllables, and words—the building blocks of language—toward understanding? The place to start is by finding the **main idea**. How do you do that?

main idea central message a writer is trying to get across

> Look for hints that identify the topic or subject being discussed.

> Look for words and phrases that are repeated.

> Look for a thesis statement or topic sentence that summarizes the passage.

> Look for evidence of the author's opinion on what's being written about.

VARK It!

Read/Write: After you read these four bullet points to the right, cover them with your hand and list them elsewhere. How many did you remember? How did you do it? Was it by looking for the main idea in each one?

> **Outside of a dog, a book is man's best friend.**
> **Inside of a dog, it's too dark to read.**
>
> *Groucho Marx, American comedian, actor,*
> *and singer (1890–1977)*

How do you know whether the main idea is worth buying into? Where can you find the evidence that supports the idea and makes it believable?

> Look for statistics, testimony from an expert, or examples.

And how do you detect inferences?

> See whether you can uncover a generalization that could be made after reading the passage.

> Ask how the passage overall relates to you.

Read Right!

What do we know about reading? How *should* you tackle your many reading assignments in college? Consider these twelve essential points:[6] As you read, put checkmarks next to items you see as potential areas of improvement for yourself as a reader.

1. _____ **Understand what being a good reader is all about.** Reading isn't a race. Remember the old children's story about the tortoise and the hare? The turtle actually won the race because he plodded along, slowly and steadily, while the rabbit zipped all over the place and lost focus. The moral of that story applies to reading, too. Reading is a process; understanding is the goal. The point isn't simply to make it through the reading assignment by turning pages every few minutes so that you can finish the chapter in a certain amount of time. Reading requires you to back up occasionally, just like when you back up a DVD to catch something you missed: "What did he say to her? I didn't get that."

   Students sometimes mistakenly think that good readers are speed-readers, when it's really about focus.[7] Science fiction writer Isaac Asimov once wrote, "I am not a speed reader. I am a speed understander." On the other hand, reading too slowly can be a problem, too. If you chew (with your eyes) on every word and huff and puff along as you go, your mind can wander. Before you know it, you've let a thousand other thoughts intervene, as Katie Alexander did, and you have no idea where you are. The average reader reads at a rate of approximately 250 words per minute, with a 70 percent comprehension rate. Time yourself on an upcoming paragraph in this chapter, and then see whether you can talk through what you've just read and convince yourself that you understand it.[8] The point is to be efficient so that you can actually get all your reading done for all your classes.

Keeping a Reading Log

Is there a book you'd really like to read? Perhaps it's a book about which people say, "Oh, the book is much better than the movie!" Perhaps it's an author you've heard about: a famous politician, actor, or singer. Select a book to read for pleasure this month, and keep a reading log of how many pages you read each day and how long you stick with it. After you finish the book, write a letter about the book and the process of reading it to your instructor and classmates. There's evidence that reading something you choose yourself can be an important force in becoming a better reader![9]

2. _____ **Take stock of your own reading challenges.** Which of the following are reading issues for you? Rank order your top five, with 1 as your most difficult challenge.[10]

___ boredom	___ surroundings	___ vision	___ fear	___ speed
___ fluency	___ comprehension	___ fatigue	___ time	___ level
___ amount	___ retention	___ interest	___ laziness	___ motivation
___ vocabulary	___ attitude toward reading	___ finding the main point	___ estimating reading time	___ reading everything the same way

Many people find reading challenging. You may have worked with an impatient teacher as a youngster, or you may have been taught using a method that didn't work well for you—factors that still cause you problems today. Reading involves visually recognizing symbols, transferring those visual cues to your brain, translating them into meaningful signals—recording, retaining, and retrieving information (here's where your memory kicks in)—and finally using these meanings to think, write, or speak. Reading challenges can be caused by *physical factors* (your vision, for example) and *psychological factors* (your attitude). If you want to become a better reader in the future, it's a good idea to assess honestly what's most challenging about the process for you right now.[11]

3. _____ **Adjust your reading style.** You shouldn't read a magazine (flip through and find something interesting) the same way you scan a quick text message or devour a novel that you just can't put down. Reading requires flexibility. Contrast these two situations: reading the menu on the wall at your local fast-food joint and poring over the menu at a fancy, high-end restaurant. You'd just scan the fast-food menu in a few seconds, wouldn't you? You wouldn't

> 66 99
>
> **Perhaps the most valuable result of all education is the ability to make yourself do the thing you have to do, when it ought to be done, whether you like it or not.**
>
> *Thomas Henry Huxley, British biologist (1825–1895)*

read word by word and ask: "Is the beef in that burger from grass-fed cattle?" "What, exactly, is in the 'special sauce'?" If you did, the counter clerk would probably blurt out, "Look, are you going to order something or not?" That kind of situation requires quick skimming. But you'd take some time to study the menu at a pricy restaurant you might go to with friends and family to celebrate a special occasion. It's an entirely different situation, and the information is more complicated. And if it's a fancy French restaurant, you might even need to ask the definitions of some terms like *canard* (duck) or *cassoulet* (a rich, hearty stew). That kind of situation requires slow, considered study, word by word. You're going to pay for what you choose, and you want the best results on your investment. That's true about college, too. You're investing in your college classes, so reading right is important!

You'll face an enormous amount of reading in your combined college classes. The question is, what's fast food (to carry through with the example) and what's fine dining? According to research on reading, good readers know the difference and adjust their reading styles.[12]

Reading a popular new detective novel is something you could whip through, but reading the first chapter of your philosophy textbook would require more concentration. Likewise, some of the reading you'll do in college is fast food. You just need to skim to get the main points and then move on to the next homework item on your agenda. However, much of the reading you'll do in college is fine dining. That's why it's important to devote more time to reading and studying than you think you'll actually need. You'll be able to "digest" what you're reading much better.

4. _____ **Have a "conversation" with the author.** In every book you read, the author is trying to convince you of something. Take this book, for example. We have been engaged in a conversation all the way through. What do you know about me? What am I trying to persuade you to think about or do? Even though I'm not right in front of you in person on every page, you are forming impressions of me as you read, and I'm either convincing you to try the suggestions in this book or I'm not. As you read any book, argue with the author ("That's not how I see it!"), question her ("What makes you say that?"), agree with her ("Yes, right on!"), relate something she said earlier to something she's saying now ("But what about …?"). Instead of just coloring with your yellow highlighter, scribble comments in the margins, or keep a running commentary in a notebook. Reading is an active process, not a passive one in which the words just float by you. In fact, mark up this page right now! How do you decide what's really important? One thing you can do is ask your instructor in this course to show you his or her mark-ups in this book, and see whether the two of you agree on what's important.

commentary a record of your opinion

5. _____ **Dissect the text.** Whether you did it virtually online or physically in a real lab, dissecting or cutting up those little critters in your biology class helped you figure out what was what. The ability to dissect text is important in reading. As you read and make notes in the margins,

It matters, if individuals are to retain any capacity to form their own judgments and opinions, that they continue to read for themselves.

Harold Bloom, literary critic

Marginal Notes

Go back through the section of this chapter on reading that you've just finished. Make notes to yourself in the margins (or on another sheet of paper) about why you underlined a word, phrase, or section. Why did you consider that part to be important? Knowing the answers to these questions is more important than the act of "coloring."[13]

VARK It!

Multimodal (Kinesthetic/ Aural): Use Google images to find an online cartoon to print out and bring to class. If there is time in class, present the specific aspects of cultural literacy behind the humor.

---

cultural literacy core knowledge—things that everyone knows—that helps put things into context and give them meaning

---

write "what" and "why" statements. Try it: beside each paragraph on this page, write a one-sentence summary statement, a "what" statement. Put the author's words into your own words. Then write another sentence that focuses on why the paragraph is included. Does the paragraph contain *evidence* to make a point? Is it an *example* of something? If you can tackle this recommendation, you'll do wonders for yourself when exam time rolls around.

6. _____ **Make detailed notes.** You'll be much more likely to actually master a challenging reading assignment if you keep a notebook beside you and take full-blown notes as you read. Go back and forth, detailing main points and supporting evidence. Or go online and use a note-taking tool like evernote.com. The old rule of thumb still applies: read, close the book, and write down what you remember. Then go back into the book and check.[14] The physical act of writing or typing can help you remember it later.

7. _____ **Put things into context.** Reading requires a certain level of what's called cultural literacy. Authors assume their readers have a common background. They refer to other books or current events, or historical milestones, and unless you know what they're referring to, what you're reading may not make sense to you. An example you might be familiar with is how the television show *Seinfeld* made real words that everyone now knows and uses, out of fake ones: *yada yada yada*, for example. Those words are now part of our cultural literacy that have meaning for you and everyone you know, probably, but may not for people from another culture. They know the literacy of their own culture instead.

8. _____ **Don't avoid the tough stuff.** Much of the reading you'll do in college includes complicated sentences that are difficult to work your way through. When you read complex passages aloud, you may stumble because you don't immediately recognize how the words are linked into phrases. But practicing reading aloud is one way you can become more conversant with difficult language. Many instructors teach their students a common approach to reading and studying called SQ3R:

Survey—Skim to get the lay of the land quickly.

Question—Ask yourself "what," "why," and "how" questions. What is this article or chapter about? Why is it included? How might I use this information?

Read (1)—Go ahead now and read the entire assignment. Make notes in the margins or even create a study guide for yourself.

Recite (2)—Stop every now and then and talk to yourself. See whether you can put what you're reading into your own words.

> **Parents should play an inestimable role in children's learning to read and learning to love to read.**
>
> —*Barbara Swaby, Literacy expert*

Review (3)—When you've finished, go back and summarize what you've learned.

Try it right now with this section of the chapter, "Read Right."

Survey—What is this section of the chapter about, generally? When you preview a chapter or section of a textbook, look for color, highlighting, italics, layout, bullets—anything that communicates, "This is important!"

Question—What's the point of including it? Why is it here? How can it help you?

Read (1)—Now read the bullets in this section carefully, making "what" and "why" comments in the margins.

Recite (2)—At the conclusion of each bullet, summarize the point out loud, and decide whether this is an item you should put a checkmark next to, indicating that it's something you should work on.

Review (3)—When you're finished with the whole section, see whether you can summarize what you've learned from reading it.

9. _____ **Learn the language.** Every discipline has its own perspective and its own vocabulary. In many of the introductory classes you take, you'll spend a good deal of time and effort learning terms to be used in classes you'll take later. In order to study *advanced* biology, everyone has to learn the same language in *introductory* biology. You can't be calling things whatever you want to call them. You call it a respiratory system, but your classmate calls it a reproductive system. In college you will be introduced to various subjects or disciplines as you take what are often called general education or core courses. It's important to get to know a discipline.

10. _____ **Bring your reading to class.** Some of your instructors will infuse the outside course readings into their lectures. They may preview the readings in class, talk about their importance, or create reading worksheets for use in small groups. If they don't, however, it's up to you to integrate them. Bring up the reading in class, ask questions about it, and find out how it relates to particular points in the lecture. Doing so is an important part of being responsible for your own learning.

11. _____ **Ask for a demonstration.** If a textbook reading assignment for a course baffles you, ask your instructor for a mini-lesson in how to proceed. Sometimes all it takes is for the teacher to give the entire class (or just you) some pointers. For example, the instructor may help you come up with "what" and "why" statements or tell you where she would stop to write something in the notebook she keeps beside her.

VARK It!

Visual: Can you close your eyes and picture an important page you've already read in this chapter? Why do you think you remembered it? Was it the arrangement of text, a quote, or a photo? Remember to use visual cues to learn course material.

> **Reading is to the mind what exercise is to the body.**
>
> *Joseph Addison, British politician and writer (1672–1719)*

12. _____ **Be inventive!** Students who are the best readers invent strategies that work for them. Perhaps you're an auditory learner. Reading assignments aloud might drive people you live with crazy (so find a place where you can be alone), but it might be the perfect way for you to learn. If you're a kinesthetic learner, you might make copies of particular passages from your textbook and lecture notes, and build your own scrapbook for a course. Or cut up the instructor's lecture notes into small puzzle pieces and reassemble them. Using what you know about yourself as a learner is a big part of college success, so don't just do what everyone else does or even follow your instructor's advice word for word, if it doesn't work for you. Figure out what does, and then do it!

EXERCISE 8.5

Channel Chooser

Today's wide array of technology options requires that we choose how to communicate on a minute-by-minute basis. Your grandparents used to make long-distance calls (which were expensive) or write snail-mail letters. Besides talking face-to-face, those were the primary options. Today, you can call someone, fire off a text, send an e-mail or Tweet, or post on his Facebook wall, for example. The particular choices you make send a message about you and whether you are a competent communicator. The bottom-line question is this: Is one channel more appropriate than another for a specific message? Look at the following scenarios, decide which particular communication channel you'd choose for each situation, and then explain why. Here's an example:

A student employee who has worked with you for two years wins a prestigious college award. You want to congratulate her. Which channel would you choose, and why?

a. Phone call

b. Text message

c. E-mail

d. Facebook post

e. Written note

f. Face-to-face conversation

g. Tweet

h. Other

E. I'd send her a handwritten note because that's more personal and special.

Exercise 8.5 Continued

Now try some on your own. Be prepared to defend your choices during a class discussion.

1. You need your instructor's approval on the thesis statement you've written for your first essay in English class. You're having trouble coming up with something. _____

2. You want to break up with your romantic partner of six months. You just found out something disappointing that makes you feel hurt and angry. _____

3. You want to let other students know about an exciting campus event this weekend. It is free and open to everyone. _____

4. Your last college tuition bill contained a major error. It's a big mess. _____

5. The low grade you earned on your history paper counted for a large portion of your overall grade and may put you on academic probation. You need to ask your instructor to reconsider. _____

6. You want to tell your boss you're not coming in to work today because something came up. _____

7. You want to thank your favorite professor for a great learning experience this term. _____

Write Right!

Although your reading skills will be critical, they are only one of the several types of communication skills you will need in college. Good writing skills will be essential, too. The question we'll explore next is how to build the writing skills you'll need. If you can do that, you're well on your way to successful outcomes.

An old Doonesbury cartoon may very well hang on the wall in the Writing Center on your campus. It shows two college students. One is tapping away at a typewriter and mutters, "Man, have I got a lot of papers due!" as he types the paper's opening: "Most problems, like answers, have finite resolutions. The basis for these resolutions contain many of the ambiguities which conditional man daily struggles with. Accordingly, most problematic solutions are fallible. Mercifully, all else fails; conversely hope lies in a myriad of polemics. …" The other student is looking over his shoulder and asks, "Which paper is this?" to which the writer replies, "Dunno, I haven't decided yet." Obviously, cranking out college papers just for the sake of getting them done isn't the best idea. But, unfortunately, it happens.

Why do some students put off writing assignments? Is it because they worked with a cranky writing teacher in the past? Are they afraid of producing something less than perfect? Have they been unsuccessful at previous writing projects? Or, like Katie, do they simply dislike writing? As shown in the cartoon dialogue above, it's tempting to start with something so general that it could work for literally any paper. Or you may fall into a boring habit, like starting every paper with the dictionary definition for whatever you're writing about. Or perhaps you don't even get that far. You may simply stare at the blank screen until it's time to do something else and move on.

When you have an important writing assignment to do, how do you get started? Many students just sit down at their computers and start typing at midnight the night before the paper is due—hoping for a flash of inspiration—and thereby end up sabotaging themselves. They avoid the upfront work and rationalize that they work better under pressure or they enjoy the adrenaline rush of a tight deadline. But ask yourself this: Would you invite your girlfriend out for dinner before the prom and then just drive around with her until you find a restaurant that looks inviting? Would you start your vacation by going to the airport and wandering around until you see an alluring destination at one of the gates? Of course not! Why then would you sit down at your computer at midnight and just start typing? Sure, eventually you will have filled enough pages to reach the assignment's required length, but it's not just about quantity; it's about quality. Quality writing takes patience, focus, and attention to detail. Writing and critical thinking are linked. When you write, you're thinking on paper. Doing it well will help you become a better critical thinker and learner in all your courses.[15]

Writing as a Process

How should the writing process work, ideally? It should involve three basic stages: prewriting, writing, and rewriting.

Prewriting

Think of this analogy: When you speak, you may not know exactly which words will come out, but you have some idea of what you want to say before you open your mouth, right? Just as you prethink what you're going to say, you must prewrite what you're going to put down on paper. In order to do that, you must ask yourself questions like these:

1. **What is the assignment asking me to do?** Let's say one assignment asks you to summarize interviews with three English instructors on campus, to find out what makes them effective teachers. And another assignment asks you to compare and contrast teaching English with teaching math. You'd go about these two writing papers differently. Zero in on the verbs in the assignment—*summarize* versus *compare* and *contrast,* in this case. The specifics of the assignment must be crystal clear to you, and if you're given a choice of topic, pick something that really interests you.

2. **Who is my audience, and what do I want them to know or do?** You write differently for different audiences—for your composition class or for your blog on being a college student, for example. If you're writing for your blog readers, you may aim for catchy phrasing, short sentences, and an intriguing title. Once you know who you're writing to or for, then you can ask: *What do I want them to know? Am I trying to inform, persuade, or entertain them?* You'll write differently, depending on your specific purpose.

3. **Can I compose a strong thesis statement?** Your paper's thesis statement should be the specific argument you're making, summarized into one sentence, ideally. For example, in your paper about good teaching, you might begin with a thesis statement like, "Being a good English teacher requires knowledge, patience, and enthusiasm." Formulating a strong thesis is half the battle.

thesis your main points, summed up in a sentence (or two); what you intend to "prove" in your paper

4. **Have I done enough research?** If you've followed the guidelines provided in your instructor's handout about the assignment, ask: Do I have enough support for my thesis? Have I gathered enough statistics, expert testimony, and examples to persuade my reader?

5. **Set in-between target dates for the three stages of writing, even if your instructor doesn't.** Some instructors will ask to see your work at each stage of the writing project. If you try to print your paper at 9:50 A.M. for your 10 A.M. class, you can count on something going wrong, like your printer cartridge shriveling up or your hard drive plummeting to an untimely death. To beat the odds, schedule in-between deadlines for yourself for prewriting, writing, and rewriting to keep the project moving along.

VARK It!

Kinesthetic: Think about a writing assignment coming up in another class. Insert in-between target dates for prewriting, writing, and rewriting in your planner or cell phone calendar.

EXERCISE 8.6

Getting Started

The mystery writer Agatha Christie once said, "The secret of getting ahead is getting started." Look at the topics below, and choose one of them. Write the first paragraph for an essay on the topic. If you do this exercise in class, your instructor may only give you one minute, for example, to get something down on paper. When it comes to getting started, one of the biggest challenges is commitment. You have an idea that could go in a dozen different directions, but in order to get started, you have to settle on one direction and run with it. If you do this exercise on your own, set a timer so that you're forced to commit to something. Give it your best effort, and use correct grammar and spelling. The point of the exercise is to practice getting started, which is sometimes the most difficult part of a writing assignment.

A. Why I will (won't) be quitting Facebook

B. Why I love to read (or don't)

C. Why writing is good therapy (or why writing stresses me out)

D. Why public speaking is (or isn't) my strong suit

Now look back at what you have written. Give your paragraph a grade (based on your own standards), or trade with a classmate who chose the same option (A, B, C, or D), and explain the grade you've assigned to him or her. What is the grade based on? Does the writing have a topic sentence that can be identified? Is there a clear thesis statement? If your instructor thinks there is time, try another option. Practicing the art of getting started (when the threat is low because no real grade will be assigned) can be a helpful exercise.

Writing

Have you ever experienced writer's block, or nowadays, the "tyranny of the blank screen"? You sit down to write and suddenly go blank? Whatever you call it, you'll be relieved to know there are ways around it.

Some professional writers resort to downright weird strategies to get themselves going. Victor Hugo supposedly wrote in his study at the same time every day—naked! His servant was ordered to lock away all Hugo's clothes until he had finished each day's writing.[16] Apparently, the method worked—look at *Les Misérables.* The paperback version has 1,488 pages! But this technique may not be well received by the people you live with. Just write freely about whatever comes into your head, whether it's on target or not. But how do you start doing that? Take a look at these techniques for starting the writing process.

1. **Begin by writing what's on your mind.**

   I'm having trouble starting this paper because there's so much to talk about in terms of good teaching. When I think back over all the English teachers I've ever had, a few really stand out. Mrs. Hampton, in seventh grade, was definitely the worst teacher ever, but Mr. Evans, in eighth grade, was the complete opposite. Just what was it that made him so good? I think it was his knowledge, patience, and enthusiasm. Maybe identifying these three characteristics will help me decide what makes a good English instructor in college.

   Now stop and look at what you've written. Based on your "stream of consciousness," you now have the beginnings of a paper about how being a teacher requires knowledge, patience, and enthusiasm. You're on your way.

2. **Begin with the words, "The purpose of this paper is . . ."** and finish the sentence. You may be surprised by what comes out of your fingertips.

3. **Work with a tutor in your campus Writing Center.** Sometimes talking through the assignment with someone else can help, particularly if that person is a writing expert. Or talk it through with a family member.

4. **Change the audience.** If it helps, assume you're writing your paper to someone who sharply disagrees with you or to a middle school student who just asked you a question. Sometimes thinking about your audience—instead of the topic in the abstract—helps you zero in on the writing task.

5. **Play a role.** Imagine yourself as a nationally-known education guru or a network newscaster deciding what to include on the evening news. Separate yourself from the task, and see it from another perspective.

Rewriting

Rewriting is often called "revision," and that's a powerful term. It means not merely changing, but literally re-seeing, re-en*vision*ing your work. Sometimes students think they're

> I must write it all out, at any cost. Writing is thinking. It is more than living, for it is being conscious of living.
>
> *Anne Morrow Lindbergh, American writer and aviation pioneer (1906–2001)*

> **A C essay is an A essay turned in too soon.**
>
> *John C. Bean, Professor of English, Seattle University*

revising when they're actually just editing: tinkering with words and phrases, checking spelling, changing punctuation. But the word revision actually means more than that. It means making major organizational overhauls, if necessary. According to many writing experts, that's what you must be willing to do. You're on a search and destroy mission, if that's what it takes.[17] Try these suggestions for rewriting to see whether they work for you:

1. **Leave it alone.** To help you see your paper as others will see it, set it aside for a while. If you can wait an hour, a day, or a weekend before revising, you'll have distanced yourself long enough to see your writing for what it is, and then improve it. Of course, this suggestion isn't meant to serve as an excuse for a late paper ("I couldn't turn my paper in today because I need to wait before I rewrite."). That won't fly. But coming back later can provide "Aha!" moments. (*What? I wrote that? What was I thinking?*)

2. **Ask for feedback.** One way of discovering how your writing will affect others is simply to ask them. Share your writing before it becomes final.

3. **Edit ruthlessly!** Cutting a favorite phrase or section may feel like lopping off an arm or a leg. But sometimes it must be done. The goal here is to produce the best paper possible, even if it's painful!

4. **Decide on an organizational format.** If you were writing about the three qualities of good English instructors, you'd want to use a *topical* format. Your paper would be organized into three major chunks. If you were writing about the differences between good English instructors and good math instructors, you'd use a *compare and contrast* format. If you were going to present solutions to other instructors about the problems in making English and math classes more exciting, you'd use a *problem-solution* format. Decide how best to present your information, and then follow the format you choose.

5. **Proofread, proofread, proofread!** You may think you have just written an unbelievable essay, but if it's full of mistakes, your instructor may pay more attention to those than to your paper's brilliant ideas. Sometimes it also helps to proofread out loud. Somehow, hearing the words, especially if you're an aural learner, makes errors more obvious. Be proud of the document's final appearance—paper clean, type dark and crisp, margins consistent, headings useful, names and references correct, no spelling errors. And remember that spellcheck, for all its convenience, can let you down. If the word you use is an actual one, but not the right on, it will give its approval, regardless. (Did you catch the spelling error in that last sentence? Spellcheck didn't.)

VARK It!

Visual: Think about all the organizational formats you know about. Can you develop symbols that help you understand them, like these?

■■■ or ⟷ or ?/☺

What's in an A?

Take a look at this first-year student's essay and offer the writer advice.

Assignment: Describe a problem you have faced as a first-year student and identify a possible solution.

Last summer, I worked for a bank in my hometown to earn money for college. I was told to show up for the interview at 8:30 A.M. I usually don't get up that early, so on Thursday night, I set my alarm clock, my cell phone alarm, and my clock radio to make sure I didn't miss it. Afterward, I thought that I had really hit it off with the interviewer. When I first got the job on a Friday, I was thrilled. Imagine me working for a bank! I thought that sounded like a prestigious job. When I told my Dad about getting the job, he said that he thought banks really shouldn't hire young people because they don't know the value of money. I decided he was probably kidding around.

But after my first week at Citizen's National Bank, I found myself bored stiff. Counting bills and tallying numbers really aren't that interesting. I did meet this girl named Nicole, and she was kind of cool, but everyone else at the bank was a little standoffish, including my supervisor, Ned. I didn't want to have a strained relationship with my supervisor, so I was friendly with him and serious about getting my work done. But by the following Wednesday, I was ready to quit. I heard about an opening at the coffee shop close to my house that included free food. So that's where I ended up. The moral of this story is to only take a job if you are really interested in the work. And I've definitely decided not to major in accounting.

What's the main problem with this essay? The writer has written about a problem she faced as a first-year student. The essay contains no grammatical errors. But is it likely to earn an A? Actually, the assignment calls for a problem-solution organizational pattern. Instead, it follows a chronological pattern (and then this happened, and then this . . .). What is the writer's thesis statement? Is it the next-to-the last sentence? *Only take a job if you are really interested in the work.* Instead of telling a story from start to finish, how would the essay change if the writer had asked a question like this: What mistakes do students make when looking for a job to help them pay for college? Then the writer could have organized the essay around the thesis statement (only take a job if you are really interested in the work) and found evidence, including her own experience, to back up the claim. Paying attention to the specific requirements of an assignment is the first step in earning a good grade.

One more tip. Throughout these three stages, be prepared to move fluidly from one to the other at the slightest provocation. If you're rewriting and you come across some prewriting information (as in *new research*) copy it down and fit it in. If in the prewriting stage you think of writing that strikes you as powerful—a good argument or a well-constructed phrase—write it down.[18]

Build a Better Paper: The Seven C's

In many ways, writing is like building. But instead of using nails, planks, and sheetrock to construct our communication, we use words, sentences, and paragraphs. Here are seven suggestions—all of which begin with C to help you remember them.[19]

1. **Be Clear.** Unfortunately, the English language gives you endless opportunities to write something quite different from what you mean. You can flip through your thesaurus and use a word that sounds good, but isn't recognizable (as in *profundity*, below), or you can write a convoluted sentence that can't be understood. Compare the problems in these two sentences, both of which are unclear:

> *The profundity of the quotation overtook its author's intended meaning.*

> *The writing was profound, but on closer examination, not only was it devoid of content but it was also characterized by a preponderance of flatulent words.*

Yes, many of us will be able to figure out what these sentences mean, though perhaps we'll need to check the dictionary. Sometimes beginning college students decide they must write to *impress* rather than to *express*. They assume instructors like this kind of complicated writing. They think it sounds more academic. Instructors see through that trick. Mean what you say, and say what you mean.

2. **Be Complete.** Ask yourself what your reader needs to know. Sometimes we're so close to what we're writing that we leave out important information, or we fail to provide the background the reader needs to get our meaning. Put yourself in your reader's shoes (or in this case, eyes).

3. **Be Correct.** If your writing has many grammatical, spelling, and punctuation errors, readers may get the sense that you don't know what you're writing about either. If grammar and punctuation aren't your strong points, ask someone you know who's a crackerjack writer to look over your first draft.

4. **Be Concise.** In the past, you may have used tricks like enlarging the font or increasing the margins to fill an assigned number of pages. But college students sometimes face the opposite problem: they find that writing less is more challenging than writing more. Think of this formula: A given idea expressed in many words has relatively little impact. But that same idea expressed in few well-chosen and well-combined words can stick in your memory. You could say:

> *"Whether or not a penny, or any amount of money, is earned or saved, it has the same or at least a similar value, fiscally speaking, in the long run."*

Compare that writer's tendency to "run off at the mouth" with Ben Franklin's concise expression:

> *"A penny saved is a penny earned."*

5. **Be Compelling.** Your writing should be interesting, active, and vivid, so that people want to read what you have to say. Compare these two headlines. Which article would you want to read?

> *Protests against tuition increases have been led by community college student leaders.*

> *Student leaders urge campus-wide protests over tuition hikes.*

What's another word for Thesaurus?

—Steven Wright, American comedian

The sentences create different images, don't they? The first sentence makes the situation sound like something that happens every day. The second sentence uses the active voice *(leaders urge campus-wide protests)* instead of the passive voice *(protests have been led)*, and the second sentence uses a more descriptive verb *(urge versus lead)* and noun *(hikes versus increases)*. Of course, you can go too far *(Campus leaders spearhead fiery student fury over radical tuition upsurge)*. But this principle is a good one to remember.

EXERCISE 8.8

Paper Submission Checklist

Before you turn in a written assignment, make sure you go through this checklist. Consider it to be "insurance" that your paper is fully ready. If you checked the "No" box for any item, explain why in the margin. For example, if you checked "no" for item 3 under "Structure," you might write that the assignment required your opinion, rather than research.

Structure

	Yes	No
1. Did you use a normal-sized font (12-point) and one-inch margins?	☐	☐
2. Did you follow APA or MLA stylesheet rules if doing so was a part of your assignment?	☐	☐
3. Did you include a list of references (bibliography)?	☐	☐
4. Did you number the pages, as instructed, format the title page correctly, and so on?	☐	☐

Content:

1. Reread the assignment. Did you do what the assignment asked you to do?	☐	☐
2. Did you write for the appropriate audience? (Are you writing for your instructor or for another student or group of students, for example?)	☐	☐
3. Does your paper have a clear thesis statement?	☐	☐
4. Did you do enough research?	☐	☐

5. Circle the organizational pattern you used:

problem–solution, chronological, topical, cause and effect, other (please explain).

_____

6. Is your writing clear, complete, correct, concise, compelling, courteous, and convincing? Circle the "C's" that are particularly strong.	☐	☐

Process

1. Have you received feedback on your paper, either formally from a campus Writing Center tutor or informally from someone you know who is a good writer?	☐	☐
2. Have you edited your paper after reading and rereading it (after allowing some time to pass), or after reading it aloud?	☐	☐

3. Other (as indicated by your instructor): _____

4. Based on the grading criteria your instructor has discussed for this paper, what grade would you assign it? Why?   Ⓐ Ⓑ Ⓒ Ⓓ Ⓕ

_____

_____

6. **Be Courteous.** Courtesy is important in any kind of writing. E-mail and texts are often places where people are discourteous to one another in writing—perhaps because distance gives them courage or they're just plain cranky. Having a meltdown on paper or your computer screen is rarely the right choice.

7. **Be Convincing.** You'll be a more successful writer if you support your views with solid evidence and credible testimonials. Give specific examples to illustrate your point—anecdotes, testimonials from experts, experiences, analogies, facts, statistics—and your writing will be more persuasive.

Keep these seven C's in mind. The secret to learning to think in college is to become a better writer. As you're learning critical thinking skills, you'll also become a more clear, complete, correct, concise, compelling, courteous, and convincing writer.

BOX 8.1 ## Ten Ways to Oust Speaking Anxiety

High anxiety. It's the curse of many a speaker. Although doing your best on a writing assignment can certainly generate stress, giving a presentation is an even more personal, more immediate look at you and your work. There you are, up front, doing your thing. If you can harness your anxiety and actually look forward to opportunities to speak, you'll build more confidence and get better at doing it. See whether you think the items on this checklist of fear-suppressing suggestions might work for you.

1. **Ready, set, go.** Being unprepared will cause your anxiety to skyrocket, and winging it won't help your presentation fly! The best antidote to anxiety is to prepare, prepare, prepare!

2. **Dress for success.** Confidence in your physical appearance can increase your confidence overall. Wearing a tee shirt that makes a questionable statement or displays a swear word to get attention won't help your grade. Dress up a little; show the audience they're worth the extra effort!

3. **Lighten up.** Humor can ease tensions, both for your audience and for you. But say something funny that occurs to you at the moment, rather than repeating a joke you read on the Internet.

4. **Don't be a mannequin.** Move around. Use gestures. Look at your audience. Talk as if you were having a conversation with each individual in the room alone. Be real, be yourself, and you'll feel more confident. Let your personality shine through.

5. **Practice in your presentation room.** Doing so can help put you at ease during your actual speech.

6. **Find some guinea pigs.** When you practice your presentation, do it in front of a live audience to prepare yourself for natural distractions, like people coughing or sneezing. Practice in front of your best friend or your family. Research indicates your grade is likely to go up.[20]

7. **Channel your energy.** Harness your fear, and turn it into positive energy that makes you more dynamic.

8. **Visualize success.** When you see yourself giving your presentation in your mind's eye, visualize success, not failure.

9. **Remember that mistakes are made to be corrected.** If disaster strikes, remember that how you handle it is what's important. Perhaps you fear making a "tip of the slung." Don't worry; instead, make the most of a few moments of lightheartedness!

10. **If you can't shake it, fake it.** If your nerves get the better of you, fake it. Pretend you're confident. Before you know it, your confidence may actually begin to rise.

In a Manner of Speaking . . .

When your assignment involves a presentation, instead of or in addition to, a paper, your public speaking skills will be on the line. You may be thinking something like this: *I'm not going to be a public speaker. I'm going to be a surgeon. I'll spend all my time hunched over an unconscious person lying on an operating table. All I'll need to know how to do is hold a scalpel with a steady hand.* But is that really true? What about the communicating you'll need to do with totally conscious hospital administrators, other doctors, and patients before and after surgery?

Most people think of public speaking as an episode, a one-time event. You stand up to give a speech, and when you're finished, you sit down. But actually, there's a sense in which all the speaking we do is public. By contrast, what would *private* speaking be? Thinking? On the job, you'll communicate with others every day. Unless you join a profession that requires you to take a vow of silence, you'll be speaking publicly all the time!

When you prepare for a presentation in one of your classes, what is your primary goal? To impress your instructor? To amaze your classmates? To get your presentation over with? How about to give the very best presentation you can give?

Many of the suggestions in this chapter apply to both writing and speaking. As both a writer and a speaker, you should be clear, complete, correct, concise, compelling, courteous, and convincing. You should choose an organizational pattern and use it to help your audience understand what you're saying. (Unlike reading a written paper, they only have one chance to hear your words go by.) You must have a strong thesis in a speech, just as you must in a paper. But let's examine some other advice that relates primarily to speaking. Use these suggestions to create winning presentations that set you apart in all your courses.[21]

1. **Purpose.** What is the purpose of your presentation? Often the purpose is given to you directly by your instructor: Prepare a five-minute speech *to inform.* . . . But other assignments will allow you to select your own purpose: "The Trials and Tribulations of a Student Mom" (to inform), "Sustainability in an Age of Materialism" (to persuade), "Five Sure-Fire Ways to Flunk Out of College . . . Not!" (to entertain), "How Being Class President Can Change Your Life" (to inspire). Knowing exactly what you're trying to accomplish helps!

2. **People.** Who will be your listeners? Generally, you'll be speaking to an audience of students in your classes, right? But what are their specific characteristics as they relate to your purpose? For example, if you're addressing parents and friends at graduation, you might create a different speech than the one you'd present to your co-members of a student club.

3. **Place.** Where will you deliver your presentation? The location of your presentation may affect its tone and style. A presentation you might give to a group of tourists at a national park would allow

VARK It!

Visual: Map the 7 C's for writing with the 7C's for speaking. Can you connect any dots between items in the two sets?

> **The trouble with talking too fast is you may say something you haven't thought of yet.**
>
> *Ann Landers, syndicated advice columnist (1918–2002)*

alphaspirit/Shutterstock.com; Dmitriy Shironosov/Shutterstock.com

FIGURE 8.1

Storyboarding a PowerPoint

you to be informal, and your visual aid would be the scenery around you. But if you gave the same presentation as a geography major to high school seniors, you'd be more formal and scholarly, using a PowerPoint presentation or maps in the classroom.

4. **Preparation.** How should you prepare your speech? Developing the content of a speech is often similar to writing a paper. You'll need to develop a thesis statement and find support for each point by researching examples, statistics, and expert testimonies. Depending on the assignment, you might write out your speech or create a set of PowerPoint slides with talking points. Or you may find it helpful to create a storyboard, a map, or flowchart of your slides on paper before moving to the screen (see Figure 8.1). Then, after you know your basic format, you'll need to come up with an attention-grabbing introduction and a memorable conclusion. Or think about it this way: One of the best ways to prepare is

to make sure your presentation is SHARP. SHARP stands for <u>s</u>tories, <u>h</u>umor, <u>a</u>nalogies ("this" is like "that"), <u>r</u>eferences (or quotes), and <u>p</u>ictures/visuals.[22] SHARP is a good formula for a successful presentation, one that your audience will remember. Imagine that you decided to give a presentation about "exiting from college and finding a job." You might start with a horrendous story (S) about a plane trip you just took, where you ran through three airports but missed all three connections (H); compare a plane trip to the journey in college toward a "career destination" (A); include the quote "Map out your future, but do it in pencil. The road ahead is as long as you make it. Make it worth the trip" (Jon Bon Jovi); and include this photo you took with your cell phone camera on the plane.[23] You'd have the makings of a very SHARP presentation.

5. **<u>P</u>lanning.** What planning should you do? For example, are visual aids available, or do you need to bring your own? Is there a plug in the room, if you need one? Should you bring a backup of your presentation on a flash drive? Should you test the LCD projector to make any necessary adjustments? Many a speaker has been unnerved at the last minute by some overlooked detail.

6. **<u>P</u>ersonality.** How can you connect with the audience? How can you demonstrate your competence, charisma, and character to your listeners? Eye contact is important. Look at each person individually, if possible. Inspire trust by telling a story or relating your topic to some aspect of your own experience. Rather than playing a role, act natural and be yourself.

7. **<u>P</u>erformance.** This last P relates to delivering your presentation. Rehearsal is important (although too much rehearsal can make your presentation sound singsongy and memorized). Beware of bringing a full written draft to the podium. If you do, you may be tempted to read it, which is the last thing you want to do. Aim for a dynamic delivery, both verbally and nonverbally, that helps keep your listeners listening.

One final thing: After you've finished a paper or presentation, you're not really done. It's time to sit back and think about what you've accomplished. Are you pleased with your work? What have you learned? What will you do differently next time? If you do this every time you finish a project, you'll build your skills over time and take them with you to your other college classes, a university, or the world of work.

BOX 8.2

PowerPoint or PowerPointless? Five Ways to Make Your PowerPoint Pop

College presentations usually involve visual aids, often electronic ones. These e-tools can serve as helpful cues for you during your presentation. Although you'd never want to simply read your slides to an audience, glancing quickly at a slide can serve as a cue card and remind you of what you want to say. But how professionally your visual aids are created and used can make or break your presentation—and your grade. Your instructor may allow you to use Keynote (for Macs), Prezi (an online tool that moves and shows the relationships between concepts), or PowerPoint, the industry standard. Each of these tools has pros and cons, but the one we'll concentrate on here is PowerPoint. PowerPoint is an excellent and neutral tool. How you use it makes all the difference. Bulleted words or phrases with the same PowerPoint background, one after the other, aren't nearly as engaging as SHARP ones, Prezi's (prezi.com), or Keynote presentations delivered from your iPad, using an iPhone app as a slide advancer. Start to perfect your skills now by considering these five ways to make your PowerPoint "pop."

1. **DO use your whole brain.** When it comes to designing PowerPoint presentations, the challenge is to combine useful information with attractive design. Think of it as using both sides of your brain—your logical left hemisphere and your creative right hemisphere. For example, if you're giving a presentation on teaching young children, you might want to use a font that looks like this (children's writing) on your title slide. (Just make sure it's legible from a distance. A good rule of thumb is to use 24-point font size or larger and keep your fonts simple unless you have a particular reason to change them.) You also might want to include a high-quality graphic like this one here.

2. **DO use color to your advantage.** Choose an attractive color scheme and stick to it. That doesn't mean that every background on every slide must be the same. In fact, if you do that, your listeners may die of boredom. But if your title slide is blue, orange, and white, then use one, two, or all three of these colors in some hue or shade on every slide. Some speakers create PowerPoint presentations that seem fragmented and messy because the individual slides aren't connected visually.

3. **DON'T crowd your slides with text.** Your listeners won't pay attention to you if they're spending all of their time reading. Be kind, and spare them the trouble by limiting the text on your slides. Some of the most deadly PowerPoint presentations are those in which the speaker turns around, faces the screen, and flies through slide after slide. The only way your listeners can live through that is if oxygen masks drop from the overhead compartments!

4. **DON'T let your slides steal the show.** Always remember that YOU are the speaker. Your slides shouldn't be so fascinating that your audience ignores you. Gunshots and screaming sirens shouldn't be used as sound effects unless, of course, you're speaking on gun control or ambulance response times. Any special effects should be used sparingly to make a point, rather than to shock your listeners.

5. **DO include a bibliography slide, both for words and images.** Some students assume that plagiarism only pertains to writing papers. Not so! Always give credit where credit is due. List your references, either on individual slides (if you use a direct quote, cite it) or on one slide at the end.

ardni/Shutterstock.com

CONTROL: *"DISCIPLINED" READING*

Here are paragraphs from three different textbooks. You will need to know the answers to these six questions by the time you finish reading each paragraph. Notice that it's important to read each discipline's paragraph differently, and it also helps to annotate what's important alongside, especially so that you'll remember when you study for exams. Be prepared to discuss your reponses to this exercise in class.

Paragraph A

1. What are the pro's of of the way police departments are organized?

2. What are the con's?

Paragraph B

3. What is learned helplessness?

4. Where does learned helplessness come from?

Paragraph C

5. What does the word "process" mean?

6. Is the process always used exactly as shown? Why or why not?

(When you read assignments for your classes, skipping ahead to the questions that will be asked of you afterward can be a good way to make sure you read more closely.) Below each paragraph, list the topic, the main idea, and suggestions for how this textbook should be read.

Paragraph A (Criminal Justice)

This pro-con format helps me separate the paragraph into two parts.

Police administrative organization has both its pros and cons. Because most departments are civil service organizations, administrators must rise through the ranks to get to command positions. To be promoted, they must pass a battery of tests, profiles, interviews, and so on. Most police departments employ a time-in-rank system for determining promotion eligibility. This means that before moving up the administrative ladder, an officer must spend a certain amount of time in the next lowest rank; a sergeant cannot become a captain without serving an appropriate amount of time as a lieutenant. This system has both benefits and shortcomings. On the plus side, it is designed to promote stability and fairness and to limit favoritism. The chief's favorite cannot be promoted over a more experienced officer who is better qualified. Once earned, a rank can rarely be taken away or changed if new management takes over. The rank system also protects police agencies from losing talented officers trained at public expense to other departments who offer more money or other incentives. On the downside, the rank system restricts administrative flexibility. Unlike in the private sector, where the promotion of talented people can be accelerated in the best interests of the company, the time-in-rank system prohibits rapid advancement. A police agency would probably not be able to hire a computer systems expert with a Ph.D. and give her a command position in charge of its data-analysis section. The department would be forced to hire the expert as a civilian employee under the command of a ranking senior officer who might not be as technically proficient.

Topic: _____

Main idea: _____

Reading suggestions: _____

Adapted from Siegel, L. & Worrall, J. (2011). *Essentials of Criminal Justice,* 8e. Belmont, CA: Wadsworth, Cengage Learning, pg. 95.

Paragraph B (Psychology)

Research supports the notion that college students who feel helpless are less likely to persist, more likely to give up easily, and as a result earn poor grades and report unhappiness. Adults and adolescents who react to stress by feeling at a loss to do anything about the situation are more prone to depression and other stress problems. Learned helplessness also has been documented in children with a history of reading failure. It can develop in elderly people in nursing homes who are not given choices about their daily activities and routines. In all of these situations, the expectation of failure and lack of control are what influence one's perceived level of stress, one's subsequent response to stress, and ultimately, one's mental and physical health.

I think this paragraph is an example of a cause-effect organizational pattern. Blue = causes. Yellow = effects.

Topic: _____

Main idea: _____

Reading suggestions: _____

Adapted from Pastorino, E., & Doyle-Portillo, S. (2012). *What is psychology?* Belmont, CA: Wadsworth Cengage Learning, p. 519.

Paragraph C (Nursing)

A process is a series of steps or acts that leads to the accomplishment of some goal or purpose. The purpose of the nursing process is to provide care for clients that is individualized, holistic, effective, and efficient. The nursing process is not linear but involves overlapping steps that build on each other (see Figure 5-1). In actual practice, there may not be a definite beginning or end to each step. Work in one step may begin before work in the preceding step is completed. The nursing process is dynamic and requires creativity for its application. The steps remain the same, but the application and results will be different in each client situation.

Memorize the definition of process and the graphic for the next exam!

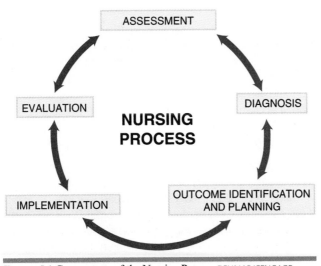

FIGURE 5-1 Components of the Nursing Process DELIMAR/CENGAGE LEARNING

Topic: _____

Main idea: _____

Reading suggestions: _____

Adapted from DeLaune, S., & Ladner, P. (2011). *Fundamentals of Nursing*, 4e. Clifton Park, NY: Delmar, Cengage Learning, p. 79.

CURIOSITY: *HINTS ON PRONUNCIATION FOR FOREIGNERS*

I take it you already know
Of laugh and bough and cough and dough?
Others may stumble but not you,
On hiccough, thorough, laugh and through.
Well done! And now you wish, perhaps,
To learn of less familiar traps?

Beware of heard, a dreadful word
That looks like beard and sounds like bird,
And dead: It's said like bed, not bead—
For goodness' sake don't call it "deed"!
Watch out for meat and great and threat
(They rhyme with suite and straight and debt.)

A moth is not a moth in mother
Nor both in bother, broth in brother
And here is not a match for there
Nor dear and fear for bear and pear,
And then there's dose and rose and lose—
Just look them up—and goose and choose,
And cork and work and card and ward,
And font and front and word and sword,

And do and go and thwart and cart—
Come, come, I've hardly made a start!
A dreadful language? Man alive.
I'd mastered it when I was five.

Anonymous

Go ahead. Try reading the preceding poem aloud. Even if English is your first language, you probably had to pause and think about how to say a word occasionally. Most anyone would. English isn't exactly the easiest language in the world to learn, non-native English speakers say. It's filled with perplexing irregularities. Think about the raw courage it would take to pursue a college degree by reading and writing in a language other than your native tongue. If English is your first language, could you do it in German or Arabic or Hindi? That being acknowledged, what strategies can ESL (English as a second language) students use to help with challenging reading assignments?

1. Remember that spoken English differs from the written English you'll find in textbooks and academic articles. In casual conversation, you'll hear, "And she's … like, 'Wow!' and I'm . . . like, 'Really?'" If you read that in a book, you'd have no idea what the speakers were communicating about. But if you're standing next to the conversationalists in the hallway, you have a chance of figuring it out. Learning to speak informally in conversation is very different from learning to read scholarly discourse. When you read, there's no body language to rely on or real-live author around to whom you can address questions.

2. Ask your English-speaking friends and instructors to coach you. For example, ESL speakers sometimes struggle with the hundreds of idioms found in English. Idioms are groups of words with a particular, nonliteral meaning. For example, "I have a frog in my throat" means your voice is hoarse, not that you literally have swallowed a green amphibian. Considering how many idioms English has and how freely English speakers use them without consciously thinking about it, non-native speakers may find learning them all to be a challenge.

3. Use the Internet or an online course to improve your language skills. According to one study, international students in an online course made significant gains in their

language skills, compared with a control group of students who sat through the same course in a classroom. Online courses provide good exposure and practice in your reading and writing skills via e-mail, web searching, threaded discussions, and online postings.[24]

4. Try explaining what you're reading to someone else. Talking something through while you're reading, especially with a native English speaker, can help you clarify meanings on the spot—and may help the other student achieve better comprehension, too.

5. Mark up the textbook so that you can pursue difficult passages in greater detail later. Insert question marks in the margin. Read with your English–native tongue dictionary in front of you. If you get completely stuck, find another book that may explain the concepts differently.

What can English speakers learn from strategies intended for ESL students?

_____

_____

_____

CAREER OUTLOOK: _COMMAND CRUCIAL CONVERSATIONS_

Imagine this: You're appealing to your professor to change an exam grade: "Why did you give me a D? Now I'm going to lose my scholarship." "Open mouth, insert foot." Often during challenging conversations, you know intuitively that your communication choices are crucial. You also know intuitively (by that sinking feeling in the pit of your stomach) when you've said the wrong thing. Unfortunately, by implying that your poor grade is your professor's fault, you've probably "failed the test." You're unlikely to get the results you were seeking. There are ways in which crucial conversations are tests of our communication skills, and it's clear that most of us don't always know how to get the "grade" we want.

When is a conversation crucial instead of just plain important? Crucial conversations are said to be those with results that could potentially change the quality of your life. According to experts, crucial conversations have three components: high stakes, strong emotions, and differing opinions—a potentially toxic triangle.[25]

At times like these, results are on the line, and sometimes our communication skills don't rise to the occasion. We underreact with silence; overreact with a meltdown; or choose a safe, but inappropriate, medium (like sending a text message that says, "The wedding is off," for example). Other times, we somehow get it right. The question is this: How do we develop the communication skills we need for these inevitable crucial conversations? When we're at our best, we demonstrate a willingness to speak up when we disagree, deal with issues head-on rather than resorting to the "silent treatment," and dive into dreaded conversations with bravery and resolve rather than fear. Underneath it all is this advice: "Engage brain before opening mouth." Intentionality and planning make a crucial conversation work.[26]

In your coming career, crucial conversations will be nothing short of crucial. When you're seeking an opportunity, responding to criticism, giving your boss feedback, asking a difficult teammate to cooperate, or requesting help, your career may be on the line. How well you communicate will make all the difference.

Can the lesson you just identified be applied to your future career in the workplace? If so, how?

_____

_____

_____

CHALLENGE: REALITY CHECK

How much did you learn? At the beginning of this chapter, you filled out a "Readiness Check" that asked how you thought this chapter would relate to you, and how you would relate to it. Now, fill out this "Reality Check" to find out.

1. This chapter discusses several reasons why reading skills are important. Can you identify one of them?

2. What does *SQ3R* stand for?

3. Identify the three stages involved in the writing process.

4. List three of the seven "P" items to consider in order to give better presentations.

5. How long did it take? _____ hours _____ minutes. Before you began this chapter, you were asked to predict how long it would take you to complete it (total time, even if you read it in more than one sitting). Was your estimate on target, or will you revise it for the next chapter you'll read? _____

step 3 INSIGHT *Now* What Do You Think?

At the beginning of this chapter, Katie Alexander, a frustrated and disgruntled student, faced a challenge. Now after reading this chapter, would you respond differently to any of the questions you answered about the "FOCUS Challenge Case"? Using what you learned in the chapter, write a paragraph ending to Katie's case study. What are some of the possible outcomes for Katie?

step 4 ACTION Your Plans for Change

1. What, in particular, from this chapter will you put to the test immediately in some other class?

2. In what ways might the information in this chapter help you become more successful in this class? What results are you expecting and how will you achieve them?

chapter 9

Developing Memory, Taking Tests

READINESS CHECK

How this chapter relates to YOU

1. When it comes to memorizing material for tests and taking exams in college, what do you find most challenging, if anything?

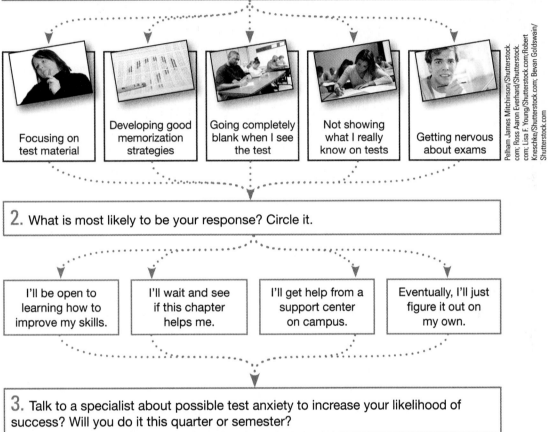

Focusing on test material

Developing good memorization strategies

Going completely blank when I see the test

Not showing what I really know on tests

Getting nervous about exams

2. What is most likely to be your response? Circle it.

I'll be open to learning how to improve my skills.

I'll wait and see if this chapter helps me.

I'll get help from a support center on campus.

Eventually, I'll just figure it out on my own.

3. Talk to a specialist about possible test anxiety to increase your likelihood of success? Will you do it this quarter or semester?

Example: Talk to a specialist about possible test anxiety. Yes!

How YOU will relate to this chapter

What are you most interested in learning about? Put checkmarks by those topics.

☐ How your memory works like a digital camera

☐ How to improve your memory, using 20 different techniques

☐ Why you should change your thinking about tests

☐ What to do before, during, and after a test

☐ What text anxiety is and what to do about it

☐ How to take different kinds of tests differently

☐ How cheating can hurt your chances for success

● How motivated are you to learn more about getting the right start in college? (5 = high, 1 = low) ____

● How ready are you to read now? ____

(If something is in your way, take care of it if you can; zero in and focus.)

● How long do you think it will take you to complete this chapter? If you start and stop, keep track of your overall time. ____ hour(s) ____ minutes

KEVIN BAXTER

Darko Kovacevic/Shutterstock.com

©Larry Harwood Photography. Property of Cengage Learning.

A s he got ready for work one morning, it finally hit him. He took a long, close look at himself in the mirror, and frankly, he didn't like what he saw. Kevin Baxter was a forty-year-old father of three who was dissatisfied with his life. Yes, he earned a decent income as a construction foreman, and yes, his job allowed him to work outdoors. To Kevin, being cooped up in an office from eight to five every day was something he'd always wanted to avoid. Being outdoors, where you could see the sky, feel the sunshine, and breathe fresh air, was what made him feel alive. The world outside was where he wanted to be, yet at the same time, he knew the world inside his head was withering away. Kevin realized he hadn't really learned much since high school. *I feel brain-dead; that's the best way to describe it,* he frequently thought. *I've run out of options, and I'm stuck.*

Clearly, dropping out of college his first semester twenty-two years ago had been the wrong decision for him. But at the time, he'd convinced himself that he wasn't college material. Besides, college had seemed so expensive, and he desperately wanted to be on his own and begin a life with Carol, his high school sweetheart. Unfortunately, that hadn't worked out well, either. Now he was a single dad whose children lived out of state. He very rarely saw them. Nothing had quite turned out as he had planned.

But in a way, his divorce had jolted him into a midlife crisis. He needed to change things, and going back to college to earn a degree in architecture was the right decision for him now. He was sure of it. Working in construction, he frequently saw flaws in the architects' plans, and he'd often come up with better ideas. *This is a chance to start over again,* he thought to himself, *and I'm going to do it right this time.* So at forty, he quit his construction job and enrolled in his county community college. His first-term courses consisted of

Nadezda/Shutterstock.com

Buturlimov Paul/Shutterstock.com

Ingvar Bjork/Shutterstock.com

Dmitriy Shironosov/Shutterstock.com

Introduction to Architectural Design, Introduction to Philosophy, Introduction to Rhetoric and Writing, and Introduction to Art. For Kevin, college would be an introduction to many new things. Underneath it all, he had to admit that he was proud of himself. *Going back to college at forty takes guts,* he congratulated himself. Who knows? He might even transfer to a four-year school to get an engineering degree before it was all over.

But halfway into the term, Kevin's confidence was shaken. Although he'd been a construction foreman on huge projects, after he got his first midterm exam back, he wondered, *Am I too old to learn new things? I keep up with the reading, come to every class, do my assignments conscientiously, and study until I'm blue in the face! But things just don't seem to stick.* His exam didn't reflect the time he was investing, and frankly, he was embarrassed. Younger students without his years of experience were outperforming him. *That* bothered him. Kevin was getting discouraged about school and his academic capabilities.

Without a doubt, his most challenging class was philosophy. What did Socrates, Plato, Aristotle, Galileo, and Descartes have in common, and what separated them? Philosophy was unlike anything he had ever tried to learn. He'd read a chapter four, five, or six times, and feel sure he knew it,

but when he faced the exam, it seemed as if he'd never studied at all. Of course, it didn't help that while he was trying to focus, his kids would call to talk about their problems or a telephone solicitor would interrupt his reading. It was getting to the point that exams in any class made him break out in a cold sweat. He just couldn't figure it out. He'd always been known as an unflappable guy, and he never had problems at work remembering details, like ordering materials and managing multiple construction teams. But trying to memorize the differences between Plato, Aristotle, and Socrates was hard for him, and many of the new terms he was learning didn't really seem to have any relevance to his life. More than once on the exam, he just couldn't come up with a term he thought he had memorized.

Kevin hated to admit it, but doubts were beginning to creep in. Maybe being a construction foreman was as far as he could ever go in life, and he should have left well enough alone. Maybe college was the last place he should be. Maybe he should have been satisfied with what he'd already achieved, instead of putting everything on the line for more.

© Cengage Learning

| Course Schedule |
| Community College |
| FALL SEMESTER |
| Baxter, Kevin |

Course ID	Course Title	Hrs	Days	Meeting Times	Bldg	Room	Meeting Dates	Stat
ARCH 100	INTRO TO ARCHITECTURAL DESIGN	3.0	T	0500PM-0830PM	SCI BLDG	210	AUG 16 - DEC 16	ENRO
PHIL 101	INTRO TO PHILOSOPHY	3.0	M	0705-1020PM	MAIN HALL	105	AUG 16 - DEC 17	ENRO
COMM 180	INTRO TO RHETORIC AND WRITING	3.0	S SU	0800AM-0400PM	MAIN HALL	412	OCT 2 - OCT 23	ENRO
ART 110	INTRO TO ART	3.0	R	0705-1020PM	MAIN HALL	300	AUG 16 - DEC 17	ENRO
	Credit Load:	12.0						

REACTION What Do *You* Think?

1. Do you have anything in common with Kevin? If so, how are you managing the situation so that you can be successful?
2. Why is Kevin experiencing problems remembering course content for exams in his philosophy class? List three reasons you identify from the case study.
3. Identify three memory techniques that Kevin should use to help him memorize all the names and terms he needs to know.
4. Does Kevin have test anxiety? Why or why not?

Memory: The *Long* and *Short* of It

EXERCISE 9.1

Subjective Memory Test

How would you rate your memory overall?

	Excellent		Good		Poor
	1	2	3	4	5

A. How often do the following general memory tasks present a problem for you?

	Never		Sometimes		Always
1. Names	1	2	3	4	5
2. Where I've put things	1	2	3	4	5
3. Phone numbers I've just checked	1	2	3	4	5
4. Words	1	2	3	4	5
5. Knowing whether I've already told someone something	1	2	3	4	5
6. Forgetting things people tell me	1	2	3	4	5
7. Faces	1	2	3	4	5
8. Directions	1	2	3	4	5
9. Forgetting what I started to do	1	2	3	4	5
10. Forgetting what I was saying	1	2	3	4	5
11. Remembering what I've done (lock the door, etc.)	1	2	3	4	5

B. How often do the following academic memory tasks present a problem for you?

	Never		Sometimes		Always
12. What I've just been reading	1	2	3	4	5
13. What I read an hour ago	1	2	3	4	5
14. What I read last week	1	2	3	4	5
15. Assignment/exam due dates	1	2	3	4	5
16. Appointments with instructors	1	2	3	4	5
17. Assignment details	1	2	3	4	5
18. Factual information for exams	1	2	3	4	5
19. Theoretical information for exams	1	2	3	4	5
20. Information from readings for exams	1	2	3	4	5
21. Information from in-class lectures for exams	1	2	3	4	5
22. Including everything I should study for exams	1	2	3	4	5

These informal assessments may help you understand your own perception of how well your memory works. The lower your score on each portion, the better you perceive your memory to be. Do your scores for Part A and Part B differ? The general tasks in Part A are presented in the order of concern reported by older adults cited in one study (with the top items perceived as most problematic).[1] Are your priorities similar? Did your numbers drop as you went down the list?

In one recent study in which college students were asked which aspects of memory they most wanted to improve among general and academic tasks, the top three items were improving schoolwork or study skills, remembering what was read, and remembering specific facts and details.[2] Understandably, the academic aspects of memory were those most personally valued. Is that true for you, too? Are the items in Part B generally higher priorities for you now as a college student?

Most of us may not even realize just how important memory is. We talk about our memories as if they were something we own. We say we have good memories or bad memories, just like we have a crooked smile or a nice one. But no one would ever say, "Hey, that's one nice-looking memory you've got there!" in the same way they'd say, "Wow, you have a really nice smile!" Memory isn't a thing; it's a process. You can't see it or touch it or hold it. Even one specific memory has many different features: You can remember something by what you saw, smelled, heard, or felt. And even within one of these categories, individuals may differ in what they recall. You may be able to hum the movie's theme song, but your friend may remember conversations between the main characters almost word for word.

Don't believe it when someone claims to have a one-size-fits-all, magic formula to help you unlock the secrets of your memory. It isn't that easy. Still, there are techniques that can help you do your best academically. We can only begin to grasp the rich complexities of memory by understanding it as a process. However, it's important to recognize first that mastering memory depends on the answers to several questions like these:[3]

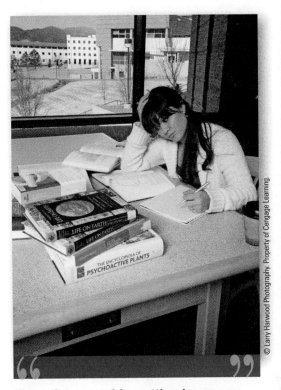

66 99

The existence of forgetting has never been proved: We only know that some things don't come to mind when we want them.

Friedrich Nietzsche, German philosopher (1844–1900)

1. **Who is learning?** An algebra instructor and a beginning algebra student would approach memorizing the main points of an article on math differently.

2. **What needs to be learned?** How you learn your lines for a play would differ from how you learn to recognize paintings for your art appreciation test.

3. **How will learning be tested?** Learning information to *recall* uses different memory techniques than learning information to *recognize*. Recognition requires that you select from several possibilities; recall requires that you come up with memorized information on your own.

4. **How long must the information be remembered?** Learning your multiplication tables as a child is something that must remain with you throughout your life. You use it on a daily basis to do routine things like figure how much it will cost you to fill up your gas tank.

Test Your Memory

For a more objective assessment of your memory, try this test. Study the following list of words for up to one minute. Then cover them with your hand and see how many you can remember and list them in the right-hand column.

theory	_____
rehearsal	_____
student	_____
bone	_____
frostbite	_____
camera	_____
rose	_____
calculus	_____
lecture	

How many words were you able to remember? Which words did you forget? Unfamiliar words? Words that had no meaning in your life? What memory techniques did you use to help you remember? Specific strategies to help you master your memory are worth learning.

VARK It!

Visual: Draw a mind map to help you connect and remember the words in Exercise 9.2.

The Three R's of Remembering: Record, Retain, Retrieve

Improving your memory is easier if you understand how it works. Memory consists of three parts:

> Your sensory memory

> Your working memory (called short-term memory by some psychologists)

> Your long-term memory

These three parts of the memorization process are connected to these three memory tasks, the "Three R's of Remembering"[4]:

> Recording

> Retaining

> Retrieving

We'll compare the three R's of remembering to the process involved when taking pictures with a digital camera: record, retain, retrieve.

© chris brignell/Alamy

I have a photographic memory but once in a while I forget to take off the lens cap.

Milton Berle, comedian (1908–2002)

FIGURE 9.1

Your Memory as a Digital Camera

The 3R's of Remembering: Record   Retain   Retrieve

Step 1
Click, View, and Save or Delete

Step 2
Transfer and Store

Step 3
Locate and Use

Your Working Memory: Record

To understand the way your memory works, it may be helpful to use a digital camera as a metaphor (Figure 9.1). The first thing you have to do is focus on whatever you want to take a picture of. That's obvious, but it requires that you slow down, clear your mental "deck," and focus. After you've focused your camera on your subject, you're ready to take a picture, right? But with a digital camera, you don't just click and walk away. You actually click and then review the picture on the small viewing screen to decide whether you want to save it or delete it.

Similarly, *recording* sensory impressions involves an evaluation process that takes place in your short-term or *working memory*. Your working memory is like a review screen, where you review recently acquired sensory impressions. In fact, your working memory is often involved in the focus process.

The problem with working memory is that the length of time it can hold information is limited. You probably don't remember what you ate for dinner last Monday, do you? You'd have to reconstruct the memory based on other clues. Where was I? What was I doing? Who was I with?

The other problem with working memory is that it has limited capacity. It fills up quickly and then dumps what it doesn't need. If you look up a number in the campus directory, you can usually remember it long enough to walk over to the phone, right? A few minutes after you've dialed, however, the number is gone. Current estimates are that you can keep something in working memory for one to two minutes, giving your brain a chance to do a quick review, selecting what to save and what to delete.[5] Look at these letters and then close your eyes and try to repeat them back in order.

SAJANISMOELIHHEGNR

Can't do it? This task is virtually impossible because the string contains eighteen letters. Researchers believe that working memory can recall only seven pieces of information, plus or minus two.[6] (There's a reason why telephone numbers are prechunked for us.) Chunking these eighteen letters into five units helps considerably. Now look at the letters again and try to recall all eighteen.

SAJA NISM OELI HHEG NR

If we rearrange the letters into recognizable units, it becomes even easier, right?

AN IS MAJOR ENGLISH HE

And if the words are rearranged to make perfect sense, the task becomes simple.

VARK It!

Multimodal: Use your multimodal preference to your advantage by combining memorization techniques such as drawing diagrams *and* summarizing written notes.

VARK It!

Read/Write: Try another example like the one here in the book to see whether you understand this concept. Can you memorize this list of letters?

HADCEEHISSITHYROESTT

What would make it easier?

The principle of chunking is also used to move information from your working memory to your long-term memory bank, and it's used in memorization techniques described later in this chapter.

Your Long-Term Memory: Retain and Retrieve

Once your camera's memory card gets full, you probably transfer the photos to your computer, or you print them out and put them in photo albums or picture frames. However, before you do that, you generally review the photos, decide how to arrange them, where to put them, whether to print them, and so forth. In other words, you make the photos memorable by putting them into some kind of order or context.

Just as you must transfer photos from your camera's memory stick to a more permanent location with more storage room, you must transfer information from short-term, or working, memory to long-term memory. You retain the information by transferring it, and this transfer takes place if you review and use information in a way that makes it memorable. It is this review process that we use when we study for a test. You transfer information to long-term memory by putting the information into a context that has meaning for you, linking new information to old information, creating stories or using particular memory techniques, or organizing material so that it makes sense. You can frame material you're learning by putting a mental border around it, just as you put pictures into frames.

Your long-term memory is the computer in which you store new knowledge until you need to use it. However, although the memories in long-term memory aren't easily disturbed, they can be challenging to retrieve.[7] Ideally, you'd like your memories to be readily available when you want to retrieve them, just like the pictures or digital images that you have transferred to your computer or put in a photo album. You can click on them to view them again, arrange them into a slideshow, or send them to your friends as attachments. If you just dump your photos onto your hard drive or print them out and then put them into a box, with no organization or labeling system, how easy will it be to find a specific photo? Difficult, right? Retrieving information from your long-term memory can be equally challenging if you haven't organized your information or created mental labels that will help you retrieve them later. Good recall often depends on having a good storage system. The remainder of this chapter will be about how to *retain* information by transferring it from working memory into long-term memory and how to *retrieve* information when you need to.

VARK It!

Kinesthetic: Demonstrate three memory techniques that work for you, in front of classmates, and let them guess what you're portraying.

A memory is anything that happens and does not completely unhappen.

Edward de Bono, creative thinking expert and author of Lateral Thinking: Creativity Step by Step

VARK It!

Read/Write: Use your preference for writing to your advantage. Write a story or case study to help memorize important info. Then think about strategies that could have improved your results.

Twenty Ways to Master Your Memory

What can you do to sharpen your memory for the test taking you'll do in college? Try the following twenty techniques, grouped into five major categories (to help you remember them). As you consider each one, think about what you know about your own learning style. Of course, memorizing means more than simply

Make it stick[8] **Rehearse and practice.**	**1. Rehearse.** Practice makes better. Repeat or re-read things over and over again. It helped you learn your multiplication tables as a child, but re-reading a chapter over and over, for example, especially when you don't understand parts of it, isn't the best strategy. But rehearsal and repetition can help in some instances. **2. Overlearn.** If you practice something so much that it becomes almost second-nature, then you get to the point where you can do it on "auto pilot." The more you over-practice, the better at it you may become.[9] **3. Space it out.** Instead of studying algebra for six straight hours, break it up. For a week before the exam, study an hour a day instead.[10] **4. Separate it.** If you're taking two social science courses and notice some overlap in the content, study psychology on Mondays and sociology on Wednesdays. Or find another way to distinguish and separate, like making your own compare and contrast chart.[11] **5. Mind the middle.** People tend to remember what they're introduced to *first* and what they heard *last*. Information in the middle can get lost unless you pay particular attention to it.[12]
Make it meaningful **Ask: How does this relate to me?**	**6. Feel.** Emotions are powerful motivators. If reading a novel for your English class makes you cry or laugh or actually feel fear, your memory can light up.[13] But be advised: Generating feelings may take some effort. You may be used to reacting neutrally to what you're learning in school. **7. Connect.** As you study, connect the dots. "Oh, we talked about this in another class this week. I remember." Connecting one thing to something you already know helps you know where to "file" it in your brain. **8. Personalize.** What does what you're trying to learn have to do with you? Remember *Pride and Prejudice*? You may think of it as a 1813 Jane Austin book, which it is, but does any of it remind you of you and your family? You may be surprised at similarities you begin to notice between the Bennet family described in the novel and your own, especially in terms of human relationships.
Make it mnemonic **Use a proven system.**	**9. Spell.** Acronyms work. If someone asks you how much RAM your new computer has, they're talking about <u>R</u>andom <u>A</u>ccess <u>M</u>emory. The word RADAR, which everyone knows, stands for <u>Ra</u>dio <u>D</u>etecting <u>a</u>nd <u>R</u>anging. Shortcuts like these can help us lock in information. **10. Locate.** Sometimes "placing" things can help us remember. If your classmates always sit in the same seats every week, you may learn their names by connecting them with their locations. **11. Narrate.** World Memory Championship Masterminds remember by creating a story and then connecting parts of the story to specific things they're trying to memorize. Make up a story, for example, about "theory," "rehearsal," "student," etc. to remember the list of words in Exercise 9.2. **12. Peg.** In the Peg System, you learn a list of rhyming words (used as "pegs") to hang items on in your memory.[14] Create mental stories to go along with them. For example, the most common "pegs" are: One—bun six—sticks Two—shoe seven—heaven Three—tree eight—gate Four—door nine—wine Five—hive ten—hen If you're trying to memorize, the first ten American presidents for your American History class, you might imagine George Washington standing in line at a fast food restaurant ordering a cheeseburger on a <u>bun</u>. Then think of John Adams with big, old-fashioned buckles on his <u>shoes</u> and Thomas Jefferson dressed as a lumberjack sawing down a <u>tree</u>, etc. Once you learn the rhyming pegs, you can memorize any kind of list by making up mental images to remember the items. Try it with the words in Exercise 9.2.
Manipulate it **Work with the material.**	**13. Mark it up.** As you read this book (or any other one, for that matter), mark all over it. Write your reactions in the margins, highlight things, circle and underline. Actually putting things on paper tells you what you think and feel, instead of ignoring a vague impression.[15] **14. Mark it down.** Sometimes trying to remember something isn't really all that important at all. In that case, write it down, and then go about your business doing other things until you need it. Save your memory for something more important. **15. Organize.** Another way to manipulate information is by moving it around. Create a chart that clearly defines the three major branches of government for your political science class, for example. Organizing information can help you "own" and hold onto it. **16. Picture.** Draw a mind map or create an elaborate picture that includes all the things on your memorization list. Visual learners do well with this option. **17. Act.** Put motions to your memorizing. Deliver Martin Luther King's "I Have Dream" speech in front of the mirror, as if you were him. Chances are you'll be much more likely to remember the main points if you learn them kinesthetically by putting them into motion. **18. Produce.** Put things into your own words.[16] Redeliver the instructor's lecture. Stop while you're reading and explain aloud what you've just read. When you take ownership of information, it becomes incorporated into your learning. **19. Test.** Make a practice test for yourself or a classmate. When you do this, you must ask yourself what's important enough to be included. You may just get a preview of the actual test!
Make it funny **Be silly and creative.**	**20. Mock it.** Think about how easy it is to remember your favorite comedy scenes. Create a David Letterman-like top ten list of why Shakespeare's tragedies are tragic. To remember that Romeo was a Montague and Juliet was a Capulet, and not the other way around, write a silly limerick: *There once was a girl named Cap* *Who fell for a guy and was hap* *But her family and his* *Wouldn't stand for the biz* *So they both ended up playing taps.* Set it to music. Be imaginative. We tend to remember what's bizarre, funny, or even obscene![17]

FIGURE 9.2

Twenty Ways to Master Your Memory

VARK It!

Aural: Recite the twenty ways out loud to let yourself hear the information.

being able to "regurgitate" back what you've learned. Most exams will supply you with a new problem and ask you to analyze it or apply information you've learned to a new situation. But developing your memory will underlie these tasks, too, so expanding your repertoire of memorization strategies is a major key to doing your best on tests. You can't analyze a new problem, if you don't remember how you solved the one you studied.

Testing 1, 2, 3...*Show What You Know*

All the memorizing you do in college leads to one thing—or so it seems—tests. And often tests feel like nothing more than a big hassle. Are they worth it? Exactly what do they prove?

Let's face it, life would be very different without grades in college, time clocks on the job, or performance reviews throughout your career, wouldn't it? You wouldn't have to show up at work if you didn't feel like it, and you'd get a paycheck anyway. You wouldn't have to do a good job because no one would care. And you wouldn't have to write papers, give presentations, or take tests in college. What a wonderful world that would be—or would it? Realistically, it would probably bring total chaos.

accountability understanding the consequences of doing a good job or a poor one

Life's not like that. Results count. Accountability is the bottom line. Achievement is taken seriously. You may be thinking, "I'll never have to take another test once I get out of here," but exams are actually realistic representations of life's requirements. The experience of taking a test is similar to running a critical meeting or giving a high-stakes presentation on the job. You'll need to walk into the room, ready to show what you know, and answer unanticipated questions. Tests are inevitable; so rather than complain about them, perhaps we should change the way we think about them.

The first step of test taking, of course, is to make sure you're prepared. All of the information in this chapter is worthless if you haven't gone to class or read the textbook or taken good notes during lectures. Miracles, by their very definition, are in very short supply. Nothing can substitute for being

conscientious dedicated to doing your best

conscientious about your work. Think about preparing for an exam as you would for running the 26-mile, 385-yard Boston Marathon. You'd have to work for months to develop the stamina you would need to finish successfully. You wouldn't want to just show up for kicks and wing it. If you did, at the very least, you'd probably pull a muscle. At the very worst, they'd carry you away on a stretcher.

The same principle holds true for exams in college. In order to have the stamina required and avoid the "injury" of not doing well, tests require this same kind of step-by-step, long-term preparation. Using specific test-taking strategies, like the ones discussed in this chapter, improve your test scores, change your attitude about tests, and boost your self-confidence.[18]

Think about taking tests as a three-stage project with a beginning, middle, and end. What do you do *before* the test to get ready? What do you do *during* the test to do your best? What do you do *after* the test to ensure a productive learning experience you can use for future exams?

Before the Test: Prepare Carefully

As you read the upcoming sections about *before, during,* and *after* a test, evaluate how many of these suggestions apply to you. Put a plus sign (+) in front of each item you already do regularly and a check mark (✓) in front of items you could start doing more regularly to improve your test-taking skills.

Wakako Tsuchida wins the 2011 Boston Marathon Women's Wheelchair Division

1. _____ **Begin preparing for an exam on the first day of class.** Nothing can replace consistent, regular study before and after each class. If you work along the way, then when it comes time for the exam, you will be much more ready and much less in need of last-minute heroics. Keep up with the reading, even if there are things you'd rather be doing, and make a study schedule for yourself leading up to each exam.

2. _____ **Identify the days and times of all your exams for the whole term up front.** At the beginning of the term, record the days and times of all the exams in all your courses—even finals, which will seem very far off—in your planner, cell phone, or online calendar. You'll thank yourself many times over for completing this essential task.

3. _____ **Find out exactly what the test will cover.** There's nothing more terrifying than having a classmate next to you say something like this before the exam begins, "I can't believe this test covers the entire first six chapters," when you thought it only covered the first four chapters. Clarify whether handouts will be included, previous quiz questions—anything you're not sure of. Phone, text, or e-mail other students, or better yet, ask your instructor questions like these: How long will the test be? What material will it cover? Which topics are most important? It's also a good idea to ask about criteria that will be used in grading. Do punctuation and grammar count? Will you be asked to turn in your notes or draft so that the instructor can see your work? Will there be an in-class review? All these questions are usually fair game.

   criteria standards

4. _____ **Understand that specific types of preparation are required for specific types of tests.** As described in later sections in this chapter, objective and subjective tests should be approached differently, and online tests require that you know the answers to important questions up front. For example, will the test time out? Must you complete the exam once you start, or can you save your answers and come back to finish later? Should you compose essay answers elsewhere and paste them into the online exam so that you don't lose all your work in case of a technology hiccup?

5. _____ **Begin serious reviewing several days before the test.** The best strategy is paying regular attention to class material, just as you take care of other things you care about, like your car or your dog. After each lecture, work with your notes, revising, organizing, or summarizing them. Then several days before the exam, step up your effort. Divide up the work

by days or study blocks. Begin putting your lecture notes and reading notes together. Make flashcards, outlines, charts, summaries, tables, diagrams—whatever works for your learning style and fits the material.

6. _____ **Maximize your memory.** Research indicates that specific techniques, like the ones discussed in this chapter, help transfer information from short-term to long-term memory. Remember to "Make It Stick" (rehearse, overlearn, space it out, separate it, and mind the middle), "Make It Meaningful" (feel, connect, and personalize), "Make It Mnemonic" (spell, locate, link or narrate, and peg), "Manipulate It" (mark it up, mark it down, organize, picture, act, produce, and test), and "Make It Funny" (mock it). Go back to Exercise 9.2 and try using several of the twenty memory techniques to master the list. Do some techniques work better than others for you?

7. _____ **Manage your energy so that you're ready to focus and work quickly.** You've heard it before, but if you're exhausted or feverish, you're not as likely to "show what you know" as you will if you're healthy and rested. "All-nighters" are something students brag about, but they catch up with you, and they're a bad habit to get into. According to one expert, "For every hour of sleep we lose, we drop one IQ point."[19] A series of all-nighters during midterms or final exams can seriously impair your intellectual performance. It's also a good idea to get everything ready the night before so that you remove as much hassle as you can from test day, and arrive early, but not too early. Find a good seat and get situated, but don't allow your anxiety to skyrocket while you're waiting.

8. _____ **Don't give in to a nonproductive, negative attitude.** Emotions are contagious. Stay away from other students who are freaked out or pessimistic about the exam. Think—and feel—for yourself. Make sure your self-coaching is productive ("I've studied this section for an hour; if it's on the exam, I'll nail it."), rather than punishing ("I'm so stupid. Why didn't I keep up with the reading?").

9. _____ **Study with other students.** When you teach something to someone else, you must first learn it thoroughly yourself. Why not study with other students? You can take turns teaching one another, comparing class notes, and making practice exams for each other. For most of us, talking things through helps us figure them out as we go. But don't wait to be invited; take responsibility and start a study group yourself. And if you're concerned that a study group of several students may degenerate into a social club, study with just one other person—find a study buddy and commit to doing the work.

> If you would hit the mark, you must aim a little above it.

Henry Wadsworth Longfellow, American poet (1807–1882)

10. _____ **Don't pop pills to stay awake.** You may know students who use Ritalin, Adderall, Vicodin, and OxyContin as study aids. This is a bad idea. When these drugs are used for the wrong reasons, they can help you stay awake for hours and enter a dreamy state. The potential side effects include insomnia, nausea or vomiting, dizziness, palpitations, headaches, tremors, and muscle twitching—even seizures. With such horrible potential health risks staring you in the face, not to mention possible legal sanctions if you obtain these drugs without a prescription, why not make things simple? Just study.[20]

11. _____ **Don't let open-book or take-home tests lull you into a false sense of security.** What could be easier than an open-book test? What could be better than taking a test in the comfort of your own home? Actually, these two types of tests require more preparation than you'd expect. Time is the issue here. If you're unfamiliar with the material, flipping through pages of notes or skipping around in the textbook won't help. Create a reference guide or page tabs for yourself so that you can find various topics in your notes or textbook and use your time efficiently.

12. _____ **Remind yourself of your long-term goals.** Why are you going to college? All this hard work is worth something, or you wouldn't be doing it. Keep your sights on the finish line! Enjoy the feeling of accomplishing something now that contributes to your goal-oriented success later.

13. _____ **Don't mess with success.** If you're doing well and earning the grades you deserve, don't discard what is working for you. Honestly assess the efficiency and effectiveness of your current practices, and then decide what ideas from this chapter you should add to your test-taking preparation routine.

VARK It!

Kinesthetic: If you have a friend taking a similar course at another school, make a Skype date to study together long distance.

Cramming: Does "All or Nothing" Really Work?

Imagine yourself as the actor in the following scenarios. Compare these situations to cramming for tests.

> You haven't called your significant other since last year. Suddenly you appear at her door with candy, flowers, concert tickets, and dinner reservations at the most exclusive restaurant in town. You can't understand why she isn't happier to see you.

> You don't feed your dog for several months. When you finally bring him a plate loaded with ten T-bone steaks to make up for your neglect, you notice he's up and died on you. Oops!

Of course, these situations are ridiculous, aren't they? How could anyone ever neglect such basic necessities of life? There's an important point to be made here. Many things in life require continuous tending. If you ignore them for a time, catching up is next to impossible. Your college courses should be added to the list.

Believe it or not, some students give themselves permission to follow this all-or-nothing principle of cramming in their academic work. They sail along without investing much time or energy in their studies, and then they try to make up for

> " **For fast-acting relief, try slowing down.** "

—LILY TOMLIN, COMEDIAN

Reason 9: They stress out.

Stress—a six-letter dirty word. We complain about it and try to avoid it. Often, it overtakes our lives and causes us to lose our focus. Of course, some stress is good for you. Olympic athletes, for example, subject themselves to unbelievable stress, and they achieve excellence. It's true that stress can produce results. Short-term stress—giving a speech or doing a tough math problem in your head—can actually bring out the best in you. But long-term stress such as living through a devastating hurricane or taking care of a sick relative can take its toll. Short-term stress "revs up" your immune system and protects you, but long-term or chronic stress tears it down, making you more vulnerable to illness.[21] What's so stressful about college? Plenty! Grades, workload, exams, tough classes, finances, family problems that interfere with your academic work—you name it. You can't get rid of stress in your life, but what *can* you do about it so that you don't lose your focus when you need it most? Sometimes you can (1) Change the stressful situation, (2) Change your reaction to stress, (3) Keep up with your schoolwork so that falling behind doesn't become a major stressor, or (4) Become a better problem solver. And above all, remember why you're doing this. Keep your focus sharp!

Keep a stress diary for a week. Record what causes you stress each day and how strongly you react. How high was your stress level? What did you do about it? After a week, you'll have good information about what causes you stress and how you handle it. Summarize your results, what you learned in doing this experiment, and what actions you can take in the future to better manage the stress in your life.

	Cause(s) of Stress	H = high, M = medium, L = low
Sunday	_____	[ ]
Monday	_____	[ ]
Tuesday	_____	[ ]
Wednesday	_____	[ ]
Thursday	_____	[ ]
Friday	_____	[ ]
Saturday	_____	[ ]

Summarized results: _____

_____

Lessons learned: _____

_____

Future actions: _____

_____

Photos.com/Jupiterimages; Photos.com/Phil Date; Photos.com/Matthew Valentine; Photos.com/Stockbyte

lost time right before an exam by cramming. The word *cram* provokes a distinct visual image, and rightly so. Picture yourself packing for a vacation in a warm, sunny place and hardly being able to close your suitcase because it's crammed full. You can't decide what to bring so you bring everything you can think of.

The same holds for cramming for a test. You try to stuff your brain full of information, including things you won't need. Because you haven't taken the time to keep up with learning as you go, you try to learn everything at the last minute. Cramming is an attempt to overload information into your unreliable working memory. It's only available for a very short time. However, there are other reasons why cramming is a bad idea:

> Your anxiety level will rise quickly.

> Your sleep will suffer.

> Your immune system may go haywire.

> You may oversleep and miss the exam altogether.

Despite the warnings here, most students cram at some time or other while taking college courses, and doing so may even give them a temporary high and make them feel like they're suffering for a cause.[22] But generally, slow and steady wins the race.[23]

Test Taking: High Anxiety?

EXERCISE 9.3

Test Anxiety Survey

What is test anxiety? What are the symptoms? Do you have it? Fill out the following informal survey to determine whether you may have test anxiety. For each of the twelve statements, rate your degree of agreement or disagreement.

1	2	3	4	5
Disagree Completely	Disagree Somewhat	Unsure	Agree Somewhat	Agree Completely

1. I cringe when I suddenly realize on the day of an exam that a test is coming up. _____

2. I obsess about the possibility of failing an upcoming exam. _____

3. I often experience disappointment, anger, embarrassment, or some other emotional reaction during an exam. _____

4. I think that instructors secretly get enjoyment from watching students squirm over exams. _____

5. I experience physical symptoms such as an upset stomach, faintness, hyperventilation, or nausea before an exam. _____

6. I tend to zone out during exams; my mind goes blank. _____

7. I feel extreme pressure to please others by doing well on exams. _____

8. If I'm honest, I'd have to admit that I really don't know how to study for tests. _____

9. I'd much rather write a paper or give a presentation than take an exam. _____

10. I usually fear that my exam grade will be lower than that of other students. _____

11. After taking an exam, I obsess on my performance, going over and over questions that I think I may have missed. _____

12. I convince myself that I'm not good at taking exams even though I often do fairly well on them. _____

TOTAL (add up your score) _____

If your score equals 49–60, you are a likely candidate for test anxiety. For suggestions on how to manage your anxiety, read on.

If you scored between 37 and 48, you have some signs of anxiety and may need help in managing your stress level.

If you scored 36 or below, you most likely experience a normal amount of anxiety and have already developed coping skills to help you.

Test anxiety—what is it? And more importantly, does it affect you? Although most people think of test anxiety as a negative, the truth is, it's natural to be anxious before, during, and even after an exam. Most everyone is. In fact, some anxiety is useful. The adrenaline rush that accompanies anxiety can keep you alert and focused.

But for some students, like Kevin Baxter, test anxiety takes over and sabotages their efforts. They may say, "I knew it all before the test, but when I saw the questions, everything I knew vanished before my very eyes." These students experience fainting spells or even gastric distress that requires them to make a quick exit from the room. Some of them may be reacting to prior bad

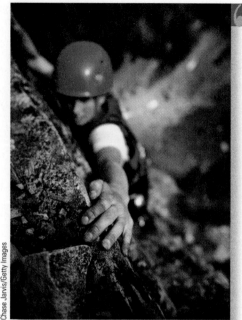

> Positive thinking will let you do everything better than negative thinking will.
>
> *Zig Ziglar, motivational speaker and author*

experiences with exams. Others may put intense pressure on themselves because they're perfectionists. Clearly, there's evidence from medical science that too much anxiety can work against you. Corticosterone, a hormone released during times of extreme stress, can actually hurt your ability to retrieve information from long-term memory.[24] Regardless of the reason, the first part of the solution is understanding exactly what test anxiety is. It has four different, but related, components in terms of what you think, feel, and do, as well as how your body reacts:[25]

cognitive thinking

emotional feeling

behavioral doing

physiological your body reacting with physical symptoms

> cognitive **aspects**—nonproductive thoughts that run through your head before, during, and after an exam ("I have to get an A on this test. If I don't, I'll flunk out of school.")

> emotional **aspects**—negative feelings you experience related to the exam (disappointment, frustration, sadness, and so on)

> behavioral **aspects**—observable indications of stress (fidgeting, drumming your fingers on the desk, and so on)

> physiological **aspects**—unhelpful physiological reactions (dry mouth, butterflies in your stomach, your heart pounding in your chest, and so on)

VARK It!

Visual: Draw a pie chart showing how the four aspects of test anxiety affect you.

Because you can't expect the tests you take in college to change for your sake—to reduce your anxiety—the possibility for change must come from within *you*. Consider these suggestions as they relate to the four indicators of test anxiety.

Cognitive

> **Understand your testing strengths and challenges, based on your learning style.** Although research indicates that most students prefer multiple-choice tests over essay tests, you have your own strengths and preferences.[26]

> **Don't catastrophize!** Stop yourself from engaging in negative, unproductive self-talk. It's easy to imagine worst-case scenarios: "If I fail this exam, I'll probably fail the exams in all my courses and flunk out of college, and if I don't go to college, I'll probably end up as a homeless person, begging for change on the street." Negative thinking can easily spiral downward, and before you know it, you're thinking about major life catastrophes and the end of the world. Although some exams do have crucial outcomes, it's important to put things in perspective.

Emotional

> **Monitor your moods.** Your emotions change based on many factors; they vary by type, intensity, and timing.[27] If you eat well and get enough sleep before an exam, your moods are more likely to be stable than if you

skip meals, give in to sugar highs and lows, and pull all-nighters. An eight-hour sleep debt will cause your mood to take a nosedive.[28]

> **"Park" your problems if you can.** When you go into a store, you leave your car outside in the parking lot and come back to it when you're finished shopping. Think about how that example can relate to taking a test. Park your problems for a while. Focus on your work, and challenge yourself to do your best.

Behavioral

> **Relieve some stress with physical activity.** Expend some of that extra, pent-up energy before the exam. Sprint to class or take a walk to clear your head in the hour before the test begins.

> **"Step out of your life" by spending time outdoors.** Being in the outdoors is liberating. It's easy to forget that when you're spending large amounts of time in classrooms or at work.

Physiological

> **Teach yourself how to relax.** Relaxation training can be used to overcome test anxiety. As simple as it sounds, that may involve learning how to breathe. Watch a new baby sleep, and you'll see instinctive, deep, even breathing in which only the baby's stomach moves up and down. As adults, when we're anxious, we breathe rapidly and shallowly, which doesn't sufficiently oxygenate our brains.

> **Seek help from a professional.** An expert who works with anxiety-ridden college students can diagnose your problem and help you visualize success or take steps to overcome your fears.

Reduce Math Anxiety and Increase Your Test Scores

Let's zero in on a particular type of test anxiety that plagues many college students. Honestly, most people feel some twinge of anxiety about working a complex set of math problems on an exam. But if your level of anxiety interferes with your test success, you may suffer from math anxiety. One expert estimates that roughly 20 to 25 percent of college students are in that category.[29] And some estimates are that as many as 85 percent of college students in introductory math classes experience some degree of math anxiety.[30]

If you're one of them, admitting the problem is the first step. Next, it's important to understand how math anxiety can work against you during exams so that you can do something about it. The most effective strategies to cope are direct and uncomplicated.[31]

Think back; perhaps you can pinpoint where your fears began. It may have been a teacher or a class or a particular test. Experts believe math anxiety is *learned* and that it's up to you to "unlearn" it.

Why and how does math anxiety affect people? Try this experiment: multiply 86×7. To arrive at the answer, you must first multiply 6×7, make note of the 2, and carry the 4. Then you must multiply 7×8 and add the 4 to arrive at 602. Notice the steps involved in this simple math problem. You have to keep certain numbers in your head while you continue to work through it, which is often the case with math. Your working memory allows you to pull it off.

Working memory is your short-term, temporary-storage, limited-space memory. It's the memory you use to hold certain pieces of information—your brain's scratchpad—keeping them available for you to work with and update.[32] A task like multiplying 639×924 would be too much for most people's working memories, but some people have more capacity than others. Here's the kicker: math anxiety actually eats up your working memory.

Why? Managing anxiety takes up working memory space that could be used to solve math problems. When you reduce your anxiety, you have more room to use your working memory productively. Math anxiety also causes people to take longer to do math and to make more mistakes.[33] It's not the case that you use up your working memory because you think and think and think about how to work the problem and get the right answer. Instead, your working memory is hijacked by negative thoughts, causing you to choke.[34]

The solution? Practice for stressful exams under pressure. Set a timer, and tell yourself you must finish before it goes off. Make a game of it: for every question you miss on a practice exam, you must put a quarter in the kitty and pay off your friend, spouse, or mom. In other words, practicing in an equally stressful environment (or nearly so) can help during the actual test.[35] Because math anxiety is a learned fear, it can be unlearned.

As you study for math tests, keep these five suggestions in mind.[36]

1. **Get to know your calculator (like it's your best friend).** If your instructor allows you to use a calculator in class, learn its functions inside and out. Even though today's calculator can do amazing things, it won't help you much during an exam if you don't know how to use it. Your graphic calculator can plot graphs, solve several equations at once, and you can even program it to run customized applications. But it can't do those things on its own; it requires you to run it. So part of your study strategy should be to learn what your calculator can do and become so familiar with it that using it is almost second-nature.

2. **Concentrate on *comprehension*, not *memorization*.** Memorizing formulas or rules is fine, but it won't help you if you don't know how to apply them. This formula, $a^2 + 2ab + b^2 = (a + b)^2$, is a good thing to know about factoring in algebra, but on a test it wouldn't help you factor $w^2 + 8w + 16$ unless you knew exactly how to apply the formula, step by step. Here's a sample practice problem, showing the steps you should learn to feel comfortable with:

Problem:
Simplify: $5(a - 4) + 3 = 8$

Solution:

Step 1: Remove the brackets	**Step 2: Isolate variable a**
$5a - 20 + 3 = 8$	$5a = 8 - 3 + 20$
	$5a = 25$
	$a = 25/5$
	$a = 5$
	Answer: $a = 5$

VARK It!

Visual: Picture your working memory. Can you think of a metaphor for it (for example, a bucket, a sponge, etc.)? Can you see how math anxiety could use up part of it?

VARK It!

Kinesthetic: Try setting a timer and taking a practice test you've exchanged with a friend. Does the practice situation feel somewhat stressful with the timer ticking?

3. **Maximize opportunities to practice.** Homework isn't just busywork; it's practice so that you can succeed. Besides homework, you can find countless web sites with practice tests online. Here's an example of a question you might encounter on a test:

Question: There are 2,000 liters of water in a swimming pool. Water is filling the pool at the rate of 100 liters per minute. How much water, in liters, would be in the swimming pool after m minutes?

Answer: The amount of water added to the pool after m minutes will be 100 liters per minute times m, or $100 \times m$. Because we started with 2,000 liters of water in the pool, we add this to the amount of water added to the pool to get the expression $2,000 + (100 \times m)$.

Having experience reformulating problems like this means that you know how to extract the math from the words used to describe the math. If you can translate a word problem into a mathematical expression, then you can easily plug in any value to get an answer, given a specific value for m. But in order to do that, you need to understand what you're doing. "Practice makes perfect" may be hard to actually accomplish, but it's important to keep practicing in small chunks. Most experts recommend that you take math classes that meet more than once a week, just for the regular practice.

4. **Make flash cards.** The simple act of creating the flashcards will help commit the information to your memory. And if no one is available to help you go through the flash cards, go through them yourself, and write down the answers as you go.

$$\frac{a/c}{b/c} = \frac{a}{b}$$

The act of writing this fact on a flashcard reminds you to look for commonalities in the denominator and numerator.

5. **Hit the "redo" button.** Mistakes are invitations to "do it right" the next time. For example, if you get a homework problem wrong, figure out why, rework the problem, write down a sentence about the right way to solve it, and then work a similar problem to prove to yourself that you understand now. Don't just skip it or convince yourself that you'll probably get it right next time. It's called "self-regulated learning," and it works.[37]

During the Test: Focus and Work Hard

During an exam, the heat is on! Do you use these strategies? If not, which ones can you incorporate to improve your performance? Put a plus sign (+) in front of each item you already do regularly and a check mark (✓) in front of items you could start doing more regularly to improve your test-taking skills.

1. _____ **Jot down what you don't want to forget right away.** When you first receive your exam, turn it over and jot down everything you want to make sure you remember—mnemonic devices, charts you've created—assuming, of course, that writing on the test is allowed. Some students treat the exam itself as if it were a sacred document, but marking up your exam is usually allowed. Circle key words and strike through answers you eliminate.

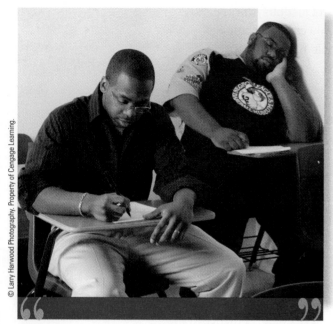

We all have ability. The difference is how we use it.

Stevie Wonder, singer and composer

VARK It!

Read/Write: When you preview an exam, make a quick list of problems or questions that seem impossible. Just acknowledging the hardest questions may give your memory a jump start.

2. _____ **Preview the exam.** Just going through all the questions may help you review terms you know. And you'll notice which questions are easier and which are harder right away. It's also likely that reading sample questions will trigger your memory and help you come up with information you need. After the first few minutes, you may relax a bit, and answers will come to you more easily.

3. _____ **Start with what you know.** Make sure you get credit for answers you know; don't waste time early on struggling with the more difficult questions. This strategy will also boost your confidence and help you relax. Studies show that running up against extremely difficult test questions at the beginning of a test can actually hurt your ability to answer simpler questions later on.[38]

4. _____ **Weigh your answers.** Allocate your time based on the relative weight of the questions. Don't wrestle with one question for ten minutes when it's only worth one point. Go on to one that's worth more.

5. _____ **Read directions thoroughly.** Misreading or skipping the directions altogether can be a lethal mistake. Remember that your instructor can't read your mind. ("But that's not what I meant!") Slow down and make sure you understand what you're being asked to do.

6. _____ **Read questions carefully.** Sometimes skipping over a word in the sentence (or filling one in where there isn't one) will cause you to jump to a false conclusion. Don't let your eyes (or your brain) play tricks on you!

7. _____ **If the test has a mixed format, complete the multiple-choice questions first.** Often instructors create exams using both *objective* (multiple-choice, true-false) questions and *subjective* questions (fill in the blank, essay). Generally, objective questions ask you to *recognize* answers from several alternatives, and subjective questions ask you to *recall* answers from memory. A multiple-choice question may remind you of something you want to include in an essay. Keep a pad of paper nearby during the exam. Jot down ideas as you answer multiple-choice questions. You'll feel more confident and do a better job if you keep a running list of ideas that occur to you as you go.

8. _____ **Explain your answer to a confusing question in the margin of your test.** You may point out a problem your instructor wasn't aware of or get partial credit.

9. _____ **Change your answers if you're convinced you're wrong.** Despite advice you've probably always received from teachers and classmates alike, changing answers when you're sure you've made a mistake is usually a good idea, not a bad one. In one study, less than 10 percent of students made changes that decreased their scores, whereas 74 percent made changes that increased their scores.[39]

10. _____ **Ask your instructor for clarification.** If the exam appears to have a typo or something seems strange, ask your instructor to clarify for you. Of course, if you ask for the definition of a word that is a clue, you probably won't get an answer, but if you have a legitimate question, don't be afraid to ask.

11. _____ **Pay attention to "aha" moments.** Don't let your "aha" moments turn into "oh, no" moments. If you remember something you couldn't think of earlier, go back to that question and finish it right away.

12. _____ **Don't give in to peer pressure.** If, while you're working away, you look around and see that many students are leaving because they're already finished, don't panic. Take as much of the allowed time as you need. Everyone works at a different rate.

13. _____ **Save time for review.** When you're finished, go back over all your answers. Make sure you've circled the right letter or filled in the correct bubble. Be certain you've made all the points you intended to make in your essay. Look at your work critically, as if you were the instructor. Careless errors can be costly!

14. _____ **Be strategic about taking online tests.** Often tests posted online are timed. If you're taking a distance education course or a class-room course with an online test component, watch for e-mail announcements that tests have been posted, and note particular instructions. When will the test expire and disappear? Can you reenter the test site and redo answers before you hit the submit button? Can you take tests together with other students? With online tests, of course, the other recommendations in this chapter for true-false or multiple-choice tests apply as well.

Taking Objective Tests

Many of the exams you'll take in college will be objective, rather than subjective, tests. Let's examine the best strategies for taking objective tests.

True-False: Truly a 50–50 Chance of Getting It Right?

> Exam questions that test your ability to remember are always more challenging than questions that test your ability to recognize the right answer. T or F?

True-false tests may seem straightforward, but they can be tricky. You assume you have a 50–50 chance of answering correctly. But don't forget, you also have a 50–50 chance of answering incorrectly. Sometimes the wording of the statements makes the *process*

I am easily satisfied with the very best.

Winston Churchill, Prime Minister of England (1874–1965)

of taking true-false tests more challenging than their *content*. Consider these helpful guidelines:

> **Watch for parts of statements that make the entire statement false.** The statement must be all true to be "true," and a few words may make an otherwise true statement "false." Here's an example:

> Derek Bok, who was president of Harvard University for thirty years, once said, "If you think education is expensive, try ignorance." T or F

The main part of the statement is true; the quotation does belong to Derek Bok. But Bok wasn't president of Harvard for a full thirty years, making the entire statement false.

> **Assume statements are true until you can prove them false.** Statistically, exams usually contain more true answers than false ones. You have a better than 50 percent chance of being right if you guess "true." But teachers vary; yours may not follow the norm.

> **Watch for *absolutes*; they often make a statement false.** Words like *always, never,* and *entirely* often make otherwise true statements become false. "You can *always* get an A on an exam if you study for it." Unfortunately, no.

> **Look for *qualifiers*; they often make a statement true.** On the other hand, words like *sometimes, often,* and *ordinarily* often make statements true. "You can *sometimes* get an A on an exam if you study for it." Fortunately, yes.

> **Remember that negatives can be confusing.** Is this statement true or false? "Students who don't lack motivation are likely to excel." "Don't lack" really means "have," right?

Multiple Choice or Multiple Guess? Taking the Guesswork Out

> Which of the following statements is (are) true?
>
> a. Richard Greener, who became Harvard's first African American graduate in 1870, later became a lawyer, educator, and distinguished U.S. consul and diplomat.
>
> b. Elizabeth Blackwell, who graduated from Geneva Medical College in New York, was the first woman in the United States to earn a medical degree.
>
> c. Oberlin College was the first U.S. college to admit women and the last to admit African American students on an equal footing with Caucasians.
>
> d. a and b
>
> e. a, b, and c

Are multiple-choice tests difficult for you? Often what's difficult about multiple-choice tests has more to do with the structure of the test than the content. Studying for these tests requires a particular approach, and if you master the approach, you'll find taking multiple-choice tests to be much easier. You can actually think of them as similar to true-false tests. [The correct answer to the question, by the way, is (d).]

> **Think of answers on your own before reading your choices.** You may get hung up on the wording of an answer. Answer it on your own so that you can recognize it, no matter how it's worded. You may want to do this by covering up the alternatives first and then going ahead after you know what you're looking for. Sometimes the alternatives will differ by only one or two words. It's easy to become confused.

> **Line up your test and answer sheet.** This sounds like a simple suggestion, but getting off a line can be very disruptive when you have to erase like crazy and start over!

> **Determine the TPI (time per item).** Divide the number of questions by the allotted time. If there are seventy-five questions to answer in an hour, you know that you'll need to work faster than one question per minute. Remember to save some time for review and revision at the end, too.

> **Don't decide answers based on the law of averages.** If you flip a coin three times, and it comes up "heads," most of us assume it's probably time for "tails" to come up next. Likewise, on exams, if you've answered (d) for three questions in a row, you may think it's time for an (a), (b), or (c). It may not be.

> **Use a process of elimination and guess if there's no penalty.** Some instructors subtract points for wrong answers, but if you do guess, guess wisely. And don't skip questions. Always mark something unless you're penalized for doing so. Take a look at this example:

Before you write an answer on an essay test, you should do all but the following:

a. Read all the questions.

b. Begin with the hardest question.

c. Look at what the questions are asking you to do, specifically.

d. Underline key words in the question.

You know that you should do (a). Reading all the questions before you start is a must. You know that option (d) makes sense, and so does (c). But you're not quite sure about option (b). You can eliminate (a), (c), and (d), so (b) must be the right answer based on a process of elimination. As you work, eliminate answers that you know are incorrect by marking through them ~~like this~~.

> **Look for highly similar pairs.** Sometimes two options will differ by a single word or the order of words. Often one of these is the right choice.

> **Look for contradictory answers.** If two statements are complete opposites, one of them is often the right choice.

> **Watch out for tricks intended to separate the prepared from the unprepared!** For example, avoid answers that are true in and of themselves,

but not true when attached to the first part of the question being asked. For example, imagine this question option on a multiple-choice exam:

> Global warming is considered to be a serious issue among some scientists because:
>
> a. Former President Bill Clinton describes global warming as a greater threat to the world than terrorism.

While Clinton did say this in a 2006 speech, it is not the reason for scientists' concern, so (a) isn't the correct answer.[40] Two other tips: generally, when numbers are in each alternative, choose numbers in the middle range. Choosing answers that are longer and more descriptive usually pays off, too.

> **Consider each answer as an individual true-false question.** Examine each option carefully, as if you had to decide whether it is true or false, and use that process to decide which answer is correct.

EXERCISE 9.4

Multiple-Choice Test

Answer the following multiple-choice questions. Beneath each question, identify which of the principles of test taking from this chapter you are using to identify the correct answer.

1. "I know of no more encouraging fact than the unquestionable ability of man to elevate his life by conscious endeavor." These words were said by:

   a. Bill Clinton

   b. Abraham Maslow

   c. Ronald Reagan

   d. Henry David Thoreau

   _____

2. Which of the following statements about the ACT test is not true?

   a. The ACT includes 215 multiple-choice questions.

   b. ACT results are accepted by virtually all U.S. colleges and universities.

   c. Students may take the ACT test as many times as they like.

   d. None of the above.

   _____

3. Which of the following suggestions about preparing for college is (are) true?

   a. Get involved in co-curricular activities in high school.

   b. Always take challenging courses that show your effort and ability.

   c. Involve your family in your decisions and preparation for college.

   d. Find a mentor, a teacher, or a counselor who can give you good advice.

   e. All of the above.

   _____

[Answer key: (d), (d), (e)]

- **Be careful about "all of the above" or "none of the above" options.** Although instructors sometimes make these options the correct ones, it's also possible they resort to these options because making up enough possible answers is challenging.

- **Watch for terms that have been emphasized.** Look for key terms that appeared in your lecture notes and in chapters of the text. These words may provide links to the correct answer. Remember when taking multiple-choice tests that you are looking for the *best* answer, not simply the *right* one.[41]

> Knowing is not enough; we must apply. Willing is not enough; we must do.

Johann Wolfgang von Goethe, German writer and scholar (1749–1832)

Short-Answer, Fill-in-the-Blank, and Matching Tests

Short-answer tests are like essay tests, which we'll discuss shortly, in many ways. You're required to come up with an organized, thoughtful answer on your own. But instead of a long essay, you only need to write a paragraph or two. Is that easier? It may be, but sometimes it's just as hard or harder to say what you need to say in fewer words. Generally, however, the suggestions for essay tests hold.

For fill-in-the-blank tests, first think the statement through. What does it mean? Try inserting different words. Which one sounds best? Which one was used during lectures or appeared in the textbook? If one word looks awkward, try another one. Although it's not a completely reliable hint, look at the number of words, placement of spaces, and length of the space. If you don't know the exact terminology the question is looking for, insert your own words. You may at least earn partial credit.

Matching tests require particular strategies, too. First of all, you must determine whether items should be used only once or if they can be reused. If it's not clear from the test directions, ask for clarification. Match the items you're certain about first and cross them out if once only is the rule. If you mismatch an item early on, all your subsequent choices will be wrong, too.

Taking Subjective Essay Tests

> Essay Question: Please discuss the value of brain research in relation to our current knowledge of how learning takes place.

Essay questions are difficult for some students because details are required. Rather than being able to *recognize* the correct answer, you must be able to *recall* it totally from your own memory. Here are some recommendations you should consider:

- **Save enough time for essays.** If the test has a mixed format with different types of questions, it's important to save enough time to write well-thought-through essays. Often objective questions such as multiple-choice or true-false only count a point or two, but essay questions often count into the double digits.

> **Read all the questions before you start.** To sharpen your focus and avoid overlap, give yourself an overview of all the questions before you start writing.

> **Make brief notes.** Somewhere on the exam or on scratch paper, write a brief plan for your responses to essay questions. A few minutes of planning may be time well spent. As you plan your answer, keep basic questions in mind—*who, what, when, where,* and *why*—as an organizing framework.

thesis your main point

> **State your thesis up front.** How will you handle this question? What's your plan of attack? Your first paragraph should include your basic argument in a thesis statement.

assertions statements you claim to be true

> **Provide support for your thesis.** Writing an answer to an essay question requires you to make assertions. However, it's not enough that you assert things; you must try to prove that they are true. If your thesis asserts that college students cheat more today than they did when your parents went to college, you must present evidence—statistics, examples, or expert testimony—to demonstrate that what you're asserting is true.

> **Zero in on the verb.** The heart of an essay question is its verb. Take a look at this list and think about how each verb dictates what is required:

Analyze—break into separate parts, and examine or discuss each part

Compare—examine two or more things, and find the similarities and differences (usually you emphasize the similarities)

Contrast—find the differences between two or more things

Critique, criticize, or evaluate—make a judgment, describe the worth of something

Define—provide the meaning (usually requires a short answer)

Describe—give a detailed account, listing characteristics or qualities

Discuss—describe a cause/effect relationship, the significance of something, the pros and cons, or the role played by someone or something

Enumerate—list qualities, characteristics, events, and so on

Explain—similar to discuss

Illustrate—give concrete examples

Interpret—comment on, give examples, provide an explanation for, discuss

Outline—describe the plot, main ideas, or organization of something

Prove—support an argument with evidence from the text or class notes

Relate—show the relationship or connection between two things

State—explain in precise terms

Summarize—give a condensed account of key points, reduce to the essential components

Trace—describe a process or the development of something

VARK It!

Kinesthetic: Act out three verbs on this list, and see whether your study partner or classmates can guess which ones you're portraying.

Understanding "Verb-age"

What would you emphasize in your written response to these essay questions about this chapter, based on the verb used in each question? For each question, write the first several sentences of an answer to demonstrate how you might respond, just like the student's example in number 1.

1. **Critique** this chapter of FOCUS on developing memory and taking tests.

   To me, this is the best chapter of FOCUS I've read so far. I never actually realized it before, but I have symptoms of all four aspects of test anxiety. Many students do. I usually think negatively about how well I'll do, feel frustrated, get fidgety, and get an upset stomach. To me, this one section of the chapter makes it worthwhile to read . . .

2. **Summarize** this chapter of FOCUS on developing memory and taking tests.

3. **Outline** this chapter of FOCUS on developing memory and taking tests.

4. **Analyze** this chapter of FOCUS on developing memory and taking tests.

5. **Compare** this chapter of FOCUS with an earlier chapter.

> **Use terms from the course.** Perhaps more than any other type of exam, an essay test allows you room to truly display your knowledge. Use the opportunity! Reflect new terms you have learned, and tie your answer directly to course content.

> **Rifle your answer, don't shotgun.** Here's an analogy: A shotgun fires many small metal pellets. A rifle fires a single bullet. When writing an essay answer, some students write down everything they know, hoping that something will be correct. You may actually lose points by doing this. It's better to target your answer and be precise.

> **Generalize if you're unsure of small, exact details.** You can't quite remember, was it 1884 or 1894? The best idea is to write, "Toward the end of the nineteenth century" instead of choosing one of the two and being wrong.

> **Follow all the rules.** When answering an essay question, it's important to be as concise yet thorough as possible. Number your ideas ("There are *three* major . . . "). Avoid slang ("Wordsworth elaborated . . . " not "Wordsworth *jazzed up* the poem."). Refer to researchers or authors or noteworthy people by their last names ("Jung wrote . . . " not "Dr. Carl Jung wrote . . . ").

> **Watch your grammar.** The reason why its important, to do this, is because many student's dont and there answers are marked wrong. They wish they would of done better afterwards. (You get the point.)

> **Write an answer that corresponds to how much the question is worth.** It's important to be concise, but generally, if one essay answer is worth 10 points and another is worth 25 points, your instructor will expect you to write more for the question that's worth more. A more detailed, thorough response is what is called for, but make sure you're adding content, not just padding your answer.

> **Put down what you do know.** If you see a question you didn't predict, don't panic. If you've studied, you know *something* that might help give you partial credit even if you don't know the answer in full.

> **Proofread and make sure your handwriting can be read.** Although most instructors will count the number of points you covered and use specific standards, grading essays requires instructors to use their own judgment. A good essay answer is taken less seriously if it's littered with mistakes or a real mess to read. This is the real world; neatness counts. Anything you can do to create a positive impression may work in your favor.

> **If you run out of time, jot down any remaining points in the time that's left.** You may not get full credit, but partial credit is better than none.

> **Include a summary statement at the end.** Your essay answer should read like a real essay with an introduction, a body, and a conclusion. Don't just stop mid-sentence without wrapping things up.[42]

Don't Cheat Yourself!

VARK It!

Read/Write: Find an online article about a highly publicized case of corporate cheating, and bring it to class to read.

What if you were in one of these situations? How would you respond?

> Many students in your math class get through the homework by sharing answers on their Facebook pages. The instructor doesn't know, and the course isn't all that interesting anyway.

> A friend of yours stores all the names and dates she'll need to know for her history exams on her cell phone. With just one click she can call up whatever information she needs. "Try it," she says. "Everyone else does it, and you'll feel cheated if you don't cheat. If you don't do what other students do, you'll graduate with so-so grades, and you'll never be able to compete for the jobs you've always wanted. Besides, getting away with it here just helps prepare you for the business world where things are *really* cutthroat!"

> You hear about an entrepreneurial student who operates an underground paper-writing service. For $20 a page, he will guarantee you the grade you want (based on the grade you already have going in the course so that your paper won't raise the instructor's suspicions), and he "doctors" each sentence so that the source can't be found on the Internet. You have four papers, a presentation, and an exam all due the same week, and one or two papers would only run you around $150 to $200. That's not all that much considering the tips you make as a server. Hmm....

> **For nothing can seem foul to those that win.**
>
> *William Shakespeare, British poet and playwright (1564–1616)*

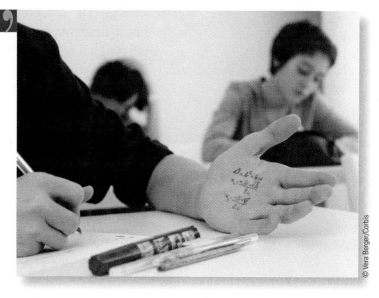

How did you respond to these three scenarios? Are you aware of cheating schemes at your school? Could students you know be the ones these scenarios were written about? Notice that these students have practical-sounding reasons for what they are doing. If you want to cheat, it's not hard, and you can always blame someone else. What's the harm? You get better grades, your teachers think they're doing a good job, your school brags about the fine academic record of its students, and you pat yourself on your back for skillfully managing a very busy, demanding life. Everyone wins, right? Wrong.

According to some studies done fifty years ago, one in five college students admitted to cheating. Today's figures range from 75 to 90 percent. Here's some straight talk about cheating:[43]

1. **Remember that cheating snowballs.** What started as secretly pocketing some kid's toy or glancing at your neighbor's reading test in grade school turns into writing a math formula between your fingers or hiding the names of the constellations under your shirt cuff in middle school. Then these violations as a kid turn into full-fledged, sophisticated rule-breaking as students "download their workload" in high school and knowingly violate their school's Academic Integrity Policy in college. Where does it stop?

2. **Instead of saving time, cheating can take time.** Everyone is busy. Most students are working at jobs for pay in addition to taking classes. How can anyone get everything done that needs to get done? But instead of devising elaborate cheating schemes, which take time to design, why not just use that time to study?

3. **If you cheat now, you'll pay later.** Sooner or later, cheating will catch up with you. You may get past your math instructor this time, and you may even get good grades on others' work you turn in as your own. But someday your boss will ask you to write something, do some research, or use a skill a student is expected to have mastered in college, and you won't know where to start.

4. **If you do get caught, cheating may do you in.** Some students cheat because they know other students have gotten away with it. Cheating for them is a thrill, and not getting caught is like winning or beating the system. Roll the dice and see what happens, they say. But you should know that instructors are in the know these days. Academic hallways are abuzz with faculty talk about cheating. If you do get caught, your academic career may come to an abrupt halt.

5. Cheating is just plain wrong. You may or may not agree with this point, but it deserves some serious consideration. How would you like to be cheated out of money that's owed you or days off that are due you? The Golden Rule may sound old-fashioned, but the fact that it's been around for a long time with roots in a wide range of world cultures tells you something. "Intellectual Property" and "Academic Integrity" may not be as tangible as money you deserve or eight hours of free time, but they are things that are increasingly protected by every college.

ethical standards agreements about what is right and wrong

What are your personal *ethical standards*? Are you willing to cut corners? Would you cheat to achieve top grades in college? What kind of "devil's bargain" would you be willing to strike?

Some students today believe that technology is a tool, and using technology to avoid work isn't cheating, it's just plain smart. Some experts call it the "technological detachment phenomenon." These students think: schoolwork is just busywork, so if you download homework answers, buy a paper online, or collaborate with other students over the Internet when the assignment calls for your own work, you're just saving valuable time. They think the pervasiveness of technology somehow justifies cheating. But cheating, no matter how you do it, is still cheating—and the person you're cheating most is yourself. One student went to a campus computer lab and happened to find another student's homework saved there. So he changed the name to his own name, and turned the assignment in as his own. But he mistakenly forgot to change the name on one page. Busted.[44]

If you're tempted, remember this. Learning is about *doing,* not figuring out ways *not to do,* and sooner or later, cheating costs you—big time! Don't cheat yourself out of learning what you need to learn in college. Learning is not all about *product*—the exams, papers, grades, and diplomas themselves—it's about *process,* too. The process involves gaining skills that will prepare you for life after college. That's a goal worth working toward.

You can't go through life devising elaborate schemes, hiring someone else to do your work for you, or rationalizing about finding a way to beat the system because you're too busy to do your own work. Cheating in your college classes now just makes it that much easier to risk cheating your employer—and yourself—later on the job. Look through newspapers or watch the evening news to see who's been caught lately. It's a competitive world out there, but more and more companies find that having a good reputation, which comes from being honest, is good business. Integrity starts now: *earn what you learn.*[45]

After the Test: Continue to Learn

After you finish an exam and get your results, you may be thrilled or discouraged. Regardless, exams can be excellent learning experiences if you take these steps. Put a plus sign (+) in front of each item you already do regularly and a check mark (✓) in front of items you could start doing more regularly to improve your test-taking skills.

Non scholae sed vitae discrimus. **(We do not learn for school, but for life.)**

—Lucius Annaeus Seneca, Roman philosopher and statesman (4 B.C.–A.D. 65)

1. _____ **Analyze your results.** Conduct a thorough analysis of your test results. For example, an analysis like this one might tell you what kinds of questions are most problematic for you.

Type of Question	Points Earned/Right	Points Deducted/Wrong	Total
Multiple-Choice	32	3	35
Fill-in-the-Blank	15	2	17
True-False	20	8	28
Essay	10	10	20
Total	77	23	100

Or analyze your results by comparing how many lecture questions there were versus textbook questions to find out where to concentrate your efforts on future tests. Or do an analysis by chapter to tell you where to focus your time when studying for the final exam.

2. _____ **Read your instructor's comments and take them to heart.** After an exam, ask yourself: What was the instructor looking for? Was my writing ability part of the issue? Does the test make more sense now than it did while I was taking it? Are there instructor's comments written on the test that I can learn from? What do the results of this exam teach me about preparing differently, perhaps, for the next test?

3. _____ **Explain your grade to yourself.** Where did you go wrong? Did you misread questions? Run out of time? Organize essay answers poorly? Does the grade reflect how much time you studied? If not, why not? Did test anxiety get the better of you? On the other hand, if you studied hard and your grade reflects it, that's an explanation, too!

4. _____ **Be honest.** It's easy to get caught up in the blame game: "I would have gotten a better grade if the exam had been fairer, if the test had been shorter, if the material hadn't been so difficult, if I'd had more time to study...." Your instructors have heard every excuse in the book: "My dog ate my notes," "A relative died," "A family emergency made it impossible to study," "My hard drive crashed"—you name it. Of course, sometimes crises do overtake events. But rather than pointing fingers elsewhere if you're disappointed with your results, take a close look at what you can do differently next time.

5. _____ **Make a specific plan for the next test.** Most courses have more than one exam. You'll probably have an opportunity to apply what you've learned and do better next time.

6. _____ **Approach your instructor politely if you believe your exam has been mismarked.** Sometimes teachers make mistakes. Sometimes

VARK It!

Visual: Try creating a chart like the one above for one of your recent tests. What does it teach you?

VARK It!

Kinesthetic: Role play being a coach and give yourself some pointers. What would you tell yourself about improving your test results?

they're interrupted while grading and forget to finish reading an essay answer, or the answer key is wrong, or they make a mistake adding up points. Even if the scoring is correct, it may be a good idea to approach your instructor for help about how to improve your next test score.

7. _____ **Reward yourself for good (study) behavior.** After you've worked hard to prepare and the exam is over, reward yourself—take in a movie, go out with friends, do something to celebrate your hard work.

Deepen Your Learning

The final point this chapter will make about memory and tests is this: in a classic study conducted in the mid-1970s, two Swedish scholars decided to find out the difference between effective and ineffective learners. They gave students this task: read an essay, summarize it, and solve a problem. Then they interviewed the students to find out how they had approached the task.

The interviews revealed two types of learners. One group of students said things like, "I just tried to remember as much as I could" or "I just memorized what I read." Other students said, "I tried to look for the main idea" or "I looked for the point of the article." The professors who conducted the study then characterized the difference between *surface-level processing,* looking at words and numbers alone, and *deep-level processing,* searching beneath the surface for underlying meaning.[46] To become a truly focused learner, you must process information as you go. Dig deep for increased learning, better test results, and greater success!

Deepen Your Memory

Surface-level processing
just skims the surface.

Deep-level processing
goes deep.

Nathan B Dappen/Shutterstock.com; Elisei Shafer/Shutterstock.com

FIGURE 9.3

Memory Processing: Skipping a Stone versus Deep Sea Diving

The Four C Factors: Just how motivated are YOU?

 CONTROL: *YOUR TOUGHEST CLASS*

Think about your most challenging class this term. Identify one key challenge you face in this class that relates to this chapter. Now develop a step-by-step action plan to deal with this one challenge.

For example, let's say your math class is your most challenging. Your action plan might look like this:

1. Reread the sections of the chapter on preparing for tests and test anxiety.

2. Meet with my instructor to discuss my problems in his class.

3. Show him this action plan, and ask for his suggestions.

4. Keep a journal of my progress to note improvement, and meet with him four more times this term.

Now do the same for your most challenging class.

1.

2.

3.

4.

How might outlining your action plan affect your success? Why?

_____

_____

_____

 CURIOSITY: *ACT ON YOUR MEMORY*

Have you ever watched a movie, wondering how *do* actors learn all those lines? Do they have superhuman memory powers?

Actually, what actors are most concerned with is convincing you that they're not playing a role. But actors' contracts require them to be absolutely precise in conforming to the script, so how do they do it? Studying how actors learn their parts with precision has confirmed what learning experts know about memory.[47]

Most actors aren't memory experts, but they do use the memory techniques described in this chapter. They manipulate the lines, elaborate on them to themselves, relate the lines to experiences or feelings of their own, or try writing or saying the lines themselves, rather than just reading them. Four of the techniques used by actors may also be useful to you as you try to commit course material to memory. Maybe you've even tried some of these techniques.

Chunking: Actors chunk their material into beats. For example, an actor might divide a half-page of dialogue into three beats: to flirt, to sweet-talk, and to convince. In other words, the character would first flirt with the other actor, then sweet-talk him to lower his guard, and then convince him to do something he might not want to do. The results? Three chunks to remember instead of twelve lines of double-spaced text.

Goal Setting: Notice that the chunks are based on goals, a strategy that also works well when you're studying. Actors ask themselves goal-oriented questions such as these: "Should I be flirting with him here?" "Am I trying to sweet-talk him?" "Should I be trying to convince him to do something he doesn't really want to do?" In the same way, you can ask yourself, "Am I trying to learn the underlying formula so that I can work other problem sets?" or "Should I be coming up with my own reasons for why the play is considered to be Shakespeare's best comedy?" When you ask yourself goal-oriented questions while you study, you steer your actions, as actors do, toward learning.

Moving: Going through the motions while rehearsing their lines helps actors memorize them. Imagine the hypothetical actor whose goals were to flirt, to sweet-talk, and to convince, glancing toward the other actor from across the room, moving closer and smiling, and then touching his arm while making the persuasive case. The actor must know the meanings behind the movements to give meaning to the lines. (She could be glancing across the room to give a dirty look instead of to flirt, for example.) The meanings are tied to the movements, which are tied to the lines, and the lines become committed to memory. When you study, moving around may help you learn. Even if you're not primarily a kinesthetic learner, pieces of information become tied to motions in ways that help you recall information.

Meaning: "Say what you mean" and "mean what you say" was Lewis Carroll's advice in *Alice's Adventures in Wonderland*. When actors concentrate on truly meaning what they're saying, they learn their lines more easily than they do when they simply try to memorize them. As you study course material, do the same thing. Imagine you need to communicate the information to someone you know who needs it. Put emotion into it. In a sense, when you do this, you become an actor, and as a result you "learn your lines."

Do you see how movement could help you learn subject matter that has often been challenging for you? How could becoming "an actor" help you learn?

_____

_____

_____

CAREER OUTLOOK: *FAIL FORWARD*

There's no doubt about it: Failure isn't fun. But have you ever read the professional backgrounds of highly successful people? Believe it or not, most of them didn't skyrocket to the top. If you graphed their careers, you'd see just as many lows as highs. Their histories are littered with failures.

Although it's a radical departure from what most people think—that to fail is to "crash and burn"—try thinking of failure as forward motion. You're moving along toward a goal when you suddenly trip and fall forward. The act of falling isn't fun, but at least you end up further along than you were beforehand.

Instead of "falling forward," try to wrap your brain around the concept of "failing forward." What would that one attitude tweak do for you? It might change everything.

For example, one thing it might do is to help you be more realistic about yourself. Nobody is exceptional at everything, but most of us are pretty good at multiple things. Maybe you're good at remembering key dates for your history class, but not so great at remembering equations for your calculus class. And even though one comes more easily than the other, you still wouldn't consider yourself to be a history genius. You're moderately good at it.

The question is: How can you creatively combine the things you're moderately good at into one package? Realizing your value by creatively piecing together your unique talents is the secret. Acting on that one realization can propel you and your career forward.

Perhaps you've heard the old quotation, "Good things come to those who wait." In today's competitive career world, that's hardly the case. The action won't move toward you, and luck won't come knocking at your door. You have to move to where the action is to attract luck. You will fail at some things; there's no doubt about that. But when you do fail, look around to see where you've landed. Are you ahead of where you were? Take note, collect yourself, get out the superglue, and piece together your own success. Over time, failing forward can not only provide the best lessons but also advance your career in ways you can't possibly anticipate now.

Think about a college class in which you've not succeeded or not done as well as you hoped you would. What lessons did you learn?

_____

_____

_____

CHALLENGE: REALITY CHECK

Can you answer these questions about test taking and studying now that you've read the chapter?

1. What are the three "R's" of remembering?

2. This chapter names twenty ways within five different categories to master your memory. Can you identify five of the twenty ways?

3. What are the four components of test anxiety?

4. Identify three hints to managing your time during tests.

5. How long did it take? _____ hours _____ minutes. Before you began this chapter, you were asked to predict how long it would take you to complete it (total time, even if you read it in more than one sitting). Was your estimate on target, or will you revise it for the next chapter you'll read?_____

step 3 INSIGHT *Now* What Do You Think?

At the beginning of this chapter, Kevin Baxter, a frustrated and discouraged returning adult student, faced a challenge. Now after reading this chapter, would you respond differently to any of the questions you answered about the "FOCUS Challenge Case"? Using what you learned in the chapter, write a paragraph ending to Kevin's case study. What are some of the possible outcomes for Kevin?

step 4 ACTION Your Plans for Change

1. Which type of test do you find most difficult—multiple-choice, true-false, or essay, for example? Within that particular portion of the chapter, which strategies that you read about will you try on your next exam?

2. Many students have negative attitudes toward tests. What could they do to change their outlook and learn to see tests as opportunities, rather than threats?

3. What piece of helpful information about memorizing or test-taking, based on your own experience, would you add to this chapter? How has it changed the way you prepare for or actually take tests?

Building Relationships, Valuing Diversity

READINESS CHECK

How this chapter relates to YOU

1. When it comes to building relationships and valuing diversity in college, what do you find most challenging, if anything?

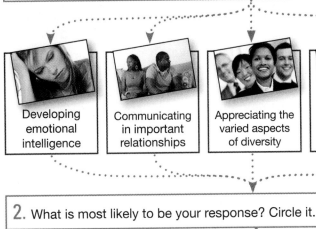

| Developing emotional intelligence | Communicating in important relationships | Appreciating the varied aspects of diversity | Developing cultural intelligence | Understanding the impact of globalization |

2. What is most likely to be your response? Circle it.

| I'll be open to learning how to improve my skills. | I'll see whether this chapter helps me. | I'll pay particular attention to these issues in my classes. | Eventually, I'll just figure it out on my own. |

3. What would you have to do to increase your likelihood of success? Will you do it this quarter or semester?

Example: Find a mentor, counselor, or instructor to talk about these issues. Yes!

How YOU will relate to this chapter

What are you most interested in learning about? Put checkmarks by those topics.

☐ Whether your emotional intelligence can be improved

☐ How to improve communication with people you care about

☐ Why diversity enriches our lives

☐ What cultural intelligence is and why it's important

☐ How globalization changes our world

• How motivated are you to learn more about getting the right start in college? (5 = high, 1 = low) ____

• How ready are you to read now? ____ (If something is in your way, take care of it if you can, zero in, and focus).

• How long do you think it will take you to complete this chapter? If you start and stop, keep track of your overall time. ____ hour(s) ____ minutes

Kia Washington

Jupiterimages/Photos.com

At first, Kia Washington was frustrated. Then she was scared. Then she was furious. How could her husband, James, manage to get laid off after only six months on the job? It had been a good job, too, in the construction industry, and it qualified them for their first house loan. A home of their own was a dream come true for Kia, especially after moving around as a military spouse for the first three years of their marriage. Now, how would they possibly afford it? To make matters worse, it wasn't long before Kia found out that she was staring possible unemployment in the face, too, at the manufacturing plant in town.

Recently, there had been talk of starting a family; maybe it would help bring some stability to their relationship, they'd even thought. But now that seemed out of the question. So Kia had enrolled at the community college close to home, in their nursing program, to become a pediatric nurse and work with children. Nursing was a stable profession, and jobs were plentiful. Security was what Kia wanted most in her life.

Financial turmoil had put considerable stress on their already rocky marriage, but there were other outside stressors, too. Both families had objected to an interracial marriage, but Kia and James didn't care. "It's not about race or the color of someone's skin," Kia remem-

Tiplyashin Anatoly/
Shutterstock.com

bered telling her mother. "It's about what's inside." Most of their friends were totally fine with the idea, but their families seemed to be stuck in another decade. And now, with talk about starting a family, they had turned up the heat again. *Why can't they be more open-minded*, Kia often thought. She was accepting of other family members' differences, like her older brother William's gay relationship. Her family had never accepted Will's boyfriend even though he and his partner had been in a stable relationship for five years. *Inclusiveness*, as she once heard it called, was not her family's strong suit.

Growing up, Kia's family life had been rocky. Her parents, who probably cared for each other deep down, just couldn't get along. As a child, Kia sometimes hid in her

©Larry Harwood Photography. Property of Cengage Learning.

©Cengage Learning

Nursing Degree Requirements

	(18 credits)
...lucation	
Human Anatomy and Physiology I	4 credits
Human Anatomy and Physiology II	4 credits
Microbiology (with lab)	4 credits
English Composition I	3 credits
Human Growth and Development	3 credits
	(14 credits)
...mester	
...03 Pharmacology Calculations	3 credits
...09 Fundamentals	8 credits
...12 Basic Concepts of Pharmacology	2 credits
...08 Nutrition	1 credit
	(20 credits)
...Concepts	9 credits
	7 credits

bedroom to wait out the arguments. Their decision to divorce had actually come as a relief. Despite trouble at home, Kia had been a very good student in high school. Perhaps because home was a difficult place, she threw herself into her studies. She liked to read anything she could get her hands on, and doing homework had been a good escape. But her family had no money, so college was never part of the plan. Instead, it was a plan she was now making for herself. So far, the only real problem looked like it would be finding a lab partner in her anatomy and physiology class. No one had approached her about teaming up yet. She hoped it wasn't because she was the only minority student in the class. On the other hand, she had to admit that she kept to herself and hadn't really spoken up in class at all. Was that it?

Regardless, the one constant in her life had been James. When she looked back, she wasn't quite sure how she and James ended up together. They were very different people, beyond just being of different races. But throughout all of her high school years, Kia and James had been inseparable. James also happened to look like a movie star, and he was the funniest person Kia knew. So when they graduated, getting married seemed to be the natural next step. Some of the time, they got along fairly well, and fights were over quickly. Whenever a conflict came up, Kia exploded and James just took it. He was the proverbial nice guy

and she often felt as if she were on an emotional roller coaster. Often her temper got the best of her. Trying to communicate her way through a disagreement never seemed worth it to Kia. Fighting had been a fact of life with her parents, and Kia had never learned how to "fight fair." She'd spit out a few rude comments and then walk away. Fortunately, James never seemed to hold a grudge.

But two weeks ago, they'd had the worst fight ever on the phone, about the layoff. Suddenly, she heard herself yelling into the phone, saying things she knew she'd regret. James managed to get the words "control freak" out, and then this time he hung up. His texts and calls suddenly stopped, and he hadn't been home since. And she had missed her anatomy and physiology class both weeks since then because she was so upset about the fight. *Why does this have to be so hard*? Kia kept asking herself. All she wanted to do was make a better future for herself. But right now the most important thing she had to do was get through the *present. My life is a soap opera*, she thought. And to anyone watching right now, she was right.

Real Estate Agent

Michelle Jenson
Residential Specialist
Accredited Buyer Representative (ABR)

515-555-1531 ext. 1200
Cell: 515-555-1822
Fax: 515-555-1582

Call me when want to see sou

Budget for this Month	
Car Insurance	$100
Car Payment	$200
	$150
Groceries	$650
Rent	$150
Utilities	$350
Cell phones, Internet	$1600
Total	

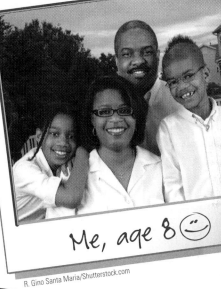

Me, age 8 ☺

BIOLOGY LAB ASSIGNMENT: ENZYME

Lab Objectives

1. Measure the rate of an enzyme.
2. Calculate rate.
3. Describe titration.
4. Collect and graph data.
5. Make hypotheses based on data.

DATA TABLE

	Initial H_2O_2 in Beaker before Catalase	Remaining H2O2 in Beaker after Catalase
10 seconds	10 mL	
30 seconds	10 mL	9 mL
60 seconds	10 mL	7 mL
90 seconds	10 mL	4 mL
120 seconds	10 mL	2 mL
180 seconds	10 mL	1 mL
	10 mL	0 mL

GRAPH

2 REACTION What Do *You* Think?

1. Do you have anything in common with Kia? As you read her story, do you identify with portions of it—or do you know anyone else in college who would?

2. Kia's life is complicated, just like the lives of many college students. Identify five specific problems described in this case study that could interfere with her college success.

3. To have done so well in school, Kia must be an intelligent person. But is her emotional quotient (EQ) different from her intelligence quotient (IQ)? Why or why not?

4. Kia's relationship with James is an important one in her life. What is she doing to contribute to the problems? Will the relationship survive? If so, what would it take?

5. Identify three things Kia should do to get her college success and her life on track.

The Heart of College Success

EXERCISE 10.1

How Would You Respond?

Read these five scenarios and identify your most likely reactions.[1]

1. You peer over a classmate's shoulder and notice she has copied your online response from a class chat and submitted it as her paper in the course, hoping the instructor won't notice. What do you do?
   a. Tell the student off to set the record straight, right then and there.
   b. Tell the instructor that someone has cheated.
   c. Ask the student where the research for the paper came from.
   d. Forget it. It's not worth the trouble. Cheaters lose in the end.

2. You're riding on a plane that hits a patch of extreme turbulence. What do you do?
   a. Grab hold of the person in the next seat and hold on for dear life.
   b. Close your eyes and wait it out.
   c. Read something or watch the movie to calm yourself until things improve.
   d. Panic and lose your composure.

3. You receive a paper back in your toughest course and decide that your grade is unacceptable. What do you do?
   a. Challenge the instructor immediately after class to argue for a better grade.
   b. Question whether you're really college material.
   c. Reread the paper to honestly assess its quality and make a plan for improvement.
   d. Deemphasize this course and focus on others in which you are more successful.

4. While kidding around with your friends, you hear one of them tell an offensive, racial joke. What do you do?
   a. Decide to ignore the problem and thereby avoid being perceived as overly touchy.
   b. Report the behavior to your advisor or an instructor.
   c. Stop the group's conversation. Make the point that racial jokes can hurt and that it's important to be sensitive to others' reactions.
   d. Tell your joke-telling friend later that racial jokes offend you.

5. You and your romantic partner are in the middle of a heated argument, and you're losing your temper. What do you do?
   a. Stop, think about what you're trying to communicate, and say it as clearly and neutrally as possible.
   b. Keep at it because if the issue generated that much emotion, it must be important to get to the bottom of it.
   c. Take a twenty-minute time out and then continue your discussion.
   d. Suggest that both of you apologize immediately and move on.

College is a time of transition; it can be an emotionally challenging time. Even if you're a returning student who's been on your own for years, college will require you to make some major adjustments in your life. Trying to do so without the internal resources you need may be overwhelming, as it was for Kia Washington in the "FOCUS Challenge Case." When it looked as if the relationship that was most important to her was falling apart, so did she.

> **Our emotions are the driving powers of our lives.**
>
> *Earl Riney, American clergyman (1885–1955)*

©Larry Harwood Photography. Property of Cengage Learning

Here's a fundamental truth: College isn't just about your head. Yes, academics are the reason you're in college, but your heart plays a critical role in your success, too. From friends to family members, to professors, to romantic partners, how you handle relationships can make or break you academically. Emotional reactions to troubling circumstances have the raw potential to stop you dead in your tracks. As may be the case for Kia Washington, who most likely has the *academic* skills required for success, *nonacademic* issues can interfere.

In college and in life, your EQ (emotional quotient), or *emotional intelligence*, can be just as important as your IQ (intelligence quotient). Studies show that first-year students often feel overwhelmed and lonely. Begin now to refine the emotional skills you'll need to face whatever challenges come your way.

Perhaps you've found yourself in settings such as those described in Exercise 10.1. You might need more actual details to make the best choice in these five scenarios, but according to some experts, choice (c) is the most emotionally intelligent one in each case. Do you agree? How do *you* make decisions such as these? What constitutes an emotionally intelligent response?

What Is Emotional Intelligence?

Many experts believe that intelligence takes many forms. Rather than a narrow definition of intelligence, they believe in Multiple Intelligences: Linguistic, Logical-Mathematical, Spatial, Kinesthetic, Musical, Interpersonal, Intrapersonal, and Naturalistic.[2] Emotional intelligence may well be a combination, at least in part, of *intrapersonal* and *interpersonal* intelligences.

Emotional intelligence is a set of skills that determines how well you cope with the demands and pressures you face every day. How well do you understand yourself, empathize with others, draw on your inner resources, and encourage the same qualities in people you care about? Emotional intelligence involves having people skills, a positive outlook, and the capacity to adapt to change. Emotional intelligence can propel you through difficult situations.

The bottom line? New research links emotional intelligence to college success, and learning about the impact of EI in the first year of college helps students stay in school.[3] Or consider this research finding: strong emotional intelligence helps you achieve a higher GPA when you take online courses.[4] That makes sense because the self-discipline required is related to the very definition of EI.

As you read about the five scales of emotional intelligence, begin thinking about yourself in these areas. As each scale is introduced, ask yourself whether you agree or disagree with the sample statement from a well-known emotional intelligence instrument as it pertains to you.[5]

VARK It!

Read/Write: Summarize the definition of emotional intelligence in a 140-character tweet. Some people think using Twitter can potentially help you condense your thoughts and make you a better writer.

Intrapersonal Skills (Self-Awareness)

"It's hard for me to understand the way I feel." Agree or disagree?

Are you in tune with your emotions? Do you fully realize when you're anxious, depressed, or thrilled? Or do you just generally feel up or down? Are you aware of layers of emotions? Sometimes we show *anger,* for instance, when what we really feel is *fear.* (For example, Kia was in the habit of screaming angrily at her husband, James, when she probably desperately feared losing him.) Are you emotionally strong on your own, rather than depending on others for your happiness? Do you realize that no one else can truly make you happy, that you are responsible for creating your own emotions? How well do you understand yourself and what makes you tick?

Interpersonal Skills (Relating to Others)

"I'm sensitive to the feelings of others." Agree or disagree?

Are you aware of others' emotions and needs? Do you communicate with sensitivity and work to build positive relationships? Are you a good listener? Are you comfortable with others, and do you have confidence in your relationships with them?

Stress Management Skills

"I feel that it's hard for me to control my anxiety." Agree or disagree?

Can you productively manage your emotions so that they work *for* you and not *against* you? Can you control destructive emotions? Can you work well under pressure? Are you in control, even when things get tense and difficult?

Adaptability Skills

"When trying to solve a problem, I look at each possibility and then decide on the best way." Agree or disagree?

Are you flexible? Do you cope well when things *don't* go according to plan? Can you switch to a new plan when you need to? Do you manage change effectively? Can you anticipate problems and solve them as they come up? Do you rely on yourself and adapt well?

General Mood

"I generally expect things will turn out all right, despite setbacks from time to time." Agree or disagree?

Are you optimistic and positive most of the time? Do you feel happy and content with yourself, others, and your life in general? Are you energetic and self-motivated? Do people tell you you're pleasant to be around?

Source: From EQ-i:HEd. Used by permission of Multi-Health Systems Inc.

resilience the ability to bounce back from difficulties

learned optimism a way of thinking that helps you stay optimistic and potentially improves your mental and physical health

Emotional intelligence affects every part of our lives. For example, researchers study related concepts: "hardiness," "resilience," and "learned optimism."[6] Some people are more resistant to stress and illness. Hardy, resilient, optimistic people are confident, committed to what they're doing, feel greater control over their lives, and see hurdles as challenges. Emotional intelligence is part of the reason why.

> **Managing your emotions is an inside job.**
>
> *Doc Childre and Howard Martin, performance experts*

Looking back at the "FOCUS Challenge Case," we can see that Kia Washington probably lacks strong emotional intelligence. Her level of skill in these five areas may help explain her difficulty controlling her moods, communicating with James, managing stress, adjusting to college, and being positive and optimistic about working through her problems. Will she be academically successful? What do you think?

Emotional intelligence and its five scales are important in all aspects of life, including your future career.[7] When *Harvard Business Review* first published an article on the topic in 1998, it attracted more readers than any article in the journal's previous forty years. When the CEO of Johnson & Johnson read it, he ordered copies for the company's 400 top executives worldwide.[8]

Why? Emotional intelligence is a characteristic of true leaders. Immediately after the first shock of the September 11, 2001, tragedy, the world tuned in to a press conference with New York's Mayor Rudy Giuliani. He was asked to estimate the number of people who had lost their lives in the World Trade Center collapse that day, and his reply was this: "We don't know the exact number yet, but whatever the number, it will be more than we can bear." In that one sentence, Giuliani demonstrated one of the most important principles of true leadership. Leaders inspire by touching the feelings of others.[9]

Can Emotional Intelligence Be Improved?

Everyone wants well-developed emotional intelligence, but how do you get it? Can EI be learned? Although researchers admit that genes definitely play a role, most experts believe that emotional intelligence can be increased. One of the most convincing pieces of evidence is from a study that followed a group of students over seven years. Students assessed their emotional intelligence, selected particular areas to strengthen, and then each created an individual plan to develop them. Seven years later, their competencies remained high.[10]

If you believe what this chapter says about the importance of emotional intelligence and college success, you're probably asking yourself what you can do

> **VARK It!**
>
> **Visual:** To help you remember the five EI scales, select a photo or image of your own to represent each one.

about it. Are the skills related to emotional intelligence something *you* can work to improve?[11] And if so, how?

Seek honest input from others. It's hard to be objective about yourself. But it is possible to ask for the opinions of others who interact with you regularly. How do they see you? Use other people as coaches to help you see which aspects of your emotional intelligence need strengthening.

Find an EI mentor. A mentor on the job is someone who's older and more experienced than you are and can help you navigate your way through tough problems and manage your college or professional career. Mentors help, and an EI mentor—someone with EI skills you admire—can provide you with important advice about handling challenging emotional situations. Develop a personal relationship with someone whose wisdom you admire, be honest about your problems, and follow the guidance you get.

What's going on in the inside shows on the outside.

Earl Nightingale, success consultant

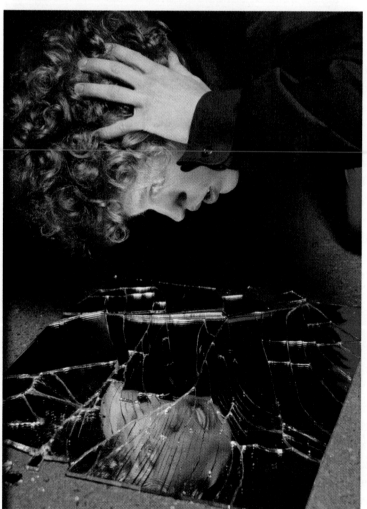

© Robert Recker/Corbis

Complete an assessment tool. Other than just feeling up or down, or thinking back on on how you handled problems when they came up, is there a way to know more about your own emotional intelligence? The oldest and most widely used instrument to measure emotional intelligence is the Emotional Quotient Inventory, the EQ-i, from which the sample statements for the five scales we have been discussing come. The instrument asks you to respond to various statements by indicating that they are "very seldom true of me" to "very often true of me," and the results provide you with a self-assessment of your emotional intelligence on each of the five major scales and subscales within them.

As a part of the course for which you're using this textbook, you may have an opportunity to complete the EQ-i or a similar instrument. Check your college's Counseling Center, too, to see if it offers EI assessment tools for students. You can also locate plenty of informal instruments online. They may not be valid, however, so be cautious about fully trusting their results.

Work with a counselor to learn more. Some areas of emotional intelligence may be too challenging to develop on your own. You may need some in-depth, one-on-one counseling to work on areas that need enrichment. Recognize that doing so isn't a bad thing. Instead, you are taking advantage

Sharpen Your FOCUS

> " **People are lonely because they build walls instead of bridges.** "
>
> —JOSEPH F. NEWTON, WELL-KNOWN CROSS COUNTRY COACH AND AUTHOR

Reason 10: They don't have enough support.

A famous Barbara Streisand song starts like this, "People, people who need people . . . are the luckiest people in the world." Don't we *all* need people? Building relationships is a critical part of our lives because many of our most basic needs can only be met by other people. It takes people to fulfill our need to belong, for example, and people to meet our need to be held in high esteem by others.

With that in mind, take a look at this formula: relationships ↓ = ability to focus ↓. Do you agree? We need healthy, productive relationships in our lives, and when a major problem or conflict erupts, it's easy to get derailed. We may stress out, lose sleep, overindulge, obsess, and temporarily lose our ability to focus. *"Should I have said that?" "Did he take that the wrong way?" "Why can't I stop thinking about the stupid fight we had last night?"* In one study of college students' sleeping habits, worrying about relationships was the reason most often cited for not getting enough sleep.[12] Remember this advice: To keep your focus sharp, keep your relationships strong. It's hard to focus when a problem relationship pushes to the forefront of your mind.

TRY It!

Think about the three most important relationships in your life—your romantic partner, your mom, your best friend, or your kid brother, for example. Fill in their names on the lines below. Put a + (things are great!), ✓ (things are okay), or – (this relationship needs work!) beside each entry. If any of the three relationships earned a minus sign, list three ways in which you may be contributing to the problems in the relationship—and what you can do to improve the relationship and thereby improve your ability to focus.

1) _____ 2) _____ 3) _____

a.   a.   a.

b.   b.   b.

c.   c.   c.

---

of the resources available on your campus and working toward the growth that can come during your college years.

Be patient with yourself. Learning to become more sensitive to someone else's emotions in a close relationship isn't something you can get better at overnight, using cookbook techniques. Building emotional skills is a gradual process that involves becoming aware, acting on your new awareness, and noting the results over time.

Keep at it: Developing your emotional intelligence should be a long-term goal. It's safe to say that EI is something all of us can strengthen, if we're willing to work at it. Relationships that are important to us require the best of our emotional intelligence skills. In fact, studies show that the way in which we provide emotional support is strongly related to how satisfied we are with our relationships.[13]

BOX 10.1 # What Is This Thing Called Love?

Ah, romance. ... Relationships—they're what makes the world go 'round. Although 80 percent isn't a hard and fast number, Brian Tracy has a point in his quote below. Relationships count, and for many of us, romantic ones count as much or more than others.

Most of us have strong ideas about what we want in someone else: good looks, intelligence, or honesty, for example. But if your parents, a friend, or a previous partner were to put your profile on a matchmaking website, what would they say about you? What qualities do you bring to a relationship—loyalty, humor, caring?

Anthropologist Helen Fisher defines love in ways you may not have thought about before: the psychological and physiological characteristics of love. Fisher asked her 437 American subjects to agree or disagree with statements about their romantic partners such as "My heart races when I hear _____'s voice" and "When I'm in class/at work my mind wanders to _____." Interestingly, Fisher found that neither age, gender, sexual orientation, religion, nor ethnic group made a difference. Love is love, she found. Participants in the study shared characteristics such as these five.[14]

1. **Extreme energy.** When you're in love, your heart pounds, you are breathless, you feel as if you could "leap over tall buildings with a single bound." Your brain is "hopped up" on chemicals, and you have energy to spare.

2. **Imagined betterment.** Although most people in love can easily point out faults in their romantic partners, they tend to persuade themselves that these characteristics are unimportant, unique, or even charming.

3. **Interfering thoughts.** People in love spend huge amounts of time thinking about their partners. No matter how hard they try to think about other things, their thoughts return to him or her. In some studies, participants report that they spend more than 85 percent of their waking hours thinking about their romantic partners.[15]

4. **Mood swings.** Lovers soar to the heights of happiness and sink to the depths of despair, based on their romantic partners' responses. "She loves me; she loves me not" is a constant, realistic worry.

5. **Hypersensitivity.** People in love continuously watch and wait for clues about how their romantic partners feel about them. They hover by the phone or computer, and search endlessly for a meaningful sign, reinterpret a facial expression, or translate a word or phrase into a sign they've been waiting for.

When you're newly infatuated with someone, your brain has higher than usual levels of dopamine and norepinephrine, chemicals that result in the characteristics just explained. Scientists also believe that lovers have lower levels of serotonin in their brains. These three chemicals appear to be the physiological basis for passionate, exhilarating, romantic love. You can't eat, you can't sleep, you're madly in love. However, later in life, after years of marriage, perhaps, these chemicals are overtaken by others. None of us could tolerate the chemicals associated with the craziness of being madly in love forever! Wild passion is replaced by feelings of contentment and security. However, many couples remain "in love" for twenty, thirty, fifty, or more years. They may even describe themselves as more in love than when they first met. In one remarkable study, couples married more than twenty years rated themselves higher on romantic love than couples married only five years. Researchers noted that some long-term couples' results looked like those of high school seniors![16]

The chemistry of love points to a truth worth noting: Love is not just an emotion. Chemicals increase and decrease; emotions come and go. Commitment is more than attraction or emotion. It's a *decision* to invest—and continually *reinvest*—in a relationship. As Fisher writes, "Don't assume the relationship will last forever; build it one day at a time. And never give up."

> **Eighty percent of life's satisfaction comes from meaningful relationships.**
>
> *Brian Tracy, personal and career success author*

© Larry Harwood Photography. Property of Cengage Learning.

Communicating in Important Relationships

Friends

Think of all the kinds of communicating you do—and with whom. For example, you have friends you care about. You may think the primary thing friends help you do is fill up your spare time. But new research shows that friends can actually help you fight illness and depression, boost your brain power, and even prolong your life. In one study, students were taken to the bottom of a steep hill while wearing a heavy backpack. They were asked to guess how steep the hill was. Students standing next to friends, rather than by themselves, thought the hill looked much less steep, and friends who had known each other longer guessed it was even less steep. Researchers wrote that "People with stronger friendship networks feel like there is someone they can turn to. Friendship is an undervalued resource. The consistent message of these studies is that friends make your life better." If that's true, then how you communicate with them is more important than you may even realize.[17]

> I'm very loyal in relationships. Even when I go out with my mom I don't look at other moms.
>
> *Garry Shandling, comedian*

Family

Or consider family members. These people make up the core of who you really are. Your kid brother may drive you crazy at times, and a parent may seem to smother you, but generally, these people care about you most. Often we "let it all hang out" with family members, perhaps because we know they'll overlook our flaws. When we're tired or stressed, this is often where we "veg" or vent. But because of the central, lasting role they play in our lives, they deserve more quality communication than we sometimes give them.

Classmates/Instructors

Classmates and instructors, too, deserve your best communication, even when you disagree with what they're saying in class. You may see your instructors as either friendly or unfriendly, but you'll need to make the first move to get to know them, rather than the other way around. Take the initiative to meet them during their office hours, and bring up points from class that you'd like to know more about.

You'll want to get to know your classmates, too, to make your classes more engaging. You're likely to work with them on class projects. Do some of your best communicating here. Chances are your group-mates—and the group's grade—will depend on it. Participate, do your part, and keep your word. No one will appreciate it if you promise to come to every planning meeting outside of class and turn out to be a no-show every week. Group work in your college classes is a great place to practice the exact skills that are required of you in the workplace. Whatever the type of important relationship—friends, family, classmates, or instructors—how you communicate is vital. Some would go so far as to state this broad opinion: the quality of your communication directly affects the quality of your life. Do you agree?

> Piglet sidled up to Pooh from behind. "Pooh!" he whispered." "Yes, Piglet?" "Nothing," said Piglet, taking Pooh's paw. "I just wanted to be sure of you."
>
> *A. A. Milne, British author (1882–1956)*

Romantic Partners

Beyond friends, family, classmates, and instructors, think about how very important communication is in romantic relationships. If you're in a romantic relationship right now, you may have wondered from time to time whether it's truly a good one. In one study, 94 percent of college students reported having been in love, and over one-third reported three or more past love relationships.[18] Perhaps it was love at first sight, and you immediately announced to your friends or family that this was the one for you. Instead, perhaps right now you're with someone you've never really gotten to know very well; you're going through the motions. The relationship is convenient, fun for the time being, but you're just filling up time with someone you're not really interested in, long term. If you're not in a romantic relationship at all right now, perhaps you're on the lookout for someone with potential. If you look around at others' relationships, you only see what those two people choose to display. It's not easy to know exactly what characterizes a healthy relationship. What does it take? A study of 21,501 couples across the country compared the answers of the happiest couples to those of the unhappiest.[19] The areas of maximum difference between the two groups were found on responses like the following.

	Happy Couples	Unhappy Couples
1. My partner is a very good listener.	83%	18%
2. My partner does not understand how I feel.	13%	79%
3. We have a good balance of leisure time spent together and separately.	71%	17%
4. We find it easy to think of things to do together.	86%	28%
5. I am very satisfied with how we talk to each other.	90%	15%
6. We are creative in how we handle our differences.	78%	15%
7. Making financial decisions is not difficult.	80%	32%
8. Our sexual relationship is satisfying and fulfilling.	85%	29%
9. We are both equally willing to make adjustments in the relationship.	87%	46%
10. I can share feelings and ideas with my partner during disagreements.	85%	22%

[Note: numbers do not total 100 percent because of the study's design.]

Look at the highest percentages in the "Happy Couples" column. These results point to an all-important truth: Communication is at the heart of every quality relationship.

In relationships we sometimes communicate in ways that aren't productive. The work of communication specialist Deborah Tannen focuses on miscommunication between men and women. Remember the *Seinfeld* episode in which George's date asks him whether he'd like to come up to her apartment for coffee when he takes her home? George completely misses the point and replies that he never drinks coffee late at night. She meant, "Would you like to continue our date?" but he took the question at face value. Later he kicked himself for being so slow witted. Trying to "listen between the lines" in romantic relationships is a challenge. We say one thing and mean another, or we hope romantic partners can read our minds and then resent it when they do.

Productive Communication

The classic work of psychiatrist Dr. George Bach and others can help relational partners communicate more openly and honestly and meet conflict head on. He described types of "crazymaking" that cause communication breakdowns and, at their worst, relationship failures. See whether you recognize people you know—romantic partners or even friends—in these six types of crazymakers.[20]

"Crazymaking" communicating in dishonest, underhanded, and, in the long term, damaging ways

> The TRAPPER: *Trappers* play an especially dirty trick by requesting a desired behavior from the other person and then attacking when the request is met.

> The BLAMER: *Blamers* are more interested in whose fault the problem is than they are in solving it.

> The MINDREADER: *Mindreaders* try to solve the problem by telling their partners what they're *really* thinking.

> The GUNNYSACKER: *Gunnysackers* save grudges. They fill up proverbial gunnysacks and then dump all the contents on their partners at some "opportune" moment.

> The HIT-AND-RUN FIGHTER: *Hit-and-run fighters* attack and then leave the scene quickly, without giving their partners a chance to explain or defend themselves.

> The "BENEDICT ARNOLD": *Benedict Arnolds* like to stir up trouble behind the scenes by playing "let's you and someone else fight."

If you think you're a victim of crazymaking communication, what should you do about it? Try these five suggestions:

1. **Step back and try to figure out the situation.** Is the crazymaker making a request of you (to be more open, reliable, or responsible, for example)? If so, is the request reasonable, and are you willing?

2. **Become aware of the feelings behind the crazymaking.** Is your partner feeling powerless or afraid, for example?

3. **Try not to respond with anger, even though it's difficult.** Piling more wood on the fire certainly won't help to put it out.

4. **Check out your assumptions with the other person.** Ask, "Are you feeling frustrated? Is that what this is about? What would you like me to do?"

5. **Try and reach a mutually agreeable solution by changing communication patterns that aren't productive.** Once you've identified any unproductive communication habits, you can work on improving your skills as well as your relationships. The following five suggestions are a place to start. These recommendations work for any type of close relationship—friends or romantic partners.

Choose wisely. When it comes to selecting someone you may want to build a future with, as a friend or romantic partner, don't settle. Seek someone who shares your values, whose background is compatible, but who is different enough to make life interesting. Choose someone who values productive communication as much as you do.

Let go of unrealistic expectations. Remember that although people live happily ever after in movies, what's really true is that all relationships have ups and downs. We're human; we make mistakes as communicators. One blip on the screen, as they say, doesn't necessarily indicate that the whole program should be scrapped. Instead, working on problems together strengthens your relationship.

Don't ignore small problems. You take your car in for a checkup every so many thousand miles to prevent major breakdowns. It's a good idea to do the same with relationships you care about. Keep the channels of communication open, and talk about small issues before they turn into giant ones. Experts say that doing interesting new things together—going on a vacation, for example— can trigger renewed romantic love.[21] In the same way, going through an intense experience with a friend may strengthen your relationship.

Pay attention to your own communication. You can't change someone else, but you can change your own communication: "Although it takes two to have a relationship, it takes only one to change its quality."[22] Get rid of an annoying behavior or change your conflict style. Be more tolerant of someone else's communication faults, too. Communicate your needs; relationships aren't guessing games. Check, don't assume. Remember that listening is one of the highest compliments you can pay someone. (You're important to me!) Instead of attacking, own your emotions by using the X-Y-Z formula: When you do X in situation Y, I feel Z. ("When you tease me [X] in front of other people [Y], I feel embarrassed and never know how to react [Z]" as opposed to "You always embarrass me! Stop it, will you?")[23] Working to increase your emotional intelligence doesn't mean denying all negative feelings; that would mean cutting off part of your psyche! How you choose to communicate those negative feelings is where the "paying attention" comes in. It's also often best to work through difficult problems in face-to-face settings when you can. Texts, e-mails, and Facebook posts aren't always the most productive way to communicate when a message is really sensitve and important.

Take the high road. Don't give in to momentary temptations that may lead to regret and possibly the end of a relationship with great potential. Without trust as the foundation of your communication, little else matters. If your friend is truly your friend, don't join in when someone else is badmouthing her. And if you've promised yourself to someone, keep your promise.[24]

©Larry Harwood Photography, Property of Cengage Learning.

> **At the extreme, we are so enmeshed in our connections that we neglect each other.**
>
> *Sherry Turkle, from* Alone Together: Why We Expect More from Technology and Less from Each Other

Managing Conflict: Life Is Not a Sitcom

Bad relationships can hurt your job performance, your finances, your physical and mental health—even your life span.[25] Conflict with romantic partners, or with anyone you're close to—family or friends, for example—can bring on major stress that affects your academic performance, not to mention your overall happiness.[26]

Unfortunately, movies and television often communicate—subtly or not so subtly—that conflict can be resolved by the end of the show. Just lighten up or settle down and you can resolve almost any problem. And if you can't, just swallow, take a deep breath, and move on. But life isn't like that, nor should it be. Managing the conflict in your life takes time, energy, and persistence. It requires understanding your natural tendencies, considering why you communicate as you do, and making good choices as a communicator.

If you've ever monitored yourself during a particularly heated conflict, you may remember doing something like this: yelling in anger at someone at the top of your lungs, being interrupted by a phone call and suddenly communicating calmly and quietly to the caller, and then returning to the original shouting match after you hang up.

Why? We make *choices* as communicators. Sometimes our choices are productive ones, and sometimes they aren't. It's important to remember that we *do* choose what we say and how we behave. Our choices affect both the *process*—how things go during the conflict—and the *product*—how it turns out in the end. Negative choices produce destructive conflict that includes personal attacks, name calling, an unwillingness to listen, or the crazymaking strategies described earlier in this chapter. Positive choices are much more likely to bring productive conflict that helps us learn more about ourselves, our partners, and our relationships.

VARK It!

Read/Write: The next time you're involved in an important conflict, try writing down your thoughts on paper before discussing them out loud.

EXERCISE 10.2

What's Your Conflict Style?

For each of the following statements, please rate your response on a scale of 1 to 5, with 1 representing "strongly agree" and 5 representing "strongly disagree."

Strongly Agree	Agree	Not Sure	Disagree	Strongly Disagree
1	2	3	4	5

1. _____ I usually end up compromising in conflict situations. (CO)

2. _____ Someone always loses in a conflict. (CP)

3. _____ I usually let other people "win" in conflicts because I often feel less strongly about the outcome than they do. (AC)

4. _____ When I really care about a relationship, I devote unusual amounts of time and energy into coming up with creative solutions so that each of us can get what we want. (CL)

5. _____ "Don't rock the boat" is a good philosophy. (AV)

6. _____ "Winning" in conflict situations gives me a real "high." (CP)

7. _____ Sacrificing what I want so that someone else can achieve a goal is often worth it. (AC)

8. _____ It's possible for both parties to "win" in conflict situations. (CL)

9. _____ Sometimes you have to settle for "part of the pie." (CO)

10. _____ I try to avoid conflict at all costs. It's not worth it. (AV)

Now find a partner in class and compare your responses. Circle the items on which the two of you differed most, for example, where one of you marked a "1" and the other a "5." See whether you can explain your own choice and also come to understand your partner's thinking. On how many items did you differ? If the answer is "several" or "many," you might experience substantial conflict as coworkers or romantic partners.

People often come at conflicts using differing styles. Not only do you disagree on the topic at hand—whatever it is—but you approach conflict itself differently. This quick quiz is based on a well-known, five-part model of conflict styles (see Figure 10.1). In our version of the model, the horizontal axis is labeled "Concern for Other" (or cooperativeness) and the vertical axis is labeled "Concern for Self" (or assertiveness).[27]

Where are your highest scores? Notice the letters at the end of the ten statements.

If you like to win and care most about your own goals, you compete (CP).

If you care more about the other person's goals, and give in, you accommodate (AC).

If you don't care about your goals or your partner's, you avoid (AV).

If you care somewhat about both and are willing to settle for "part of the pie," you compromise (CO). Strictly speaking, when you compromise, neither of you gets exactly what you want.

If you care about your own goals and your partner's, and you're willing to devote the time and energy required to reach a win–win solution, you collaborate (CL).

What's your style? Do you have a conflict style you're most comfortable with? Do you fall into the habit of using one style, even if it's not productive in particular situations? Flexibility is the key to managing conflicts productively, and if the relationship really counts, collaboration is the ideal.

FIGURE 10.1

Conflict Management Styles

© 2014 Cengage Learning

Just like healthy relationships, unhealthy ones have identifying characteristics, too. Although every relationship can teach us something important about future ones, some red flags are worth our attention. Here are three to think about.[28] If you see these danger signals, it may be time to end the relationship or to devote more time and energy toward improving it.

Danger signal 1: "All we ever do is fight!" This point seems obvious, but sometimes it's so obvious that it's overlooked. All some couples talk about is how much they disagree or how wrong things are between them. As a general rule, if 50 percent or more of what you talk about is devoted to managing conflict, sit up and take notice. When so much of your time is spent walking on eggshells to avoid conflict, getting things out on the table during conflict, or smoothing things over afterward, there's little time or energy left to talk about anything else.

Danger signal 2: "Let's dig in deeper!" Can you imagine anyone saying something like this: "We've been going out for two years now, but we're just not getting along. I think if we got engaged, we'd both be more committed." Or consider a couple who is unhappily married, who say, "Maybe we should have a baby. That would bring us closer together." Whoa! Statements such as these are danger signals. Relationships should escalate (or reach the next level of commitment) when we're satisfied with them, when we find them fulfilling, and when we are ready to take the next step together. Trying to force intimacy doesn't work. Although this point makes sense, it's surprising how many couples fall into this trap.

Figure 10.2 provides a visual example of a traditional pattern of relationship stages in our society. (Of course, the steps don't always occur in this order,

FIGURE 10.2

Moving to the Next Stage

© 2014 Cengage Learning

©Larry Harwood Photography. Property of Cengage Learning.

nor are they even these particular steps.) At each step, the couple is making a decision about staying together. Ideally, relationships should escalate naturally along Line A; however, sometimes people mistakenly force themselves to escalate unnaturally along Line B.

Danger signal 3: "This relationship just isn't worth it!" From two unique individuals, a third thing—a unique relationship—is born. The relationship you create with one person is different from the one you'll create with anyone else. Not only are *you* different in many ways, but *your relationship* with each of these individuals is unique, too. Relationships, like individuals, have their own attitudes, values, and sensitivities.

At some point, you may decide that a relationship just isn't worth it anymore. The costs outweigh the rewards. The relationship is suffocating or lifeless. You find yourself thinking about having a relationship with someone else, or you're actually on the lookout for a new one. It may be best to face this fact squarely and end the dissatisfying relationship honestly, rather than allowing another one to develop in secret. When relationships end, the quality and quantity of communication between the two people change. But as the golden oldie goes, "Breaking Up Is Hard to Do," and applying all the emotional intelligence you can muster will help you through it.

> **The difference between friendship and love is how much you can hurt each other.**
>
> *Ashleigh Brilliant, author and cartoonist*

EXERCISE 10.3

Part I: 25 Things We Have in Common

Conflict is based on differences. Two people each want different things—or two people want the same thing, but only one can have it. But when you think about it, we have many things in common as human beings. Try this experiment: work with three classmates (in a group of four), and when your instructor announces, "Go," begin listing things that all four of you have in common. The first group to reach 25 items wins! After the exercise, discuss the kinds of things you listed and how easy or hard it was to create a list of 25 different items.[29]

Part II: What's the Difference?

Now find a single partner to work with on this part of the exercise. Individually, list all the various ways in which you differ: age, height, gender, eye color, birth place, and so on. When your instructor calls "time," read your lists aloud. The point of the exercise is to begin a discussion on the meaning of diversity, to explore its many different facets—beyond just external appearance—and to appreciate the fact that each individual is unique.[30] Now look back at Part I of this exercise, "25 Things We Have in Common." Was it easier to find commonalities or differences? Why?

Diversity Makes a Difference

EXERCISE 10.4

Your Views on Diversity

What are your views on diversity? Look at the following ten statements, and indicate the extent to which you agree or disagree.

Strongly Agree	Agree	Not Sure	Disagree	Strongly Disagree
1	2	3	4	5

1. Race is still a factor in hiring decisions today. _____
2. Multiculturalism implies that all cultures have equally valid viewpoints. _____
3. Workforce diversity improves the quality of work. _____
4. The number of male versus female corporate CEOs is nearing the halfway mark in the United States. _____
5. In some situations, sexual orientation is a justifiable basis for discrimination. _____
6. All cultures tend to see the rest of the world through their own cultural lens. _____
7. Feminism is a set of beliefs held by females. _____
8. A global perspective ensures objectivity. _____
9. Religious persecution is a thing of the past. _____
10. There is less racism in the United States today than there was ten years ago. _____

As you continue reading this section of the chapter, search for points relating to these topics. Also, your instructor may wish to use these ten items to begin a discussion in class.

You see a sticker on a passing car's bumper: "Celebrate Diversity." Diversity is a word that's used often these days. But what does it mean? Diversity is a term that relates to differences between human beings based on race, ethnicity, age, culture, physical features and abilities, mental capability, socio-economic status, religion, politics, sexual orientation, geographic region, gender identity, and points of view.

diversity the ways in which people differ from one another

You may be American, male, white, 21, heterosexual, tall, athletic, smart, good-looking, and from a well-to-do family—and inadvertently, without ever realizing it, think anyone who isn't like you is somehow "less" than you are. It's not that you intend to look down on others. In fact, some of these traits identified above aren't chosen ones; they're qualities a person is born with or grew up with. But others unlike you may see you very differently. You see yourself as "fortunate;" they may see you as "privileged." Perceptions are important in discussions about diversity. Perceptions influence our interactions with others, and sometimes perceptions can lead to bias. Let's take a closer look:

perceptions an awareness of people, things, and qualities around you

Type of Diversity	Possible Perceptions	Things to Consider
Age Diversity	"Those youngsters with all the tattoos and piercings! What do they know?"	Trends change, and outward expressions vary from one generation to the next.
	"Older drivers! They're so slow!"	Reaction times slow down, and vision can worsen.
Gender Diversity	"I'm all for women's rights, but a female president? I'm not sure we're ready for that!"	Actually, in recent presidential races several women rose to prominent roles at the top of their parties.
	"Why would a guy want to be a nurse? That's a woman's job."	Nursing is a top career field for men or women, now and in the future.
Geographic Diversity	"The South is so backwards."	Southerners are proud of their traditions.
	"Northerners are such snobs."	Regional accents can carry particular stereotypes.
Physical Diversity	"Boy, if I only had a handicapped sticker, I could park anywhere on campus."	Physical challenges warrant access capability.
	"That professional signer in class is really distracting!"	In-class signers help deaf students follow lectures and discussions—like a language translator.
Sexual Orientation Diversity	"Call me homophobic, but all *my* friends are straight."	Homophobia can be a highly negative hidden bias.
	"Bisexual? How can somebody be attracted to both sexes? That's just not normal!"	College is a time to become aware of differences, including things you may never have been exposed to.
Religious Diversity	"Religious people are unthinking."	Religious beliefs are highly personal, and spirituality in some form can bring balance and meaning.
	"I'm glad I was raised believing in the right religion."	Although it can be natural to see your family traditions as "right," realize that others may feel equally strong about theirs.

© 2014 Cengage Learning

You must look into people, as well as at them.

Lord Chesterfield,
British statesman (1694–1773)

Each of us is a unique human being. Some of us are taller, some are shorter, some are older, some are younger. Some aspects of our uniqueness are visible. It's not hard to tell the difference between someone who's five feet tall and someone who's seven feet tall or someone who's twenty years old versus someone who's eighty. But other aspects of our uniqueness aren't as obvious. Would people necessarily know your religion, your sexual orientation, or even your race just by looking at you? If you had a stack of photos—a headshot of every student who attends your school—could you sort them by race into the same stacks they'd sort themselves into? Anyone can tell an Asian American from an African American just by looking. Or so they may think.

Race is often the first thing people think of when they hear the word *diversity*. But some experts say race is a relatively modern idea. Centuries ago, people tended to classify other people by status, religion, or language, for example, not by race. Actually, most of us are a blend of ethnicities, and how we perceive ourselves may be different from the way others see us. People may assume that a Pacific Islander with light brown skin, dark hair, and dark eyes, for example, is Hispanic. And a classmate you may assume is white may think of himself as black. Or consider this: If you have a Chinese mother and a white father, you may not know which "race box" to check on standard forms. Should you choose Mom or Dad?[31] Biologists tell us that there's more variation within a race than there is between races. Race isn't biological, they say, but *racism* is real.[32]

Although you or some of your classmates may have grown up in communities with less racial, ethnic, or cultural diversity than others, you have probably experienced the multicultural nature of our society in many different ways, even in terms of food, music, and clothing, for example. The media have introduced you to aspects of diversity, and perhaps you've even traveled to other parts of the United States or the world yourself.

EXERCISE 10.5

Facing the Race Issue

Take a look at the faces below. Can you categorize them into common racial types: White, Black, Hispanic/Latino, Native American, or Asian? After you've identified each one, check the answers below. How accurate were you? Does this activity confirm the point above that although race is used as a common identifier, it isn't an easy or accurate way to classify people?[33]

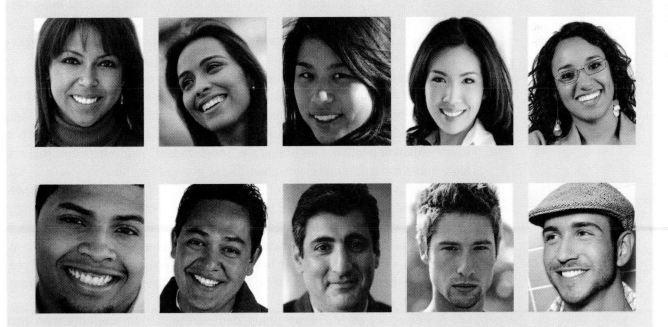

Answers: (top row): B, H, NA, A, H and (bottom row): B, H, H, W, W.

From top left: iStockphoto.com/Jacom Stephens; iStockphoto.com/billnoll; iStockphoto.com/Thomas Gordon; iStockphoto.com/Goldmund; iStockphoto.com/Jacom Stephens; iStockphoto.com/Lisa Marzano; iStockphoto.com/Jason Lugo; iStockphoto.com/Roberto A Sanchez; iStockphoto.com/TriggerPhoto; iStockphoto.com/LajosRepasi

©Larry Harwood Photography. Property of Cengage Learning.

But here's the challenge: Have experiencing diversity and learning about it in school truly made a difference in the way you think and act? Do you choose to diversify your awareness, your relationships, and yourself as a person? Do you think that discrimination no longer exists in our multicultural society?

Many college students today do believe that racial discrimination is no longer a problem. *Been there; done that*, they've concluded. We may think of ourselves as more "highly evolved" than Americans of past decades, but are we? If you see an interracial couple like Kia and James, do you take a second look without even thinking about it? Are we truly bias-free in this day and age?

tolerance a fair, objective attitude toward differences

ethnicities groups of people who share a culture, language, and possibly a religion

discrimination bias that results in unfair treatment

According to a recent survey, "helping to promote racial understanding" was considered "essential" or "very important" by only slightly more than one-third of incoming first-year students.[34] In another study, students were asked to identify the five most critical and two least critical outcomes of a college education from a list of sixteen possibilities. Tolerance and respect for people of other races, ethnicities, and lifestyles were identified as among the least important goals for college learning.[35] Why do you think they responded that way? Do they think they've already achieved these goals, or do they think they're less important for other reasons?

stereotypes commonly held unfavorable beliefs about people

If you conducted a survey on your campus to find out whether discrimination exists, you might be surprised at the results. Research continues to show that minority students report experiencing discrimination at higher rates than majority students. Many of us downplay the prejudice all human beings harbor to one extent or another. Our brains are "programmed" to group people that are alike and standardize our views about these groups, resulting in stereotypes. Sometimes, we feel safe around others like us and fear those unlike us. Appreciating individuals for what they are, instead of stereotyping, could drastically change the way we think and act. If you open up your thinking to new possibilities, all kinds of new options present themselves. Imagine a band made up of only trombones, a meal with nothing but string beans, a song played on one note, or a world where everyone looks exactly like you. Diversity enriches our lives. Prejudice stunts our thinking.

proactive planning ahead, rather than simply reacting

A University of Michigan study demonstrated that students who had more positive interactions with diverse peers, and in particular took a college course on diversity, were more likely to be academically self-confident, more personally proactive, and more likely to develop better critical thinking skills.[36] Learning to deal effectively with diversity can actually change you as a college student! Prejudice, or looking down on people just because they are different, isn't a good vantage point. If a classmate who's unlike you were the son or daughter of a famous actor, would that change your view? Prejudice sneaks up on us and limits our ability to grow as human beings.

prejudice a general, unfavorable opinion held without specific evidence

Appreciate the American Mosaic

It's becoming more and more impossible to draw clear lines between what separates us physically. Actress Jessica Alba has a mother with French and Danish roots and a Mexican-American father; Keanu Reeves is Hawaiian, Chinese, and Caucasian; Mariah Carey is Black, Venezuelan, and Caucasian; and Johnny Depp is Cherokee and Caucasian.[37] The woman in the photo below is Noemie Lenoir, who is of African and European descent and one of the world's highest paid mixed-race models. Most of us are a blend, but diversity is about more than physical appearance. Each of us is a unique human being.

Actually, college is a perfect time to learn more about diversity—in the classroom and beyond it. Classrooms are becoming more diversely populated; it's true. Diversity in higher education gives you an opportunity to expand your world view and develop empathy for others who have vastly different experiences.

Aside from meeting students who are different from you in college, taking advantage of diversity can help you become a more sophisticated thinker, one who can see problems from multiple perspectives, and a better prepared employee, ready to hit the ground running in today's highly diverse workplace. Appreciating diversity also helps us become better citizens. Diversity is what our society is based on. In a democratic society such as ours, citizens must be able to recognize and endorse creative solutions to complex problems. A former chief justice of the U.S. Supreme Court, Charles Evans Hughes, once said, "When we lose the right to be different, we lose the privilege to be free."

One mistake many college students make is not taking advantage of what diversity offers them. Because people often tend to feel comfortable with others like them they join groups of people just like themselves, based on religion, sexual orientation, or majors, for example. You can choose to belong to the Young Republicans; the Gay, Lesbian, Bisexual, Transgender (GLBT) student group; or the Chemistry Honor Society. Joining a group of like students assures you a place where people accept you for who you are, and you feel comfortable. Think about the groups you belong to and what they say about you.

> **We have become not a melting pot, but a beautiful mosaic. Different people, different beliefs, different yearnings, different hopes, different dreams.**
>
> *Jimmy Carter, thirty-ninth president of the United States*

Venturelli/WireImage/Getty Images

Circles of Awareness

Each of us has a cultural identity. How do we see ourselves, and how do others see us? Write your name in the center of the drawing, and then label each of the surrounding circles with a word that represents a group you identify with. You may use categories like age, gender, ethnicity, social, political, and so forth. After your drawing is labeled, your instructor will ask you to circulate around the room and find three classmates who have listed at least three of the same subgroups. After that, you will be asked to find three students who listed at least three categories that you did not. In the second group you formed, based on differences, use the activity to discuss diversity, differences among individuals and groups, and how awareness can change behavior. Look over everyone's list, and to diversify your thinking, select one group on someone else's list, but not on yours. Find out more about that group or decide to attend a group meeting to raise your awareness of what you think the group is like, and what it's actually like.[38]

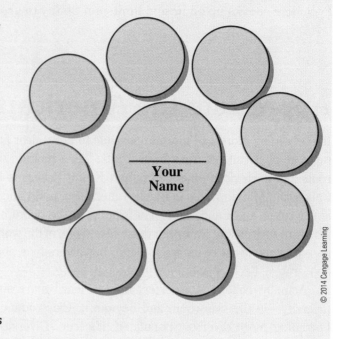

© 2014 Cengage Learning

Your Name

Of course, being comfortable and feeling accepted are important. But instead, imagine choosing to join groups composed of very different types of people. Consider what philosopher and educator John Dewey once said, "Conflict . . . shocks us out of sheep-like passivity," or the words of a famous American lawyer, Louis Nizer, who once put it like this: "Where there is no difference, there is only indifference." Valuing diversity relates directly to your empathy skills and your emotional intelligence. What about stretching ourselves to learn fully what diversity has the potential to teach us?[39]

Imagine you were engaged in a service-learning project for a class, working in your local soup kitchen. It's easy to criticize a homeless person and think, "Why doesn't he just get a job?" But when you actually sit down and share a bowl of soup across the table, you might see things differently. You might hear stories of personal illness, family tragedy, unbelievable trauma—a list of bad luck coincidences you'd never even think of. Rather than assigning all homeless people to a group with a negative label, learn more about the individuals that make up that group. You might change your views.

One professor says this: "I tell my students to keep in mind that everything they see is a snapshot. That guy drinking from a bottle in a paper bag, he's a photograph. How did he get to where he is? From there, we can share some of the rage at the inherent injustice that awaits so many of our poor children as they grow up. As we examine people, the snapshots become a motion picture that links the past, present, and future—what was, what is, what can be."[40]

Choose a stereotype you recognize, one you suspect you believe if you're honest, and decide what you can do to test it. Ask yourself whether it affects your thinking and actions. For example, are you aware of these facts about continuing stereotypes in our culture?

> **Sexism is still an issue in corporate America.** In 2012, twenty of America's top 500 companies were run by a woman, up from one out of forty in 1995. Then, only one of those companies had a female CEO; by 2003, seven did. Experts predict that by 2020, it could be one in five; however, the numbers are still lopsided.[41]

> **Racism is still an issue in hiring decisions.** A recent Gallup poll asked: "Do you feel that racial minorities in this country have job opportunities equal to whites, or not?" Among whites, the answer was 55 percent yes and 43 percent no. (The rest were undecided.) Among African Americans, the answer was 17 percent yes and 81 percent no. You might also be shocked to read about an experiment in which fake applicants of one race were 50 percent more likely to be called for interviews than applicants of another race, based solely on whether their names sounded like they belonged to a particular racial group! As one *Wall Street Journal* reporter noted, "Someday Americans will be able to speak of racial discrimination in hiring in the past tense. Not yet."[42]

> **Discrimination and stereotypes persist.** Students with disabilities report a "chilly classroom climate" for students with disabilities in higher education.[43] According to one college president, "With all [the change in racial demographics], diversity has become the largest issue behind unrest on campus, accounting for 39 percent of student protests."[44] A recent study of closeted and out gay and lesbian college students reported that these students perceived unfair treatment and a need to hide their identity from most other students. Both groups reported experiencing a similar amount of antigay attacks.[45] In 2010, 6628 total hate crime incidents were reported in the United States, according to the U.S. Department of Justice. Racially motivated crimes accounted for approximately 47 percent; religious bias accounted for 20 percent; bias against sexual orientation for 19 percent; bias against disabilities for .6 percent; and bias against ethnicity or national origin accounted for 13 percent.[46] People still harm one another out of hatred for differences they may not understand.

Diversity makes a difference, and as educator Adela A. Allen once wrote, "We should acknowledge differences, we should greet differences, until difference makes no difference anymore." What can we do about it? Raising awareness is a first step on the road to recognizing the reality and the richness of diversity.

VARK It!

Read/Write: Write a short paragraph about diversity, using fictitious names, that shows prejudice you've experienced or witnessed.

What's Your CQ?

Diagnosing Your Cultural Intelligence[47]

These statements reflect different aspects of cultural intelligence. For each set, add up your scores and divide by four to arrive at an average. As you answer, think about your answers in each category as they compare to the other two categories.

Rate how much you agree with each statement, using this scale:
1 = strongly disagree   2 = disagree   3 = neutral   4 = agree   5 = strongly agree

____ Before I interact with people from a new culture, I think about what I'm going to communicate.

____ If I come up against something unexpected in a new culture, I use the experience to think about how I should respond in other cultures in the future.

____ I plan how I'm going to relate to people from a different culture before I even meet them.

____ When I'm communicating in a new culture, I have a clear sense of whether things are going well or not.

____ **Total divided by 4 = ____ COGNITIVE CQ**

____ It's easy for me to change my body language (eye contact or posture, for example) to match that used by people from a different culture.

____ I can change my expression when I need to interact with people from another culture.

____ I can modify my speech (for example, accent or tone) when interacting with people from another culture.

____ I can easily change the way I act when a cross-cultural situation seems to require it.

____ **Total divided by 4 = ____ PHYSICAL CQ**

____ I have confidence that I can deal well with people from another culture.

____ I am certain that I can make friends with people from a culture that's different from mine.

____ I can adapt to the lifestyle of another culture when I need to fairly easily.

____ I am confident that I can deal with a cultural situation, even if it's unfamiliar.

____ **Total divided by 4 = ____ EMOTIONAL/MOTIVATIONAL CQ**

Generally, an average lower than three identifies an opportunity for improvement, and an average greater than 4.5 identifies a true CQ strength.

An advertisement for an international bank gets the point across well. It shows a picture of a grasshopper. Below the grasshopper are these three sentences that describe three different cultural views of grasshoppers: USA—Pest, China—Pet, Northern Thailand—Appetizer.[48] One insect, three cultural perspectives. Americans tend to shoo away pesky grasshoppers. But if you travel to China, be careful of stepping on one that may be someone else's beloved pet. And if you travel to Northern Thailand, try not to look disgusted when you see fried grasshoppers on the appetizer plate.

America   **China**   **Northern Thailand**

iStockphoto.com/Antagain; iStockphoto.com/Diane Diederich   iStockphoto.com/Antagain; iStockphoto.com/jclegg   iStockphoto.com/Antagain; iStockphoto.com/frytka

Just as individuals have emotional intelligence, they also have cultural intelligence. Some of us are more naturally sensitive to cultural differences, and we know how to handle ourselves. But all of us can grow our cultural intelligence with training and preparation. EQ relates to self-awareness and relationship skills; CQ relates to awareness and responses to other cultures (and subcultures of our own culture). EQ and CQ are linked.

Here's a definition: cultural intelligence is an outsider's seemingly natural ability to interpret someone's unfamiliar and ambiguous gestures the way other people of that culture would.[49] CQ has three components that involve your head, your body, and your heart. All three work together to help you interact in a foreign culture—or a subculture that's new to you within your own larger culture. Think, for example, about taking a job in a new culture, either by transferring overseas or by entering an organization with different rules: "Casual Fridays," "Bring Your Dog to Work Day," "Follow Strict Communication Rules and Always Go Through Your Boss," or "Choose Your Own Project to Work on One Day a Week" (if you work for Google). These rules might be different for you, and you'd need good CQ skills to adapt. Or think about entering a subculture you're unfamiliar with: like being "straight" and having a gay best friend, or marrying someone of another ethnicity, like Kia and James did. CQ can be broken down into three parts, all of which work together:

1. **Cognitive quotient (head):** Do you understand the differences between another culture and your own? Before entering a new culture, do you think before you act? Do you learn about the culture in advance of interacting with its members so that you don't make embarrassing mistakes?

2. **Physical quotient (body):** Do you watch for behaviors that are different in other cultures? Do you mimic the gestures and customs of the people? Do you shake hands correctly? Do you notice whether the culture is "high touch" or "low touch"? Do you adopt their habits so that you earn their trust?

VARK It!

Kinesthetic: Tour your campus to find examples of art, music, or literature from other cultures.

VARK It!

Aural: Talk with an international student on your campus about how college life in the United States differs from what a student would experience in his or her home country.

3. **Emotional/motivational quotient (heart):** Do you empathize with people from this culture? Can you imagine what it's like to be a member of this culture? Do you want to connect despite your differences? This aspect of CQ is thought to be most like EQ.

VARK It!

Kinesthetic: If you have a Facebook account, look at the pages of three people you know who have traveled to another country. Can you find examples of cultural differences they describe?

To have good CQ skills, you must be more than a "mimic," simply repeating what you see and hear in another culture. You must be a "chameleon," taking on what it's like to be a member of that culture. You must—through your head, your body, and your heart—prove to others that you have entered their world. Not only are CQ skills important within the American culture, they're also important in today's global society. How culturally intelligent are you? CQ is a natural extension of EQ, and the suggestions for how to improve your EQ apply to strengthening your CQ. If your cognitive quotient is low, read up about other cultures. If your physical quotient is low, watch for differences in gestures or movements and find out what they mean. If your emotional/motivational quotient is low, ask others for input, for example, or find a CQ mentor.

Think Globally; Act Locally

Sustainability the practice of meeting our needs now without compromising the ability of future generations to meet theirs (Brundtland Commission of the United Nations, March 20, 1987)

The 1972 United Nations international conference on the human environment in Stockholm was the origin of the phrase "Think Globally, Act Locally." Perhaps you've heard it. Simply put, it originally meant "Do what you can to 'save the environment.'"

Today the phrase takes on added meaning. True, recycling is becoming the norm, and sustainability is the goal of modern corporations. But beyond environmental concerns, the world is characterized by networks of connections across continents and distances. As citizens of the world, we are all connected, if not geographically, then economically, militarily, socially, financially, and technologically. The General Electric website allows users to select from forty different languages. Google offers an interface in over 130 languages.[50] By 2003, 66 percent of all e-commerce spending originated outside of the United States, and now nearly two-thirds of all Internet users live in Asia and Europe.[51] A famous song title once made the claim: "We Are the World."

The education you get now must prepare you to solve the problems of the future. It will require you to look beyond the walls of your classrooms and refine your skills in terms of how relationships work, how diversity impacts our lives, and how to be culturally intelligent. It will require you to think and act both globally *and* locally. The course for which you're using this textbook is a good place to start.

We have not inherited the world from our fore-fathers—we have borrowed it from our children.

Kashmiri proverb

BOX 10.2 # Service-Learning: Learning by Serving

One of the best ways to learn about diversity in college is by serving others. Instead of spending all your time in a classroom, imagine a class on aging in which you team up with an elder in your community and work together on a project. You might help a senior write her memoirs, for example, or help an elderly man create a family tree for the next generation. You might be wondering, How would that work? What could we possibly have in common–especially if you're an 18-year-old teamed up with an 88-year-old? You might be surprised.

Campus Compact, a national organization with nearly 1200 member two- and four-year colleges, estimates that college student volunteering is worth $9.1 billion to the communities they serve.[52]

Beyond the dollars calculated, college students' community service provides invaluable support. Literally thousands of college students volunteered to help with Hurricane Katrina and Rita relief efforts in 2005, for example, to help displaced victims of one of the country's worst natural disasters ever.

However, here's an important point: community service and service-learning aren't quite the same thing.[53] Service-learning is specifically about the learning. It's a learning experience in which you connect what you're learning in the classroom for credit with what you're learning in the community. You're applying what you're learning, which may change your perspective. "Service, combined with learning, adds value to each and transforms both."[54] While you're engaged in a service-learning experience, you'll also be engaged in critical reflection or focused thinking about what you're doing. Critical reflection is like critical thinking, recalling or looking back at the service experience and writing about what you're learning in a continuous, connected, challenging, and contextualized way.[55] That's not the same thing as donating your time for a good cause, as important as that is, in terms of you and your own personal development and the lives of the people you help.

Search out these opportunities to learn and appreciate diversity by serving other people.

Brand X Pictures/Getty Image

> **We make a living by what we get, but we make a life by what we give.**
>
> *Winston Churchill, Prime Minister of England (1874–1965)*

CONTROL: *YOUR TOUGHEST CLASS*

Imagine you are preparing for an exam in your anatomy and physiology class, just as our case study character Kia Washington will be doing. Students often describe A&P as a very challenging course, one that requires a great deal of reading, studying, and memorizing. Read the following excerpt from Kia's A&P textbook, and prepare, as she will, using the steps below. As you study the list of terms in this passage from the book, make sure you understand what you are reading. Don't just skip over things that look too complicated. Instead, really give it a try.

Connective Tissue Functions

Connective tissue has many and varied functions:

1. **Support:** Bones support other tissues of the body. On top of bones we find muscle, nerves, blood vessels, fat, and skin. Cartilage supports our nose and forms the bulk of the structure of our ear.

2. **Nourishment:** Blood carries nutrients to the cells of our body. Synovial membranes in joint capsules nourish the cartilage found on top of bones.

3. **Transportation:** Blood transports gases, enzymes, and hormones to cells.

4. **Connection:** Tendons connect muscles to bone, and ligaments connect bone to bone.

5. **Movement:** Muscles through tendons pull on bones, and bones move our bodies through our environment.

6. **Protection:** Bones protect vital organs of the body like the heart, lungs, brain, and spinal cord. Blood cells, especially the white blood cells, protect us from foreign microorganisms and tissue injury.

7. **Insulation:** Adipose tissue (fat) insulates us from excessive heat loss and excessive increases in temperature.

8. **Storage:** Bone stores the mineral salts calcium and phosphorous. Adipose tissue stores the high-energy molecules of fat to be used and converted to adenosine triphosphate when necessary.

9. **Attachment and separation:** Connective tissue attaches skin to underlying muscle. It also forms layers around and between organs.

[From Rizzo, D. C. (2012). *Introduction to anatomy and physiology.* Clifton Park, NY: Delmar, Cengage Learning, pp. 106–108.]

Follow these steps to prepare for a practice test:

1. *Annotate* this excerpt. Write questions or explanations or draw pictures, if it helps, in the margin.

2. *Memorize* the list using a memorization strategy that makes sense to you. Repeating the terms over and over again may not be enough. After you have memorized the nine terms, list them here. Keep your hand over the passage so that you're not tempted to look back. Can you do it?

_____

_____

_____

3. *Test* yourself. See whether you know what the nine terms mean. Again, without looking back at the passage, match the terms to their descriptions. After you have finished (but not before), look at the answer key to see how well you did.

_____ **1.** Storage

_____ **2.** Insulation

_____ **3.** Movement

_____ **4.** Attachment and separation

_____ **5.** Protection

_____ **6.** Transportation

_____ **7.** Connection

_____ **8.** Support

_____ **9.** Nourishment

a. brings gases, enzymes, and hormones to cells

b. attaches muscles to bone, and bone to bone

c. keeps vital organs safe

d. holds up other parts of our bodies

e. carries nutrition

f. helps make us mobile

g. helps keep temperatures steady

h. holds onto fats and helps converts them for use

i. connects skin to muscle and keeps organs apart

Answer key: 1-h, 2-g, 3-f, 4-i, 5-c, 6-a, 7-b, 8-d, 9-e

4. How well did you do? What might you have done differently, if anything, to improve your practice test score?

_____

_____

_____

CURIOSITY: *BUILD RELATIONSHIPS, ONE DROP AT A TIME*

After the Korean War, the U.S. Army's chief psychiatrist studied the psychological warfare used against 1,000 American prisoners of war who had been kept at a North Korean camp. He made a startling discovery: negativity kills.[56]

The prisoners had not been treated cruelly. They were given food, water, and shelter. They hadn't been tortured, yet many American soldiers died in the camp. They weren't surrounded by barbed wire and armed guards, yet no one ever tried to escape. Many of these men died of extreme hopelessness caused by a total removal of emotional support. All positive letters from home were withheld, but negative ones telling of relatives passing away or wives divorcing their husbands were delivered right away. Eventually, many of these American prisoners simply gave up. They died of "give-up-itis," as they called it, raising the overall death rate in the camp to the highest American POW death rate in U.S. history.

The record of what happened raised this fundamental question, described in *The New York Times and Wall Street Journal* bestseller *How Full Is Your Bucket?* If negativity can have such a devastating impact, what can positivity do? That's where the analogy of buckets and dippers begins. Most of us will never endure the kind of psychological warfare these soldiers did, but all of us can examine the negativity we inflict on others and, by contrast, the positivity we can bring to others' lives.

How Full Is Your Bucket? by Tom Rath and Donald Clifton claims that each of us has an invisible bucket; we function at our best when our buckets are full. We each also have an invisible dipper. In every interaction, we use our dipper to fill others' buckets or to dip from them. The principle of the book is simple; following its advice, however, is challenging. Consider these five recommendations for filling rather than dipping:

1. **Dip less.** Get in the habit of listening to yourself. Are your words cynical, insensitive, or critical? If so, push the pause button and rephrase what you're trying to communicate.

2. **Bring out the best.** By filling others' buckets, we set off a chain reaction that comes back to us.

3. **Make more than one best friend.** Whoever said people are only allowed one best friend? High-quality relationships improve the quality of your life.

4. **Fill a drop at a time.** Giving a small unexpected gift is a great way to fill someone else's bucket. It needn't be much: a token, a trinket, a compliment, or a thank you.

5. **Apply the Golden Rule backward.** Rather than "Do unto others as you would have them do unto you," try this: "Do unto others as they would have you do unto them." Paying attention to this one thing can make a big difference.

How full is your bucket? In the most important relationships in your life, are you filling or dipping? Is there a relationship in which you need to change?

_____

_____

_____

CAREER OUTLOOK: *MAKE IT PERSONAL*

Have you ever been accused of taking things personally? Your Mom looks askance at your new, multitone hair color or your ever-so-stylish "runway" outfit, or your roommate makes a confusing, offhanded comment about something that's dear to your heart. "How dare she?" you think to yourself! When you tell the story to your best friend, she provides a reality check, "Oh, lighten up. You don't have to take it personally."

People count. We care about what they think of us. But what about the often overlooked reverse point of view? They care, too. People prop us up, validate us (or not), and meet our personal needs—and we do the same for them. Even though we know it, we don't always show it. It explains why some very intelligent, highly capable people fail and why misunderstandings are common. It's not so much that people always take things personally; it's that they sometimes forget to make things personal.

Consider this scenario: You're on a team with a colleague who's a bear to work with. She may be the hardest worker in the company, have the best ideas, and sport a sales record that no one can touch. But ultimately, she fails miserably in your organization and moves to another one . . . again. She moves from job to job, and she just can't figure out why she's not seen as successful. But to her, the job is all about the work. The people she works with are invisible to her. She doesn't realize that the people are how the work gets done. According to one career expert, "There's a simple reason for it: we rarely take the time to pause, breathe, and think about what's working and what's not. There's just too much to do and no time to reflect." Making things personal is about listening carefully to the layers of communication and remembering that people count. Actually, it's less about time and more about mindset. Appreciate your differences, explore your commonalities, and above all, remember that work, like the rest of life, is about building productive relationships.[57]

Here's a recommendation: At the end of every workday, take five minutes to reflect not only about the work but also about your coworkers. Ask yourself these three questions:

1. What went well today and what didn't?

2. What lessons from today will help me do a better job tomorrow?

3. Who contributed to my success? Is there someone I should update or thank? If so, do it.[58]

Doing so will not only help you do your best, but it will do the same for others. Remembering to "make it personal" will affect your career more positively than you can possibly imagine now.

Think about a time that you were involved in a college project (a group presentation, for example) when things either did or didn't work well. Which principles you've just read about were (or would have been) important?

_____

_____

_____

CHALLENGE: *REALITY CHECK*

How much did you learn? At the beginning of this chapter, you filled out a "Readiness Check" that asked how you thought this chapter would relate to you and how you would relate to it. Now, fill out this "Reality Check" to find out.

1. What is emotional intelligence, and how does it relate to college success?

2. Identify one of the five basic conflict styles.

3. Describe three benefits of valuing diversity.

4. In your own words, define *CQ*.

5. How long did it take? _____ hours _____ minutes. Before you began this chapter, you were asked to predict how long it would take you to complete this chapter (total time, even if you read it in more than one sitting). Was your estimate on target, or will you revise it for the next chapter you'll read?_____

step
3 INSIGHT *Now* What Do You Think?

At the beginning of this chapter, Kia Washington faced a series of challenges as a new college student. Now after reading this chapter, would you respond differently to any of the questions you answered about the "FOCUS Challenge Case"? Using what you learned in the chapter, write a paragraph ending to Kia's case study. What are some of the possible outcomes for Kia?

step 4 ACTION Your Plans for Change

1. Do you fall into any of the communication traps you read about in this chapter? If so, which ones? What will you do to change the way you communicate in important relationships?

2. This chapter asserts that diversity makes a difference. Do you believe that statement? In what ways can learning to appreciate diversity change how you interact with others? How can these communication skills pay off in the future? What will you do to refine them further?

3. Is cultural intelligence something you've ever thought about before? What role might it play in your future personal or professional life?

11 chapter

Choosing a College Major and Career

How this chapter relates to YOU

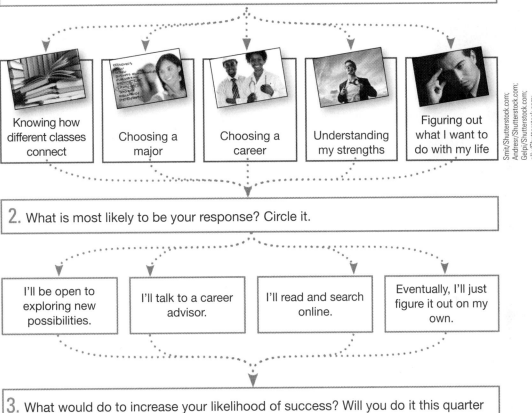

1. When it comes to choosing a college major and career, what do you find most challenging, if anything?

| Knowing how different classes connect | Choosing a major | Choosing a career | Understanding my strengths | Figuring out what I want to do with my life |

Smit/Shutterstock.com;
Andresr/Shutterstock.com;
Gelpi/Shutterstock.com;
olly/Shutterstock.com;
Blend Images/Shutterstock.com

2. What is most likely to be your response? Circle it.

| I'll be open to exploring new possibilities. | I'll talk to a career advisor. | I'll read and search online. | Eventually, I'll just figure it out on my own. |

3. What would do to increase your likelihood of success? Will you do it this quarter or semester?

Example: Talk to a career advisor on campus. Yes!

How YOU will relate to this chapter

What are you most interested in learning about? Put checkmarks by those topics.

☐ Why "college in a box" isn't an accurate view of coursework

☐ How the disciplines connect in the Circle of Learning

☐ How to choose a major and career

☐ How to follow your bliss, conduct research, and take a good look at yourself

☐ What a SWOT analysis is

☐ How to analyze your "Academic Anatomy"

● How motivated are you to learn more about getting the right start in college? (5 = high, 1 = low) ___

● How ready are you to read now? ___ (If something is in your way, take care of it if you can, zero in and focus.)

● How long do you think it will take you to complete this chapter? If you start and stop, keep track of your overall time. ___ hour(s) ___ minutes

©Larry Harwood Photography. Property of Cengage Learning.

Ethan Cole

Jorge Folha/Shutterstock.com

One thing was certain: Ethan Cole was unsure. Unsure of his abilities, unsure of which major to choose, unsure of what he wanted to do with his life, unsure of himself. Unsure of almost everything.

Ethan came from a good family, and he actually got along pretty well with his parents. They both had decent jobs, worked long hours, and overall they had been good to him. Compared with many of his friends, he came from a "happy home." But frankly, his parents weren't all that interested in the details of his life. When he announced one day as a high school senior that he wanted to go to the community college in town, they said, "What for?" When he said he didn't know, they replied, "Well, you'll figure it out." And that was that. He enrolled the next day.

The only thing Ethan was sure of was that skateboarding was his life right now. It's all he wanted to do and all he ever thought about. He'd look at a curve on a window frame or an arc in a picture and imagine what skating on it would feel like. All his friends were skateboarders, too, and he read skateboarder magazines and dreamed of the day he might even go pro. He

realized not many people make a living at it, but a few really talented athletes did, and maybe—just maybe—he'd be one of them. Recently, he'd found out about the largest concrete skatepark on the globe, Black Pearl in the Grand Cayman Islands—62,000 square feet! He'd made a promise to himself to skate there someday. *Life couldn't get much better than that,* he thought.

But school . . . that was a different story. Schoolwork had never captured his attention. In primary school, his physician had diagnosed him with Attention Deficit Disorder (ADD). *No wonder I don't like school,* he remembered thinking then. But finally knowing why he couldn't focus didn't change his attitude. He still hated sitting in a classroom.

Despite these challenges, his parents had always told him he was smart. "You can do anything you want to do," they'd said. "Look at you: you're a

© Larry Harwood Photography. Property of Cengage Learning.

TheSupe87/Shutterstock.com

Manuel Fernandes/Shutterstock.com

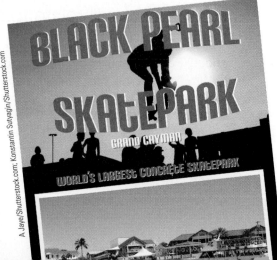

A Jaye/Shutterstock.com; Konstantin Sutyagin/Shutterstock.com

BLACK PEARL SKATEPARK
GRAND CAYMAN
WORLD'S LARGEST CONCRETE SKATEPARK

good-looking kid with plenty of talents. The world is your oyster!" *What a funny phrase,* he'd always thought when they said that. By the time he finally learned what it meant, he totally believed it. His life would become whatever he chose to make of it.

The problem was there were too many choices. How could anyone decide what he wanted to be when he was only nineteen? Ethan remembered liking geometry; he was good at creative writing; he played the drums like a real jazz musician; and he was an incredible artist. *But what do you do with* that *combination of skills?* he'd asked himself more than once. What possible college major and career would really fit him? He'd spent plenty of time on career websites to try and figure it out.

He'd managed to pull decent grades his first term—a B average—at the community college close to home. He'd taken Geography, Interpersonal Communication, Drawing 101, and Study Skills, and while he'd done well,

none of the course material really sparked a genuine interest. His instructors didn't take much of an interest in him either. His Study Skills instructor was friendly and tried to get him interested in class, and he knew the material could really help him. But frankly, Ethan just wasn't motivated when it came to school.

Instead, Ethan skateboarded every minute he could. He preferred skateboarding to studying any day of the week, and when it came to actually choosing a major—much less his classes for the next term—he was clueless. The one thing that did interest him was a certificate in entrepreneurship. It was all about starting a business of your own. Now that sounded intriguing. Ethan didn't quite fit any molds, and doing his own thing might just be "his thing!"

But the more he thought about it, dropping out sounded like a good idea, too. He could get a job delivering pizzas, think about his life, and try to figure it all out. He'd have nobody to tell him what to do, nobody to hold him accountable, nobody to pressure him, nobody to force him into making decisions—and plenty of free time to skateboard.

Study Skills (ID 102)
Course Syllabus

INSTRUCTOR: Anna Morgan
OFFICE: 342 Smith Hall
HOURS 9 a.m.-12 p.m. Mon-Thurs

TEXT: *FOCUS on Community College Success* by Constance Staley

COURSE OBJECTIVES: This course is designed to give you the tools
more productive, and a more successful learning experience. The
to make you a better student by building your study skills and e
strategies.

EXPECTATIONS: Students are expected to be respectful of instruct
Assignments should be turned in on time unless you have a va
due date. Please see me if you have any questions. Water bott
but no food or sugary drinks are permitted. Please turn off y
come to class.

GRADING: 100 Possible Points.
-Participation: 10 Points.
-Final Presentation: 20 Points.
-Final Exam: 20 Points.
-Assignments(3) and Quizzes (2): 50 Points (10 each)

GRADES: 100-90 = A   89-80 = B   79-70 = C   69-60

Course Schedule

WEEK 1:	Overview and PreTest
WEEK 2:	Managing Time and Stress
WEEK 3:	Reading Skills
WEEK 4:	Test Taking
WEEK 5:	Listening and Memory
WEEK 6:	Diversity
WEEK 7:	Effective Writing

Facts about Learning Disabilities

Quick Facts

- 1 in 7 Americans has a learning disability
- 80% of students with learning disabilities have reading problems
- Learning disabilities can be genetic
- Multiple learning disabilities can occur at the same time

Types of LDs

- Dyslexia- trouble understanding written words
- Dyscalculia- trouble grasping mathematical concepts
- Dysgraphia- trouble writing letters or words
- Aural and Visual Processing Disorders

1. Do you have anything in common with Ethan? If so, how are you managing the situation so that you can be successful?
2. In your view, what will become of Ethan? What are his prospects for the future? Do you think he'll decide on a career and finish college? Why or why not?
3. Why is Ethan experiencing problems? Are these problems serious? Should they hold him back? List all the problems you can identify.
4. Which majors and careers might Ethan be well suited for? If you were an academic advisor, what advice would you give him?
5. Who would you send Ethan to on your campus for help? What are his options? What do you think he should do at this point?

What's the Connection?

College is about becoming an educated person—learning how to think, solve problems, and make decisions. College is much more than the "sum of its tests." It's about developing yourself as a person and becoming well educated. What does it mean to be well educated? Simply put, being well educated is about the pursuit of human excellence.[1]

Colleges help societies *preserve the past* and *create the future*. Studying the history of the U.S. Constitution in a political science course as opposed to studying potential cures for cancer in a cell biology course are concrete examples. Colleges help us look back (preserve the past) and look ahead (create the future).

College in a Box?

Have you ever thought about the fact that college courses appear to exist in discrete "boxes"? Schools tend to place courses in academic departments, and your class schedule reflects these divisions. For example, your schedule this term might look something like the one in Figure 11.1.

This organizing system helps you keep things straight in your head, and it also helps your school organize a complex institution. Instructors normally work in one department or another. And classes are categorized into particular academic disciplines.

academic discipline a branch of learning, instruction, or emphasis

VARK It!

Aural: What courses are you taking this term? How would your "College in a Box" look? As you read this section, talk through the problems with this approach.

FIGURE 11.1

Most Schools Compartmentalize Learning

	M	T	W	Th	F
9–10	ENG			COMM	
10–11		MATH			
11–12			PSYCH		PSYCH

© Cengage Learning

But something students often wonder about is how to connect the dots. What's the big picture? Knowledge isn't quite as neat as departments and boxes; it's messy. It overlaps and merges. Despite the divisions and abbreviations colleges use to divide up knowledge, you might be able to take a somewhat similar course in visual art as an art course, a computer science course, or a communication course. You've probably noticed that you sometimes hear something discussed in one of your classes that's also being discussed in another one. Knowledge is interconnected. College in a Box isn't an accurate way of looking at things.

Even though each academic discipline has its own history and identity and way of asking questions and finding answers, the disciplines aren't as distinct as your class schedule might lead you to believe.

> It takes courage to grow up and become who you really are.

e. e. cummings, American poet (1894–1962)

How Do the Disciplines Connect?

The Circle of Learning (see Figure 11.2) illustrates the interconnectedness of knowledge. Although this circle could be drawn in many different ways, using many different traditional academic disciplines, here is an example to get you thinking.[2]

It works like this. Let's start at the top of the circle with *math,* which is a basic "language" with rules and conventions, just like spoken language. You manipulate numbers and operations and functions, just as you manipulate sounds and words and sentences. Now, move clockwise around the circle.

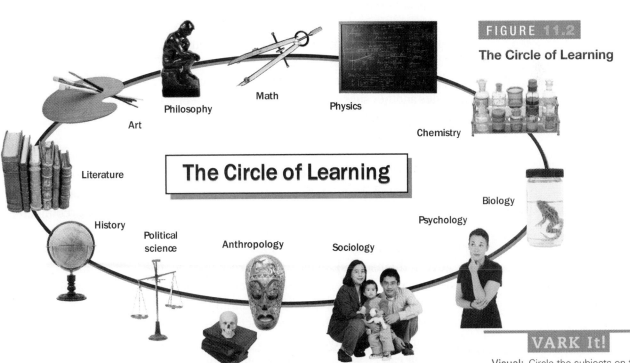

FIGURE 11.2

The Circle of Learning

The Circle of Learning

Art · Philosophy · Math · Physics · Chemistry · Biology · Psychology · Sociology · Anthropology · Political science · History · Literature

CLOCKWISE: Travis Klein/Shutterstock; Image Source/Jupiter Images; Hemera Technologies/Jupiterimages; Hemera Technologies/Jupiterimages; Hemera Technologies/Jupiterimages; Jupiterimages; PhotosToGo.com; OlegD/Shutterstock.com; Photos.com; Sebastian Kaulitzki/Shutterstock.com; Photos.com; aquatic creature/Shutterstock.com; originalpunkt/Shutterstock.com

VARK It!

Visual: Circle the subjects on the Circle of Learning chart that you enjoy most. Are they clustered together or at opposite ends of the circle? What could this tell you about choosing a major or career?

David Chasey/Getty Images

> **Never mistake knowledge for wisdom. One helps you make a living; the other helps you make a life.**
>
> *Sandra Carey, consultant and lobbyist*

Math is the fundamental language of *physics,* one branch of which studies atomic and subatomic particles. When atoms combine into molecules, such as carbon dioxide, the academic discipline involved is called *chemistry*. Chemicals combine to create living organisms studied in *biology* courses. Living organisms don't just exist; they think and behave, leading to the study of *psychology*. They also interact in groups, families, and societies, which you study in *sociology*. You can also study units of living beings throughout time and across cultures in the discipline of *anthropology*. These units—people—who live and work together are typically governed or govern themselves, leading to *political science*. Let's keep going.

When an account of peoples and countries and their rulers is recorded, you study *history*. These written accounts, sometimes factual or sometimes fictional (for pleasure or intrigue) comprise the study of *literature*. Literature is one way to record impressions and provoke reactions—poetry is a good example—through the use of words. But images and symbols can do the same things—enter *art*. A particular question artists ask is "What is beauty?" otherwise known as aesthetics, which is also a particular topic of study in *philosophy*. Philosophy also includes another subspecialty called number theory, one of the earliest branches of pure mathematics. And now we're all the way around the Circle of Learning, arriving right back at *math*.

That's a quick rundown. Of course, many academic disciplines don't appear on this chart, but they could and should. The point isn't which disciplines are represented. Instead, the Circle of Learning demonstrates that academic disciplines are interconnected because knowledge itself is interconnected. *Anthropology* (understanding people throughout time and across cultures) can provide an important foundation for *political science* (how people are governed or govern themselves), and *history* (a record of peoples and countries and rulers) can easily be the basis for *literature*. Using what you're learning in one discipline can lead to deeper understanding in another, and although some of your instructors will help you connect the dots, putting it all together is basically your responsibility.

In your career, you'll need to use knowledge without necessarily remembering in which course you learned it. You'll be thinking critically and creatively, solving problems, and calling upon all the skills you're developing in all the courses you're studying in college. The bottom line is that connections count. Recognize them, use them, and strengthen them to reinforce your learning.

How to Choose a Major and a Career

Like many students, you probably put value in how well college prepares you for a profession.[3] Choosing a college major and directing yourself toward a prospective career can be stressful. Many students feel pressure to make the right decision—and make it right now! You might hear conflicting advice from family members that put a high priority on financial success above other important factors, for example, and feel overwhelmed by the number of possibilities from which to choose.[4] You may know what you want to do with the rest of your life right now, but many of your classmates don't, and even if they *say* they do, they may well change their minds. Yes, these decisions are important, but there's evidence that you don't have to have it all figured out right away.[5] Where do you start? The decision-making process should involve these critical steps. If you're still deciding, or even if you think you already have, consider how they apply to you.

The self is not something that one finds. It's something one creates.

Thomas Szasz, Professor Emeritus in Psychiatry, State University of New York Health Science Center, Syracuse

Step 1: Follow Your Bliss

In an ideal world, which major and career would you choose? Don't think about anything except the actual content you'd be studying. Don't consider career opportunities, requirements, difficulty, or anything else that might keep you from making these choices in an ideal world. What are you passionate about? If it's skateboarding, think about which

---

Sharpen Your FOCUS

"The laws of science do not distinguish between the past and the future."
—STEVEN W. HAWKING

Reason 11: They have unrealistic expectations.

It's easy to lose your focus when you aren't realistic. You may think you can finish a paper in half an hour when it's really going to take a minimum of three hours. When you're not present and honest, you can lose your focus. You may even get discouraged and give up.

Think back on what you actually accomplished today. Did you pay attention to the things and people that are most important to you? Did you make progress toward the future you're trying to create?

TRY It!

Keep track of how realistic you were about your time this week and be prepared to be accountable to your instructor and classmates next week. Keep a journal of each day's biggest accomplishment and most distracting obstacle, and see whether you recognize patterns. Create one pointer of your own to share with your classmates.

Example:

Monday I thought I would study for an exam in the evening, but a new TV show started, and I watched it (just like I knew I would...) That was an obstacle, but on the other hand, I did finish a paper for another course later on. Pointer: Be honest about my tendencies and pat myself on the back when I finish something important!

_____

_____

> *Follow your bliss and be what you want to be. Don't climb the ladder of success only to find it's leaning against the wrong wall.*
>
> *Dr. Bernie Siegel, physician and writer*

majors might apply. Majoring in physics would help you understand skateboard "flight paths," spin, and angles. Majoring in landscape architecture would allow you to design skateparks. Majoring in journalism would put you in a good position to write for a skateboarding magazine.

Like Ethan Cole from the "FOCUS Challenge Case," you may be wondering what to do with your life. Perhaps the *idealist* in you has one potential career in mind and the *realist* in you has another. The $300,000 salary you'd earn as a surgeon may look very compelling until you consider the years of medical school required after college, the time invested in an internship and residency, and the still further years of specialization. It takes long-term commitment, dedication, and resources—yours or borrowed ones—to make that dream come true. Do these factors lessen the appeal?

Perhaps there's conflict between your ideal career and someone else's idea of an ideal career for you. Comedian Robin Williams once said, "When I told my father I was going to be an actor, he said, 'Fine, but study welding just in case.'"

And perhaps you just don't know yet. If that's the case, don't panic. Despite the increased pressure these days to choose the right major because of rising tuition and a changeable economy, Ethan Cole is right: It's hard to have it all figured out from the start.[6]

One thing is certain: You'll be a happier, more productive person if you do what *you* want to do *and* pursue it vigorously. When it comes to success, ability (*Can* you do it?) and effort (Are you *willing* to invest what it takes?) go hand in hand. Whatever your motivation, remember this. It's unusual for people to become truly successful halfheartedly. There are undeniable emotional and psychological components involved in success. Wayne Gretzky, called the greatest player in the history of hockey, once said, "God gave me a special talent to play the game . . . maybe he didn't give me a talent, he gave me a *passion*."

Having said that, what if your "bliss" just isn't feasible? You'd give anything to play for the NBA, but you're five foot two and female. You dream of being a rock star, but you can't carry a tune. Then it may be time to set aside the dream and get real. Maybe then it's time to translate—or shift—your dreams into goals.

When the statistics are against you, achieving success isn't impossible, but it might take more than expert skill. It might also take some luck, very specific planning, and perseverance.

Step 2: Conduct Preliminary Research

Has it ever occurred to you that you may not have all the facts—accurate ones—about your ideal major? Do you know what it *really* takes? Have you gotten your information from qualified sources—or are you basing your opinion on your friend's reaction to one course he took?

VARK It!

Kinesthetic: When you have some free time, go online and look up successful people who have achieved your dream. How did they translate their dreams into goals?

Try an experiment. Choose three majors you're considering, one of which is your ideal major, and send yourself on a fact-finding mission. To find out whether you're on target, get the answers to the following ten questions for each of the three possibilities. Go to the physical location (department) where each major is housed, and interview an instructor. The experiment requires legwork; don't just let your fingers do the clicking.

VARK It!

Read/Write: Consider a possible college major or career option and create a list of reasons why it would or wouldn't be a good choice for you.

1. What is the major or certificate?

2. Who is the interviewee?

3. What is the name of the academic department where this major is housed? Where are the department offices physically located on campus?

4. Which introductory courses in this major would give you information about your interests and abilities?

5. Which specialized courses in this major interest you? (List three.)

6. What courses do you have to complete before you can major in the subject?

7. How many students major in this discipline on your campus?

8. Which required course in the major do students usually find most challenging? Which is most engaging? Which is most valued? Why?

9. How would the interviewee describe the reputation of this department on campus? What is it known for?

10. From the interviewee's perspective, why should a student major in this discipline?

After you complete your interviews, review the facts. Did you change any of your opinions based on what you learned?[7]

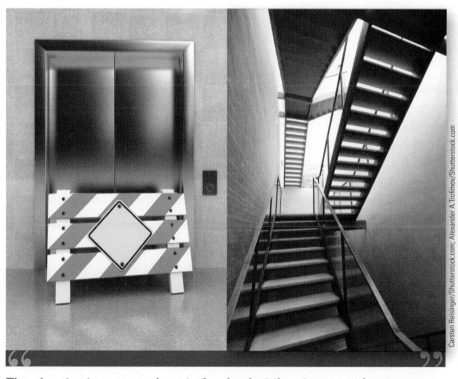

Carsten Reisinger/Shutterstock.com; Alexander A.Trofimov/Shutterstock.com

The elevator to success is out of order, but the steps are always open.

Zig Ziglar, American author, salesman, and motivational speaker

Step 3: Take a Good Look at Yourself

What Are Your Job Preferences?

Take a good look at yourself and answer the following questions about how you prefer to work. Rank each item 1 or 2 based on your general preference. Although many careers, if not most, require both, your task is to decide which of the two you prefer.

I prefer to work at a job:

1. Alone	_____	With other people	_____
2. Indoors	_____	Outdoors	_____
3. With people	_____	With equipment or materials	_____
4. Directing/leading others	_____	Being directed/led by others	_____
5. Producing information	_____	Managing information	_____
6. In an organized, step-by-step way	_____	In a big-idea, big-picture way	_____
7. Starting things	_____	Completing things	_____
8. Involving a product	_____	Involving a service	_____
9. Solving challenging problems	_____	Generating creative ideas	_____
10. Finding information	_____	Applying information	_____
11. Teaching/training others in groups	_____	Advising/coaching others one-on-one	_____

Now look at your eleven first choices. Identify several career fields that come to mind that would allow you to achieve as many of them as possible.

Here's a bottom-line question: For you—as Dr. Bernie Siegel would say—what *is* the "right wall" to lean your ladder of success on? How do you know? Many first-year college students don't know. They don't have enough experience under their belts to plan for a lifetime. They're in college to *discover*. It all comes down to questions this book has been asking you all along: Who are you? And what do you want? If you're unsure of how to proceed in your decision making, follow these recommendations to see whether they help you bring your future into focus.

Send in the SWOT Team! A SWOT analysis is an excellent way to begin taking a good look at yourself in relation to your future. SWOT stands for Strengths, Weaknesses, Opportunities, and Threats. SWOT analyses are typically used in business, but creating one for yourself may be useful when it comes to deciding on a college major and a career. Make a chart with four sections, label each one, and fill them in as objectively as you can.

> **Strengths** are traits that give you a leg up. These are talents you can capitalize on and qualities you can develop.

- **Weaknesses** are traits that currently work against you. You can, however, work to reduce or eliminate them.

- **Opportunities** are conditions or circumstances that work in your favor, like a strong forecast for the future of your prospective career.

- **Threats** are conditions that could have bad effects. Some of these factors are beyond your control; however, sometimes you can figure out ways to make them matter less.

As you create your own chart, begin with two basic questions:

What kinds of forces will impact your potential career?

Internal—forces inside you, such as motivation and skill

External—forces outside you that may affect your success: the job market or economy, for example

What kind of influence can these forces exert?

Positive—some forces will give you a boost toward your goals.

Negative—other forces will work against you.[8]

VARK It!

Read/Write: Before you look carefully at Figure 11.3, make a list of the pros and cons of being a professional skateboarder. Compare your list with what's on the chart here in the chapter.

Let's complete a SWOT analysis for Ethan and his dream of becoming a professional skateboarder. Of course, you might say that, technically, he doesn't need an academic degree for that particular career. But if he wants to pursue related, more traditional careers—design a new skatepark or write for a skateboard magazine, for example—he would need knowledge from design and writing to finance and marketing. Besides, college isn't just about jobs, it's about living a fuller life as a well-educated person.

Look back at the "FOCUS Challenge Case," and see whether you agree with the basic SWOT analysis shown in Figure 11.3.

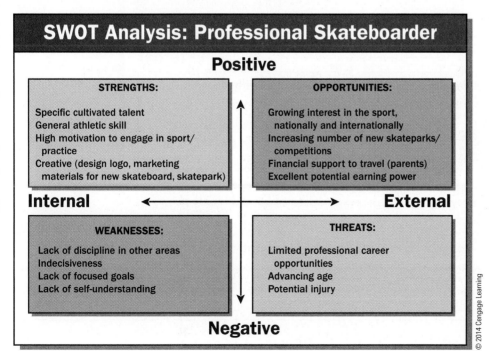

FIGURE 11.3

SWOT Analysis

Looking at his SWOT analysis, what would you conclude? Is professional skateboarding a good career for him? In your view, do the opportunities outweigh the threats? For example, does the possibility of earning big bucks outweigh the risks of possible injuries? If not, could he move toward other potential careers, perhaps some that also involve skateboarding? "Ethan remembered liking geometry, he was good at creative writing, he played the drums like a real jazz musician, and he was an incredible artist." Do you see potential majors for him in college? Sports management? Kinesiology? Architecture? Journalism? Jazz studies? Creative writing? What should Ethan do?

EXERCISE 11.2

SWOT Analysis:

Looking at the model in Figure 11.3, try doing a SWOT Analysis of a career you're considering. If you have no idea where to begin, choose the career of someone you know—a friend or family member. Carefully analyze the Strengths, Weaknesses, Opportunities, and Threats as you see them. It may help to Google the career for specifics and check information-rich, accurate sites like OOH (Occupational Outlook Handbook), compiled by the U.S. Bureau of Labor Statistics. After you're done, write your conclusions below, and share your results in class, if asked. Is the career you've analyzed worth pursuing in your view?

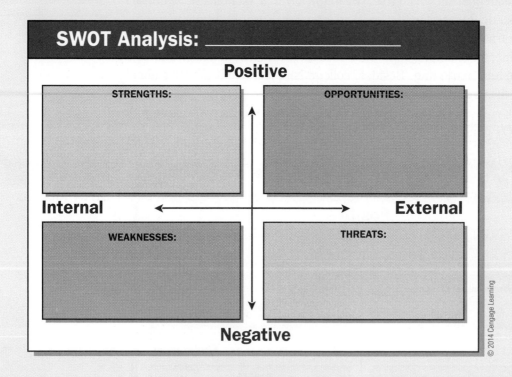

SWOT Analysis: _____

Positive

STRENGTHS:

OPPORTUNITIES:

Internal ←————→ **External**

WEAKNESSES:

THREATS:

Negative

© 2014 Cengage Learning

1. _____

2. _____

3. _____

Step 4: Consider Your Major versus Your Career

Which comes first, the chicken or the egg? The major or the career? Silly question? The obvious answer, of course, is that you must first major or earn a certificate in something in college before you can build a career on it. But the question isn't as straightforward as it seems.

Should you choose a major based on an intended career? Perhaps you know you want to be a science teacher, first and foremost. You don't know whether to get an associate's degree in physical science or an associate of arts degree in teaching. You like all sciences, but teaching is your real interest. If you major in science, which one should you emphasize (see Figure 11.4)?

Or instead, should you choose a major first, and then decide on a career? Say you made a firm decision to major in chemistry when your favorite science teacher did "mad scientist" experiments for the class in eighth grade. But at this point, you're not certain of the professional direction you'd like to pursue. Chemistry is your passion, but should you apply your chemistry degree as a forensics expert, a pharmaceutical salesperson, a chemical technician, or a teacher (see Figure 11.5)? You could enter some of these career fields with an associate's degree, but others might require transferring to a four-year school.

So which comes first—major or career? It depends.[9] The answer sounds uncertain, and it's meant to. Although some professional degree programs put you into a particular track right away (nursing, for example), generally either direction can work well. Doors will open and close for you, and as

VARK It!

Kinesthetic: Go on a "field trip" to the Career Center on your campus. Collect resources you find there, and bring them to class.

FIGURE 11.4

Which Science Should a Science Teacher Major In?

FIGURE 11.5

Which Career Should a Chemistry Major Choose?

Hemera Technologies/Jupiterimages; Hemera Technologies/Jupiterimages; Hemera Technologies/Jupiterimages; Hemera Technologies/Jupiterimages; Hemera Technologies/Jupiterimages; Hemera Technologies/Jupiterimages

you gain more knowledge and experience, you'll narrow your focus. As you learn more about your chosen major, you'll also learn about its specific career tracks. But it's important to remember that a major doesn't have to lock you into one specific career. And you can always narrow or refocus your area of emphasis by earning your bachelor's degree and continuing your education beyond that.[10]

What's Your Academic Anatomy? Thinking about your academic anatomy is a simple way to begin to get a handle on what you find fulfilling. If you had to rank order the four parts of you listed in Figure 11.6, what would you put in first place? Second, third, and last? To get yourself thinking, ask these questions:

1. Do you find fulfillment by using your *head*? Do you enjoy solving complex problems or thinking through difficult situations? Do you like to reason things out, weigh evidence, and think critically? Someone working toward a paralegal certificate might fit this category.

2. Do you find it satisfying to work with matters of the *heart*? Are you the kind of person others come to with problems because you listen and care? Does trying to make others happy make you happy? A nursing major might be what students with this preference choose, for example.

3. Do you like to create things with your *hands*? Do you enjoy making art? Doing hands-on projects? Building things out of other things? A drafting major who designs and builds models might be what students with this preference choose, for example.

VARK It!

Aural: Have a conversation with a student who's majoring in something very different from you. What does she or he think about the "Academic Anatomy" approach and that major?

FIGURE 11.6

What's Your Academic Anatomy?

Another way of analyzing your preferences is by considering your "Academic Anatomy." What do you find most satisfying? Working with your

Head?
Heart?
Hands? or
Whole Body?

Hemera Photo Objects/Jupiterimages

4. Do you excel at physical activities that involve your *whole body*? Are you athletic? Do you like to stay active, no matter what you're doing? A physical therapy major who goes on to work in a rehabilitation facility helping stroke victims relearn to walk might be what students with this preference choose, for example.

Now look at your academic anatomy rankings. Of course, the truth is that "all of you" is involved in everything you do. And achieving balance is important. But what are your priorities? This type of simple analysis can be one way of informing you about who you are and where you should be headed.

However, no system for choosing a major is perfect. In fact, most are imperfect at best. Here are four things to consider:

1. Sometimes students who don't select a likely major based on their "anatomical preferences" can still be successful. A whole-body person (like Ethan Cole probably is) may decide to major in art (using his hands). But he'll have to find other ways to meet his whole-body needs unless he becomes a sculptor involved in creating large constructed projects.

© Larry Harwood Photography. Property of Cengage Learning.

Are you fit company for the person you wish to become?

Anonymous

How to Choose a Major and a Career   315

2. You may intentionally choose an unlikely major. Perhaps art (using your hands) comes so naturally to you that you decide to major in science (using your head). You need the challenge to stay fully involved in getting your education. Although it may sound unlikely, it's been known to happen.

3. You may choose an unlikely major because one particular course turns you on. You had no idea majoring in this subject was even possible, and you didn't know what it entailed. But you find studying it fascinating—so you shift gears to focus all your attention on it.

4. You may be equally engaged, no matter what. You love subjects that require using your head, hands, heart, and whole body. The anatomy of learning is less important to you than other factors—a teacher whose enthusiasm is contagious, for example.[11]

Ethan's rankings would probably go something like this: (1) whole body, (2) hands, (3) heart, and (4) head. And just because "head" is in last place for him doesn't mean he's doomed in college. A career as a financial analyst sitting behind a desk probably wouldn't be his cup of tea, for example. But it may well be yours. As you decide, you may want to consider whether your choice is "anatomically correct."

Whatever major or career you're aiming for–or still looking for–make sure you follow the four steps outlined in this chapter to create the future you want.

EXERCISE 11.3

Get a Job!

Bring an employment ad from a newspaper or Internet website to class, perhaps for a job that's related to your prospective career. After carefully considering your individual ads in small groups of three or four, create an employment ad for the "job" of college student. For example, "_____ College seeks applicants with excellent skills in oral and written communication, problem solving, time management, and technology, for positions as professional students preparing for a variety of future opportunities...." Your ad should list particular job requirements, benefits, information about your institution, and so on, and be as much like a real ad as possible. When your group is finished constructing its ad, present it to the entire class.[12]

CONTROL: *YOUR TOUGHEST CLASS*

Think about your most challenging class this semester. Is it a general education course or one required for your major? If it's a general education course, make a list of all the ways this course can help you either to further your career or to become a well-educated person. If this course is one in your major, ask yourself why the challenge is so great. Do you understand the course content? Do you see how it connects with the content in other courses? Do you keep up with readings and assignments? Can you follow your instructor's teaching style? Send your instructor in this class an e-mail indicating your specific efforts to do your best and detailing your progress.

In what ways will asking these questions about your classes now *help you in your career* later?

_____

_____

_____

CURIOSITY: *FOCUS YOUR I'S*

Some experts on growing up in our society say it's difficult to transition into adulthood. For many college students today, childhood was where they were given many opportunities: baseball, tennis, soccer, art, music, dance, travel. Their parents—with whom they have close ties—desperately want to help their children become successful. Many parents want to help solve their children's problems for them—with the best of intentions. They may be so eager to help that they try to motivate them with "ladder talk": "If you do well in your community college classes, then you can get admitted to the big university, and if you graduate with a high grade point average there, you can get into a really good law school, and if you do well there, you'll be offered a job with a prestigious firm, and if you prove yourself to your superiors there, eventually you'll make partner." See how it goes—up the ladder of success? This type of communication, which is intended to encourage, can actually discourage some students. Such a long chain of challenging hurdles looks like an impossible dream.

Mel Levine, author of *Ready or Not, Here Life Comes*, says, "We are in the midst of an epidemic of work-life unreadiness because an alarming number of young adults are unable to find a good fit between their minds and their career directions. … Because they are not finding their way, they may feel as if they are going nowhere and have nowhere to go."[13]

How can anyone have nowhere to go with thousands of different occupations or careers to choose from, with countless alternative job titles—for a mind-blowing number of options?[14] The truth is that some students start college and become overwhelmed. Sometime during the first year, or possibly later, they take a step back and announce in so many words, "There are too many choices. I refuse to choose at all."[15]

Here's another tough issue many college graduates face when entering the world of work. Many of them have already decided that work is boring because their part-time jobs in high school and college were boring. They don't want to climb the ladder of success. They'd like to skip the bottom and start somewhere closer to the top rung. But every job involves some element of grunt work, even those at the top. No job is round-the-clock fun, and in every new job, eventually the honeymoon is over, and the tough challenges begin. The simple truth is this: building a career takes time, persistence, dedication, and focus. Seemingly overnight successes like J. K. Rowling of Harry Potter fame are rare; steady progress toward a goal is the norm.[16]

So what does it take to launch your career successfully? You'll need to focus your I's on four things: Inner direction, Interpretation, Instrumentation, and Interaction—the four I's of career-life readiness. Here's what they mean:[17]

Inner direction. How accurate is your view of yourself? Are you honest about your potential? You must first understand the inner you before you can direct it toward a career that fits.

Interpretation. You must interpret the information and apply it in your own way, which demonstrates whether you do (or don't) understand what is involved.

Instrumentation. In your career, you'll need a toolkit filled with different kinds of abilities—engaging in high-level thinking, brainstorming, problem solving, making decisions, tapping your creativity, and cultivating both hard (technical) and soft (interpersonal) skills. And not only must you know how to use each of these tools, but you'll need to know when and why.

Interaction. Business (or any profession) isn't just about facts and figures. It's about people, values, and relationships. People will be what help you build your career. Without people to buy, sell, trade, consume, or produce, there is no business.

The more you focus your I's, the better prepared you'll be for the career challenges ahead.

Regardless of whether you are a younger student coming from high school or an older student coming or returning to college, what are some ways you can focus your I's right now during your college career?

_____

_____

_____

CAREER OUTLOOK: *ZOOM IN, ZOOM OUT*

Perhaps the most common question asked during hiring interviews is this one: "Where do you see yourself in five years?" Undoubtedly, it's a tough question. In today's uncertain economy, the most honest answer is "Are you kidding—who knows? I'm not even sure what I'll have for dinner tonight." Five years seems like forever. Although your imaginary answer may be the most truthful one, it's not necessarily smart.[18]

One thing that trips up many first-year college students is thinking that they have to have it all figured out—now. They think there should be a linear path between their major and their career.[19] For example, a student should enter college having declared a business major, earn business degree, and then land a good job in the business world. "On a clear day," as the old song goes, "you can see forever." It should be that easy.

Realistically, clarity typically unfolds as you go. Many students don't have a particular major or a career in mind. When things become increasingly foggy during their "trip" through college, they lose their way or maybe even give up. Rather than being linear, the path is often nonlinear. You work toward success by keeping two concurrent perspectives in mind: zooming out on your big-picture goals and zooming in on the "up close and personal" details of managing yourself on a daily basis. While you're in college, you must be able to zoom in on your individual courses and zoom out to your overall degree plan. The same principle definitely holds in your career.[20]

So when the time comes and the interviewer asks you the inevitable question, "Where do you see yourself in five years?" take this advice:

1. Reflect on what you will say beforehand.

2. Figure out what the interviewer is trying to learn about you. Does she expect a full-blown answer, or is she just trying to see how you think?

3. Shorten the time frame so that you can answer: "I'm not really sure how many years it will take, but I do know that I want to join an organization just like this one and work on a highly creative team to learn all I can. Challenges are important to me."

On the other hand, don't:

1. Make up something so far-fetched that even you don't believe what you're saying.

2. Identify the exact job you want in the future. ("Honestly? I'd like your job. Are you planning to retire in the next five years?")

3. Feel obliged to answer the question literally, even if you don't really know for sure. Turn the question into one you can answer, communicating what you want the interviewer to know about you.[21] Although you're being asked to zoom out, instead zoom in on who you are and what you want. It's important to keep both perspectives in mind in your journey toward success.

Think about how you would answer the question identified in this section if you were applying for a job you could get today. When you finish your degree or certificate, would you expect your answer to be different in some ways? Might it be the same in some ways?

_____

_____

_____

CHALLENGE: REALITY CHECK

How much did you learn? At the beginning of this chapter, you filled out a "Readiness Check" that asked how you thought this chapter would relate to you and how you would relate to it. Now, fill out this "Reality Check" to find out.

1. What does college in a box mean?

2. What is a SWOT analysis, and how might it help you choose a major and career?

3. How can you try on a career before actually entering it?

4. What does the term *academic anatomy* mean?

How long did it take? _____ hours _____ minutes. Before you began this chapter, you were asked to predict how long it would take you to complete this chapter (total time, even if you read it in more than one sitting). Was your estimate on target, or will you revise it for the next chapter you'll read?_____

INSIGHT *Now* What Do You Think?

At the beginning of this chapter, Ethan Cole, a confused and discouraged student, faced a challenge. Now after reading this chapter, would you respond differently to any of the questions you answered about the "FOCUS Challenge Case"? Using what you learned in the chapter, write a paragraph ending to Ethan's case study. What are some of the possible outcomes for Ethan?

step 4 **ACTION** Your Plans for Change

1. Where are you when it comes to choosing a major or career? If you haven't decided yet, what specific information from this chapter will you use? If you've already decided, had you already taken these suggestions into account? Will you change any of your plans?

2. Do you know someone working in a career field that is disillusioned or disappointed with the choice he or she made? How will you know your decision is a wise one? What can you do to make sure?

chapter 12 Creating Your Future

READINESS CHECK

How this chapter relates to **YOU**

1. When it comes to creating a future for yourself, what, if anything, do you find challenging?

Launching a career

Writing an impressive resume

Interviewing successfully

Knowing whether to continue my education

Figuring out what's next for me

2. What's is most likely to be your response? Circle it.

| I'll concentrate on learning new skills. | I'll see whether this chapter helps me. | I'll talk with an instructor or advisor. | Eventually, I'll just figure it out on my own. |

3. What would you have to do to increase your likelihood of success? Will you do it this quarter or semester?

Example: Find a role model to talk with about these issues. Yes!

How **YOU** will relate to this chapter

What are you most interested in learning about? Put checkmarks by those topics.

☐ How to launch a career
☐ How to write a résumé
☐ How to interview successfully
☐ What to consider if you're thinking of continuing your education
☐ How to put what you've learned in college to good use
☐ How to think about the future

- How motivated are you to learn more about getting the right start in college? (5 = high, 1 = low) ___

- How ready are you to read now? ___ (If something is in your way, take care of it if you can, zero in and focus.)

- How long do you think it will take you to complete this chapter? If you start and stop, keep track of your overall time. ___ hour(s) ___ minutes

Anthony Lopez

Anthony Lopez was average in nearly every sense of the word. He played T-ball as a kid, but not particularly well. He didn't like school much, but he went when he felt like it. He didn't have many friends except for a few kids that lived in the eight city blocks that made up his neighborhood. He was even sandwiched between two older brothers and two younger sisters. His brothers were successful—one was an attorney and the other a doctor. Somehow, deep inside himself, Anthony knew that measuring up would be hard for him. Maybe that's why he decided to make his mark in his own way.

You could say that Anthony's kid sister, Gina, was his closest friend. Even though she was four years younger, the two of them would pal around the neighborhood. They could laugh over absolutely anything, and their specialty was pulling pranks on all the other neighborhood kids. For a while, the two of them were inseparable. Whenever you saw Gina, you knew that Anthony was close by.

But as Anthony got older, things changed. The trouble started in middle school. His mom, who worked more than one job to keep the family afloat, was worried that he was getting in with the wrong crowd. But Anthony wasn't worried. His friends knew where to get cigarettes and alcohol—even drugs. When he was with them, he imagined the other kids looked up to him and his tough-guy friends. By the time high school rolled around, Anthony already had a record. Eventually, he dropped out, left home, and basically lived on the streets. When he needed money, he snatched a purse or wallet. He lost contact with his family, and there seemed to be no turning back. Drugs were a way of life for him, and he began sinking deeper and deeper into a life that most people predicted wouldn't turn out well.

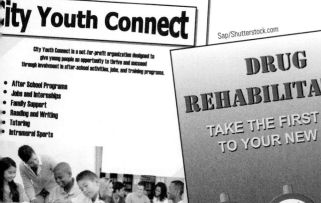

City Youth Connect

City Youth Connect is a not-for-profit organization designed to give young people an opportunity to thrive and succeed through involvement in after-school activities, jobs, and training programs.

- After School Programs
- Jobs and Internships
- Family Support
- Reading and Writing
- Tutoring
- Intramural Sports

Contact Nicky Russo
2015 East Front St

DRUG REHABILITATION

TAKE THE FIRST STEP TO YOUR NEW LIFE

Criminal Search- County

Name: Lopez, Anthony   **DOB:** 7-10-1989   **SSN:** XXX-XX-XXX

RESULT: RECORD FOUND

STATE/COUNTY:	VERIFIED INFORMATION
Case #:	T3-13145
Filing Date:	8-18-08
Offense Date:	8-03-08
Disposition Date:	9-05-08

Charges:

(MISDEMEANOR) PETTY LARCENY - THEFT

But that was then, and this was now. Anthony's life probably would have been headed in the wrong direction entirely, if it hadn't been for several wakeup calls, including seeing his little sister, Gina, on the street one day. He tried to talk with her, but she was so high that she didn't even recognize him. Anthony saw that she was repeating his worst mistakes, which troubled him deeply. The stark realization that he might be ruining her life in addition to his own shocked him back into reality.

Now Anthony was part of an inner-city youth organization for kids like him. The group's leader, Nicky Russo, had once been a gang member himself. He reached out to Anthony, and Anthony responded. Anthony was on a mission to find Gina and get her into the group. Anthony's life was changing, and his life's goal was becoming clear: to help other people like him. He decided to earn his GED and enroll in the best community college he could find to earn an associate's degree in social services. And that's exactly what he did.

As he sat in his favorite class, Urban Social Issues, Anthony realized that he had made the right choice. So much of what he heard his instructor lecturing about had been a part of his own past. As he got deeper into the associate's program, Anthony learned that an associate's degree in social services was a general degree that prepared graduates for many types of jobs. But what if he wanted to be an actual social work-

er? He learned that the need for social workers was very high, working with young children to older adults. He was taking classes like Racial, Ethnic, and Minority Groups and Sociology of the Family.

Even though the classes were hard, it wasn't long before Anthony was totally engrossed, and he knew he wanted to continue his education. With an associate's degree in social services, he could certainly work more knowledgeably alongside Nicky in the inner city. But what if he transferred to a four-year school for a bachelor's degree in sociology? What if he wanted to earn a master's degree in social work to specialize and become a school or hospital social worker? What if he wanted to conduct research and teach, like his community college instructors? What would getting a Ph.D. require, and should he even be thinking that far ahead? A million questions were forming in his mind.

What did the future hold for Anthony? Right now, he couldn't answer that question. But he did know that his future would be different from the future he might have had without college. What had always been true about Anthony was now true in the best possible sense: Anthony would make his mark.

Scholastic Studio 10/Getty Images

© Cengage Learning

© Cengage Learning

Sociology Program Comparison

	Bachelor Degree
Ethnic Relations	
City in a Global Society	
Societal Change and Development	
Environmental Sociology	
Global Sociology	
Sociological Analysis	
Classical Theories of Society	
Contemporary Theories of Society	
Sociological Field Methods	
Gender and Society	
Global Sociology	
Quantitative Methods	
Regression and Multivariate Data Analysis	
Policy Issues in Education	
Economics of Educational Policy	
Public Policy	
Demographic Analysis	
Evaluation of Educational Programs	
Race and Class in American Cities	
Masters Thesis Project	
Qualitative Research	
Sociological Analysis	

Philip Lange/Shutterstock.com

An urban sociology text that helps you understand the past, present & future of cities around the globe

Klemewski · Thomas

FOURTH EDITION

Cities, Change & Conflict

A POLITICAL ECONOMY OF URBAN LIFE

SOCIAL SERVICES
ASSOCIATE OF ARTS DEGREE

The AA degree with an emphasis in Sociology is designed to provide a better understanding of how humans act and interact in social settings. The program offered provides an excellent foundation for students seeking to continue their education in Sociology, either pursuing a Bachelor's or Master's degree.

First Semester	
	3
ENGL 101 English Composition I	3
SOC 101 Introduction to Sociology	3
Science Elective	3
Humanities Elective	12
Total Credits	

Second Semester	
	3

1. Do you have anything in common with Anthony? If so, how are you managing the situation so that you can be successful?

2. Anthony appears to be headed toward a life of service. Do you know anyone like him who has turned his or her life around? Describe the situation.

3. What are the pros and cons of continuing his education beyond an associate's degree?

4. In your view, should he continue his education beyond a two-year degree? Why or why not?

What's the Next Step?

You've done it. You've nearly finished your first term of college. Perhaps at this point, you're even jumping ahead to when you finish all of your courses. Then what? Yogi Berra, the baseball giant, is known for having a way with words. His advice was, "When you come to a fork in the road, take it." *Which one?* you ask. Precisely! (Yogi Berra is said to have been giving directions to his New Jersey home, and both streets worked equally well.)

After you achieve your community college goals—whether you're taking a few targeted classes for a particular reason or earning a certificate or associate's degree—you'll come to a fork in the road. Should you take the fork leading toward pursuing a particular career right away or the fork leading toward continuing your education? This chapter won't answer the question *for* you, but it will give you some things to think about. Just as was the case with Yogi Berra's famous advice, both forks in *your* road will lead you toward the same thing: *your* future. What you decide to do and when you decide to do it will be up to you.

VARK It!

Visual: Draw a mind map that shows the various "forks" in your future. Where might you go, and why? Provide some possibilities and reasons.

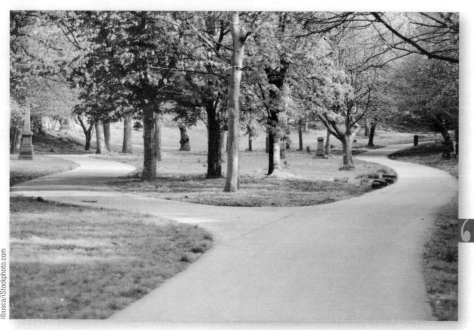

illbusca/iStockphoto.com

> When you come to a fork in the road, take it.

Yogi Berra, baseball player and manager

Launching a Career: Plan Your Work and Work Your Plan

Career Auction

Assume you have $100,000 to spend on the following items. In a few minutes, your instructor will begin a real-live auction, putting one item at a time up for auction. Before the auction begins, budget your money in the first column. You may select as many items as you wish to bid on, but you may not place all your money on any single item. As the group auction proceeds, fill in the appropriate amounts that are actually spent by members of the class for each item.

	BUDGETED AMOUNT	WINNING BID
1. Becoming the CEO of a leading Fortune 500 company	_____	_____
2. Being a top earner in your career field	_____	_____
3. Being the number-one expert in your profession	_____	_____
4. Having good friends on the job	_____	_____
5. Being your own boss	_____	_____
6. Creating a good balance between productive work and a happy family life	_____	_____
7. Having opportunities for travel and adventure in your job	_____	_____
8. Doing work you find fully satisfying	_____	_____
9. Working in a beautiful setting	_____	_____
10. Being a lifelong learner so that your career can develop and change over time	_____	_____

Let's assume, for now, that you decide to go straight into your chosen career field after community college. You've been focused all along, earned your degree, and now you're ready to find a job that fits your new skills, your personality—*you*! "Fit" is the key word in that last sentence. Where you choose to launch your career and who you work with will be critical factors in your job satisfaction.

The two questions posed early in this book resurface now: "Who are you?" and "What do you want?" Working your way through *FOCUS*, you have learned more about who you are (although this is a lifelong quest). In this final chapter, we'll deal with "What do you want?" The answer to that question can be just as important.

What do you really want from a career? What's important to you? Even though your views may change over time, it's important to start thinking about them now. In Exercise 12.1, item 4, "Having good friends on the job," may be a top priority now, but item 5, "Being your own boss," may be more

> I always wanted to be somebody, but I should have been more specific.
>
> *Lily Tomlin, comedian*

appealing a few years down the road, after you have some additional work experience under your belt. Maybe you already prepared for a career once, but something has changed. The field you entered has transformed over time, so that you need to retool. Or a career that attracted you earlier turned out to be much less engaging than you expected. Or your family has grown and you need a career that brings in more resources. That's what community colleges are for. You may be older than the students sitting around you, but you deserve the same educational opportunities. Interestingly, according to research, the most important factor in job satisfaction isn't any of the ten items in Exercise 12.1. The number one contributor to job satisfaction, statistically speaking, is the quality of your relationship with your boss.[1] Here are some suggestions to help you launch the career you're aiming for.

Try on a Career for Size

If all your jobs thus far have been just that—*jobs*—to help you pay the bills, how do you know what you want in a *career*? A career is different from a job. It's a profession you've chosen and prepared for. Perhaps you've had more than a string of jobs, and your career is well underway, but now you'd like to go in a different direction. Or perhaps you haven't launched your career yet. Exactly how *do* you launch a new career? You have to start somewhere, so perhaps you'd search online or through actual newspaper want ads. There are plenty of career exploration websites online. Check out these career mega websites to explore some options:

> Careerbuilder.com

> Monster.com

> The Occupational Outlook Handbook (www.bls.gov/oco/)

> Americasjobexchange.com/

> Career-Journal.com

> US.jobs/ (by the National Labor Exchange)

> USAJobs.gov

> TrueCareers.com

> AllJobSearch.com[2]

VARK It!

Multimodal (Kinesthetic/ Aural): Visit a few of these websites with another student from class. As you're browsing, discuss the specific benefits of each website.

You can Google and surf to your heart's content.

But you may be likely to read something like this: "Opening in . . . (anything). Experience required." Isn't that the way it always goes? You have to *have* experience in order to get a job that will *give* you experience. This problem is one many people face. Sure, you have experience. It's just not the right kind. Perhaps you've bagged fries, mowed yards, bussed tables, and chauffeured pizzas up to this point. If that's not the kind of experience the posted opening is looking for, how do you get the right kind? Or perhaps you're in school to switch career fields. You have experience, but it won't help you go in a different direction. The process of job-hunting includes many different steps. Here are some things for you to consider doing during your time in college. One important suggestion is to try a job on for size. Take a look at the three possibilities described in Figure 12.1.

It is not what we get but who we become, what we contribute . . . that gives meaning to our lives.

Anthony Robbins, motivational speaker and author

These experiences help you in three ways. First, they allow you to test a potential career field. The actual day-to-day work may be exactly what you expected, or not. They show you whether that particular career field is one you'd really be interested in. *I had no idea this field was so cutthroat, hectic, dull . . . exciting, stimulating, invigorating. . . .* A thumbs-down can be just as informative as a thumbs-up. At least you can remove one option from your list. Second, internships, co-ops, and service-learning opportunities give you experience to list on your résumé. And third, they help you make connections with others in the field, and sometimes they even lead to employment.

The key to successful trial experiences such as internships is the relationship between you and your sponsor in the host organization. If you're not being given enough to do, or not allowed to test your skills in a particular area, speak up. The answer may be put in terms of company policy, or you're "not quite ready for prime time." Nevertheless, you must communicate about these kinds of important issues. No one can read your mind! As you work toward launching your career, keep up with the latest information. Read up on résumé writing and interviewing, networking, hot career fields, and the latest employment trends. Use the information in this chapter to pique your interest, and search further on your own.

	Description: What is . . . ?	What kind of experience do I get?	Why would I want to do it?	How do I get involved?
An Internship	An internship is an opportunity for you to work alongside a professional in a career field of interest to you, and to learn from him or her.	Your supervisor will mentor you, and you'll get a clearer picture of what the career field is like.	Some majors will require you to complete an internship as a part of your program, for licensure or certification, for example.	Internships may be offered through your academic major department, or through a central office on campus, or sometimes you can pursue one on your own through the Internet or personal connections.
A Co-op Program	Co-op programs allow you to take classes and then apply what you've learned on the job, either after or while you take classes.	You may take classes for a term and then work full-time for a term. You can test a career field.	A potential employer can get a sense of your potential, and you can gain practical experience to put on your résumé.	Your advisor will be able to tell you whether your program has co-op opportunities.
Service-Learning	Some classes contain service-learning experiences in which you volunteer your time.	A service-learning component built right into the syllabus can give you valuable, practical experience.	The emphasis is on hands-on learning and connecting what you're learning in class with what you're experiencing out of class. If you take a class on aging, for example, you may work with a senior citizen at an assisted living facility to apply what you're learning in class.	If you're particularly interested in hands-on learning, ask your advisor to recommend classes with service-learning components that will benefit you.

FIGURE 12.1

Three Ways to Try a Job on for Size

Group Résumé[3]

Your instructor will provide a sheet of newsprint and several markers per team of three to four students. Your job is to work on the floor, desktops, or somewhere with sufficient space to create a group résumé, highlighting all the characteristics you bring with you as a group that can help you succeed in college. Your combined group qualifications may look like this:

Qualifications:

- 27 combined years of work experience
- background in four different industries
- familiarity with Word, PowerPoint, Photoshop, and Excel
- proven research skills
- eagerness to learn
- well-developed time management skills
- interest in networking with others

After each team has completed the task, hang the newsprint sheets on the walls to create a gallery and present your group résumé to the rest of the class.

Build a Portfolio of Your Best Work

Even though it feels good to progress through your degree plan, and move on from one course to another, it's important to keep a record of each class. A potential employer may want to know exactly what you learned in Principles of Web Design, so that she can tell if what you learned matches the way her company does things. An interviewer may ask you about the course you were most successful in. You don't want to stammer and say, "Uh, let me get back to you on that. . . ." You want to sound knowledgeable. Build a portfolio of your best work. Your community college may have a formal way to help you do that through a course management system like Blackboard or an online electronic portfolio requirement, for example. If not, begin compiling a portfolio of your own. Keep copies of your best papers or other assignments, and write a summary of how each assignment relates to your career goals. If a prospective employer asks you about your writing skills, you can produce a paper on the spot. Or if you bring a laptop with you to an interview, you can access your best PowerPoint presentation or show a website you designed yourself.

VARK It!

Kinesthetic: Build a portfolio of your best work from each learning style. For example, include your best essay, best recorded (video or audio) presentation, and so on.

Network, Network, Network!

The old saying is partially true: "It's not *what* you know, it's *who* you know." Who you know *is* important, but what you know is important, too. Another version

Don't follow your dreams; chase them.

Richard Dumb

iStockphoto.com/Michael Svoboda

"To dare is to lose one's footing momentarily. To not dare is to lose oneself.

Soren Kierkegaard, Danish philosopher and theologian (1813–1855)

of the saying, which is more accurate, goes like this: "It's not who you know, it's who you know, knows (and who THEY know)." If you're a Facebook addict, put these skills to work as you start to launch your career. Online sites help you "hook up" professionally with people who can help you, like LinkedIn (www.linkedin.com), where you can build an online network of contacts, contacts of your contacts, and so forth. In minutes, you can find thousands of people who know people who work in the industry you're interested in. According to the site, you can connect, stay informed about your contacts and industry, and find the people and knowledge you need to achieve your goals. And of course, instead or in addition, you can network with real people in person, too. Ask people you know about who they know that works in your career field, contact these people, meet for coffee, for example, and pursue networking the old-fashioned (but highly effective) way.[4]

Write the Right Résumé

Interestingly, today companies may receive hundreds of applications for particular positions. Some experts say that instead of simply looking at resumes, companies may request and look at your social media presence on Facebook, LinkedIn, blogs, YouTube, and so forth. This trend has already begun.[5] However, learning how to write a written resume is still a vital skill for most of the jobs you might apply for.

In today's competitive world, when literally hundreds of people may be applying for one choice position, how should a résumé be written? Can a résumé be solid, but not stuffy? Professional, but still personal? Thorough, but brief? Actually, there's more than one way to write a résumé, depending on how much experience you have in the career field you'd like to work in.

> **Skills Approach:** If your work experience has little to do with the career field you'd like to enter, but you've learned important skills you could transfer to your new job, use a *skills* approach, as shown in Marcus Brown's resume.

> **Chronological Approach:** If you have a work history that's relevant, use a chronological approach (that details job by job what you've done), as shown in Jennifer Ortega's resume.

Take a look to see whether you can detect the differences between these two sample applicants' résumés. Assume they earned the same degree and are applying for the same job.

chronological arranging information in time order beginning with the most recent job

© Larry Harwood Photography. Property of Cengage Learning.

VARK It!

Visual: Draw a diagram of how networking might help you in the future. For example, draw a line from you to your instructor, and from your instructor to a business professional he or she knows.

MARCUS BROWN
1234 Aspen Way, Apartment 105
Great Bluffs, CO 89898
(555) 987-6543
mbrown@gbcc.edu

CAREER OBJECTIVE
To obtain a position as a web designer for a large health care organization

EDUCATION
Great Bluffs Community College, Great Bluffs, CO
Certificate in Web Design
GPA 3.2/4.0
Personally financed 100% of college tuition by working two jobs

HONORS
Selected for City Council Outstanding Leadership Award (College Division), 2012
Awarded Technology Scholarship, GBCC Foundation

SUMMARY OF ACADEMIC COURSEWORK

Introduction to Web Graphics   Web Development Software
Introduction to Web Multimedia   Electronic Commerce
Principles of Web Design   Emerging Technologies

SKILLS
Technology
Do part-time freelance work, web-page design
Work in Word, PowerPoint, Excel, Access, Macromedia Flash, Dreamweaver, Java, HTML,
    PHP, Adobe Acrobat, and Photoshop
Graphics
Designed flyers and posters for campus events for GBCC Office of Campus Activities
Writing
Wrote columns for GBCC student online newsletter

EMPLOYMENT HISTORY
Server, Pancake Heaven, 2008–2009
Cashier, Toyland, 2008–present
Ticket Taker, Movies at the Mall, 2008–present

REFERENCES (available on request)

It's likely that Marcus Brown is a traditionally aged college student. Notice that he has little experience in the field he'd like to work in after getting his certificate in Web Design. Contrast his résumé with the following one, where Jennifer Ortega has considerable experience working in the IT field. Rather than using a skills approach, her résumé uses a chronological approach that shows everything she's done that's related to the job she's applying for.

You may automatically assume that Jennifer has the advantage over Marcus, but the health care company with the opening may be looking for fresh,

JENNIFER ORTEGA
789 Breckenridge Court, Apartment C
Great Bluffs, CO 89898
(555) 333-9999
jortega@gbcc.edu

CAREER OBJECTIVE

To obtain a position as a web designer in a large health care organization

> Jennifer has had several jobs in the IT field. On her résumé, she lists what she did in each one that might be useful in the job she wants.

EMPLOYMENT HISTORY

2009–present   Technology Helpdesk Manager, Central College
· Developed new phone answering system that increased the unit's responsiveness by 50%
· Oversaw a staff of 10 student technology experts
· Installed software and made troubleshooting visits to approximately 15 faculty offices per week

> Numbers are important and memorable! Notice how they stand out.

2008–2009   IT Supervisor, Great Bluffs School District 1
· Coordinated software maintenance in 12 elementary school administrative offices
· Managed a team of 8 technology employees
· Installed financial software to improve budget management at the K-6 level

2004–2008   Sales staff member, Tech 4 U, Great Bluffs, Colorado
· Earned Salesperson of the Quarter Award, Jan–Mar, 2008
· Recognized with Sales and Service Award, June 2008
· Initiated store display rearrangement

> Notice that Jennifer gives specific dates and has listed a variety of things to discuss with an interviewer.

EDUCATION

Great Bluffs Community College, Great Bluffs, CO
Certificate in Web Design
GPA 3.2/4.0
Personally financed 100% of college tuition

HONORS

Selected as the student body representative to GBCC faculty government
Earned a place on the GBCC Dean's Honor Role each term

> Note that there are many different ways to say the same thing. Jennifer has noted that she was selected as the student representative. She has chosen particular wording to emphasize that this was an honor.

SUMMARY OF ACADEMIC COURSEWORK

Introduction to Web Graphics   Web Development Software
Introduction to Web Multimedia   Electronic Commerce
Principles of Web Design   Emerging Technologies

SKILLS

Technology
Do part-time freelance work, web-page design
Work in Word, PowerPoint, Excel, Access, Macromedia Flash, Dreamweaver, Java, HTML, PHP, Adobe InDesign, Acrobat, and Photoshop

> Notice that Jennifer starts each phrase with a verb to emphasize action, and that all verbs are in the same tense (past or present).

Graphics
Design brochures for local health care organizations as a freelancer:
    Forest Hills Rehabilitation Center, Mercy Hospital, and Sunnydale Senior Center

Writing
Write brochure content after consulting with management at these organizations

REFERENCES (available on request)

© 2014 Cengage Learning

Cover Letter Critique

When you submit a résumé, either in person, through the mail, or online, you should send a well-written cover letter along with it that briefly outlines your qualifications for the job, expresses your interest, and gives the person who reviews your résumé some idea of who you are. Take a look at the following cover letter from Marcus Brown and critique it. What has he done right, and what has he done wrong?

---

15 September

To Whom It May Concenr,

I'd like to apply for your opening at Anderson-Wallace Healthcare Industries. I have heard a lot about your company and it sounds great. A friend of mine works there, and he said his starting salary was unbelieveable. What exactly do you do at your company? He's told me a few things, but I'm eager to learn more!

As you can see from my résumé, I don't have much experience. But I have just earned my web design certificate from GBCC, and I did pretty well. I want to start my career at a great company like yours.

I hope to hear from you soon.

Warmly,

Marcus Brown

After finding the mistakes Marcus made, rewrite this letter to bring to class or submit to your instructor.

new talent, and Marcus should capitalize on his web design freelance work or get an actual internship with a professional web designer. Everyone has to start somewhere. Do your best with whichever approach fits you. Finally, remember that you can hire a professional to write a résumé for you, but if you read up on résumé writing and follow the suggestions here, you can do just fine on your own. Hiring a professional or going through an employment agency can be helpful, but they can also be expensive propositions. And if they promise you the moon ("You'll have a new job at the starting salary of your dreams in just one week!"), be wary.

Interview at Your Best

By now, you have probably already been interviewed several times to get a job. But when you're ready to launch your career, you'll be facing interviews for the new job you really want, the one you prepared for by earning a certificate or degree. Often interviewers aren't particularly skilled at asking questions. They haven't been trained on how to interview prospective employees, so they just ask whatever questions come to them. And often, interviewees don't quite know what they're doing either. Of course, you should always be honest, but there are various ways to communicate the same information. Telling an interviewer you "like to work alone" sounds antisocial. But if you say you "like to really focus on what you're doing without distractions," you show dedication to your work ethic. You also need to be aware of real pitfalls to avoid. See what you think of these suggestions.

1. **Play up the positive, and downplay the negative.** A trap question interviewers sometimes ask is "What's your worst fault?" Although you may be tempted to say the first thing that comes to mind, that could be a big mistake. "Umm . . . sleeping too much! I really like to sleep in. Sometimes I sleep half the day away." Not good. But some faults you could identify might actually be seen as strengths: "I have a little too much nervous energy. I'm always on the go. I like to stay busy."

2. **Stay focused.** "Tell me about yourself" is a common question interviewers ask. How much time do you have? Most of us like to talk about ourselves, but it's important to stay on track. Think possible questions through in advance, and construct some hypothetical answers. Keep your answers job focused: what your long-term career goals are, how this job can help you prepare, what you liked about your last job. You don't need to go into your family background or your personal problems. And it's always a bad idea to bash a previous job or former boss. The interviewer may worry that you'll bring whatever didn't work there with you to this new job.

3. **Don't just give answers, get some.** A job interview is like a first date. Find out what you need to know. If the job is one you're interested in long term, ask questions such as these three key ones:

   > **What does this company value?** Listen to the answer. Hard work? New ideas? Communication skills? The answer will tell you about the personality of the company.

   > **What's a typical day like for you?** Ask the interviewer. An answer such as "I get up at 5:00 A.M., get here at 6:30 A.M., and go home around 7:00 P.M.—and then I do paperwork all evening" tells you something. This may—or may not—be the job or the company for you.

   > **What happened to the last person in this job?** If you find out he was promoted, that's one thing. But if you learn he was fired or quit, see whether you can find out why. Maybe he had job performance problems, or maybe this is an impossible job that no one could do well. Listen to the interviewer. She may be looking for an opportunity to tell you things she thinks are important, too.

4. **Watch for questions that seem to come out of left field.** Some companies like to get creative with their interviewing. Microsoft, for example, is known for asking problem-solving questions, such as "If you could remove any of the fifty states, which would it be? Be prepared to give specific reasons why you chose the state you did." There is no right or wrong answer, although some answers are better than others. ("We should just nuke state X. I had a bad experience there once" would probably concern some people, and naming Washington state, where Microsoft is located, might be a bad choice.) The interviewer just wants to hear how you can think critically and give reasons for your answers.[8] Remember: Today's interviewers are looking for more than technical skills; they're looking for critical thinking skills, problem-solving skills, and creativity.[9]

5. **Don't start off with salary questions.** Make sure the first question out of your mouth isn't "So tell me about the salary again? Any way to notch that up

VARK It!

Aural: Interview someone in your intended career field. Be prepared to report back to class or e-mail your instructor the results.

a bit?" The last thing you want to do is give the interviewer the idea you're in it for the money. Of course, you are, but not just for that. More importantly, in every job you have, you'll gain experience and knowledge that will always better prepare you for every job that will be a part of your long-term career. Don't start negotiating a salary until you've actually been offered a job.

6. **Negotiate wisely.** If the interviewer asks you to name a salary figure, be careful. Saying "I could probably live on $30,000," when the actual figure the interviewer is authorized to start with is $38,000, has just given the employer the option to lower the salary, based on your expectations. A good rule of thumb is: Never name a number. It's always best to ask the interviewer what the salary range for the job is. It's also good to research the salaries of similar jobs, and it's even better to have another job offer you're considering, so you have choices. Otherwise, you're not negotiating; you're begging.[10]

7. **Know what you're dealing with.** One of the easiest ways to blow a job interview is by doing nothing. Candidates who don't do their homework usually don't pass an interview. If the interviewer asks, "So what do you know about the company?" and you reply, "Oh, not much, but I'm a fast learner," you'll be perceived to care very little about the outcome of the interview. Go online to read up about the place you'd like to work. Your knowledge, and therefore your interest, will show. And it goes without saying (although here it is, anyway) that you should arrive early, dress professionally, overprepare, and send a follow-up thank-you note or e-mail.[11]

Continuing Your Education

Like Anthony Lopez, perhaps you're exploring the idea of continuing your education. Typically, the more education you get, the more money you can make, the more you can do, and the more responsibility you have. Figure 12.2 summarizes both earnings and unemployment rates by educational level achieved, but the decision to continue is yours and yours alone. You know yourself and your interests best.

FIGURE 12.2

Education Pays

Source: Bureau of Labor Statistics. (2012, March 23). Available at http://www.bls.gov/emp/ep_chart_001.htm.

	Associate's Degree in Social (Human) Services	Bachelor's Degree in Sociology (or a related field)	Master's of Social Work (MSW)	Ph.D. in Sociology (or Doctorate of Social Work)
Average Time to Complete:	2 years	4–5 years	2 years beyond a bachelor's degree	3–4 years beyond a master's degree
Average Number of Required Courses:	Approximately 20	Approximately 40	10 courses and 900 hours of supervised field experience or internship	10 (plus dissertation)
Type of Work:	Social Service Assistant or Aid: work with social workers, pharmacists, psychologists, etc. Varying levels of responsibility. Help people in need.	Social Worker (although an MSW is increasingly required): help clients cope with disabilities (like substance abuse or homelessness). Work in schools, public health agencies, hospitals, etc., and visit clients in their homes.	Social Worker clinical work: supervise other social workers, manage case loads. Must pass state licensure exam. May wish to go into private practice at least part-time. May specialize in such areas as • Child, family, or schools • Medical and public health • Mental health and substance abuse	Professor, High-level administrator, researcher: May teach at the college or university level, conduct research, or run a health-care or nonprofit organization, for example.
Future Demand:	Higher than average. Expected growth of 28 percent between 2010 and 2020.	Favorable (varies by type of specialization).	Favorable, much faster than average (varies by type of specialization).	Generally good for faculty positions (although varies by type of specialization and preference for full- or part-time work).
Median salary:	$28,200 (as of May 2010)	$42,480 (as of May 2010)	$48,140 and higher (as of May 2010)	$62,050 (for all full-time college professors as of May 2010)

FIGURE 12.3

An Educational Career Path[12]

There are two mistakes one can make along the road to truth . . . not going all the way and not starting.

Buddha (c. 563–483 B.C.)

By the end of the "FOCUS Challenge Case," Anthony was considering four alternatives: an associate's degree, a bachelor's degree, a master's degree, and a Ph.D. Each level of these four educational paths has distinct differences he needs to know about. Anthony seems to have "found his bliss," and his heart is in the work. He is convinced that being a social worker is the right career field for him. He is motivated, engaged in what he's learning, and looking forward to a career of service. But at what level? Figure 12.3 lists some basic considerations for Anthony. Can you compare his choices to ones you may be considering?

If Anthony thinks he may wish to take the first step beyond getting his associate's degree, he must begin planning now. Sometimes students who transfer to a four-year institution experience what's called "transfer shock." Courses can be taught differently, classes can be larger, and in a class with several hundred students, the atmosphere can seem more impersonal. According to research, math and science courses, in particular, may seem (and be) harder.[13] The campus itself may have a very different feel to it, and transfer students can feel lost and isolated, which can hurt their academic performance. Anthony must work closely with his community college advisor and an advisor at the school where he plans to transfer, to make sure his credits are transferable. His goal should be to make the process as seamless as possible by visiting the new campus now and talking with advisors and professors there. Take control of the situation: Ask for help, if you need it, and get involved in campus life.[14]

The important thing for Anthony—and for you—is to determine what you really want. Many different educational and career paths exist. Don't feel pressure from others to continue your education if you know that decision isn't right for you—or isn't right for you *now*. Think about your goals in life, what you want to achieve, and what kind of work you would find most fulfilling, and then decide which educational level is right for you.

EXERCISE 12.4

Circling the Right Career[15]

Different people are motivated by different types of careers. Think of motivation as three overlapping circles, with one circle labeled "Service," one labeled "Power," and one labeled "Money." Anthony Lopez is choosing a career that focuses primarily on service. Power and money are not particularly important to him, it seems. Think of six different careers (several of which you may be considering), and place them on the chart wherever you think they belong. Start with careers that you think belong primarily in one circle, and then brainstorm some careers that overlap into two (money and power, for example). Can you think of any careers that contain elements of all three circles? Then compare notes with your classmates. Where would you put the career you think you would find most fulfilling?

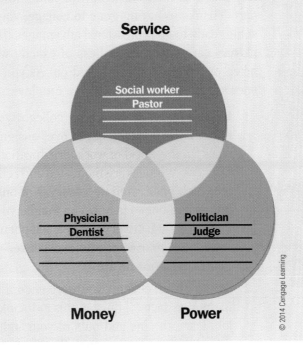

> **Time is the quality of nature that keeps events from happening all at once. Lately it doesn't seem to be working.**
> —ANONYMOUS

12. They lack time management skills

Your time management skills are something a prospective employer will be interested in. An interviewer may ask you: "How good are you at focusing when you have to juggle several different projects?" or "This is a fast-paced company. Are you willing to work overtime?" It seems that most jobs today require a significant—sometimes frantic—investment of your time and energy. When requests are coming at you from all sides on the job, how will you fare? Can you sharpen your focus and prioritize?

TRY It!

At the beginning of each day, decide on three things that must get done, no matter what. Check back at the end of the day to see how successful you've been. If you're a stay-at-home mom, it may be preparing three nutritious meals for your kids. If you're in the workforce, it may be making continual progress on a big project with a deadline. When everything seems to be happening at once, you have to decide which of those things are most important. Try it tomorrow.

Priority 1:

Priority 2:

Priority 3:

Put What You've Learned to Good Use: Ten Things Employers Hope You Will Learn in College

You must motivate yourself EVERY DAY!

Matthew Stasior, motivational speaker

Regardless of which fork in the road you choose—launching a career or transferring to a four-year school—college teaches many lessons, and they're not all about the subject matter in your classes. Much of the academic professionalism you've developed in college can easily translate into career professionalism, with some thought and application on your part. Thanks to having gone to college, you can begin your career with some ready-to-go professional advantages. Here is a set of ten things employers care about, regardless of exactly which college courses you've taken or degree you've worked on. As you evaluate, think about which ones are already in place for you. Employers want you to:

1. **Exhibit a work ethic.** In college, you demonstrated your work ethic. Perhaps you labored over assignments to produce your best work. In the world of work, organizations prefer to hire winners, not slackers. Winners are motivated and reliable. They know how to kick into high gear when necessary. Not only is day-to-day performance important, but so is how you handle yourself at crunch time. Someone once said, "Every job is a self-portrait of the person who did it. Autograph your work with excellence." Your work ethic says a great deal about who you are.

2. **Study up.** In college, you were encouraged to learn deeply, not just memorize facts. Transfer this principle to the workplace. On the job, learn the ins and outs of your industry. If you are an automotive mechanic, know more than just about the nuts and bolts and

transmissions of the cars you work on. Learn about the automobile maker's history, what the company stands for, its vision and values, and the reputation it has earned from customers. It's easy to get tunnel vision and lose sight of the bigger picture.

3. **Prove you're a problem solver.** While taking your college classes, you learned problem-solving skills. Some of those problems were personal (*Who can I get to watch my kids at the last minute?*), and some were academic (*Why* was *Edgar Allen Poe so "dark"?*). On the job, everyone values the person who comes up with a workable solution when everyone else is stumped. And your boss will value you more if you come up with solutions yourself. Instead of, *What should I do about X?* say, *We're facing Problem X. Should I do A, B, or C?* You've proven that you've already thought about the problem and generated three possible solutions and demonstrated that you can think on your own.

Goals are the fuel in the furnace of achievement.

Brian Tracy, Eat that Frog

4. **Speak and write well.** Your college career may have put more emphasis on these skills than any others. In today's world of abbreviated text messages (AYS = Are you serious?) and empty conversation ("And she's . . . like so . . . you know . . . whatever . . ."), you can become a super star on the job by just speaking and writing well. And in addition to speaking and writing, learn to listen to what's *really* being said and why. With practice, you can listen past the bravado or baloney and get to the *real* message. That's important!

5. **Polish your people skills.** Your college instructors may have assigned group projects in your classes to help you learn teamwork skills. Good teamwork skills are key to a successful career in anything! People can be difficult to work with, yet *people* are the way work gets done.

6. **Learn the rules of the game.** In school—and throughout your life—you have learned what's sometimes called "The Hidden Curriculum": things everyone knows, more or less, but never learned formally. For example, most people know that it's not polite to tell off-color jokes to people you've just met or smack your gum while giving a speech. In the same way, on the job, the "grapevine," or informal network, is important to understand. To be successful, you must be tuned in. Understand the culture of the organization you work for. What does it value? Who holds the power? Where do you fit in, and what can you contribute?

When one door closes, another opens. But often we look so long, so regretfully, upon the closed door that we fail to see the one that has opened for us.

Helen Keller, American author, activist, and lecturer (1880–1968)

7. **Know how to gather information and use it.** In college, you're asked to develop your research skills. It's easy to think that each paper for a class is just another assignment to check off the list, when, actually, you're developing skills that will be critical to your success later. You don't just string together pieces of information when you do research for your college classes. You analyze research through the "eyes" of the problem you're trying to address and *your* perspective on it. You weave ideas together to make an argument.

8. **Understand that numbers count.** Unfortunately, math gets a bad rap. Many people approach math classes in college with "fear and loathing," when, actually, math is a key to success in the world of work. If you can understand spreadsheets or figure out the budget, you'll be ahead of the game. Some people de-emphasize the importance of financial skills by referring to them as "bean counting" or "number crunching," but people who know how to apply math on the job are highly sought after.

9. **Go for extra credit.** In some of your courses, your instructors may give extra credit. You could be allowed to do something extra, beyond the requirements on the syllabus, to raise your grade. But what's extra credit in terms of your career? On the job, you have "extra credit" when your abilities stand out. You speak German and no one else does, so when something needs translating, you're the go-to person. Or you're so exceptional at PowerPoint that you're affectionately referred to as the "PowerPoint King."

10. **Manage your time, your attention, and yourself.** College is about self-responsibility. You're in charge of your education; you call the shots. If you manage your time and money, you can focus as you should on your courses. If you "spend" unwisely—in either area—you lose your focus and your performance slips. In your career, the same will be true. Your ability to manage time, your attention, and yourself will affect your personal and professional future.[16]

What Ifs

Life is full of "what ifs?" isn't it? What if you had dated someone else? What if you took the other job? What if things were different?

What If College Isn't Right for You?

What if you decide, after a term or two, that college isn't right for you? Perhaps your heart just isn't in it, and neither is your head. If so, know that you aren't alone. That realization comes to many students. The important question to ask yourself is whether you're really making the right decision, not just getting discouraged if college seems too challenging. Remember that "College is a team sport," and use all of the campus resources available to you before you abandon your efforts. But something other than college may also be the right decision for you—right now at this particular point in your life. However, this kind of decision is one you shouldn't make lightly.

> " Every adversity, every failure, every heartache carries with it the seed of an equal or greater benefit. "

Napoleon Hill, author, Keys to Success: The 17 Principles of Personal Achievement *(1883–1970)*

What If You Can't Finish a Degree Now?

Even though you have dreams and goals, sometimes "life happens." A turn of events changes everything, a new job consumes all of your time and energy, or someone needs you. Don't feel like a failure if that happens. Take time off, regroup, and come back when you can. Going to college expands your thinking and gives you a whole new take on life. Beyond a certificate or diploma, the learning that takes place in college changes you forever—and it's worth the investment in your future.

My, How You've Grown! Goodbye and Good Luck!

Remember Aunt Ruth (or whatever her name was)? Every time she visited when you were a kid, she remarked about how much you'd grown. Or when you went to visit her, she'd measure you and mark a notch on the wall to compare your height now to the one from last year's visit. She loved watching you grow, and the fact that she noticed made you feel special.

There's no doubt about it. In this first term of college, you have grown. You have gained new perspectives, new insights, and new ways of thinking about things. Like Aunt Ruth, others may notice. If those close to you are threatened by these changes, reassure them that your newfound knowledge hasn't made you think less of them. Remember the words of writer M. L. Boren, "You should have education enough so that you won't have to look up to people; and then more education so that you will be wise enough not to look down on people." If they are proud of you and your accomplishments, and have supported you along the way, thank them!

The important thing is to keep learning and never stop. Continuing to learn—whether in college or in life—is what will determine who you are and what you will become. Learn new things, update your goals, and reinvent yourself. This book, and the course for which you're reading it, have begun that process. Now the rest is up to you!

> People succeed in as many ways as there are people. Some can be completely fulfilled with destinations that are much closer to home and more comfortable. But if you long to keep going, then I hope you are able to follow my lead to the places I have gone. To within a whisper of your own personal perfection. To places that are sweeter because you worked so hard to arrive there. To places at the very edge of your dreams.

Michael Johnson, American sprinter

CONTROL: *THE BEST IS YET TO COME*

As you read at the beginning of *FOCUS*, "One thing is sure: College will change you. Most every high-intensity experience full of opportunity does." As you've read this book, what have you learned about yourself? How have you become better at controlling your learning, your time, and your ability to focus? Look at the first page for each of the chapters you have read. What did you mark in terms of "How this chapter relates to you" and "How you will relate to this chapter"? Where did your greatest learning leaps occur? Write a summary statement here about what you have learned and how you have changed. Where do your biggest challenges still lie? Include areas that you still would like to improve upon in your statement. If you wrote a case study about yourself early on, take this opportunity to analyze it in terms of what you have learned. Remember, based on the gains you're making now, at the beginning of your college career, the best is yet to come.

_____

_____

_____

CURIOSITY: *WHAT'S THE BIG IDEA?*

In terms of creating your future, there's one big idea you need to know. In fact, it's not just big; it's huge. "Whatever captures your attention controls your life." That's a sweeping statement, so where's the evidence?

Here's a sample: Several years ago, two consultants were hired to observe infants and toddlers at DisneyWorld. Their task, assigned by park executives, was to find out what most captured children's attention in the theme park. It didn't take long for the consultants to figure out that what captured their attention wasn't the cuddly Disney characters in costume, the wildest rides with the longest lines, or the magical sights and sounds all around them. It was their parents' cell phones, especially while their parents were on them. What the children wanted, it seems, was their parents' attention, and while parents were on their phones, their attention wasn't on their children. Because their parents were captivated, kids wanted to be in on it.[17] The parents probably didn't even realize that what they were doing was affecting their children. After all, they were taking time off and spending money to show their children a good time.

We've all probably been guilty of allowing distractions to control us: texting during an oh-so-romantic dinner, an intimate conversation with a best friend, a class in which the professor is delivering a well-prepared lecture, or a key meeting when we think the boss isn't looking. But the fact that our attention is elsewhere is a dead giveaway that something else is more important at that moment. Being aware of where we're focusing our attention isn't really that easy because our brains become wired, eventually. "Attention shapes the brain," says one expert.[18] The more attention you pay to something, the more neurons your brain builds to pay attention to that thing.

Even though we may be unaware, our distractions often show our true priorities. As this book has asserted all along: It's about focus, and focus takes awareness. The bad news is that the human brain wanders about half the time; the good news is our brains can actually be trained to focus.[19] "Giving undivided attention is the first and most basic ingredient in any relationship. It is impossible to communicate, much less bond, with someone who can't or won't focus on you. At the same time, we often fail to realize how what we focus on comes to control our thoughts, our actions, and indeed, our very lives."[20]

As you create your future, think about who—or what—in your life could benefit from more attention. Write your thoughts here.

_____

_____

_____

CAREER OUTLOOK: *KEEP YOUR BALANCE*

You're a winner. You're working hard as a highly motivated, ultra-competent employee. Your boss is impressed—so much so that you get promoted. Your new position requires you to work harder, and before you know it, you're promoted again. This cycle keeps repeating itself, and over time, you have success written all over you. You're well on your way to mapping out a great future.

There's an underlying question worth exploring, however. Why are you working so hard? Is it because you're passionate about your work? Perhaps it fuels you, gives you purpose, direction, and fulfillment. You love it.

But what if your success isn't about fulfillment at all? What if it's about moving up, making more money, reveling in the prestige? What if you actually dislike your work? One work-life balance expert asks, why do people "work long hard hours at jobs they hate to enable them to buy things they don't need to impress people they don't like"?[21] Good question. The why of success is fundamentally important.

If you ever lose your professional balance, take charge of your own future. Your company is unlikely to say, "You know what? You've been working far too hard. You need to chill for a few weeks." Corporations won't fix things for you. You must take control and assume responsibility for living the type of life you want to live. For example, make a rule for yourself that evenings are for family or your romantic partner, and stick to it. Or make a pact that you'll only check your e-mail once a day on weekends so that you can let your mind "idle" for a while.

A recent study asked dying people to identify their biggest regrets. "Their most common regret? 'I wish I'd had the courage to live a life true to myself, not the life others expected of me.' Their second most common regret? 'I wish I didn't work so hard.' There are two ways to address these regrets. One, work less hard and spend your time living a life true to yourself, whatever that means. Or two, work just as hard—harder even—on things you consider to be important and meaningful. If you put those two regrets together, you realize that what people really regret isn't simply working so hard, it's working so hard on things that don't matter to them. If our work matters to us, if it represents a life true to us. . . . then we will have lived more fully."[22]

What does balance *mean to you as a college student? What will it mean in your anticipated career?*

_____

_____

_____

How much did you learn? At the beginning of this chapter, you filled out a "Readiness Check" that asked how you thought this chapter would relate to you and how you would relate to it. Now, fill out this "Reality Check" to find out.

1. What is *networking* and how can it help you?

2. Why is your continuing your education potentially important?

3. Why is it advantageous to build a portfolio of your best work?

4. List three of the things employers hope you learn in college.

5. How long did it take? _____ hours _____ minutes. Before you began this chapter, you were asked to predict how long it would take you to complete this chapter (total time, even if you read it in more than one sitting). Was your estimate on target? Have you become more realistic in your estimates over time?_____

step 3 INSIGHT *Now* What Do You Think?

At the beginning of this chapter, Anthony Lopez faced a series of challenges as a new college student. Now after learning from this chapter, would you respond differently to any of the questions you answered about the "FOCUS Challenge Case"? Using what you learned in the chapter, write a paragraph ending to Anthony's case study. What are some of the possible outcomes for Anthony?

step 4 ACTION Your Plans for Change

1. Identify one new thing you learned in reading this chapter. Why did you select the one you've selected? How will it affect what you do in your college classes?

2. How will this chapter change how you approach your future, no matter which fork of the road you choose as a next step? What will be most challenging for you?

3. How do you plan to increase your skills in college so that you can be more successful in your next step?

INFORMATION ABOUT YOU

Name _____

Student Number _____ Course/Section _____

Instructor _____

Gender _____ Age _____

Although you have not quite completed your first term as a college student, we're interested in your reactions to college so far: how you have spent your time, what challenges you've experienced, and your general views about what college has been like. Please answer thoughtfully.

NOTE: Questions 1–10 were asked on the Entrance Interview and need not be repeated here. The numbering below begins with number 11 so that the Entrance and Exit Interview results can be compared, if you or your instructor would like to do that. It may be interesting to see how your original expectations of college compare to your actual experience. Note, too, that the Exit Interview contains several added questions at the end about your future education.

YOUR COLLEGE EXPERIENCE

Your Reactions to College

11. **Which of the following reasons to finish your college degree seem important to you now? (Check all that apply.)**

_____ I want to build a better life for myself.

_____ I want to be well off financially in the future.

_____ My friends are going to college.

_____ It is expected of me.

_____ I want to continue learning.

_____ I am unsure of what I might do instead.

_____ I want to build a better life for my family.

_____ I need a college education to achieve my dreams.

_____ My family is encouraging me to continue.

_____ I want to prepare for a *new* career.

_____ The career I am pursuing requires a degree.

_____ other (please explain)

12. **How did you find you learned best in college? (Check all that apply.)**

_____ by looking at charts, maps, graphs

_____ by listening to instructors' lectures

_____ by reading books

_____ by going on field trips

_____ by looking at color-coded information

_____ by listening to other students during in-class discussions

_____ by writing papers

_____ by engaging in activities

_____ by looking at symbols and graphics

_____ by talking about course content with friends or family

_____ by taking notes

_____ by actually doing things

13. The following sets of opposite descriptive phrases are separated by five blank lines. Put an X on the line between the two that best represents your response, like this: For me, high school was easy _____:___X___:_____:_____:_____ hard

My first term of college:

challenged me academically   _____:_____:_____:_____:_____ was easy

was very different from high school   _____:_____:_____:_____:_____ was a lot like high school

was exciting   _____:_____:_____:_____:_____ was dull

was interesting   _____:_____:_____:_____:_____ was uninteresting

motivated me to continue   _____:_____:_____:_____:_____ discouraged me

was fun   _____:_____:_____:_____:_____ was boring

helped me feel a part of this school   _____:_____:_____:_____:_____ made me feel like an outsider

14. How many total hours per week did you study outside of class for your college courses?

____ 0–5   ____ 6–10   ____ 11–15   ____ 16–20   ____ 21–25
____ 26–30   ____ 31–35   ____ 36–40   ____ 40+

15. Now what do you expect your grade point average to be at the end of your first term of college?

____ A+   ____ A   ____ A–   ____ B+   ____ B
____ B–   ____ C+   ____ C   ____ C–   ____ D or lower

Your Strengths, Personality, and Interests

16. Which of these *strengths* or personal characteristics contributed to your college success? (Check all that apply.)

____ a. I am good at building relationships.

____ b. I can usually convince others to follow my plan.

____ c. I like to win.

____ d. I work toward future goals.

____ e. I like to be productive and get things done.

____ f. I have a positive outlook on life.

____ g. I'm usually the person who gets things going.

____ h. I enjoy the challenge of learning new things.

____ i. I am focused.

____ j. I can usually look at a problem and figure out a plan of action.

____ k. I work to keep everyone happy.

____ l. I'm a take-charge kind of person.

____ m. I help other people develop their talents and skills.

____ n. I'm a very responsible person.

____ o. I can analyze a situation and see various ways things might work out.

____ p. I usually give tasks my best effort.

17. How confident are you now in yourself in each of the following areas? (1 = very confident, 5 = not at all confident)

____ overall academic ability   ____ technology skills

____ mathematical skills   ____ physical well being

____ leadership ability   ____ writing skills

____ reading skills   ____ social skills

____ public speaking skills   ____ emotional well being

____ study skills   ____ teamwork skills

18. For each of the following pairs of descriptors, which set sounds most like you based on what you've learned about yourself this term? (Please choose between the two options on each line and place a checkmark by your choice.)

____ Extraverted and outgoing   or   ____ Introverted and quiet

____ Detail-oriented and practical   or   ____ Big-picture and future-oriented

____ Rational and truthful   or   ____ People-oriented and tactful

____ Organized and self-disciplined   or   ____ Spontaneous and flexible

19. *FOCUS* is about 12 different aspects of college life. Which did you find to be most interesting as they applied to your academic success? (Check all that apply.)

____ Getting the right start	____ Learning styles and studying
____ Building dreams, setting goals	____ Thinking critically and creatively
____ Managing time, energy, and money	____ Engaging, listening, and note-taking in class
____ Learning online	____ Developing memory, taking tests
____ Reading, writing, and presenting	____ Choosing a college major and career
____ Building relationships, valuing diversity	____ Creating a future

Your Challenges

20. Of the 12 aspects of college life identified in the previous question, which were most challenging to apply to yourself in your academic work? (Check all that apply.)

____ Getting the right start	____ Learning styles and studying
____ Building dreams, setting goals	____ Thinking critically and creatively
____ Managing time, energy, and money	____ Engaging, listening, and note-taking in class
____ Learning online	____ Developing memory, taking tests
____ Reading, writing, and presenting	____ Choosing a college major and career
____ Building relationships, valuing diversity	____ Creating a future

21. Which one of your current classes was most challenging this term and why?

Which class? (course title *or* department and course number) _____

Why? _____

Did you succeed in this course? ____ yes ____ no ____ Somewhat (please explain): _____

22. Please mark your *top three areas of concern* relating to your first term of college by placing 1, 2, and 3 next to the items you choose (with 1 representing your top concern).

____ I did not fit in.	____ My social life interfered with my studies.
____ I did have difficulty making friends.	____ My studies interfered with my social life.
____ I was not academically successful.	____ My instructors did not care about me as an individual.
____ My performance disappointed my family.	____ I may not finish my degree.
____ My personal life interfered with my studies.	____ I did not manage my time well.
____ My studies interfered with my personal life.	____ I was bored in my classes.
____ I had financial difficulties.	____ I felt intimidated by my instructors.
____ My job(s) interfered with my studies.	____ I was overwhelmed by all I had to do.
____ My studies interfered with my job.	____ other (please explain) _____

Your Future

23. How certain are you now of the following (1 = totally sure, 5 = totally unsure)?

_____ Finishing your degree or certificate

_____ Finishing your degree or certificate at this school.

_____ Sticking with the major you've chosen.

_____ Continuing on to work toward a bachelor's or advanced degree

24. What are you most looking forward to after this semester/quarter?

25. Did you achieve the outcomes you were hoping to achieve at the beginning of this first semester/quarter? Why or why not?

> You may gain some personal insights if you compare the questions in this "Your College Experience" section of the Exit Interview with the matching questions from the "Your College Expectations" section in the Entrance Interview at the front of the book. Or your instructor may ask you to write about your Insights and intended Actions. Now continue on to these final questions about "Your Next Steps."

YOUR NEXT STEPS

26. Looking ahead, how satisfied do you expect to be with your decision to attend this school?

_____ very satisfied _____ satisfied

_____ somewhat dissatisfied _____ very dissatisfied

_____ not sure

27. Which of the following statements best reflects your educational intentions?

_____ I plan to stay at this school until I complete my degree.

_____ I plan to transfer to another institution (please identify which one _____).

_____ I plan to stop out of college for awhile (to work, for example) and then return to this school.

_____ I plan to drop out of college.

28. If you are thinking about transferring to another institution, why would you do so? Check all that apply.

_____ This school does not offer my intended major (which is _____). _____ This school is too small.

_____ This school is too large. _____ This school is too expensive.

_____ I don't feel I fit in. _____ I want to go to a school in another location.

_____ I think I might like another school better. _____ I want to be closer to my boy/girlfriend.

_____ I want to be closer to my friends. _____ I will change job locations.

_____ I want to transfer from a two-year to a four-year institution. _____ other (please explain)

29. What was the biggest difference between what you thought college would be like and what it was actually like for you?

30. How have you changed most over this first semester/quarter? In what ways are you different now that you've been in college? How will this introductory semester/quarter affect or change your future college experience?

CHAPTER 1

1. Paulson, K., & Boeke, M. (2006). *Adult learners in the United States: A national profile.* Washington, DC: American Council on Education.

2. Carey, K. (2007). America's best community colleges: Why they're better than some of the "best" four-year universities. *Washington Monthly.* Available at http://www.washington-monthly.com/features/2007/0709.careyessay.html.

3. Knowles' Andragogy. Available at http://www.learningandteaching.info/learning/knowlesa.htm.

4. Barrier busters: *Community college students . . . by the numbers. Lumina Foundation Focus.* From The American Association of Community Colleges, based on material in the National Profile of Community Colleges: Trends & Statistics, Phillippe & Patton, 2000. Available at http://www.luminafoundation.org/publications/focus_archive/winter_2006/cc_students.html; Documentary shows struggles of nontraditional community college students. (2007, July 20). Available at http://newsroom.ucr.edu/news_item.html?action=page&id=1634; Matthews, D. (2009, February). A stronger nation through higher education. *A Special Report from Lumina Foundation for Education.* Available at http://www.luminafoundation.org/publications/A_stronger_nation_through_higher_education.pdf; CCSSE, 2006 findings. *Act on fact: Using data to improve student success.* Available at http://www.ccsse.org/center/resources/docs/publications/CCSSENationalReport2006.pdf; (2012). *Collegeboard.com.* Available at http://professionals.collegeboard.com/guidance/college/community-college; (2011). 2011 fact sheet. *American Association of Community Colleges.* Available at http://www.aacc.nche.edu/AboutCC/Documents/FactSheet2011.pdf.

5. Balderrama, A. (2009, May 1). The ten best jobs requiring two-year degrees. Available at http://www.careerbuilder.com/Article/CB-1366-Job-Search-10-Best-Jobs-Requiring-Two-Year-Degrees/?ArticleID=1366&cbRecursionCnt=1&cbsid=960a4ed9fa914960bc395ac1534070d9-322921368-w0-6&ns_siteid=ns_us_g_percentage_of_jobs_re_-.

6. Crosby, O. (2002–2003, Winter). Associate degree: Two years to a career or jump start to a bachelor's degree. *Occupational Outlook Quarterly,* 2–13. Available at http://www.bls.gov/opub/ooq/2002/winter/art01.pdf.

7. What's the Difference between an Associate Degree and a Certificate? *Brookhaven College.* Available at http://www.brookhavencollege.edu/studentsvcs/advising/faq.aspx#q17.

8. Certificate program vs. associate's degree—What's the difference? *Top Colleges Blog.* Available at http://www.top-colleges.com/blog/2007/04/11/certificate-program-vs-associates-degree/.

9. Different paths for different majors. (2007, January/February). Datanotes: *Achieving the Dream.* Available at http://www.achievingthedream.org/_pdfs/datanotes/datanotes-janfeb-2007.pdf.

10. Marchand, A. (2010, 29 March). 6 strategies can help entering community-college students succeed. *The Chronicle of Higher Education.* Available at http://chronicle.com/article/6-Strategies-Can-Help-Entering/64871.

11. Hart Research Associates. (2010, January 20). *Raising the bar: Employers' views on college learning in the wake of the economic downturn.* Available at http://www.aacu.org/leap/documents/2009_EmployerSurvey.pdf.

12. Shoenberg, R. (2005). *Why do I have to take this course? A student guide to making smart educational choices.* Association of American Colleges and Universities. Washington, DC: AAC&U.

13. Linda Foltz and the Student Success Center advisors at the University of Colorado at Colorado Springs; Jennifer Sengenberger and Wayne Artis, Pikes Peak Community College; Kocel, K. C., (2008, March 12). Advising first-generation college students for continued success. Kocel, K. (2008, March 12). *The Mentor: An Academic Advising Journal.* Available at http://www.psu.edu/dus/mentor/080312kk.htm; Knight, T. M. (2000, May 17). Planting the seeds of success: Advising college students with disabilities. *The Mentor: An Academic Advising Journal.* Available at http://psu.edu/dus/mentor/000517tk.htm.

14. The challenges of remedial education: Views of 3 presidents. (2006, October 27). *The Chronicle of Higher Education.* Available at http://chronicle.com/article/The-Challenges-of-Remedial/32361/.

15. Developmental education and student success. (2006, September/October). *Datanotes: Achieving the Dream.* Available at http://www.achievingthedream.org/_pdfs/DataNotes/DataNotes-SeptOct-2006.pdf.

16. Crews, D. M., & Aragon, S. R. (2004). Influence of a community college developmental education writing course on academic performance. *Community College Review, 32*(2), 1–18.

17. Settle, J. S. (2011). Variables that encourage students to persist in community colleges. *Community College Journal of Research and Practice, 35,* 281–300.

18. Dweck, C. S. (2006). *Mindset: The new psychology of success.* New York: Random House. pp. 104–105.

19. Employment Projections—2008–2018 Summary. Available at http://www.bls.gov/news.release/ecopro.nr0.htm.

20. Rampell, C. (2009, July 13). Preparing today's workers or tomorrow's jobs. *The New York Times.* Available at http://economix.blogs.nytimes.com/2009/07/13/preparing-todays-workers-for-tomorrows-jobs/.

21. (2006, July). Fact Sheet. Community Colleges: Challenges and Benefits. *Achieving the Dream.* Available at http://www.lee.edu/atd/pdf/FS-ChallengeBenefit.pdf.

22. Greenstone, M., & Looney, A. (2012, February 26). Where is the best place to invest $102,000—in stocks, bonds, or a college degree? *Brookings.* Available at http://www.brookings.edu/papers/2011/0625_education_greenstone_looney.aspx.

23. Leonhardt, D. (2011, June 25). Even for cashiers, college pays off. *The New York Times.* Available at http://www.nytimes.com/2011/06/26/sunday-review/26leonhardt.html.

24. (2006, July). Fact Sheet. Community Colleges: Challenges and Benefits. *Achieving the Dream.* Available at http://www.lee.edu/atd/pdf/FS-ChallengeBenefit.pdf.

25. Omara-Otunnu, E. (2006, July 24). Conference examines transition from high school to college. University of Connecticut *Advance.* Available at http://advance.uconn.edu/2006/060724/06072407.htm.

26. Hoachlander, G., Sikora, A. C., Horn, L., & Carroll, C. D. (2003, June). Community college students: Goals, academic preparation and outcomes. *National Center for Education Statistics.* Available at http://nces.ed.gov/pubs2003/2003164.pdf.

27. Pascarella, E. T., Pierson, C. T., Wolniak, G. C., & Terenzini, P. T. (2004). First-generation college students: Additional evidence on college experiences and outcomes. *Journal of Higher Education, 75*(3), 249–284.

28. Tyler, M. D., Johns, K Y. (2009). From First-Generation College Student to First Lady. *Diverse Issues in Higher Education Psychology, 25*(25). Available at http://diverseeducation.com/article/12184/.

29. Community college: Myth vs. reality. *The College Board.* Available at http://www.collegeboard.com/student/csearch/where-to-start/150494.html; (2000, August 17). These famous people of color got their start at a community college. *Black Issues in Higher Education.* Available at http://findarticles.com/p/articles/mi_m0DXK/is_/ai_65229406; 2006); Notable alumni. *American Association of Community Colleges.* Available at http://www.aacc.nche.edu/AboutCC/alumni/Pages/default.aspx.

30. Bal, F. T., Zhang, S., & Tachlyama, G. T. (2008). Effects of a self-regulated learning course on the academic performance and graduation rate of college students in an academic support program. *Journal of College Reading and Learning, 39*(1), 54–73; O'Gara, L., Karp, M. M., & Hughes, K. L. (2009). Student success courses in the community college: An exploratory study. *Community College Review, 36*(3), 195–218. Derby, D. C. (2007). Predicting degree completion: Examining the interaction between orientation course participation and ethnic background. *Community College Journal of Research and Practice, 31*(11), 883–894; Duggan, M. H., & Williams, M. R. (2011). Community college student success courses: The student perspective. *Community College Journal of Research and practice, 35*(1), 121–143.

31. McCarron, G. P., & Inkelas, K. K. (2006). The gap between educational aspirations and attainment for first-generation college students and the role of parental involvement. *Journal of College Student Development, 47*(5), 534–549.

32. Martinez, J. A., Sher, K. J., Krull, J. L., & Wood, P. K. (2009). Blue-collar scholars? Mediators and moderators of university attrition in first-generation college students. *Journal of College Student Development, 50*(1), 87–103; Collier, P. J., & Morgan, D. L., (2008). Is that paper really due today? *Higher Education, 55*(4), 425–446.

33. Cox, R. D. (2009). *The college fear factor: How students and professors misunderstand one another.* Cambridge, MA: Harvard University Press.

34. http://www.counselingcenter.illinois.edu/?page_id=142.

CHAPTER 2

1. Multi-tasking adversely affects brain's learning, UCLA psychologists report. (2006, July 26). *ScienceDaily.* Available at http://www.sciencedaily.com/releases/2006/07/060726083302.htm.

2. Bregman, P. (2010, May 20). How (and why) to stop multitasking. *Harvard Business Review.* Available at http://blogs.hbr.org/bregman/2010/05/how-and-why-to-stop-multitaski.html; "Infomania" worse than marijuana. *BBC News.* Available at http://news.bbc.co.uk/2/hi/uk_news/4471607.stm.

3. Seven, R. (2004, November 28). Life interrupted. *Pacific Northwest,* seattletimes.com. Available at http://seattletimes.nwsource.com/pacificnw/2004/1128/cover.html; Richtel, M. (2010, June 6). Addicted to technology and paying a price. *The New York Times.* Available at http://www.nytimes.com/2010/06/07/technology/07brain.html?ref=yourbrainoncomputers; Richtel, M. (2010, August 24). Digital devices deprive brain of needed downtime. *The New York Times.* Available at http://www.nytimes.com/2010/08/25/technology/25brain.html?ref=yourbrainoncomputers.

4. Hamilton, J. (2008, October 9). Multitasking teens may be muddling their brains. *NPR: Your Health.* Available at http://www.npr.org/templates/story/story.php?storyId=95524385; Tierney, J. (2009, May 5). Ear plugs to lasers: The science of concentration. *The New York Times.* Available at http://www.nytimes.com/2009/05/05/science/05tier.html?scp=1&sq="ear plugs to lasers: the science of concentration"&st=cse; Tugend, A. (2008, October 25). Multitasking can make you lose . . . um . . . focus. *The New York Times.* Available at http://www.nytimes.com/2008/10/25/business/yourmoney/25shortcuts.html?pagewanted=all; Walls, C. (2006, March 19). genM: The multitasking generation. *Time.* Available at http://www.time.com/time/magazine/article/0,9171,1174696,00.html.

5. Spielberg finally to graduate. (2002, May 15). *BBC News.* Available at http://news.bbc.co.uk/2/hi/entertainment/1988770.stm.

6. Staley, C. (2003). "Spending Time." In *50 ways to leave your lectern.* Beverly, MA: Wadsworth, p. 54.

7. Davis, J. R. (1993), *Better teaching, more learning.* Phoenix, AZ: Oryx Press.

8. French, B. F., & Oakes, W. (2003). Measuring academic intrinsic motivation in the first year of college: Reliability and validity evidence for a new instrument. *Journal of the First-Year Experience, 15*(1), 83–102; French, B. F. Executive summary of instruments utilized with systemwide first-year seminars. Policy Center on the First Year of College; French, B. F., Immerkus, J. C., & Oakes, W. C. (2005). An examination of indicators of engineering students' success and persistence. *Journal of Engineering Education, 94*(4), 419–425.

9. Based on Harrell, K. (2003). *Attitude is everything: 10 life-changing steps to turning attitude into action.* New York: HarperBusiness.

10. Dweck, C. S. (2000). *Self-theories: Their role in motivation, personality, and development.* New York: Psychology Press, p. 1.

11. Berglas, S. & Jones, E. E. (1978). Drug choice as a self-handicapping strategy in response to non contingent success. *Journal of Personality and Social Psychology, 36,* 405–417; Jones, E. E. & Berglas, S. (1978). Control of attributions about the self through self-handicapping strategies: The appeal of alcohol and the role of underachievement. *Personality and Social Psychology Bulletin, 4,* 200–206; Dweck, C. S. (2006). *Mindset: The new psychology of success.* New York: Random House.

12. Dweck, C. S. (2000). *Self-theories: Their role in motivation, personality, and development.* New York: Psychology Press; Dweck, *Mindset.*

13. Robins, R. W., & Pals, J. (2002). Implicit self-theories of ability in the academic domain: A test of Dweck's model. *Self and Identity, 1,* 313–336.

14. Mangels, J. A., Butterfield, B., Lamb, J., Good, C. D., & Dweck, C. S. (2006). Why do beliefs about intelligence influence learning success? A social cognitive neuroscience model. *Social Cognitive and Affective Neuroscience, 1*(2), 75–86.

15. Bauer, A. R., Grant, H., & Dweck, C. S. (2006). *Personal goals predict the level and impact of dysphoria.* Unpublished manuscript.

CHAPTER 3

1. Leamnson, R. (1999). *Thinking about teaching and learning: Developing habits of learning with first year college and university students.* Sterling, VA: Stylus.

2. Shuster, W. G. (2001). *Less stress? Yes! Jewelers' Circular Keystone, 172*(2), 98.

3. Caine, R. N., & Caine, G. (1994). *Making connections: Teaching and the human brain.* Menlo Park, CA: Addison Wesley.

4. Brandt, R. (1998). *Powerful learning.* Alexandria, VA: Association for Supervision and Curriculum Development, p. 29.

5. Campbell, B. (1992). Multiple intelligences in action. *Childhood Education, 68*(4), 197–201; Gardner, H., & Hatch, T. (1989). Multiple intelligences go to school: Educational implications of the theory of multiple intelligences. *Educational Researcher, 18*(8), 4–9; Gardner, H. (1983). *Frames of Mind: The Theory of Multiple Intelligences.* New York: Basic Books.

6. Griggs, L., Barney, S., Brown-Sederberg, J., Collins, E., Keith, S., & Iannacci, L. (2009). Varying pedagogy to address student multiple intelligences. *Human Architecture: Journal of the Sociology of Self Knowledge 7*(1), 55–60.

7. Armstrong, T. (2000). *MI and cognitive skills.* Available at http://www.ascd.org/publications/books/100041/chapters/MI_and_Cognitive_Skills.aspx.

8. Davis, B. (2009). *Tools for teaching,* 2nd ed. San Francisco: Jossey-Bass, p. 273.

9. Fleming, N. D. (1995). I'm different; not dumb: Modes of presentation (VARK) in the tertiary classroom. In A. Zeimer (Ed.), *Research and development in higher education, Proceedings of the 1995 Annual Conference of the Higher Education and Research Development Society of Austral-Asia (HERDSA), HERDSA, 18,* 308–313; Fleming, N. D., & Mills, C. (1992). Not another inventory, rather a catalyst for reflection. *To Improve the Academy, 11,* 137–149. Available at http://www.ntlf.com/html/lib/suppmat/74fleming.htm.

10. Fleming, I'm different; not dumb.

11. Fleming, N. D. (2005). *Teaching and learning styles: VARK strategies.* Christchurch, NZ: Microfilm Limited.

12. Based on DiTiberio, J. K., & Hammer, A. L. (1993). *Introduction to type in college.* Palo Alto, CA: Consulting Psychologists Press.

13. Tessler, L. G. (1997). How college students with learning disabilities can advocate for themselves. *LD OnLine.* Available at http://www.ldonline.org/article/6136.

14. Mangrum, C. T., & Strichart, S. S. (Eds.) (1997). *Peterson's guide to colleges with programs for students with learning disabilities.* Princeton, NJ: Peterson's Guide.

15. Strichart, S. S., & Mangrum, C. T. II. (2002). *Teaching learning strategies and study skills to students with learning disabilities, attention deficit disorder, or special needs,* 3rd ed. Boston: Allyn and Bacon; *Learning Disabilities Online.* Available at http://ldonline.org; Sousa, D. A. (2001). *How the special needs brain learns.* Thousand Oaks, CA: Corwin Press.

16. Soldner, L. B. (1997). Self-assessment and the reflective reader. *Journal of College Reading and Learning, 28*(1), 5–11.

17. VanBlerkom, M. L, & VanBlerkom, D. L. (2004). Self-monitoring strategies used by developmental and non-developmental college students. *Journal of College Reading and Learning, 34*(2), 45–60.

18. Melchenbaum, D., Burland, S., Gruson, L., & Cameron, R. (1985). Metacognitive assessment. In S. Yussen (Ed.), *The growth of reflection in children.* Orlando, FL: Academic Press. p. 5.

19. Hall, C. W. (2001). A measure of executive processing skills in college students. *College Student Journal, 35*(3), 442–450; Taylor, S. (1999). Better learning through better thinking: Developing students' metacognitive abilities. *Journal of College Reading and Learning, 30*(1), 34–45.

20. Learning to learn. *Study Guides and Strategies.* Available at http://www.studygs.net/metacognition.htm.

21. Simpson, M. L. (1994/1995). Talk throughs: A strategy for encouraging active learning across the content areas. *Journal of Reading, 38*(4), 296–304.

22. How Air Traffic Control Works. *How Stuff Works.* Available at http://travel.howstuffworks.com/air-traffic-control.htm.

23. Glenn, D. (2010, February 7). How students can improve by studying themselves. *The Chronicle of Higher Education.* Available at http://chronicle.com/article/Struggling-Students-Can/ 64004/?sid=pm&utm_source= m&utm_medium=en.

24. Elias, M. (2004, April 5). Frequent TV watching shortens kids' attention spans. *USA Today.* Available at http://www.usatoday.com/news/health/2004-04-05-tv-kids-attention-usat_x.htm.

25. Carey, B. (2010, September 6). Forget what you know about good study habits. *The New York Times.* Available at http://www.nytimes.com/2010/09/07/health/views/07mind.html?_r=1&pagewanted=1&ref=homepage&src=me.

26. Bol, L., Warkentin, R. W., Nunnery, J. A., & O'Connell, A. A. (1999). College students' study activities and their relationship to study context, reference course, and achievement. *College Student Journal, 33*(4), 608–622.

27. When students study makes a difference too. (2005, November). *Recruitment & Retention.*

28. Trainin, G., & Swanson, H. L. (2005). Cognition, meta-cognition, and achievement of college students with learning disabilities. *Learning Disability Quarterly, 28,* 261–272.

29. Guibert, S. (2012, March 23). Learning best when you rest: Sleeping after processing new info most effective. *Science Daily.* Available at http://www.sciencedaily.com/releases/2012/03/120323205504.htm.

30. Doidge, N. (2007). *The brain that changes itself: Stories of personal triumph from the frontiers of brain science.* New York: Viking.

31. *Newsweek* writer with Ian Yarett. (2011, January 10 & 17). Can you build a better brain? *Newsweek,* pp. 40–45.

32. Jozefowicz, C. (2004, May-June). Sweating makes you smart. *Psychology Today.* Available at http://www.psychologytoday.com/ articles/200405/sweating-makes-you-smart; Wu, A., Ying, Z., & Gomez-Pinilla, F. (2004). Dietary omega-3 fatty acids normalize BDNF levels, reduce oxidative damage, and counteract learning disability after traumatic brain injury in rats. *Journal of Neurotrauma, 21,* 1457–1467; PT Staff. (1998, March-April). Brain Boosters. *Psychology Today, Alzheimer's Association.* (2004). Stay mentally active. *alz.org.* Available at http://www.alz.org/we_can_help_stay_mentally_active.asp.

33. Springer, M. V., McIntosh, A. R., Winocur, G., & Grady, C. L. (2005). The relation between brain activity during memory tasks and years of education in young and older adults. *Neuropsychology, 19*(2), 181–192.

34. http://dictionary.reference.com/browse/grit.

35. Halvorson, H. G. (2011, February, 25). Nine things successful people do differently. *Harvard Business Review Conversation.* Available at http://blogs.hbr.org/cs/2011/02/nine_things_successful _people.html#; Duckworth, A. L.; Peterson, C.; Matthews, M. D.; Kelly, D. R. (2007). Grit: Perseverance and passion for long-term goals. *Journal of Personality and Social Psychology, 92*(6), 1087–1101; Mangan, K. (2012, August 5). Traits of the 'get it done' personality: Laser focus, resilience, and true grit. *The Chronicle of Higher Education.* Available at http://chronicle.com/article/Traits-of-the-Get-it-Done/133291/.

CHAPTER 4

1. Sakai, J. (2012, March 15). A wandering mind reveals mental processes and priorities. *Science Daily.* Available at http://www.sciencedaily.com/releases/2012/03/120315161326.htm.

2. Coleman, J. (2012, February 22). Faced with distraction, we need willpower. *HBR Blog Network*. Available at http://blogs.hbr.org/cs/2012/02/faced_with_distraction_we_need.html.

3. Saunders, F. (2009, November–December). Multitasking to distraction. *American Scientist*. Available at http://www.americanscientist.org/issues/pub/multitasking-to-distraction.

4. Khawand, P. (2009). *The accomplishing more with less workbook*. On the Go Technologies, LLC.

5. Austin, C. (2010). Go with the flow: Fresh ideas for managing time. *Prezi.com*. Available at http://prezi.com/7gypurup9uke/go-with-the-flow/.

6. Rafter, M. V. (2012, February 23). Siri says it's time to get to work. *Workforce.com*. Available at http://www.workforce.com/article/20120223/NEWS02/120229973/siri-says-its-time-to-get-to-work#.

7. Eade, D. M. (1998). Energy and success: Time management. *ClinicianNews,* July/August. Available at http://www.adv-leadership-grp.com/articles/energy.htm.

8. Loehr, J., & Schwartz, T. (2003). *The power of full engagement: Managing energy, not time, is the key to high performance and personal renewal.* New York: Free Press.

9. Bittel, L. R. (1991). *Right on time! The complete guide for time pressured managers.* New York: McGraw-Hill, p. 16.

10. DeMaio, S. (2009, March 25). The art of the self-imposed deadline. *Harvard Business Review.* Available at http://blogs.hbr.org/demaio/2009/03/the-art-of-the-selfimposed-dea.html.

11. Bittel, *Right on time!* p. 16.

12. Loehr, *The power of full engagement.*

13. Astin, A. W., Astin, H. S., Lindholm, J. A., & Bryant, A. N. (2005). *The spiritual life of college students: A national study of college students' search for meaning and purpose.* Los Angeles: Higher Education Research Institute, UCLA; http://spirituality.ucla.edu/; Crosby, J. (2010, April 4). College students struggle with religion and spirituality. *Cape Cod Times.* Available at http://www.capecodonline.com/apps/pbcs.dll/article?AID=/20100404/LIFE/4040307/-1/NEWSMAP.

14. Allen, D. (2012, March 17). When technology overwhelms, get organized. *New York Times.* Available at http://www.nytimes.com/2012/03/18/business/when-office-technology-overwhelms-get-organized.html?pagewanted=1&nl=todaysheadlines&emc=edit_th_20120318.

15. Based on Covey, S. R., Merrill, A. R., & Merrill, R. R. (1996). *First things first: To live, to love, to learn, to leave a legacy.* New York: Free Press, 37.

16. Fortino, M. (2001). *E-mergency.* Groveland, CA: Omni Publishing. Also see The American Time Use Survey results at http://www.bls.gov/news.release/atus.nr0.htm.

17. Hobbs, C. R. (1987). *Time power.* New York: Harper & Row, pp. 9–10.

18. Based on Berglas, S. (2004, June). Chronic time abuse. *Harvard Business Review*, 90–97.

19. Solomon, L. J., & Rothblum, E. D. (1984). Academic procrastination: Frequency and cognitive- behavioral correlates. *Journal of Counseling Psychology, 31,* 503–509.

20. Hoover, E. (2005, December 9). Tomorrow I love ya! *The Chronicle of Higher Education, 52*(16), A30–32.

21. Ferrari, J. R., McCown, W. G., & Johnson, J. (2002). *Procrastination and task avoidance: Theory, research, and treatment.* New York: Springer Publishing.

22. Hoover, Tomorrow I love ya!.

23. Khawand, P. (2009). *The accomplishing more with less workbook.* On the Go Technologies, LLC.

24. Sandholtz, K., Derr, B., Buckner, K., & Carlson, D. (2002). *Beyond juggling: Rebalancing your busy life.* San Francisco: Berrett-Koehler Publishers.

25. Adapted from Sandholtz et al., *Beyond juggling.*

26. Farrell, E. F. (2005, February 4). More students plan to work to help pay for college. *The Chronicle of Higher Education, 51*(22), A1. Available online at http://chronicle.com/weekly/v51/i22/22a00101.htm.

27. McFaddon, L. (2009, August 20). 8 major benefits of new credit card law. *Bankrate.com.* Available at http://www.bankrate.com/finance/credit-cards/8-major-benefits-of-new-credit-card-law-1.aspx.

28. See FinAid at http://www.finaid.org/loans/studentloandebtclock.phtml.

29. Ludlum, M., Tilker, K., Ritter, D., Cowart, T., Xu, W., & Smith, B. C. (2012). Financial Literacy and Credit Cards: A Multi Campus Survey. *International Journal of Business and Social Science, 3*(7), 25–33. Available at http://www.ijbssnet.com/journals/Vol_3_No_7_April_2012/3.pdf; http://moneyland.time.com/2012/04/12/college-students-are-credit-card-dunces/.

30. Choosing a credit card. *The Federal Reserve Board.* Available at http://www.federalreserve.gov/pubs/shop/default.htm.

31. Muller, K. New credit card laws (2009) and students. *ezine@rticles.com.* Available at http://ezinearticles.com/?New-Credit-Card-Laws-(2009)-And-Students&id=2410035; Miranda. (2009, May 21). Credit CARD Act of 2009: How it affects you. *Personaldividends.com.* Available at http://personaldividends.com/money/miranda/credit-card-act-of-2009-how-it-affects-you.

32. Kantrowitz, M. (2007). *FAQs about financial aid.* FinAid: The Smart Student Guide to Financial Aid. Available at http://www.finaid.org/questions/faq.html; Jevita Rogers, Director of Financial Aid, University of Colorado, Colorado Springs.

33. Nathan, R. (2005). *My freshman year: What a professor learned by becoming a student.* Ithaca, NY: Cornell University Press.

34. Fried, J., & Hanson, D. (2010). *Rework.* New York: Crown Business, p. 25–26.

35. Rock, D. (2009). *Your brain at work: Strategies for overcoming distraction, regaining focus, and working smarter all day long.* New York: HarperCollins Business.

CHAPTER 5

1. Perry, J. (1995–2008). *Procrastination and perfectionism. Philosophy Talk @Stanford.* Original essay reposted at http://people.tribe.net/aecb0f57-afa4-49a6-a13f-cbc588cd0923/blog/d75959db-01a7-4121-8b6f-ce3a18ddb9a7.

2. Halx, M. D., & Reybold, E. (2005). A pedagogy of force: Faculty perspective of critical thinking capacity in undergraduate students. *The Journal of General Education, 54*(4), 293–315.

3. Walkner, P., & Finney, N. (1999). Skill development and critical thinking in higher education. *Teaching in Higher Education, 4*(4), 531–548.

4. Diestler, S. (2001). *Becoming a critical thinker: A user friendly manual.* Upper Saddle River, NJ: Prentice Hall.

5. Arum, R. & Roksa, J. (2011). *Academically adrift: Limited learning on college campuses.* Chicago: University of Chicago Press.

6. Falcione, P. A. (1998). *Critical thinking: What it is and why it counts*. Millbrae, CA: California Academic Press.

7. Paul, R. (2005). The state of critical thinking today. *New Directions for Community Colleges*, 27–38.

8. Nosich, G. M. (2005). Problems with two standard models for teaching critical thinking. *New Directions for Community Colleges*, 59–67.

9. Twale, D., & Sanders, C. S. (1999). Impact of non-classroom experiences on critical thinking ability. *NASPA Journal, 36*(2), 133–146.

10. Thomas, C., & Smoot, G. (1994, February/March). Critical thinking: A vital work skill. *Trust for Educational Leadership, 23*, 34–38.

11. Kaplan-Leiserson, E. (2004). Workforce of tomorrow: How can we prepare *all* youth for future work success? *Training & Development, 58*(4), 12–14. 13. Based in part on Brookfield, S. D. (1987). *Developing critical thinkers: Challenging adults to explore alternative ways of thinking and acting*. San Francisco: Jossey-Bass.

12. Van den Brink-Budgen, R. (2000). *Critical thinking for students*, 3rd ed. Oxford: How to Books; Ruggiero, V. R. (2001). *Becoming a critical thinker*, 4th ed. Boston: Houghton Mifflin.

13. Blakey, E., & Spence, S. (1990). Developing metacognition. *ERIC Digest*. Available at http://www.ericdigests.org/pre-9218/developing.htm.

14. Florida, R. (2002). *The rise of the creative class: And how it's transforming work, leisure, community and everyday life*. New York: Basic Books, xii.

15. Sternberg. R. J. (2004). Teaching college students that creativity is a decision. *Guidance & Counseling, 19*(4), 196–200.

16. Rowe, A. J. (2004). *Creative intelligences: discovering the innovative potential in ourselves and others*. Upper Saddle, NJ: Pearson Education, pp. 3–6, 34.

17. Michalko, M. (2001). *Cracking creativity: The secrets of creative genius*. Berkeley, CA: Ten Speed Press.

18. Adapted from Adler, R., & Proctor, R. F. II (2011). *Looking out/ Looking in*. (13th ed.) New York: Holt, Rinehart, and Winston, pp. 110–116.

19. Douglas, J. H. (1977). The genius of everyman (2): Learning creativity. *Science News, 111*(8), 284–288.

20. Harris, R. (1998). Introduction to creative thinking. *Virtual-Salt*. Available at http://www.virtualsalt.com/crebook1.htm.

21. Eby, D. Creativity and flow psychology. Available at http://talentdevelop.com/articles/Page8.html.

22. Schwartz, T., Gomes, J., & McCarthy, C. (2010) *The way we're working isn't working: The four forgotten needs that energize great performance*. New York: Free Press, 149.

23. Schwartz, T., Gomes, J., & McCarthy, C. (2010) *The way we're working isn't working: The four forgotten needs that energize great performance*, 147–149.

CHAPTER 6

1. Dahlstrom, E., de Boor, T., Grunwald, P., & Vockley, M. (2011). National study of undergraduate students and information technology. *Educause*. Available at http://net.educause.edu/ir/library/pdf/ERS1103/ERS1103W.pdf.

2. Jaschik, S. (2008, April 7). Distance ed continues rapid growth at community colleges. *Inside Higher Ed*. Available at http://www.insidehighered.com/news/2008/04/07/distance.

3. Bollet, R. M., & Fallon, S. (2002). Personalizing e-learning. *Educational Media International, 39*(1), 39–45; Barber, S., in Shank, P. (Ed). (2011). *The online learning idea book: Proven ways to enhance technology-based and blended learning, vol 2*. San Francisco: Pfeiffer.

4. Guess, A. (2007, September 17). Students' "evolving" use of technology. *Inside Higher Ed*. Available at http://www.insidehighered.com/news/2007/09/17/it; (2007, September). Key findings: The ECAR study of undergraduate students and information technology, 2007. *Educause*. Available at http://net.educause.edu/ir/library/pdf/ERS0706/ekf0706.pdf; Smith, S. D., Salalway, G., & Caruso, J. B. (2009, October). Key findings: The ECAR study of undergraduate students and information technology, 2009. *Educause*. Available at http://net.educause.edu/ir/library/pdf/EKF/EKF0906.pdf.

5. Roach, R. (2004). Survey unveils high-tech ownership profile of American college students. *Black Issues in Higher Education, 21*(16), 37.

6. Jones, S., & Madden, M. (2002, September 15). The Internet goes to college: How students are living in the future with today's technology. *Pew Internet*. Available at http://www.pewinternet.org/PPF/r/71/report_display.asp.

7. *Internet World Stats*. Available at http://www.internetworldstats.com/stats.htm.

8. Billout, G. (2008, July/August). Is Google making us stupid? *The Atlantic.com*. Available at http://www.theatlantic.com/magazine/print/2008/07/is-google-making-us-stupid/6868/.

9. (2010, June). Social insecurity. *Consumer Reports: Best and worst computers*, 24–27.

10. Holson, L. M. (2010, May 8). Tell-all generation learns to keep things offline. *The New York Times*. Available at http://www.nytimes.com/2010/05/09/fashion/09privacy.html.

11. (2010, June). Social insecurity. *Consumer Reports: Best and worst computers*, pp. 24–27.

12. Kelly, W. E., Kelly, K. E. & Clanton, R. C. (2001). The relationship between sleep length and grade-point average among college students. *College Student Journal, 35*(1), 84–86; Stein, R. (2005, October 9). Scientists finding out what losing sleep does to a body. *The Washington Post*. Available at http://www.washingtonpost.com/wp-dyn/content/article/2005/10/08/AR2005100801405.html; Frisinger, C. (2009, October 24). Not getting enough sleep is more serious than you think. *The News Argus*. Available at http://www.thenewsargus.com/2.5246/not-getting-enough-sleep-is-more-serious-than-you-might-think-1.799912.

13. New Media Consortium. (2012). *NMC horizon report: 2012 higher education edition*. Available at http://www.nmc.org/publications/horizon-report-2012-higher-ed-edition.

14. Dahlstrom, E., de Boor, T., Grunwald, P., & Vockley, M. (2011). National study of undergraduate students and information technology. *Educause*. Available at http://net.educause.edu/ir/library/pdf/ERS1103/ERS1103W.pdf.

15. Dahlstrom, E., de Boor, T., Grunwald, P., & Vockley, G. (2011). National study of undergraduate students and technology. *Educause*. Available at http://net.educause.edu/ir/library/pdf/ERS1103/ERS1103W.pdf.

16. http://compnetworking.about.com/od/dns_domainnamesystem/a/domain-name-tld.htm; http://lists.econsultant.com/top-10-domain-name-extensions.html; http://webfoot.com/advice/email.domain.php.

17. Top 15 most popular search engines, April 2012. *eBiz/MBA: The eBusiness Knowledgebase*. Available at http://www.ebizmba.com/articles/search-engines.

18. Caruso, J. B., & Salaway, G. (2007, September). Key findings: The ECAR study of undergraduate students and information technology, 2007. *Educause.* Available at http://net.educause.edu/ir/library/pdf/ERS0706/ekf0706.pdf.

19. Trunk, P. (2008, July/August). Show me the blog. *Wild Blue Yonder,* p. 44.

20. New Media Consortium. (2012). *NMC horizon report: 2012 higher education edition.* Available at http://www.nmc.org/publications/horizon-report-2012-higher-ed-edition.

21. (1998). What is research? Available at http://danroh89.wordpress.com/2010/01/19/research-methodology-2---reading-1/ (from *Practical Research* by P. D. Leedy and J. D. Ormrod).

22. Fitzgerald, M. A. (2004). Making the leap from high school to college. *Knowledge Quest, 32*(4), 19–24; Ehrmann, S. (2004). Beyond computer literacy: Implications of technology for the content of a college education. *Liberal Education.* Available at http://www.aacu.org/liberaleducation/le-fa04/le-fa04feature1.cfm; Thacker, P. (2006, November 15). Are college students techno idiots? *Inside Higher Ed.* Available at http://www.insidehighered.com/news/2006/11/15/infolit.

23. Christina Martinez, Reference Librarian, University of Colorado, Colorado Springs.

24. Ableson, H. Ledeen, K., & Lewis, H. (2008). *Blown to bits: your life, liberty, and happiness after the digital explosion.* Boston, MA: Pearson Education, Inc.

25. Thacker, P. (2006, November 15). Are college students techno idiots? *Inside Higher Ed.* Available at http://www.insidehighered.com/news/2006/11/15/infolit.

26. Ibid.

27. Based on Wood, G. (2004, April 9). Academic original sin: Plagiarism, the Internet, and librarians. *The Journal of Academic Librianship, 30*(3), 237–242.

28. Facebook addiction is needless, yet compelling. *The Volante Online.* Available at http://media.www.volanteonline.com/media/storage/paper468/news/2005/10/05/Opinion/Facebook.Addiction.Is.Needless.Yet.Compelling-1008873.shtml.

29. Greenfield, D. N. (1999). *Virtual addiction.* Oakland, CA: New Harbinger Publications; Yair, E., & Hamburger, A. (2005). *The social net.* Oxford: Oxford University Press; Young, K. S. (1998). *Caught in the net.* New York: John Wiley.

30. Cassagrande, J. (2010). *It was the best of sentences, it was the worst of sentences.* Berkeley, CA: Ten Speed Press.

31. Selberg, A. (2011, March 19). Teaching to the text message. *The New York Times.* Opinion Pages. Available at http://www.nytimes.com/2011/03/20/opinion/20selsberg.html.

Chapter 7

1. Marchand, A. (2010, 29 March). 6 strategies can help entering community-college students succeed. *The Chronicle of Higher Education.* Available at http://chronicle.com/article/6-Strategies-Can-Help-Entering/64871.

2. Burchfield, C. M., & Sappington, J. (2000). Compliance with required reading assignments. *Teaching of Psychology, 27*(1), 58–60; Hobson, E. H. (2004). *Getting students to read: Fourteen tips.* IDEA Paper No. 40, Manhattan, KS: Kansas State University, Center for Faculty Evaluation and Development; Maleki, R. B., & Heerman, C. E. (1992). *Improving student reading.* IDEA Paper No. 26, Manhattan, KS: Kansas State University, Center for Faculty Evaluation and Development. Most Idea

Center papers available at http://www.theideacenter.org/research-and-papers/idea-papers.

3. Marburger, D. R. (2001). Absenteeism and undergraduate exam performance. *Journal of Economic Education, (32)*, 99–109; Romer, D. 1993. Do students go to class? Should they? *Journal of Economic Perspectives* 7(Summer), 167–74.

4. Perkins, K. K., & Wieman, C. E. (2005). The surprising impact of seat location on student performance. *The Physics Teacher, 43*(1), 30–33. Available at http://scitation.aip.org/journals/doc/PHTEAH-ft/vol_43/iss_1/30_1.html?bypassSSO=1.

5. Armbruster, B. B. (2000). Taking notes from lectures. In R. F. Flippo & D. C. Caverly (Eds.), *Handbook of college reading and study strategy research.* Mahwah, NJ: Erlbaum, pp. 175–199.

6. Hughes, C. A., & Suritsky, S. K. (1993). Notetaking skills and strategies for students with learning disabilities. *Preventing School Failure, 38*(1).

7. Staley, C. C., & Staley R. S. (1992). *Communicating in business and the professions.* Mahwah, NJ: Erlbaum, pp. 229–236.

8. Kiewra, K. A., Mayer, R. E., Christensen, M., Kim, S., & Risch, N. (1991). Effects of repetition on recall and note-taking: Strategies for learning from lectures. *Journal of Educational Psychology, 83,* 120–123.

9. Brock, R. (2005, October 28). Lectures on the go. *The Chronicle of Higher Education, 52*(10), A39–42; French, D. P. (2006). iPods: Informative or invasive? *Journal of College Science Teaching, 36*(1), 58–59; Hallett, V. (2005, October 17). Teaching with tech. *U.S. News & World Report, 139*(14), 54–58; *The Horizon Report.* (2006). Stanford, CA: The New Media Consortium.

10. Adapted from Mackie, V., & Bair, B. Tips for improving listening skills; *International Student and Scholar Services.* University of Illinois at Urbana–Champaign. Available at http://www.isss.illinois.edu/publications/english/englang.html#listen.

11. Adapted from *Effective listening skills. Elmhurst College Learning Center.* Available at http://www.elmhurst.edu/library/learningcenter/Listening/listening_behaviors_survey.htm.

12. Palmatier, R. A., & Bennett, J. M. (1974). Note-taking habits of college students. *Journal of Reading, 18,* 215–218; Dunkel, P., & Davy, S. (1989). The heuristic of lecture notetaking: Perceptions of American and international students regarding the value and practices of notetaking. *English for Specific Purposes, 8,* 33–50.

13. Armbruster, *Handbook of college reading and study strategy research.*

14. Van Meter, P., Yokoi, L., & Pressley, M. (1994). College students' theory of note-taking derived from their perceptions of note-taking. *Journal of Educational Psychology, 86,* 323–338.

15. Davis, M., & Hult, R. (1997). Effects of writing summaries as a generative learning activity during note taking. *Teaching of Psychology 24*(1), 47–49; Boyle, J. R., & Weishaar, M. (2001). The effects of strategic notetaking on the recall and comprehension of lecture information for high school students with learning disabilities. *Learning Disabilities Research & Practice 16*(3); Kiewra, K. A. (2002). How classroom teachers can help students learn and teach them how to learn. *Theory into Practice 41*(2), 71–81; Kiewra, How classroom teachers can help students learn and teach them how to learn; Aiken, E. G., Thomas, G. S., & Shennum, W. A. (1975). Memory for a lecture: Effects of notes, lecture rate and informational density. *Journal of Educational Psychology, 67,* 439–444; Hughes, C. A., & Suritsky, S. K. (1994). Note-taking skills of university students with and without learning disabilities. *Journal of Learning Disabilities, 27,* 20–24.

16. Bonner, J. M., & Holliday, W. G. (2006). How college science students engage in note-taking strategies. *Journal of Research in Science Teaching, 43*(8), 786–818.

17. Pauk, W. (2000). *How to study in college.* Boston: Houghton Mifflin.

18. Montis, K. K. (2007). Guided notes: An interactive method of success in secondary and college mathematics classrooms. *Focus on learning problems in mathematics, 29*(3), 55–68.

19. Pardini, E. A., Domizi, D. P., Forbes, D. A., & Pettis, G. V. (2005). Parallel note-taking: A strategy for effective use of Webnotes. *Journal of College Reading and Learning, 35*(2), 38–55. Available at http://www.biology.wustl.edu/pardini/TeachingMaterials/JCRL_spring2005_pardini.pdf.

20. Glenn, D. (2009, May 1). Close the book. Recall. Write it down. *The Chronicle of Higher Education.* Available at http://chronicle.com/article/Close-the-Book-Recall-Write/31819.

21. De Simone, C. (2007). Applications of concept mapping. *College Teaching, 55*(1), 33–36.

22. Kiewra, How classroom teachers can help students learn and teach them how to learn.

23. Porte, L. K. (2001). Cut and paste 101. *Teaching Exceptional Children, 34*(2), 14–20.

24. Adapted from Staley, C. (2003). *50 ways to leave your lectern,* Belmont, CA: Wadsworth, p. 116.

25. Craik, F. I. M., & Watkins, M. J. (1973). The role of rehearsal in short-term memory. *Journal of Verbal Learning and Verbal Behavior, 12,* 599–607.

26. Based on Staley, *50 ways to leave your lectern,* pp. 80–81.

27. Selby, J. (2004). *Quiet your mind.* Makawao, Maui: HI: Inner Ocean Publishing.

28. Ancowitz, N. (2010, June 24). How to increase your self-promotion intelligence, or SPQ. *Psychology Today.* Available at http://www.psychologytoday.com/blog/self-promotion-introverts/201006/how-increase-your-self-promotion-intelligence-or-spq.

29. Hanson, M. (2009, June 17). Is bragging good for your career? *LiveCareer.* Available at http://www.livecareer.com/news/Career/Is-Bragging-Good-for-Your-Career-_$$00858.aspx.

Chapter 8

1. Rogers, M. (2007, March–April). Is reading obsolete? *The Futurist,* 26–27; Waters, L. (2007, February 9). Time for reading. *The Chronicle of Higher Education, 53*(23), 1B6.

2. Caverly, D. C., Nicholson, S. A., & Radcliffe, R. (2004). The effectiveness of strategic reading instruction for college developmental readers. *Journal of College Reading and Learning, 35*(1), 25–49; Simpson, M. L., & Nist, S. L. (1997). Perspectives on learning history: A case study. *Journal of Literacy Research, 29*(3), 363–395.

3. Colarusso, K. (2000). Using a faculty survey of college-level reading and writing requirements to revise developmental reading and writing objectives. Kellogg Institute final report, practicum 1999 (ERIC Document Reproduction Service No. ED448823).

4. English language. *Wikipedia.* Available at http://en.wikipedia.org/wiki/English_language.

5. The sounds of English and the International Phonetic Alphabet. *Antimoon.com.* Available at http://www.antimoon.com/how/pronunc-soundsipa.htm.

6. Bean, J. C. (1996). *Engaging ideas: The professor's guide to integrating writing, critical thinking, and active learning in the classroom.* San Francisco: Jossey-Bass; Wood, N. V. (1997). College reading instruction as reflected by current reading textbooks. *Journal of College Reading and Learning, 27*(3), 79–95.

7. Saumell, L., Hughes, M. T., & Lopate, K. (1999). Underprepared college students' perceptions of reading: Are their perceptions different than other students? *Journal of College Reading and Learning, 29*(2), 123–125.

8. Smith, B. D. (2006). *Breaking through college reading.* New York: Pearson Education, Inc., p. 351.

9. Paulson, E. J. (2006). Self-selected reading for enjoyment as a college developmental reading approach. *Journal of College Reading and Learning, 36*(2), 51–58.

10. Buzan, T. (1983). *Use both sides of your brain.* New York: E. P. Dutton.

11. Ibid.

12. Sternberg, R. J. (1987). Teaching intelligence: The application of cognitive psychology to the improvement of intellectual skills. In J. B. Baron & R. J. Sternberg (Eds.), *Teaching thinking skills: Theory and practice.* New York: Freeman, pp. 182–218.

13. Based on Bean, *Engaging ideas.*

14. Glenn, D. (2009, May 1). Close the book. Recall. Write it down. *The Chronicle of Higher Education.* Available at http://chronicle.com/free/v55/i34/34a00101.htm.

15. McCarroll, C. (2001). To learn to think in college, write—a lot. *Christian Science Monitor, 93*(177), 20.

16. De Vos, I. (1988, October). Getting started: How expert writers do it. *Training & Development Journal,* 18–19.

17. Bean, J. C. (1996). *Engaging ideas: The professor's guide to integrating writing, critical thinking and active learning in the classroom.* San Francisco: Jossey-Bass.

18. Portions of this section are based on Staley, C., & Staley, R. (1992). *Communicating in business and the professions: The inside word.* Belmont, CA: Wadsworth.

19. Portions based on Staley & Staley, *Communicating in business and the professions.*

20. Smith, T. E., & Frymier, A. B. (2006). Get "real": Does practicing speeches before an audience improve performance? *Communication Quarterly, 54*(1), 111–125.

21. Engleberg, I. N. (1994). *The principles of public presentation.* New York: HarperCollins; Daley, K., & Daley-Caravella, L. (2004). *Talk your way to the top.* New York: McGraw-Hill.

22. Decker, K. (9 May, 2012). Airline-inspired analogies. *Decker Blog.* Available at http://decker.com/airline-inspired-analogies/.

23. Ibid.

24. Al-Jarf, R. S. (2002). Effect of online learning on struggling ESL college writers. San Antonio, TX: National Educational Computing Conference. Available at http://scholar.google.com/scholar?hl=en&lr=lang_en&q=cache:nUFnaTizpjgJ:dwc.hct.ac.ae/elearning/Research/SaudiResearchESL.pdf+ESL+college+success+recommendations.

25. VitalSmarts. Crucial conversations explained in 2 minutes. *Youtube.* Available at http://www.youtube.com/watch?v=qHRF8q3ltRw.

26. Patterson, K., Grenny, J., McMillan, R. & Switzler, A. (2011). *Crucial conversations: Tools for talk when stakes are high,* second edition. Excerpt available at http://www.leadershipnow.com/leadershop/0194-6excerpt.html.

1. Bolla, K. I., Lindgren, K. N., Bonaccorsy, C., & Bleecker, M. L. (1991). Memory complaints in older adults: Fact or fiction? *Archives of Neurology, 48,* 61–64.

2. Higbee, K. L. (2004). What aspects of their memories do college students most want to improve? *College Student Journal, 38*(4), 552–556.

3. Higbee, K. L. (1988). *Your memory: How it works and how to improve it* (2nd ed.). New York: Prentice Hall.

4. Ibid.

5. Nairine, J. S. (2006). *Psychology: The adaptive mind.* Belmont, CA: Wadsworth/Thomson Learning.

6. Miller, G. A. (1956). The magical number seven plus or minus two: Some limits on our capacity for processing information. *Psychological Review, 63,* 81–97; Raman, M., McLaughlin, K., Violato, C., Rostom, A., Allard, J.P., & Coderre, S. (2010). Teaching in small portions dispersed over time enhances long-term knowledge retention. *Medical Teacher, 32,* 250–255.

7. Narayanan, K. The neurological scratchpad: What is working memory? (2004, July 7). *Brain Connection.com.* Available at http://brainconnection.positscience.com/topics/?main=fa/working-memory; *Human memory.* Available at http://www.cc.gatech.edu/classes/cs6751_97_winter/Topics/human-cap/memory.html; Kerry, S. (1999–2002). Memory and retention time. *Education Reform.net.* Available at http://www.education-reform.net/memory.htm; Goodhead, J. (1999). The difference between short-term and long-term memory [On-line].

8. Rozakis, L. (2003). *Test-taking strategies and study skills for the utterly confused.* New York: McGraw Hill; Meyers, J. N. (2000). *The secrets of taking any test.* New York: Learning Express; Ehren, B. J. *Mnemonic devices.* Available at http://www.athens.edu/academymodules/a304/support/xpages/a304b0_20600.html; Lloyd, G. (1998–2004). Study skills: Memorize with mnemonics. *Back to College.* Available at http://www.back2college.com/memorize.htm; Raman, M., McLaughlin, K., Violato, C., Rostom, A., Allard, J.P., & Coderre, S. (2010). Teaching in small portions dispersed over time enhances long-term knowledge retention. *Medical Teacher, 32,* 250–255.

9. Willingham, D. T. (2004). Practice makes perfect—but only if you practice beyond the point of perfection. *American Educator.* Available at http://www.aft.org/newspubs/periodicals/ae/spring2004/willingham.cfm.

10. Raman, M., et al. Teaching in small portions.

11. Tigner, R. B. (1999). Putting memory research to good use: Hints from cognitive psychology. *College Teaching, 47*(4), 149–152.

12. Murdock, B. B., Jr. (1960). The distinctiveness of stimuli. *Psychological Reports, 67,* 16–31; Neath, I. (1993). Distinctiveness and serial position effects in recognition. *Memory & Cognition, 21,* 689–698.

13. Cahill, L. (2003). Similar neural mechanisms for emotion – induced memory impairment and enhancement. *Proceedings of the National Academy of Sciences, 100*(23), 13123–13124. Available at http://www.pnas.org/cgi/content/full/100/23/13123.

14. Higbee, *Your memory.*

15. Bean, J. (1996). *Engaging ideas.* San Francisco: Jossey-Bass.

16. Higbee, *Your memory.*

17. Berk, R. A. (2002). *Humor as an instructional defibrillator.* Sterling, VA: Stylus; Berk, R. A. (2003). *Professors are from Mars®, students are from Snickers®.* Sterling, VA: Stylus.

18. Dodeen, H. (2008). Assessing test-taking strategies of university students: developing a scale and estimating its psychometric indices. *Assessment & Evaluation in Higher Education, 33*(4), 409–419.

19. Coren, S. (1996). *Sleep thieves.* New York: Free Press; Cox, K. (2004, October 14).

20. Grant, K. B. (2003, September 4). Popping pills and taking tests. *The Ithacan Online.* Available at http://www.ithaca.edu/ithacan/articles/0309/04/news/2popping_pill.htm.

21. Segerstrom, S. C., & Miller, G. E. (2004). Psychological stress and the human immune system: A meta-analytic study of 30 years of inquiry. *Psychological Bulletin, 130*(4), 601–630. Available at http://www.apa.org/pubs/journals/releases/bul-1304601.pdf; (2004, July 4). Stress affects immunity in ways related to stress type and duration, as shown by nearly 300 studies. *APA Press Release.* Available at http://www.apa.org/news/press/releases/2004/07/stress-immune.aspx.

22. Brinthaupt, T. M., & Shin, C. M. (2001). The relationship of academic cramming to flow experience. *College Student Journal, 35*(3), 457–472.

23. Tigner, R. B. (1999). Putting memory research to good use: Hints from cognitive psychology. *Journal of College Teaching, 47*(4), 149–152.

24. Small, G. (2002). *The memory bible.* New York: Hyperion.

25. (2010). Test anxiety. *University of Oregon Counseling and Testing Center.* Available at http://counseling.uoregon.edu/dnn/SelfhelpResources/StressandAnxiety/TestAnxiety/tabid/337/Default.aspx.

26. Tozoglu, D., Tozoglu, M. D., Gurses, A., & Dogar, C. (2004). The students' perceptions: Essay versus multiple-choice type exams. *Journal of Baltic Science Education, 2*(6), 52–59.

27. Schutz, P. A., & Davis, H. A. (2000). Emotions and self-regulation during test taking. *Educational Psychologist, 35*(4), 243–256.

28. Coren, *Sleep thieves.*

29. Perina, K. (2002). Sum of all fears. *Psychology Today.* Available at http://www.psychologytoday.com/articles/pto-20021108-000001.html.

30. Perry, A. B. (2004). Decreasing math anxiety in college students. *College Student Journal, 38*(2), 321–324.

31. Perry, Decreasing math anxiety in college students.

32. Jonides, J., Lacey, S. C., & Nee, D. E. (2005). Processes of working memory in mind and brain. *Current Directions in Psychological Science, 14*(1), 2–5.

33. Ashcraft, M. H., & Kirk, E. P. (2001). The relationships among working memory, math anxiety, and performance. *Journal of Experimental Psychology: General. 130*(2), 224–237.

34. Beilock, S. L., Kulp, C. A., Holt, L. E., & Carr, T. H. (2004). More on the fragility of performance: Choking under pressure in mathematical problem solving. *Journal of Experimental Psychology: General, 133*(4), 584–600.

35. Mundell, E. J. (2005, March 9). Test pressure toughest on smartest. *Healingwell.com.* Available at http://news.healingwell.com/index.php?p=news1&id=524405.

36. Based partially on Arem, C. (2003). *Conquering math anxiety,* second edition. Belmont, CA: Brooks/Cole.

37. Glenn, D. (2010, February 7). How students can improve by studying themselves. *The Chronicle of Higher Education.* Available at http://chronicle.com/article/Struggling-Students-Can-Imp/64004/.

38. Firmin, M., Hwang, C., Copella, M., & Clark, S. (2004). Learned helplessness: The effect of failure on test-taking. *Education, 124*(4), 688–693.

39. Heidenberg, A. J., & Layne, B. H. (2000). Answer changing: A conditional argument. *College Student Journal, 34*(3), 440–451.

40. See http://news.bbc.co.uk/2/hi/uk_news/scotland/glasgow_and_west/4755297.stm.

41. Preparing for tests and exams. (2007). *York University.* Available at http://www.yorku.ca/cds/lss/skillbuilding/exams.html#Multiple.

42. Taking exams. *Brockport High School.* Available at http://www.frontiernet.net/~jlkeefer/takgexm.html. Adapted from Penn State University; On taking exams. *University of New Mexico.* Available at http://www.unm.edu/~quadl/college_learning/taking_exams.html; Lawrence, J. (2006). Tips for taking examinations. *Lawrence Lab Homepage.* Available at http://cobamide2.bio.pitt.edu/testtips.htm; The multiple choice exam. (2003). *Counselling Services, University of Victoria.* Available at http://www.coun.uvic.ca/learning/exams/multiple-choice.html; General strategies for taking essay tests. *GWired.* Available at http://gwired.gwu.edu/counsel/asc/index.gw/Site_ID/46/Page_ID/14565/; Test taking tips: Guidelines for answering multiple-choice questions. *Arizona State University.* Available at http://neuer101.asu.edu/additionaltestingtips.htm; Landsberger, J. (2007). True/false tests. *Study Guides and Strategies.* Available at http://www.studygs.net/tsttak2.htm; Landsberger, J. (2007). Multiple choice tests. *Study Guides and Strategies.* Available at http://www.studygs.net/tsttak3.htm; Landsberger, J. (2007). The essay exam. *Study Guides and Strategies.* Available at http://www.studygs.net/tsttak4.htm; Landsberger, J. (2007). Short answer tests. *Study Guides and Strategies.* Available at http://www.studygs.net/tsttak5.htm; Landsberger, J. (2007). Open book tests. *Study Guides and Strategies.* Available at http://www.studygs.net/tsttak7.htm; Rozakis, L. (2003). *Test-taking strategies and study skills for the utterly confused.* New York: McGraw-Hill; Meyers, J. N. (2000). *The secrets of taking any test.* New York: Learning Express; Robinson, A. (1993). *What smart students know.* New York: Crown Trade Paperbacks.

43. *Plagiarism.org.* Available at http://www.plagiarism.org/facts.html; A cheating crisis in America's schools. (2007, 29 April). *ABC News.* Available at http://abcnews.go.com/Primetime/story?id=132376&page=1.

44. Young, J. R. (2010, March 28). High tech cheating abounds, and professors bear some blame. *The Chronicle of Higher Education.* Available at http://chronicle.com/article/High-Tech-Cheating-on-Homew/64857/; Gabriel, T. (2010, August 1). Plagiarism lines blur for students in digital age. *The New York Times.* Available at http://www.nytimes.com/2010/08/02/education/02cheat.html?_r=1&src=me&ref=homepage.

45. Caught cheating. (2004, April 29). *Primetime Live,* ABC News Transcript. Interview of college students by Charles Gibson; Zernike, K. (2002, November 2). With student cheating on the rise, more colleges are turning to honor codes. *The New York Times,* p. Q10, column 1, National Desk; Warren, R. (2003, October 20). Cheating: An easy way to cheat yourself. The Voyager via U-Wire. *University Wire (www.uwire.com)*; Thomson, S. C. (2004, February 13). Heyboer, K. (2003, August 23). Nearly half of college students say Internet plagiarism isn't cheating. *The Star-Ledger Newark, New Jersey*; Kleiner, C., & Lord, M. (1999).

46. Tagg, J. (2004, March-April). Why learn? What we may really be teaching students. *About Campus,* 2–10; Marton, F., & Säljö, R. On qualitative differences in learning: I-Outcome and process. (1976). *British Journal of Educational Psychology, 46,* 4–11.

47. Noice, H., & Noice, T. (2006). What studies of actors and acting can tell us about memory and cognitive functioning. *Current Directions in Psychological Science, 15*(1), 14–18.

CHAPTER 10

1. Some situation topics are suggested at Hay Group Transforming Learning EI Quiz. *Haygroup.com.* Available at http://www.haygroup.com/leadershipandtalentondemand/Demos/EI_Quiz.aspx.

2. Gardner, H. (1993). *Multiple intelligences: The theory in practice.* New York: Basic Books; Checkley, K. (1997). The first seven … and the eighth: A conversation with Howard Gardner. Expanded Academic ASAP (online database). Original Publication: *Education,* 116.

3. Parker, J. D. A., Duffy, J. M., Wood, L. M., Bond, B. J., & Hogan, M. J. (2005). Academic achievement and emotional intelligence: Predicting the successful transition from high school to university. *Journal of the First Year Experience & Students in Transition 17*(1), 67–78; Schutte, N. S., & Malouff, J. (2002). Incorporating emotional skills content in a college transition course enhances student retention. *Journal of the First Year Experience & Students in Transition 14*(1), 7–21.

4. Berenson, R.; Boyles, G.; Weaver, A. (2008). Emotional intelligence as a predictor for success in online learning. *International Review of Research in Open and Distance Learning, 9*(2), 1–16; Zeidner, M., & Roberts, R. (2010). Coping mediates the relationship between emotional intelligence (EI) and academic achievement. *Contemporary Educational Psychology,* 36 (2011) 60–70.

5. EQ-i:HEd, Multi-Health Systems, Inc. North Tonawanda, NY. Available at http://www.mhs.com. Used with permission.

6. Turning lemons into lemonade: Hardiness helps people turn stressful circumstances into opportunities. (2003, December 22). *Psychology Matters.* Available at *APA Online* at http://www.apa.org/research/action/lemon.aspx; Marano, H. E. (2003). The art of resilience. *Psychology Today.* Available at http://www.psychologytoday.com/articles/pto-20030527-000009.html; Fischman, J. (1987). Getting tough: Can people learn to have disease-resistant personalities? *Psychology Today, 21,* 26–28; Friborg, O., Barlaug, D., Martinussen, M., Rosenvinge, & J. H. Intelligence. *International Journal of Methods in Psychiatric Research, 14*(1), 29–42; Schulman, P. (1995). Explanatory style and achievement in school and work. In G. M. Buchanan & M. E. P. Seligman (Eds.), *Explanatory style* (pp. 159–171). Hillsdale, NJ: Lawrence Erlbaum; American Psychological Association. (1997). Learned optimism yields health benefits. *Discovery Health.* Available at http://health.discovery.com/centers/mental/articles/optimism/optimism.html.

7. Cherniss, C. (2000). *Emotional Intelligence: What it is and why it matters.* Paper presented at the Annual Meeting of the Society for Industrial and Organizational Psychology, New Orleans, LA. Available at http://www.eiconsortium.org/reports/what_is_emotional_intelligence.html.

8. Ibid.

9. Goleman, D. (2002, June 16). Could you be a leader? *Parade Magazine,* pp. 4–6.

10. Boyatzis, R. E., Cowan, S. S., & Kolb, D. A. (1995). *Innovation in professional education: Steps on a journey from teaching to learning.* San Francisco: Jossey-Bass.

11. Saxbe, D. (2004, November/December). The socially savvy. *Psychology Today.* Available at http://www.psychologytoday.com/articles/pto-3636.html.

12. Kelly, W. E. (2003). Worry content associated with decreased sleep length among college students: Sleep deprivation leads to increased worrying. *College Student Journal, 37*, 93–95.

13. Knox, D. H. (1970). Conceptions of love at three developmental levels. *The Family Coordinator, 19*(2), 151–157; Fisher, *Why we love;* Cramer, D. (2004). Satisfaction with a romantic relationship, depression, support and conflict. *Psychology and Psychotherapy: Theory, Research and Practice, 77*(4), 449–461.

14. Fisher, H. (2004). *Why we love.* New York: Henry Holt.

15. Ibid.

16. Beach, S. R. H., & Tesser, A. (1988). Love in marriage; a cognitive account. In R. J. Sternberg & M. L. Barnes (Eds.), *The Psychology of Love* (pp. 330–355). New Haven, CT: Yale University Press; Hatfield, E., & Walster, G. W. (1978). *A new look at love.* Lanham, MD: University Press of America.

17. Parker-Popel, T. (2009, April 20). What are friends for? A longer life. *The New York Times.* Available at http://www.nytimes.com/2009/04/21/health/21well.html?_r=1; Ybarra, O., Burnstein, E., Winkielman, P., Keller, M. C., Manis, M. Chan, E., & Rodriguez, J. (2008). Mental exercising through simple socializing: Social interaction promotes general cognitive functioning. *Personality and Social Psychology Bulletin, 34*, 248–259.

18. Knox, D., Schacht, C., & Zusman, M. E. (1999, March). Love relationships among college students. *College Student Journal, 33*(1), 149–154. Available at http://findarticles.com/p/articles/mi_m0FCR/is_1_33/ai_62894068/.

19. Schwartz, P. (2003, May–June). Love is not all you need. *Psychology Today.* Available at http://www.psychologytoday.com/articles/200302/love-is-not-all-you-need.

20. Bach, G. R., & Goldberg, H. (1974). *Creative aggression: The art of assertive living.* Garden City, NJ: Doubleday; Bach, G. R, & Wyden, P. (1972). *The intimate enemy: How to fight fair in love and marriage.* New York: Avon; Bach, G. R., Deutsch, R. M., (1985). *Stop! You're driving me crazy.* New York: Berkley Publishing Group; Tucker-Ladd, C. E. (1996–2006); *Driving each other crazy. Psychological self-help.* Available at http://psychologicalselfhelp.org/Chapter9/chap9_90.html.

21. Fisher, *Why we love.*

22. Fisher, R., & Brown, S. (1988). *Getting together: Building a relationship that gets to yes.* Boston: Houghton Mifflin, p. xi.

23. Wilmot, W. W., & Hocker, J. L. (2010). *Interpersonal conflict* (8th ed.). New York: McGraw Hill.

24. Based in part on Marano, H. (2002). Relationship rules. *Psychology Today.* Available at http://www.psychologytoday.com/articles/200410/relationship-rules.

25. Dakss, B. (2006, March 3). Study: Bad relationships bad for heart. *CBS News.* Available at http://www.cbsnews.com/2100-500194_162-1364889.html. (2005, December 5) Unhappy marriage: Bad for your health. *WebMD.* Available at http://www.webmd.com/sex-relationships/news/20051205/unhappy-marriage-bad-for-your-health. Based on Keicolt-Glaser, J. (2005). *Archives of general psychiatry, 62*, 1377–1384.

26. Dusselier, L., Dunn, B., Wang, Y., Shelley, M. C., & Whalen, D. F. (2005). Personal, health, academic, and environmental predictors of stress for residence hall students. *Journal of American College Health, 54*(1), 15–24; Hardigg, V., & Nobile, C. (1995). Living with a stranger. *U.S. News & World Report, 119*(12), 90–91. Available at http://www.usnews.com/usnews/edu/articles/950925/archive_032964_print.htm; Nankin, J. (2005). Rules for roomies. *Careers & Colleges, 25*(4), 29.

27. Thomas, K. (1977). Conflict and conflict management. In M. D. Dunnette (Ed.), *Handbook of industrial and organizational psychology*, 889–935 Chicago: Rand McNally; Kilmann, R., & Thomas, K. W. (1975). Interpersonal conflict handling behavior as reflections of Jungian personality dimensions. *Psychological Reports, 37*, 971–980; Rahim, M., & Magner, N. R. (1995). Confirmatory factor analysis of the styles of handling interpersonal conflict: First-order factor model and its invariance across groups. *Journal of Applied Psychology, 80*, 122–132; Wilmot, W. W., & Hocker, J. L. (2001). *Interpersonal conflict* (6th ed.). New York: McGraw Hill. Kilmann, R. H., and K. W. Thomas. (1977). Developing a Forced Choice Measure of Conflict-Handling Behavior: The MODE Instrument, *Educational and psychological measurement, 37*(2), 309–325.

28. Miller, G. R., & Steinberg, M. (1975). *Between people: A new analysis of interpersonal communication.* Chicago: Science Research Associates.

29. Staley, C. (2003). *50 ways to leave your lectern,* Belmont, CA: Wadsworth, p. 32.

30. Staley, C. (2003). *50 ways to leave your lectern.* Belmont, CA: Wadsworth, p. 67. Based on Defining "Diversity." (1995). In B. Pike & C. Busse, *101 games for trainers* (p. 11). Minneapolis: Lakewood Books.

31. Fulbeck, K. (2010). *Mixed: Portraits of multiracial kids.* San Francisco: Chronicle Books.

32. *Race, the power of an illusion.* PBS. California Newsreel. Available at http://www.pbs.org/race/000_General/000_00-Home.htm.

33. Based on "Sorting People" activity at http://www.pbs.org/race/002_SortingPeople/002_00-home.htm.

34. Wyer, K. (2007). Today's college freshmen have family income 60% above national average, UCLA survey reveals. *UCLA News.* Available at http://www.heri.ucla.edu/PDFs/PR_TRENDS_40YR.pdf</URL.

35. Humphrey, D., & Davenport, A. (2004, Summer/Fall). What really matters in college: How students view and value liberal education. *Liberal Education.* Excerpt: Diversity and civic engagement outcomes ranked among least important. Available at http://www.diversityweb.org/Digest/vol9no1/humphreys.cfm.

36. Laird, T. F. (2005). College students' experiences with diversity and their effects on academic self-confidence, social agency, and disposition toward critical thinking. *Research in Higher Education, 46*(4), 365–387.

37. Bucher, R. D. (2004). *Diversity consciousness: Opening our minds to people, cultures, and opportunities* (2nd ed.). Upper Saddle River, NJ: Pearson Education.

38. Based on Nilsen, L. B. (1998). The circles of awareness. *Teaching at Its Best.* Bolton, MA: Anker Publishing; Bucher, R. D. (2008). *Building cultural intelligence: Nine megaskills.* Upper Saddle River, NJ: Pearson.

39. Carnes, M. C. (2005). Inciting speech. *Change, 37*(2), 6–11.

40. Lyons, P. (2005, April 15). The truth about teaching about racism. *The Chronicle of Higher Education, 51*(32), B5.

41. Epstein, G. (2005, June 5) More women advance, but sexism persists. *College Journal from the Wall Street Journal;* Leahey, C. (2012, July 18). Update: Fortune 500 women CEOs hits a record 20. *CNN Money.* Available at http://postcards.blogs.fortune.cnn.com/2012/07/18/fortune-500-women-ceos-2/.

42. Wessel, D. (2003, September 9). Race still a factor in hiring decisions. *College Journal from the Wall Street Journal.* Available

at http://usearch.mnscu.edu/news/fw/fw4522FutureWork.html.

43. Beilke, J. R., & Yssel, N. (1999). The chilly climate for students with disabilities in higher education. *College Student Journal, 33*(3), 364–372.

44. Parker, P. N. (2006, March–April). Sustained dialogue: How students are changing their own racial climate. *About Campus, 11*(1), 17–23.

45. Gortmaker, V. J., & Brown, R. D. (2006). Out of the college closet: Differences in perceptions and experiences among out and closeted lesbian and gay students. *College Student Journal, 40*(3), 606–619.

46. FBI releases 2010 hate crime statistics. (2010, November 14). *FBI, Department of Justice.* Available at http://www.fbi.gov/news/pressrel/press-releases/fbi-releases-2010-hate-crime-statistics.

47. Based on Earley, P. C., & Mosakowski, E. (2004, October). Cultural intelligence. *Harvard Business Review,* p. 143.

48. Earley, P. C., & Mosakowski, E. (2004, October). Cultural intelligence. *Harvard Business Review,* 139–146; Early, C. P., Ang, S., & Tan, J. (2006) CQ: *Developing cultural intelligence at work.* Stanford, CA: Stanford University Press; Osborn, T. N., (2006). *"CQ": Another aspect of emotional intelligence.* Available at http://www.teaminternational.net/resources/docs/cultural%20intelligence.pdf.

49. Earley, P. C., & Mosakowski, E. Cultural intelligence.

50. Ten things we know to be true. *Google Company.* Available at http://www.google.com/about/company/philosophy/.

51. Advertising, Marketing, & Communications. (2010). *Quicksilver Translate.* Available at http://www.quicksilvertranslate.com/customers/industry-solutions/advertising- branding-and-marketing.

52. Farrell, E.F. (2005, August 5). Student volunteers are worth billions. *The Chronicle of Higher Education,* 51(48), A33; 2011 annual survey executive summary: Deepening the roots of civic engagement. *Campus Compact.* Available at http://www.compact.org/wp-content/uploads/2008/11/2011-Annual-Survey-Executive-Summary.pdf.

53. Zlotkowski, E. (1999). Pedagogy and engagement. In R. G. Bringle, R. Games, & E. A. Malloy (Eds.). (1999). *Colleges and Universities as Citizens* (pp. 96–120). Needham Heights, MA: Allyn & Bacon.

54. Honnet, E. P., & Poulsen, S. J. (1989). *Principles of good practice for combining service and learning: A Wingspread special report.* Racine, WI: The Johnson Foundation. Available at http://servicelearning.org/filemanager/download/Principles_of_Good_Practice_for_Combining_Service_and_Learning.pdf/.

55. Eyler, J., Giles, Jr., D. E., & Schmiede, A. (1996). *A practitioner's guide to reflection in service learning: Student voices and reflections.* Nashville, TN: Vanderbilt University Press.

56. Rath, T., & Clifton, D. O. (2004). *How full is your bucket?* New York: Gallup Press.

57. Bregman, P. (2010, July 21). How to avoid (and quickly recover from) misunderstandings. *Harvard Business Review Blog.* Available at http://blogs.hbr.org/bregman/2010/07/how-to-avoid-and-quickly-recov.html; Bregman, P. (2011, January 3). The best way to use the last five minutes of the day. *Harvard Business Review Blog.* Available at http://blogs.hbr.org/bregman/2011/01/the-best-wayto-use-the-last-f.html.

58. Ibid.

CHAPTER 11

1. Gregory, M. (2003, September 12). A liberal education is not a luxury. *The Chronicle of Higher Education, 50*(3), B16.

2. Staley, R. S., II. (2003). In C. Staley, *50 ways to leave your lectern* (pp. 70–74). Belmont, CA: Wadsworth.

3. Farrell, E. F. (2006, December 12). Freshmen put high value on how well college prepares them for a profession, survey finds. *The Chronicle of Higher Education.* Farrell, E. F. (2007, January 5). Report says freshmen put career prep first. *The Chronicle of Higher Education, 53*(18), A32. Available at http://chronicle.com/article/Report-Says-Freshmen-Put-Ca/19260/; Bok, D. (2010, January 31). College and the well-lived life. *The Chronicle of Higher Education.* Available at http://chronicle.com/article/Collegethe-Well-Lived-/63789/.

4. Associated Press (2007, January 22). Polls say wealth important to youth. *NewsOK.* Available at http://newsok.com/article/3002446; Schwartz, B. (2004, January 23). The tyranny of choice. *The Chronicle of Higher Education, 50*(20), B6.

5. Berrett, D. (2012, June 3). Changing majors is no big deal if the timing is right, studies find. *The Chronicle of Higher Education.* Available at http://chronicle.com/article/Changing-Majors-Is-No-Big-Deal/132105/.

6. Koeppel, D. (2004, December 5). Choosing a college major: For love or for the money? *The New York Times,* section 10, p. 1, column 4. Available at http://www.nytimes.com/2004/12/05/jobs/05jmar.html?ex=1259989200&en=51dcc14fa52a65e7&ei=5090&partner=rssuserland; Dunham, K. J. (2004, March 2). No ivory tower: College students focus on career. *Wall Street Journal* (Eastern Edition), pp. B1, B8. Available at http://online.wsj.com/article/SB107818521697943524.html.

7. Based in part on Gordon, V. N., & Sears, S. J. (2004). *Selecting a college major: Exploration and decision making,* 5th ed. Upper Saddle River, NJ: Pearson Education.

8. Based on Hansen, R. S., & Hansen, K. Using a SWOT analysis in your career planning. *Quintessential Careers.* Available at http://www.quintcareers.com/SWOT_Analysis.html.

9. Rowh, M. (2003, February–March). Choosing a major. *Career World, 31*(5), 21–23.

10. Ezarik, M. M. (2007, April–May). A major decision. *Career World, 35*(6), 20–22.

11. Rask, K. N., & Bailey, E. M. (2002). Are faculty role models? Evidence from major choice in an undergraduate institution. *The Journal of Economic Education, 33*(2), 99–124.

12. Based on Staley, *50 ways to leave your lectern,* p. 82.

13. Levine, M. (2005). *Ready or not, here life comes.* New York: Simon & Schuster, p. 4; Levine, M. (2005, February 18). College graduates aren't ready for the real world. *The Chronicle of Higher Education, 51*(24), B11.

14. Farr, M. & Shatkin, L. (2007). *O*Net Dictionary of occupational titles.* (2007). Indianapolis, IN: Jist Works. Or see *O*Net Online* (Occupational Information Network) at http://www.onetonline.org/.

15. Based on Schwartz, The tyranny of choice.

16. See J. K. Rowling Biography at http://www.biography.com/people/jk-rowling-40998.

17. Levine, *Ready or not, here life comes.*

18. Gallo, A. (2011, March 18). Where Will You Be in Five Years? *HBR Blog Network.* Available at http://blogs.hbr.org/hmu/2011/03/where-will-you-be-in-five-year.html.

19. Brooks, K. (2009). *You Majored in What?* New York: Viking.

20. Kanter, R. M. (2011, March). Managing yourself: zoom in, zoom out. *Harvard Business Review Magazine*. Available at http://hbr.org/2011/03/managing-yourself-zoom-in-zoom-out/ar/1.

21. Gallo, A. (2011, March 18). Where will you be in five years? *HBR Blog Network*. Available at http://blogs.hbr.org/hmu/2011/03/where-will-you-be-in-five-year.html.

CHAPTER 12

1. Goldhaber, G. M. (1986). *Organizational communication* (4th ed.). Dubuque, IA: Wm. C. Brown, p. 236. In Staley, R. S., II, & Staley, C. C. (1992). *Communicating in business and the professions: The inside word*. Belmont, CA: Wadsworth.

2. See *Top Job Search Websites* at http://www.quintcareers.com/top_10_sites.html.

3. Staley, *50 ways to leave your lectern*, p. 33. Based on "Group Resume." (1995). In M. Silberman, *101 ways to make training active* (pp. 49–50). Johannesburg: Pfeiffer.

4. McConnon, A. (2007, August 30). Social networking is graduating—and hitting the job market. *BusinessWeek*. pp. IN 4, IN 6.

5. Stewart, J. (2012, March 23). Working: No resume needed. *GPB News*. Available at http://www.gpb.org/news/2012/03/23/working-no-resume-needed.

6. Giang, V. (2012, April 9). What recruiters look at during the 6 seconds they spend on your resume. *Business Insider*. Available at http://articles.businessinsider.com/2012-04-09/news/31311078_1_recruiters-study-decision.

7. Why sneaky resume tactics may no longer aid job hunters. (2009, March 10). *Vault Blogs.com*. Available at http://blogs.vault.com/blog/resumes-cover-letters/why-sneaky-resume-tactics-may-no-longer-aid-job-hunters/.

8. *Job interviews get creative*. (2003, August 22). *NPR*. Available at http://www.npr.org/templates/story/story.php?storyId=1405340.

9. Vance, E. (2007, February 2). College graduates lack key skills, report says. *The Chronicle of Higher Education, 53*(22), A30.

10. Ashler, D. (2004). *How to get any job with any major*. Berkeley, CA: Ten Speed Press.

11. Pollak, L. (2007). *Getting from college to career*. New York: HarperCollins.

12. *Occupational Outlook Handbook 2012–2013*. Available at http://www.bls.gov/ooh/Community-and-Social-Service/Social-and-human-service-assistants.htm and http://www.bls.gov/ooh/Community-and-Social-Service/Social-workers.htm.

13. Cedja, B. D., Kaylor, A. J., & Rewey, K. L. (1998). Transfer shock in an academic discipline: The relationship between students' majors and their academic performance. *Community College Review, 26*(3), 1–13.

14. Thurmond, K. (2007). Transfer shock: Why is a term forty years old still relevant? *National Academic Advising Association (NACADA)*. Available at http://www.nacada.ksu.edu/clearinghouse/AdvisingIssues/Transfer-Shock.htm; Rhine, T. J., Milligan, D. M., & Nelson, L. R. (2000). Alleviating transfer shock: Creating an environment for more successful transfer students. *Community College Journal of Research and Practice, 24*, 443–452.

15. Idea from Wallace, P. C. (2005). *Life 101*. New York: iUniverse, p. 3.

16. Coplin, B. (2003). *10 things employers want you to learn in college*. Berkeley, CA: Ten Speed Press.

17. Anderson, K. (2012, June 5). What captures your attention controls your life. *HBR Blog Network*. Available at http://blogs.hbr.org/cs/2012/06/what_captures_your_attention_c.html.

18. Hanson, R. (2009). *Buddha's brain: The practical neuroscience of happiness, love, and wisdom*. Oakland, CA: New Harbinger Publications.

19. Sakai, J. (2012, March 15). A wandering mind reveals mental processes and priorities. *Science Daily*. Available at http://www.sciencedaily.com/releases/2012/03/120315161326.htm.

20. Anderson, K. What captures your attention controls your life.

21. Marsh, N. (2011, February). How to make work-life balance work. *TedTalks*. Available at http://www.ted.com/talks/nigel_marsh_how_to_make_work_life_balance_work.html.

22. Bregman, P. (2010, July 30). Don't regret working too hard. *HBR Blog Network*. Available at http://blogs.hbr.org/bregman/2010/07/dont-regret-working-too-hard.html.

Index

Note: numbers followed by (b) indicate boxes; by (f) indicate figures.

A

A-B-C method, 95–96
Ability, effort vs., 39–40
    defined, 39
Absolutes, defined, 252
Academic, defined, 4
Academic achievement, critical thinking
        and, 130
Academic advisor, 12
Academic anatomy, 314–315
Academic disciplines, defined, 304
Academic Intrinsic Motivation Scale
        (AIMS), 34–35
Academic professionalism, 7–9
    college as daily obligation, 7
    choosing to go to class, 7
    college email's, 9
    engagement in school, 10
    "Ostrich Syndrome," 8
    groups, working in, 9
    respect and, 8
    rules and policies, 8
    taking charge, 8–9
    time investment, 9
Academic relevant questions, 192
Academic rankings, 315–316
Academic responsibility. *See*
        Responsibility
Academic Search Premier, 156
Academic success, 23f, 67, 84, 203
Accomplishments, acknowledging, 102
Accountability, defined, 240
Accuracy, in information literacy, 146,
        157, 159
Acronyms, defined, 239f
Act, memory and, 239f
Action
    in CRIA system, 33
    plan of, 129
Active-learning lecturer, defined, 178
Actors, memory and, 243, 264
Adams, Franklin P., 156
Adaptability skills, 272
Addison, Joseph, 212
Adequacy, defined, 121
Adler, Mortimer, 55
Advisor, academic, 12
Affordability, of Internet, 146
Age diversity, 286
AIMS. *See* Academic Intrinsic Motivation
        Scale (AIMS)
Alertness, relaxed, 53

Alexander, Katie, 200–202
Allen, David, 103
All-over-the-map lecturer, defined, 178
Alternating, time/energy and, 102
Altshuler, Michael, 98
American mosaic, 289–291
American Psychological Association
        (APA), 163
Analogy, defined, 163
Analysis, SWOT, 310–312
Analytical decision making, 128
Analyze, defined, 116, 256
Answers, searching for, 134
Anthropology, defined, 306
Antivirus program, 142
Anxiety
    blocking, brain and, 52
    concentration and, 44
    contributing factors, 98, 100
    cramming and, 244
    math, 247–249
    perfectionists and, 98
    procrastination and, 100
    reduction, 246, 247, 248
    sleep and, 244
    speaking, 221b
    test, 244–247
    usefulness of, 245
APA. *See* American Psychological
        Association (APA)
Aptitude
    versus attitude, 37–38
    defined, 37
Arguments
    acceptance of, 117
    analyzing, 120–121
    bad, 122
    contradictory, 120
    deductive, 120
    inductive, 120
    propositions, 120
Aristotle, 121
Art, defined, 306
Ask
    connections and, 51
    defined, 210
    explained, 191–192
    learning and, 54, 55
    questions and, 191–193
Assertions, defined, 256
Assessment tools, 274
Assignments, learning and, 71, 72

Associate's degree, 6–7, 10, 11, 21
Assumptions, 121–122
Attendance, 76, 173
Attention, 13
Attention management, 84
Attention span, 71–72
Attitude
    adjustments, 38
    aptitude versus, 37–38
    defined, 37
    goals and, 38
    learning and, 38, 54
    tests and, 240, 242
Audiences, and writing, 214, 216
Audiovisual resources, 156
Aural learning strategy, 61, 70f
    defined, 60
    example for, 61, 72
    listening and, 181
    multimodal, 158
    multiple intelligences and, 66
    notes and, 181
    See also VARK
Authors, citing, 160–161
Authority, in information literacy, 159–160
Availability, on Internet, 145

B

Bach, Richard, 41
Bachelor's degree, 7, 10, 21
Backing up electronic work, 143
Balance, 82–83
    alternating strategy, 102
    bundling strategy, 103
    career outlook, 343
    critical thinking and, 130
    outsourcing strategy, 102–103
    simplifying strategy, 103
    techflexing strategy, 103
    time and, 102
    work and, 325
Barrett, Collean C., 161
Baxter, Kevin, 232–233
Bean, John C, 217
Behavioral, defined, 246
Behavioral aspects, of test anxiety, 247
Behavioral decision making, 129
Benedict Arnolds, defined, 279
Berle, Milton, 236
Bernard, Claude, 55
Berra, Yogi, 11, 324

Bias, 74, 117
Biology, 209, 211, 304, 305, 306
Bing, 151
Blackboard, 143, 145, 149, 151
Blamers, defined, 279
Blended, defined, 140
Blessings, attitude and, 38
Blessington, Marguerite, 163
Bloch, Robert, 142
Blocking, classes and, 18, 85, 91
Blogs, defined, 151
Bloom, Harold, 209
Bodily-kinesthetic intelligence, 57, 59
Body language, 174, 195
Body rhythm, energy and, 87–88
Bookmark, defined, 159
Book(s)
    buying, 18
    note-taking by, 189
Boorstin, Daniel, 76
Boss, relationship with, 229, 326, 339
Brain
    fatigue, 31
    focus and, 52, 85, 149
    hardwire connections, 51
    improving activity in, 78
    learning and, 50–53
    listening and, 176
    love and, 276
    majors/careers and, 229
    memory and, 127
    mind maps and, 186–187f
    multitasking and, 31
    notes and, 190
    sleep and, 247
    use of, 51
    wellness and, 78, 149
    See also Mind maps
The Brain That Changes Itself (Doldge), 78
Brainstorming, 124–125
Brilliant, Ashleigh, 284
Buddha, 336
Bundling, 103
Burn-out, 89
Bush, George H. W., 288
Business Source Premier, 156
Buttons, pushing, 130
Buzan, Tony, 60

C

Cage, John, 133
Calculators, 248
Calming, mind distractions, 175, 195–196
Campus Compact, 320
Campus resources, 17–20
Campus Security, 20

Camtasia, 151
Capra, Frank, 133
Car and Driver, 61
Card catalog, 155–156
    defined, 155
Career outlook feature
    balance in life, 343
    classes and, 44
    conversations, command of, 229
    defined, 36, 37, 44
    doctor for, 45
    expectations, 45–46
    failure and, 264–265
    future goals, 318–319
    grit and, 78–79
    jobs and, 36, 37, 318–319
    knowing yourself, 45–46
    lawyer for, 114–115
    personal involvement and, 298–299
    psychologist for, 110
    relationships and, 298–299
    social (human) services, 336f
    SPQ and, 196–197
    thinking and, 135
    time management and, 111
    work versus progress, 111
    writing and, 166–167
Careers
    as accounting assistant, 82
    AIMS and, 36–37
    as architect, 232
    as chemical technician, 314f
    chemistry major and, 314f
    choosing, 307–316
    as day care owner, 170–171
    defined, 326
    early childhood development, 170–171
    as entrepreneur, 303
    as forensic scientist, 48, 314f
    interview for, 333–334
    job vs., 316
    launching, 325–326
    as legal assistant, 115
    major versus, 313–316
    motivation for, 339
    as nurse, 268
    as paralegal, 114–115
    options for, 326
    as pharmaceutical salesperson, 314f
    preferences and, 310–312
    preliminary research on, 308–309
    reading disabilities and, 200–201
    as recording artist, 29
    as skateboarder, 302–303, 311
    as science teacher, 313f
    as social worker, 322, 323, 336f
    as teacher, 313f, 314f

    as web designer, 138, 331, 332, 333
    See also Internships; Jobs
Career center, 19
Carey, Sandra, 306
Carlson, Dawn, 102
Carter, Jimmy, 289
Carver, George Washington, 172
Case studies, 25b–26
Catastrophic attitude, tests and, 246
Cell phone, 8, 16, 110, 174
Cell phone calendars, 92, 94
Certificates, 7, 21
C-Factors, 36, 37, 44
Challenge reaction insight action system
    (CRIA) system, 31–33
Challenge(s)
    adjustment of, 53
    in AIMS, 36, 37
    constructive responses to, 38
    in CRIA system, 32
    focusing as, 30–31
    learning and, 30, 32, 35–36
    successful people and, 39
    talk through, 71
"Challenge/Reaction" feature
    critical thinking and, 115, 135
    diversity and, 268–269, 299
    dreams/goals and, 28–30, 46
    engaging and, 170–172
    information literacy and, 140
    future success, 322–323
    learning styles, 47–50, 79
    listening and, 170–172, 197
    majors/careers and, 302–303, 319
    memory and, 232–234
    note-taking and, 170–172
    plagiarism and, 139–140, 167
    to not procrastinate, 82–83, 111
    online learning and, 138–140, 167
    reading/studying and, 200–202
    relationships and, 268–269, 299
    seven C's and, 218–220
    seven P's and, 222–224
    SWOT analysis, 319
    technology and, 138–140
    tests and, 232–234, 265
    thinking critically and creatively,
        114–116, 136
    time/energy and, 81–84, 112
Cheating, 162, 258–261
Chemistry, defined, 306
Chesterfield, Lord, 286
Chew on, defined, 207
Chicago Manual of Style, 163
Child care, 19
Choices
    attitude and, 38

career, 65, 110, 307–308, 336
classes and, 8
communication and, 229, 281
conflict and, 281–282f
focus and, 303, 317
learning and, 55
multiple choice tests, 253
negative, 252, 281
nonstop, 103, 110
negotiation and, 335
personality types and making, 110
relationships and, 281–282
strategic, 67
Chronological approach, for résumé,
330–332f
Chunking, memory and, 237–238, 264
Churchill, Winston, 251
Circle of Awareness, 290
Circle of Learning, 305–306
Claims, 119
case study, 126–127
considering, 122
See also Evidence
Clarity, in writing, 218
Class
choosing to go to, 8
materials for, 174
online. *See* Learning online
skipping, 92
time, 72, 175, 182
See also Focused listening
Classmates, relationships with, 277
Classrooms/classes
control factor in, 44
diversity in, 289
online, 140–144
seating strategy, 174
C-learning, 140–141
Cognition, defined, 68
Cognitive
aspects, of tests anxiety, 246
defined, 246
development, 171, 184–186f, 187f
Cognitive quotient (CQ), 292–294
Cohen, Leonard, 67
Cole, Ethan, 302–303
Coleridge, Samuel Taylor, 205
College
back to, after a break, 5
as a "box," 304–305
benefits of, 21
community (*See* Community
college)
dropping out of, 340
managing, 340
obstacles in, 21–22
overview, 304–305

purpose of, 4–6
success, 20–24, 270–271
College success courses, 23
Comfort, and learning, 66–67
Commentary, 195
defined, 209
Communicating
emotional connections and, 88
with instructors, four C's and, 229
productive, 279–280
in relationships, 277–280
technology options, 212–213
Community college
admission, of, 14–15
advisors, relationships with, 12
convenience, 17
educational goals and, 7, 10–11, 21, 30
engagement and, 172
orientation courses, 23
people attending, 5–6, 22
reasons for, 4
technology and, 145, 151, 152b
tests and, 15
variety in, 5, 15
Community, learning, 142
Compare, defined, 256
Compare and contrast format, 214, 217
defined, 217
Compelling writing, 219–220
Components, break-down of project, 100
Comprehension, tests and, 248
Computer help desk, 18
Concentration, defined, 10
Conceptual decision making, 128
Conciseness, in writing, 219
Conclusion
hasty, 124
Myers-Briggs Type Indicator® (MBTI)
and, 65
Concreteness, in FOCUS, 43
Conflict, 281–284
managing, 280
in relationships, 283–284
style of, 281–282f
Confucius, 202
Confusion, learning and, 51
Connecting, memory and, 239f
Conscientious, defined, 240
Constructive responses, defined, 38
Content, learning and, 71
Content-intensive lecturer, defined, 178
Context, reading and, 205
Continuing education, 335–337
Contradictory, defined, 120
Contrast, defined, 256
Control/controlling
in AIMS, 36, 37

classes and, 44, 77–78, 134–135,
164–165, 194–195, 296–297
managing vs., 30
online classes and, 140–141
of procrastination, 100
of spending, 105, 107
time management and, 76, 86, 97, 98
Convincing writing, 221
Co-ops, 328f
Core, defined, 10
Core values, self-assessment, 41
Cornell system, 185, 186f
Counselors, 18, 274–275. *See also* Advisor
Course management systems, 16, 141,
145, 150
defined, 151
Coursework, planning, 11
Courtesy, in writing, 221
Cover letter, 333
Coverage, in information literacy, 160
Cowell, Simon, 42
Cramming, 76–77, 243–244
"Crazymaking," defined, 279–280
Creative style, 131–132
Creative thinking
as thinking outside the box, 130–133
blockage of, 132
overview, 113, 134–135
ways to improve, 132–133
Creativity
acceptance of, 132
four styles of, 131–132
hunches and, 133
ideas, generation/flow, 132, 133
mistakes and, 133
overcomplexify, 132
perspectives and, 132–133
"right" answer, 133
self-concept and, 133
study of, 133
visual mind and, 132
Credit Card Act of 2009, 106
Credit cards, 106–107
Credit history, 107
Credit reports, 107
Credits, advisor and, 13
CRIA system. *See* Challenge reaction
insight action system (CRIA) system
Criteria, 125, 159–160
defined, 241
Critic, defined, 116
Critical searching skills, 159–160
Critical thinking
academic achievement and, 130
becoming better at, 117, 130
defined, 117
four-part model of, 118–129

Critical thinking (*Continued*)
   importance of, 117–118
   information literacy and, 159–160
Critical Thinking Pyramid, 122, 123f
Criticize, defined, 256
Critique, defined, 256
Cultural intelligence, 292
Cultural literacy, defined, 210
Cummings, e. e., 305
Curiosity
   in AIMS, 36, 37
   careers and, 317–318
   choices and, 110
   in learning, 54
   memory and, 263–264
   relationships and, 297–298
Currency
   defined, 145
   in information literacy, 159

D

Databases, defined, 156
Day care owner, career as, 170, 171
Deadlines, 72, 94
De Bono, Edward, 238
Decision making, 127–129
   analytical, 128
   behavioral, 129
   conceptual, 128
   directive, 128
   emotions and, 54
   major/career and,
      Myers-Briggs Type Indicator® (MBTI)
         and, 65
   overview, 127–128
Deductive arguments, 120
Deep learner, defined, 32
Deep-level processing, 262
Deep practice, 134–135
Define
   defined, 158, 256
   in information literacy, 157–159
   in problem-solving, 124
Degree
   associate's, 6–7, 10, 11, 21, 336f
   bachelor's, 7, 10, 21, 336f
   finishing, 341
   master's, 336f
   Ph.D., 336f
   plan, 10–11
   two-year, 6–7
Degree plan, 10–11
Demonstration, reading and, 211
Describe, defined, 211, 256
Details
   information literacy and,
      153, 161

studying and, 71
tests and, 255, 257
Developmental, defined, 15
Developmental courses, 14–15
Dewey Decimal system, 155–156
Dictionary, 179, 201, 205, 229
Directions, 250
Directive decision making, 128
Disability, learning, 18, 67
Discrimination
   defined, 288
   persistence of, 288, 291
   racial, 288, 291
Discipline, 101
Disciplines, academic, 304–306
Discuss, defined, 256
Distance education, defined, 140
Diversity, 285–289
   age, 286
   in classrooms, 289
   defined, 285
   gender, 286
   geographic, 286
   life management options and, 30–31
   media and, 287
   overview, 285–287
   personal views on, 285–286
   physical, 286
   race and, 287–289
   relationships and, 278–279
   religious, 286
   sexual orientation, 286
   success and, 289
Downloading workloads, 162–164. *See also*
      Plagiarism; Sources, citing
Drawings, memory and, 59, 182,
      186, 192
Dreams
   defined, 41
   goals and (*See* Goals)
   major/career and, 30, 42, 308
Dropbox, defined, 152b
Dropping a class, 13, 18
Drugs, and studying, 243
Dumb, Richard, 329

E

Earning potential, 21
"Easy" listening, 175–176
Editing, 181, 217
   defined, 217
Education
   continuing, 335–337, 341
   distance, 140
Educational Resources Information Center
      (ERIC), 156

Effort, ability vs., 39–40
Einstein, Albert, 77
Either/or thinking, 124
E-learning, 140–144. *See also* Learning
      online
   adjustment to, 141–143
   versus C-learning, 140–141
   control, how and when you learn,
      140–141
   obstacles, addressing, 143
   strategies for, 141–143
Eliot, T. S., 71
E-mails
   C-factors and, 166–167
   from instructors, 9
Emotional appeal, 123
Emotional aspects, of test anxiety,
      246–247
Emotional energy, 86
Emotional connections, 88
Emotional issues, 130
Emotional intelligence, 271–273
   improvement, 273–276
Emotional Quotient (EQ), 294
Emotional Quotient Inventory (EQ-i), 274
Emotions. *See also* Feelings
   interpersonal skills and, 272
   learning and, 54
   memory and, 239f
   relationships and, 88, 275, 276, 280
   self-awareness and, 272
   stress and, 272
   tests and, 242, 246–247
   thinking and, 130
Employers, 118, 131, 147, 338. *See also*
      Interviews
   skills desired by, 338–340
Employment, 316, 327, 331, 332, 333
Energy
   emotional, 88
   direction of, 65
   dynamics of, 87, 89
   love and, 276b
   managing, 242
   mental, 173
   physical, 87–88
   renewal, 88
   as resource, 86–87
   spiritual, 86, 88
   tests and, 242, 243, 247
Energy management, 86
Engagement/engaging, 10, 172–174
   choosing, 174
   rules of, 172–174
English, reading and, 204–205
English as a Second Language (ESL), 179b
Enumerate, defined, 256

Environment
  academic, 179b
  concerns for, 58
  learning, 142
  lecturer styles and, 178
  online classes and, 140, 142
Epictetus, 4
EQ. *See* Emotional Quotient (EQ)
EQ-i. *See* Emotional Quotient Inventory
    (EQ-i)
ERIC. *See* Educational Resources
    Information Center (ERIC)
ESL. *See* English as a Second Language
    (ESL)
Essays
  writing, 218, 218
  questions, 255–258
  tests, 255–258
Ethical
  standards, defined, 260
  use of research, 162
  See also Plagiarism, 164
Ethnicities, defined, 288
Evaluate
  defined, 256
  evidence, 122
  options, 125
  results, 127
Evidence
  defined, 119
  evaluating, 119–122, 123, 124
  on note-taking, 181, 193
  reading and, 206–207, 221, 223f
  test of, 120–121
  writing and, 218, 221
Examples
  arguments, 120–121
  Cornell System, 186f
  Mind Map, 187f
  lecture styles and, 196
  note-taking and, 182, 183, 188f,
    190f, 195
  PowerPoint, 187f, 223f
  timeline, 189f
Excuses, for procrastination,
    92b, 100
Expectations, careers and, 307
Expenses, tracking, 107
Exhaustion, studying and, 149
Experience, 327–328f, 330
Experts, defined, 51
Explain, defined, 256
External forces, defined, 311
Extra credit, 9, 340
Extrinsic motivation
  defined, 33
  learning and, 36

F

FAQs of new students, 17–19
Facebook, 143, 145, 149, 152, 165
Facebook profile, 147
Facilitators, defined, 178
Facione, Peter, 125
Facts, defined, 122
Faculty member, 12, 13. *See also* Advisor
Failure, 264–265
False authority, 123
False cause and effect, 123
False statements, 252
Family members, relationships
    with, 277
Faulty reasoning, 122–124, 126
Fears, overcoming of, 101
Feedback
  learning and, 55, 133
  writing and, 217
Feelings. *See also* Emotions,
  learning and, 54, 65
  memory and, 239f, 246
Fees, for credit cards, 107
Ferraro, Geraldine, 140
Feynman, Richard P., 162
Fill in the blank questions, 188, 255
Fill in the blank tests, 255
Financial
  aid, 108b
  advice for economic troubles, 107
Fine print, for credit cards, 107
First-year seminar course, 23
Fit, in FOCUS, 43
Flash, 151
Flash cards, 59, 72, 76, 249
Flexibility, in actions, 117
Flow, defined, 133
Flow: The Psychology of Optimal Experience
    (Csikszentmihalyi), 133
FOCUS, defined, 37
Focus
  engagement and, 174
  factors of, 37
  goals and, 43
  information and, 116
  memory and, 237, 244, 249–251,
    256, 257
  sharpening of, 44, 117
  time management and, 84–86
Focused listening, 175–176
Focused thinking
  critical thinking and, 117, 119f
  defined, 116
  pyramid, 123f
Focusing, 30–31, 177
Ford, Henry, 9
Four I's, 317–318

Four-part model of critical thinking,
    118–129
  decision making, 127–129
  evaluation, 128–129
  problem solving, 124–127
  reasoning, 119–124
Foxfire, 157
Free time, 89–90
Friends, relationships with, 277
Frick, James. W., 104

G

Gardner, Howard, 58
GED. *See* General education development
    (GED)
Gender diversity, 286
General education courses, 7
General education development (GED),
    defined, 4
Generalization
  arguments and, 120, 124
  conclusions and, 120
  essay tests and, 257
  reading and, 207
Geographic diversity, 286
Gestures, 175
Global awareness, 294
The Global Internet Economy (Kogut), 156
Goal setting, 42–43
  memory and, 264
Goals
  ability and, 39
  attitude and, 38
  CRIA system and, 32–33
  defined, 41
  developing, 42–43
  dreams vs., 42
  effort and, 39–40
  in FOCUS, 43
  future and, 25, 42, 324
  learning and, 68
  long-term, 43, 243
  major/career and, 42
  motivation and, 34–35
  overview, 27
  portfolio and, 329
  realistic, 101
  setting, 43–44, 101
  short-term, 43
  values and, 41–42
  what you want to achieve, 30
Google, 139, 151, 157
Google Docs, 161
Google Scholar, 156
Grade point averages (GPAs), 13–14
  defined, 13
Grading scale, 14

Graduate, first generation, 24
Grammar
    tests and, 258
    writing and, 219
Gretzky, Wayne, 18
Groups, 9
Guided notes, 188
Gunnysackers, defined, 279

H

Hale, Edward Everett, 22
Handouts, 182, 187–188
Hands, major/career and, 315, 316
Hard listening skills, defined, 176–177
Hard work, e-learning and, 141
Hardiness, 272, 273
Harvard Business Review, 273
Hasty conclusion, 124
Head, major/career and, 314, 315f, 316
Health, engagement and, 174
Health services, 18
Heart, major/career and, 294, 314,
    315f, 316
Help
    needing, 17–19
    professionals and, 247
High school, college transition after, 4–5
High school diploma, 4, 21
Hill, Napoleon, 341
History
    credit, 107
    defined, 107
Hit and run fighters, defined, 279
Holmes, Oliver Wendell, 131
Holtz, Lou, 39
Honesty, as a learning strategy, 76, 274
Horner, Martina, 30
Humor, 221, 224
Hunches, and creative thinking, 133
Huxley, Thomas, 132–133, 208
Hybrid, defined, 140
Hypersensitivity, and love, 276b

I

Ideal student concept, 37
Ideas. *See* Creative thinking
Illustrate, defined, 59, 256
Imaginative creative style, 131
iMovie, 151
Impending, defined, 192
Inaccuracy, of Internet, 146
Inductive arguments, 120
Inferences, defined, 206
Information
    gathering, 340
    learning and, 60–63

perception and processing of, 60–61
    styles and, 61–63
Information Age, 159
Information literacy, 156–162
    components, 157–162
    define, 157–159
    ethics and, 162
    locate, 159
    organize, 160–161
    select, 159–160
    steps, 158f
Information, resources for, 20
Injustice, defined, 291
Inner direction, 89
Innovative creative style, 131
Insight
    as benefit of college, 21
    in CRIA system, 32–33
    learning and, 50, 69
Inspiration creative style, 131
Instructors, relationships with, 142, 277
Instrumentation, 318
Intelligence
    ability/effort and, 39–40
    bodily-kinesthetic, 57, 59
    cultivation, 40
    cultural, 292
    defined, 58
    emotional, 271–273
    interpersonal, 57, 59
    intrapersonal, 57, 59, 272
    kinesthetic, 61, 64, 66, 67, 70f
    learning and, 40
    linguistic, 56, 59, 69
    logical-mathematical, 56
    multiple, 56–58
    musical, 57, 58, 59
    naturalistic, 58, 59
    spatial, 56, 59
    theories of, 39
    weaker, development of, 60
Intelligence quotient (IQ), 58
Intelligence-oriented study techniques,
    58–59
Intentional learners, 70–72
Intentional plagiarism, 162
Interaction, 118, 285, 288, 318
Interactivity, on Internet, 145
Interference
    love and, 276b
    memory and, 77
Internal forces, defined, 311
Internet
    benefits of, 145–146
    critical searching on, 159–160
    dangers of, 146, 147
    downloading workloads, 162–164

information literacy and, 157–161
    overdependence upon, 166
    pros/cons of, 145–148
    phishing, spam, spyware, and viruses, 147
Internet domain extensions, defined, 151
Internships, 327–328f
Interpersonal intelligence, 57, 59, 66
Interpersonal skills, 272, 318
Interpret, defined, 256
Interpretation, 318
Interviews
    career choices and, 308
    for jobs, 318–319, 333–335
Intrapersonal intelligence, 57, 58, 59
Intrapersonal skills, 272
Intrinsic motivation, 272
    defined, 36
    learning and, 36
    scale, 34–35
Intuitive creative style, 131
Inventing, 132, 212
Ionesco, Eugene, 54
ISpy.com page, 148f
IQ. *See* Intelligence quotient (IQ)

J

James, William, 94
Job growth, 21
Job preferences, 310
Jobs
    advertisement for, 316
    defined, 326
    hunting, 327
    school as, 72
    study of the industry, 338–339
    trying out, 328
Jobs, Steve, 145
Johnson, Derek, case study, 82–83
Johnson, Michael, 341
Jones, Dario, 138–139
Journals, 151, 156
Judgments, 175
Jung, Carl, 65

K

Kahn, Alice, 147
Kaiser, Henry J., 14, 188
Keller, Helen, 339
Kennedy, Florynce, 160
Keynote, 225b
Key terms, 255
Key words, 182, 186
Kierkegaard, Soren, 330
"Killer B's," 101, 109
Kinesthetic intelligence, 61, 64, 66, 67, 70f
Kinesthetic learning strategy, 61.
    See also VARK

Knowledge
  brain and, 51
  core, defined, 210
  critical thinking and, 130
  learning and, 54–55
  major/career and, 305, 306, 311, 335
  mistakes and, 133
  memory and, 238
  personal insights, action and, 33
  as power, 116
  studying and, 54–55, 66, 76
  on tests, 240, 257
Ko, Tammy, case study, 48–49

L

Laboauf, Michael, 184
Landers, Ann, 222
Language
  attitude and, 39b
  body, 174, 195
  listening and, 179b
  note taking and, 195
  reading and, 204–205, 206, 210–211, 228–229
  writing and, 219
Law of averages, 253
Laziness, Internet and, 146
Learned optimism, defined, 272
Learners
  deep, 32
  defined, 40
  intentional, 70–72
Learning
  brain and, 50–52
  C-, 140
  cheating and, 258–260
  Circle of, 305–306
  comfort, 66–67
  compartmentalization of, 304f
  conditions for, 52–55
  E-, 140–144
  employers and, 118, 131, 338–340
  engagement and, 86–89, 172–174
  focus of, 54
  information and, 60–64, 156–162
  intelligence and, 40, 60–63
  lifelong, 21, 261–262
  memory and, 235, 238
  note-taking and, 180–191
  overview, 47, 50–51
  passive, 54
  personality and, 64–67
  self-regulated, 249
  service-, 295b, 328f
  successful people and, 39–41
  tests and, 235, 242, 246, 262

  to think, 21, 48, 114, 116
  VARK and, 61–63
  views on, 50
Learning center, 65
Learning community, defined, 142
Learning curve, defined, 10
Learning disability, 18, 67b
Learning environment, 142
Learning online, 137–68
  C factors and, 164–167
  case study of, 138–140
  downloading workloads, 162–164
  e-learning, 140–144
  information literacy and, 156–162
  overview, 137, 167–168
  research skills and, 154–156
  technological skills and, 144–154
Learning points, attitude and, 38
Learning strategy, 61–63. *See also* VARK
Learning style, 47–80
  defined, 60
  listening and, 61, 70f
  MBTI and, 65–66
  memory and, 69, 70f
  note-taking and, 182
  study style and, 69
  styles of, 66, 72
  tests and, 51, 70f, 77
  theory, 61
  See also VARK
Lecture notes, 141, 142, 193–194
Lecture styles, 178, 194–195
Legal assistant, career as, 115
Les Misérables, 216
Library, 155–156
Library of Congress, 155–156
Lifelong learning, 21
Lincoln, Abraham, 21
Lindbergh, Anne Morrow, 216
Linguistic intelligence, 56, 58, 59
LinkedIn, 330
Linking mnemonic, 239f, 242, 249
Listening
  "easy," 175–176
  ESL and, 179b
  with focus, 175–177
  focused, defined, 175
  hard, 176–177
  note-taking skills and, 180–181
Listening skills
  improving, 175–176
  note-taking and, 180–181
  soft, 176
Listening styles, 178
Literacy
  cultural, 210
  information, 156–162

Literature, defined, 306
Locate
  in information literacy, 158f, 159
  memory and, 239f
Loci mnemonic system, 239f
Logic, 120
Logical-mathematical intelligence, 56, 58
Longfellow, Henry Wadsworth, 242
Long-term goals, 43
Long-term memory, 238
Lopez, Anthony, 322
Lubbock, Sir John, 84

M

Magazines, 61, 118, 156
Main idea, 182, 206–207
Main points, note-taking and, 182
Major, choosing, 13, 313–316
Management
  attention, 84
  energy, 85, 86–89
  money, 104–106
  time (*See* Time management)
Managing, 181
  of conflict, 95–96
  controlling vs., 30
  of personal life, 102–112
  of stress, 245, 248
Manipulating, 193
Manlius, 214
Marginal notes, 210
Mark it down, memory and, 239f
Mark it up, memory and, 239f
Marketplace of ideas, defined, 5
Marx, Groucho, 207
Master study plan, 70–72
Master's degree, 323, 335f, 336f
Matching tests, 255
Math
  described, 306
  importance of, 340
  note-taking example, 190f
  as a skill, 340
Math anxiety, 247–249
Mayer, Jeffrey, 84
MBTI. *See* Myers-Briggs Type Indicator® (MBTI)
McElveen-Hunter, Bonnie, 253
Meaning
  inferences and, 206, 264
  learning and, 262
  memory and, 194
  thinking and, 116
  word context and, 205, 210, 228
  writing and, 219

Media,
  benefits of, 145
  dangers of, 147
  diversity and, 287
  employers and, 330
  Internet as, 145
Memorization, tests and, 236, 239f, 248
Memory, 231–266
  aids, 182
  deepen your, 262
  failure, 127
  humor in, 239f
  improving, 239f
  intelligence-specific, 58
  learning and, 235
  limits of, 69
  long-term, 194
  manipulating, 239f
  mastering, 238–240
  maximizing, 242
  mnemonic devices for, 239f
  musical, 59
  note-taking and, 182, 185, 194
  overview, 235
  questions and, 235
  sensory, 236, 237
  short-term, 236, 237, 238, 242. (*See also*
    Working memory)
  subjective tests, 234
  testing, 240
  tests and, 236
  three R's of remembering and, 236–238
  working, 236, 237–238, 248
Mental energy, 173
Mentor, 24b, 274
Metacognition
  defined, 68, 129
  reading and, 68
  studying and, 68–69
  thinking and, 129
Microsoft Excel, defined, 151
Microsoft Powerpoint, defined, 151
Microsoft Word, defined, 151
Milne, A. A., 277
Mind maps, 186–187f
Mindreaders, defined, 279
Mind the middle, memory and, 239f
Mistakes
  advisors' and, 12–13
  common, among students, 12–13
  capitalizing on, 132
  math anxiety and, 248, 249
  research, 157b
MLA. *See* Modern Language Association
    (MLA)
Mnemonic devices, 239f, 242, 249
Mobile apps, defined, 152b

Mock it, memory and, 239f
Modern Language Association (MLA), 163
Money
  management, 104–106
  time as, 104
Monty Python Flying Circus, 119
Moodle, 143, 151
Moods
  EI and, 272
  love and, 276b
  tests and, 246–247
Moore, Desiree, case study, 114–115
Motivation, 34–37
  careers and, 337
  C-Factors and, 36–37, 44–46
  creating, 52
  defined, 35
  in FOCUS, 37
  intrinsic self-assessment scale, 34–35
  overview, 36–36
Motivational quotient, 292, 294. *See also*
    Emotional quotient (EQ)
Moving, memory and, 239f, 264
Mozart, 58
Multimodal,
  defined, 64
  uses of, 64
Multiple intelligences, self-assessment,
    56–58
Multiple-choice questions, 49, 250,
    253–254
Multiple-choice tests, 72, 252–255
Multitasking, 31
  defined, 31, 85
  "focused," 109, 191
Musical intelligence, 57, 58, 59
Myers-Briggs Type Indicator® (MBTI),
    65–66

N

Narration, memory and, 239f , 242
Naturalistic intelligence, 58, 59, 60
Negatives, defined, 87f
Negativity, in attitudes, 15, 38, 54, 242, 297
Netiquette, 153–154
Networking, 85, 147, 329–330
Newspapers, 156, 260
Nietzsche, Friedrich, 235
Nightingale, Earl, 274
Notebooks, 174
Notes
  general goals for, 182
  guided, 188
  information literacy and, 142,
    160–161, 164
  lecture, 141, 142

  marginal, 73, 172, 189, 209, 210
  online, 142
  reading and, 161
  tests and, 256
Note-taking
  by book, 189
  Cornell system of, 185, 186f
  guided notes for, 188
  on instructor-provided handouts, 182,
    187–188
  lecture notes for, 141, 142
  listening skills and, 180–181
  math example, 190f
  mind maps for, 186–187f
  outlining as, 184–185
  parallel, 188
  PowerPoint miniatures for, 187
  by system/subject, 181–182, 189–190
  timeline example, 189f
Note-taking 4-M, 194
Note-taking skills, 180
Novice, defined, 180–181, 194
Number theory, defined, 306
Nurse, career as, 10, 268
Nutrition and study, 88

O

Objective questions, 250, 255
Objective tests, 251–255
Objectivity, defined, 160
Obligation, college as, 7
O'Conner, Marie, 72
Online classes, 140–144
  adjustments for, 141–143
  control of, 140–141
  example of, 143–144
  overview, 140–141, 168
Online degree, 138–139
Online research, 166
Online tests, 241, 251
Open-book tests, 243
Open mind, toward classes, 175
Opportunities
  defined, 311
  learning and, 21, 67, 77, 141–143
  making use of, 67
  missed, 203
Opposition, in critical thinking, 130
Optimism
  learned, 272
  realistic, 135
Orators, defined, 178
Orben, Robert, 40
Organizational formats, 217
Organizational pattern, 180, 218,
    220, 222

Organize
    in information literacy, 142, 158f,
        160–161
    memory and, 239f
    online courses, 143
    tools for, 161
"Ostrich Syndrome," 8
Outlining/outline, 184–185
    defined, 256
Outlook, career in AIMS, 37
Outside activities, tests and, 247
Outsourcing, 102–103
Overdependence, of Internet, 146
Overgeneralization, critical thinking
        and, 124
Overcomplexify, creative thinking and, 132
Overlearning, 239f
Oversimplification, critical thinking and, 124
Ownership, in FOCUS, 43124

P

Papers
    purpose of, 216
    submission checklist, 220
Parallel note-taking, 188
Paraphrasing, 193–194
Passive learning, 54
Patience, with self, 275
Patterns
    learning and, 54
    organizational, 180, 218, 220, 222
"PCP Syndrome: Parking Lot, Class,
        Parking Lot," 17–20
PDF files, 152b
Peck, M. Scott, 173
Peer pressure, 251
Peg system, 239f, 242
People pleasers, 98
People skills, 339
Perceive, defined, 60
Perceptions, defined, 285
Perfectionists, 98
Performers, defined, 40
Persistence
    careers and, 318
    conflicts and, 281
Personal attack, 123
Personal life, managing, 102–103
Personal time, managing. See Time
        management
Personal meaning, learning and, 54
Personal relevant questions, 192
Personality, 64–67
Personalize, memory and, 239f
Perspectives, creative thinking and,
        132–133

Ph.D., 226, 323, 336
Philosophy, defined, 233, 306
Phishing, 147
Physical activity, tests and, 247
Physical diversity, 286
Physical energy, 52, 86
Physical factors, for reading, 208
Physical quotient, 293–294
Physical state, learning and, 54
Physics, defined, 306
Physiological, defined, 246
Physiological aspects of test anxiety, 247
Picasso, Pablo, 60
Pictured, memory and, 239f
Pillow Method, 132
Plagiarism, 164
    author credit and, 146
    avoiding, 158f
    copying and, 155, 157
Plan of action, 129
Planner, 92–93
Planning ahead, advisor and, 13–14, 18
Planning strategies, thinking and, 129
Platform, defined, 143
Podcasts, defined, 152b
Political science, defined, 304
Portfolio, 329
Posture, 292
Powell, Colin, 33
*The Power of Full Engagement: Managing
        Energy Not Time, Is the Key to High
        Performance and Personal Renewal*
        (Loehr/Schwartz), 86
PowerPoint miniatures, 187–188
PowerPoint presentation, 141, 145,
        151, 161
    storyboarding, 223f
    tips for, 226b
Practice, tests and, 249
Predictors, defined, 22
Preemptives, 22, 98
Prefixes, 204, 205
Prejudice, defined, 289
Prep time, 175
Preparation
    engagement and, 172, 173, 176
    for presentations, 224
    study strategies and, 70f, 76–77
    for tests, 70f, 241–243
Prerequisites
    defined, 13
    skipping, 13
Present, in information literacy, 163
Presentations
    in information literacy, 151
    PowerPoint and, 225b
    public speaking and, 222–225

Prewriting, 214–215
Prezi, 225b
Primary sources, defined, 203–204
Priority
    choice of, 41, 307, 338
    developing, 95–96
Proactive, defined, 288
Problematic time management ("P's"),
        98–101
Problem solving, 124–128
    brainstorming, 124–125
    choice of solution, 125, 127
    definition, 124
    evaluation of options, 125
    implementation, 127
    skills, 339
Problem-solution format, 128, 218
Problems, ignoring, 13, 247
Process
    defined, 227
    learning as a, 50–51, 53
    memory as a, 235
    reading as a, 207
    research as a, 155
    See also Writing, (as process)
Process of elimination, 253
Processing
    deep-level, 262
    memory and, 262
    surface-level, 262
Procrastinating, 13
Procrastination, 99–102
    excuses for, 92b, 100
    projects, breakdown of, 100
    starting projects, 100
    issue resolution, 100
    realistic goals and, 101
    "Killer B" and, 101
    progress observation and, 101
    fears, overcoming and, 101
    discipline and, 101
    accomplishments, acknowledging, 102
Procrastinators, 98
Produce, memory and, 239f
Product, described, 181, 260, 281
Productive communication, 279–280
Productive skills, 122
Progress, observation of, 101
Pronunciation, for foreigners, 228–229
Proofreading, 217, 258
Proposition, defined, 120
Prove, defined, 256
Psychological factors, for reading, 208
Psychology, defined, 306
PsycINFO™, 156
Public Safety Office, 20
Publius Syrus, 86

Q

QR codes, defined, 152b
Qualifiers, defined, 252
Quality, energy and, 86
Quantity, energy and, 86
Questions
   asking, 191–193
   employment interviews, 333–334
   essay, 255–258
   fill in the blank, 188, 250, 255, 261
   interview, 255, 334–335
   listening and, 175, 178, 180, 191
   major/career and, 340, 343
   metacognition and, 68
   multiple-choice, 253–254
   note-taking and, 172, 174, 181,
      182, 183
   objective, 250, 251–255
   reading and, 179, 210, 211
   in SQ3R, 211
   subjective, 255–258
   on tests (See Time per item (TPI))
   tests and, 250
   true-false, 251–252
   value of, 192

R

Race, 286–289
Racial discrimination, 288, 291
Racism, 287, 291
Rapid-fire lecturer, defined, 178
Reaction, in CRIA system, 32
Reading
   authors and, 209
   basics of, 207
   challenges of, 208, 210, 185, 189
   discipline and, 226–227
   dissecting text, 209–210
   engagement and, 172–173
   ESL and, 204, 228–229
   four C's and, 226–229
   importance of, 202–203
   knowledge about, 210
   instructors and, 211
   language and, 211
   LD and, 67b
   lecture styles and, 178
   master study plan and, 71, 72
   memory and, 208
   metacognition and, 68–69
   note-taking and, 161, 210
   paragraphs and, 205, 210
   in SQ3R, 210–211–211
   stress and, 53, 244 245, 246
   strategies, 212
   studying and, 207–213
   tests and, 244

Reading log, 208
Reading skills, 203–207
Reading style, 208–209
Read/write learning strategy, 61, 70f.
   See also VARK
Real world, relationship to, 65
Reasoning, 119–124
   assumptions and, 121–122
   claims and, 122, 126–127
   faulty reasoning, 122–124
   overview, 119–121
Ramen, Rachel Naomi, 177
Recall, learning information to, 70, 181,
      193, 194, 235
Receptive skills, 122
Recite, reading and, 210, 211
Recognize, learning information to, 70f,
      181, 185, 193
Recording, 59, 208, 236, 237–238
Rehearsal, 224, 239f
Relate, defined, 256
Relationships
   American mosaic and, 289–291
   with boss, 293
   communicating in, 88, 276–280
   conflict in, 281–284
   EI and, 273
   with friends, 277
   interpersonal skills, 272
   love, 276b
   romantic, 278–279
   stress and, 272
   stages in, 283f
Relaxation training, 247
Relaxed alertness, defined, 53
Relearning, defined, 193
Relevancy, 120
Religious diversity, 286
Remedial, 15
Remediation, 15
Remembering, three R's of, 236–238
   long-term memory and, 238
   working memory record, 237–238
Repetition, learning and, 51, 239f
Research
   on attention span, 71, 84
   on brains, 31, 78
   on career choices, 308–309
   classes, missing, 173
   communication, 24b
   college benefits, 21, 78
   conducting, 154–155
   data selection, 159–160
   defined, 155, 157–159
   on degrees, 335f
   on discrimination, 288
   on EI, 271, 272, 273

   on examples of things, 32
   on exercise, 52
   on friends, 277
   on grades, 221b, 227
   on hope, 38
   on illness, 277
   information literacy and, 156–162
   Internet studies for, 74
   on job satisfaction, 326
   on learning state, 53
   libraries, 155–156
   locating information, 159
   on love, 276b
   on manipulation of information, 193
   on memory, 237, 242
   mindsets, 40
   mistakes, 157b
   multitasking, 31
   on note-taking, 194
   online, 147, 166
   organization, 160–161
   procrastination, 100
   on reading, 194
   on recruiters, 331
   on relationships, 276b, 277
   on salaries, 335f
   scholarly, 204
   on sleep, 88, 149
   on speaking anxiety, 221b
   on stress, 53–54
   on studying, 72, 193, 194
   for success, 154–155
   on talent, 134–135
   talking to yourself, 71
   on tests, 246
   on things going wrong, 32
   writing and, 194
Research skills, 154–156
Resilience, defined, 272
Resolution of problems, 100
Resource(s)
   audiovisual, 156
   campus, 17–20
   energy as, 86–89
Respect, toward college, 8
Responsibility
   academic, 10–20
   attitude and, 38
   degree plan, 10–11
   listening and, 175
Résumé, 329, 330–333
Retaining, 238
Retrieving, 238
Review/reviewing
   memory and, 237, 238
   note-taking and, 94, 181,
      185, 193

online classes and, 142
podcasts and, 152b, 177
studying and, 211
tests and, 238, 250, 251, 253
Review-the-text lecturer, defined, 178
Revision, defined, 216–217
Rewriting, 216–218
Road and Track, 61
Robbins, Anthony, 327
Rogers, Will, 51
Roles, and writing, 216
Romantic relationships, 278–279
Roosevelt, Eleanor, 122
Royal, Darnell, 185
Rules and policies
    of life, 339
    of specific college, 8
Russell, Bertrand, 117

S

Salaries, 82, 335f
Sanchez, Sylvia, case study, 28–30
Schedules
    academic disciplines and, 304
    conflicts of, 95–96
    fixed activities, 94
    flextime, 96
    keeping up with, 141
    monitor, 95
    study, 241
    studying and, 17, 72, 90, 91, 92, 94–95
    success and, 71, 91–95
Scholarly research, defined, 204
Scope, defined, 145
Search engines, defined, 151
Seating strategy, 174
Seinfeld, 210, 278
Select, in information literacy, 157, 158f,
    159–160
Self-awareness, 272. *See also* Intrapersonal
    Skills
Self-concept, 133
Self-criticism, 133
Self-discipline, 137, 200, 204, 271
Self-handicapping, defined, 40
Self-Promotion Intelligence (Quotient).
    See SPQ
Self-regulated learning, 249
Senses
    defined, 60
    studying and, 61, 76
Sensory memory, 236, 237
Sensory preferences, 63–64
Separate it, memory and, 239f
Seven C's, for writing, 218–221
Service-learning, 295b, 328f

Sexism, 291
Sexual orientation diversity, 286
Shakespeare, William, 50
Shandling, Garry, 277
Shaw, George Bernard, 120, 130
Shifting the burden of proof, 124
Short-answer tests, 255
Short-hand system, in note-taking, 183
Short-term goals, 43
Short-term memory, 236, 237, 238, 242.
    See also Working memory
Simplifying, 103
Skills approach, for résumé, 330–332f
Sleep, 87–88, 149, 244
Social insecurity, 147
Social worker, career as, 323, 336f, 337f
Sociology, defined, 306
Soft listening skills, defined, 176
Software, defined, 151
Solutions. *See* Problem solving
Sounds, reading and, 204
Sources, citing, 163–164
Space it out, memory and, 239f
Spam, 146, 153
Spatial intelligence, 56, 59, 60
Speaking, 16b, 70f, 174, 221, 339
Speech patterns, 175
Spellcheck, 205, 217
Spelling
    acronyms and, 239f
    e-mails and, 153
    reading and, 204
    writing and, 215, 217, 219
Spending logs, 105–106
Spielberg, Steven, 31
Spiritual energy, 86
SPQ (Self-Promotion Intelligence
    Quotient), 196–197
Spyware, 147
Stacks, defined, 156
Staley, Constance, 85
Starting projects, 100
Stasior, Matthew, 338
State, for learning, 53–54
    defined, 256
Statistics
    claims and, 122
    ideas and, 207
    PowerPoint and, 223
    research, 215
    speeches and, 223
    thesis and, 256
    writing and, 221
Stereotypes, defined, 288
    persistence of, 291
Straw man, 124
Steinem, Gloria, 214

Stevenson, Adlai, 175
Strengths, defined, 310, 311f
Stress
    assessing, 53–54
    attention and, 31
    choices and, 110
    emotional intelligence and, 272
    illness and, 88, 272
    learning and, 53–54
    managing, 24b, 52, 103, 110, 272, 273
    reading and, 53, 244 245, 246
    relationships and, 268, 272, 277, 281
    sleep and, 244
    spirituality and, 89
    studying and, 244
    tests and, 244
    time management and, 85, 103
    See also Test anxiety
Stress management skills, 53–54
Stretch, in FOCUS, 43
Sticklers, and learning, 71
Student, ideal concept, 37
Students
    as learning community, 142
    online advice from, 141–142
    studying with, 242
Study breaks, 71–72
Study buddy, 242
Study plan, master, 70–72, 76
Study schedule, 91–95
Study techniques, 58, 72
Studying
    C factors and, 77–80
    cramming and, 76–77, 243–244
    disciplined, 73–75
    explanation of, 68
    learning and, 69–70
    metacognition and, 68–69
    reading and, 51, 61, 62–63, 69, 71, 72
    tests and, 70f, 72
    strategies, 70f, 71–72
    style, 69
Style
    creative, 131–132
    learning (*See* Learning style)
    lecture, 178
    listening, 178–179b
    reading, 208–209
Subject, note-taking by, 189–190
Subjective essay tests, 253, 255–258
Subjective memory tests, 234
Subjective questions, 250
Submissions, of papers, 220
Substance, learning and, 54
Success
    academic, 23f, 67, 84, 270–271
    defined, 20

Success (*Continued*)
  EI and, 271, 273
  information literacy and, 156–162
  major/career and, 317–318, 327, 339
  relationships/diversity and, 285–289
  research skills and, 154–156
  schedule and, 91–95
  tests and, 243
Suffixes, 204–205
Summarize, defined, 157, 256
Summarizing, 157, 163, 194, 214
Summary, defined, 184
Summary statement, 184, 194, 258
Supplementary materials, defined, 178
Support, 275
Support centers, 18
Surface-level processing, 262
Sustainability, defined, 294
Swaby, Barbara, 211
SWOT analysis, 310–312
Syllables, reading and, 204–205
Syllabus, 17
  analyzing, 16b
  checking, 172
  master, 17
Szasz, Thomas, 307

T

Tablet computing, defined, 152b
Take charge, of education, 8–9, 52–55
  internal initiation, 52
  external encouragement, 52
  motivation and, 53–55
Take stock, defined, 32
Take-home tests, 243
Talent, 134–135
The Talent Code, 134
Talking, in class, 174
Tangent, defined, 192
Teamwork, 9
Techflexing, 103
Technology
  advantage of, 149
  applications, 150–151
  campus resources and, 18
  cheating and, 162, 260
  definitions for, 151–152
  e-mail netiquette, 153–154
  lecture recordings, 177
  plagiarism and, 162–164
  podcasts, 177
  time management and, 103, 149, 260
  use, 149
  videocasts, 177
  See also Technology skills
Technology ownership, 149

Technology skills, 144–154
  Internet use, 145–149
  overview, 144–145
Technology use, 149
Television, 88, 159, 179
"Term on a Page" calendar, 92, 93–94
Test anxiety, 244–247
  math, 247–249
  survey, 245
Test scores, increasing, 247–249
Testimony
  evidence and, 119
  presentations and, 223f
  reading and, 207
  writing and, 215, 256
Tests
  before, 240, 241–249
  during, 240, 249–251
  after, 240, 260–262
  cheating on, 258–260
  cramming, 243–244
  fill in the blank, 255
  matching, 255
  memorizing and, 239f, 240
  multiple-choice, 250, 252–255
  objective, 251–255
  online, 241, 249, 251
  open-book, 243
  note-taking and, 256
  short-answer, 255
  showing knowledge on, 240
  subjective essay, 255–258
  take-home, 255–258
  true-false, 251–252
  See also Memory
Textbook websites, defined, 151
Themes, 175
Thesis statements
  defined, 215, 256
  for essay tests, 256
  presentations and, 223
  reading and, 206
  successful, 218
  writing and, 215
Thinking, 116
  creative, 116, 130–133
  critical (*See* Critical thinking)
  defined, 116
  either/or, 124
  focused, 116
  overview, 113
  reading and, 132
  rethinking, 116
  tests and, 116, 118
Threats
  defined, 311
  spreading, 153

SWOT analysis and, 311, 312
Three R's of remembering, 236–238
Time
  assignments and, 72
  cheating and, 259
  class, 33
  dreams/goals and, 41, 43
  employment and, 338
  flextime, 96
  free, 72, 89–90
  investment, 9
  prep, 176
  studying and, 71, 72, 76
  tests, 253, 258
  use of, over a lifetime, 97
  wasting, 97–98
  zones, 95f–96
Time management, 84–86
  money as, 104–106
  obligations and, 102
  online classes, 143
  rushing and, 177
  to-do list, 95–97
  use of, 97–98
  See also problematic time management
    ("P's"), 98–101
Time per item (TPI), 253, 258
To-do list, 95–97, 110
Tolerance, defined, 288
Tomlin, Lily, 326
Topical format, defined, 217
TPI. *See* Time per item (TPI)
Trace, defined, 256
Tracy, Brian, 339
Training, relaxation, 247
Transfer shock, 337–338
Trappers, defined, 279
Triage, as learning strategy, 76
Trojan horses, defined, 152b
True-false questions, 251–252
True-false tests, 251–252
Trust, in critical thinking, 130
Turkle, Sherry, 280
Turning points, attitude and, 38
Tutors, 9, 18, 125, 179
  writing and, 216
Two-way inferences, 206
Two-year degree, 6–7

U

Understanding, reading and, 207
Unemployment rates, 21
Unintentional plagiarism, 157b, 162–163
Unwarranted assumption, 123
Urgency, defined, 95
Usefulness, in FOCUS, 43

V

Values, 41–42. 37–38
  defined, 41
  See also Goals
Variety
  in community college, 15
  of sources, 160
  studying and, 66, 72
VARK, learning and, 61–63, 64
Verb, tests and, 256–257
Verify, in critical thinking, 130
Virtual Private Network (VPN),
    defined, 152b
Viruses, 152b
Visual learning strategy, 61, 70f.
    See also VARK
Visual mind and, 132
Vocabulary, reading and, 205
Von, Lindsey, 58
Von Goethe, Johann Wolfgang,
    101, 255
VPN. *See* Virtual Private
    Network (VPN)

W

Washington, Kia, 268–269
Weaknesses, defined, 60
Web 2.0, defined, 152b
Web designer, career as, 138, 331, 332, 333
Web logs, defined, 151

Websites
  bookmarks for, 159
  for careers, 326
  dates for, 159
  evaluation of, 159–160
  Google and, 158
  for learning disabilities, 67
  surveys on, 74
  textbook, 151
  types of, 151
What ifs, 131
  FAQs and, 18, 20
White, Rachel, case study, 170–171
A Whole New Mind, 132
Wikipedia, 139, 158
Wikis, defined, 151
Williams, Darnell, case study, 2–3
WilsonWeb OmniFile Full Text Mega, 156
Wisdom, as benefit of college, 21
Wonder, Stevie, 250
Words
  attitude and, 39b
  reading and, 205
Work
  C-factors in, 164–167
  downloading, 162–164
  hard-, 141, 249–251
  in groups, 161
  learning and, 50, 175, 243
  managing, 102–103, 105, 111
  online classes and, 141, 143–144

Work ethic, 338
Working memory, 237–238
Worms, defined, 152b
Wright, Stephen, 240
Write learning strategy. *See* Read/write
    learning strategy
Writing
  block, 215
  in information literacy, 152–154
  jobs and, 339
  memory and, 219
  note-taking and, 182
  online communications, 152–154
  plagiarism and, 139–140, 167
  as process, 214–215
  research for, 215
  seven C's and, 218–221
  stages of, 214, 215, 218
  target dates for, 215
  topics and, 215
  See also Essays; Prewriting; Rewriting
Writing skills, 213–214

Y

Yahoo, defined, 151
YouTube, defined, 151

Z

Ziglar, Zig, 246, 309

Fostering Opportunity, Cultivating Unparalleled Success

ACA 122
STUDENT RESOURCE
WORKBOOK

Name: _____

Section: _____

Semester/Year: _____

Nash Community College • www.nashcc.edu

522 N. Old Carriage Road • Post Office Box 7488
Rocky Mount, North Carolina 27804-0488
Telephone: (252) 443-4011 • Fax: (252) 451-8401

Contents

ACA 122 ASSIGNMENTS AT A GLANCE...3

ASSIGNMENTS 4

  ACA Scavenger Hunt 5

  Core Assessment 1 7

      Contact Information Verification Form 9

      WebAdvisor Basics...11

      Nash CC Student Email 12

      Basic College E-mail Etiquette 13

      Moodle Basics..14

      How to Upload a Picture to Moodle (iPad Views) 15

  Core Assessment 2 16

      SMARTEST Goals Worksheet: Core Assessment 2...20

      Semester-by-Semester Plan of Study 23

      Advisor Questionnaire 24

  Core Assessment 3 25

  Core Assessment 4 29

  Core Assessment 5 35

      Note Taking Reflection Form 37

  Core Assessment 6 45

SESSION HANDOUTS AND INFORMATION...51

  Find an Expert 52

  Social Contract 53

  Envision Excellence 54

  Calendar Activity...59

  Responsibility Model 61

  Case Studies 63

  Note Taking Checklist..67

  Cornell Note Paper..68

  PowerPoint Miniatures 70

  Master Study Plan...755

  Emotional Intelligence 79

  SWOT Analysis 82

RESOURCE INFORMATION 844

  NCC Tutorial Service Options...85

  Student Organizations 86

  Steps to Apply for Financial Aid 88

TRANFER PORTFOLIO...89

MAP OF CAMPUS 99

CALENDAR 100

ACA 122 ASSIGNMENTS AT A GLANCE

ASSIGNMENT	DUE DATE	SUBMITTED ☑	GRADE	NOTES
Scavenger Hunt				
Core 1: Course Management				
Core 2: Goal Setting				
Core 3: Study Skills				
Core 4: Tutorial/Library				
Core 5: Note Taking				
Core 6: Test Taking				
Portfolio Part 1				
Portfolio Part 2				
Portfolio Part 3				
Portfolio Part 4				

 Username & Password Information:

Program/Resource:	Username:	Password:
NCC Student E-mail	@st.nashcc.edu	
Moodle		
WebAdvisor		
CFNC.org		
Smart Thinking		

CORE ACA ASSIGNMENTS

- **Scavenger Hunt**
- **Core Assessment 1 Course Management System**
- **Core Assessment 2 Goal Setting**
- **Core Assessment 3 Study Skills**
- **Core Assessment 4 Tutorial and Learning Resources**
- **Core Assessment 5 Note Taking**
- **Core Assessment 6 Test Taking**

*See Transfer Portfolio for additional assignments.

ACA Scavenger Hunt

Name: _____

Directions: Visit each location on campus and gather the requested information. If you do the scavenger hunt with a partner, each student should still complete and turn in separate copies with original signatures where requested.

Library:

What are the hours of operation? _____

List 2 magazine titles that are available in the library: _____

_____

List 2 DVD titles that are available in the library: _____

_____

Are the computers in the library available for students for any course work and internet research? _____

What is the current username and password used to access library resources from home? Username: _____ Password: _____

Signature of library employee: _____

Bookstore:

What are the hours of operation? _____

Name 5 things you can buy in the bookstore other than books. _____

_____

Advising:

What is your advisor's name and office number? _____

List your advisor's office hours: _____

Obtain a copy of your degree checklist. Degree checklists can often be found outside of the department chair's door and/or online on the College's website.

Website:

Go to the college website home page and locate the portal of links shown to the right. (It's located in the upper right hand corner.) Click on **Student Email**. What do you do if you need login help with your *student email*? _____

Home | Contact Us | WebAdvisor
Employee Email | Student Email | Moodle
Faculty/Staff Resources

Click on the **Moodle** link. Find the instructions on how to recover your Moodle password. What is the first step? _____

_____

Username | |
Password | | Login
☐ Remember username
Forgotten your username or password?

Prospective Students

Students

Finally, click on the **WebAdvisor** link. Select the Students menu. Find and select the link with the question "What's my password?" From the options listed, which statement would you click on if you forgot your password?

_____

COMMUNITY From the college website's home page, locate and hold the cursor over the word "Community." Choose the "EmploymeNCC" link. Click the "Students Find Jobs!" blue button.

List one of the two NCC contact names listed: _____

Register if you are interested by selecting "Click Here to Register."

From the college website's home page, locate and hold the cursor over the "About NCC" (Located at the bottom left hand corner of the changing banner photo.) Choose the "Bookstore" link from the list. This takes you to the online bookstore. In the "Books" drop down menu in the upper left, select "Textbooks & Course Materials." Find for the current textbook to COM 231. Select the current term; the department is COM; the course number is 231, pick any section; click SUBMIT.

List the title of the book: _____

How much is the book if purchased new? _____ Used? _____

Current Students From the College's website, click on the "Current Students" tab.

What is the e-mail address for the Financial Aid office?

_____

Next, locate the orange "Students" tab on the bottom right hand side of the screen. Select the "Campus Tutoring" option. Locate the PAL Tutor Connection Program. Student's interested in tutoring need to complete what?

_____

Math Assessment Center:
(Locate the testing center on the first floor of the S&T building.)
What does a student need in order to make up a test? _____
What are the hours that the testing center is available for make-up testing?

_____

What personal item should be left in your book bag or at the front desk?

_____

Signature of center employee: _____

Student and Enrollment Services (SES):
 If you do not already have a student ID, get your ID made at Student and Enrollment Services.
List at least one service that SES provides: _____

_____

Signature of SES employee: _____

Miscellaneous:
Where is the campus radio station located? _____
What is the name of the building where the cashier's office is located? _____
Where do you go to eat on campus? _____
Where is lost and found located? _____
Where is Cosmetology located? _____
What is the minimum GPA required to maintain financial aid? _____

Core Assessment 1   Due Date: _____

Course Management System Learning Outcome:
Students will access and utilize a campus course management system.

In-Class Assignment: Locate the WebAdvisor, Student Email and Moodle links from the Nash Community College website, successfully log in and complete the following tasks.

Complete the following tasks in **WebAdvisor:**

☐ 1. Access WebAdvisor and log in. (See page 11 in workbook for access and log in information.) If it is your first time logging in you will be asked to change your password. Be sure to select something you can remember. (Consider using the same password for all your campus accounts.) If you need your WebAdvisor password reset, you can do so directly from WebAdvisor before logging in. Select the "Student" menu, click on the link, "What's my password?" and follow the instructions.

☐ 2. After successfully logging into WebAdvisor, select the "STUDENTS MENU," then select "My Profile."

☐ 3. What is the name of your advisor? _____

☐ 4. What is your 7 digit student ID? _____

☐ 5. Here, when viewing the "My Profile" screen, you will see the most current personal information that NCC has for you on record.
Verify your address and phone number. Complete the "Contact Information Verification Form" found on page 9 in this workbook. Turn in the form to your instructor.

      If your contact information was incorrect when you selected "My Profile," select OK at the bottom of the screen. This will take you back to the "Students Menu." Select "Student Forms." Select, "Change of Contact Information." Complete the Change of Contact Information Form and select, "Submit."

☐ 4. Obtain a printout of your Program Evaluation. From the student menu, click on "Program Evaluation" located on the right hand side of the screen under "Academic Profile." Print. **Do not turn this into your instructor! Keep this in a safe place, you will need this for the Core Assessment 2: Goal Setting project.**

Complete the following tasks in **Student Email:**

☐ 1. Access Student Email and log in. (See page 12 in this workbook for access and log in information.)

☐ 2. Using quality e-mail etiquette (see page 13 in this workbook), send your ACA instructor an e-mail introducing yourself <u>and</u> describing your favorite thing about Nash Community College.

To Lisa Cooper ×   Cc

Introduction & ACA Assignment

☐ 3. Using quality e-mail etiquette, compose an e-mail of introduction to your advisor and in the "CC" line, include your ACA instructor. You can locate your advisor's e-mail address by typing their name in the "To" line. In the "Subject" line, type "Introduction and ACA assignment." <u>Be sure to introduce yourself, let them know they are your advisor and that you look forward to working with them.</u>

Complete the following tasks in **Moodle:**

☐ 1. Access Moodle and log in. (See page 14 in this workbook for access and log in information.) Select this specific course from the list, "ACA College Transfer Success."

☐ 2. To review specific information about this course, Access the course "Syllabus" from the General Welcome block.

☐ 3. Select the "Scavenger Hunt Quiz" under assignments from the Session 2 block and take the quiz.

☐ 4. Enter the " 💬 On Campus Helpful Advice Forum" under assignments from the Session 2 block. Post a reply and feel free to respond to other student posts. Note that this is a single simple discussion forum. Just to make you aware, there are different types of forum formats instructors can use, such as allowing you to start a new discussion topic.

☐ 5. If you haven't already done so, add a picture to your profile. Follow the instructions on page 15 of this workbook. There is also a how-to video located in the Moodle Session 2 block. (Your instructor MAY award extra credit to students who add a profile picture!)

☐ 6. Access grades. From the Settings block under "Course Administration," select Grades. Make sure "user report" is selected. This gives you detailed information on the specific course. Print a copy and submit to your ACA instructor. Note, the "overview report" shows you an overview of all the courses you are enrolled in.

☐ 7. After completing every item for this entire Core Assessment 1, open the " 📣 Core Assessment 1 Reflection Questionnaire" under assignments from the Session 2 block. Complete and submit.

Documentation of Completion

The instructor will have:

1. the completed "Contact Information Verification Form"
2. the e-mail "introduction" sent from the student
3. the e-mail sent to the student's advisor (cc instructor)
4. printout of grades from Moodle
5. submission of completed Reflection Form Questionnaire via Moodle
6. completion of Scavenger Hunt quiz in Moodle
7. participation in a Forum in Moodle

Contact Information Verification Form

Complete and submit this form to your ACA instructor.

Name: _____

Record the phone number **displayed** in WebAdvisor from the student menu under "My Profile."

_____

Is that information correct? Yes _____   No _____

If NO, please:
1. Record the correct phone number to best reach you: _____
                              -and-
Select "Student Forms." Under the STUDENTS MENU. Select, "Change of Contact Information." Complete the Change of Contact Information Form and select, "Submit."

Note: ALL changes of address, phone or major need to be submitted to Student and Enrollment Services on a timely basis. Change of Contact Information forms are located in WebAdvisor at all times.

****

I attest that I have verified my contact information and made any necessary corrections by completing a Change of Information Form and submitting it to Student and Enrollment Services.

_____
Signature

ACA Course Management System
CORE ASSESSMENT 1 EVALUATION RUBRIC

STUDENT NAME_____

Student submits Contact Information Verification Form	10	
Student sends introduction e-mail to instructor.	10	
Introduction e-mail is well-developed including required information, and elaboration.	0-10	
Student sends e-mail to advisor.	10	
Student demonstrates quality e-mail etiquette.	0-10	
Student completes Scavenger Hunt Quiz in Moodle.	10	
Student responds to a discussion forum prompt in Moodle.	10	
Student's discussion forum response demonstrates care and thought and/or student posts multiple times.	0-10	
Student submits print out of grades from Moodle.	10	
Student completes CA1 Reflection Questionnaire in Moodle.	10	
TOTAL POINTS	(0-100)	
LETTER GRADE		
RUBRIC SCORE	(0-4)	

GRADE RANGE	RUBRIC SCORE	DESCRIPTION
90-100	4	Exceeds Expectations
80-89	3	Meets Expectations
60-79	2	Partially Meets Expectations
1-59	1	Did Not Meet Expectations
0	0	Did Not Attempt Assignment

<u>WebAdvisor Basics</u>

WebAdvisor is the portal that Nash Community College uses to allow students to register for classes, review financial aid information, and review grades online. WebAdvisor processes registration requests based on class availability and is able to determine if course prerequisites have been met. WebAdvisor is accessed with a secure username and password. This helps the college keep student information confidential and secure.

Where can I find WebAdvisor?

How do I Log In to WebAdvisor?

1. All student accounts (current and new) must be activated prior to logging into WebAdvisor. New student activation will begin the first day of class.

2. Go to www.nashcc.edu. Follow the directions above by clicking on the "Student Portal" button on the Nash CC homepage. Click on WebAdvisor, and then click "Log In".

3. Your **username** is your first initial, middle initial, last name and the last 3 digits of your student ID (all lowercase, no spaces, no punctuation).
   Example: Name: John Allen Smith   Student ID: 2563244   Username: jasmith244.

4. Your **password** is Ncc plus your date of birth using 2 digits each for month, day, and year (no spaces, no punctuation). Example: John's Birthday: February 6, 1981, Password: Ncc020681. You will be able to change this password after your first successful login.

5. Once you click "Submit" it will say that your "password has expired". Re-enter your username and password and enter in a new password **(Your password needs to be between 6 and 9 characters and must have both letters and numbers)**.

6. Click "Students" to access your information.

*If you are unable to log in or have forgotten your password, click on "Students" and "What is my User ID?" or "What is my password?" For verification purposes, they will be sent to your Student Email.

Nash CC Student Email

Gmail (Student Email) is Nash Community College's official means of communication to students. You will receive important information about your Financial Aid, updates from your instructors, and any other valuable information that you will be responsible for knowing while you are at Nash CC through Student Email.

Get in the habit of checking your Nash CC Student Email on a daily basis!

How to Log-in to Student Email:

1. Go to www.nashcc.edu. Follow the directions above by clicking on the "Student Portal" button on the Nash CC homepage.
2. Next, click on the "Student Email" button. This will take you straight to the Student Email log in screen.
3. Your **username** is your first initial, middle initial, last name and the last 3 digits of your student ID   (all lowercase, no spaces, no punctuation).
   Example: Name: John Allen Smith   Student ID: 2563244   Username: jasmith244.
4. Your **password** is Ncc plus your date of birth using 2 digits each for month, day, and year (no spaces, no punctuation). Example: John's birthday is February 6, 1981—Password: Ncc020681. You will be able to change this password after you first successful login.
5. Once you have entered your login information, click 'Sign In'
6. After you have read the Terms of Service, click "I accept". Continue to my account.
7. You will be asked to set a new password.
8. Enter your initial password, then enter your new password twice. Try to choose a strong password. The password strength can be determined by looking at the bar on the right of the password fields.
9. Click the 'Submit' button. You will be taken to your new inbox.
* For log in assistance, in the Student Portal, click on "Log In Help" under Student Email. At the top of the page, you can submit a help ticket for forgotten passwords.

Basic College E-mail Etiquette

Subject line: Always use a meaningful subject to help the recipient know the content of the message. Failure to do so with an instructor might result in the message being discarded as spam.

Greeting: Just like a written letter, open your e-mail with a greeting like Dear Dr. West or Dear Mrs. Cooper.

Identify yourself: Your instructors (or advisor) may have over one hundred students in any given semester. Put your name and the course at the beginning of the e-mail to help identify who you are and the subject for which you are requesting information.

Grammar: Always use correct spelling, grammar, and punctuation in an e-mail. Do not use text messaging abbreviations. Avoid typing an e-mail in all capital letters, which is often perceived as yelling. Spell check and proofread the message before you send it.

Length: Use short paragraphs, be concise, and get to the point. Do not make the e-mail longer than it needs to be for your question or concern.

Purpose: Make sure that e-mail is an appropriate venue for your concern. If you really need to meet face-to-face with your instructor, send an e-mail to set up an appointment, but save the rest of the conversation for when you meet with them. Don't try to use e-mail to replace a face-to-face conversation if the face-to-face meeting is what is really needed.

Courtesy: "Speak" to people electronically in the same manner you would speak to them face-to-face. Re-read the e-mail to ensure that the tone is what you intended.

Closing: Always end a message with your name and basic contact information, particularly if your peers or instructor need to respond to you. Consider including your first and last name, phone number, and e-mail address

References

Email Etiquette: http://owl/english/purdue.edu/owl/resource/636/01.
Fundamentals of College Email Etiquette:
http://school.tips.net/Pages/T007953_Fundamentals_of_College_Email_Etiquette.html
SCC Email Etiquette and Appropriate Use of Distribution Lists:
http://www.scc.losrios.edu/FacultyStaffPublications_and_Marketing_Guide/E-mail/SCC_Email_Etiquette_and_Appropriate_Use_of_Distribution_Lists.htm
eMail Etiquette: http://www.dawsoncollege.qc.ca/info-desk/web-tutorials/email-etiquette

MOODLE Basics
What is Moodle?

Moodle is an online course management system that can be used for all classes, including online, hybrid, virtual, and on campus- classroom based courses. Instructors will post course syllabi, grades, assignments, and documents in Moodle.

Where can I find Moodle?

How do I Log In to Moodle?

1. As a student, you will be able to access your Moodle course(s) on the first day of class each semester. (If you are taking an online course, you will be required to log into Moodle and complete an Enrollment Verification Activity—the due date for this assignment will be posted in Moodle. Students who do not complete this assignment by the due date will be dropped from the online course—this does not include hybrid courses).

2. Go to www.nashcc.edu. Follow the directions above by clicking on the "Student Portal" button on the Nash CC homepage. Click Moodle and under "Log In" you will type in your username and password.

3. Your username is your first initial, middle initial, last name and the last 3 digits of your student ID (all lowercase, no spaces, no punctuation). Example: Name: John Allen Smith Student ID: 2563244 Username: jasmith244.

4. Your password is Ncc plus your date of birth using 2 digits each for month, day, and year (no spaces, no punctuation). Example: John's Birthday: February 6, 1981, Password: Ncc020681. You will be able to change this password after your first successful login.

5. Once you click "Login" you will be prompted to change your password. For security purposes, please do not share this password with anyone.

*If you fail to log in successfully go to the Online Support Center—located on the Moodle home page.

Moodle Basics: How to Upload a Picture to Moodle (iPad Views)

1 To upload a picture select your name to edit your profile.

2 Lisa Cooper

Select Edit profile.

3

Take Photo or Video

Choose Existing

*

From the file picker, from upload a file, select browse, from the iPad you can choose to take a photo or choose an existing photo.

* NOTE – You can take a photo of yourself in class with the iPad camera and it will appear on the camera roll for you to upload. OR you can select any picture or icon from the internet and save it to the camera roll on the iPad and upload it to Moodle as described.

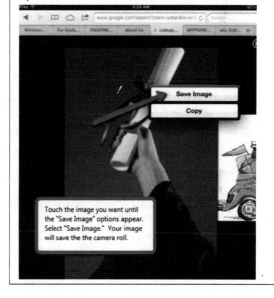

Save Image

Copy

Touch the image you want until the "Save Image" options appear. Select "Save Image." Your image will save the camera roll.

5 Camera Roll

Select photo you want.

81 Photos, 2 Videos

6 Select Update profile.

Core Assessment 2   Due Date: _____

Goal Setting Learning Outcome:

Students will set personal and academic goals, explore career options, and develop a semester-by-semester plan of study through degree completion.

1. SMARTEST Goals Worksheets

Complete the SMARTEST Goals Worksheet for your academic/ professional life and personal life found on pages 20-22 in this workbook. Submit completed worksheets to the instructor at the end of the class period.

2. Career Assessment (Complete in–class as time and technology permit)

☐ Complete the **"Interest Profiler"** under the *Learn About Yourself* menu from the "Plan for a Career" tab at CFNC.org

a. In Moodle, from the Session block under assignments access the link " 🖼 Interest Profiler from CFNC. Org." For your reference here is the direct link to the CFNC Interest Profiler: https://www1.cfnc.org/Plan/For_A_Career/Learn_About_Yourself/Learn_About_Yourself.aspx

b. Select the Interest Profiler button. You will be prompted to set up an account first to complete the "Interest Profiler." After setting up your account, you should be re-directed back to the "Interest Profiler."

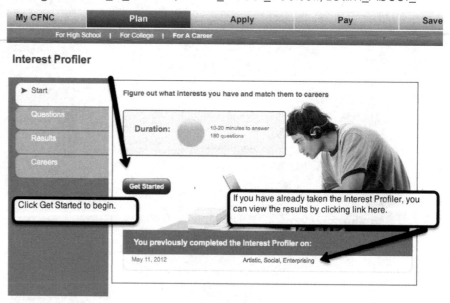

☐ Type a minimum 5 sentence reflection regarding your results in the space provide at the bottom of your results page.

☐ Print out the results, review and submit a copy to your instructor.

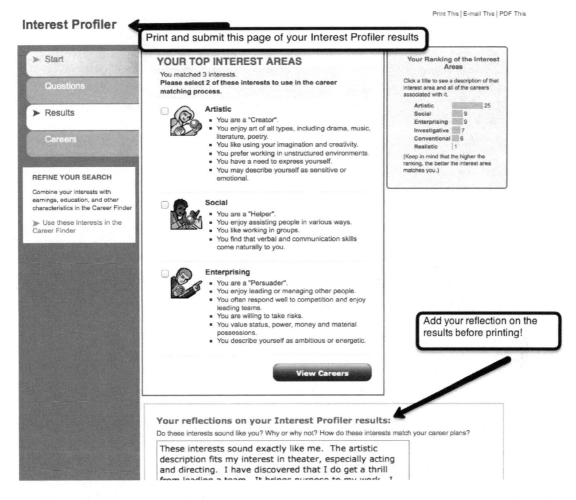

Out-of-Class Assignment

3. Semester-by-Semester Plan of Study

☐ **Make an appointment** with your advisor before the registration period to create a plan of study.

☐ **Bring** the 4 following items to the meeting with your advisor:
   a) <u>Degree checklist</u> - Degree checklists can often be found outside of the department chair's door and/or online on the College's website.
   b) <u>Program Evaluation</u> - **You should have printed this while completing Core Assessment 1.** The Program Evaluation can be found on WebAdvisor. To do so, click on "Students." "Program Evaluation" is on the right hand side of the screen under "Academic Profile."
   c) <u>Advisor Questionnaire</u> – A hard copy is located on a page 24 in the workbook. An electronic copy can be found in Moodle under assignments in the Session block, titled "ⓦ Advisor Questionnaire."
   d) <u>Semester-by-Semester Plan of Study Form</u>: Brainstorm ideas for future semesters' coursework, and consider any transfer plans, if applicable, before the meeting. A hard copy of the form is located in your workbook on page 23. An electronic

copy can be found in Moodle under assignments in the Session block titled " Semester-by-Semester Plan of Study Form."

☐ **At the meeting, work jointly** with your advisor to develop your **Semester-by-Semester Plan of Study** through graduation.
    a) Take from the meeting a hardcopy of the completed Semester-by-Semester Plan of Study.
    b) Ask if your advisor can e-mail you a copy of the Semester-by-Semester Plan of Study so that each has an electronic file for future reference and modification.
    c) Ask your advisor to complete the Advisor Questionnaire and give it back to you for submission.

Advisor Responsibilities:

1. The advisor and student should jointly develop a plan of study for the student through degree completion. Each individual should leave the meeting with a copy of the Semester-by-Semester Plan of Study.
2. Ideally, the advisor should e-mail the student a copy of the Semester-by-Semester Plan of Study so that each has an electronic file for future reference and modification.
3. The advisor will complete the Advisor Questionnaire and return it to the student at the meeting.

Helpful Hints:

1. Make an appointment with your advisor in advance. **Keep the appointment!** If an emergency arises, contact the advisor to reschedule.
2. Come prepared with all of the documents mentioned above: Degree Checklist, Program Evaluation, Plan of Study, and Advisor Questionnaire.

Documentation needed for completion of assignment:

1. SMARTEST Goals Worksheets
2. copy of "Interest Profiler" results from CFNC.org
3. completed Semester-By-Semester Plan of Study
4. completed Advisor Questionnaire

ACA Goal Setting
CORE ASSESSMENT 2 EVALUATION RUBRIC

STUDENT NAME_____

Student Completes all portions of the SMARTEST Goals Worksheets with thought & care	0-30	
Student completes "Interest Profiler" Career Assessment	15	
Student's "Interest Profiler" includes a thoughtful reflection.	0-10	
Student completes signed Plan of Study Form.		
• Completes form for one semester	15	
• Completes form through degree completion	15	
Student meets with advisor to develop plan of study.	15	
TOTAL POINTS	(0-100)	
LETTER GRADE		
RUBRIC SCORE	(0-4)	

CORE EVALUATION RUBRIC

GRADE RANGE	RUBRIC SCORE	DESCRIPTION
90-100	4	Exceeds Expectations
80-89	3	Meets Expectations
60-79	2	Partially Meets Expectations
1-59	1	Did Not Meet Expectations
0	0	Did Not Attempt Assignment

SMARTEST Goals Worksheet: Core Assessment 2

NAME: _____ DATE_____

My Academic/Professional Goal: _____

_____

My Personal Goal: _____

_____

Complete this worksheet to make sure your goals are the **SMARTEST!**

S- Specific	*What exactly do you want to accomplish? Be as specific as possible. For example, a general goal would be, "Get in shape" but a specific goal would say, "Get in shape by joining a health club and working out 3 days a week."* **Academic/Professional Goal:** **Personal Goal:**
M-Measurable	*How will you know when you have reached this goal? Be concrete.* **Academic/Professional Goal:** **Personal Goal:**
A-Achievable	*Is achieving this goal realistic with effort and commitment? Have you got the resources to achieve this goal? If not, how will you get them? Who are the people you can go to for help?* **Academic/Professional Goal:** **Personal Goal:**

R- Relevant	*Why is this goal important to your life? What are the benefits to achieving this goal?*
	<u>Academic/Professional Goal:</u>
	<u>Personal Goal:</u>
T-Time-bound	*When will you achieve this goal? With no time frame tied to it there's no sense of urgency. "Someday" won't work. But if you anchor it within a timeframe, "by May 1, 2016", then you've set your mind into motion to begin.*
	<u>Academic/Professional Goal:</u>
	<u>Personal Goal:</u>
E-Exhibit	*How will you display your goals so that you are reminded of them every day?*
	<u>Academic/Professional Goal:</u>
	<u>Personal Goal:</u>

S-Specific Action Step	*What smaller steps need to be taken to get you to your goal?*
	Academic/Professional Goal:

Action Step	Expected Completion Date
O	
O	
O	
O	
O	

Personal Goal:

Action Step	Expected Completion Date
O	
O	
O	
O	
O	

T- Target Obstacles	*What are some obstacles you might face and what steps can you take to meet these challenges?*
	Academic/Professional Goal:

Potential Obstacles	Potential Solutions

Personal Goal:

Potential Obstacles	Potential Solutions

Semester-by-Semester Plan of Study

Student Name:	ID #
Major:	Code:
Advisor:	Phone #

Semester	
Total	

Semester	
Total	

Semester	
Total	

Semester	
Total	

Semester	
Total	

Semester	
Total	

Semester	
Total	

Semester	
Total	

Semester	
Total	

Total Credit Hours:

Advisor Signature: Student Signature:

Date: Click here to enter a date.

Advisor Questionnaire

Advisor:

Student:

ACA Instructor:

Date of Meeting:

Did the student bring any of the following to the meeting?

Departmental Degree Check sheet	☐ YES	☐ NO
Printout of Program Evaluation	☐ YES	☐ NO
Semester-By-Semester Plan of Study	☐ YES	☐ NO
with some ideas filled-in	☐ YES	☐ NO

ADVISOR, COMPLETE AND RETURN TO STUDENT AT THE MEETING

_____

Advisor Signature

Core Assessment 3   Due Date: _____

Study Skills Learning Outcome:
Students will define and explain strategies for effective studying.

Name: _____

Directions: Complete the following tasks in order to gain a true understanding of the type of learner you are, how you learn best, and ways you can improve your academic performance.

1. **VARK Learning Style Assessment:** Complete the assessment in order to identify your primary VARK learning style.

   a. In Moodle, find and click on the "VARK Learning Style Assessment" under Session 4.
   b. This will open a new window, read the directions and take the assessment. It is only 16 questions, answer them honestly. Then click, OK.
   c. A new window with your results will show, print this page.
   d. You will submit the results page to your instructor on the due date.
   e. Determine your VARK Learning Style by looking at the numbers on your results page. Circle the learning style with the largest number.
   f. Which learning style did you circle? _____
   g. You have now identified your VARK Learning Style!

2. **Learning Style Research:** Conduct research on your primary learning style.

   a. Complete the graphical organizer on pages 27 & 28 in an effort to obtain a deeper understanding and identify strategies and characteristics.
   b. You will share this research and knowledge with your classmates.

ACA Study Skills
CORE ASSESSMENT 3 EVALUATION RUBRIC

Student Name: _____

Learning Style Evaluated: ☐ Visual ☐ Aural ☐ Read/Write ☐ Kinesthetic

VARK Learning Style Assessment		
Student completes and submits the VARK Learning Styles Assessment.	20	
Learning Style Research		
Student appropriately defines his/her preferred learning style.	0-10	
Student appropriately identifies strengths of his/her preferred learning style.	0-10	
Student appropriately identifies weaknesses of his/her preferred learning style.	0-10	
Student appropriately identifies characteristics of his/her preferred learning style.	0-10	
Student appropriately identifies study tips for his/her preferred learning style.	0-10	
Student completes reflection on preferred learning style.	0-10	
Using learned information about his/her preferred learning style, the student develops a plan for success in an additional course in which they are enrolled.	0-10	
Student's assignment demonstrates a higher level of thought and depth of understanding for the study process and learning style.	0-10	
TOTAL POINTS	(0-100)	
LETTER GRADE		
RUBRIC SCORE	(0-4)	

GRADE RANGE	RUBRIC SCORE	DESCRIPTION
90-100	4	Exceeds Expectations
80-89	3	Meets Expectations
60-79	2	Partially Meets Expectations
1-59	1	Did Not Meet Expectations
0	0	Did Not Attempt Assignment

Learning Style Research

Directions: Using your primary learning style, complete the following graphical organizer in an effort to obtain a deeper understanding and identify strategies and characteristics.

What type of learner are you?

Definition:

(Define/Explain your learning style.)

Strengths:

(Identify 3 strengths that are typical for your learning style.)

1.

2.

3.

Characteristics of my learning style:

(Identify 5 characteristics of your learning style.)

1.

2.

3.

4.

5.

Weaknesses:

(Identify 3 weaknesses that are typical for your learning style.)

1.

2.

3.

Study Tips...
for my learning style:
(Identify 10 study tips for your learning style.)

1.

2.

3.

4.

5.

6.

7.

8.

9.

10.

Learning Style Reflection:
(Were you classified as the type of learner that you thought you were? After doing research, do you agree or disagree with your results?)

_____

_____

_____

_____

_____

_____

Applying Your Knowledge

Identify a course (other than ACA) you are currently taking:

_____

How will you use the knowledge you've gained to ensure success in the course listed above?

_____

_____

_____

_____

_____

_____

_____

_____

_____

_____

Core Assessment 4

Tutorial and Learning Services Learning Outcome:

Students will locate and utilize academic tutorial and learning resource services.

Academic Tutorial In-Class Assignment: Access the online tutorial services provided and complete the following tasks.
DUE: Class Session 9

1. **Study Stack   (online –** www.studystack.com**) –** Here you can use pre-made flash cards from numerous subjects or create your very own flash cards, depending upon your desired content, allowing for very focused review. You can also take practice quizzes, study the flash cards, or even play games to learn the content.

   ☐ Access Study Stack by visiting www.studystack.com.

   ☐ Register as a new user by clicking "Free Sign Up" located on the upper right hand side of the screen.   You are only asked to provide a username, password, and e-mail address. (Suggestion, use your college email username and password.)

   ☐ Write your username here:

   _____.

   ☐ Write your password here:

   _____.

   ☐ Once you have created an account, click on "Home" in the upper left corner to return to the homepage.

   ☐ If you needed to access flash cards for Science, what five types of science are available?

   1. _____.
   2. _____.
   3. _____.
   4. _____.
   5. _____.

   ☐ Type "ACA 115" in the search bar.
      1. Select "ACA 115: Core 4 | Chapter 3: Learning Styles and Studying
      2. Study the flash cards by clicking them to flip and display the definition.
      3. How many terms are there? _____
      4. Scroll to the bottom of the page and view the numerous icons that can be used to study the terms. Try the "Matching" icon and play. Record how long it took you to complete. _____ (Timer is at the bottom of the matching list)
      5. Now try the "Quiz." How did you do? Record your score here: _____.
      6. Try "Hangman" or "Crossword". Did you get them correct? _____.
      7. FYI- You can create your own flash cards by clicking the "Create your own flashcards" link.

2. **SAS Curriculum Pathways and Writing Reviser** (online - www.sascurriculumpathways.com) - SAS Curriculum Pathways and WritingReviser is a free, self-help resource to assist students in five main subject areas: English, Math, Science, Social Studies and Spanish. There are interactive tutorials and resources for each subject. In addition, SAS Writing Reviser provides assistance with writing assignments.

   Username: nccstudent
   No password is required

   SAS Curriculum Pathways   WritingReviser

   ☐ From The Moodle Session block under assignments click on: " SAS Curriculum Pathway & Writer Reviser. " Log in as directed above.

   ☐ Under "Browse Resources" listed on the left hand side of the screen, record the 5 main categories listed: English Language Arts, _____, Science, _____ _____, _____.

   ☐ Under the Science category, select "Cells". From the list of resources, find the "Cell Sizes" resource and read the description of the resource. (This video may not play due to the plug-ins needed.) What question would you be able to answer after watching the video based upon the description? _____
   _____

3. **Smarthinking** (online – www.smarthinking.com) - Smarthinking is the online tutoring service provided for Nash Community College students. Smarthinking can provide assistance with math, writing, chemistry, physics, accounting, economics, anatomy and physiology, biology, Spanish, nursing, and allied health.

   Username: nash0405
   Password: livetutors

   ☐ From The Moodle Session block under assignments click on:" Smarthinking online tutoring services."

   ☐ Use the above username and password to begin. You will be asked to set up your own account with a username and password. Do so now. (Suggestion, use your college email username and password in order to remember.)

   ☐ Once you are logged in you will be at the home page. Complete the list of buttons found at the home page and fill in the blanks.
   1. **Writing Center** – Have your _____ reviewed by a tutor.
   2. _____ _____ - Chat _____ with a _____ tutor.
   3. _____ _____ - Schedule to _____ with a _____ tutor in the _____.
   4. **Offline** _____ - Send a _____ an academic _____.

   ☐ Select the "Drop-In Tutoring" button. Why are some subjects grayed out?
   _____

   ☐ List one subject available for a live tutor right now: _____

   ☐ From the menu options at the top of the page, select, "Scheduled Tutoring."

   ☐ Scheduled sessions must be reserved _____ hours in advance.

   ☐ Name a subject listed that you might schedule a tutor for: _____

   ☐ From The Moodle Session block under assignments click on: Sample session for Smarthinking.

   ☐ Select and watch the nursing tutorial. (Note, flash is needed to view. Best watched from a PC.) Bonus question...What two hormones does the Thyroid gland secrete? _____ and _____.

o   Visit the Nash Community College Library website: www.nashcc.edu/library

Library

o   There are 8 icons that represent a variety of databases and resources that are available to you as a student of Nash Community College.

Which icon would you select to...

1.   Find a library book? _____

2.   Obtain 24 hour assistance? _____

3.   Read an electronic version of a book? _____

4.   Explore international facts? _____

o   Select the NC Live icon.   **What is the username and password used to access library resources from home?**

SEARCH
NC
live
.org

   Username: _____

   Password: _____

o   From the NCLIVE homepage, go to the search box and input:

   | Note Taking Habits |

   1.   How many results did you get? _____

o   Now try the search again, but this time **INCLUDE** quotation marks.

   | "Note Taking Habits" |

   2.   How many results did you get? _____

o   Choose the following article:

   Assisting students to avoid plagiarism

By clicking on the ▣ icon to the right of the blue title link, complete the following:

1. Author(s): _____

2. Source: _____

3. Volume & Issue: _____

4. Date the article was written: _____

5. Read the Abstract and answer the following question: This study looked at secondary school students from what country? _____

6. Now, click on the actual article. (The blue title of the article is the link) Find the "Cite" button and select it. ▤ Cite

Find the MLA citation format for this article and record it here:

_____

_____

_____

Describe briefly the importance of citing sources:

_____

_____

When is it appropriate to cite sources?

_____

_____

o Return to the NC Live homepage by clicking on the NC Live icon in the upper left corner of the screen.

NC LIVE

o Here you will be able to choose links to numerous databases specific to many content areas.

Books & Literature
novels, poetry, criticism, plays, Worldcat

History & Biography
WWII, Civil War, presidents, world history

Business & Management
small business, company info, Morningstar, WSJ

Hobbies & Interests
books, auto repair, gardening

1. Dependent upon your current major or career goal, which database link would best supply you with information? _____

2. If you were told to write an essay on World War II, which database link would provide you with resources? _____

o Select the Current Issues database link. Then, select the CQ Researcher Online link. **CQ Researcher is a great database for finding topics and articles on current events.**

　　1.　What is today's Featured Report? _____

o Click on the Pro/Con tab. (This can be used to obtain information on both sides of the topic.) List the two experts that are part of the pro/con debate.

　　2.　Pro: _____
　　3.　Con: _____

o View the Hot Topics listed on the right side of the screen. Select a topic.

　　4.　What topic did you select? _____
　　5.　Each article begins with a topic question. What is your article's topic question?

　　　_____

CORE ASSESSMENT 4 EVALUATION RUBRIC

ACA Tutorial & Learning Resource Services

Student accesses Study Stack.	5	
Student completes the Study Stack portion of the assignment accurately.	0 -15	
Student accesses SAS Curriculum Pathways and Writing Reviser.	5	
Student accesses Smarthinking.	5	
Student completes the Smarthinking portion of the assignment accurately.	0 -15	
Student answers Smarthinking bonus question accurately.	2	
Student accesses the library website and correctly completes the database and resource information on the form.	0-10	
Student accesses NC Live and completes a search for "Note Taking Habits."	0-10	
Student utilizes information from selected article and correctly completes the information on the form.	0-10	
Student includes MLA citation and satisfactorily explains the importance of citing sources.	0-10	
Student accesses CQ Researcher from NC Live and correctly completes the information as indicated on form.	0-15	
TOTAL POINTS	(0-100)	
LETTER GRADE		
RUBRIC SCORE	(0-4)	

GRADE RANGE	RUBRIC SCORE	DESCRIPTION
90-100	4	Exceeds Expectations
80-89	3	Meets Expectations
60-79	2	Partially Meets Expectations
1-59	1	Did Not Meet Expectations

| 0 | 0 | Did Not Attempt Assignment |

Core Assessment 5   Due Date: _____

Note Taking Learning Outcome
Students will demonstrate effective note taking skills.

Directions: This assignment asks you to demonstrate effective note taking skills during a lecture.

1) You will apply one of the note taking methods discussed in class while taking notes during an in-class exercise.
2) You will submit a copy of the notes taken during the in-class exercise.
3) Complete and submit the Note Taking Reflection form on pages 37 & 38. The Note Taking Reflection Form should be answered in full sentences and in detail.
4) The entire Core Assessment will be graded based upon the level of effective note taking demonstration as well as the detail and care in your reflection responses.

Alternate assignment for absentees: Alternatively, if you are absent from class this day, take notes from the reading in the text book from pages 172 to 181 using either Cornell, Mindmap, Outlining or PowerPoint Miniatures (found on page 103 of this workbook) and submit your notes along with the Note Taking Reflection Form found on page 37 & 38 of the workbook.

Documentation of Completion for either option:

1. Turn in a copy of the lecture or reading notes to the instructor.
2. Complete the Note Taking reflection form and turn in with your notes.

ACA Note Taking
CORE ASSESSMENT 5 EVALUATION RUBRIC

STUDENT NAME_____

Student completes in-class lecture note exercise or alternative textbook notes if absent from class.	5	
Student demonstrates ability to apply and understand selected note-taking technique by showing obvious consistency and diligence while completing the in-class lecture note exercise or alternative textbook notes.	0 - 20	
Student completes the Note Taking Quiz in Moodle.	10	
Student submits completed note taking reflection form	5	
Students' reflection of current note taking methods as well as completed improvement plan demonstrates an understanding of the note taking process and its impact.	0 - 30	
Students' open-ended reflection questions demonstrate an understanding of the note taking process and its impact.	0 - 30	
TOTAL POINTS	(0-100)	
LETTER GRADE		
RUBRIC SCORE	(0-4)	

GRADE RANGE	RUBRIC SCORE	DESCRIPTION
90-100	4	Exceeds Expectations
80-89	3	Meets Expectations
60-79	2	Partially Meets Expectations
1-59	1	Did Not Meet Expectations
0	0	Did Not Attempt Assignment

<u>Note Taking Reflection Form</u> - **Page 1 of 2**

Directions: After completion of Note Taking Core Assessment 5 activity, answer the following in full sentences and in detail. The assignment will be graded based on the level of detail in your responses. Attach a copy of your notes.

Name:

1. Which note taking assignment option did you complete?

☐ Cornell system

☐ Mind mapping

☐ PowerPoint miniatures

☐ Outlining

2. Using what you have learned from each of the 6 types of note-taking, identify your current 3 most challenging courses. Evaluate the content delivery method and teaching style of the instructor, reflect upon your current note taking methods, and identify the note taking methods you may need to apply.

Course: _____	Course: _____	Course: _____
Content Delivery Method / Teaching Style: _____ _____ _____	Content Delivery Method / Teaching Style: _____ _____	Content Delivery Method / Teaching Style: _____ _____
Current Note Taking Method: _____ _____	Current Note Taking Method: _____ _____	Current Note Taking Method: _____ _____
Ways to improve Note Taking in this course: _____ _____ _____ _____ _____ _____ _____ _____	Ways to improve Note Taking in this course: _____ _____ _____ _____ _____ _____ _____ _____	Ways to improve Note Taking in this course: _____ _____ _____ _____ _____ _____ _____ _____

3. From your perspective, what are the positives of this method? If you did not find any positives, elaborate on why.

4. From your perspective, what negatives did you encounter? If you did not find any negatives, elaborate on why.

5. Will you use this lecture or reading note taking method again? Why or why not?

How to Make a Mind Map®

The 'Laws of Mind Mapping' were originally devised by Tony Buzan when he codified the use of imagery, color and association and coined the phrase 'Mind Mapping'. In the intervening 30 plus years, there have been many variations on the original 'Mind Map ' and the widespread usage of mapping software of various sorts, has dramatically changed what is possible.   The summary below is based on Buzan's structure (a 'Mind Mapping, how to' - details available in his many books) but we believe that whilst this structure is great for establishing well-structured maps that can be used in many different ways, variations on these rules or 'laws' are often sensible and appropriate - as long as they are based on an understanding of why the laws exist and what they are trying to help the mind mapper to achieve.

The Mind Map below was produced using iMindMap.

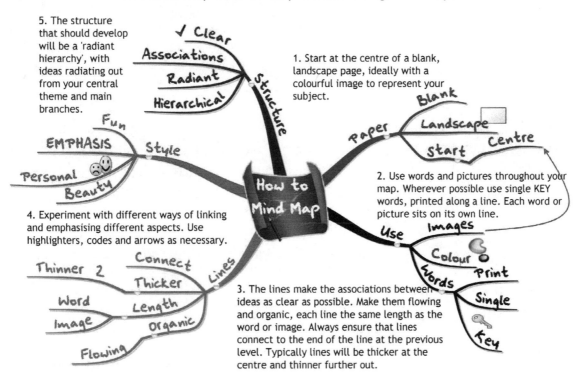

5. The structure that should develop will be a 'radiant hierarchy', with ideas radiating out from your central theme and main branches.

1. Start at the centre of a blank, landscape page, ideally with a colourful image to represent your subject.

2. Use words and pictures throughout your map. Wherever possible use single KEY words, printed along a line. Each word or picture sits on its own line.

4. Experiment with different ways of linking and emphasising different aspects. Use highlighters, codes and arrows as necessary.

3. The lines make the associations between ideas as clear as possible. Make them flowing and organic, each line the same length as the word or image. Always ensure that lines connect to the end of the line at the previous level. Typically lines will be thicker at the centre and thinner further out.

1. Take a blank piece of paper, A4 or larger.	Blank paper allows 360° of freedom to express the full range of your cortical skills, whereas pre-drawn lines restrict the natural flow of your thoughts.
2. Use the paper in landscape orientation.	Words and images have more space in the direction we write, so they don't bump into margins as quickly.
3. Start in the center.	Thoughts start in the center of our mental world. The Mind Map page reflects this!
4. Make a central image that represents the topic about which you are writing/thinking: • Use at least three colors. • Keep the height and width of the central image to approx. 2" or 5 cm (proportionately larger for bigger paper). • Allow the image to create its own shape (do not use a frame).	A picture is worth a thousand words. It opens up associations, focuses the thoughts, is fun and results in better recall: • Colors stimulate the right cortical activity of imagination as well as capturing and holding attention. • This size gives plenty of space for the rest of your Mind Map, while making it large enough to be the clear focus of the topic. • The unique shape makes it more memorable and enjoyable. A frame makes the center a monotony of shape and disconnects the branches.
5. The main themes around the central image are like the chapter headings of a book: • Print this word in CAPITALS or draw an image. • Place on a line of the same length • The central lines are thick, curved and organic i.e. like your arm joining your body, or the branch of a tree to the trunk. • Connect directly to the central image.	The main themes, connected to the central image on the main branches, allow their relative importance to be seen. These are the Basic Ordering Ideas (BOIs) and aggregate and focus the rest of the Mind Map: • Printing (versus cursive) allows the brain to photograph the image thus giving easier reading and more immediate recall. • Word length equals line length. An extra line disconnects thoughts, length accentuates the connection. • Curved lines give visual rhythm and variety and so are easier to remember, more pleasant to draw and less boring to look at. Thicker central lines show relative importance. • Connected to the image because the brain works by association not separated, disconnected lines.

6. Start to add a second level of thought. These words or images are linked to the main branch that triggered them. Remember: • Connecting lines are thinner. • Words are still printed but may be lower case.	Your initial words and images stimulate associations. Attach whatever word or image is triggered. Allow the random movement of your thought; you do not have to 'finish' one branch before moving on: • Connected lines create relationships and a structure. They also demonstrate the level of importance, as from a branch to a twig. • The size and style of the letters provide additional data about the importance and meaning of the word/image.
7. Add a third or fourth level of data as thoughts come to you: • Use images as much as you can, instead of, or in addition to the words. • Allow your thoughts to come freely, meaning you 'jump about' the Mind Map as the links and associations occur to you.	Your brain is like a multi-handed thought-ball catcher. The Mind Map allows you to catch and keep whatever 'thought ball' is thrown by your brain.
8. Add a new dimension to your Mind Map. Boxes add depth around the word or image.	To make some important points stand out.
9. Sometimes enclose branches of a Mind Map with outlines in color: • Enclose the shape of the branch and hug the shape tightly. • Use different colors and styles.	The outlines will create unique shapes as you find in clouds and will aid your memory: • These provide immediate visual linking. They can also encourage follow-up and remind you of action you need to take. • They can also show connection between branches by using the same color outline.
10. Make each Mind Map a little more: • BEAUTIFUL • ARTISTIC • COLOURFUL • IMAGINATIVE and • DIMENSIONAL	Your eyes and brain will be attracted to your Mind Map: • It will be easier to remember. • It will be more attractive to you (And to others as well).
11. Have fun! Add a little humor, exaggeration or absurdity wherever you can.	Your brain will delight in getting the maximum use and enjoyment from this process and will therefore learn faster, recall more effectively and think more clearly.

The Cornell Note-taking System

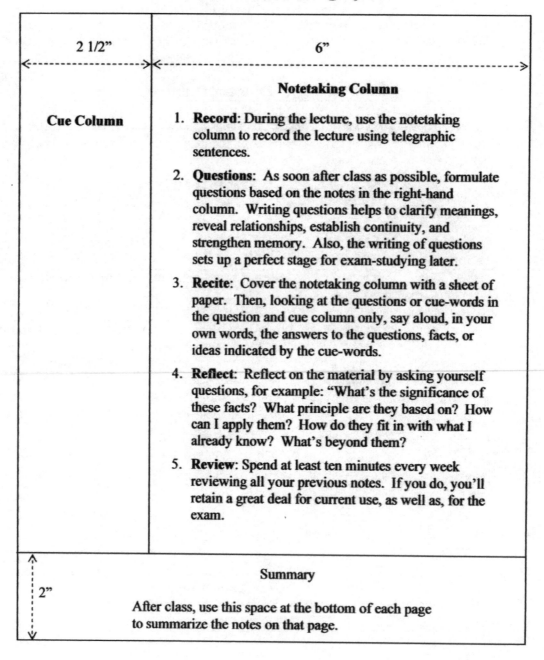

Cue Column

2 1/2"

6"

Notetaking Column

1. **Record**: During the lecture, use the notetaking column to record the lecture using telegraphic sentences.

2. **Questions**: As soon after class as possible, formulate questions based on the notes in the right-hand column. Writing questions helps to clarify meanings, reveal relationships, establish continuity, and strengthen memory. Also, the writing of questions sets up a perfect stage for exam-studying later.

3. **Recite**: Cover the notetaking column with a sheet of paper. Then, looking at the questions or cue-words in the question and cue column only, say aloud, in your own words, the answers to the questions, facts, or ideas indicated by the cue-words.

4. **Reflect**: Reflect on the material by asking yourself questions, for example: "What's the significance of these facts? What principle are they based on? How can I apply them? How do they fit in with what I already know? What's beyond them?

5. **Review**: Spend at least ten minutes every week reviewing all your previous notes. If you do, you'll retain a great deal for current use, as well as, for the exam.

Summary

2"

After class, use this space at the bottom of each page to summarize the notes on that page.

Adapted from _How to Study in College 7/e_ by Walter Pauk, 2001 Houghton Mifflin Company

Structure of Three-Column Math Notes
from
ON COURSE: STRATEGIES FOR CREATING SUCCESS IN COLLEGE AND IN LIFE,
STUDY SKILLS PLUS EDITION by Skip Downing p. 168

Three Column Math Notes		
Problem	**Solution**	**Explanation**
Write down the math problem.	*Write the steps used to solve the problem.*	*Write in your own words how to do each step.*

Example Using Three Column Math Notes

Problem	Solution			Explanation
Find the first 5 *multiples* of 12 and 18		12	18	Set up a table to organize your work.
	1			
	2			
	3			
	4			
	5			

		12	18	Multiply 12 by each number in column 1. Write the answer in column 2.
	1	**12**		
	2	**24**		
	3	**36**		
	4	**48**		
	5	**60**		

		12	**18**	Multiply 12 by each number in column 1. Write the answer in column 3.
	1	12	**18**	
	2	24	**36**	
	3	36	**54**	
	4	48	**72**	
	5	60	**90**	
		12	**108**	

The Outlining Method

Dash or indented outlining is a traditional note taking method that can work for most subjects except for some science classes such as physics or math.
- The information which is most general begins at the left with each more specific group of facts indented with spaces to the right.
- The relationships between the different parts is carried out through indenting.
- No numbers, letters, or Roman numerals are needed.

Method

Listen and then write in points in an organized pattern based on space indention. Place major points farthest to the left. Indent each more specific point to the right. Levels of importance will be indicated by distance away from the major point. Indention can be as simple as or as complex as labeling the indentations with Roman numerals or decimals. Markings are not necessary as space relationships will indicate the major/minor points.

Advantages

Well-organized system if done right. Outlining records content as well as relationships. It also reduces editing and is easy to review by turning main points into questions.

Disadvantages

Requires more thought in class for accurate organization. This system may not show relationships by sequence when needed. It doesn't lend to diversity of a review attach for maximum learning and question application. This system cannot be used if the lecture is too fast.

When to Use

The outline format can be used if the lecture is presented in outline organization. This may be either deductive (regular outline) or inductive (reverse outline where minor points start building to a major point). Use this format when there is enough time in the lecture to think about and make organization decisions when they are needed. This format can be most effective when your note taking skills are super sharp and you can handle the outlining regardless of the note taking situation.

Example:

I) **Extrasensory perception**
   A) **-definition: means of perceiving without use of sense organs.**
   B) **-three kinds -**
      1) **-telepathy: sending messages**
      2) **-clairvoyance: forecasting the future**
      3) **-psychokinesis: perceiving events external to situation**
   C) **-current status -**
      1) **-no current research to support or refute**
      2) **-few psychologists say impossible**

Core Assessment 6   Due Date: _____

Test-Taking Learning Outcome:
Students will identify and describe test taking strategies.

In-Class Assignment: Identify and describe test taking strategies through classroom activities dealing with test anxieties, preparation for testing, and test integrity. Complete the following tasks:

1. Complete Exercise 9.3 Test Anxiety Survey on page 47 of this student workbook, to determine your level of anxiety. On page 48 of the student workbook, complete a 6-8 sentence reflection on the survey results.

2. Read the True/False section of Chapter 9 on pages 251 & 252 of the textbook. Pay close attention to the two tips that specifically discuss "absolutes" and "qualifiers." Use the worksheet on page 49 of this workbook to categorize key words into absolutes and qualifiers that can be clues to the correct answer in a true/false format. After completing the worksheet, add and categorize 3 additional words.

3. Form small groups in class and choose from one of the following activities to demonstrate your understanding of test-taking techniques and strategies.
   a. Develop at least 10 game show questions on test-taking strategies. The questions should contain a combination of true/false, multiple choice, and fill-in-the-blank questions. Consult pages 241-262. Your group will create a game show such as Jeopardy, Family Feud, or Are You Smarter than a Fifth Grader to play with the class. Each group will turn in its test-taking strategy questions and answer key.
   b. Collaborate with your group to develop what you consider to be the ten most important tips from the before, during, and after the test sections in your textbook. Consult pages 241-243, 249-251, and 260-262. Create a skit, song, or cheer based upon the top ten list and perform it for your classmates. Each group will turn in its top ten test-taking strategy tips.
   c. Create a visual display such as a Mind Map, poster, or graphic organizer that outlines 10 strategies and/or suggestions for taking multiple choice, true/false, essay, short answer, fill in the blank, and matching tests. Consult pages 251-258. Exhibit your visual display to your classmates and submit your creation to your instructor.

Out-of-Class Assignment: Identify one of your most challenging current courses. Using information on that course and your knowledge of your upcoming final exam, presentation, or essay; apply your preferred VARK learning style and complete the Master Study Plan on page 73 and 74 75-78 of the student workbook to create a detailed plan for your success.

Documentation of Completion:

1. Surevy and reflection on test anxiety
2. Worksheet on key words
3. 10 item list from small group project

Student completes Test Anxiety Survey Plan	5	
Student completes reflection on Test Anxiety Survey results.	5	
Students' reflection is thoughtful and contains a minimum of 6-8 sentences.	0-10	
Student thoughtfully completes Key Word exercise and includes at least 3 additional key words.	0-10	
Student appropriately contributes and participates in a small group to complete a test-taking activity.	0 - 15	
Student submits documentation of completed test-taking activity, demonstrating thoughtful understanding and application of appropriate test-taking strategies. (Game Show questions, Top Ten List, or visual display.)	0 - 20	
Student submits completed Master Study Plan.	5	
Student thoughtfully completes Master Study Plan, demonstrating the ability to apply and understand techniques and strategies for success based upon their VARK learning style.	0 - 30	
TOTAL POINTS	(0-100)	
LETTER GRADE		
RUBRIC SCORE	(0-4)	

ACA Test-Taking Skills
CORE ASSESSMENT 6 EVALUATION RUBRIC

STUDENT NAME: _____

Group Members: _____

GRADE RANGE	RUBRIC SCORE	DESCRIPTION
90-100	4	Exceeds Expectations

80-89	3	Meets Expectations
60-79	2	Partially Meets Expectations
1-59	1	Did Not Meet Expectations
0	0	Did Not Attempt Assignment

Test Taking: High Anxiety?

Name: _____

Exercise 9.3 Test Anxiety Survey

What is test anxiety? What are the symptoms? Do you have it? Fill out the following informational survey to determine whether or not you may have test anxiety. For each of the twelve statement, rate your degree of agreement or disagreement.

1	2	3	4	5
Disagree Completely	Disagree Somewhat	Unsure	Agree Somewhat	Agree Completely

____4__ 1.   I cringe when I suddenly realize on the day of an exam that I forgot about the test.

____2__ 2.   I obsess about the possibility of failing an upcoming exam.

____2__ 3.   I often experience disappointment, anger, embarrassment, or some other emotional reaction during an exam.

____4__ 4.   I think that instructors secretly get enjoyment from watching students squirm over exams.

____1__ 5.   I experience physical symptoms such as an upset stomach, faintness, hyperventilation, or nausea before an exam.

____1__ 6.   I tend to zone out during exams; my mind goes blank.

____1__ 7.   I feel extreme pressure to please others by doing well on exams.

____1__ 8.   If I'm honest, I'd have to admit that I really don't' know how to study for tests.

____4__ 9.   I'd much rather write a paper or give a presentation that take an exam.

____2__ 10.   I usually fear that my exam grade will be lower than that of other students.

____2__ 11.   After taking an exam, I obsess on my performance, going over and over questions that I think I may have missed.

____3__ 12.   I convince myself that I'm not good at taking exams even though I often do fairly well on them.

_____ **TOTAL (add up your score)**

If your score equals 49-60, you are a likely candidate for test anxiety.

If you scored between 37-48, you have some signs of anxiety and may need help in managing your stress level.

If you scored 36 or below, you most likely experience a normal amount of anxiety and have already developed coping skills to help you.

TEST-TAKING HIGH ANXIETY REFLECTION

Take a moment to think about what your results from the Test-Taking Anxiety Survey mean for you as a student. Complete a 6-8 sentence reflection paragraph discussing your results, areas of concern and steps you could take to help reduce your test-taking anxiety or outline those behaviors you practice to help you cope with test taking anxiety.

NAME: _____ TEST ANXIETY SCORE: _____

_____

_____

_____

_____

_____

_____

_____

_____

_____

_____

_____

_____

_____

_____

_____

_____

_____

_____

_____

True/False Exercise

Name: _____

Read the True/False section of Chapter 9 on pages 251 & 252 of the textbook. Pay close attention to the two tips that specifically discuss "absolutes" and "qualifiers." Categorize the key words into absolutes and qualifiers that can be clues to the correct answer in a true/false test question. Absolutes tend to make the answer false and qualifiers tend to make the answer true. After completing the worksheet, add and categorize 3 additional words.

Key Word	Absolutes	Qualifiers
Always		
Sometimes		
Only		
A few		
Commonly		
Never		
Biggest		
More		
Might		
May		
100%		
Least		
Frequently		
Typically		
Without a doubt		
Nobody		
Better		
Entirely		
Smartest		
Smarter than		
No one		
Largest		
Larger than		
Average		
All		
Most		
Worst		
Everyone		
Occasionally		
Everybody		

NOW, ADD YOUR OWN WORDS

SESSION HANDOUTS
AND INFORMATION

Find an Expert

Find someone in our group with expertise in each of the areas described. As you circulate around the room, introduce yourself, fill in your interviewee's first name below, describing your own experience as it relates and something in particular your interviewee knows about the subject that you don't. Find someone...

1. Who knows a lot about **cars**?
   Name: _____

2. Who has had a piece of **writing published**?
   Name: _____

3. Who is a **fast food** junkie?
   Name: _____

4. Who knows how **families** work as a result of having five or more siblings?
   Name: _____

5. Who knows the campus because a **friend or sibling previously attended**?
   Name: _____

6. Who's had a stellar career in **high school athletics**?
   Name: _____

7. Who's never gotten anything but **A's in math**?
   Name: _____

8. Who studied **art or dance** growing up?
   Name: _____

9. Who knows the food service industry well from working as a **server**?
   Name: _____

10. Who is a relationship expert as a result of a **long-lasting romance**?
    Name: _____

Finally, what kind of expertise do you hope to develop during your first term in college?

_____

Social Contract

In groups, discuss the behaviors you would like to see all class members exhibit that promote learning and foster a meaningful class experience. What behaviors should students avoid? Record those items you would like to see included in a class social contract that we will all agree to abide by. Here is a sample, however, focus on your desires for the most optimum class environment!

Sample In-Class Social Contract

- We are comfortable exploring tangents, but we will not get upset when the teacher reins us back in to move on. Anyone in the class is allowed to remind us to get back on task.
- Everyone is responsible to the rest of us for having done the reading.
- Only attack ideas, not people in the class.
- We can all make a mistake with the language we use, but some words are just too surprising and you should avoid them. Four-letter words and anything racist will upset a lot of us.
- Using your laptop is okay, but not for computer games, social networking sites, stuff unrelated to class. If you're on those, sit further back in the room so we aren't seeing it from behind you.
- No cell phones should be on during class. Annoying rings and texting notices are too much.
- Only ask for a paper extension if you really are deathly ill. Otherwise the rest of us are likely to resent it.

Record your group's suggestions for a class social contract. When complete, Access the " Social Contract Shared Google Document" in your Moodle Session 1 block to submit your suggestions. As a class you will collaborate to finalize the document.

Envision Excellence

Excellence in academics is often measured in terms of grades, with an "A" grade representing the highest achievement. Consider what it takes to be a successful student. First individually, then in small groups, do the following activities.

1. INDIVIDUALLY: Answer these 2 questions.
   - What makes someone an "A" student?

   - What qualities does "A" work possess?

2. INDIVIDUALLY: Read the article from NISOD Innovation Abstracts *Calatrello's Highly Unscientific Theory of Halves: A Primer for Student Success.* As you read the article, circle key terms and underline important details.

3. IN GROUPS: Write a 20/20 reflection from the article. As a group summarize the article in 20 words.

Record your 20 word summary here:

4. IN GROUPS: Compare your answers to the first question, what qualities makes an A student. Then answer the following question:
   - What are the behaviors of successful students? Record at least 7. Be prepared to share answers to the whole class.

5. INDIVIDUALLY: After the whole class discussion, consider the behaviors listed on the board and select at least 3 successful student behaviors you will commit to this semester and complete the following sentence:

This semester I _____ *will commit to* _____

_____

_____

_____

_____.

Choices of Successful Students

SUCCESSFUL STUDENTS...	STRUGGLING STUDENTS...
1. ... accept **PERSONAL RESPONSIBILITY** seeing themselves as the primary cause of their outcomes and experiences.	1. ... seeing themselves as Victims, believing that what happens to them is determined primarily by external forces such as fate, luck, and powerful others.
2. ... discover **SELF-MOTIVATION**, creating positive energy in their lives by discovering personally valuable goals and dreams.	2. ... having difficulty sustaining motivation, often feeling depressed, frustrated, and/or resentful about a lack of purpose in their lives.
3. ... master **SELF-MANAGEMENT**, consistently planning and taking purposeful actions in pursuit of theirs goals and dreams.	3. ... seldom identify specific actions needed to accomplish a desired outcome. And when they do, they tend to procrastinate.
4. ... employ **INTERDEPENDENCE,** building mutually supportive relationships that help them achieve their goals and dreams (while helping others do the same).	4. ... are solitary, seldom requesting, even rejecting, offers of assistance from those who could help.
5. ... gain **SELF-AWARENESS**, consciously employing behaviors, beliefs, and attitudes that keep them on course.	5. ... make important choices unconsciously, being directed by self-sabotaging habits and outdated life scripts.
6. ... adopt **LIFE-LONG LEARNING**, finding valuable lessons and wisdom in nearly every experience they have.	6. ...resist learning new ideas and skills, viewing learning as fearful or boring rather than as mental play.
7. ... develop **EMOTIONAL INTELLIGENCE**, effectively managing their emotions in support of their goals and dreams.	7. ... live at the mercy of strong emotions such as anger, depression, anxiety, overwhelm or a need for instant gratification.
8. ... **BELIEVE IN THEMSELVES**, seeing themselves as capable, loveable and unconditionally worthy human beings.	8. ... doubt their competence and personal value, feeling inadequate to create their desired outcomes and experiences.

From Skip Downing: *On Course: Strategies for Creating Success in college and in life.* Houghton Mifflin

24 Hour Time Management Boxes

6am	7am	8am	9am	10am	11am

5am	**To Do:**	12noon

4am		1pm

3am		2pm

2am	**Notes:**	3pm

1am		4pm

12midnight		5pm

11pm	10pm	9pm	8pm	7pm	6pm

6am	7am	8am	9am	10am	11am

5am	**To Do:**				12noon
4am					1pm
3am					2pm
2am	**Notes:**				3pm
1am					4pm
12midnight					5pm

11pm	10pm	9pm	8pm	7pm	6pm

Calendar Activity

Assignment: Add you school related events and the NCC shared calendar to your Google Calendar.

1. Watch the video tutorial on Moodle found in Session 5 block under assignments: How to use Google calendar video tutorial. (Your instructor may opt to show to entire class.)
2. From Moodle access the NCC Google Calender ID found in the Session 5 block under asissignments.

Click to watch video

Click here to locate and copy the calendar ID

3. Copy the ID. <u>For iPad users</u>, touch and hold the screen for a few a seconds to pull up the copy option. You will have to adjust the size of the area so you only capture the ID in blue. Then tap the copy button.

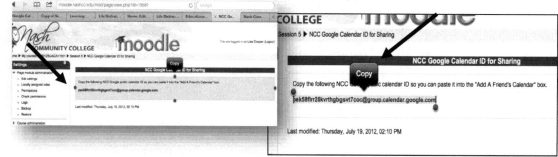

4. Now leave Moodle and log in to your student gmail account and access the Google calendar.

Make sure YOU are logged in (and not a previous student!)

5. <u>For iPad users,</u> you want your calendar to display in "desktop" view NOT "mobile."

On the iPad, to switch from mobile view to desktop view, click desktop view at the bottom of the screen and select cancel when you get the warning.

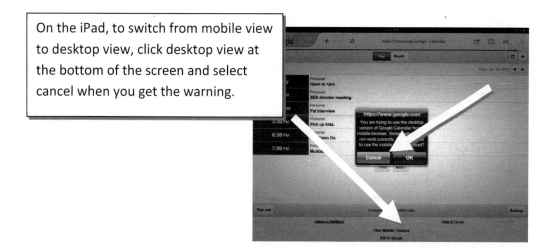

6. With your Google calendar open, paste the NCC Calendar ID in the box under "Other Calendars." <u>For iPad users,</u> touch the box until the paste option appears, then tap paste. And press enter (or Go on the iPad.)

7. You have added the NCC Calendar! Be sure it is selected so all the NCC events appear.
8. Now it's time to add your academic events! Consult your syllabi and activity calendars from all the other courses in which you are enrolled.
9. **ADD EVENTS!** Add *all* due dates such as tests, papers or projects for each class. You can even add smaller personal due dates that help prepare for tests or papers such as complete study guide, revise notes, start research, select topic, etc. Don't forget all the Core Assessments and assignments for ACA!

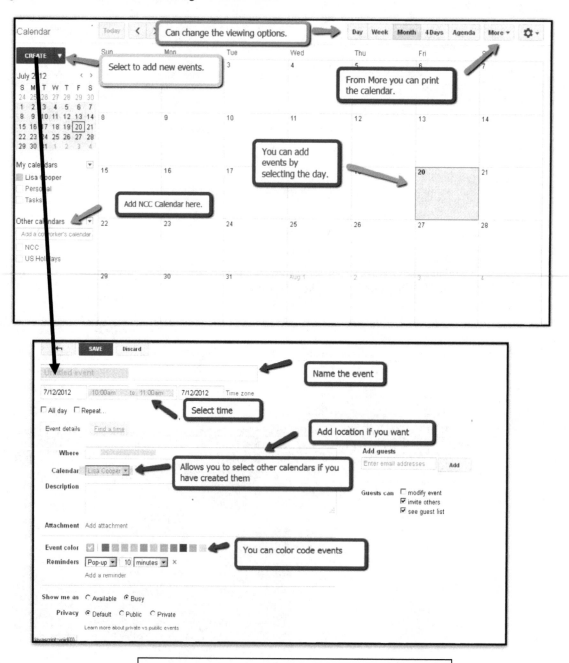

YOU CAN PRINT YOUR CALENDAR WHEN COMPLETE

Responsibility Model

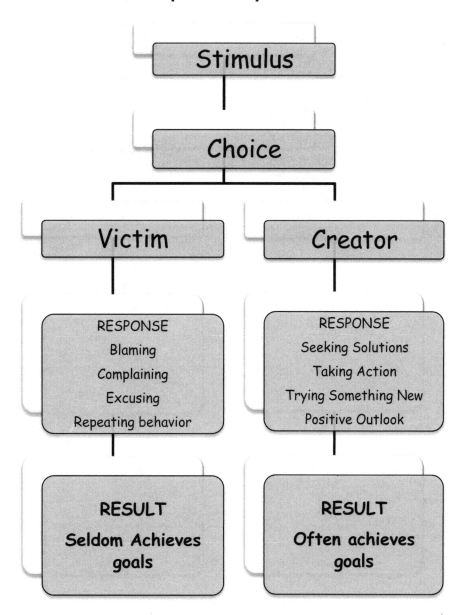

The key ingredient of personal responsibility is choice. Numerous times each day, you come to a fork in the road and must make a choice. Even not making a choice is a choice. Some choices have a small impact: Shall I get my hair cut today or tomorrow? Some have a huge impact: Shall I stay in college or drop out? The sum of the choices you make from this day forward will create the eventual outcome of your life. **The Responsibility Model** shows what the moment of choice looks like. In that brief moment between stimulus and response, we can choose to be a Victim or a Creator. At critical forks in the road, Victims waste their energy and remain stuck, while Creators use their energy for improving their outcomes and experiences.

The Language of Responsibility

Victim Language	Creator Language
Victim Language *Victims believe that their outcomes and experiences are determined by forces beyond their control, such as powerful others and luck. They believe they are merely pawns in the chess game of life. Their language is characterized by blaming, complaining, and excusing.*	**Creator Language** *Creators believe that their outcomes and experiences are the natural consequences of their choices. They believe they are chess masters who **create, promote**, or **allow** all that happens in their lives. Their language is characterized by **ownership** and **action** plans.*
1. I'm terrible in this subject.	*I find this course challenging, so I'll start a study group and ask more questions in class.*
2. The instructor is so boring he puts me to sleep.	*I'm having difficulty staying awake in this class, so I'm going to ask permission to record lectures. Then I'll listen to them a little at a time and take detailed notes.*
3. This course is a stupid requirement.	*I'm going to ask my instructor to help me see how this course will benefit me in the future.*
4. I couldn't get the assignment because I was absent.	
5. I can't help talking or texting in class.	
6. I couldn't come to class because I had to go to the dentist for a checkup.	
7. I work nights so didn't have time to do my homework.	
8. My friend got me so angry, I can't even study for the exam.	
9. I'll try to do my best this semester.	
10. I hate group projects because people are lazy and I always end up doing most of the work.	
11. If they'd do something about the parking on campus, I wouldn't be late so often.	
12. I am failing my online class because the site is impossible to navigate.	
13. I'm too shy to ask questions in class even when I'm confused.	
14. I wish I could do better in math, but I just can't.	

Case Study in Critical Thinking:
<u>Strange Choices</u>

"Do your students make really strange choices?" Professor Assante asked.

The other professors looked up from their lunches. "What do you mean?" one asked.

At the beginning of each class, I give short quizzes that count as 50 percent of the final grade," **Professor Assante** replied. "One of my students comes late to every class, even though I keep telling her that there is no way she can pass the course if she keeps missing the quizzes. But, she still keeps coming late! What is she thinking?"

"That's nothing," **Professor Buckley** said "I've got a really bright student who attends every class and offers great comments during discussions. But the semester is almost over, and he still hasn't turned in any assignments. At this point, he's too far behind to pass. Now that's what I call a strange choice."

"You think that's strange, **Professor Chen** said, "I'm teaching composition in the computer lab. Last week I sat down next to a woman who was working on her essay, and I suggested a way she could improve her introduction. I couldn't believe what she did. She swore at me, stormed out of the room, and slammed the door."

Professor Donnelly chimed in. "Well, I can top all of you. In my philosophy class, participation counts for one-third of the final grade. I've got a student this semester who hasn't said a word in twelve weeks. Even when I call on him, he just shakes his head and says something under his breath that I can't hear. One day after class, I asked him if he realized that if he didn't participate in class discussions, the best grade he could earn is a D. He just mumbled, "I know.' Now there is a choice I don't get!"

"How about this!" **Professor Egret** said. "I had a student last semester with a B average going into the final two weeks. Then he disappeared. This semester, I ran into him on campus, and asked what happened. 'Oh' he said, 'I got burned out and stopped going to my classes.' 'But you only had two more weeks to go. You threw away thirteen weeks of work,' I said. You know what he did? He shrugged his shoulders and walked away. I wanted to shake him and say, 'What is wrong with you?'"

Professor Fanning said, "Talk about strange choices. Last week I had four business owners visit my marketing class to talk about how they promote their businesses. Near the end of the period, a student asked if the business owners had ever had problems with procrastination. While the panelists were deciding who was going to answer, I joked, 'Maybe they'd rather answer later.' Okay, it was weak humor, but most of the students chuckled, and then one panelist answered the question. The next day I got a call from the dean. The student who'd asked the question about procrastination told him I'd mocked her in front of the whole class, and now she's going to drop out of college. I had videotaped the class, so I asked her if she'd be willing to watch the tape. Later she admitted I hadn't said what she thought I had, but she still dropped out of school. What is it with students today and their bizarre choices?"

Listed below are all the professor's students. Choose the one you think made the strangest choice and speculate why this student made the choice. Dive deeper than the obvious answers such as "He's probably just shy." Why do you suppose he is shy? What past experiences might the inner conservation of this Inner Critic and Inner Defender sound like? What emotions might he often feel? What beliefs might he have about himself, other people, or the world? In what other circumstances (e.g. work, relationship, and health) might a similar choice sabotage his success?

_____ Professor Assante's Student
_____ Professor Buckley's Student
_____ Professor Chen's Student
_____ Professor Donnelly's Student
_____ Professor Egret's Student
_____ Professor Fanning's Student

Diving Deeper: Recall a course you once took in which you made a choice that your instructor might describe as "strange." Explain why you made that choice. Dive deep, exploring what really caused your choice.

Case Study in Critical Thinking: The Late Paper

Professor Freud announced in her syllabus for Psychology 101 that final term papers had to be in her by noon on December 18. No student, she emphasized would pass the course without a completed term paper turned in on time. As the semester drew to a close, **Kim**, had an "A" average in Professor Freud's psychology class, and she began researching her term paper with excitement.

Arnold, Kim's husband, felt threatened that he had only a high school diploma while his wife was getting close to her college degree. Arnold worked the evening shift at a bakery, and his coworker **Philip** began teasing that Kim would soon dump Arnold for a college guy. That's when Arnold started accusing Kim of having an affair and demanding she drop out of college. She told Arnold he was being ridiculous. In fact, she said, a young man in her history class had asked her out, but she had refused. Instead of feeling better, Arnold became even angrier. With Philip continuing to provoke him, Arnold became sure Kim was having an affair, and he began telling her every day that she was stupid and would never get a degree.

Despite the tension at home, Kim finished her psychology term paper the day before it was due. Since Arnold had hidden the car keys, she decided to take the bus to the college and turn in her psychology paper a day early. While she was waiting for the bus, **Cindy**, one of Kim's psychology classmates, drove up and invited Kim to join her and some other students for an end-of-semester celebration. Kim told Cindy she was on her way to turn in her term paper, and Cindy promised she'd make sure Kim got it on time. "I deserve some fun," Kim decided, and hopped into the car. The celebration went long into the night. Kim kept asking Cindy to take her home, but Cindy always replied, "Don't be such a bore. Have another drink." When Cindy finally took Kim home, it was 4:30 in the morning. She signed with relief when she found that Arnold had already fallen asleep.

When Kim woke up, it was 11:30 A.M., just thirty minutes before her term paper was due. She could make it to the college in time by car, so she shook Arnold and begged him to drive her. He just snapped, "Oh sure, you stay out all night with your college friends. Then, I'm supposed to get up on my day off and drive you all over town. Forget it." "At least give me the keys," she said, but Arnold merely rolled over and went back to sleep. Panicked, Kim called Professor Freud's office and told **Mary**, the secretary, that was having car trouble. "Don't worry," Mary assured Kim, "I'm sure Professor Freud won't care if your paper's a little late. Just be sure to have it here before she leaves at 1:00." Relieved, Kim decided not to wake Arnold again; instead, she took the bus.

At 12:15, Kim walked into Professor Freud's office with her term paper. Professor Freud said, "Sorry, Kim, you're fifteen minutes late." She refused to accept Kim's term paper and gave Kim an "F" for the course.

Listed before are the characters in this story. Rank them in order of their responsibility for Kim's failing grade in Psychology 101. Give a different score to each character. Be prepared to explain your choices.

Most responsible ← 1 2 3 4 5 6

_____ **Professor Freud**, the teacher
_____ **Kim**, the psychology student
_____ **Arnold**, Kim's husband
_____ **Philip**, Arnold's coworker
_____ **Cindy**, Kim's classmate
_____ **Mary,** Professor Freud's secretary

DIVING DEEPER: Is there someone not mentioned in the story who may have also bear responsibility for Kim's failing grade?

The "Who Stays?" Problem

The Dilemma

Enrollment has been cut back at this college. As a member of the board, it is your responsibility to rank the following ten students according to who deserves to remain in this college, number 1 being the most deserving. Each of these students has been enrolled for about seven weeks. Descriptions of their pre-college situations and performances, as well as the circumstances of their college career, thus far, are listed.

Factors to Keep in Mind

Each student's potential, abilities, or capabilities
Each student's motivation to preform
The degree of difficulty in conquering problems
The availability of services to help overcome those problems
The outcome of his or her education: how badly each wants to achieve
The probability of successful completion of a college education

The Students

Angela: Extremely intelligent; senior class valedictorian; has won awards in the National Science Fair for exhibits; received a full scholarship from a national company to the college of her choice; has much difficulty relating to others on a social basis; has definite plans to major in chemistry; an out-of-state student; is having great difficulty adjusting to dorm life; is homesick.

Albert: An All-State quarterback in high school plans to play college football on a full scholarship; scored extremely poorly on the college admittance tests although his high school were average; has no major; plans to become a coach; poor classroom attendance.

Jill: Ranked in the middle of her graduating class; did fair in high school math; did poorly in high school science; parents pushed her toward her declared major in biology; doing poorly in these college subjects; has good study habits; high capabilities in English; lives at home; family problems are developing

Carolyn: A divorced mother with two children; 24 years old; has returned to college to continue her college education after dropping out six years earlier; is working and raising her family; commutes; major is a two year degree in secretarial sciences; receives financial aid

Dominique: An exchange student from Venezuela; lives in a men's dorm; visiting our college for one semester; has already earned a degree in his own country; doing very well academically; involved in several campus organizations; self-supported; here to experience our lifestyle; not working toward any major.

Thomas: Outgoing and well-liked among his peers; poor grades; studied little in high school and has few study skills; undecided on major; his parents pay for his education; an in-state student, lives on campus; enjoys the college party life most of all.

Howard: Ranked in the top 5 percent of his graduating class; out-of-state student; lives on campus; came from an influential family in a small town; was "Mr. Popular" in high school; is having a terrible time adjusting to college life; very homesick; grades are dropping as time passes; uninvolved in campus life; has much potential that could be used.

Gina: An accounting major; dropped all but 9 hours of classes; very poor classroom attendance; extremely active in her sorority; poor grades; parents pay for everything; in town student; lives on campus; her parents donate a scholarship each year.

Evelyn: 63 years old; worked in a daycare center for the past 15 years; prior to that was a housewife and mother; is working toward a degree in child psychology; receiving financial aid for returning students over 60; doing well academically.

Karl: Average grades; commutes; works 20 hours a week to pay for his education; is aiming for a degree in engineering; would like to get involved in more activities on campus but does not have the time; high potential in math; hard worker.

Only the top 5 students will be allowed to remain in school.
Who will stay? Who will go?

1.

2.

3.

4.

5.

6.

7.

8.

9.

10.

Note Taking Checklist

Listening, Engaging and Note-taking

Step 3: What are my choices?

- ☐ Assemble appropriate supplies- paper, pencil, etc.
- ☐ Do the assigned reading
- ☐ Complete homework assignments before attending class
- ☐ Go over notes from previous class sessions
- ☐ Prepare a list of questions
- ☐ Eliminate distractions- don't sit with your best friend, turn off cell phone, etc.
- ☐ Attend every class – show up physically!
- ☐ Posture counts- sit up in class
- ☐ Arrive early and choose a good seat
- ☐ Don't talk while others are speaking
- ☐ Be organized (ID your notes)
- ☐ Listen actively for key concepts, main ideas supporting material
- ☐ Write down examples or key words from stories that will help anchor the main points
- ☐ Note whether a handout accompanies lecture materials
- ☐ Listen and look for gestures and statements that communicate, "This is important" or "Be sure to include this in your notes."
- ☐ Ask and answer questions- Speak up!
- ☐ When in doubt, write it down
- ☐ Watch for visual cues
- ☐ Stay focused! (Take a deep breath, keep the worries and to-do lists at bay)
- ☐ Take notes with this system: _____
- ☐ Speed up note-taking—consult shorthand list on page 183
- ☐ Record the class if needed
- ☐ Polish notes within 24 hours
- ☐ Manipulate your notes (For example, fill in charts, draw diagrams, retype notes, create a mind map, underline, highlight, organize, copy notes to flash cards, cut up a copy of your notes and put it back together again – work with your notes!
- ☐ Paraphrase – put your notes in your own words
- ☐ Summarize your notes

☐ Compare notes

Cornell Note Paper

FOCUS	Name:
	Class:
	Date:
Topic/Objective:	Essential Question:

Questions/Main Ideas:	Notes:

Summary:

FOCUS

	Name:
	Class:
	Date:
Topic/Objective:	Essential Question:

Questions/Main Ideas:	Notes:

Summary:

PowerPoint Miniatures

Using Lecture Notes

Manipulating involves working with your notes by typing them out later.

Paraphrasing is the process of putting your notes into your own words.

Summarizing is a process of writing a brief overview of all of your notes from one lecture.

Exercise 7.4:
Note-Taking 4M

© 2012 Wadsworth, Cengage Learning

Get Engaged in Class

What actually correlates with success are not grades, but 'engagement' — genuine involvement in courses and campus activities. Engagement leads to 'deep learning,' or learning for understanding. That's very different from just memorizing stuff for an exam, then forgetting it.
John Merrow, reporter, USA Today

© 2012 Wadsworth, Cengage Learning

Dare to Prepare

1. Look ahead.
2. Do the assigned reading.
3. Show up physically.
4. Show up mentally.
5. Choose your seat strategically.
6. Bring your tools.
7. Don't sit by your best friend.
8. Posture counts!
9. Maintain your health.
10. Focus.

© 2012 Wadsworth, Cengage Learning

The Rules of Engagement

1. **Be aware that gab is not a gift.**
   In class, talking while others are speaking is inappropriate.

2. **Control Your Hunger.**
   Get in the habit of eating before or after class and not during.

3. **Turn off your cell phone, please!**
   Yes, we can hear your phone vibrating, too. And texting in class shows where your attention *really* is.

4. **Better late than never?**
   Arriving late and leaving early disturbs students and instructors.

5. **Actively choose to engage, not disengage.**
   You must make a conscious decision to become engaged.

© 2012 Wadsworth, Cengage Learning

Soft vs. Hard Listening

SOFT Listening Skills:
- Used in emotionally charged situations.
- You must be accepting, sensitive, and nonjudgmental.
- You don't have to assess, analyze, or conclude.

HARD Listening Skills:
- Used in classroom/educational situations.
- Pay close attention and think critically.
- Evaluate, analyze, and make decisions about new information.

© 2012 Wadsworth, Cengage Learning

Listening with Focus

➤ Calm yourself.
➤ Be open.
➤ Don't make snap judgments.
➤ Assume responsibility.
➤ Watch for gestures that say "Here comes something important!"

➤ Listen for speech patterns that subtly communicate "Make sure you include this in your notes!"
➤ Uncover general themes or roadmaps for each lecture.
➤ Appreciate your instructor's prep time.

"You cannot truly listen to anyone and do anything else at the same time."
M. Scott Peck, American author

Exercise 7.1: Listening

© 2012 Wadsworth, Cengage Learning

Adapt to a Variety of Lecture Styles

The Rapid-Fire Lecturer   The Slow-Go Lecturer   The All-Over-the-Map Lecturer   The Content-Intensive Lecturer

The Review-the-Text Lecturer   The Go-Beyond-the-Text Lecturer   The Active-Learning Lecturer

Exercise 7.2: Multitasking

© 2012 Wadsworth, Cengage Learning

Ask and You Shall Receive

Have you ever decided NOT to ask a question in class because you thought:

* I don't want to look stupid.
* I must be slow. Everyone else seems to be understanding.
* I'm too shy.
* I'll get the answer later from the text.
* I don't think my question is important.
* I don't want to interrupt the lecture; the instructor's on a roll.
* I'm sure the instructor knows what he's talking about. He must be right.

The next time you find yourself in a situation where you don't understand something, consider these points:

1. Remember that you're not in this alone.
2. Ask academically relevant questions when the time is right.
3. Save personally relevant questions for later.
4. Build on others' questions.

© 2012 Wadsworth, Cengage Learning

QUIZ TIME!

© 2012 Wadsworth, Cengage Learning

Intentionally Left Blank

Master Study Plan

What is my learning style: _____

This means I should:

_____

_____

EXAM I AM PREPARING FOR:	
DAY & DATE of EXAM:	
WHAT WILL THE TEST COVER? • How long will it be? • Is there a study guide? • What content is covered? • What materials, text, should I use? • What types of questions will be on it? Objective: multiple choice, T/F, matching; Subjective: fill-in-the-blanks, short answer or essay	

Best location for me to study:	
Best time for me to study:	
Do I need to study alone, or with others?	
Anything else I should do to make sure my study time is effective?	
Challenges or distractions I may encounter:	Possible solutions to overcome these challenges:
Study Strategies I use	Study Strategies I will try:

CONTENT I NEED TO LEARN	BEST STRATEGY TO USE (Consult your VARK list, Memory Devices or search online)

HOW DO I KNOW WHEN I AM DONE STUDYING CHECKLIST?

☑	Item to-do	Goal Date:
	Find out when, where & how long the test will be	
	Find out what it will cover, request a study guide	
	Schedule my study times	
	List the content I need to learn and select the study strategies I will use	
	Gather all the supplies and reading materials I will need	

STUDY SCHEDULE

I should start studying on: _____

INCLUDE ON YOUR CALENDAR *When* you will study and *What* you will accomplish (i.e. make note cards, create quiz, read & take notes, review notes, re-organize notes, make a chart or drawing, create and practice a mnemonic and device, etc.) Use the template provided or put on your own personal calendar.

Monday	Tuesday	Wednesday	Thursday	Friday	Saturday	Sunday

Components of Emotional Intelligence

One of psychology's open secrets is the relative inability of grades, IQ, or SAT scores, despite their popular mystique, to predict unerringly who will succeed in life... At best, IQ contributes about 20 percent to the factors that determine life success, which leaves 80 percent to other forces... IQ offers little to explain the different destinies of people with roughly equal promises, schooling, and opportunity.   *Daniel Goleman*

1. **<u>EMOTIONAL SELF-AWARENESS</u>: Knowing your feelings in the moment.** Self-awareness of one's own feelings as they occur is the foundation of emotional intelligence and is fundamental to effective decision making. Thus, people who are keenly aware of their changing moods are better pilots of their lives. For example, emotional self-awareness helps you deal effectively with feelings of overwhelm instead of attempting to escape them by watching television.

2. **<u>EMOTIONAL SELF-MANAGEMENT</u>: Managing strong feelings**. Emotional Self-Management enables people to make wise choices despite the pull of powerful emotions. People who excel at this skill avoid making critical decisions during times of high drama: instead they wait until their inner storm has calmed and then make considered choices that contribute to their desired outcomes and experiences. For example, emotional self-management helps you resist dropping an important class simply because you got angry at the teacher. It also helps you make a choice (e.g., writing a term paper) that offers delayed benefits instead of a choice (e.g. attending a party) that promises instant gratification.

3. **<u>SOCIAL AWARENESS</u>: Empathizing accurately with other people's emotions.** Empathy is the fundamental "people skill." Those with empathy and compassion are more attuned to the subtle social signals that reveal what others need or want. For example, social awareness helps you notice and offer comfort when someone is consumed by anxiety or sadness.

4. **<u>RELATIONSHIP MANAGEMENT</u>: Handling emotions in relationships with skill and harmony.** The art of relationships depends, in large part, upon the skill of managing emotions in others. People who excel at skills such as listening, resolving conflicts, cooperating and articulating the pulse of a group do well at anything that relies on interacting smoothly with others. For example, relationship management helps a person resist saying something that might publicly embarrass someone else.

After Math

When **Professor Bishop** returned mid-term exams, he said, "In 20 years of teaching math, I've never seen such low scores. Can anyone tell me what the problem is?" He ran a hand through his graying hair and waited. No one spoke. "Don't you people even care how you do?" Students fiddled with their test papers. They looked out of the window. No one spoke.

Finally, Professor Bishop said, "Okay, Scott, we'll start with you. What's going on? You got a 35 on the test. Did you even *study*?" **Scott**, 18, mumbled, "Yeah, I studied. But I just don't understand math." Other students in the class nodded their heads. One student muttered, "Amen, brother."

Professor Bishop looked around the classroom. "How about you Elena? You didn't even show up for the test." **Elena**, 31, sighed. "I'm sorry, but I have a lot of other things besides this class to worry about. My job keeps changing my schedule, I broke a tooth last week, my roommate won't pay me the money she owes me, my car broke down, and I haven't been able to find my math book for three weeks. I think my boyfriend hid it. If one more thing goes wrong in my life, I'm going to scream!"

Professor Bishop shook his head slowly back and forth. "Well, that's quite a story. What about the rest of you?" Silence reigned for a full minute. Suddenly **Michael**, 23, stood up and snarled, "You're a damn joke, man. You can't teach, and you want to blame the problem on us. Well, I've had it. I'm dropping this stupid course. Then I'm filing a grievance. You better start looking for a new job!" He stormed out of the room, slamming the door behind him.

"Okay, I can see this isn't going anywhere productive," Professor Bishop said. "I want you all to go home and think about why you're doing so poorly. And don't come back until you're prepared to answer that question honestly." He picked up his books and left the room. Elena checked her watch and then dashed out of the room. She still had time to catch her favorite show in the student lounge.

An hour later, Michael was sitting alone in the cafeteria when his classmates Scott and **Kia**, 20, joined him. Scott said, "Geez, Michael, you really went off on Bishop! You're not really going to drop his class are you?" "Already did!" Michael snapped as his classmates sat down. "I went right from class to the registrar's office. I'm outta there!"

I might as well drop the class myself, Kia thought. Ever since she was denied entrance to the nursing program, she'd been too depressed to do her homework. Familiar tears blurred her vision.

Scott said, "I don't know what it is about math. I study for hours, but when I get to the test, I get so freaked it's like I never studied at all. My mind just goes blank." Thinking about math, Scott started craving something to eat.

"Where do you file a grievance against a professor around here, anyway?" Michael asked. "I have no idea," Scott said. "What?" Kia answered.

Michael stood and stomped off to file a grievance. Scott when to buy some French fries. Kia put her head down on the table and tried to swallow the burning sensation in her throat.

Listed below are the characters in this story. Rank them in order of their emotional intelligence. Give a different score to each character. Be prepared to explain your choices.

Most emotionally intelligent < 1 2 3 4 5 > Least emotionally intelligent

__Professor Bishop   __Scott   __Elena   __Michael   __Kia

Diving Deeper: Imagine that you have been asked to mentor the person whom you ranked number 5 (least emotionally intelligent). Other than recommending a counselor, how would you suggest that this person handle his or her upset in a more emotionally intelligent manner?

From Downing, On Course: Strategies for Success in College and in Life, Houghton Mifflin

ASSESSING EMOTIONAL INTELLIGENCE

Your Character:_____ Average of Four Scores:_____

Low Emotional Intelligence <- 1 2 3 4 5 6 7 8 9 10 -> High Emotional Intelligence

Emotional Self-Awareness: Knowing your feelings in the moment.
Character's specific behavior(s) that influenced your score.

Emotional Self-Management: Managing strong feelings.
Character's specific behavior(s) that influenced your score.

Social Awareness: Empathizing accurately with other people's emotions.
Character's specific behavior(s) that influenced your score.

Relationship Management: Handling emotions in relationships with skill and harmony. Character's specific behavior(s) that influenced your score.

SWOT Analysis

Strengths	Opportunities
Weaknesses	**Threats**

How can you minimize weaknesses and threats and capitalize on strengths and opportunities?

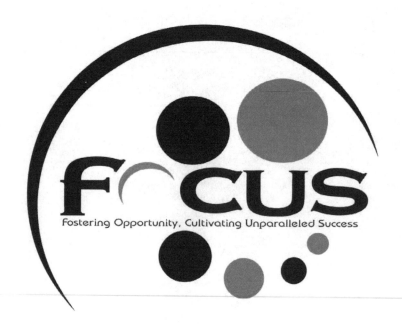

RESOURCE INFORMATION

NCC Tutorial Service Options

1. **Math Tank** (S&T building 7106)-Individual tutorial assistance is available for math homework. Computerized programs are available for developmental math. Math re-testing is also conducted here.

2. **PAL (Peer Assisted Learning) Tutor Connection Program**
   PAL Tutor Connection Program is an appointment based peer tutoring initiative that connects students who need extra support with Peer Tutors who have demonstrated proficiency in select courses. Students interested in tutoring can fill out a PAL Tutor Connection Request Form found on the Nash website under the "Students" tab/Academics/Campus Tutoring. For more information about the PAL Tutor Connection Program contact: Student & Enrollment Services, 252-451-8219

3. **Smarthinking** (online – www.smarthinking.com) - Smarthinking is the online tutoring service provided for Nash Community College students. A handout with additional details for accessing this resource is located in CampusCruiser. Smarthinking can provide assistance with math, writing, chemistry, physics, accounting, economics, anatomy and physiology, biology, Spanish, nursing, and allied health.
   Username: nash0405
   Password: livetutors
   ** After logging the first time with the above information, you will be asked to set up an account and create your own log in and password.

4. **SAS Curriculum Pathways and Writing Reviser** (online - www.sascurriculumpathways.com) - SAS Curriculum Pathways and WritingReviser is a free, self-help resource to assist students in five main subject areas: English, Math, Science, Social Studies and Spanish. There are interactive tutorials and resources for each subject. In addition, SAS Writing Reviser provides assistance with writing assignments.
   Username: nccstudent
   No password is required

Student Organizations

Nash Community College realizes the role of student organizations in enhancing a student's college experience. These organizations provide the students and the college with regional, state, and national exposure via participation in their respective chapter affiliations and campus social activities.

Artistic Designers Club

The Artistic Designers Club is an organization for students who are enrolled in cosmetology courses at Nash Community College. The club encourages and provides opportunities for development of leadership skills and accountability in the cosmetology field.
Advisor: Karey Parker
Phone: 451-8377
Email: kparker@nashcc.edu

Criminal Justice Club

The Criminal Justice Club gives students the opportunity to gain exposure to the professional realm of law enforcement, courts, and corrections.
Advisor: Carmi Guyette
Phone: 451-8375
Email: cguyette@nashcc.edu

Culinary Club

The Culinary Club is designed to encourage students in the Culinary or Hotel and Restaurant Management (HRM) programs to polish and perfect skills learned in the Culinary and HRM curriculum.

Advisor: Co Advisor:
Don Sexauer   Carlos Quagliaroli
Phone: 451-8362   Phone: 451-8366
Email: Email:
dsexauer@nashcc.edu cquagliaroli@nashcc.edu

Drama Club

The Drama Club encourages support and participation in activities of theater interest. This includes participation in campus productions at Nash Community College as well as supporting and participating in activities which enhance theatrical development.
Advisor: Lisa Cooper
Phone: 451-8223
Email: lcooper@nashcc.edu

Early Childhood Education Club

The Early Childhood Education Club is an organization for students who are pursuing a degree or certificate in Early Childhood. Students are encouraged to become actively involved in local, state and national professional activities in Early Childhood Development.
Advisor: Sarah Prezioso
Phone: 451-8317
Email: sprezioso@nashcc.edu

Gamma Beta Phi Society

GBP is the honor society on campus. Students must have a 3.0 or higher cumulative grade point average, must have earned 12 or more semester hours in a major at NCC. Membership drives are held in September and February of each semester.
Advisor: Natasha Neal
Phone: 451-8256
Email: nneal@nashcc.edu

M.A.L.E.

Men Achieving Leadership and Excellence (M.A.L.E.) promotes academic, personal & professional success for minority males at Nash CC.
Advisor: Keith Smith
Phone: 451-8264
Email: ksmith@nashcc.edu

Math & Science Club

The Math & Science Club provides opportunities to develop leadership, critical thinking and advocacy skills in mathematics and science.
Advisor: Kochi Angar   Co Advisor: Dave Beamer
Phone: 451-8396   Phone: 451-8334
Email: kangar@nashcc.edu Email: dbeamer@nashcc.edu

Metal Workers Club

The Metal Workers Club is an organization to promote skills, technology and knowledge for students in the Machining, Welding, and Industrial Systems Technology programs.
Advisor: George Shook   Co Advisor: Jay Manning
Phone: 451-8283   Phone: 451-8270
Email: gshook@nashcc.edu Email: jamanning@nashcc.edu

Nash Community Lambda Association of Students and Supporters (NCLASS)

NCLASS is an organization with a goal to provide outreach, support, information, and resources for gay, lesbian, transgender, and bisexual students, faculty and staff, and for their families or friends. The club also provides information and resources for the College on issues regarding sexuality and sexual orientation while promoting a culture of fairness and equality for all NCC students and a social outlet for members and their friends.
Advisor: Sarah Prezioso
Phone: 451- 8317
Email: sprezioso@nashcc.edu

Phi Beta Lambda

PBL is an organization open to all curriculum students who are interested in the business field. PBL is the college-level counterpart of FBLA.
Advisor: Nakisha Floyd
Phone: 451-8299
Email: nfloyd@nashcc.edu

Phi Theta Kappa

Phi Theta Kappa is an international honor society that recognizes and encourages scholarship among 2-year college students. Students must have completed a minimum of twelve (12) semester hours of non-developmental course work and have earned a cumulative grade point average of 3.50 or higher.
Advisor: Robin Latham
Phone: 451-8213
Email: rlatham@nashcc.edu

Published Ink

Published Ink is a club which is open to any curriculum student at NCC who has an interest in writing, visual arts, marketing or publication. Its main purpose is to foster the production of creative writing and visual arts among the students of the College. By offering seminars and workshops, the club seeks to help students refine their skills. The club strives to produce a juried literary and visual arts magazine once a year.
Advisor: Robin Latham   Co- Advisor: Debbie Lee
Phone: 451-8213   Phone: 451-8388
Email: Email:
rlatham@nashcc.edu   dlee@nashcc.edu

Rock Solid Fellowship

Rock Solid Fellowship is a Christian organization open to all curriculum students who desire to worship Christ at Nash Community College through Bible studies, outreach, and various activities.
Advisor: Lori Sherick
Phone: 451-8483
Email: lsherick@nashcc.edu

Student Government Association (SGA)

The Student Government Association (SGA) is the primary organization responsible for providing activities and opportunities such as blood drives, fall/spring festivals, campus events and student talent shows. Through a democratic system of government, SGA enhances the formal educational experience and protects the rights and privileges of all students. Every curriculum student at NCC is a member of SGA and may attend all meetings.
Advisor: Kara Deans
Phone: 451-8218
Email: kdeans@nashcc.edu

Student Ambassadors

The Nash Community College Foundation sponsors a Student Ambassador program for selected individuals who demonstrate leadership, scholarship, and strong written and oral communication skills. Ambassadors represent Nash Community College at foundation events and a wide variety of school functions. Ambassadors assist the college during times such as registration and open house. Ambassador applications are available in the spring. In the spring of each year, a selection committee appointed by the Nash Community College Foundation Executive Director interviews and selects the ambassadors. Ambassadors receive a scholarship and serve the college in the subsequent school year.
Interim Advisor: Cheryl Gordon
Phone: 451-8230
Email: cgordon@nashcc.edu

Student Nurses' Association

The Student Nurses' Association is a pre-professional organization for student nurses at NCC. Membership is open to nursing and pre-nursing students.
Advisor: Cheryle Traish
Phone: 451-8211
Email: ctraish@nashcc.edu

Steps to Apply for Financial Aid

1. Apply for a Pin Number

   If you do not have a pin number to apply for federal aid, apply on the following website: www.pin.ed.gov . You may request a pin number at that time or have them to email one to you. You must have an active email address for your pin number to be sent to you. If you are a dependent student, a parent must apply for a pin number also. Please place your pin number in a safe place, because this will be your pin number as long as you received financial aid.

2. Fill out the FAFSA (Free Application for Federal Student Aid) for the current year
   a. Complete the application at www.fafsa.ed.gov
   b. Select "Start Here"
   c. For accurate tax information utilize the feature for the IRS Data Retrieval Tool. Nash Community College strongly recommends all students, parents, and spouses (if applicable) to use the IRS Data Retrieval Tool. In order to do so, all parties must have already filed the previous year taxes at least three weeks prior to filling out the FAFSA.
   d. **NCC's school code---008557**
   e. If you filled out your FAFSA without a pin number, print out the signature page and mail it to the address on the same page. Your application will be processed faster if you use your pin number.
   f. Submit your FAFSA. The website produces a confirmation page that you have successfully transmitted your FAFSA. You may note the confirmation number and your estimated Expected Family Contribution (EFC).
   g. This confirmation is not an award letter. You must be approved by the institution you will be attending.
   h. Check your campus e-mail (given by NCC's admissions office) for further documentation that may be required by NCC's Financial Aid Department.
   i. Submit all required documentation.
   j. Await an Award notification by e-mail and mail (check your WebAdvisor account for updates as well).

TRANSFER PORTFOLIO

Transfer Portfolio
Part I: Exploring your Transfer School

This section of the portfolio will help you gather information from your transfer school. Don't worry if you have not decided on a transfer school yet; this section will help you make that choice as well! Fill in all blanks where required and check each item off as you complete it. Even if you think you have already selected a four year institution to transfer to, it's always best to have options and a "Plan B." Please, utilize the CFNC.org information to explore additional schools. You must choose 2 institutions to explore for this portion of your portfolio.

1. Log on to CFNC.org and click on the Plan Tab; then, click Plan for College. Visit the Explore Postsecondary Schools link and the Explore Programs and Majors link to find out more about NC Colleges and the majors they offer. You may also wish to visit the Plan for a Career section of the website and explore various resources there to help you hone in a specific career field.

2. Identify two institutions that you are considering transferring to:

Option 1: _____

Option 2: _____

Portfolio Scoring Rubric for Part I: Exploring Your Transfer School

Student utilizes CFNC.org's resources and identifies two options as transfer institutions.	10	
Student thoroughly and accurately answers all virtual tour questions about "Option 1" institution.	0-30	
Student thoroughly and accurately answers all virtual tour questions about "Option 2" institution.	0-30	
Student thoughtfully completes reflection based upon their exploration of both institutions.	0-30	
Total Score for Portfolio Part 1		

3.   Start by touring your "Option 1" school virtually; as you do so, complete answer these questions:

- What school are you "touring"? _____
- Do you qualify for in-state or out-of-state tuition rates? _____
- Based on the answer above, what is the current tuition for your status (in or out-of state)? _____
- Should you choose to live on campus, what is the current cost of room and board? _____
- What is the minimum GPA for a transfer student application? _____
- Provide the school's transfer office contact information (i.e. phone number, email, contact person, etc.)

  Name: _____

  Phone Number: _____   E-mail: _____
- What is the application fee? _____
- What other documents need to be submitted with your application? _____

  _____

- What major at this institution best matches with your career goals? _____
- How many total credit hours are required for you to obtain a degree in this area? _____
- Please list one contact person (name, phone number, and email) for your desired major:

  Name: _____

  Phone Number: _____   E-mail: _____
- List 2 on-campus housing options (i.e. dorm names) for transfer (i.e. junior-level) students: _____

  _____

- What is the name and location of your transfer school's library? _____
- What are the hours of the library? _____
- What sort of tutorial services does your transfer school offer for students? _____

  _____

- List 2-3 campus activities your transfer school offers that you might be interested in participating in at this school: _____

  _____

  _____

4. Start by touring your "Option 2" school virtually; as you do so, complete answer these questions:

- What school are you "touring"? _____
- Do you qualify for in-state or out-of-state tuition rates? _____
- Based on the answer above, what is the current tuition for your status (in or out-of state)? _____
- Should you choose to live on campus, what is the current cost of room and board? _____
- What is the minimum GPA for a transfer student application? _____
- Provide the school's transfer office contact information (i.e. phone number, email, contact person, etc.)

  Name: _____

  Phone Number: _____ E-mail: _____
- What is the application fee? _____
- What other documents need to be submitted with your application? _____

  _____
- What major at this institution best matches with your career goals? _____
- How many total credit hours are required for you to obtain a degree in this area? _____
- Please list one contact person (name, phone number, and email) for your desired major:

  Name: _____

  Phone Number: _____ E-mail: _____
- List 2 on-campus housing options (i.e. dorm names) for transfer (i.e. junior-level) students: _____

  _____
- What is the name and location of your transfer school's library? _____
- What are the hours of the library? _____
- What sort of tutorial services does your transfer school offer for students? _____

  _____
- List 2-3 campus activities your transfer school offers that you might be interested in participating in at this school: _____

  _____

  _____

5.   Based upon the knowledge you have gained from exploring the above institutions, reflect on the choice you have made. Do you believe that you have made the right decision about where to transfer? Has your opinion changed about either school? Are you undecided about where to go? Why or why not?

_____

_____

_____

_____

_____

_____

_____

_____

_____

_____

_____

_____

_____

_____

_____

_____

Transfer Portfolio
Part II: College Culture at Your Transfer School

This portion of the portfolio will allow you to explore the culture of the specific college/university you wish to transfer to after your time at NCC by talking to an actual student who attends that college/university.

Please notify your instructor immediately if you have trouble locating a student to interview.

Interview Directions: You may interview a current student or a recent alumni (graduated within the past five years) of the school you wish to transfer to. If you do not know anyone who is a current student or graduate of your transfer school, then start by contacting the school's admissions office. Most schools have student ambassadors who you can speak to in order to complete this portion of the portfolio.

You will find some suggested questions on the back of this page; you are welcome to ask these questions, but you are certainly not limited to them. After conducting your interview, please summarize and reflect upon your conversation. Your summary should be typed, double-spaced and approximately 350-500 words.

Basic Interview Information:

Name of Interviewee: _____   Interview Date: _____

Interviewee was: Current Student   Alumni

Interview conducted: Phone   Email   Face-to-face

__Attach a typed summary of your interview, summarizing your conversation with your interviewee.__

Portfolio Scoring Rubric for Part II: College Culture at Your Transfer School

Student provides basic interviewee information.	20	
Student types summary of interview.	20	
Student's summary is thorough and provides a thoughtful reflection of his/her interview.	0-60	
Total Score for Part 2		

Potential Interview Questions

- Why did you choose to attend this college?

- What would you change about the college?

- What would you fight to keep unchanged at your college?

- What do you think makes your school distinctive?

- What are the major campus issues?

- Have you been challenged in your coursework?

- How large are your classes?

- What do students do on the weekend?

- How effective is the faculty advising system?

- How is the relationship between the students and the surrounding community?

- How important is the Greek system?

- Does the student body have a voice in the university?

- Have you ever met the college president?

- If you had to select a college again, would you make the same choice?

- How many years will it take/did it take to earn your degree?

- Additional Questions I Want To Ask:

_____

_____

_____

Transfer Portfolio
Part III: Financial Literacy

In this section of the portfolio, you will explore the financial realities of being a student at your transfer school. Fill in all blanks and check each item off as you complete it.

1.   **Assessing the Biggest Expense:**
   - What is your transfer school's yearly tuition? _____

2.   **Reviewing Financial Aid:**
   - Are you currently receiving financial aid (Pell Grant, Student Loans, or Scholarships) here at NCC? _____

*If you answered <u>yes</u>, continue with the following bullet points, then move on to #3.

   - Check and see what aid you have utilized by visiting www.nslds.ed.gov. If you have received Pell grant funding, you will see what percent you have remaining to use as a transfer student.
   - My percent of Pell used to date is: _____
   - Have you completed your FASFA for the current school year? _____
   - When do you need to complete your FASFA for the next school year? _____

*If you answered <u>no</u>, continue with the following bullet points prior to moving onto #3.

   - It is imperative to have a solid plan to be able to afford tuition and additional costs at any transfer institution.
   - What is your plan to cover the costs of your degree? _____
   _____
   - What will be your course of action if your previous plan fails? _____
   _____

3.   **Looking at Student Loans:**
   - Do you plan to apply for student loans at your transfer school? _____

   If you answered <u>yes</u>, continue with the bullet points under 3.
   If you answered <u>no</u>, move on to 4.

   - What amount do you plan to borrow? _____
   - Based on your FASFA, do you currently qualify for Direct Subsidized* or Direct Unsubsidized* student loans or will you need to borrow from a private lender**? _____

* There is a loan limit at the two year level; therefore, your status in terms of subsidized or unsubsidized loans could change at a four year school. For this reason, it is recommend students always apply (or re-apply) for aid and let the individual school review their information.
**According to CFNC.org: "private, loans for education are offered by both for-profit and not-for-profit lenders. These loans are not backed by the federal government. They should be used to supplement, not replace other financial aid.
Before you borrow an alternative loan: First look for grants and scholarships; then apply for federal loans; then research alternative loans options.
Make sure you understand the terms and conditions: Is the interest rate variable? (Later rate changes could mean higher monthly payments); are payments delayed while you're in school? (If you can, making payments while in school will actually save you money. When you wait to start, the total amount you pay back will be higher because interest charges will accrue.); does it require a co-signer (another person who agrees to be legally responsible for paying your loan if you don't)?
If you've considered it carefully – and don't borrow more than you really need -- an alternative loan can be a good option.

4.   **Assessing Scholarship Opportunities**: There are a variety of needs-based and merit-based scholarships available to college transfer students. There are also scholarships available based on certain groups you may belong to, religious affiliations you may have, etc. Two great places to start researching scholarship opportunities are CFNC.org and your transfer school's website.

After conducting your research, list at least 3 scholarships you qualify for:

1. Scholarship Name: _____
   Scholarship Amount: _____
   What is needed to apply (i.e. reference letters, transcripts, essay, etc.):
   _____
   _____

2. Scholarship Name: _____
   Scholarship Amount: _____
   What is needed to apply (i.e. reference letters, transcripts, essay, etc.):
   _____
   _____

3. Scholarship Name: _____
   Scholarship Amount: _____
   What is needed to apply (i.e. reference letters, transcripts, essay, etc.):
   _____
   _____

Portfolio Scoring Rubric for Part III: Financial Literacy

Student provides cost of transfer school's tuition and reviews financial aid status.	0-20	
Student assesses student loan options.	0-20	
Student explores and provides information on three scholarship opportunities.	0-60	
Total Score for Part 3		

Transfer Portfolio
Part IV: Completing Your Mock Entrance Essay

Congratulations! You've made it to the last section of the College Transfer Success Portfolio. In this section of the portfolio, you will complete the Career Readiness Certificate and complete an entrance essay.

Career Readiness Certification (CRC): Submit the certificate that you received after previously completing the CRC or report to the designated testing site during this course to complete the test.

Complete a mock application essay*:

The essay demonstrates your ability to write clearly and concisely on a selected topic and helps you distinguish yourself in your own voice. What do you want the readers of your application to know about you apart from courses, grades, and test scores?

Choose one of the following options and write an essay (minimum of 1 page, typed, double spaced, 12 point font), using the prompt to inspire and structure your response.

- Some students have a background or story that is so central to their identity that they believe their application would be incomplete without it. If this sounds like you, then please share your story.
- Recount an incident or time when you experienced failure. How did it affect you, and what lessons did you learn?
- Reflect on a time when you challenged a belief or idea. What prompted you to act? Would you make the same decision again?
- Describe a place or environment where you are perfectly content. What do you do or experience there, and why is it meaningful to you?
- Discuss an accomplishment or event, formal or informal, which marked your transition from childhood to adulthood within your culture, community, or family.

Attach your typed mock application essay.

Portfolio Scoring Rubric for Part IV: Completing Your Mock Entrance Essay

Student completes or submits Career Readiness Certificate.	50	
Student writes mock application essay.	10	
Student's essay is appropriately written, speaks to the writing prompt and is free of grammatical errors.	0-40	
Total Score for Part 4		

Mk	Room # Series	Description	Contains
A	2000, 2200	Building A	Student & Enrollment Services, Library, Classrooms, Offices, Information Technology
B	2100	Building B	Classrooms, Offices, Learning Center
B&I	1000	Business & Industry Center	Bookstore, Cashier, Administrative Offices, Continuing Education, Brown Auditorium, Culinary
C	3000	Building C	Classrooms, Offices, Shops
CO		Commons	Midway Cafe
D1, D2	4000	Building D	Classrooms, Offices, Nursing, Humanities
E	5000	Building E	Maintenance, Classrooms, Offices
CDC	6000	Child Development Center	Child Care, Offices, Early Childhood Education
EC		Early College	High School
F		Electric Line Construction Technology Training Field	Electric Line Construction Training
POPAT		Police Officer's Physical Agility Training	Burn Laboratory
S&T	7000	Science & Technology Center	Classrooms, Offices, Radio, Biology, Chemistry

Eastern Ave.

Rocky Mount & Nashville

Connector Road

POPAT

Old Carriage Road

Rocky Mount Hwy 64 Raleigh

CLK	Clock Tower
P1-P10	Parking Areas
PIC	Picnic Shelter
AMP	Myrtle Carter Henry Amphitheater

August 2015

Sun	Mon	Tue	Wed	Thu	Fri	Sat
26	27	28	29 Last day of Summer Cla	30 Faculty/Staff Workdays	31	Aug 1
2	3 Faculty/Staff Workdays	4	5	6 Last Day to Pay for fall WebAdvisor closes for f	7	8
9	10 Faculty/Staff Workday	11 Faculty/Staff Profession:	12 Extended Registration for Fall 2015 WebAdvisor opens for e	13	14 WebAdvisor closes for e	15
16	17 First Day of Classes	18	19	20	21	22
23	24	25	26	27	28	29
30	31	Sep 1	2	3	4	5

September 2015

Sun	Mon	Tue	Wed	Thu	Fri	Sat
30	31	Sep 1	2	3	4	5
6	7 College Closed-Labor [	8	9	10	11	12
13	14	15	16	17	18	19
20	21	22	23	24	25	26
27	28	29	30	Oct 1	2	3

October 2015

Sun	Mon	Tue	Wed	Thu	Fri	Sat
27	28	29	30	Oct 1	2	3
4	5	6	7	8	9	10
11	12 Fall Break-No Classes	13	14	15	16	17
18	19	20	21	22	23	24
25	26	27	28	29	30	31

November 2015

Sun	Mon	Tue	Wed	Thu	Fri	Sat
Nov 1	2	3	4	5	6	7
8	9	10	11 College Closed-Veterar	12	13	14
15	16	17	18	19 Registration for Spring 2016	20	21
22	23	24 No Classes-Faculty Workdays	25	26 College Closed-Thanksgiving Holiday	27	28
29	30 Last day to Withdraw fro	Dec 1	2	3	4	5

December 2015

Sun	Mon	Tue	Wed	Thu	Fri	Sat
29	30	Dec 1	2	3	4	5
	Last day to Withdraw fro					
6	7	8	9	10	11	12
13	14	15	16	17	18	19
			Last day of classes	Faculty/Staff Workdays		
20	21	22	23	24	25	26
	College Closed-Christmas Holidays					
27	28	29	30	31	Jan 1	2
	College Closed-Faculty/Staff Conservation Days				College Closed-New Ye	

January 2016

Sun	Mon	Tue	Wed	Thu	Fri	Sat
27	28	29	30	31	Jan 1	2
	College Closed-Faculty/Staff Conservation Days				College Closed-New Ye	
3	4	5	6	7	8	9
	Faculty/Staff Workday	Extended Registration for Spring 2016				
10	11	12	13	14	15	16
	First Day of Classes					
17	18	19	20	21	22	23
	College Closed-MLK Ho					
24	25	26	27	28	29	30

February 2016

Sun	Mon	Tue	Wed	Thu	Fri	Sat
31	Feb 1	2	3	4	5	6
7	8	9	10	11	12	13
14	15	16	17	18	19	20
21	22	23	24	25	26	27
28	29	Mar 1	2	3	4	5

March 2016

Sun	Mon	Tue	Wed	Thu	Fri	Sat
28	29	Mar 1	2	3	4	5
6	7	8	9	10	11	12
13	14	15	16	17	18	19
20	21	22	23	24	25 College Closed-Good F	26
27	28 Easter Break-No Curriculum Classes	29	30	31	Apr 1	2

April 2016

Sun	Mon	Tue	Wed	Thu	Fri	Sat
27	28	29	30	31	Apr 1	2
	Easter Break-No Curriculum Classes					
3	4	5	6	7	8	9
10	11	12	13	14	15	16
			Registration for Summer 2016 & Fall 2016			
17	18	19	20	21	22	23
					Last day to Withdraw or	
24	25	26	27	28	29	30

May 2016

Sun	Mon	Tue	Wed	Thu	Fri	Sat
May 1	2	3	4	5	6	7
8	9	10 Last day of Classes-Foll	11 Faculty/Staff Workdays	12 Graduation-GED/Adult H / Nurses' Pinning	13 Graduation-Curriculum	14
15	16 Faculty/Staff Workdays	17	18	19	20	21
22	23 Extended Registration or Summer 2016	24	25 First Day of Classes-SU	26	27	28
29	30 College Closed-Memori	31	Jun 1	2	3	4

June 2016

Sun	Mon	Tue	Wed	Thu	Fri	Sat
29	30 College Closed-Memori	31	Jun 1	2	3	4
5	6	7	8	9	10	11
12	13	14	15	16	17	18
19	20	21	22	23	24	25
26	27	28	29	30	Jul 1	2

July 2016

Sun	Mon	Tue	Wed	Thu	Fri	Sat
26	27	28	29	30	Jul 1	2
3	4 College Closed-July 4th	5 College Closed-Faculty/Staff Conservation Days	6	7	8	9
10	11	12	13 Registration for Fall 2016	14	15	16
17	18	19 Last day to withdraw	20	21	22	23
24	25	26	27 Last day of Classes Su	28	29	30
31	Aug 1	2	3	4	5	6